ARCTIC OCEAN

New Siberian Is.

Novaya Zemlya

Bering Sea

NORWAY
SWEDEN
FINLAND
Helsinki
Oslo
Stockholm
Copenhagen
DEN.
BELO.
POLAND
Warsaw
GERMANY
Berlin
Vienna
Kiev
ROMANIA
Bucharest
BULGARIA
Istanbul
GREECE
TURKEY
Athens
Rome
Mediterranean Sea
Tripoli
Alexandria
Cairo
LIBYA
EGYPT
Arkhangelsk

St. Petersburg
(Leningrad)
Yekaterinburg
Moscow

RUSSIA

Novosibirsk

Irkutsk

KAZAKHSTAN

MONGOLIA

Ulan Bator

Vladivostok
Sapporo

N. KOREA
Peking
Dalian
S. JAPAN
Tokyo
Chungking
Shanghai
Osaka
Pusan

PACIFIC

GEORG.
ARM.
AZ.
Baku
UZBEKISTAN
KIRGHIZIA
Tashkent
TURKMENISTAN
TAJIKISTAN
SYRIA
Baghdad
Tehran
AFGHANISTAN
Kabul
Islamabad
Lahore
IRAQ
IRAN
JORDAN
ISRAEL
KUWAIT
PAKISTAN
Karachi
BAHRAIN
Delhi
BANGLA-
DESH
Dacca
Hanoi
TAIWAN
Hong Kong

OCEAN

Tropic of Cancer

Wake I.
(U.S.)

SAUDI
Mecca
ARABIA
U.A.E.
OMAN
Ahmadabad
INDIA
Calcutta
BURMA
(MYANMAR)
LAOS
Northern
Marianas

20

RED SEA
YEMEN
Bombay
Rangoon
Bay of
Madras
Bengal
THAILAND
VIETNAM
Manila
Marshall Is.

NIGER
CHAD
Khartoum
SUDAN
Arabian
Sea
Bangkok
CAM-
BODIA
PHILIPPINES

Kano
Ndjamena
DJIB.
Addis Ababa
SOMALI
REP.
Phnom
Penh
Ho Chi Minh
City

NIGERIA
Lagos
CAMEROON
CENTRAL
AFRICAN
REPUBLIC
Douala
ETHIOPIA
SRI LANKA
Federated States
of Micronesia

EQUATORIAL
GUINEA
GABON
CONGO
ZAÏRE
UGANDA
KENYA
Colombo
MALAYSIA
BRUNEI
Equator
Kiribati

RWANDA
Nairobi
Mogadishu
Maldives
Kuala
Lumpur
Singapore

CABINDA
Kinshasa
BURUNDI
TANZANIA
Mombasa
Seychelles
INDIAN
Padang
Sumatra
Borneo
New
Guinea
PAPUA
NEW GUINEA
Solomon Is.
Tuvalu
(Ellice Is.)

Luanda
ANGOLA
Dar-es-Salaam
INDONESIA
Jakarta
Surabaya
Port Moresby

ZAMBIA
MALAWI
MOZAMBIQUE
OCEAN
Coral
Sea
Vanuatu

Harare
ZIMBABWE
Antananarivo
MADAGASCAR
Mauritius
Darwin
Fiji

NAMIBIA
BOTSWANA
SWAZ.
Johannesburg
LES.
SOUTH
AFRICA
Durban
Alice Springs
AUSTRALIA
New
Caledonia
(Fr.)
Tropic of Capricorn

Cape Town

Crozet Is.
(Fr.)
Kerguelen Is.
(Fr.)
Perth
Adelaide
Sydney
Canberra
Melbourne
Brisbane
Auckland

Tasmania
Hobart
NEW
ZEALAND
Christchurch

Dunedin

SOUTHERN OCEAN

60

DEPENDENCY
AUSTRALIAN DEPENDENCY
ADÉLIE LAND
from Greenwich

20
40
60
80
100
120
140
160
180

PHILIP'S

ENCYCLOPEDIC
WORLD
ATLAS

COUNTRY BY COUNTRY

PHILIP'S

ENCYCLOPEDIC WORLD ATLAS

COUNTRY BY COUNTRY

BCA

LONDON · NEW YORK · SYDNEY · TORONTO

CONTENTS

Compiled by:
RICHARD WIDDOWS

Editor: Caroline Rayner

Assistant Editors:
Alan Lothian, Helen Dawson,
David Cheal, Richard Dawes

Design: Andrew Sutterby,
Peter Burt, Karen Stewart,
Gwyn Lewis

Maps prepared by:
B.M. Willett, David Gaylard,
Ray Smith, Jenny Allen

Index prepared by:
Byte and Type Limited,
Birmingham, UK

Information on recent
changes to flags provided and
authenticated by the Flag
Institute, Chester, UK

This edition published 1992 by
BCA by arrangement with
George Philip Limited,
59 Grosvenor Street, London
W1X 9DA

© 1992 George Philip Limited

CN 6027

Printed in Hong Kong

WORLD STATISTICS: COUNTRIES

This alphabetical list includes the principal countries and territories of the world. If a territory is not completely independent, then the country it is associated with is named. The area figures give the total area of land, inland water and ice. Units for areas and populations are thousands. The annual income is the Gross National Product per capita in US dollars. The figures are the latest available, usually 1989-91.

Country/Territory	Area km² Thousands	Area miles² Thousands	Population Thousands	Capital	Annual Income US $
Afghanistan	652	25	16,433	Kabul	450
Albania	28.8	11.1	3,250	Tiranë	1,000
Algeria	2,382	920	24,960	Algiers	2,060
American Samoa (US)	0.20	0.08	39	Pago Pago	6,000
Andorra (Fr/Spain)	0.45	0.17	52	Andorre-la-Vella	
Angola	1,247	481	10,020	Luanda	620
Anguilla (UK)	0.40	0.09	8	The Valley	
Antigua & Barbuda	0.44	0.17	77	St John's	4,600
Argentina	2,767	1,068	32,322	Buenos Aires	2,370
Armenia	29.8	11.5	3,300	Yerevan	
Aruba (Neths)	0.19	0.07	60	Oranjestad	6,000
Australia	7,687	2,968	17,086	Canberra	17,080
Austria	83.9	32.4	7,712	Vienna	19,240
Azerbaijan	86.6	33.4	7,100	Baku	
Azores (Port)	2.2	0.87	260	Ponta Delgada	
Bahamas	13.9	5.4	253	Nassau	11,510
Bahrain	0.68	0.26	503	Manama	6,500
Bangladesh	144	56	115,594	Dacca	200
Barbados	0.43	0.17	255	Bridgetown	6,540
Belau (US)	0.46	0.18	15	Koror	
Belgium	30.5	11.8	9,845	Brussels	15,440
Belize	23.0	8.9	188	Belmopan	1,970
Belorussia	208	80.1	10,300	Minsk	
Benin	113	43	4,736	Porto-Novo	360
Bermuda (UK)	0.05	0.02	61	Hamilton	25,000
Bhutan (India)	47.0	18.1	1,517	Thimphu	190
Bolivia	1,099	424	7,400	La Paz/Sucre	620
Botswana	582	225	1,291	Gaborone	2,040
Brazil	8,512	3,286	153,322	Brasilia	2,680
Brit. Antarctic Terr. (UK)	1,709	660	0.3	Stanley	
Brit. Ind. Oc. Terr. (UK)	0.08	0.03	3		
Brunei	5.8	2.2	266	Bandar Seri Begawan	6,000
Bulgaria	111	43	9,011	Sofia	2,210
Burkina Faso	274	106	9,001	Ouagadougou	330
Burma (Myanmar)	677	261	41,675	Rangoon	500
Burundi	27.8	10.7	5,438	Bujumbura	210
Cambodia	181	70	8,246	Phnom Penh	300
Cameroon	475	184	11,834	Yaoundé	940
Canada	9,976	3,852	26,522	Ottawa	20,450
Canary Is. (Spain)	7.3	2.8	1,700	Las Palmas/S. Cruz	
Cape Verde Is.	4.0	1.6	370	Praia	890
Cayman Is. (UK)	0.26	0.10	27	Georgetown	
Central African Republic	623	241	3,039	Bangui	390
Chad	1,284	496	5,679	Ndjamena	190
Chile	757	292	13,386	Santiago	1,940
China	9,597	3,682	1,139,060	Beijing	370
Colombia	1,139	440	32,987	Bogotá	1,240
Comoros	2.2	0.86	551	Moroni	480
Congo	342	132	2,271	Brazzaville	1,010
Costa Rica	51.1	19.7	2,994	San José	1,910
Croatia	56.5	21.8	4,680	Zagreb	
Cuba	111	43	10,609	Havana	3,000
Cyprus	9.3	3.6	702	Nicosia	8,040
Czechoslovakia	128	49	15,678	Prague	3,140
Denmark	43.1	16.6	5,140	Copenhagen	22,090
Djibouti	23.2	9.0	409	Djibouti	1,000
Dominica	0.75	0.29	83	Roseau	1,940
Dominican Republic	48.7	18.8	7,170	Santo Domingo	820
Ecuador	284	109	10,782	Quito	960
Egypt	1,001	387	53,153	Cairo	600
El Salvador	21.0	8.1	5,252	San Salvador	1,100
Equatorial Guinea	28.1	10.8	348	Malabo	330
Estonia	44.7	17.3	1,600	Tallinn	
Ethiopia	1,222	472	50,974	Addis Ababa	120
Falkland Is. (UK)	12.2	4.7	2	Stanley	
Faroe Is. (Den)	1.4	0.54	47	Tórshavn	22,090
Fiji	18.3	7.1	765	Suva	1,770
Finland	338	131	4,986	Helsinki	26,070
France	552	213	56,440	Paris	19,480
French Guiana (Fr)	90.0	34.7	99	Cayenne	2,500
French Polynesia (Fr)	4.0	1.5	206	Papeete	6,000
Gabon	268	103	1,172	Libreville	3,220
Gambia, The	11.3	4.4	861	Banjul	260
Georgia	69.7	26.9	5,500	Tbilisi	
Germany	357	138	79,479	Berlin/Bonn	17,000
Ghana	239	92	15,028	Accra	390
Gibraltar (UK)	0.007	0.003	31	-	4,000
Greece	132	51	10,269	Athens	6,000
Greenland (Den)	2,176	840	60	Godthåb	6,000
Grenada	0.34	0.13	85	St George's	2,120
Guadeloupe (Fr)	1.7	0.66	344	Basse-Terre	7,000
Guam (US)	0.55	0.21	119	Agana	6,000
Guatemala	109	42	9,197	Guatemala City	900
Guinea	246	95	5,756	Conakry	480
Guinea-Bissau	36.1	13.9	965	Bissau	180
Guyana	215	83	796	Georgetown	370
Haiti	27.8	10.7	6,486	Port-au-Prince	370
Honduras	112	43	5,105	Tegucigalpa	590
Hong Kong (UK)	1.1	0.40	5,801	-	11,540
Hungary	93.0	35.9	10,344	Budapest	2,780
Iceland	103	40	255	Reykjavik	21,150
India	3,288	1,269	843,931	Delhi	350
Indonesia	1,905	735	179,300	Jakarta	560
Iran	1,648	636	58,031	Tehran	2,450
Iraq	438	169	18,920	Baghdad	2,000
Ireland	70.3	27.1	3,523	Dublin	9,550
Israel	27.0	10.4	4,659	Jerusalem	10,970
Italy	301	116	57,663	Rome	16,850
Ivory Coast	322	125	11,998	Abidjan	730
Jamaica	11.0	4.2	2,420	Kingston	1,510
Japan	378	146	123,537	Tokyo	25,430
Jordan	89.2	34.4	4,009	Amman	1,240
Kazakhstan	2,717	1,049	16,700	Alma Ata	
Kenya	580	224	24,032	Nairobi	370
Kirghizia	199	76.9	4,400	Bishkek	
Kiribati	0.72	0.28	66	Tarawa	760
Korea, North	121	47	21,773	Pyongyang	900
Korea, South	99.0	38.2	43,302	Seoul	5,400
Kuwait	17.8	6.9	2,143	Kuwait City	16,380
Laos	237	91	4,139	Vientiane	200
Latvia	63.1	24.4	2,700	Riga	
Lebanon	10.4	4.0	2,701	Beirut	2,000
Lesotho	30.4	11.7	1,774	Maseru	470
Liberia	111	43	2,607	Monrovia	500
Libya	1,760	679	4,545	Tripoli	5,800
Liechtenstein	0.16	0.06	29	Vaduz	33,000
Lithuania	65.2	25.2	3,751	Vilnius	
Luxembourg	2.6	1.0	384	Luxembourg	28,770
Macau (Port)	0.02	0.006	479	-	2,000
Madagascar	587	227	11,197	Antananarivo	230
Malawi	118	46	8,556	Lilongwe	200
Malaysia	330	127	17,861	Kuala Lumpur	2,340
Maldives	0.30	0.12	215	Malé	440
Mali	1,240	479	8,156	Bamako	270
Malta	0.32	0.12	354	Valletta	6,630
Martinique (Fr)	1.1	0.42	341	Fort-de-France	4,000
Mauritania	1,025	396	2,050	Nouakchott	500
Mauritius	1.9	0.72	1,075	Port Louis	2,250
Mexico	1,958	756	86,154	Mexico City	2,490
Micronesia, Fed. Stat. (US)	0.70	0.27	103	Kolonia	
Moldavia	33.7	13.0	4,400	Kishinev	
Monaco	0.002	0.0001	29	-	20,000
Mongolia	1,567	605	2,190	Ulan Bator	400
Montserrat (UK)	0.10	0.04	13	Plymouth	
Morocco	447	172	25,061	Rabat	950
Mozambique	802	309	15,656	Maputo	80
Namibia	824	318	1,781	Windhoek	1,000
Nauru	0.02	0.008	10	Domaneab	
Nepal	141	54	18,916	Katmandu	170
Netherlands	41.9	16.2	15,019	Amsterdam	17,330
Neths. Antilles (Neths)	0.99	0.38	189	Willemstad	6,000
New Caledonia (Fr)	19.0	7.3	168	Nouméa	4,000
New Zealand	269	104	3,429	Wellington	12,680
Nicaragua	130	50	3,871	Managua	800
Niger	1,267	489	7,732	Niamey	310
Nigeria	924	357	108,542	Lagos (Abuja)	270
Norway	324	125	4,242	Oslo	23,120
Oman	212	82	1,502	Muscat	5,220
Pakistan	796	307	112,050	Islamabad	380
Panama	77.1	29.8	2,418	Panama City	1,830
Papua New Guinea	463	179	3,699	Port Moresby	860
Paraguay	407	157	4,277	Asunción	1,110
Peru	1,285	496	22,332	Lima	1,160
Philippines	300	116	61,480	Manila	730
Poland	313	121	38,180	Warsaw	1,700
Portugal	92.4	35.7	10,525	Lisbon	4,890
Puerto Rico (US)	8.9	3.4	3,599	San Juan	6,470
Qatar	11.0	4.2	368	Doha	15,860
Réunion (Fr)	2.5	0.97	599	St-Denis	
Romania	238	92	23,200	Bucharest	1,640
Russia	17,068	6,593	147,440	Moscow	
Rwanda	26.3	10.2	7,181	Kigali	310
St Christopher/Nevis	0.36	0.14	44	Basseterre	3,330
St Lucia	0.62	0.24	151	Castries	1,900
St Pierre & Miquelon (Fr)	0.24	0.09	6	St Pierre	
St Vincent/Grenadines	0.39	0.15	116	Kingstown	1,610
San Marino	0.06	0.02	24	San Marino	
São Tomé & Príncipe	0.96	0.37	121	São Tomé	380
Saudi Arabia	2,150	830	14,870	Riyadh	6,230
Senegal	197	76	7,327	Dakar	710
Seychelles	0.46	0.18	67	Victoria	4,670
Sierra Leone	71.7	27.7	4,151	Freetown	240
Singapore	0.62	0.24	3,003	Singapore	12,310
Slovenia	20.3	7.8	1,940	Ljubljana	
Solomon Is.	28.9	11.2	321	Honiara	580
Somalia	638	246	7,497	Mogadishu	150
South Africa	1,221	471	35,282	Pretoria	2,520
Spain	505	195	38,959	Madrid	10,920
Sri Lanka	65.6	25.3	16,993	Colombo	470
Sudan	2,506	967	25,204	Khartoum	450
Surinam	163	63	422	Paramaribo	3,050
Swaziland	17.4	6.7	768	Mbabane	820
Sweden	450	174	8,618	Stockholm	23,680
Switzerland	41.3	15.9	6,712	Bern	32,790
Syria	185	71	12,116	Damascus	990
Taiwan	36.0	13.9	20,300	Taipei	6,600
Tajikistan	143	55.2	5,300	Dushanbe	
Tanzania	945	365	25,635	Dar es Salaam	120
Thailand	513	198	57,196	Bangkok	1,420
Togo	56.8	21.9	3,531	Lome	410
Tokelau (NZ)	0.01	0.005	2	Nukunonu	
Tonga	0.75	0.29	95	Nuku'alofa	1,010
Trinidad & Tobago	5.1	2.0	1,227	Port of Spain	3,470
Tunisia	164	63	8,180	Tunis	1,420
Turkey	779	301	57,326	Ankara	1,630
Turkmenistan	488	188	3,600	Ashkhabad	
Turks & Caicos Is. (UK)	0.43	0.17	10	Grand Turk	
Tuvalu	0.03	0.01	10	Funafuti	600
Uganda	236	91	18,795	Kampala	220
Ukraine	604	233	51,800	Kiev	
United Arab Emirates	83.6	32.3	1,589	Abu Dhabi	19,860
United Kingdom	244	94	57,405	London	16,070
United States of America	9,373	3,619	249,928	Washington	21,700
Uruguay	177	68	3,094	Montevideo	2,560
Uzbekistan	447	173	20,300	Tashkent	
Vanuatu	12.2	4.7	147	Port Vila	1,060
Vatican City	0.0004	0.0002	1.0	-	
Venezuela	912	352	19,735	Caracas	2,560
Vietnam	332	127	66,200	Hanoi	300
Virgin Is. (UK)	0.15	0.06	13	Road Town	
Virgin Is. (US)	0.34	0.13	117	Charlotte Amalie	12,000
Western Sahara (Mor)	266	103	179	El Aiun	
Western Samoa	2.8	1.1	164	Apia	730
Yemen	528	204	11,282	Sana	640
Yugoslavia (ex. Croatia/Slov.)	179	69	17,144	Belgrade	3,060
Zaire	2,345	906	35,562	Kinshasa	230
Zambia	753	291	8,073	Lusaka	420
Zimbabwe	391	151	9,369	Harare	640

WORLD STATISTICS: PHYSICAL DIMENSIONS

Each topic list is divided into continents and within a continent the items are listed in order of size. The order of the continents is as in the atlas, Europe through to South America. The bottom part of many of the lists are selective. The world top ten are shown in square brackets; in the case of mountains this has not been done because the world top 30 are all in Asia. The figures are rounded as appropriate.

WORLD, CONTINENTS, OCEANS

	km²	miles²	%
The World	509,450,000	196,672,000	
Land	149,450,000	57,688,000	29.3
Water	360,000,000	138,984,000	70.7
Asia	44,500,000	17,177,000	29.8
Africa	30,302,000	11,697,000	20.3
North America	24,241,000	9,357,000	16.2
South America	17,793,000	6,868,000	11.9
Antarctica	14,100,000	5,443,000	9.4
Europe	9,957,000	3,843,000	6.7
Australia & Oceania	8,557,000	3,303,000	5.7
Pacific Ocean	179,679,000	69,356,000	49.9
Atlantic Ocean	92,373,000	35,657,000	25.7
Indian Ocean	73,917,000	28,532,000	20.5
Arctic Ocean	14,090,000	5,439,000	3.9

MOUNTAINS

Europe		m	ft
Mont Blanc	France/Italy	4,807	15,771
Monte Rosa	Italy/Switzerland	4,634	15,203
Dom	Switzerland	4,545	14,911
Weisshorn	Switzerland	4,505	14,780
Matterhorn/Cervino	Italy/Switzerland	4,478	14,691
Mt Maudit	France/Italy	4,465	14,649
Finsteraarhorn	Switzerland	4,275	14,025
Aletschhorn	Switzerland	4,182	13,720
Jungfrau	Switzerland	4,158	13,642
Barre des Ecrins	France	4,103	13,461
Gran Paradiso	Italy	4,061	13,323
Piz Bernina	Italy/Switzerland	4,052	13,294
Ortles	Italy	3,899	12,792
Monte Viso	Italy	3,841	12,602
Grossglockner	Austria	3,797	12,457
Mulhacén	Spain	3,478	11,411
Pico de Aneto	Spain	3,404	11,168
Etna	Italy	3,340	10,958
Galdhöpiggen	Norway	2,469	8,100
Hvannadalshnúkur	Iceland	2,119	6,952
Ben Nevis	UK	1,343	4,406

Asia		m	ft
Everest	China/Nepal	8,848	29,029
Godwin Austen (K2)	China/Kashmir	8,611	28,251
Kanchenjunga	India/Nepal	8,598	28,208
Lhotse	China/Nepal	8,516	27,939
Makalu	China/Nepal	8,481	27,824
Cho Oyu	China/Nepal	8,201	26,906
Dhaulagiri	Nepal	8,172	26,811
Manaslu	Nepal	8,156	26,758
Nanga Parbat	Kashmir	8,126	26,660
Annapurna	Nepal	8,078	26,502
Gasherbrum	China/Kashmir	8,068	26,469
Broad Peak	India	8,051	26,414
Gosainthan	China	8,012	26,286
Disteghil Sar	Kashmir	7,885	25,869
Nuptse	Nepal	7,879	25,849
Elbrus	Russia	5,633	18,481
Fuji-san	Japan	3,776	12,388
Pidurutalagala	Sri Lanka	2,524	8,281

Africa		m	ft
Kilimanjaro	Tanzania	5,895	19,340
Mt Kenya	Kenya	5,199	17,057
Ruwenzori	Uganda/Zaïre	5,109	16,762
Ras Dashan	Ethiopia	4,620	15,157
Meru	Tanzania	4,565	14,977
Karisimbi	Rwanda/Zaïre	4,507	14,787
Mt Elgon	Kenya/Uganda	4,321	14,176
Batu	Ethiopia	4,307	14,130
Gughe	Ethiopia	4,200	13,779
Toubkal	Morocco	4,165	13,665

Oceania		m	ft
Puncak Jaya	Indonesia	5,029	16,499
Puncak Mandala	Indonesia	4,760	15,617
Puncak Trikora	Indonesia	4,750	15,584
Mt Wilhelm	Papua N. Guinea	4,508	14,790
Mauna Kea	USA (Hawaii)	4,208	13,806
Mauna Loa	USA (Hawaii)	4,169	13,678
Mt Cook	New Zealand	3,753	12,313
Mt Kosciusko	Australia	2,230	7,316

North America		m	ft
Mt McKinley	USA (Alaska)	6,194	20,321
Mt Logan	Canada	6,050	19,849
Citlaltepetl	Mexico	5,700	18,701
Mt St Elias	USA/Canada	5,489	18,008
Popocatepetl	Mexico	5,452	17,887
Mt Foraker	USA (Alaska)	5,304	17,401
Ixtaccihuatl	Mexico	5,286	17,342
Lucania	USA (Alaska)	5,226	17,145
Mt Steele	Canada	5,011	16,440
Mt Bona	USA (Alaska)	5,005	16,420

South America		m	ft
Aconcagua	Argentina	6,960	22,834
Illimani	Bolivia	6,882	22,578
Bonete	Argentina	6,872	22,546
Ojos del Salado	Argentina/Chile	6,863	22,516
Tupungato	Argentina/Chile	6,800	22,309
Pissis	Argentina	6,779	22,241
Mercedario	Argentina/Chile	6,770	22,211
Huascaran	Peru	6,768	22,204
Llullaillaco	Argentina/Chile	6,723	22,057
Nudo de Cachi	Argentina	6,720	22,047

Antarctica		m	ft
Vinson Massif		4,897	16,066

OCEAN DEPTHS

Atlantic Ocean		m	ft
Puerto Rico (Milwaukee) Deep [7]		9,200	30,183
Cayman Trench [10]		7,680	25,197
Gulf of Mexico		5,203	17,070
Mediterranean		5,121	16,801
Black Sea		2,211	7,254
North Sea		310	1,017
Baltic Sea		294	965
Hudson Bay		111	364

Indian Ocean		m	ft
Java Trench		7,450	24,442
Red Sea		2,266	7,434
Persian Gulf		73	239

Pacific Ocean		m	ft
Mariana Trench [1]		11,022	36,161
Tonga Trench [2]		10,822	35,505
Japan Trench [3]		10,554	34,626
Kuril Trench [4]		10,542	34,586
Mindanao Trench [5]		10,497	34,439
Kermadec Trench [6]		10,047	32,962
Peru-Chile Trench [8]		8,050	26,410
Aleutian Trench [9]		7,822	25,662
Middle American Trench		6,662	21,857

Arctic Ocean		m	ft
Molloy Deep		5,608	18,399

LAND LOWS

		m	ft
Caspian Sea	Europe	-28	-92
Dead Sea	Asia	-400	-1,312
Lake Assal	Africa	-156	-512
Lake Eyre North	Oceania	-16	-52
Death Valley	N. America	-86	-282
Valdés Peninsula	S. America	-40	-131

RIVERS

Europe		km	miles
Volga	Caspian Sea	3,700	2,300
Danube	Black Sea	2,850	1,770
Ural	Caspian Sea	2,535	1,574
Dnieper	Volga	2,285	1,420
Kama	Volga	2,030	1,260
Don	Volga	1,990	1,240
Petchora	Arctic	1,790	1,110
Dniester	Black Sea	1,400	870
Rhine	North Sea	1,320	820
Elbe	North Sea	1,145	710
Vistula	Baltic Sea	1,090	675
Loire	Atlantic	1,020	635
Thames	North Sea	335	210

Asia		km	miles
Yangtze [3]	Pacific	6,380	3,960
Yenisey-Angara [5]	Arctic	5,550	3,445
Ob-Irtysh [6]	Arctic	5,410	3,360
Hwang Ho [7]	Pacific	4,840	3,005
Amur [9]	Pacific	4,510	2,800
Mekong [10]	Pacific	4,500	2,795
Lena	Arctic	4,400	2,730
Irtysh	Ob	4,250	2,640
Yenisei	Arctic	4,090	2,540
Ob	Arctic	3,680	2,285
Indus	Indian	3,100	1,925
Brahmaputra	Indian	2,900	1,800
Syr Darya	Aral Sea	2,860	1,775
Salween	Indian	2,800	1,740
Euphrates	Indian	2,700	1,675
Vilyuy	Lena	2,650	1,645
Kolyma	Arctic	2,600	1,615
Amu Darya	Aral Sea	2,540	1,575
Ural	Caspian Sea	2,535	1,575
Ganges	Indian	2,510	1,560
Si Kiang	Pacific	2,100	1,305
Irrawaddy	Indian	2,010	1,250
Tigris	Indian	1,900	1,180

Africa		km	miles
Nile [1]	Mediterranean	6,670	4,140
Zaïre/Congo [8]	Atlantic	4,670	2,900
Niger	Atlantic	4,180	2,595
Zambezi	Indian	2,740	1,700
Oubangi/Uele	Zaïre	2,250	1,400
Kasai	Zaïre	1,950	1,210
Shaballe	Indian	1,930	1,200
Orange	Atlantic	1,860	1,155

Australia		km	miles
Murray-Darling	Indian	3,720	2,310
Darling	Murray	3,070	1,905
Murray	Indian	2,575	1,600
Murrumbidgee	Murray	1,690	1,050

North America		km	miles
Mississippi-Missouri [4]	Gulf of Mexico	6,020	3,740
Mackenzie	Arctic	4,240	2,630
Mississippi	Gulf of Mexico	3,780	2,350
Missouri	Mississippi	3,725	2,310
Yukon	Pacific	3,185	1,980
Rio Grande	Gulf of Mexico	3,030	1,880
Arkansas	Mississippi	2,340	1,450
Colorado	Pacific	2,330	1,445
Red	Mississippi	2,040	1,270
Columbia	Pacific	1,950	1,210
Saskatchewan	Lake Winnipeg	1,940	1,205
Snake	Columbia	1,670	1,040

South America		km	miles
Amazon [2]	Atlantic	6,430	3,990
Paraná-Plate	Atlantic	4,000	2,480
Purus	Amazon	3,350	2,080
Madeira	Amazon	3,200	1,990
São Francisco	Atlantic	2,900	1,800
Paraná	Plate	2,800	1,740
Tocantins	Atlantic	2,640	1,640
Paraguay	Paraná	2,550	1,580
Orinoco	Atlantic	2,500	1,550
Pilcomayo	Paraná	2,500	1,550

LAKES

Europe		km²	miles²
Lake Ladoga	Russia	18,400	7,100
Lake Onega	Russia	9,700	3,700
Saimaa system	Finland	8,000	3,100

Asia		km²	miles²
Caspian Sea [1]	Asia	371,000	143,000
Aral Sea [6]	Kazakh./Uzbek.	36,000	13,900
Lake Baikal [9]	Russia	31,500	12,200
Tonlé Sap	Cambodia	20,000	7,700
Lake Balkhash	Kazakhstan	18,500	7,100

Africa		km²	miles²
Lake Victoria [3]	E. Africa	68,000	26,000
Lake Tanganyika [7]	C. Africa	33,000	13,000
Lake Malawi [10]	E. Africa	29,000	11,000
Lake Chad	C. Africa	25,000	9,700

Australia		km²	miles²
Lake Eyre	Australia	9,000	3,500

North America		km²	miles²
Lake Superior [2]	Canada/USA	82,200	31,700
Lake Huron [4]	Canada/USA	59,600	23,000
Lake Michigan [5]	USA	58,000	22,400
Great Bear Lake [8]	Canada	31,500	12,200
Great Slave Lake	Canada	28,700	11,100
Lake Erie	Canada/USA	25,700	9,900
Lake Winnipeg	Canada	24,400	9,400
Lake Ontario	Canada/USA	19,500	7,500

South America		km²	miles²
Lake Titicaca	Bolivia/Peru	8,200	3,200

ISLANDS

Europe		km²	miles²
Great Britain [8]	UK	229,880	88,700
Iceland	Atlantic Ocean	103,000	39,800
Ireland	Ireland/UK	84,400	32,600

Asia		km²	miles²
Borneo [3]	S. E. Asia	737,000	284,000
Sumatra [6]	Indonesia	425,000	164,000
Honshu [7]	Japan	230,000	88,800
Celebes	Indonesia	189,000	73,000
Java	Indonesia	126,700	48,900
Luzon	Philippines	104,700	40,400
Mindanao	Philippines	95,000	36,700
Hokkaido	Japan	78,400	30,300
Sakhalin	Russia	76,400	29,500
Sri Lanka	Indian Ocean	65,600	25,300

Africa		km²	miles²
Madagascar [4]	Indian Ocean	587,000	226,600

Oceania		km²	miles²
New Guinea [2]	Indon./Pap. NG	780,000	301,080
New Zealand (S)	New Zealand	150,500	58,100
New Zealand (N)	New Zealand	114,400	44,200
Tasmania	Australia	67,800	26,200

North America		km²	miles²
Greenland [1]	Greenland	2,175,600	839,800
Baffin Is. [5]	Canada	508,000	196,100
Victoria Is. [9]	Canada	212,200	81,900
Ellesmere Is. [10]	Canada	212,000	81,800
Cuba	Cuba	114,500	44,200
Newfoundland	Canada	96,000	37,100
Hispaniola	Atlantic Ocean	76,200	29,400

South America		km²	miles²
Tierra del Fuego	Argentina/Chile	47,000	18,100

GENERAL NOTES

Philip's Encyclopedic World Atlas follows a geographical rather than an alphabetical sequence, starting with Europe and proceeding through Asia, Africa, Australasia and the Pacific islands, to North and South America and ending with the islands of the Atlantic Ocean. Within each continent the progression is generally west to east and north to south.

Each continent is introduced by maps of the whole region: a physical map and one showing the individual countries, a map showing the land use, and some small maps concerned with climate, natural vegetation and the distribution of population.

The size of a country's article and the size of its map tend to reflect the importance and status of the country on a world scale. This is not fixed, however, and a few small countries appear at a map scale which is larger than they would normally merit. Large countries such as Canada, the USA and Russia have maps covering a double page, while for a few densely populated areas – such as the Ruhr or southern Japan – supplementary maps have been added at a scale larger than the main country map.

The maps are all positioned with north at the top, with the lines of latitude and longitude shown and labelled. Around the edges of the maps are a series of letters and figures, used for locating places from the index.

Place names are spelled in their local forms on the maps, but in the tables and text conventional spellings are generally used. For example, Roma (Rome) will appear with the Italian spelling on the map but in the text it will be referred to as Rome. The maps were corrected up to March 1992 and any changes to place names and boundaries were incorporated up to that time.

For ease of reference, an alphabetical list of the countries described in the main text is given below. Some islands, areas or territories that are a part of a country, but separated from it, have been omitted from this list (please refer to the Index on pages 225-264 for the full listing).

Climate graphs
A climate graph has been provided for most countries, usually of the capital or most important town, and some large countries feature two or more. The temperature part shows the average monthly maximum and minimum with a red bar; the monthly average is the black dot centred in this bar. The temperature range mentioned in the climate description means the difference between the highest and the lowest temperature. Because of limited space for the text, the word 'average' has sometimes been omitted, but it should be borne in mind that nearly all climatic statistics are averages and

there can be, and usually are, significant variations from this figure.

Statistical tables
In the country fact-files certain terms have been used which may require some explanation:

AREA: The area of the whole country, including inland water areas.

POPULATION: The latest estimate or census figure is given, usually for 1991. The population of the cities is the latest estimate and as far as possible is for the total geographical urban area and not for the smaller area within strict administrative boundaries.

ANNUAL INCOME: Given in US$, this is the Gross National Product (GNP) divided by the total population – not average earnings. The GNP is the valuation of production within the country plus the balance of money flowing into and out of the country as a result of financial transactions.

FOREIGN TRADE: The latest imports and exports figures are given, usually for 1990, but there may be exceptional factors at work (for example, war or sanctions).

INFANT MORTALITY: The number of deaths under one year per 1,000 live births.

LIFE EXPECTANCY: The age to which a female or male child born today, applying current rates of mortality, could expect to live.

INTRODUCTION TO
WORLD
GEOGRAPHY

PLANET EARTH

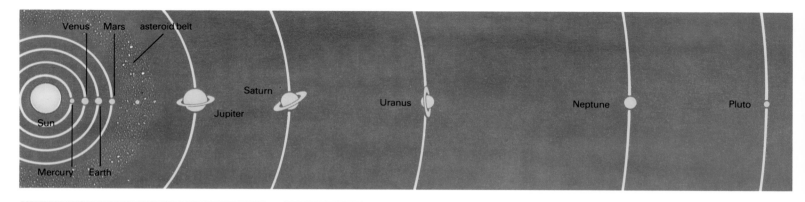

Venus Mars asteroid belt

Saturn

Uranus

Neptune

Pluto

Sun

Jupiter

Mercury Earth

THE SOLAR SYSTEM

A minute part of one of the billions of galaxies (collections of stars) that comprise the Universe, the Solar System lies some 27,000 light-years from the centre of our own galaxy, the 'Milky Way'. Thought to be over 4,700 million years old, it consists of a central sun with nine planets and their moons revolving around it, attracted by its gravitational pull. The planets orbit the Sun in the same direction – anti-clockwise when viewed from the Northern Heavens – and almost in the same plane. Their orbital paths, however, vary enormously.

The Sun's diameter is 109 times that of Earth, and the temperature at its core – caused by continuous thermonuclear fusions of hydrogen into helium – is estimated to be 15 million degrees Celsius. It is the Solar System's only source of light and heat.

PROFILE OF THE PLANETS

	Mean distance from Sun (million km)	Mass (Earth = 1)	Period of orbit	Period of rotation (in days)	Diameter (km)	Number of known satellites
Mercury	58.3	0.06	88 days	58.67	4,878	0
Venus	107.7	0.8	224.7 days	243.0	12,104	0
Earth	149.6	1.0	365.24 days	0.99	12,756	1
Mars	227.3	0.1	1.88 years	1.02	6,794	2
Jupiter	777.9	317.8	11.86 years	0.41	142,800	16
Saturn	1427.1	95.2	29.63 years	0.42	120,000	17
Uranus	2872.3	14.5	83.97 years	0.45	52,000	15
Neptune	4502.7	17.2	164.8 years	0.67	48,400	8
Pluto	5894.2	0.002	248.63 years	6.38	2,400	1

All planetary orbits are elliptical in form, but only Pluto and Mercury follow paths that deviate noticeably from a circular one. Near Perihelion - its closest approach to the Sun - Pluto actually passes inside the orbit of Neptune, an event that last occurred in 1983. Pluto will not regain its station as outermost planet until February 1999.

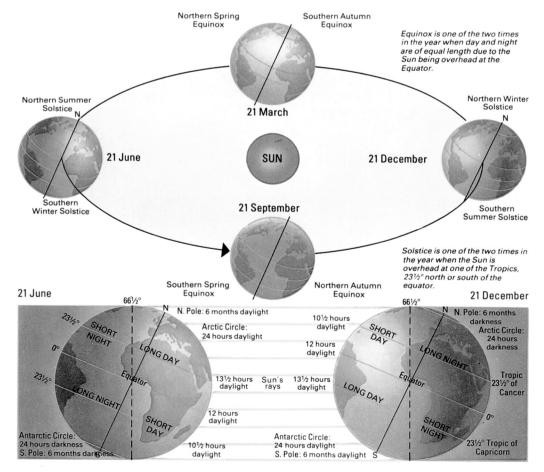

Northern Spring Equinox

Southern Autumn Equinox

Equinox is one of the two times in the year when day and night are of equal length due to the Sun being overhead at the Equator.

Northern Summer Solstice

21 March

Northern Winter Solstice

21 June

SUN

21 December

Southern Winter Solstice

21 September

Southern Summer Solstice

Southern Spring Equinox

Northern Autumn Equinox

Solstice is one of the two times in the year when the Sun is overhead at one of the Tropics, 23½° north or south of the equator.

21 June
66½°
N
23½° SHORT NIGHT
0° LONG DAY
23½° Equator LONG NIGHT
SHORT DAY
Antarctic Circle: 24 hours darkness
S. Pole: 6 months darkness

N. Pole: 6 months daylight
Arctic Circle: 24 hours daylight
10½ hours daylight
12 hours daylight
13½ hours daylight Sun's rays 13½ hours daylight
12 hours daylight
10½ hours daylight
Antarctic Circle: 24 hours daylight
S. Pole: 6 months daylight

21 December
66½°
N N. Pole: 6 months darkness
10½ hours daylight Arctic Circle: 24 hours darkness
SHORT DAY
12 hours daylight LONG NIGHT
Equator Tropic 23½° of Cancer
LONG DAY
0°
SHORT NIGHT
S 23½° Tropic of Capricorn

THE SEASONS

The Earth revolves around the Sun once a year in an 'anti-clockwise' direction, tilted at a constant angle 66½°. In June, the northern hemisphere is tilted towards the Sun: as a result it receives more hours of sunshine in a day and therefore has its warmest season, summer. By December, the Earth has rotated halfway round the Sun so that the southern hemisphere is tilted towards the Sun and has its summer; the hemisphere that is tilted away from the Sun has winter. On 21 June the Sun is directly overhead at the Tropic of Cancer (23½° N), and this is midsummer in the northern hemisphere. Midsummer in the southern hemisphere occurs on 21 December, when the Sun is overhead at the Tropic of Capricorn (23½° S).

DAY & NIGHT

The Sun appears to rise in the east, reach its highest point at noon, and then set in the west, to be followed by night. In reality it is not the Sun that is moving but the Earth revolving from west to east. Due to the tilting of the Earth the length of day and night varies from place to place and month to month.

At the summer solstice in the northern hemisphere (21 June), the Arctic has total daylight and the Antarctic total darkness. The opposite occurs at the winter solstice (21 December). At the equator, the length of day and night are almost equal all year, at latitude 30° the length of day varies from about 14 hours to 10 hours, and at latitude 50° from about 16 hours to about 8 hours.

Year: the time taken by the Earth to revolve around the Sun, or 365.24 days.

Month: the approximate time taken by the Moon to revolve around the Earth. The 12 months of the year in fact vary from 28 (29 in a Leap Year) to 31 days.

Week: an artificial period of 7 days, not based on astronomical time.

Day: the time taken by the Earth to complete one rotation on its axis.

Hour: 24 hours make one day. Usually the day is divided into hours AM (ante meridiem or before noon) and PM (post meridiem or after noon), although most timetables now use the 24-hour system, from midnight to midnight.

SUNRISE

SUNSET

THE MOON

Distance from Earth: 356,410 km - 406,685 km; Mean diameter: 3,475.1 km; Mass: approx. 1/81 that of Earth; Surface gravity: one sixth of Earth's; Daily range of temperature at lunar equator: 200°C; Average orbital speed: 3,683 km/h

PHASES OF THE MOON

| New moon | Crescent moon | Half moon, first quarter | Gibbous moon | Full moon | Waning moon | Half moon, third quarter | Old moon |

The Moon rotates more slowly than the Earth, making one complete turn on its axis in just over 27 days. Since this corresponds to its period of revolution around the Earth, the Moon always presents the same hemisphere or face to us, and we never see 'the dark side'. The interval between one full Moon and the next (and between new Moons) is about $29\frac{1}{2}$ days - a lunar month. The apparent changes in the shape of the Moon are caused by its changing position in relation to the Earth; like the planets, it produces no light of its own and shines only by reflecting the rays of the Sun.

ECLIPSES

When the Moon passes between the Sun and the Earth it causes a partial eclipse of the Sun (1) if the Earth passes through the Moon's outer shadow (P), or a total eclipse (2) if the inner cone shadow crosses the Earth's surface. In a lunar eclipse, the Earth's shadow crosses the Moon and, again, provides either a partial or total eclipse. Eclipses of the Sun and the Moon do not occur every month because of the 5° difference between the plane of the Moon's orbit and the plane in which the Earth moves. In the 1990s only 14 lunar eclipses are possible, for example, seven partial and seven total; each is visible only from certain, and variable, parts of the world. The same period witnesses 13 solar eclipses - six partial (or annular) and seven total.

Partial eclipse (1)

Total eclipse (2)

Lunar eclipse

TIDES

The daily rise and fall of the ocean's tides are the result of the gravitational pull of the Moon and that of the Sun, though the effect of the latter is only 46.6% as strong as that of the Moon. This effect is greatest on the hemisphere facing the Moon and causes a tidal 'bulge'. When lunar and solar forces pull together, with Sun, Earth and Moon in line (near new and full Moons), higher 'spring tides' (and lower low tides) occur; when lunar and solar forces are least coincidental with the Sun and Moon at an angle (near the Moon's first and third quarters), 'neap tides' occur, which have a small tidal range.

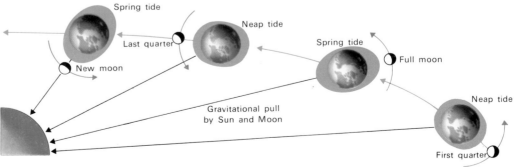

Spring tide
Neap tide
Last quarter
Spring tide
New moon
Full moon
Neap tide
Gravitational pull by Sun and Moon
First quarter

RESTLESS EARTH

THE EARTH'S STRUCTURE

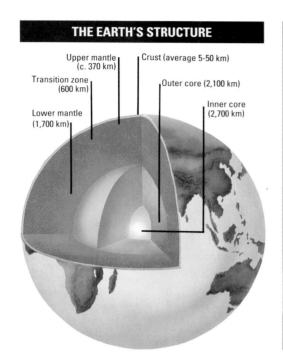

Upper mantle (c. 370 km)
Crust (average 5-50 km)
Transition zone (600 km)
Outer core (2,100 km)
Lower mantle (1,700 km)
Inner core (2,700 km)

CONTINENTAL DRIFT

About 200 million years ago the original Pangaea land mass began to split into two continental groups, which further separated over time to produce the present day configuration.

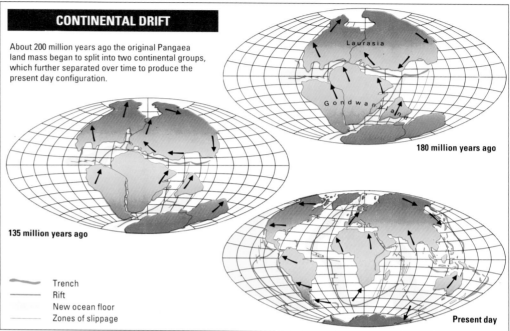

Laurasia

Gondwanaland

180 million years ago

135 million years ago

Present day

Trench
Rift
New ocean floor
Zones of slippage

EARTHQUAKES

Earthquake magnitude is usually rated according to either the Richter or the Modified Mercalli scale, both devised by seismologists in the 1930s. The Richter scale measures absolute earthquake power with mathematical precision: each step upwards represents a tenfold increase in shockwave amplitude. Theoretically, there is no upper limit, but the largest earthquakes measured have been rated at between 8.8 and 8.9. The 12–point Mercalli scale, based on observed effects, is often more meaningful, ranging from I (earthquakes noticed only by seismographs) to XII (total destruction); intermediate points include V (people awakened at night; unstable objects overturned), VII (collapse of ordinary buildings; chimneys and monuments fall) and IX (conspicuous cracks in ground; serious damage to reservoirs).

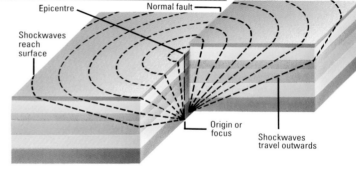

Epicentre
Normal fault
Shockwaves reach surface
Origin or focus
Shockwaves travel outwards

NOTABLE EARTHQUAKES SINCE 1900

Year	Location	Mag.	Deaths
1906	San Francisco, USA	8.3	503
1906	Valparaiso, Chile	8.6	22,000
1908	Messina, Italy	7.5	83,000
1915	Avezzano, Italy	7.5	30,000
1920	Gansu (Kansu), China	8.6	180,000
1923	Yokohama, Japan	8.3	143,000
1927	Nan Shan, China	8.3	200,000
1932	Gansu (Kansu), China	7.6	70,000
1934	Bihar, India/Nepal	8.4	10,700
1935	Quetta, India*	7.5	60,000
1939	Chillan, Chile	8.3	28,000
1939	Erzincan, Turkey	7.9	30,000
1960	Agadir, Morocco	5.8	12,000
1962	Khorasan, Iran	7.1	12,230
1963	Skopje, Yugoslavia	6.0	1,000
1964	Anchorage, Alaska	8.4	131
1968	N. E. Iran	7.4	12,000
1970	N. Peru	7.7	66,794
1972	Managua, Nicaragua	6.2	5,000
1974	N. Pakistan	6.3	5,200
1976	Guatemala	7.5	22,778
1976	Tangshan, China	8.2	650,000
1978	Tabas, Iran	7.7	25,000
1980	El Asnam, Algeria	7.3	20,000
1980	S. Italy	7.2	4,800
1985	Mexico City, Mexico	8.1	4,200
1988	N.W. Armenia, USSR	6.8	55,000
1990	N. Iran	7.7	36,000

The highest magnitude recorded on the Richter scale was 8.9, in Japan on 2 March 1933 (2,990 deaths). The most devastating quake ever was in Shaanxi (Shensi) province, central China, on 24 January 1566, when an estimated 830,000 people were killed.

* now Pakistan

DISTRIBUTION OF EARTHQUAKES

Major earthquake zones
Areas experiencing frequent earthquakes

Arctic Circle
Tropic of Cancer
Equator
Tropic of Capricorn
Antarctic Circle

Earthquakes are a series of rapid vibrations originating from the slipping or faulting of parts of the Earth's crust when stresses within build up to breaking point. They usually happen at depths varying from 8 km to 30 km. Severe earthquakes cause extensive damage when they take place in populated areas, destroying structures and severing communications. Most initial loss of life occurs due to secondary causes such as falling masonry, fires and flooding.

PLATE TECTONICS

The drifting of the continents is a feature unique to Planet Earth. The complementary, almost jigsaw-puzzle fit of the coastlines on each side of the Atlantic Ocean inspired Alfred Wegener's theory of continental drift in 1915. The theory suggested that an ancient super-continent, which Wegener named Pangaea, incorporated all of the Earth's land masses and gradually split up to form today's continents.

The original debate about continental drift was a prelude to a more radical idea: plate tectonics. The basic theory is that the Earth's crust is made up of a series of rigid plates which float on a soft layer of the mantle and are moved about by continental convection currents in the Earth's interior. These plates diverge and converge along clear margins marked by earthquakes, volcanoes and other seismic activity. Plates diverge from mid-ocean ridges where molten lava pushes upwards and forces the plates apart at a rate of up to 40mm a year; converging plates form either a trench (where the oceanic plate sinks below the lighter continental rock) or mountain ranges (where two continents collide).

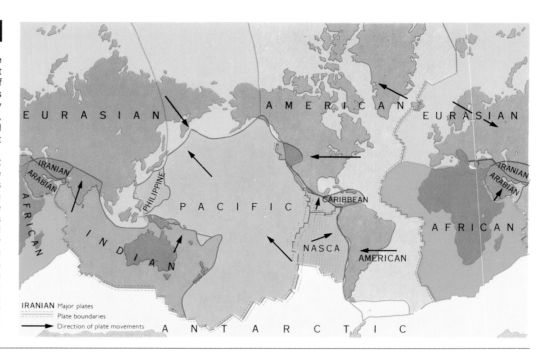

IRANIAN Major plates
Plate boundaries
Direction of plate movements

VOLCANOES

The word 'volcano' derives from the island of Vulcano off Sicily, in the Mediterranean Sea. In classical times the people of this area thought that Vulcano was the chimney of the forge of Vulcan, blacksmith of the Roman gods. Today volcanoes might be the subject of scientific study but they remain both dramatic and unpredictable, if not exactly supernatural: in 1991 Mount Pinatubo, 100 kilometres north of the Philippines capital Manila, suddenly burst into life after more than six centuries of lying dormant.

Most of the world's active volcanoes occur in a belt around the Pacific Ocean, on the edge of the Pacific plate, called the 'ring of fire'. Indonesia has the greatest concentration with 90 volcanoes, 12 of which are active. The most famous, Krakatau, erupted in 1883 with such force that the resulting tidal wave killed 36,000 people and tremors were felt as far away as Australia.

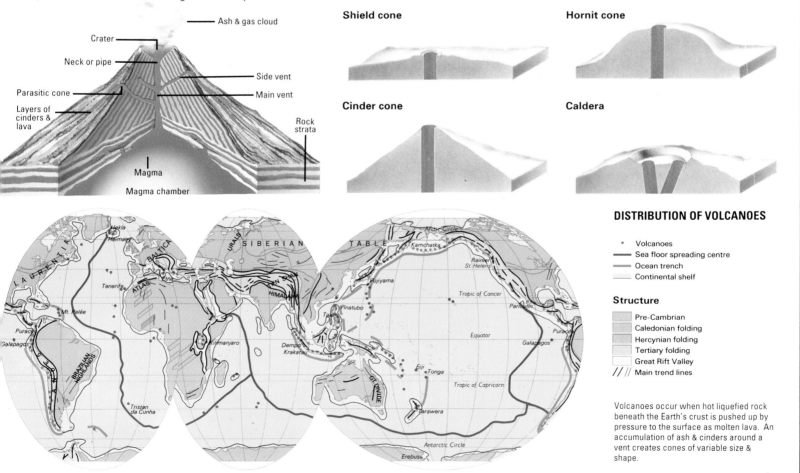

Shield cone

Hornit cone

Cinder cone

Caldera

DISTRIBUTION OF VOLCANOES

- Volcanoes
— Sea floor spreading centre
— Ocean trench
— Continental shelf

Structure

  Pre-Cambrian
  Caledonian folding
  Hercynian folding
  Tertiary folding
  Great Rift Valley
/// Main trend lines

Volcanoes occur when hot liquefied rock beneath the Earth's crust is pushed up by pressure to the surface as molten lava. An accumulation of ash & cinders around a vent creates cones of variable size & shape.

5

LANDSCAPE

Above and below the surface of the oceans, the features of the Earth's crust are constantly changing. The phenomenal forces generated by convection currents in the molten core of our planet carry the vast segments or 'plates' of the crust across the globe in an endless cycle of creation and destruction. A continent may travel little more than 25 millimetres [one inch] per year yet in the vast span of geological time, this process throws up giant mountain ranges and creates new land.

Destruction of the landscape, however, begins as soon as it is formed. Wind, water, ice and sea, the main agents of erosion, mount a constant assault that even the hardest rocks can not withstand. Mountain peaks may dwindle by as little as a few millimetres each year, but if they are not uplifted by further movements of the crust they will eventually be reduced to rubble. Water is the most powerful destroyer – it has been estimated that 100 billion tonnes of rock is washed into the oceans every year.

Rivers and glaciers, like the sea itself, generate much of their effect through abrasion – pounding the landscape with the debris they carry with them. But as well as destroying they also create new landscapes, many of them spectacular: vast deltas like the Mississippi and the Nile, or the fjords cut by glaciers in British Columbia, Norway and New Zealand.

THE SPREADING EARTH

The vast ridges that divide the Earth's crust beneath each of the world's oceans mark the boundaries between tectonic plates which are moving gradually in opposite directions. As the plates shift apart, molten magma rises from the Earth's core to seal the rift and the sea floor slowly spreads towards the continental landmasses. The rate of spreading has been calculated by magnetic analysis of the rock at 40 mm [1.5 in] a year in the North Atlantic. Underwater volcanoes mark the line where the continental rise begins. As the plates meet, much of the denser ocean crust dips beneath the continental plate and melts back to the magma.

THE SPREADING EARTH

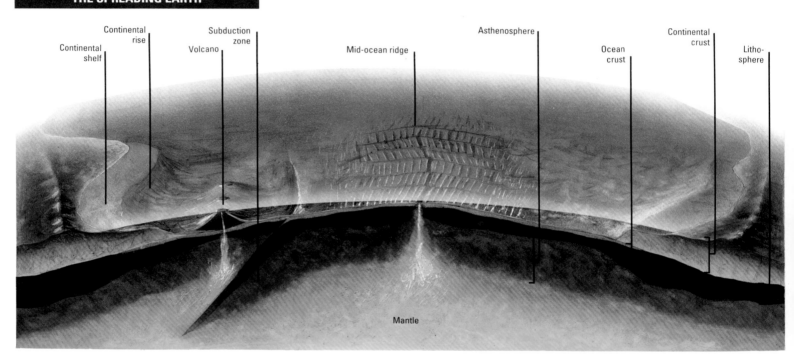

Continental shelf — Continental rise — Volcano — Subduction zone — Mid-ocean ridge — Asthenosphere — Ocean crust — Continental crust — Lithosphere — Mantle

MOUNTAIN BUILDING

Mountains are formed when pressures on the Earth's crust caused by continental drift become so intense that the surface buckles or cracks. This happens most dramatically where two tectonic plates collide : the Rockies, Andes, Alps, Urals and Himalayas resulted from such impacts. These are all known as fold mountains, because they were formed by the compression of the rocks, forcing the surface to bend and fold like a crumpled rug.

The other main building process is when the crust fractures to create faults, allowing rock to be forced upwards in large blocks; or when the pressure of magma within the crust forces the surface to bulge into a dome, or erupts to form a volcano. Large mountain ranges may reveal a combination of those features; the Alps, for example, have been compressed so violently that the folds are fragmented by numerous faults and intrusions of molten rock.

Over millions of years, even the greatest mountain ranges can be reduced by erosion to a flat landscape known as a peneplain.

Types of fold: Geographers give different names to the degrees of fold that result from continuing pressure on the rock strata. A simple fold may be symmetric, with even slopes on either side, but as the pressure builds up, one slope becomes steeper and the fold becomes asymmetric. Later, the ridge or 'anticline' at the top of the fold may slide over the lower ground or 'syncline' to form a recumbent fold. Eventually, the rock strata may break under the pressure to form an overthrust and finally a nappe fold.

Symmetric — Asymmetric — Recumbent — Overthrust — Nappe

Types of fault: Faults are classified by the direction in which the blocks of rock have moved. A normal fault results when a vertical movement causes the surface to break apart; compression causes a reverse fault. Sideways movement causes shearing, known as a strike-slip fault. When the rock breaks in two places, the central block may be pushed up in a horst fault, or sink in a graben fault.

Normal — Reverse — Strike-slip — Horst — Graben

SHAPING FORCES: GLACIERS

Many of the world's most dramatic landscapes have been carved by glaciers. During the Ice Ages of the Pleistocene Era (over 12,000 years ago) up to a third of the land surface was glaciated; even today a tenth is covered in ice. Glaciers are formed from compressed snow called névé accumulating in a valley head or cirque. Slowly the glacier moves downhill scraping away debris from the mountains and valleys through which it passes. The debris, or moraine, adds to the abrasive power of the ice.

The rate of movement can vary from a few centimetres to several metres a day but the end of the glacier may not reach the bottom of the valley: the position of the snout depends on the rate at which the ice melts. Glaciers create numerous distinctive landscape features from arête ridges and pyramidal peaks to ice-dammed lakes and truncated spurs, with the U-shape distinguishing a glacial valley from one cut by a river.

SHAPING FORCES: RIVERS

From their origins as upland rills and streams channelling rainfall, or as springs releasing water that has seeped into the ground, all rivers are incessantly at work cutting and shaping the landscape on their way to the sea. In highland regions their flow may be rapid, pounding rocks and boulders with enough violence to cut deep gorges and V-shaped valleys through softer rocks, or tumble as waterfalls over harder ones.

As they reach more gentle slopes, rivers release some of the pebbles they have carried downstream and flow more slowly, broadening out and raising levees or ridges along their banks by depositing mud and sand. In lowland plains, where the gradient is minimal, the river drifts into meanders, depositing deep layers of sediment especially on the inside of each bend, where the flow is weakest. Here farmers may dig drainage ditches and artificial levees to keep the floodplain dry.

As the river finally reaches the sea, it deposits all its remaining sediments, and estuaries are formed where the tidal currents are strong enough to remove them; if not, the debris creates a delta, through which the river cuts outlet streams known as distributaries.

Arête — Col — Ice-dammed lake — U-shaped valley — Lateral moraine — Truncated spur — Hanging valley — Crevasse — Medial moraine — Terminal moraine — Snout — Drumlins — Outwash plain

V-shaped valley — Gorge — Waterfall — Tree line — Natural levee — Meanders — Floodplain — YOUTH — MATURITY — OLD AGE — Sediment — Man-made levee

Headland — Cliff — Wave-cut platform — Wave-built terrace — Arch — Stack — Cove

SHAPING FORCES: THE SEA

Under the constant assault from tides and currents, wind and waves, coastlines change faster than most landscape features, both by erosion and by the build-up of sand and pebbles carried by the sea. In severe storms, giant waves pound the shoreline with rocks and boulders, and frequently destroy concrete coastal defences; but even in quieter conditions, the sea steadily erodes cliffs and headlands, creating new land in the form of sand-dunes, spits and salt marshes.

Where the coastline is formed from soft rocks such as sandstones, debris may fall evenly and be carried away by currents from shelving beaches. In areas with harder rock, the waves may cut steep cliffs and form underwater platforms; eroded debris is deposited as a terrace. Bays are formed when sections of soft rock are carved away between headlands of harder rock. These are then battered by waves from both sides, until the headlands are eventually reduced to rock arches and stacks.

OCEANS

THE GREAT OCEANS

Relative sizes of the world's oceans

- Pacific
- Atlantic
- Indian
- Arctic

4%
21%
49%
26%

In a strict geographical sense there are only three true oceans - the Atlantic, Indian and Pacific. The legendary 'Seven Seas' would require these to be divided at the equator and the addition of the Arctic Ocean - which accounts for less than 4% of the total sea area. The International Hydrographic Bureau does not recognise the Antarctic Ocean (even less the 'Southern Ocean') as a separate entity.

The Earth is a watery planet: more than 70% of its surface - over 360,000,000 square kilometres - is covered by the oceans and seas. The mighty Pacific alone accounts for nearly 36% of the total, and 49% of the sea area. Gravity holds in around 1400 million cubic kilometres of water, of which over 97% is saline.

The vast underwater world starts in the shallows of the seaside and plunges to depths of more than 11,000 metres. The continental shelf, part of the land mass, drops gently to around 200 metres; here the seabed falls away suddenly at an angle of 3° to 6° – the continental slope. The third stage, called the continental rise, is more gradual with gradients varying from 1 in 100 to 1 in 700. At an average depth of 5,000 metres there begins the aptly-named abyssal plain, massive submarine depths where sunlight fails to penetrate and few creatures can survive.

From these plains rise volcanoes which, taken from base to top, rival and even surpass the biggest continental mountains in height. Mount Kea, on Hawaii, reaches a total of 10,203 metres, some 1,355 metres more than Mount Everest, though only 4,205 is visible above sea level.

In addition there are underwater mountain chains up to 1,000 kilometres across, whose peaks sometimes appear above sea level as islands such as Iceland and Tristan da Cunha.

THE OCEAN DEPTHS

Average and maximum depths of the world's great oceans, in metres

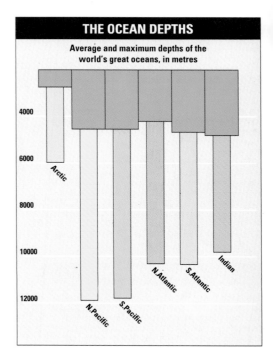

4000
6000
8000
10000
12000

Arctic
N.Pacific
S.Pacific
N.Atlantic
S.Atlantic
Indian

OCEAN CURRENTS

[Cold currents are shown in blue, warm currents in red]

WINTER IN NORTHERN HEMISPHERE

SUMMER IN NORTHERN HEMISPHERE

Moving immense quantities of energy as well as billions of tonnes of water every hour, the ocean currents are a vital part of the great heat engine that drives the Earth's climate. They themselves are produced by a twofold mechanism. At the surface, winds push huge masses of water before them; in the deep ocean, below an abrupt temperature gradient that separates the churning surface waters from the still depths, density variations cause slow vertical movements. The pattern of circulation of the great surface currents is determined by the displacement known as the Coriolis effect. As the Earth turns beneath a moving object - whether it is a tennis ball or a vast mass of water - it appears to be deflected to one side. The deflection is most obvious near the equator, where the Earth's surface is spinning eastward at 1700 km/h; currents moving poleward are curved clockwise in the northern hemisphere and anti-clockwise in the southern.

The result is a system of spinning circles known as gyres. The Coriolis effect piles up water on the left of each gyre, creating a narrow, fast-moving stream that is matched by a slower, broader returning current on the right. North and south of the equator, the fastest currents are located in the west and in the east respectively. In each case, warm water moves from the equator and cold water returns to it. Cold currents often bring an upwelling of nutrients with them, supporting the world's most economically important fisheries.

Depending on the prevailing winds, some currents on or near the equator may reverse their direction in the course of the year - a seasonal variation on which Asian monsoon rains depend, and whose occasional failure can bring disaster to millions.

FISHING

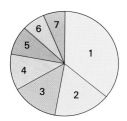

Main commercial fishing areas

Percentage of world catch

1. North Pacific 36%
2. North Atlantic 17%
3. South Pacific 14%
4. Central Pacific 11%
5. Central Atlantic 9%
6. South Atlantic 7%
7. Indian 6%

Leading fishing nations

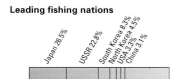

Japan 26.5% USSR 22.8% South Korea 8.3% North Korea 4.5% USA 4.3% China 3.1%

World total (1989): 14,143,923 tonnes

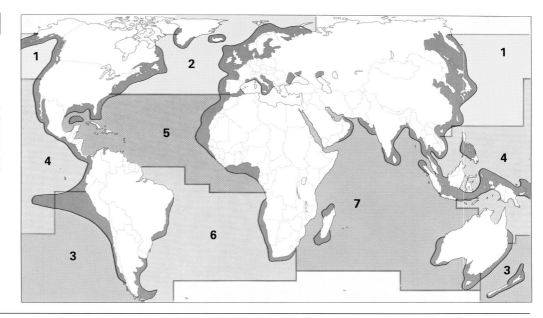

MARINE POLLUTION

Sources of marine oil pollution (1980s)

1%, 1.5%, 3%, 3.5%, 6%, 7.5%, 9%, 12.5%, 12%, 22%, 22%

- Tanker operations
- Municipal wastes
- Tanker accidents
- Bilge and fuel oils
- Natural seeps
- Industrial waste
- Urban runoff
- Coastal oil refining
- Offshore oil rigs
- River runoffs

Other

OIL SPILLS

Major oil spills from tankers & combined carriers

Year	Vessel	Location	Spill (barrels)*	Cause
1979	Atlantic Empress	West Indies	1,890,000	collision
1983	Castillo De Bellver	South Africa	1,760,000	fire
1978	Amoco Cadiz	France	1,628,000	grounding
1988	Odyssey	Canada	1,000,000	fire
1967	Torrey Canyon	UK	909,000	grounding
1972	Sea Star	Gulf of Oman	902,250	collision
1977	Hawaiian Patriot	Hawaiian Is.	742,500	fire
1979	Independenta	Turkey	696,350	collision
1976	Urquiola	Spain	670,000	grounding
1980	Irenes Serenade	Greece	600,000	fire
1989	Khark V	Morocco	560,000	fire

Other sources of major oil spills

Year	Vessel	Location	Spill (barrels)	Cause
1983	Nowruz oilfield	Persian Gulf	4,250,000 †	war
1979	Ixtoc 1 oilwell	Gulf of Mexico	4,200,000	blow-out
1991	Kuwait	Persian Gulf	2,500,000	war

* 1 barrel = 0.136 tonnes/159 lit./35 Imperial gal./42 US gal.   † estimated

RIVER POLLUTION

Sources of river pollution, USA (1987)

1%, 2%, 9%, 4%, 5%, 6%, 9%, 64%

- Agriculture
- Mining
- Forestry
- Urban runoff
- Hydro-engineering
- Construction
- Land disposal

Other

WATER POLLUTION

- Severely polluted sea areas & lakes
- Less polluted sea areas & lakes
- Areas of frequent oil pollution by shipping
- Major oil tanker spills ◤
- Major oil rig blow outs ▲
- Offshore dumpsites for industrial & municipal waste ▼
- Severely polluted rivers & estuaries

The most notorious tanker spillage of the 1980s occurred when the Exxon Valdez ran aground in Prince William Sound, Alaska in 1989, spilling 267,000 barrels of crude oil close to shore in a sensitive ecological area. This rates as the world's 28th worst spill in terms of volume.

CLIMATE

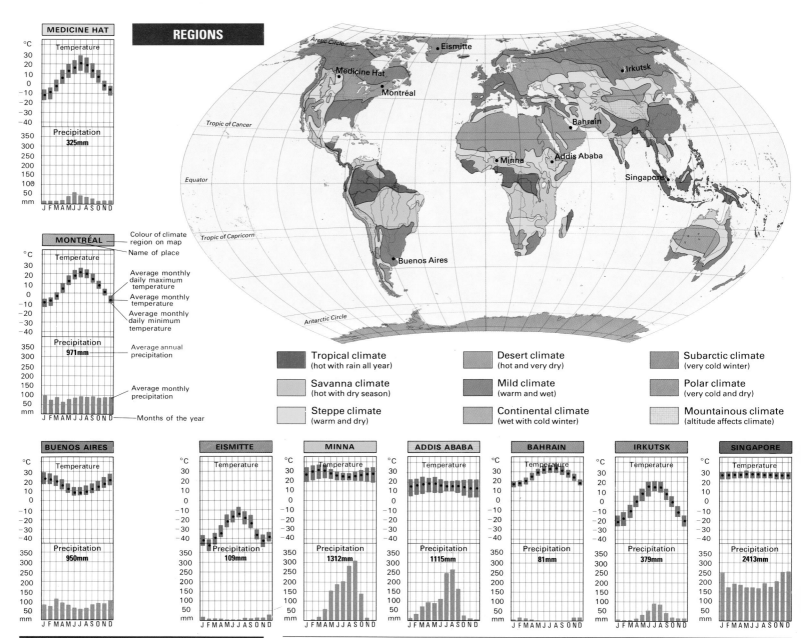

REGIONS

MEDICINE HAT

°C
Temperature
30
20
10
0
-10
-20
-30
-40

Precipitation
350 **325mm**
300
250
200
150
100
50
mm
J F M A M J J A S O N D

MONTRÉAL ——— Colour of climate region on map
——— Name of place

°C
Temperature
30
20
10
0
-10
-20
-30
-40

——— Average monthly daily maximum temperature
——— Average monthly temperature
——— Average monthly daily minimum temperature

Precipitation
350 **971mm**
300
250
200
150
100
50
mm
J F M A M J J A S O N D

——— Average annual precipitation

——— Average monthly precipitation

——— Months of the year

REGIONS

Arctic Circle
Eismitte
Medicine Hat
Montréal
Irkutsk
Tropic of Cancer
Bahrain
Minna
Addis Ababa
Equator
Singapore
Tropic of Capricorn
Buenos Aires
Antarctic Circle

Legend:

■ Tropical climate (hot with rain all year)
■ Savanna climate (hot with dry season)
■ Steppe climate (warm and dry)

■ Desert climate (hot and very dry)
■ Mild climate (warm and wet)
■ Continental climate (wet with cold winter)

■ Subarctic climate (very cold winter)
■ Polar climate (very cold and dry)
■ Mountainous climate (altitude affects climate)

BUENOS AIRES
°C
Temperature
30
20
10
0
-10
-20
-30
-40
Precipitation
350 **950mm**
300
250
200
150
100
50
mm
J F M A M J J A S O N D

EISMITTE
°C
Temperature
30
20
10
0
-10
-20
-30
-40
Precipitation
350 **109mm**
300
250
200
150
100
50
mm
J F M A M J J A S O N D

MINNA
°C
Temperature
30
20
10
0
-10
-20
-30
-40
Precipitation
350 **1312mm**
300
250
200
150
100
50
mm
J F M A M J J A S O N D

ADDIS ABABA
°C
Temperature
30
20
10
0
-10
-20
-30
-40
Precipitation
350 **1115mm**
300
250
200
150
100
50
mm
J F M A M J J A S O N D

BAHRAIN
°C
Temperature
30
20
10
0
-10
-20
-30
-40
Precipitation
350 **81mm**
300
250
200
150
100
50
mm
J F M A M J J A S O N D

IRKUTSK
°C
Temperature
30
20
10
0
-10
-20
-30
-40
Precipitation
350 **379mm**
300
250
200
150
100
50
mm
J F M A M J J A S O N D

SINGAPORE
°C
Temperature
30
20
10
0
-10
-20
-30
-40
Precipitation
350 **2413mm**
300
250
200
150
100
50
mm
J F M A M J J A S O N D

CLIMATE RECORDS

Temperature

Highest recorded temperature: Al Aziziyah, Libya, 58°C [136.4°F], 13 Sep. 1922.

Highest mean annual temperature: Dallol, Ethiopia, 34.4°C [94°F], 1960-66.

Longest heatwave: Marble Bar, W. Australia, 162 days over 38°C [100°F], 23 Oct. 1923 - 7 Apr. 1924.

Lowest recorded temperature (outside poles): Verkhoyansk, Siberia, USSR -68°C [-90°F], 6 Feb. 1933. Verkhoyansk also registered the greatest annual range of temperature: - 70°C to 37°C [-94°F to 98°F].

Lowest mean annual temperature: Polus Nedostupnosti, Pole of Cold, Antarctica, -57.8°C [-72°F].

Precipitation

Driest place: Arica, N. Chile, 0.8mm [0.3 in] per year (60-year average).

Longest drought: Calama, N. Chile: no recorded rainfall in 400 years to 1971.

Wettest place (average): Tututendo, Colombia: mean annual rainfall 11,770 mm [463.4 in].

Wettest place (12 months): Cherrapunji, Meghalaya, N.E. India, 26,470 mm [1,040 in], Aug. 1860 to Aug. 1861. Cherrapunji also holds the record for rainfall in one month: 930 mm [37 in] July 1861.

Wettest place (24 hours): Cilaos, Réunion, Indian Ocean, 1,870 mm [73.6 in], 15-16 March 1952.

Heaviest hailstones: Gopalganj, Bangladesh, up to 1.02 kg [2.25 lb], 14 Apr. 1986 (killed 92 people).

Heaviest snowfall (continuous): Bessans, Savoie, France, 1730 mm [68 in] in 19 hours, 5-6 Apr. 1969.

Heaviest snowfall (season/year): Paradise Ranger Station, Mt Rainier, Washington, USA, 31,102 mm [1,224.5 in], 19 Feb. 1971 to 18 Feb. 1972.

Pressure & Winds

Highest barometric pressure: Agata, Siberia, USSR, 1,083.8 mb [32 in] at altitude 262 m [862 ft] 31 December 1968.

Lowest barometric pressure: Typhoon Tip, 480 km [300 mls] west of Guam, Pacific Ocean, 870 mb [25.69 in], 12 Oct. 1979.

Highest recorded windspeed: Mt Washington, New Hampshire, USA 371 kph [231 mph], 12 Apr. 1934. This is three times as strong as hurricane force on the Beaufort Scale.

Windiest place: Commonwealth Bay, George V Coast, Antarctica, where gales reach over 320 kph [200 mph].

WINDCHILL FACTOR

In sub-zero weather, even moderate winds significantly reduce effective temperatures. The chart below shows the windchill effect across a range of speeds. Figures in the pink zone are not dangerous to well-clad people; in the blue zone, the risk of serious frostbite is acute.

	Wind speed (km/h)				
	16	32	48	64	80
0°C	-8	-14	-17	-19	-20
-5°C	-14	-21	-25	-27	-28
-10°C	-20	-28	-33	-35	-36
-15°C	-26	-36	-40	-43	-44
-20°C	-32	-42	-48	-51	-52
-25°C	-38	-49	-56	-59	-60
-30°C	-44	-57	-63	-66	-68
-35°C	-51	-64	-72	-74	-76
-40°C	-57	-71	-78	-82	-84
-45°C	-63	-78	-86	-90	-92
-50°C	-69	-85	-94	-98	-100

BEAUFORT WIND SCALE

Named after the 19th-century British naval officer who devised it, the Beaufort Scale assesses wind speed according to its effects. It was originally designed as an aid for sailors, but has since been adapted for use on land.

Scale	Wind speed		Effect
	kph	mph	
0	0-1	0-1	**Calm** Smoke rises vertically
1	1-5	1-3	**Light air** Wind direction shown only by smoke drift
2	6-11	4-7	**Light breeze** Wind felt on face; leaves rustle; vanes moved by wind
3	12-19	8-12	**Gentle breeze** Leaves and small twigs in constant motion; wind extends small flag
4	20-28	13-18	**Moderate** Raises dust and loose paper; small branches move
5	29-38	19-24	**Fresh** Small trees in leaf sway; crested wavelets on inland waters
6	39-49	25-31	**Strong** Large branches move; difficult to use umbrellas; overhead wires whistle
7	50-61	32-38	**Near gale** Whole trees in motion; difficult to walk against wind
8	62-74	39-46	**Gale** Twigs break from trees; walking very difficult
9	75-88	47-54	**Strong gale** Slight structural damage
10	89-102	55-63	**Storm** Trees uprooted; serious structural damage
11	103-117	64-72	**Violent Storm** Widespread damage
12	118+	73+	**Hurricane**

Conversions
°C = (°F - 32) x 5/9;   °F = (°C x 9/5) + 32;   0°C = 32°F
1 in = 25.4 mm;   1 mm = 0.0394 in;   100 mm = 3.94 in

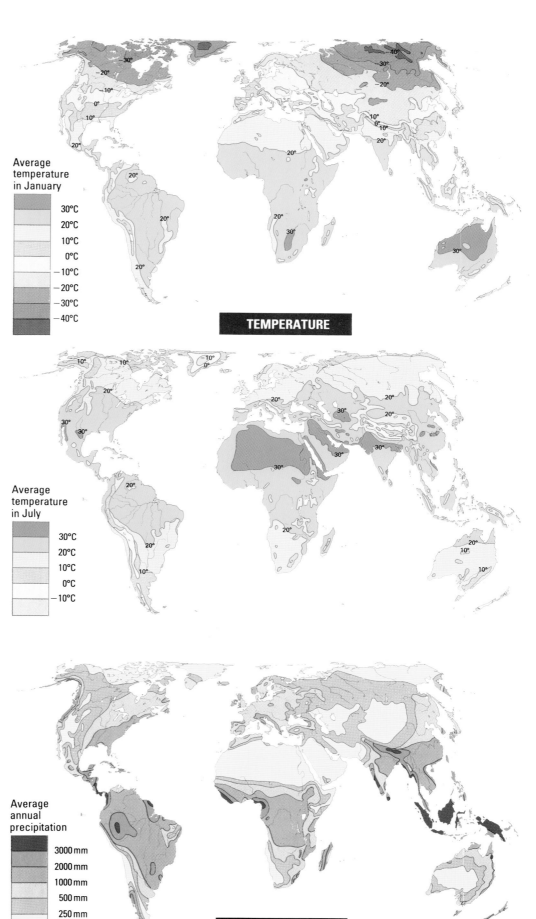

Average temperature in January

- 30°C
- 20°C
- 10°C
- 0°C
- −10°C
- −20°C
- −30°C
- −40°C

TEMPERATURE

Average temperature in July

- 30°C
- 20°C
- 10°C
- 0°C
- −10°C

Average annual precipitation

- 3000 mm
- 2000 mm
- 1000 mm
- 500 mm
- 250 mm

PRECIPITATION

WATER

THE HYDROLOGICAL CYCLE

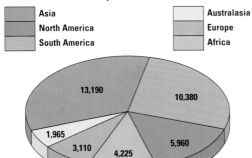

Precipitation on land

Precipitation on ocean

Evaporation from vegetation

Evaporation from soil

Evaporation from lakes & ponds

Evaporation from vegetation & streams

Evaporation from oceans

Intercepted by vegetation
Groundwater to soil
Groundwater to lakes & streams
Groundwater to vegetation
Groundwater to oceans

WATER DISTRIBUTION

The distribution of planetary water, by percentage. Oceans and icecaps together account for more than 99% of the total; the breakdown of the remainder is estimated.

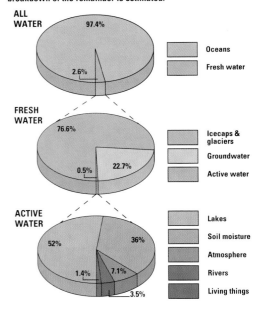

ALL WATER — 97.4%, 2.6%
- Oceans
- Fresh water

FRESH WATER — 76.6%, 0.5%, 22.7%
- Icecaps & glaciers
- Groundwater
- Active water

ACTIVE WATER — 52%, 36%, 1.4%, 7.1%, 3.5%
- Lakes
- Soil moisture
- Atmosphere
- Rivers
- Living things

WATER RUNOFF

Annual freshwater runoff by continent in cubic kilometres

- Asia
- North America
- South America
- Australasia
- Europe
- Africa

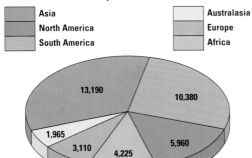

13,190 · 10,380 · 1,965 · 3,110 · 4,225 · 5,960

WATER UTILIZATION

The percentage breakdown of water usage by sector, selected countries (1980s)

Domestic · Industrial · Agriculture

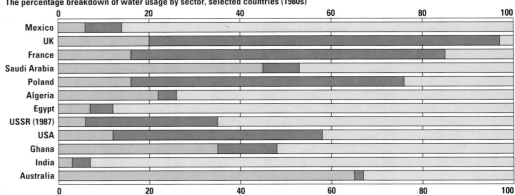

	0	20	40	60	80	100
Mexico						
UK						
France						
Saudi Arabia						
Poland						
Algeria						
Egypt						
USSR (1987)						
USA						
Ghana						
India						
Australia						

WATER SUPPLY

Percentage of total population with access to safe drinking water (latest available year, 1980s)

- Over 90%
- 75 - 90%
- 60 - 75%
- 45 - 60%
- 30 - 45%
- Under 30%

Least well provided countries (rural areas only):

Paraguay	8%	Guinea	15%
Mozambique	12%	Mauritania	17%
Uganda	12%	Malawi	17%
Angola	15%	Morocco	17%

NATURAL VEGETATION

Regional variation in vegetation

- Tundra & mountain vegetation
- Needleleaf evergreen forest
- Mixed needleleaf evergreen & broadleaf deciduous trees
- Broadleaf deciduous woodland
- Mid-latitude grassland
- Evergreen broadleaf & deciduous trees & shrubs
- Semi-desert scrub
- Desert
- Tropical grassland (savanna)
- Tropical broadleaf rainforest & monsoon forest
- Sub-tropical broadleaf & needleleaf forest

The map shows the natural 'climax vegetation' of regions, as dictated by climate and topography. In most cases, however, agricultural activity has drastically altered the vegetation pattern. Western Europe, for example, lost most of its broadleaf forest many centuries ago, while irrigation has turned some natural semi-desert into productive land.

LAND USE BY CONTINENT

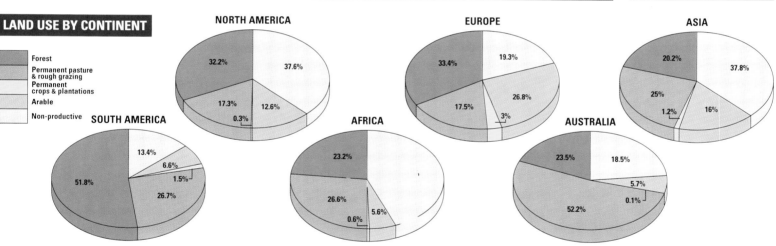

- Forest
- Permanent pasture & rough grazing
- Permanent crops & plantations
- Arable
- Non-productive

NORTH AMERICA
37.6% / 32.2% / 17.3% / 12.6% / 0.3%

EUROPE
19.3% / 33.4% / 17.5% / 26.8% / 3%

ASIA
20.2% / 37.8% / 25% / 1.2% / 16%

SOUTH AMERICA
13.4% / 6.6% / 1.5% / 51.8% / 26.7%

AFRICA
23.2% / 26.6% / 0.6% / 5.6%

AUSTRALIA
23.5% / 18.5% / 5.7% / 0.1% / 52.2%

FORESTRY: PRODUCTION

	Forest & woodland (million hectares)	Annual production (1980s average, million cubic metres)	
		Fuelwood & charcoal	Industrial roundwood
World	*4,121.4*	*1,646.1*	*1,534.8*
USSR (1988)	928.6	85.6	284.9
S. America	867.1	217.0	91.7
N. America	806.6	154.4	538.7
Africa	705.3	384.7	53.4
Asia	497.2	739.1	245.7
Europe	159.1	56.5	292.1
Australasia	158.8	8.8	28.3

PAPER & BOARD

Top producers (1988)*		Top exporters (1988)*	
USA	69,477	Canada	11,420
Japan	24,624	Finland	7,185
Canada	16,638	Sweden	6,377
China	12,645	USA	4,294
USSR	10,750	Germany	3,780

* in thousand tonnes

FORESTRY: DISTRIBUTION

- Main areas of production
- ▲ = 5% of world production of roundwood

ENVIRONMENT

Humans have always had a dramatic effect on their environment, at least since the invention of agriculture almost 10,000 years ago. Generally, the Earth has accepted human interference without obvious ill effects: the complex systems that regulate the global environment have been able to absorb substantial damage while maintaining a stable and comfortable home for the planet's trillions of lifeforms. But advancing human technology and the rapidly-expanding populations it supports are now threatening to overwhelm the Earth's ability to compensate.

Industrial wastes, acid rainfall, desertification and large-scale deforestation: all combine to create environmental change at a rate far faster than the slow cycles of planetary evolution can accommodate. Equipped with chain-saws and flamethrowers, humans can now destroy more forest in a day than their ancestors could in a century, upsetting the balance between plant and animal, carbon dioxide and oxygen, on which all life ultimately depends.

The fossil fuels that power industrial civilisation have pumped enough carbon dioxide and other so-called greenhouse gases into the atmosphere to make climatic change a near-certainty. Chlorofluorocarbons - CFCs - and other man-made chemicals are rapidly eroding the ozone layer, the atmosphere's screen against ultra-violet radiation.

As a result, the Earth's average temperature has risen by approximately 0.5°C since the beginning of the 20th century, and is still rising.

CLIMATIC CHANGE

Carbon dioxide emissions in tonnes per person per year (1980s)

High atmospheric concentrations of heat-absorbing gases, especially carbon dioxide, appear to be causing a steady rise in average temperatures worldwide - up to 1.5°C by the year 2020, according to some estimates. Global warming is likely to bring with it a rise in sea-levels that may flood some of the Earth's most densely populated coastlines.

- Over 10 tonnes of CO_2
- 5 - 10 tonnes of CO_2
- 1 - 5 tonnes of CO_2
- Under 1 tonne of CO_2

—— Coastal areas in danger of flooding from rising sea levels caused by global warming

GREENHOUSE POWER

Relative contributions to the Greenhouse Effect by the major heat-absorbing gases in the atmosphere

The chart combines greenhouse potency and volume. Carbon dioxide has a greenhouse potential of only 1 but its concentration of 350 parts per million, makes it predominate. CFC 12 , with 25,000 times the absorption capacity of CO_2, is present only as 0.00044 ppm.

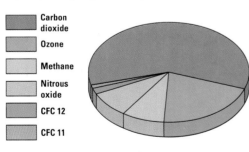

- Carbon dioxide
- Ozone
- Methane
- Nitrous oxide
- CFC 12
- CFC 11

CARBON DIOXIDE

Carbon dioxide released in millions of tonnes (1980s)

Although most of the net increase in atmospheric carbon dioxide comes from fossil fuel combustion, deforestation and changing land use also contribute.

- Fuel burning
- Deforestation

USA 1135, USSR (1987), China, Brazil, Germany, Japan, UK, India, Poland, France, Canada, Mexico

1000, 800, 600, 400, 200

GLOBAL WARMING

The rise in average temperatures caused by carbon dioxide and other greenhouse gases (1960-2020)

- assumes present trends continue
- assumes drastic emissions cuts in the 1990s

C°
+1.5
+1.0
+0.5
0
-0.5

Recorded change   Projected changes

1960 1970 1980 1990 2000 2010 2020

THE GREENHOUSE EFFECT

Carbon dioxide is increased by burning fossil fuels and cutting forests

Carbon Dioxide

Rising temperatures would melt snow and ice

Melting glacial ice could cause oceans to rise

The carbon dioxide traps the heat being reflected from the Earth, although some heat is lost

The warming increases water-vapour in the air, leading to even greater absorption of heat

Existing deserts

Areas with a high
risk of desertification

Areas with a moderate
risk of desertification

Former areas of rainforest

Existing rainforest

DEFORESTATION

Thousands of hectares of forest cleared annually, tropical countries surveyed 1981-85 & 1987-90. Loss as a percentage of remaining stocks is shown in figures on each column.

5200

1.5

3000

2000

1000

0

| 1987-90 | 1981-85 |

Brazil	India	Indonesia	Burma	Thailand	Vietnam	Philippines	Costa Rica	Cameroon
1.5 / 0.4	4.1 / 0.3	0.8 / 0.5	2.1 / 0.3	2.5 / 2.4	2.0 / 0.7	1.5 / 1.0	7.6 / 4.0	0.6 / 0.4

DESERTIFICATION

The result of overcultivation, overgrazing, and overcutting of ground cover for firewood, desertification is also caused by faulty irrigation techniques that leave land too saline or alkaline to support viable crops. Changing rainfall patterns or prolonged droughts exacerbate the process. As much as 60% of the world's croplands and rangelands are in some danger, with 6 million hectares lost altogether every year and a further 21 million rendered agriculturally worthless. Africa is especially badly hit: in Mali the Sahara advanced 350 kilometres southwards in only 20 years.

DEFORESTATION

The Earth's remaining forests are under attack from three directions: expanding agriculture, logging, and growing consumption of fuelwood, often in combination. Sometimes deforestation is the direct result of government policy, as in the efforts made to resettle the urban poor in some parts of Brazil; just as often, it comes about despite state attempts at conservation. Loggers, licensed or unlicensed, blaze a trail into virgin forest, often destroying twice as many trees as they harvest. Landless farmers follow, burning away most of what remains to plant their crops, completing the destruction.

ACID RAIN

Killing trees, poisoning lakes and rivers and eating away buildings, acid rain is mostly produced by sulphur dioxide emissions from industry, although the burning of savanna lands by African farmers has also caused acid downpours on tropical rainforests. By the late 1980s, acid rain had sterilised 4,000 or more of Sweden's lakes and left 45% of Switzerland's alpine conifers dead or dying, while the monuments of Greece were dissolving in Athens' smog. Prevailing wind patterns mean that the acids often fall many hundred kilometres from where the original pollutants were discharged.

ACID RAIN

Acid rainfall & sources of acidic emissions (1980s)

Acid rain is caused when sulphur & nitrogen oxides in the air combine with water vapour to form sulphuric, nitric & other acids.

Regions where sulphur and nitrogen oxides are released in high concentrations, mainly from fossil fuel combustion.

Major cities with high levels of air pollution (including nitrogen & sulphur emissions)

Areas of heavy acid deposition

pH numbers indicate acidity, decreasing from a neutral 7. Normal rain, slightly acid from dissolved carbon dioxide, never exceeds a pH of 5.6.

pH less than 4.0 (most acidic)

pH 4.0 to 4.5

pH 4.5 to 5.0

Areas where acid rain is a potential danger

POPULATION

DEMOGRAPHIC PROFILES

Developed nations such as the UK have populations evenly spread across age groups and, usually, a growing proportion of elderly people. Developing nations fall into a pattern somewhere between that of Kenya and the world model: the great majority of their people are in the younger age groups, about to enter their most fertile years. In time, even Kenya's population profile should resemble the world profile, but the transition will come about only after a few more generations of rapid population growth.

World

Kenya | **China**

CIS (USSR) | **Japan**

USA | **UK**

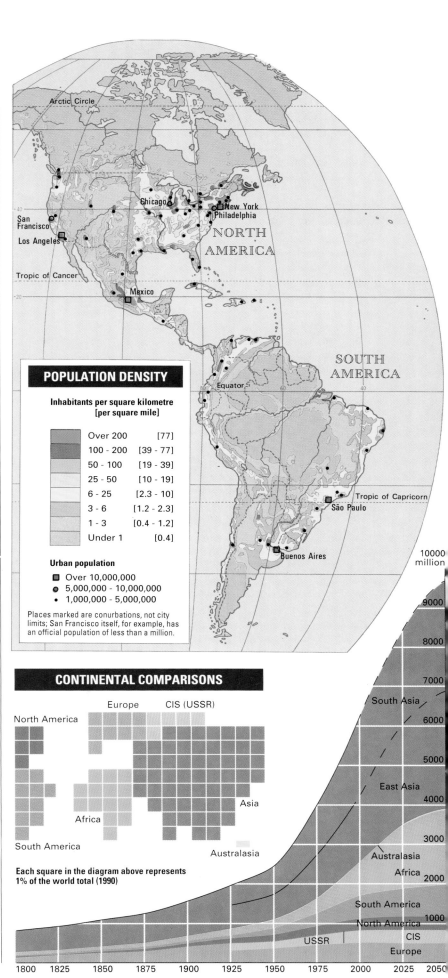

POPULATION DENSITY

Inhabitants per square kilometre [per square mile]

Over 200	[77]
100 - 200	[39 - 77]
50 - 100	[19 - 39]
25 - 50	[10 - 19]
6 - 25	[2.3 - 10]
3 - 6	[1.2 - 2.3]
1 - 3	[0.4 - 1.2]
Under 1	[0.4]

Urban population

- ■ Over 10,000,000
- ◉ 5,000,000 - 10,000,000
- • 1,000,000 - 5,000,000

Places marked are conurbations, not city limits; San Francisco itself, for example, has an official population of less than a million.

CONTINENTAL COMPARISONS

Each square in the diagram above represents 1% of the world total (1990)

MOST POPULOUS NATIONS	[in millions (1989)]					
1. China	1120	9. Pakistan	109	17. Turkey	57
2. India	812	10. Bangladesh	107	18. France	56
3. USA	250	11. Mexico	84	19. Thailand	55
4. Indonesia	179	12. Germany	79	20. Iran	55
5. Brazil	148	13. Vietnam	66	21. Egypt	53
6. Russia	147	14. Philippines	60	22. Ukraine	52
7. Japan	123	15. Italy	58	23. Ethiopia	51
8. Nigeria	109	16. UK	57	24. S. Korea	43

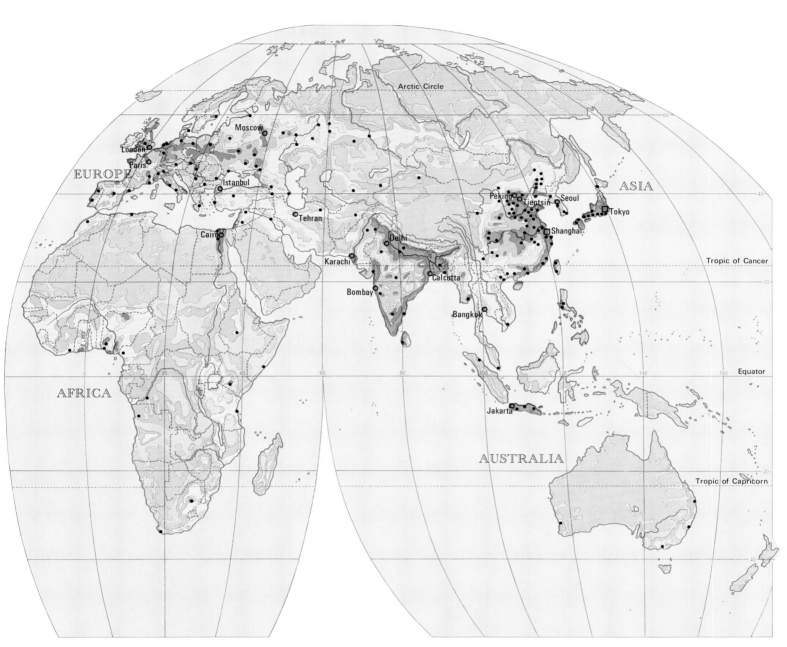

URBAN POPULATION

Percentage of total population living in towns & cities (1990)

Over 75%
50 - 75%
25 - 50%
10 - 25%
Under 10%

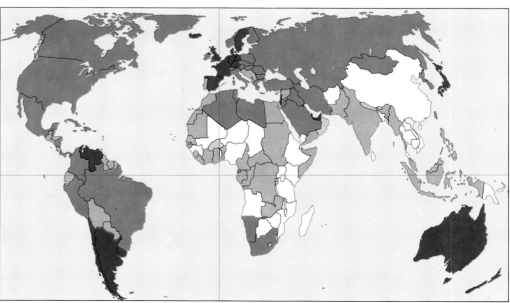

Highest urban population*

Macau	98.7%
Belgium	96.9%
Kuwait	95.6%
Hong Kong	93.2%
UK	92.5%
Israel	91.6%
Iceland	90.5%

Lowest urban population

Bhutan	5.3%
Burundi	7.3%
Rwanda	7.7%
Burkina Faso	9.0%
Nepal	9.6%
Oman	10.0%
Uganda	10.4%

* Several small countries, including Bermuda, Monaco, Singapore & Vatican City, are designated as '100% urban'

THE HUMAN FAMILY

MOTHER TONGUES

Chinese 1069 million (Mandarin 864), English 443, Hindi 352, Spanish 341, Russian 293, Arabic 197, Bengali 184, Portuguese 173, Malay-Indonesian 142, Japanese 125, French 121, German 118, Urdu 92, Punjabi 84, Korean 71.

OFFICIAL LANGUAGES

English 27% of world population, Chinese 19%, Hindi 13.5%, Spanish 5.4%, Russian 5.2%, French 4.2%, Arabic 3.3%, Portuguese 3%, Malay 3%, Bengali 2.9%, Japanese 2.3%

LANGUAGE

1	Slavic
2	Germanic
3	Celtic
4	Romance
5	Greek
6	Albanian
7	Iranian
8	Indo-Aryan
9	Armenian
10	Caucasian
11	Basque
12	Burushaskis
13	Semitic
14	Kushit
15	Berber
16	Khoisan
17	Bantu
18	Sudanese
19	E & C Sudan
20	Nilotic
21	Ural
22	Turkic
23	Mongolian
24	Tungus-Manchu
25	Japanese/Korean
26	Sinitic and other
27	Tibeto-Burman
28	Vietnamese
29	Mon-Khmer
30	Munda
31	Dravidian
32	Andamanese
33	Indonesian
34	Polynesian
35	Melanesian
36	Papuan
37	Australian Abor.
38	Ainu
39	Paleoasiatic
40	Eskimo-Aleut
41	Amerindian

RELIGIOUS ADHERENTS

Christian 1667m
  Roman Catholic 952m
  Protestant 337m
  Orthodox 162m
  Anglican 70m
  Other Christian 148m

Muslim 881m
  Sunni 841m
  Shia 40m

Hindu 663m
Buddhist 312m
Chinese folk 172m
Tribal 92m
Jewish 18m
Sikhs 17m

RELIGION

- ▲ Roman Catholicism
- Orthodox and other Eastern Churches
- • Protestantism
- Sunni Islam
- Shia Islam
- Buddhism
- Hinduism
- Confucianism
- • Judaism
- Shintoism
- Primitive religions

18

UNITED NATIONS

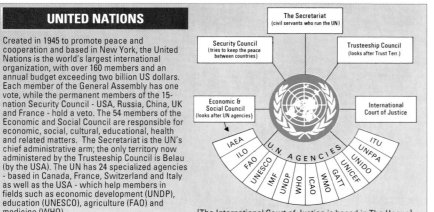

Created in 1945 to promote peace and cooperation and based in New York, the United Nations is the world's largest international organization, with over 160 members and an annual budget exceeding two billion US dollars. Each member of the General Assembly has one vote, while the permanent members of the 15-nation Security Council - USA, Russia, China, UK and France - hold a veto. The 54 members of the Economic and Social Council are responsible for economic, social, cultural, educational, health and related matters. The Secretariat is the UN's chief administrative arm; the only territory now administered by the Trusteeship Council is Belau (by the USA). The UN has 24 specialized agencies - based in Canada, France, Switzerland and Italy as well as the USA - which help members in fields such as economic development (UNDP), education (UNESCO), agriculture (FAO) and medicine (WHO).

The Secretariat
(civil servants who run the UN)

Security Council
(tries to keep the peace between countries)

Trusteeship Council
(looks after Trust Terr.)

Economic & Social Council
(looks after UN agencies)

International Court of Justice

U.N. AGENCIES
IAEA, ILO, FAO, UNESCO, IMF, UNDP, WHO, ICAO, WMO, GATT, UNICEF, UNIDO, UNFPA, ITU

[The International Court of Justice is based in The Hague]

Membership: There are 13 independent states who are not members of the UN - Andorra, Kiribati, Liechtenstein, N. Korea, S. Korea, Monaco, Nauru, San Marino, Switzerland, Taiwan, Tonga, Tuvalu and Vatican City. By 1992, the successor states of the former USSR had either joined or planned to. There were 51 members in 1945. Official languages are Chinese, English, French, Russian, Spanish and Arabic.
Funding: The UN budget for 1988-1989 was US $ 1,788,746,000. Contributions are assessed by members' ability to pay, with the maximum 25% of the total, the minimum 0.01%. Contributions for 1988-1989 were: USA 25%, Japan 11.38%, USSR 9.99%, W. Germany 8.08%, France 6.25%, UK 4.86%, Italy 3.99%, Canada 3.09%, Spain 1.95%, Netherlands 1.65% (others 23.75%).
Peacekeeping: The UN has been involved in 18 peacekeeping operations worldwide since 1945, five of which (Afghanistan/Pakistan, Iran/Iraq, Angola, Namibia and Honduras) were initiated in 1988-1989. In June 1991 UN personnel totalling over 11,000 were working in eight separate areas.

EFTA: European Free Trade Association (formed in 1960). Portugal left the 'Seven' in 1989 to join the EEC.
ACP: African-Caribbean-Pacific (1963).
COMECON: Council for Mutual Economic Assistance. Founded in 1949 by Joseph Stalin, it has been largely moribund since the political upheavals of 1989-92.

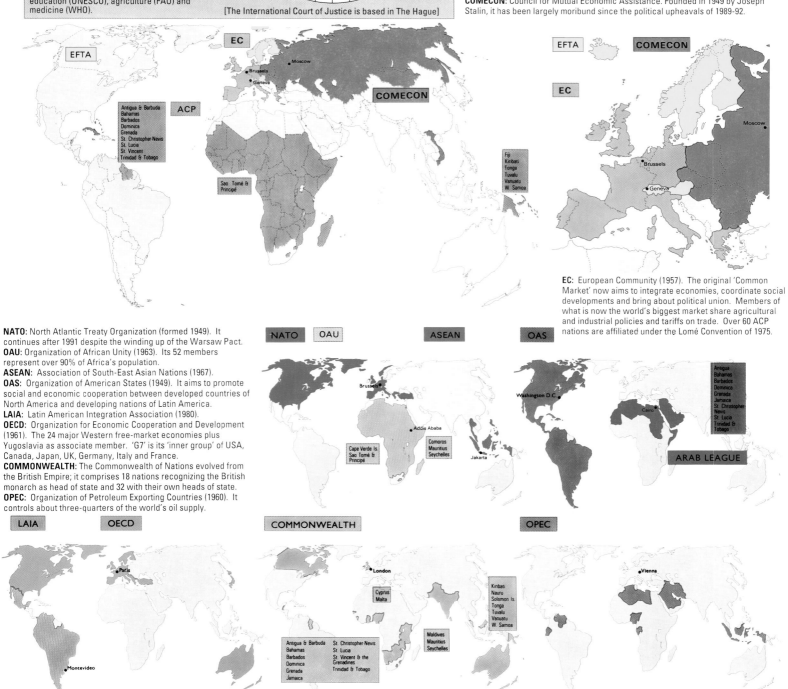

EFTA
EC
Brussels
Geneva
Moscow
COMECON
ACP
Antigua & Barbuda
Bahamas
Barbados
Dominica
Grenada
St. Christopher-Nevis
St. Lucia
St. Vincent
Trinidad & Tobago
Sao Tomé & Principé
Fiji
Kiribati
Tonga
Tuvalu
Vanuatu
W. Samoa

EFTA
COMECON
EC
Moscow
Brussels
Geneva

EC: European Community (1957). The original 'Common Market' now aims to integrate economies, coordinate social developments and bring about political union. Members of what is now the world's biggest market share agricultural and industrial policies and tariffs on trade. Over 60 ACP nations are affiliated under the Lomé Convention of 1975.

NATO: North Atlantic Treaty Organization (formed 1949). It continues after 1991 despite the winding up of the Warsaw Pact.
OAU: Organization of African Unity (1963). Its 52 members represent over 90% of Africa's population.
ASEAN: Association of South-East Asian Nations (1967).
OAS: Organization of American States (1949). It aims to promote social and economic cooperation between developed countries of North America and developing nations of Latin America.
LAIA: Latin American Integration Association (1980).
OECD: Organization for Economic Cooperation and Development (1961). The 24 major Western free-market economies plus Yugoslavia as associate member. 'G7' is its 'inner group' of USA, Canada, Japan, UK, Germany, Italy and France.
COMMONWEALTH: The Commonwealth of Nations evolved from the British Empire; it comprises 18 nations recognizing the British monarch as head of state and 32 with their own heads of state.
OPEC: Organization of Petroleum Exporting Countries (1960). It controls about three-quarters of the world's oil supply.

NATO   OAU   ASEAN   OAS
Brussels
Washington D.C.
Addis Ababa
Cairo
Cape Verde Is
Sao Tomé & Principé
Comoros
Mauritius
Seychelles
Jakarta
Antigua
Bahamas
Barbados
Dominica
Grenada
Jamaica
St. Christopher-Nevis
St. Lucia
Trinidad & Tobago
ARAB LEAGUE

LAIA   OECD   COMMONWEALTH   OPEC
Paris
London
Vienna
Montevideo
Cyprus
Malta
Maldives
Mauritius
Seychelles
Kiribati
Nauru
Solomon Is.
Tonga
Tuvalu
Vanuatu
W. Samoa
Antigua & Barbuda   St. Christopher-Nevis
Bahamas   St. Lucia
Barbados   St. Vincent & the Grenadines
Dominica   Trinidad & Tobago
Grenada
Jamaica

WEALTH

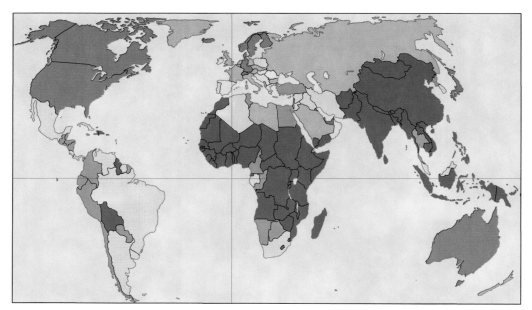

LEVELS OF INCOME

Gross National Product per capita: the value of total production divided by population (1986)

- Over 400% of world average
- 200 - 400% of world average
- 100 - 200% of world average

[World average wealth per person US $2,940]

- 50 - 100% of world average
- 25 - 50% of world average
- Under 25% of world average

WEALTH CREATION

The Gross National Product (GNP) of the world's largest economies, US $ billion (1989)

1. USA	5,237,707	21. Denmark	105,263
2. Japan	2,920,310	22. Norway	92,097
3. Germany	1,272,959	23. Saudi Arabia	89,986
4. France	1,000,866	24. Indonesia	87,936
5. Italy	871,955	25. South Africa	86,029
6. UK	834,166	26. Turkey	74,731
7. Canada	500,337	27. Argentina	68,780
8. China	393,006	28. Poland	66,974
9. Brazil	375,146	29. Thailand	64,437
10. Spain	358,352	30. Hong Kong	59,202
11. India	287,383	31. Yugoslavia	59,080
12. Australia	242,131	32. Greece	53,626
13. Netherlands	237,451	33. Algeria	53,116
14. Switzerland	197,984	34. Venezuela	47,164
15. South Korea	186,467	35. Israel	44,131
16. Sweden	184,230	36. Portugal	44,058
17. Mexico	170,053	37. Philippines	42,754
18. Belgium	162,026	38. Pakistan	40,134
19. Austria	131,899	39. New Zealand	39,437
20. Finland	109,705	40. Colombia	38,607

There are no accurate figures available for either the USSR or its successor nations.

THE WEALTH GAP

The world's richest & poorest countries, by Gross National Product per capita in US $ (1989)

1. Liechtenstein	33,000	1. Mozambique	80
2. Switzerland	30,270	2. Ethiopia	120
3. Bermuda	25,000	3. Tanzania	120
4. Luxembourg	24,860	4. Laos	170
5. Japan	23,730	5. Nepal	170
6. Finland	22,060	6. Somalia	170
7. Norway	21,850	7. Bangladesh	180
8. Sweden	21,710	8. Malawi	180
9. Iceland	21,240	9. Bhutan	190
10. USA	21,100	10. Chad	190
11. Denmark	20,510	11. Sierra Leone	200
12. Canada	19,020	12. Burundi	220
13. UAE	18,430	13. Gambia	230
14. France	17,830	14. Madagascar	230
15. Austria	17,360	15. Nigeria	250
16. Germany	16,500	16. Uganda	250
17. Belgium	16,390	17. Mali	260
18. Kuwait	16,380	18. Zaire	260
19. Netherlands	16,010	19. Niger	290
20. Italy	15,150	20. Burkina Faso	310

GNP per capita is calculated by dividing a country's Gross National Product by its population. The UK ranks 21st, with US $14,570.

CONTINENTAL SHARES

Shares of population & of wealth (GNP) by continent

POPULATION

- 58.3%
- 15.5%
- 7.1%
- 6.7%
- 12%
- 0.4%

GNP

- 32.6%
- 35.3%
- 24.7%
- 3.7%
- 2.2%
- 1.4%

- Europe
- Asia
- South America
- Australia
- Africa
- North America

INFLATION

Average annual rate of inflation (1980-1988)

- Over 50%
- 20 - 50%
- 7.5 - 20%
- 0 - 7.5%
- Negative inflation
- No data available

Highest average inflation		Lowest average inflation	
Bolivia	483%	Oman	-6.5%
Argentina	291%	Saudi Arabia	-4.2%
Brazil	189%	Kuwait	-3.9%
Israel	137%	Libya	0.1%
Peru	119%	U.A.E.	0.1%
Uganda	101%	Congo	0.8%
Nicaragua	87%	Gabon	0.9%

FOREIGN AID

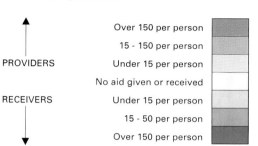

Aid provided or received, divided by total population in US $ (three-year average, 1985-1987)

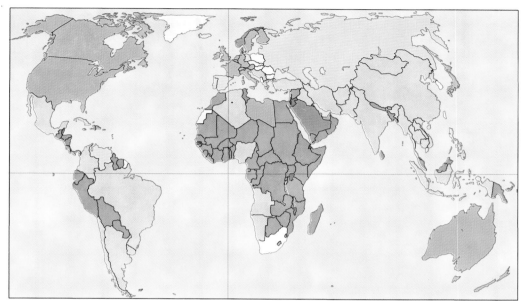

PROVIDERS
- Over 150 per person
- 15 - 150 per person
- Under 15 per person
- No aid given or received

RECEIVERS
- Under 15 per person
- 15 - 50 per person
- Over 150 per person

DEBT & AID

International debtors & the aid they receive (1989)

Although aid grants make a vital contribution to many of the world's poorer countries, they are usually dwarfed by the burden of debt that developing economies are expected to repay. In the case of Mozambique, aid amounted to more than 70% of GNP. In 1990, the World Bank rated Mozambique as the world's poorest country; yet debt interest payments came to almost 75 times its entire export earnings.

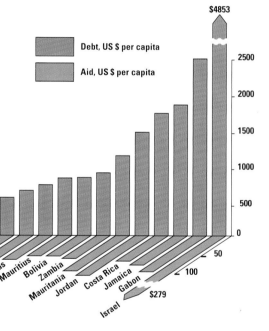

Debt, US $ per capita

Aid, US $ per capita

$4853

$279

Lesotho, Central African R., Niger, Mali, Mozambique, Somalia, Togo, El Salvador, Botswana, Senegal, Papua New Guinea, Honduras, Mauritius, Bolivia, Zambia, Mauritania, Jordan, Costa Rica, Jamaica, Gabon, Israel

DISTRIBUTION OF SPENDING

Percentage share of household spending

- Food
- Clothing
- Energy & Housing
- Medicine & Education
- Transport
- Other

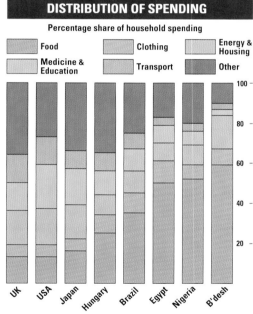

UK, USA, Japan, Hungary, Brazil, Egypt, Nigeria, B'desh

HIGH INCOME

Number of cars, televisions & telephones for each 10,000 people, selected high income countries (latest data, 1983-1988)

- Cars
- Televisions
- Telephones

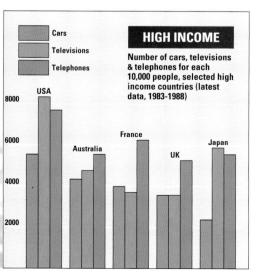

USA, Australia, France, UK, Japan

MIDDLE INCOME

Number of cars, televisions & telephones for each 10,000 people, selected middle income countries (latest data, 1983-1988)

- Cars
- Televisions
- Telephones

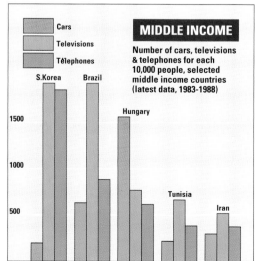

S.Korea, Brazil, Hungary, Tunisia, Iran

LOW INCOME

Number of cars, televisions & telephones for each 10,000 people, selected low income countries (latest data, 1983-1988)

- Cars
- Televisions
- Telephones

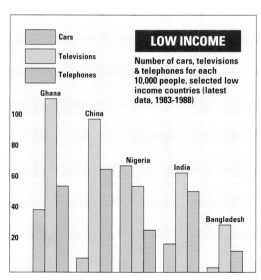

Ghana, China, Nigeria, India, Bangladesh

QUALITY OF LIFE

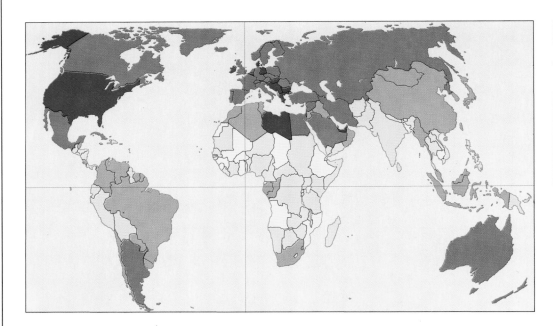

FOOD CONSUMPTION

Average daily food intake per person in kilocalories (1988)

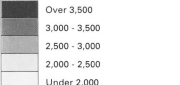

Over 3,500	[USA 3,645]
3,000 - 3,500	[UK 3,256]
2,500 - 3,000	
2,000 - 2,500	
Under 2,000	

Highest intake		Lowest intake	
Germany	3,814	C. African Rep.	1,040
UAE	3,733	Mozambique	1,595
Greece	3,688	Chad	1,717
USA	3,645	Ethiopia	1,749
Bulgaria	3,642	Guinea	1,776
Denmark	3,633	Rwanda	1,830
Ireland	3,632	Sierra Leone	1,854
Libya	3,601	Angola	1,880
Hungary	3,569	Haiti	1,902

HOSPITAL CAPACITY

Hospital beds available for each 1000 people,
(latest available year 1983-1988)

Highest capacity		Lowest capacity	
Finland	14.9	Bangladesh	0.2
Sweden	13.2	Nepal	0.2
France	12.9	Ethiopia	0.3
USSR (1986)	12.8	Mauritania	0.4
Netherlands	12.0	Mali	0.5
North Korea	11.7	Burkina Faso	0.6
Switzerland	11.3	Pakistan	0.6
Austria	10.4	Niger	0.7
Czechoslovakia	10.1	Haiti	0.8
Hungary	9.1	Chad	0.8

[UK 8] [USA 5.9]

Although the ratio of people to hospital beds gives a
good approximation of a country's health provision, it
is not an absolute indicator. Raw numbers may mask
inefficiency and other weaknesses: the high availability
of beds in North Korea, for example, has not prevented
infant mortality rates almost three times as high as in
the United Kingdom.

LIFE EXPECTANCY

Years of life expectancy at birth, selected countries (1988-89)

The chart shows combined data for both sexes. On
average, women live longer than men worldwide,
even in developing countries with high maternal
mortality rates. Overall, life expectancy is steadily
rising, though the difference between rich and poor
nations remains dramatic.

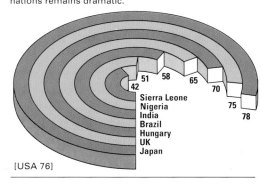

42   51   58   65   70   75   78

Sierra Leone
Nigeria
India
Brazil
Hungary
UK
Japan

[USA 76]

INFECTIOUS DISEASE

Deaths from infectious disease,
per 100,000 people,
selected countries
(latest figures, 1983-88)

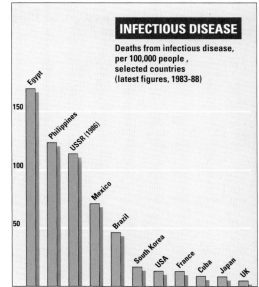

INFANT MORTALITY

Number of babies who die before the age of one year,
per thousand live births (1988)

Over 130	
100 - 130	
50 - 100	
20 - 50	
10 - 20	
Under 10	

Highest mortality		Lowest mortality	
Afghanistan	172	Iceland	3
Mali	168	Japan	5
Ethiopia	154	Finland, Sweden	6
Sierra Leone	152	Canada, Denmark	7
Somalia	151	Ireland, Netherlands	7
Malawi	149	Norway, Singapore	7
Guinea	143	Switzerland	7
Mozambique	139	Austria	8

LITERACY

Percentage of adult population unable to read or write (1988)

- Over 75%
- 50 - 75%
- 25 - 50%
- 10 - 15%
- Under 10%

Highest illiteracy		Highest female illiteracy	
Somalia	88%	Yemen	97%
Burkina Faso	87%	Burkina Faso	94%
Niger	86%	Somalia	94%
Mali	83%	Niger	91%
Mauritania	83%	Chad	89%
Yemen	82%	Mali	89%
Chad	78%	Nepal	88%
Benin	76%	Benin	84%
Nepal	76%	Guinea	83%

EDUCATION

Percentage of age group in secondary school, selected countries (1987)

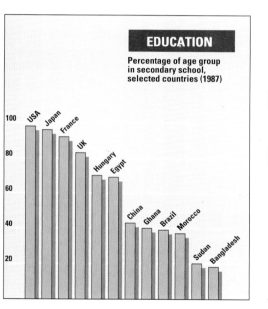

FERTILITY & EDUCATION

Fertility rates compared with female education, selected countries (1988)

- Fertility rate: number of children borne by average woman
- Percentage of female age group in secondary education

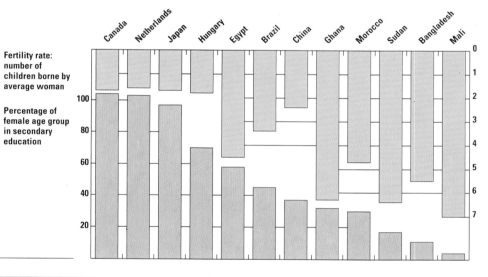

WOMEN IN THE WORKFORCE

Women in paid employment as a percentage of the total workforce (1989)

- Over 40%
- 30 - 40%
- 20 - 30%
- 10 - 20%
- Under 10%

Highest proportion		Lowest proportion	
Botswana	53%	UAE	6%
Burundi	53%	Saudi Arabia	7%
Ghana	51%	Bangladesh	7%
Burkina Faso	49%	Qatar	7%
Sweden	48%	Algeria	8%
Bulgaria	48%	Oman	8%
Barbados	47%	Libya	8%
Thailand	47%	Jordan	9%
Finland	47%	Egypt	9%

23

ENERGY

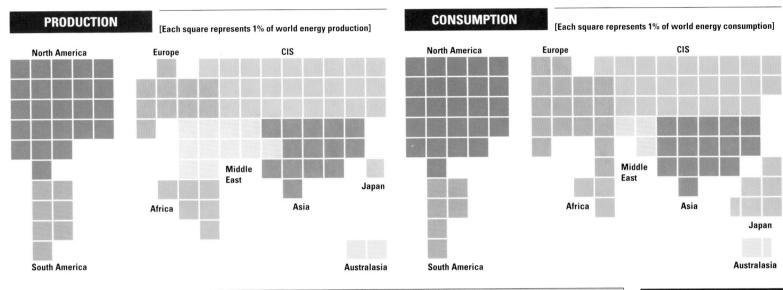

PRODUCTION [Each square represents 1% of world energy production]

North America Europe CIS
Middle East Japan
Africa Asia
South America Australasia

CONSUMPTION [Each square represents 1% of world energy consumption]

North America Europe CIS
Middle East
Africa Asia
Japan
South America Australasia

Prudhoe Bay
North Sea Yamburg
Medicine Hat Silesia Donbas
California Ruhr
Appalachians Tangshan
Texas Shanxi Chongqing
Gulf of Mexico The Gulf
Venezuela Algeria Oman Bihar
Ecuador Nigeria Sumatra
Rio Grande/ Santa Catarina Transvaal/ Natal

ENERGY BALANCE

Difference between energy production & consumption in millions of tonnes of oil equivalent (1989)

Energy deficit ↑

Over 35 MtOe
1 - 35 MtOe

Approx. balance

1 - 35 MtOe
Over 35 MtOe

Energy surplus ↓

● Major oilfields
▽ Major gasfields
▲ Major coalfields

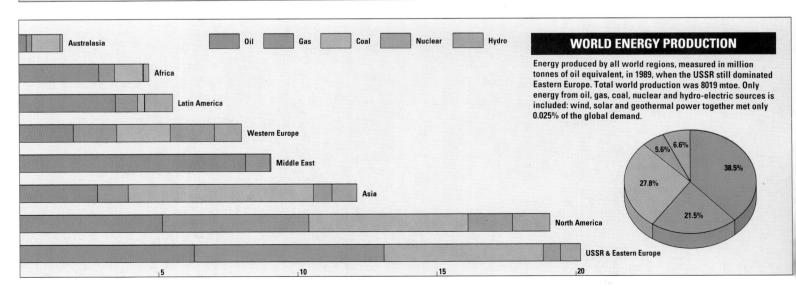

Australasia
Africa
Latin America
Western Europe
Middle East
Asia
North America
USSR & Eastern Europe

Oil Gas Coal Nuclear Hydro

WORLD ENERGY PRODUCTION

Energy produced by all world regions, measured in million tonnes of oil equivalent, in 1989, when the USSR still dominated Eastern Europe. Total world production was 8019 mtoe. Only energy from oil, gas, coal, nuclear and hydro-electric sources is included: wind, solar and geothermal power together met only 0.025% of the global demand.

6.6%
5.6%
38.5%
27.8%
21.5%

5 10 15 20

NUCLEAR POWER

Percentage of electricity generated by nuclear power stations, leading nations (1988)

1.	France 70%	11.	Germany (W) 34%
2.	Belgium 66%	12.	Japan 28%
3.	Hungary 49%	13.	Czechoslovakia.. 27%
4.	South Korea 47%	14.	UK 18%
5.	Sweden 46%	15.	USA 17%
6.	Taiwan 41%	16.	Canada 16%
7.	Switzerland 37%	17.	Argentina 12%
8.	Finland 36%	18.	USSR (1989) 11%
9.	Spain 36%	19.	Yugoslavia 6%
10.	Bulgaria 36%	20.	Netherlands 5%

The decade 1980-1990 was a bad time for the nuclear power industry. Major projects regularly ran vastly over-budget, and fears of long-term environmental damage were heavily reinforced by the 1986 Soviet disaster at Chernobyl. Although the number of reactors in service continued to increase throughout the period, orders for new plant shrank dramatically, and most countries cut back on their nuclear programmes.

HYDRO-ELECTRICITY

Percentage of electricity generated by hydro-electrical power stations, leading nations (1988)

1.	Paraguay 99.9%	11.	Laos 95.5%
2.	Zambia 99.6%	12.	Nepal 95.2%
3.	Norway............ 99.5%	13.	Iceland 94.0%
4.	Congo 99.1%	14.	Uruguay 93.0%
5.	Costa Rica 98.3%	15.	Brazil................ 91.7%
6.	Uganda 98.3%	16.	Albania 87.2%
7.	Rwanda 97.7%	17.	Fiji 81.4%
8.	Malawi 97.6%	18.	Ecuador 80.7%
9.	Zaïre 97.4%	19.	C. African Rep. 80.4%
10.	Cameroon 97.2%	20.	Sri Lanka 80.4%

Countries heavily reliant on hydro-electricity are usually small and non-industrial: a high proportion of hydro-electric power more often reflects a modest energy budget than vast hydro-electric resources. The USA, for instance, produces only 8% of power requirements from hydro-electricity; yet that 8% amounts to more than three times the hydro-power generated by all of Africa.

ALTERNATIVE ENERGY SOURCES

Solar: Each year the sun bestows upon the Earth almost a million times as much energy as is locked up in all the planet's oil reserves, but only an insignificant fraction is trapped and used commercially. In some experimental installations, mirrors focus the sun's rays on to boilers, whose steam generates electricity by spinning conventional turbines. Solar cells turn sunlight into electricity directly. Efficiencies are still low, but advancing technology could make the sun a major electricity source by 2100.
Wind: Caused by the uneven heating of the spinning Earth, winds are themselves the product of solar energy. Traditional windmills turn wind power into mechanical work; recent models usually generate electricity. But efficient windmills are expensive to build, and suitable locations are few.
Tidal: The energy from tides is potentially enormous, although only a few installations have been built to exploit it. In theory at least, waves and currents could also provide almost unimaginable power, and the thermal differences in the ocean depths are another huge well of potential energy.

FUEL EXPORTS

Fuels as a percentage of total value of all exports (1986)

- Over 75%
- 50 - 75%
- 25 - 50%
- 10 - 25%
- Under 10%

Direction of trade

- Major movements of coal
- Major movements of oil

CONVERSIONS
For historical reasons, oil is still traded in 'barrels'. The weight and volume equivalents shown below are all based on average density 'Arabian light' crude oil.

The energy equivalents given for a tonne of oil are also somewhat imprecise: oil and coal of different qualities will have varying energy contents, a fact usually reflected in their price on world markets.

1 barrel: 0.136 tonnes/159 litres/35 Imperial gallons/42 US gallons. **1 tonne:** 7.33 barrels/1185 litres/256 Imperial gallons/261 US gallons. **1 tonne oil:** 1.5 tonnes hard coal/3.0 tonnes lignite/12,000 kWh.

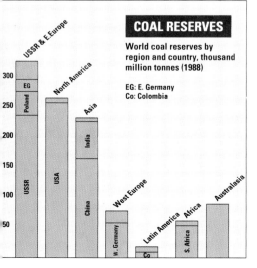

COAL RESERVES

World coal reserves by region and country, thousand million tonnes (1988)

EG: E. Germany
Co: Colombia

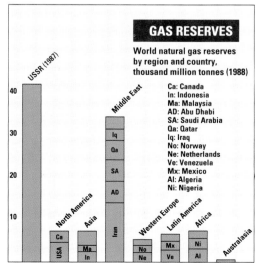

GAS RESERVES

World natural gas reserves by region and country, thousand million tonnes (1988)

Ca: Canada
In: Indonesia
Ma: Malaysia
AD: Abu Dhabi
SA: Saudi Arabia
Qa: Qatar
Iq: Iraq
No: Norway
Ne: Netherlands
Ve: Venezuela
Mx: Mexico
Al: Algeria
Ni: Nigeria

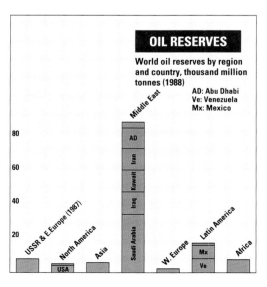

OIL RESERVES

World oil reserves by region and country, thousand million tonnes (1988)

AD: Abu Dhabi
Ve: Venezuela
Mx: Mexico

PRODUCTION

- Nomadic herding
- Primitive subsistence farming
- Intensive subsistence farming
- Tropical plantation agriculture
- Commercial ranching
- Commercial livestock & grain farming
- Commercial fruit growing & market gardening
- Forestry
- Land of little or no agricultural value

STAPLE CROPS

Separate figures for Russia, Ukraine and the other successors of the defunct USSR are not yet available

Wheat

China 16.9%, USSR 16.8%, USA 10.3%, India 10.0%, France 5.9%, Canada 4.5%, Turkey 2.9%

World total (1989): 538,056,000 tonnes

Rice

China 35.4%, India 21.2%, Indonesia 8.6%, Bangladesh 5.3%, Thailand 4.4%, Vietnam 3.6%

World total (1989): 506,291,000 tonnes

Maize

USA 40.7%, China 16.1%, Brazil 5.6%, USSR 3.6%, France 2.7%

World total (1989): 470,318,000 tonnes

Potatoes

USSR 26.0%, Poland 12.4%, China 10.9%, Germany 6.1%, USA 6.0%, India 5.2%

World total (1989): 276,740,000 tonnes

Millet

India 32.8%, China 18.7%, USSR 13.1%, Nigeria 11.5%, Niger 4.2%

World total (1989): 30,512,000 tonnes

Rye

USSR 53.9%, Poland 17.8%, Germany 11.2%, China 2.9%, Canada 2.4%

World total (1989): 34,893,000 tonnes

Soya

USA 48.9%, Brazil 22.4%, China 10.1%, Argentina 5.8%

World total (1989): 107,350,000 tonnes

Cassava

Thailand 15.9%, Brazil 15.8%, Indonesia 11.24%, Nigeria 11.19%, Zaïre 11.1%, Tanzania 4.3%, India 3.6%

World total (1989): 147,500,000 tonnes

SUGARS

Sugar cane

Brazil 22.4%, India 19.7%, Cuba 7.3%, China 5.5%, Mexico 4.0%, Pakistan 3.7%, Thailand 3.6%

World total (1989): 1,007,184,000 tonnes

Sugar beet

USSR 31.9%, Germany 8.6%, USA 7.6%, France 7.6%, Italy 4.9%, Poland 4.7%, Turkey 4.0%

World total (1989): 305,882,000 tonnes

BALANCE OF EMPLOYMENT

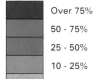

Percentage of total workforce employed in agriculture, forestry & fishing (latest available year)

- Over 75%
- 50 - 75%
- 25 - 50%
- 10 - 25%
- Under 10%

- ● Over 25% of total workforce employed in manufacturing

- ○ Over 75% of total workforce employed in service industries (eg work in offices, shops, tourism, transport, entertainment & administration)

MINERAL PRODUCTION

Separate figures for Russia, Ukraine and the other successors of the defunct USSR are not yet available

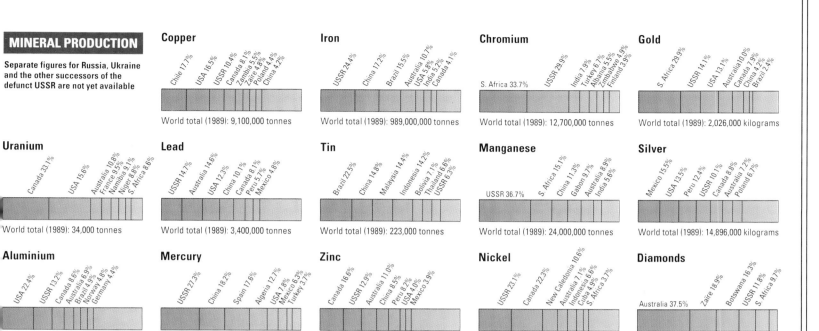

Copper
Chile 17.7% · USA 16.5% · USSR 10.4% · Canada 8.1% · Zambia 5.5% · Zaïre 4.8% · Poland 4.4% · China 4.2%
World total (1989): 9,100,000 tonnes

Iron
USSR 24.4% · China 17.2% · Brazil 15.5% · Australia 10.7% · USA 5.8% · India 5.2% · Canada 4.1%
World total (1989): 989,000,000 tonnes

Chromium
S. Africa 33.7% · USSR 29.9% · India 7.9% · Turkey 6.7% · Albania 5.5% · Zimbabwe 4.9% · Finland 3.9%
World total (1989): 12,700,000 tonnes

Gold
S. Africa 29.9% · USA 14.1% · USSR 13.1% · Australia 10.0% · Canada 7.9% · Brazil 4.2% · Brazil 2.4%
World total (1989): 2,026,000 kilograms

Uranium
Canada 33.1% · USA 15.6% · Australia 10.8% · France 9.5% · Namibia 9.1% · Niger 8.8% · S. Africa 8.6%
World total (1989): 34,000 tonnes

Lead
USSR 14.7% · Australia 14.6% · USA 12.3% · China 10.1% · Canada 8.1% · Peru 5.7% · Mexico 4.8%
World total (1989): 3,400,000 tonnes

Tin
Brazil 22.5% · China 14.8% · Malaysia 14.4% · Indonesia 14.2% · Bolivia 7.1% · Thailand 6.6% · USSR 6.3%
World total (1989): 223,000 tonnes

Manganese
USSR 36.7% · S. Africa 15.1% · Brazil 11.3% · Gabon 9.7% · Australia 8.9% · India 5.6%
World total (1989): 24,000,000 tonnes

Silver
Mexico 15.5% · USA 13.5% · Peru 12.4% · USSR 10.1% · Canada 8.8% · Australia 7.2% · Poland 6.7%
World total (1989): 14,896,000 kilograms

Aluminium
USA 22.4% · USSR 13.2% · Canada 8.6% · Australia 6.9% · Brazil 4.9% · Norway 4.8% · Germany 4.4%
World total (1989): 18,000,000 tonnes

Mercury
USSR 27.3% · China 18.2% · Spain 17.6% · Algeria 12.7% · USA 7.8% · Mexico 6.3% · Turkey 3.7%
World total (1989): 5,500,000 kilograms

Zinc
Canada 16.6% · USSR 12.9% · Australia 11.0% · China 8.5% · Peru 8.2% · USA 4.0% · Mexico 3.9%
World total (1989): 7,300,000 tonnes

Nickel
USSR 23.1% · Canada 22.3% · New Caledonia 10.6% · Australia 7.1% · Indonesia 6.6% · Cuba 4.9% · S. Africa 3.7%
World total (1989): 910,000 tonnes

Diamonds
Australia 37.5% · Zaïre 18.9% · Botswana 16.3% · USSR 11.8% · S. Africa 9.7%
World total (1989): 96,600,000 carats

MINERAL DISTRIBUTION

Light metals
● Bauxite

Base metals
□ Copper
▲ Lead
▽ Mercury
▽ Tin
◇ Zinc

Iron and ferro-alloys
● Iron
◗ Chrome
▲ Manganese
□ Nickel

Precious metals
▽ Gold
⌒ Silver

Precious stones
◆ Diamonds

STEEL PRODUCTION
Steel output in thousand tonnes (top ten countries, 1989)

USSR (1987) · Japan · USA · China · Germany · Brazil · Italy · France · UK · Czech.

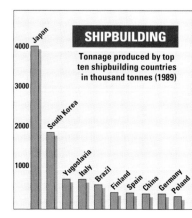

SHIPBUILDING
Tonnage produced by top ten shipbuilding countries in thousand tonnes (1989)

Japan · South Korea · Yugoslavia · Italy · Brazil · Finland · Spain · China · Germany · Poland

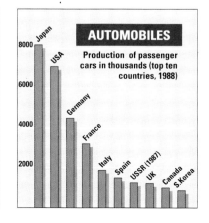

AUTOMOBILES
Production of passenger cars in thousands (top ten countries, 1988)

Japan · USA · Germany · France · Italy · Spain · USSR (1987) · UK · Canada · S.Korea

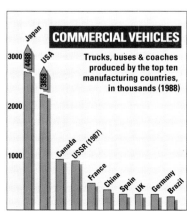

COMMERCIAL VEHICLES
Trucks, buses & coaches produced by the top ten manufacturing countries, in thousands (1988)

Japan 4488 · USA 3858 · Canada · USSR (1987) · France · China · Spain · UK · Germany · Brazil

27

TRADE

Proportion of total world exports by value (1989)

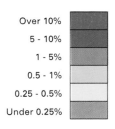

Over 10%	
5 - 10%	
1 - 5%	
0.5 - 1%	
0.25 - 0.5%	
Under 0.25%	

International trade is dominated by a handful of powerful maritime nations. The members of 'G7', the inner circle of OECD and the top seven countries listed in the diagram below, account for more than half the total. The majority of nations – including all but four in Africa – contribute less than one quarter of one per cent to the worldwide total of exports. The EC countries account for 40%, the Pacific Rim nations over 35%.

THE GREAT TRADING NATIONS

The imports and exports of the top ten trading nations as a percentage of world trade (1989). Each country's trade in manufactured goods is shown in orange.

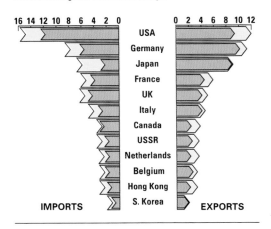

IMPORTS   USA   EXPORTS

16 14 12 10 8 6 4 2 0   0 2 4 6 8 10 12

USA
Germany
Japan
France
UK
Italy
Canada
USSR
Netherlands
Belgium
Hong Kong
S. Korea

PATTERNS OF TRADE

Thriving international trade is the outward sign of a healthy world economy, the obvious indicator that some countries have goods to sell and others the wherewithal to buy them. Despite local fluctuations, trade throughout the 1980s grew consistently faster than output, increasing in value by almost 50% in the decade 1979-89. It remains dominated by the rich, industrialized countries of the Organization for Economic Development: between them, OECD members account for almost 75% of world imports and exports in most years. OECD dominance is just as marked in the trade in 'invisibles' - a column in the balance sheet that includes among other headings the export of services, interest payments on overseas investments, tourism and even remittances from migrant workers abroad. In the UK, invisibles account for more than half all trading income.

However, the size of these great trading economies means that imports and exports usually make up only a fraction of their total wealth: in the case of the famously export-conscious Japanese, trade in goods and services amounts to less than 18% of GDP. In poorer countries, trade - often in a single commodity - may amount to 50% GDP or more.

TRADED PRODUCTS

Top ten manufactures traded, by value in billions of US $ (late 1980s)

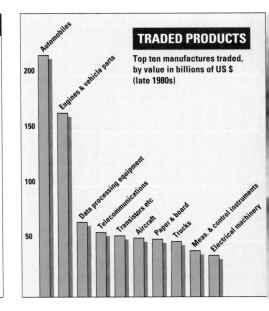

Automobiles
Engines & vehicle parts
Data processing equipment
Telecommunications
Transistors etc
Aircraft
Paper & board
Trucks
Meas. & control instruments
Electrical machinery

200
150
100
50

BALANCE OF TRADE

Value of exports in proportion to the value of imports (1988)

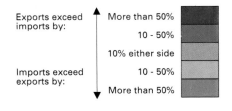

Exports exceed imports by:	More than 50%	
	10 - 50%	
	10% either side	
Imports exceed exports by:	10 - 50%	
	More than 50%	

The total world trade balance should amount to zero, since exports must equal imports on a global scale. In practice, at least $100 billions in exports go unrecorded, leaving the world with an apparent deficit and many countries in a better position than public accounting reveals. However, a favourable trade balance is not necessarily a sign of prosperity: many poorer countries must maintain a high surplus in order to service debts, and do so by restricting imports below the levels needed to sustain successful economies.

Rotterdam
New York
New Orleans
Chiba
Yokohama
Kobe Nagoya
Shanghai
Singapore

FREIGHT

Freight unloaded in millions of tonnes (1988)

- Over 100
- 50 - 100
- 10 - 50
- 5 - 10
- Under 5
- Land locked countries

Major seaports

- ● Over 100 million tonnes per year
- ○ 50-100 million tonnes per year

CARGOES

Type of seaborne freight

- Crude oil 28.2%
- Refined petroleum 8.8%
- Iron ore 9%
- Coal 8%
- Grain 5.3%
- Other 40.7%

MERCHANT FLEETS

National merchant fleets in thousand deadweight tonnes (1989). The chart records national ownership, not necessarily registry. The countries listed account for 83% of world shipping. The division of the former Soviet fleet among the USSR's successor republics was still incomplete in 1992.

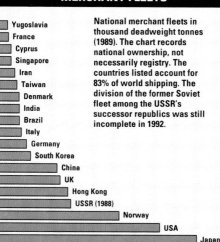

Yugoslavia
France
Cyprus
Singapore
Iran
Taiwan
Denmark
India
Brazil
Italy
Germany
South Korea
China
UK
Hong Kong
USSR (1988)
Norway
USA
Japan
Greece

20,000 40,000 60,000 80,000

WORLD SHIPPING

World merchant fleet by type of vessel and deadweight tonnage (1989)

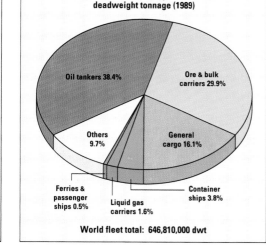

- Oil tankers 38.4%
- Ore & bulk carriers 29.9%
- Others 9.7%
- General cargo 16.1%
- Ferries & passenger ships 0.5%
- Liquid gas carriers 1.6%
- Container ships 3.8%

World fleet total: 646,810,000 dwt

THE GREAT PORTS

The world's ten busiest ports by million tonnes of shipping arrivals (late 1980s)

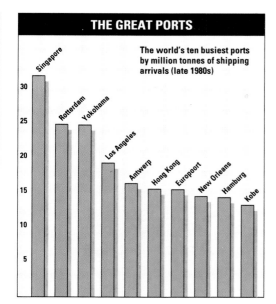

Singapore
Rotterdam
Yokohama
Los Angeles
Antwerp
Hong Kong
Europoort
New Orleans
Hamburg
Kobe

30
25
20
15
10
5

DEPENDENCE ON TRADE

Value of exports as a percentage of Gross Domestic Product (1988)

- Over 50%
- 40 - 50%
- 30 - 40%
- 20 - 30%
- 10 - 20%
- Under 10%

- ● Most dependent on industrial exports (over 75% of total exports)
- ● Most dependent on fuel exports (over 75% of total exports)
- ○ Most dependent on mineral & metal exports (over 75% of total exports)

TRAVEL & TOURISM

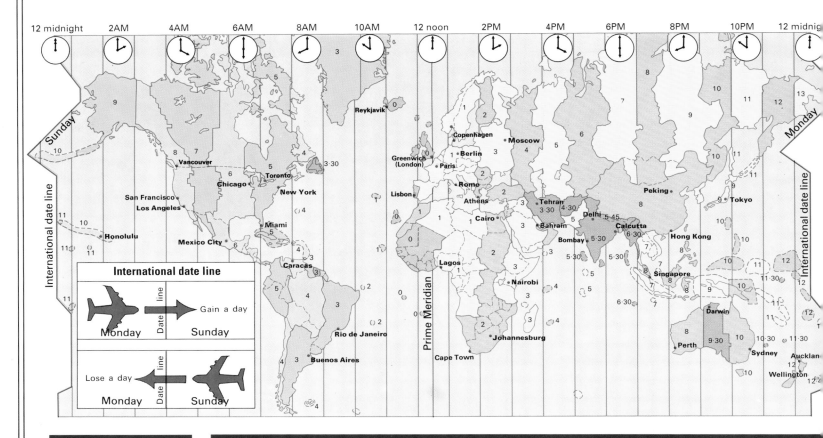

12 midnight | 2AM | 4AM | 6AM | 8AM | 10AM | 12 noon | 2PM | 4PM | 6PM | 8PM | 10PM | 12 midnig

Sunday ... Monday

International date line

Gain a day — Monday / Sunday (Date line)

Lose a day — Monday / Sunday (Date line)

TIME ZONES

Zones using GMT (Greenwich Mean Time)

Half-hour zones

Zones slow of GMT

Zones fast of GMT

The time when it is 12 noon at Greenwich

RAIL & ROAD: THE LEADING NATIONS

Total rail network ('000 km)		Passenger km per head per year		Total road network ('000 km)		Vehicle km per head per year		Vehicle km per head per year per km road network	
1. USSR (1986)	247.2	Japan	2,745	1. USA	623.3	USA	12,505	Hong Kong	4,705.7
2. USA	225.4	Switzerland	1,523	2. Brazil	167.4	Luxembourg	7,989	Kuwait	3,433.4
3. Canada	65.8	Germany (E:'87)	1,353	3. USSR (1986)	158.6	Kuwait	7,251	Jordan	1,321.4
4. India	61.8	Czech'vakia	1,286	4. India	155.4	France	7,142	UK	929.6
5. China	52.6	Poland	1,282	5. Japan	110.4	Sweden	6,991	Italy	923.4
6. Germany	41.4	USSR	1,276	6. China	98.2	Germany	6,806	Germany	843.8
7. Australia	39.3	France	1,074	7. Australia	85.3	Denmark	6,764	Netherlands	761.4
8. France	34.6	Austria	971	8. Canada	84.4	Austria	6,518	Tunisia	726.4
9. Argentina	34.1	Denmark	937	9. France	80.5	Netherlands	5,984	Iraq	657.2
10. Poland	24.2	Hungary	906	10. Germany	49.4	UK	5,738	Luxembourg	581.3
11. South Africa	23.8	Bulgaria	897	11. Poland	36.1	Canada	5,493	Japan	497.0
12. Brazil	22.1	South Africa	873	12. UK	35.2	Italy	4,852	USA	494.2
13. Mexico	20.0	Italy	722	13. Turkey	32.1	Belgium	4,821	Denmark	491.0
14. Japan	19.9	Sweden	716	14. Spain	31.8	Japan	4,476	Austria	464.9
15. UK	16.6	Germany (W:'88)	640	15. Italy	30.2	South Africa	2,776	France	459.6

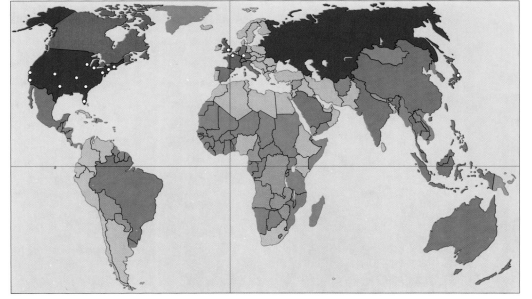

AIR TRAVEL

Passenger kilometres [the number of passengers, international & domestic, multiplied by the distance flown by each passenger from the airport of origin] (1988)

- Over 100,000 million
- 50,000 - 100,000 million
- 10,000 - 50,000 million
- 1,000 - 10,000 million
- 500 - 1,000 million
- Under 500 million

○ Major airports (handling over 20 million passengers per year)

World's busiest airports (total passengers)		World's busiest airports (international passengers)	
1. Chicago	(O'Hare)	1. London	(Heathrow)
2. Atlanta	(Hatsfield)	2. London	(Gatwick)
3. Los Angeles	(Inter'nl)	3. Frankfurt	(International)
4. Dallas	(Dallas/Ft Worth)	4. New York	(Kennedy)
5. London	(Heathrow)	5. Paris	(De Gaulle)

DESTINATIONS

- ■ Cultural & historical centres
- □ Coastal resorts
- □ Ski resorts
- ■ Centres of entertainment
- ■ Places of pilgrimage
- ■ Places of great natural beauty

Banff
Yellowstone Park
Niagara Falls
Québec
Yosemite
Aspen
Cape Cod
New York
Grand Canyon
Las Vegas
Bermuda
Disneyland
Walt Disney World
Mexico City
Miami
Bahamas
Acapulco
Cancun
Virgin Islands
Palenque
Jamaica
Hawaii
Barbados
Tahiti
Machu Picchu
Rio de Janeiro

Norway
Moscow
London
Alps
Venice
Paris
Vienna
Cote d'Azur
Florence
Costa Brava
Rome
Algarve
Athens
Costa del Sol
Rhodes
Marrakesh
Jerusalem
Canary Islands
Giza (Pyramids)
Mecca
Serengeti National Park
Mombasa
Seychelles
Victoria Falls
Mauritius
Kruger National Park

Great Wall of China
Peking
Sapporo
Tokyo
Kyoto
Kashmir
Himalayas
Agra (Taj Mahal)
Benares
Hong Kong
Goa
Bangkok
Sri Lanka
Phuket
Maldives
Penang
Singapore
Bali
Great Barrier Reef

TOURIST SPENDING

Nations spending the most on overseas tourism, US $ (1987)

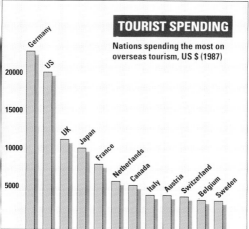

Germany, US, UK, Japan, France, Netherlands, Canada, Italy, Austria, Switzerland, Belgium, Sweden

IMPORTANCE OF TOURISM

	Arrivals from abroad (1987)	Receipts as % of GDP (1987)
1. France	36,820,000	1.4%
2. Spain	32,900,000	5.1%
3. USA	28,790,000	0.4%
4. Italy	25,750,000	1.6%
5. Austria	15,760,000	6.5%
6. UK	15,445,000	1.5%
7. Canada	15,040,000	0.9%
8. Germany	12,780,000	0.7%
9. Hungary	11,830,000	3.2%
10. Switzerland	11,600,000	3.1%
11. China	10,760,000	0.7%
12. Greece	7,564,000	4.7%

Small economies in attractive areas are often completely dominated by tourism: in some West Indian islands, tourist spending provides over 90% of total income. In cash terms the USA is the world leader: its 1987 earnings exceeded 15 billion dollars, though that sum amounted to only 0.4% of GDP.

TOURIST EARNING

Nations receiving the most from overseas tourism, US $ (1987)

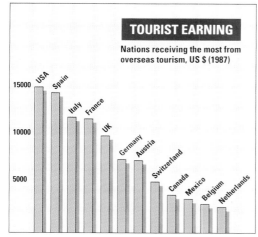

USA, Spain, Italy, France, UK, Germany, Austria, Switzerland, Canada, Mexico, Belgium, Netherlands

TOURISM

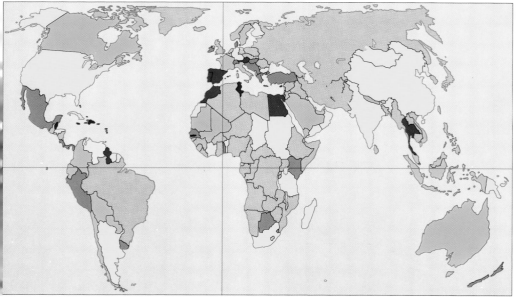

Receipts from tourism as a percentage of Gross National Product (1988)

- Over 10%
- 5 - 10%
- 2.5 - 5%
- 1 - 2.5%
- 0.5 - 1%
- Under 0.5%

Largest share of world spending on tourism

Germany	16%
USA	14%
UK	8%
Japan	7%
France	6%

Largest share of world receipts from tourism

USA	10%
Spain	9%
Italy	8%
France	8%
UK	6%

WORLD MAPS

MAP SYMBOLS

SETTLEMENTS

⬡ **PARIS**   ◼ **Berne**   ◉ **Livorno**   ● **Brugge**   ◎ **Algeciras**   ○ *Fréjus*   ○ *Oberammergau*   ○ *Thira*

Settlement symbols and type styles vary according to the scale of each map and indicate the importance of towns on the map rather than specific population figures

∴ Ruins or Archæological Sites   ⌣ Wells in Desert

ADMINISTRATION

Boundaries

――― International

―― ―― International (Undefined or Disputed)

.... Internal

National Parks

International boundaries show the *de facto* situation where there are rival claims to territory.

Country Names
NICARAGUA

Administrative Areas
KENT
CALABRIA

COMMUNICATIONS

Roads

――― Primary

⌒ Secondary

⌢⌢ Trails and Seasonal

Railways

――⌒―― Primary

⌒ Secondary

------- Under Construction

✿ Airfields

⌣⌢ Passes

⌐--⌐ **Railway Tunnels**

.... Principal Canals

PHYSICAL FEATURES

⌇ Perennial Streams

⌇⌇⌇ Intermittent Streams

⬭ Perennial Lakes

⬭ Intermittent Lakes

Swamps and Marshes

Permanent Ice and Glaciers

▲ 2259 Elevations (m)

▼ 2604 Sea Depths (m)

408 Elevation of Lake Surface Above Sea Level (m)

EUROPE

EUROPE

Second smallest of the continents, Europe is topographically subdivided by shallow shelf seas into a mainland block with a sprawl of surrounding peninsulas and off-lying islands. Its western, northern and southern limits are defined by coastlines and conventions. Of the off-lying islands, Iceland, Svalbard, the Faroes, Britain and Ireland are included. So are all the larger islands of the Mediterranean Sea, though more on the grounds of their conquest and habitation by Europeans than by their geographical proximity.

The eastern boundary, between Europe and Asia, is hard to define, and conventions differ. Geographers usually set it along the eastern flank of the Ural Mountains, the Emba River, the north shore of the Caspian Sea, the Kuma and Marich rivers (north of the Caucasus), and the eastern shores of the Azov and Black Seas, and include Turkey west of the Bosphorus. Europe extends from well north of the Arctic Circle almost to latitude 34°N, and includes a wide range of topographies and climates – from polders below sea level to high alpine peaks, from semi-deserts to polar ice-caps.

Its geological structure, and some of the forces that have shaped it, show up clearly on a physical map. In the far north lies a shield of ancient granites and gneisses occupying northern Scandinavia, Finland and Karelia. This underlies and gives shape to the rugged lowlands of this area. The highlands formed later: north and east of the platform lay a marine trough, which was raised, compressed and folded by lateral pressure about 400 million years ago to form the highlands – now well eroded but still impressive – of Norway and north-west Britain.

To the south lay another deep-sea trough, from which a vast accumulation of sediments was raised about 300 million years ago, producing the belt of highlands and well-worn uplands that stretches across Europe from Spain to southern Poland. They include the Cantabrian and central mountains of Iberia, the French Massif Central and uplands of Brittany, the Vosges, Ardennes and Westerwald, the Black Forest, the hills of Cornwall, South Wales and south-west Ireland. A third trough, the Tethys Sea, formed still further south and extended in a wide swathe across Europe and Asia. Strong pressure from a northwards-drifting Africa slowly closed the sea to form the Mediterranean, and raised the 'alpine' mountains that fringe it – the Atlas of North Africa, the Sierra Nevada of Spain, the Pyrenees, the Alps themselves, the Apennines, the Carpathians, the Dinaric Alps and the various ranges of the Balkan Peninsula.

More recently still, however, came the Ice Age. The first ice-sheets formed across Eurasia and North America from 2 to 3 million years ago; during the last million years there have been four major glacial periods in the Alps and three, maybe more, in Scandinavia. The lowland ice melted 8-10,000 years ago, and the Scandinavian and Alpine glaciers retreated, only Iceland and Svalbard keeping ice-caps. The accompanying rise in sea level finally isolated Britain.

Physically, Central Europe is divided into three clear structural belts. In the south, the Alpine fold mountains are at their highest and most complex in Switzerland and Austria, but divide eastwards into the Carpathians and the Dinaric mountains of Yugoslavia, enclosing the basin in which Hungary lies. A second belt, the central uplands, consisting of block mountains, intervening lowlands and some of Europe's greatest coalfields, stretches from the Ardennes across Germany and Czechoslovakia to thin out and disappear in Poland. The third belt, the northern lowland, broadens eastwards, and owes its relief largely to glacial deposits.

Two great rivers dominate the drainage pattern: the 1,320 km [820 ml] Rhine rises in the Alps and crosses the central uplands and northern lowland to reach the North Sea. The east-flowing 2,850 km [1,770 ml] Danube cuts right across the fold mountains at Bratislava and again at the Iron Gates (Portile de Fier) on its way to the Black Sea.

The Iberian Peninsula (586,000 sq km [226,000

sq mls]) is the largest of the three peninsulas jutting southwards from Europe into the Mediterranean Sea. Stretching through 10° of latitude it reaches to within 15 km [9.5 mls] of the African coast and extends far enough westwards to merit the title of 'the outpost of Europe'. This position is reflected in the fact that early circumnavigations of Africa and the voyages of Columbus to the New World were launched from Iberian shores.

The core of the peninsula is the Meseta plateau, a remnant of an ancient mountain chain with an average height of 600-1,000 m [1,900-3,280 ft]. Huge faulted mountain ranges, such as the Sierras de Gata, de Gredos and de Guadarrama, traverse the plateau obliquely and terminate westwards in Portugal as rocky headlands jutting into the Atlantic. Between these upthrust ranges are the wide down-warped basins of Old and New Castile. The plateau is tilted towards the west and its high eastern edge forms a major watershed that overlooks narrow, discontinuous coastal lowlands on the Mediterranean side. The main drainage is through Portugal towards the Atlantic. On its north-eastern and southern flanks the Meseta plateau drops abruptly to the Ebro and Guadalquivir (Andalusian) fault troughs; these rise on their outer sides to the lofty mountains of the Pyrenees and the Sierra Nevada respectively.

The Italian and Balkan peninsulas extend southwards into the Mediterranean Sea. In the north of Italy lies the Plain of Lombardy, drained by the River Po and its tributaries; towering above are the ranges of alpine fold mountains – southern outliers of the European Alps – that mark the boundary between Italy and neighbouring France, Switzerland and Austria. A further range of alpine mountains – the Apennines – runs through peninsular Italy and continues into Sicily.

The western Balkans are made up of alpine fold mountains, running north-west to south-east behind the western coasts – the Dinaric Alps of Yugoslavia and the Pindus Mountains (Pindos Oros) of Greece. The Balkan Mountains of Bulgaria represent the southern extension of the great arc of alpine mountains which loop round the lower basin of the Danube. Between them and the Dinaric Alps is a stable, crystalline block, the Rhodopi Massif.

Eastern Europe is a relatively huge area, stretching from the Arctic Ocean to the Caspian Sea and the Adriatic to the Urals and including the continent's two largest 'nations' – (European) Russia and the Ukraine. The most common landscape here is undulating plain, comprising coniferous forest as well as massive expanses of arable farmland, but there are impressive mountains too, notably the Carpathians, the Transylvanian Alps and, at the very eastern

corners of Europe, the Caucasus and the Urals.

The tree line in Europe – the boundary marking the northern limit of tree growth – runs north of the Arctic Circle. Only the tundra-covered northern area of Lapland and the Kola Peninsula lie beyond it. Practically all of Europe that lay south of the tree line was originally forested. North of the 60th parallel lay dark, sombre evergreen forests, dominated by spruce and pine. Since the last glacial period the evergreen forests have occupied a swathe 1,200 km [750 mls] wide across central Scandinavia and Finland, broken by marshes, moorlands and lakes, and interspersed with stands of willow and birch. Much of this forest remains today, and is still the haunt of elk, red deer and small populations of wolves, brown bears and lynx.

To the south of the coniferous forest, Europe was covered with broadleaved deciduous woodland – an ancient forest of mature oak, ash, birch, beech, sycamore, and a dozen other familiar species. Favoured by the mild damp climate, this rich forest grew in abundance over the lowlands, foothills and warmer uplands of Europe, limited in the south by dry Mediterranean summers, in Hungary and the south-west by the aridity of the plains. Virtually the first industrial resource of European man, the forest suffered a thousand years of exploitation and only remnants survive ■

EUROPE

CLIMATIC REGIONS

Mild climates
- Marine west coast
- Humid subtropical
- Mediterranean

Dry climates
- Steppe

Continental climates
- Humid continental, warm summer
- Humid continental, cool summer
- Subarctic

Polar climates
- Tundra
- Highlands

NATURAL VEGETATION

Scandinavia
Arctic Circle
Carpathians
Alps
Pyrenees
Apennines
Dinaric Alps
Balkan Pen.
Pindus
Sa. Nevada

- Coniferous forest
- Broad-leaved forest and meadow
- Evergreen trees and shrubs
- Grassland
- Steppe, moorland and semidesert
- Desert
- Alpine and tundra

ANNUAL RAINFALL

ins.	mm
80	2000
60	1500
40	1000
30	750
20	500

Arctic Circle

POPULATION

- 100 000 people

LAND USE

Reykjavík

Arctic Circle

Statfjord
Brent
Ninian
Frigg
Beryl
Forties
Ekofisk
Dan
Leman Bank

Kirkenes Ni
Kiruna
Gällivare
Boliden
Ti
Outokumpu
Helsinki

Oslo
Bergslagen
Stockholm
Mo
Fi

Moscow
Tula

Dublin

Copenhagen

Büchtereen
Berlin
Warsaw

Brussels
Ruhr

Paris
Saar

Krivoy Rog
Mn

Donbas

Hg

Berne

Vienna
Mg
Mg
Mg
Mg

Slask
Mn

Hg Idria

Ploiesti

Lisbon
Madrid

Hg
Almadén
Rio Tinto
Linares

Belgrade
Serbia
Sb

Rome

Monte Amiata
Hg

Istanbul
Cr

Athens
Ni
Mg
Hg

Sb
Cr
Sb
Cr
Fethiye

Khouribga

Projection: *Bonne*   East from Greenwich

LAND USE

	Arable land
	Arable land with permanent pasture
	Fruit trees, vineyards and market gardens
	Permanent pasture
	Woods and forests
	Rough grazing
	Non-productive land

LIVESTOCK

Beef cattle   Sheep
Dairy cattle

CROPS

Barley   Potatoes
Citrus fruits   Rice
Cotton   Rye
Date palms   Sugar beet
Flax   Tobacco
Maize   Vines
Oats   Wheat
Olives   Principal
                fishing areas

MINERALS

Asbestos   Sb Antimony
Bauxite   Cr Chrome
Copper   Mg Magnesium
Gold   Mn Manganese
Graphite   Hg Mercury
Iron ore   Mo Molybdenum
Lead   Ni Nickel
Lead and zinc   Ti Titanium
Phosphate
Salt
Silver   ## POWER
Tin   Coalfields
Uranium   Gasfields
Zinc   Oilfields
                Hydroelectric power

LAND USE

Other land
19%

Arable land and
permanent crops
30·1%

Woods and
forests 32·4%

Permanent pasture
18·5%

Total land area 472.8 million hectares
(1 168·3 million acres)

EUROPE

ICELAND

Iceland's traditional colours are blue and white. The flag's colours are a combination of those of Denmark, Norway and the coat of arms. Dating from 1915, it became the official flag on independence from Denmark in 1944.

REYKJAVIK

Temperature

Precipitation
779mm
31in

J F M A M J J A S O N D

Although the northern tip of Iceland touches the Arctic Circle, thanks to the Gulf Stream the island is relatively warm. The coldest month at Reykjavík, January, is normally 0°C [32°F], the same as Copenhagen; the warmest month is July at 12°C [54°F]. Precipitation falls on 200 days a year, 65 of them as snow. There is very high rainfall on the south coast, exceeding 800 mm [31.5 in], with half this in the north. Sunshine levels are low, being 5-6 hours from May to August. Gales are frequent most of the year.

COUNTRY: Republic of Iceland
AREA: 103,000 sq km [39,768 sq mls]
POPULATION: 255,000
CAPITAL (Population): Reykjavík (96,000)
GOVERNMENT: Republic with bicameral parliament
ETHNIC GROUPS: Icelander 97%
LANGUAGES: Icelandic (official)
RELIGIONS: Lutheran 96%, Roman Catholic 1%
NATIONAL DAY: 17 June
CURRENCY: Króna = 100 aurar
ANNUAL INCOME PER PERSON: $21,150
MAIN PRIMARY PRODUCT: Fish
MAIN INDUSTRIES: Freezing, salting, drying and smoking fish, cement, unwrought aluminium
MAIN EXPORTS: Fish products, unwrought aluminium
MAIN IMPORTS: Food and live animals, crude materials and petroleum, basic manufactures
DEFENCE: Iceland has no defence force
LIFE EXPECTANCY: Female 81 yrs, male 75 yrs
ADULT LITERACY: 99%

Situated far out in the North Atlantic Ocean, Iceland is not only the smallest but also the most isolated of the independent Scandinavian countries. Though politically part of Europe, the island (nearer to Greenland than to Scotland) arises geologically from the boundary between Europe and America – the Mid-Atlantic Ridge.

A central zone of recently active volcanoes and fissures crosses Iceland from Axarfjörður in the north to Vestmannaeyjar in the south, with a side-branch to Reykjanes and an outlying zone of activity around the Snaefellsnes peninsula in the west. During the thousand years that Iceland has been settled, between 150 and 200 eruptions have occurred in the active zones, some building up volcanic cones.

A huge eruption in 1783 destroyed pasture and livestock on a grand scale, causing a famine that reduced the Icelandic population by a quarter. More recent eruptions include the formation of a new

island – Surtsey – off the south-west coast in 1963, and the partial devastation of the town of Vestmannaeyjar-Karpstadur, on neighbouring Heimaey, ten years later. Paradoxically, Iceland is also an island of glaciers and ice-sheets, with four large ice-caps occupying 11% of the surface, and smaller glaciers.

Colonized by Viking and British farmers in the 9th century, Iceland became a dependency first of Norway, then of Denmark, though mainly self-governing with a parliament (Althing) dating from AD 930. This is thought to be the world's first parliament in the modern sense, and is certainly the oldest. Recognized as a sovereign state from 1918, Iceland was united to Denmark through a common sovereign until 1944, when it became a republic.

Since the country was formerly predominantly pastoral, with most of the population scattered in farms and small hamlets, the standard of living depended on the vicissitudes of farming close to the

Arctic Circle. Now the economy is based on deep-sea fishing; fish and fish products make up 70% of exports. About a fifth of the land is used for agriculture, but only 1% is actually cultivated for root crops and fodder. The rest is used for grazing cattle and sheep. Self-sufficient in meat and dairy products, Iceland augments its main exports with clothing such as sheepskin coats and woollen products.

Geothermal and hydroelectric power provide cheap energy for developing industries, including aluminium smelting and hot-house cultivation; and most houses and offices in Reykjavík, the capital, are heated geothermally. About a quarter of the work-force is engaged in the production of energy and manufacturing – processing food and fish, making cement and refining aluminium from imported bauxite. The population is concentrated mainly in settlements close to the coast, over half of them in or near Reykjavík ■

FAROES

In 1948 the Faroe Islands, which are part of Denmark, adopted a flag combining the local arms with the Danish arms. The cross, like that on other Scandinavian flags, is slightly off-centre.

The Faroes are a group of rocky islands situated in the North Atlantic 450 km [280 mls] from Iceland, 675 km [420 mls] from Norway and 300 km [185 mls] from the Shetlands. Like Iceland, they are composed mainly of volcanic material. They were dramatically moulded by glacial action and the landscape forms a forbidding setting for the Faroese farming and fishing settlements. Away from the villages and scattered hamlets, high cliffs are home to millions of seabirds.

Winters are mild for the latitude but the summers are cool. It is usually windy and often overcast

or foggy. Sheep farming on the poor soils is the principal occupation but salted, dried, processed and frozen fish, fishmeal and oil – from cod, whiting, mackerel and herring – comprise the chief exports. Faroese motor-vessels are found in all the deep-sea fishing grounds of the North Atlantic and the capital, Tórshavn, has ship-repairing yards. Denmark, Norway and Britain are the main trading partners.

The Faroes have been part of the Danish kingdom since 1386 and from 1851 they sent two representatives to the Danish parliament. Their own elected assembly, dating from 1852, secured a large

degree of self-government as a region within the Danish realm in 1948.

The islands left the European Free Trade Association (EFTA) when Denmark switched membership to the European Economic Community (EEC) on 1 January 1973, but did not join the community – though they do have a special associate status allowing for free industrial trade. Since 1940 the currency has been the Faroese krøna, which is freely interchangeable with the Danish krone. The people speak Faroese, official (alongside Danish) since 1948. Of the 22 islands, 17 are inhabited ■

COUNTRY: Danish self-governing region
AREA: 1,400 sq km [541 sq mls]
POPULATION: 47,000
CAPITAL (Population): Tórshavn (15,000)

NORWAY

Norway's flag has been used since 1898, though its use as a merchant flag dates back to 1821. The design is based on the Dannebrog flag of Denmark, which ruled Norway from the 14th century to the early 19th century.

The warm waters and cyclones of the North Atlantic Ocean give the western coastlands of Norway a warm maritime climate of mild winters and cool summers, although wet. The rainfall is heavy on the coast but is less inland and northwards. Inland the winters are more severe and the summers warmer. At Oslo, snow usually begins in November and is on the ground until late March. Sunshine November–January is only about one hour, but April–August is 6–8 hours per day.

One of the world's most distinctly shaped countries, the kingdom of Norway occupies the western part of the Scandinavian peninsula, from North Cape at latitude 71°N to Lindesnes at 58°N, a north-south distance of over 1,600 km [1,000 mls]. It covers an area far larger than Poland, yet has a population of less than 4.25 million, most of whom live in the southern part of the country, where the capital, Oslo, is situated.

Norway shares a short common frontier in the Arctic with Russia. Unlike her neighbours, Sweden and Finland, which are neutral, Norway is a member of NATO (North Atlantic Treaty Organization), but refused to join the EEC when Britain, Ireland and Denmark decided to enter (on 1 January 1973). As a member of the Nordic Council Norway co-operates closely with its Scandinavian neighbours on social welfare and education, and shares with Sweden and Finland membership of the European Free Trade Association (EFTA).

The sea has always been a major influence in Norwegian life. A thousand years ago Viking sailors from Norway roamed the northern seas, founding colonies around the coasts of Britain, Iceland and even North America. Today fishing, shipbuilding and the management of merchant shipping lines are of vital importance to the Norwegian economy, and its merchant ships, most of which seldom visit the home ports, earn profits which pay for a third of the country's imports.

Landscape

Norway is a rugged, mountainous country in which communication is difficult. The Norwegian landscape is dominated by rolling plateaus, the *vidda*,

SCANDINAVIA

There are several possible definitions of the term Scandinavia. In the narrow geographical sense it refers to the peninsula shared by Norway and Sweden; in a broader cultural and political sense it includes the five countries of the Nordic Council – Norway, Sweden, Denmark, Finland and Iceland. All except Finland have related languages, and all have a tradition of parliamentary democracy: Finland and Iceland are republics, while the others are constitutional monarchies.

There are also strong historical links between them, beginning in the 8th century when their ancestors, the Norsemen, colonized large parts of northern Europe. All have at different times been governed together, Sweden and Finland separating in 1809, Norway and Sweden in 1905, and Denmark and Iceland as recently as 1944.

Because of their northerly position, and their exposure to Atlantic weather systems, the Scandinavian states have a cool, moist climate not favourable to crops. However, because of the long hours of daylight in the northern summer, some surprisingly good crops are grown north of the Arctic Circle.

The Scandinavians were once among the poorest peoples of Europe, but during the last century they have become among the richest, making full use of their limited natural resources, and also seizing the opportunities which their maritime position gave them to become major shipping and fishing nations.

generally 300 to 900m [1,000 to 3,000 ft] high, above which some peaks rise to as much as 1,500 to 2,500m [5,000 to 8,000 ft] in the area between Oslo, Bergen and Trondheim. In the far north the summits are around 1,000m [3,000 ft] lower.

The highest areas retain permanent ice fields, as in the Jotunheim Mountains above Sognefjord. The Norwegian mountains have been uplifted during three mountain-building episodes during the last 400 million years, and they contain rocks of the earliest geological periods. Intrusions of volcanic material accompanied the uplifting and folding, and there are great masses of granites and gneisses – the source of Norway's mineral wealth.

There are few large areas of flat land in the country, but in the east the *vidda* are broken by deep valleys of rivers flowing to the lowlands of south-east Norway, focused on Oslo. In glacial times the whole country was covered by the great northern ice cap. When it melted about 10,000 years ago it left behind large deposits of glacial moraine, well represented around Oslo in the Raa moraines.

The coast and the islands

The configuration of the coast – the longest in Europe – helps to explain the ease with which the Norwegians took to the sea in their early history and why they have remained a seafaring nation since. The *vidda* are cut by long, narrow, steep-sided fjords on the west coast, shaped by the great northern icecap. The largest of these, Sognefjord – 203 km [127 mls] long and less than 5 km [3 mls] wide – is the longest inlet in Europe and the best known fjord.

Along the coast there are hundreds of islands, the largest group of which, the Lofoten Islands, lie north of the Arctic Circle. These islands, known as the *skerryguard*, protect the inner coast from the battering of the Atlantic breakers, and provide sheltered leads of water which the coastal ferries and fishing boats can navigate in safety.

Until recently communications along the coast were easier by boat than by land. Oslo is linked by rail to the main towns of the south, and a line reaches north to Bodö at latitude 67½°N. Roads are difficult to build and costly to maintain, and are often blocked by snow in winter and spring.

There are still several hundred ferries which carry cars across the fjords, but much money has been invested in the building of a north-south trunk road, with bridges across the fjords, to avoid the constant use of ferries. Air transport is of increasing importance and many small airstrips are in use, bringing remote communities into contact with the south.

Agriculture

With two-thirds of the country comprising barren mountains, snowfields or unproductive wastes, and one-fifth forested, less than 3% of the land can be cultivated. The barrenness of the soil, the heavy rainfall, winter snows and the short growing season restrict agriculture, especially in the north, though in the long days of summer good crops of hay, potatoes, quick-growing vegetables and even rye and barley are grown. Near the coast, farming is restricted to the limited areas of level or gently-sloping ground beside these sheltered fjords. Cattle and sheep use the slopes above them in the summer but are fed in stalls during the winter. Everywhere fish is caught in the local waters.

COUNTRY: Kingdom of Norway

AREA: 323,900 sq km [125,050 sq mls]

POPULATION: 4,242,000

CAPITAL (Population): Oslo (455,000)

GOVERNMENT: Constitutional monarchy with a unicameral legislature

ETHNIC GROUPS: Norwegian 97%

LANGUAGES: Norwegian (official), Lappish, Finnish

RELIGIONS: Lutheran 88%

NATIONAL DAY: 17 May; Independence Day (1905)

CURRENCY: Norwegian krone = 100 øre

ANNUAL INCOME PER PERSON: $23,120

MAIN PRIMARY PRODUCTS: Cereals, potatoes, livestock, fruit, timber, fish, crude oil, gas, coal, copper, iron, lead, nickel, titanium, quartz

MAIN INDUSTRIES: Mining, oil refining, minerals, shipbuilding, food processing, fishing, forestry

MAIN EXPORTS: Crude petroleum 23%, metal products 18%, natural gas 11%, machinery and transport equipment 10%, foodstuffs 8%

MAIN EXPORT PARTNERS: UK 27%, Germany 15%, Sweden 11%, Netherlands 7%

MAIN IMPORTS: Machinery and transport equipment 28%, metal and metal products 12%, raw materials including fuel 11%, foodstuffs 6%

MAIN IMPORT PARTNERS: Sweden 19%, Germany 16%, UK 9%, Denmark 8%

DEFENCE: 6.7% of national budget

TOURISM: 1,782,000 visitors per year

POPULATION DENSITY: 13 per sq km [34 per sq ml]

INFANT MORTALITY: 6 per 1,000 live births

LIFE EXPECTANCY: Female 81 yrs, male 75 yrs

ADULT LITERACY: 99%

PRINCIPAL CITIES (Population): Oslo 455,000 Bergen 211,000 Trondheim 137,000

Resources and industry

Iron and lead ores are found in the north, copper in central Norway and titanium in the south. The extent of Norway's mineral resources is not fully known, and prospecting is still revealing new deposits. Oil and natural gas from the seabed of the North Sea have made a great contribution to the Norwegian economy in recent years, and comprise more than half of the country's export earnings. Statfjord B (816,000 tonnes) is the world's biggest oil platform. Exploitation of all these reserves provides more than enough for the country's needs.

There is no coal in mainland Norway, although some is found in the islands on the Svalbard archipelago in the Arctic Ocean. The lack of coal has been partly compensated for by the development of hydroelectricity, begun in the early 20th century, when the waterfalls of streams and rivers flowing down the steep slopes above the fjords were first harnessed. Later, inland sites were developed, and the greatest concentration is in the Rjukan Valley, 160km [100mls] west of Oslo. Today Norway (which owns five of the world's highest waterfalls) derives 99% of its electricity from water power.

The availability of cheap electricity made poss-

Northern Norway is within the Arctic Circle, but owing to the Gulf Stream the winter temperatures are only just below freezing. Summers are distinctly cool with July and August temperatures around 10°C [50°F]. Inland, on the same latitude, the temperatures in the winter will be 10°C [18°F] colder, and slightly warmer in the summer. Jan Mayen and Svalbard, well within the Arctic, also benefit from the ameliorating effects of the Gulf Stream.

ible the rapid growth of the wood-pulp, paper and chemical industries, and later stimulated the metal-working industries. Many of the industrial sites are on the shores of remote fjords, where cheap electricity and deep-water access for the import of raw materials and for the export of finished products are the determining factors in choosing the location. The aluminium and chemical industries of the south-west coast are typical.

Metal-working has developed in the far north since World War II. After primary treatment iron is exported from Kirkenes to a smelter at Mo-i-Rana, on the coast just south of the Arctic Circle, which uses coal imported from Svalbard. The port of Narvik was connected by rail to the Swedish system in 1903, so that Swedish iron ore could be sent from an ice-free port to supply the iron smelters of Germany and other continental markets. This trade remains important today.

Rapid industrial development since World War II has transformed the Norwegian economy, and has ensured that the Norwegians are among the most prosperous people in Europe. Few people are very wealthy – taxation rates are high – but few are very poor, and an advanced welfare state (common to all the Scandinavian countries) provides good services even to the most isolated or rural communities. The great majority of people own their houses, and many families have second homes on the shores of fjords and lakes. Today's Norwegians are also more generous than their Viking ancestors: the nation is by far Europe's biggest donor of foreign aid per capita, with a figure of 1.1% of GNP – well above the OECD (Organization for Economic Co-operation and Development) target of 0.7%.

The pre-war economy, dependent on forestry, farming, fishing and seafaring, is still important, but the numbers employed in these industries are dwindling as more and more people move into the new industries and services in the growing towns. There are still few large towns, and all six of those with more than 50,000 population are on the coast. The largest are Oslo, Bergen and Trondheim.

Svalbard is an archipelago of 62,920 sq km [24,295 sq mls] – half as big again as Denmark – sitting halfway between the North Pole and the Arctic Circle. Despite this exposed, northerly position, the climate is tempered by the relatively mild prevailing winds from the Atlantic. By far the largest island is Spitzbergen (or Vestspitzbergen), the former also being used as the name of the whole group.

The rival claims on the islands by the Norwegians, the Dutch and the British lost their importance in the 18th century with the decline of whale hunting, but were raised again in the 20th century with the discovery of coal. A treaty signed in Paris by 40 parties in 1920 finally recognized Norwegian sovereignty in return for mining rights, and in 1925 the islands were incorporated officially into the kingdom of Norway.

Coal remains the principal product and main occupation, with mines run by Norway and the former Soviet Union, both of which produce similar amounts of coal: about 470,000 tonnes a year. Soviet citizens outnumbered Norwegians by more than 2 to 1 in 1988, when the total figure was 3,646 inhabitants. This was about 300 down on 1986.

Following the success of the North Sea projects, there is now prospecting in Svalbard for oil and natural gas. There are several meteorological stations and a research station, and other residents work on the extensive national parks and nature reserves. An airport opened in 1975 near Longyearbyen, the capital that is named after an American (J.M. Longyear), who in 1905 was the first man to mine coal on Svalbard.

Jan Mayen is a volcanic island of 380 sq km [147 sq mls], north-north-east of Iceland but actually closer to the east coast of Greenland. Desolate, mountainous and partly covered by glaciers, its dominant feature is the volcano of Beerenberg (2,277 m [7,470 ft]), which had been dormant but became active again in 1970.

The island was named in 1614 after the Dutch whaling captain Jan Jacobsz May, but 'discovered' by Henry Hudson in 1608. Though uninhabited, it was used by seal trappers and other hunters, and in 1921 Norway established a meteorological and radio station. In 1929 it was annexed into the kingdom of Norway, and today the only residents are the 30 or so staff at a weather station.

Bjørnøya (Bear Island) lies halfway between Svalbard and the Norwegian mainland, on the cusp of the Norwegian Sea and Barents Sea. Measuring 179 sq km [69 sq mls], it is uninhabited but remains the centre of important cod fisheries; after a long dispute over territorial rights it was internationally recognized as part of Norway in 1925 ■

SWEDEN

While Sweden's national flag has been flown since the reign of King Gustavus Vasa in the early 16th century, it was not officially adopted until 1906. The colours were derived from the ancient state coat of arms dating from 1364.

The kingdom of Sweden is the largest of the Scandinavian countries in both population and area. It occupies the eastern half of the Scandinavian peninsula, extending southwards to latitude 55°N and having a much smaller Arctic area than either Norway or Finland.

The 1,600 km [1,000 mls] eastern coast, along the shores of the Baltic Sea and the Gulf of Bothnia, extends from the mouth of the Torne River, which forms the border with Finland to Ystad in the south, opposite the Danish island of Bornholm and the German coast. Sweden also has a coastline facing west along the shores of the Kattegat – the strait that separates Sweden and the Jutland peninsula, which is part of Denmark.

Landscape

Sweden's share of the Scandinavian peninsula is less mountainous than that of Norway. The northern half of the country forms part of the Baltic or Fenno-Scandian Shield, a stable block of ancient granites and gneisses which extends round the head of the Gulf of Bothnia into Finland. This part of Sweden contains most of the country's rich mineral wealth. The shield land is an area of low plateaus which rise gradually westwards.

South of the plateaus area there is a belt of lowlands between the capital city, Stockholm, and the second city, Göteborg (Gothenburg). These lowlands contain several large lakes, the chief of which are Mälar, near Stockholm, and the larger Vänern and Vättern, which are situated in the middle of the lowland belt.

These are all that remains of a strait which, in glacial times, connected the Baltic with the Kattegat. Changes in land and water level during the later stages of the Ice Age led to the breaking of this connection. Now linked by canals, these lakes form an important water route across the country. South of the lakes is a low plateau, rising to 380 m [1,250 ft] above Lake Vättern and sloping gently down to the small lowland area of Skåne (Scania).

Sweden's topography was greatly affected by the Ice Age: the long, narrow lakes which fill the upper valleys of many of the rivers of northern Sweden have been shaped by the action of ice. They are the relics of a much larger lake system which was fed by water from the melting ice-sheet and provide excellent natural reservoirs for hydroelectric stations. Some of the most fertile soils in Sweden were formed from material deposited in the beds of such glacial lakes. Elsewhere, glacial moraines and deposits of boulder clay are other reminders of the impact of the Ice Age.

Forestry and agriculture

There are extensive coniferous forests throughout northern Sweden; indeed, half the country's land area is covered with trees. In the south the original cover of mixed deciduous woodland has been cleared for agriculture from the areas of better soil, the typical landscape now being farmland interspersed with forest. This is usually spruce or pine, often with birch – the national tree.

There are better opportunities for agriculture in Sweden than elsewhere in Scandinavia. Cereal crops, potatoes, sugar beet and vegetables are grown for human consumption in Skåne and in central Sweden, but by far the greatest area of cultivated land is given over to the production of fodder crops for cattle and sheep. Dairy farming is highly developed, and Sweden is self-sufficient in milk, cheese and butter production.

Industry and population

Many farmers have left the land since World War II, attracted by the higher wages and more modern life style of the towns. Sweden has been able to create a high standard of living based on industry – despite the fact that, apart from the large iron-ore deposits, many of the essential fuels and raw materials have to be imported. Most of the iron ore obtained from the mines at Kiruna and Gällivare in Arctic Sweden is exported via Narvik and Lulea to Germany.

The development of hydroelectricity has made up for the lack of oil and coal. Sweden is famous for high-quality engineering products such as ball bearings, matchmaking machinery, agricultural machines, motor vehicles (Saab and Volvo), ships, aircraft and armaments (Bofors). In addition to these relatively new industries, the traditional forest-based industries have been modernized. Sweden is the world's largest exporter of wood pulp and third largest exporter of paper and board – as well as Europe's biggest producer of softwood.

The bulk of the population lives in the lakeland corridor between Stockholm and Göteborg, or around the southern city of Malmö. These citizens, by their forebears working hard, exploiting their resources and avoiding war or occupation for nearly two centuries, now enjoy a standard of living that is in many ways the envy of most other Western countries. Sweden has by far the highest percentage figure for public spending in the OECD, with over 70% of the national budget going on one of the widest-ranging welfare programmes in the world.

In turn, the tax burden is the world's highest (some 57% of national income) and some Swedes are beginning to feel that the 'soft' yet paternalistic approach has led to over-government, depersonalization and uniformity. The elections of September 1991 saw the end of the Social Democrat government – in power for all but six years since 1932 – with voters swinging towards parties canvassing

The Gulf Stream warms the southern coastlands, but to the north continental influences take over. The February temperature in the south is just below freezing, but in the north it is –15°C [5°F]. Rainfall is low throughout Sweden, but it lies as snow for over six months in the north. The Baltic is usually frozen for at least five months, but ice is rare on the western coast. In the summer, there is little difference between the north and south, most areas experiencing between 15° and 20°C [59° to 68°F].

STOCKHOLM

COUNTRY: Kingdom of Sweden
AREA: 449,960 sq km [173,730 sq mls]
POPULATION: 8,618,000
CAPITAL (Population): Stockholm (669,000)
GOVERNMENT: Constitutional monarchy and parliamentary state with a unicameral legislature
ETHNIC GROUPS: Swedish 91%, Finnish 3%
LANGUAGES: Swedish (official), Finnish
RELIGIONS: Lutheran 89%, Roman Catholic 2%
NATIONAL DAY: 6 June
CURRENCY: Swedish krona = 100 öre
ANNUAL INCOME PER PERSON: $23,680
MAIN PRIMARY PRODUCTS: Cereals, cattle, sugar beet, potatoes, timber, iron ore, copper, lead, zinc
MAIN INDUSTRIES: Engineering, electrical goods, vehicles, mining, timber, paper, wood pulp
MAIN EXPORTS: Machinery and transport equipment 43%, paper products 11%, electrical machinery 8%, wood pulp 7%, chemicals 7%
MAIN EXPORT PARTNERS: Germany 12%, UK 11%, USA 10%, Norway 9%, Denmark 7%, Finland 7%
MAIN IMPORTS: Machinery and transport equipment 36%, chemicals 10%
MAIN IMPORT PARTNERS: Germany 21%, UK 9%, USA 8%, Finland 7%, Denmark 7%, Norway 6%
DEFENCE: 8.8% of national budget
TOURISM: 814,000 visitors per year
POPULATION DENSITY: 19 per sq km [50 per sq ml]
INFANT MORTALITY: 6 per 1,000 live births
LIFE EXPECTANCY: Female 81 yrs, male 75 yrs
ADULT LITERACY: 99%
PRINCIPAL CITIES (Population): Stockholm 669,000 Göteborg 431,000 Malmö 232,000 Uppsala 162,000

ÅLAND

Swedish settlers colonized various coastal tracts of Finland from the 12th century, and the 6.5% of the Finnish population who are Swedish-speaking include all the 24,000 people of Åland, the group of more than 6,500 islands situated between the two countries in the Gulf of Bothnia.

Although the inhabitants voted to secede to Sweden in a 1917 referendum, the result was annulled in 1921 by the League of Nations for strategic reasons and Åland (as Ahvenanmaa) remained a Finnish province. However, the islands were granted considerable autonomy and still enjoy a large degree of 'home rule' with their own flag, postage stamps and representation at the annual assembly of the Nordic Council.

Boasting many important relics of the Stone, Iron and Bronze Ages, the province's income derives mainly from fishing, farming and, increasingly, from tourism.

lower taxation. Other attractive policies appeared to include curbs on immigration and diversion of Third World aid (Sweden spends well above the OECD per capita average each year) to the newly independent Baltic states.

Other changes were in the wind, too. A founder member of EFTA – Stockholm played host to the inaugural meetings in 1960 – Sweden nevertheless applied for entry to the EEC in 1991, a move that, if successful, would almost certainly lead to Norway, Finland and Iceland following suit. Sweden remains still the key state in Scandinavia: its long experience of peace and stability, and a wide industrial base built on efficiency and quality, can be grafted on to its strategically central position and relatively large population to form the most important power among the Nordic nations.

While some say that Sweden's biggest problems could be of its own making (though contrary to belief it is Denmark that has the world's highest known suicide rate), it is possible that it will be vulnerable to forces largely beyond its control. Like its neighbours, Sweden suffers from forest-killing acid rain generated mostly by the UK and Germany, and after the shock waves from Chernobyl in 1986 the government was also forced to reconsider its electricity-generating programme, at that time more than 40% dependent on nuclear power ∎

DENMARK

The Dannebrog ('the spirit of Denmark') flag is said to represent King Waldemar II's vision of a white cross against a red sky before the Battle of Lyndanisse in 1219, and is possibly the oldest national flag in continuous use.

The climate of Denmark reflects that the country is at the meeting of Arctic, continental and maritime influences. The winters, thanks to the warm Atlantic waters, are not too cold, although there may be many nights that are below freezing. The summers are warm. January and February have about 20 frost-days, and both of these months have experienced temperatures lower than –20°C [–4°F]. The rainfall is reasonable, falling in all months with a maximum July to September.

The smallest of the Scandinavian countries (but the second largest in population), Denmark consists of the Jutland (Jylland) peninsula, which is an extension of the North German Plain, and an archipelago of 406 islands, of which 89 are inhabited. The coastline – about 7,300 km [4,500 mls] – is extremely long for the size of the country. The largest and most densely populated of the islands is Zealand (Sjaelland), which lies close to the coast of southern Sweden. In the early 1990s this will be connected to the most important island – Fünen (Fyn) – by the Storebaeltstunnel. Copenhagen (København), the capital city, lies on the narrow strait, The Sound, which leads from the Kattegat to the Baltic.

Control of the entrances to the Baltic contributed to the power of Denmark in the Middle Ages, when the kingdom dominated its neighbours and expanded its territories to include Norway, Iceland, Greenland and the Faroe Islands. The link with Norway was broken in 1814, and with Iceland in 1944, but Greenland and the Faroes retain connections with Denmark. The granite island of Bornholm, off the southern tip of Sweden, also remains a Danish possession.

Structurally, Denmark is part of a low-lying belt of sedimentary rocks extending from north Germany to southern Sweden, which are geologically much younger than the rest of Scandinavia. The surface is almost entirely covered by glacial deposits, but the underlying strata are exposed as the 122 m [400 ft] chalk cliffs on the island of Møn. Nowhere in Denmark, however, is higher than 171 m [561 ft] and the country averages just 98 m [30 ft]. Along the west coast of Jutland, facing the North Sea, are lines of sand dunes with shallow lagoons behind them.

Agriculture and industry

Denmark has few mineral resources and no coal, though there is now some oil and natural gas from the North Sea. A century ago this was a poor farming and fishing country, but Denmark has now been transformed into one of Europe's wealthiest industrial nations. The first steps in the process were taken in the late 19th century, with the introduction of co-operative methods of processing and distributing farm produce, and the development of modern methods of dairying and pig- and poultry-breeding. Denmark became the main supplier of bacon, eggs and butter to the growing industrial nations of Western Europe. Most of the natural fodder for the animals is still grown in Denmark – three-quarters of the land is cultivated and more than 60% is arable – with barley as the principal crop.

From a firm agricultural base Denmark has developed a whole range of industries. Some – brewing, meat canning, fish processing, pottery, textiles and furniture-making – use Danish products, while others – shipbuilding, oil refining, engineering and metal-working – depend on imported raw materials. The famous port of Copenhagen is also the chief industrial centre and draw for more than a million tourists each year. At the other end of the scale there is Legoland, the famous miniature town of plastic bricks, built at Billand, north-west of Vejle in eastern Jutland. It was here, in a carpenter's workshop, that Lego was created before it went on to become the world's best-selling construction toy – and a prominent Danish export. The country is also the world's biggest exporter of insulin.

People and culture

Denmark is a generally comfortable mixture of striking social opposites. The Lutheran tradition and the cradle of Hans Christian Andersen's fairy tales co-exist with open attitudes to pornography and one of the highest illegitimacy rates in the West (44%). A reputation for caring and thorough welfare services – necessitating high taxation – is dented somewhat by the world's highest recorded suicide rate.

It is, too, one of the 'greenest' of the advanced nations, with a pioneering Ministry of Pollution that has real power to act: in 1991 it became the first government anywhere to fine industries for emissions of carbon dioxide, the primary 'greenhouse'

gas. At the same time, Danes register Europe's highest rate of deaths from lung cancer.

Denmark gets on well with its neighbours and partners. On 1 January 1973, along with Britain and Ireland, it joined the EEC – the first Scandinavian country to make the break from EFTA – but it still co-operates closely on social, cultural and economic matters with its five Scandinavian partners in the Nordic Council.

Bornholm is a Danish island well away from the rest of the country and far nearer to the southern tip of Sweden (40 km [25 mls]) than to Copenhagen (168 km [104 mls]). A separate administrative region, it was occupied by Germany in World War II but liberated by the Russians, who returned it to Denmark in 1946.

Measuring 558 sq km [227 sq mls], Bornholm is composed mainly of granite and has poor soils, but deposits of kaolin (china clay) spawned a pottery industry. The principal town and ferry port is Rønne, the fishing port Neksø. Fishing and fish processing, agriculture (mainly cattle-rearing) and tourism are the main sources of income – the last-named reliant partly on the island's fine examples of fortified churches ∎

COUNTRY: Kingdom of Denmark

AREA: 43,070 sq km [16,629 sq mls]

POPULATION: 5,140,000

CAPITAL (Population): Copenhagen (1,339,000)

GOVERNMENT: Parliamentary monarchy with a unicameral legislature

ETHNIC GROUPS: Danish 97%

LANGUAGES: Danish (official)

RELIGIONS: Lutheran 91%, Roman Catholic 1%

NATIONAL DAY: 16 April; Birthday of HM the Queen

CURRENCY: Krone = 100 øre

ANNUAL INCOME PER PERSON: $22,090

MAIN PRIMARY PRODUCTS: Livestock, cereals, oil and natural gas

MAIN INDUSTRIES: Agriculture and food processing, shipbuilding, chemicals, petroleum refining

EXPORTS: $5,475 per person

MAIN EXPORTS: Meat, dairy produce, fish 27%, machinery and electronic equipment 24%, chemicals

MAIN EXPORT PARTNERS: Germany 17%, UK 12%, Sweden 11%, USA 8%, Norway 8%

IMPORTS: $5,198 per person

MAIN IMPORTS: Machinery and transport equipment 31%, chemicals 10%, foodstuffs 10% mineral fuels and lubricants 9%

MAIN IMPORT PARTNERS: Germany 24%, Sweden 12%, UK 7%, Japan 5%, USA 5%, Netherlands 5%, France 5%

DEFENCE: 7.4% of national budget

TOURISM: 1,171,000 visitors per year

POPULATION DENSITY: 119 per sq km [308 per sq ml]

INFANT MORTALITY: 6 per 1,000 live births

LIFE EXPECTANCY: Female 79 yrs, male 73 yrs

ADULT LITERACY: 99%

PRINCIPAL CITIES (Population): Copenhagen 1,339,000 Århus 258,000 Odense 174,000 Ålborg 155,000

FINLAND

Finland became an independent republic only in 1917 after separation from Russia, then in the throes of the Revolution, and the present flag was adopted soon after. The colours symbolize Finland's blue lakes and white snow.

The dominating feature of Finland's climate is the harshness and length of the winter. A third of Finland is north of the Arctic Circle and here temperatures can reach –30°C [–22°F]. Snow can lie for six months, never clearing from the north-facing slopes. Helsinki has four or five months below 0°C [32°F]. The seas and lakes nearly always freeze in winter. The summers can be hot. Rainfall is low, decreasing northwards and falling mostly late summer to winter, often as snow.

Located almost entirely between latitudes 60°N and 70°N, Finland is the most northerly state on the mainland of Europe, though Norway's county of Finnmark actually cuts it off from the Arctic Ocean. A third of Finland's total area lies within the Arctic Circle, a far higher proportion than for its two large Scandinavian partners.

The climate of the northern province of Lappi (Lapland) is not as severe as in places which lie in similar latitudes, such as Canada and Siberia, because of the North Atlantic Drift. This influence keeps the Arctic coasts of Europe free from ice all year round.

Finland enjoys a short but warm summer, with average July temperatures at Helsinki of 17°C [63°F] and 13°C [55°F] in Lapland. Because of the high latitudes, summer days are extremely long; indeed, in the Arctic region there is virtually no night throughout the month of June.

Winters are long and cold (Helsinki's January average is –6°C [21°F]) and the days are short. In severe winters the sea freezes for several miles offshore and ice-breakers have to be used to keep the ports open. Snowfall is not heavy, however, and rail and road transport is seldom badly disrupted.

Landscape

Geologically Finland is made up of a central plateau of ancient crystalline rocks, mainly granites, schists and gneisses, surrounded by lowlands composed of recent glacial deposits. In the 600 million years between the formation of these ancient rocks and the last Ice Age, the surface of the land was worn down to a peneplain, and most of central and southern Finland is below 200 m [650 ft]. However, the roots of an old mountain system running north-west to south-east can still be traced across Lapland and along Finland's eastern border with Russia. Peaks of over 1,000 m [3,000 ft] occur in northern Lapland, near the Swedish and Norwegian borders.

A tenth of the land surface is covered by lakes. Concentrated in the central plateau, they are in most cases long, narrow and shallow, and aligned in a

COUNTRY: Republic of Finland

AREA: 338,130 sq km [130,552 sq mls]

POPULATION: 4,986,000

CAPITAL (Population): Helsinki (491,000)

GOVERNMENT: Multiparty parliamentary republic with a unicameral legislature

ETHNIC GROUPS: Finnish 93%, Swedish 6%

LANGUAGES: Finnish and Swedish (official)

RELIGIONS: Lutheran 89%, Greek Orthodox 1%

NATIONAL DAY: 6 December; Independence Day (1917)

CURRENCY: Markka = 100 pennia

ANNUAL INCOME PER PERSON: $26,070

MAIN PRIMARY PRODUCTS: Timber, livestock, copper, lead, iron, zinc, fish

MAIN INDUSTRIES: Forestry, wood pulp, paper, machinery, shipbuilding, chemicals, fertilizers

EXPORTS: $4,695 per person

MAIN EXPORTS: Machinery 27%, paper and paperboard 26%, wood, lumber, cork and wastepaper 10%

MAIN EXPORT PARTNERS: Russia and other CIS nations 16%, Sweden 15%, UK 11%, Germany 11%

IMPORTS: $4,964 per person

MAIN IMPORTS: Machinery and transport equipment 44%, basic manufactures, textiles and metals 16%, petroleum and petroleum products 10%, chemicals 10%, foodstuffs 5%

MAIN IMPORT PARTNERS: Germany 17%, Russia and other CIS nations 14%, Sweden 13%

DEFENCE: 5.7% of national budget

TOURISM: 436,000 visitors per year

POPULATION DENSITY: 15 per sq km [38 per sq ml]

INFANT MORTALITY: 5 per 1,000 live births

LIFE EXPECTANCY: Female 80 yrs, male 72 yrs

ADULT LITERACY: 99%

PRINCIPAL CITIES (Population): Helsinki 987,000 Turku 263,000 Tampere 260,000 Espoo 168,000 Vantaa 151,000

THE LAPPS

Hunters, fishermen and herdsmen living in Arctic Europe, approximately 35,000 Lapps are scattered between Norway (with 20,000), Sweden and Finland, with a small group in Russia. Physically, the short, dark Lapps – or Samer, as they call themselves – are noticeably different from other Scandinavians, though their language, Saarme, is related to Finnish. They probably originated in northern Russia at least 2,000 years ago, and may have been the original inhabitants of Finland. Until the 17th century, when they first learned to domesticate reindeer, they lived entirely by hunting and fishing; thereafter, many followed a semi-nomadic life, driving their herds each summer from their winter settlements at the edge of the forest to the high pastureland.

Industrialization, especially mining and hydroelectric development and the associated roads, has badly affected nomadic herding, and it now occupies only about 10% of Lapps. Most live in fixed settlements in coastal areas, and a steady trickle migrate south, assimilating themselves into modern Scandinavian society.

north-west to south-east direction, indicating the line of movement of the ice-sheet which scoured out their basins. More than two-thirds of Finland is covered by lakes and forest – a fact that accounts for almost everything from the composition of its exports to the brilliance of its rally drivers.

The number of lakes varies from 60,000 to 185,000, depending on the source of the information and the definition used, but whatever the exact figure may be, they dominate the landscape of the southern half of Finland and contribute to its austere beauty. The Saimaa area in the south-east, near the Russian frontier, is Europe's largest inland system.

Although under increasing threat from pollution caused by wood processing and fertilizers as well as acid rain, the lakes are still rich in fish – mainly trout, salmon, pike and perch – and provide a prime source of recreation for huge numbers of Finnish people.

Forests occupy almost 60% of the land surface, the main trees being pine, spruce and birch. Forest-based products – wood pulp, sawn timber, paper and board – still constitute 40% of Finland's exports, but since World War II engineering, shipbuilding and metallurgical industries have greatly expanded. A member of EFTA, Finland saw its

economy grow at a faster rate than that of Japan during the 1980s. In 1992 Finland formally applied to become a member of the EEC.

People and culture

Between 1150 and 1809 Finland was under Swedish rule, and one of the legacies of this period is a Swedish-speaking minority of 6.5% of the total population. In some localities on the south and west coasts, Swedish speakers are in a majority and Åland, an island closer to the Swedish coast than to Finland, is a self-governing province. Many towns in Finland use both Finnish and Swedish names; for example, Helsinki is Helsingfors and Turku is Åbo in Swedish. Finnish bears little relation to Swedish or any Scandinavian language, and is closest to Magyar, the native tongue of Hungary.

While few Finns comply with the clichéd image and run around in the snow before beating their feet with birch twigs, they do try to keep warm in other ways. They consume more vodka per head than the Russians – indeed, it became a serious social problem during the 1980s – and they are the world's most committed consumers of coffee, averaging almost five cups a day ∎

EUROPE

UNITED KINGDOM

 The first Union flag, combining England's cross of St George and Scotland's cross of St Andrew, dates from 1603 when James VI became James I of England. The Irish emblem, the cross of St Patrick, was added in 1801 to form the present flag.

South-eastern England, sheltered from the ocean to the west, is one of the driest parts of the British Isles. Although rainfall varies little throughout the year, greater evaporation creates a deficit between May and August. Like other parts of north-west Europe, London has a small annual temperature range. Its record low is –10°C [14°F] and record high 34°C [93°F]. The metropolis creates its own local climate and nights are generally warmer than in the surrounding countryside.

The British Isles stand on the westernmost edge of the continental shelf – two large and several hundred small islands for the most part cool, rainy and windswept. Despite physical closeness to the rest of Europe (32 km [20 mls] at the nearest point – little more than the distance across London), Britain is curiously isolated, with a long history of political independence and social separation from its neighbours. In the past the narrow seas served the islanders well, protecting them against casual invasion, while Britons in turn sailed to explore and exploit the rest of the world. Now insularity is rapidly breaking down, and Britain is closer to federation with Europe than ever before.

The islands are confusingly named. 'Great Britain', the largest in Europe and eighth largest in the world – so named to distinguish it from 'Little Britain' (Brittany, in France) – includes the kingdoms of England and Scotland and the principality of Wales; Ireland was once a kingdom, but is currently divided into the Province of Northern Ireland, under the British Crown, and the politically separate Republic of Ireland. Great Britain, Northern Ireland, and many off-lying island groups from the Scillies to the Shetlands, together make up the United Kingdom of Great Britain and Northern Ireland, commonly known as the UK. Even isolated Rockall, far out in the Atlantic Ocean, is part of the UK, but the Isle of Man and the Channel Islands are separate if direct dependencies of the Crown, with a degree of political autonomy and their own taxation systems.

Climate

Despite a subarctic position Britain is favoured climatically. Most other maritime lands between 50° and 60°N – eastern Siberia, Kamchatka, the Aleutian Islands, southern Alaska, Hudson Bay and Labrador – are colder throughout the year, with longer winters, ice-bound coasts and a shorter growing season. Britain's salvation is the North Atlantic Drift or Gulf Stream, a current of surface water that brings subtropical warmth from the southern Atlantic Ocean, spreading it across the continental shelf of Western Europe and warming the prevailing westerly winds.

Britain's reputation for cloudiness is well merited. Mean duration of sunshine throughout the year is about 5 hours daily in the south, and only $3\frac{1}{2}$ hours daily in Scotland. At the height of summer only the south-west receives more than $7\frac{1}{2}$ hours of sunshine per day – less than half the hours available. In winter only the south coast, the Severn Estuary, Oxfordshire and a sliver of south-eastern Essex receive more than $1\frac{1}{2}$ hours per day, while many northern areas receive less than half an hour daily.

Despite a reputation for rain Britain is fairly dry. More than half of the country receives less than 750 mm [30 in] annually, and parts of Essex have less than 500 mm [20 in] per year. The wettest areas are Snowdonia with about 5,000 mm [200 in], Ben Nevis and the north-western highlands with 4,300 mm [172 in], and the Lake District with 3,300 mm [132 in].

Population and immigration

Despite insularity the British people are of mixed stock. The earliest immigrants – land-hungry farmers from the Continent – were often refugees from tribal warfare and unrest. The Belgic tribesmen escaping from Imperial Rome, the Romans themselves (whose troops included Spanish, Macedonian and probably North African mercenaries), the Angles, Saxons, Jutes, Danes and Normans, all in turn brought genetic variety; so too did the Huguenots, Sephardic and Ashkenazim Jews, and Dutch, French and German businessmen who followed them. Latterly the waves of immigrants have included Belorussians, Poles, Italians, Ukrainians and Czechs – most, like their predecessors, fugitives from European wars, overcrowding and intolerance.

During the 19th century Britain often took in skilled European immigrants through the front door while steadily losing her own sons and daughters – Scots and Irish peasants in particular – through the back. Most recent arrivals in Britain are immigrants from crowded and impoverished corners of lands once part of the British Empire, notably the West Indies, West Africa, India and Pakistan. These and their descendants now make up about 4% of the population of Britain.

Under Roman rule the population of the British island numbered half to three-quarters of a million. By the time of the Domesday Survey it had doubled, and it doubled again by the end of the 14th century. The Black Death of the late 15th century swept away one in every three or four, but numbers climbed slowly; at the Union of 1707 some 6 million English and Welsh joined about 1 million Scots under a single parliament. By 1801 the first national census revealed 8.9 million in England and Wales, 1.6 million in Scotland; Ireland missed the first two ten-year counts, but probably numbered about 5 million. In 1821 the total British population was 21 million, in 1851 31 million, and in 1921 47 million.

The rate of increase has now declined, but some parts of Britain, notably the south-east and the conurbations, are among the most heavily populated areas of the world, with higher densities only in the Netherlands and Taiwan.

England

Landscape: Visitors to England are often amazed at the variety of the landscape. Complex folding, laval outpourings, volcanic upheavals and eruptions, glacial planing, and changes of sea level have all left their marks on the present landscape.

From Northumberland to the Trent, the Pennines extend southwards as an upland with rolling hills, plateaus and fine valleys, many known as 'dales'. The range includes two western outliers – the Forest of Rossendale north of Manchester, and the Forest of Bowland in north Lancashire. To either side lie lowlands – those of Lancashire to the west and of Yorkshire and Nottingham to the east.

The Eden Valley separates the northern Pennines from Cumbria, which includes the Lake District. This is England's most striking mountain mass, a circular area of peaks, deep valleys, splendid lakes and crags. The loftiest peak is Scafell, 978 m [3,210 ft]. In the south-west Exmoor is a fine sandstone upland, and Dartmoor a predominantly granite area with many prominent tors. Elsewhere are isolated hills, small by world standards but dramatic against the small-scale background of Britain, as shown by the Malvern Hills of Worcester and the Wrekin near Shrewsbury.

Much of the English lowland consists of chalk downlands, familiar to continental visitors who enter England through Folkestone or Dover as the famous chalk cliffs. These are the exposed coastal edge of the North Downs, whose scarped northern slope forms a striking feature in the Croydon area of Greater London. The North Downs continue westwards through Surrey to the Hampshire Downs, then south and east as the South Downs, emerging at another coastal landmark – Beachy Head.

There is a northwards extension of downland through the Berkshire and Marlborough Downs to

THE CHANNEL ISLANDS

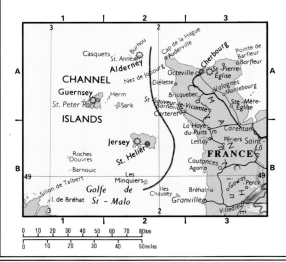

Lying 16 to 48 km [10 to 30 mls] from the French coast, the Channel Islands are a British dependency covering an area of only 200 sq km [78 sq mls]. The largest are Jersey with 115 sq km [45 sq mls] and 75,000 inhabitants, and Guernsey, with 78 sq km [30 sq mls] and 55,000 people. The other islands – Alderney, Sark and others – are small, with fewer than 2,000 residents.

The only part of the Duchy of Normandy retained by the English Crown after 1204, and the only part of Britain occupied by the Germans in World War II, the islands have their own legal system and government, with lower taxation than that of Britain. This, combined with a favourable climate and fine coastal scenery, has attracted a considerable number of wealthy residents, notably retired people, and established Jersey and Guernsey as offshore financial centres.

The main produce is agricultural, especially early potatoes, tomatoes and flowers for Britain, and the countryside has a vast number of glasshouses. Jersey and Guernsey cattle are famous breeds, introduced to many countries. Holidaymakers visit the islands in large numbers during the summer months, travelling by air or by the various passenger boats, especially from Weymouth. English is the official language but French is widely spoken.

ISLE OF MAN

Covering 590 sq km [227 sq mls], the Isle of Man sits in the Irish Sea almost equidistant from County Down and Cumbria, but actually nearer Galloway in Scotland. The uplands, pierced by the corridor valley from Douglas to Peel, extend from Ramsey to Port Erin. Mainly agricultural, the island is now largely dependent on tourism. Douglas, the capital, has over a third of the population. The IOM is a dependency of the British Crown with its own legislative assembly, legal system and tax controls.

the Chilterns then north again into East Anglia to disappear under the edge of the fens near Cambridge. Formerly forested, the downlands were cleared early for pasture and agriculture, and now provide a rich and varied mixture of woodlands, parklands, fields and mostly small settlements. Chalk appears again in the wolds of Lincolnshire and Yorkshire, emerging at Flamborough Head.

Older rocks, predominantly limestones, form the ridge of the Cotswold Hills, and the rolling, hilly farmlands of Leicestershire, the Lincoln Edge (cut by the River Witham at Lincoln), and finally the North York Moors. In these older rocks are rich iron deposits, mined by Cleveland to supply ores for the steel towns of the Tees Estuary until 1964, and still mined in the Midlands.

England is drained by many fine rivers, of which the greatest are the Thames, the Severn, the fenland Ouse, the Trent, and the great Yorkshire Ouse that receives its tributaries from the many picturesque valleys – the Dales – of the Pennine flank. There are many smaller rivers, and a large number of the old towns that dot England at intervals of 20 km [12 mls] or so were built at their crossing points – generally where dry ground existed above marshes and gave firm sites for building.

Agriculture: England has a rich variety of soils, derived both locally from parent rocks and also from glacial debris or 'drift'. During the 12,000 and more years since the ice retreated, soils have been enriched, firstly by such natural processes as flooding and the growth of forests, latterly by the good husbandry of many generations of farmers. Husbandry improved particularly from the 18th century onwards; the Industrial Revolution was accompanied by an agricultural revolution that resulted in massive increases in crop yields and in the quality of livestock.

Through the 18th and 19th centuries farming became more scientific and more specialized; as the demands from the towns grew, so did the ability of English farmers to meet increasing markets for food. The eastern counties, particularly East Anglia and Holderness (now part of Humberside), became the granaries of England, while the rich, wet grasslands of the west and the Midlands turned pastoral – Cheshire cheese is a famous product of this specialization. There were other local products – the hops of Kent and Hereford, the apples of Worcester, and the fine wools that continued to be the main product of the chalk downlands. In south Lancashire potatoes and vegetables became major crops for sale in the markets of the growing northern industrial towns; market gardening and dairying on a small scale developed near every major settlement, taking advantage of the ready market close at hand.

Scenically England still gives the impression of being an agricultural country. Less than 10% of the area is rough moorland, about 5% is forest, and about another 10% is urban or suburban, leaving roughly three-quarters under cultivation of one kind

or another. Yet only 3% of the working population is currently employed in agriculture, a figure that has declined drastically in recent years. Loss of rural populations has been an inevitable result of agricultural rationalization and improvements in farming methods. Those who deplore this trend might reflect that, though English farming formerly employed many more labourers, it supported them at little more than subsistence level.

Industry and urbanization: England had important reserves of coal, the major fields being on either side of the Pennines (Yorkshire, Lancashire, Northumberland and Durham), in the Midlands (Derbyshire and Nottinghamshire) and in South Wales. These coalfields and extensive reserves of iron ore – now largely defunct – were the basis of the Industrial Revolution of the 18th century, and the industrial growth of the 19th century, which together resulted in major changes in the English landscape.

Areas which previously had only small populations rose to industrial greatness. Perhaps the most striking example was Teesside where, following the exploitation of the Cleveland iron ores, the town of Middlesbrough grew from a small port (7,000 population in 1851) to a large manufacturing centre. Today Middlesbrough and its neighbouring settlements have almost 400,000 inhabitants. Similarly, small mill villages in Lancashire and Yorkshire grew into large towns while the West Midlands pottery towns and villages coalesced into the urban areas of Stoke-on-Trent.

Although the coalfields of the north saw the greatest local expansion of population, London and England's other major ports, such as Liverpool and Bristol, also developed as export markets flourished. These developments were accompanied by significant improvements in communications, including the building of an extensive canal network (with

NORTH SEA OIL

The discovery of gas and oil in the North Sea in the 1960s transformed Britain from an oil importer into the world's fifth largest exporter within a decade. Gas from the new fields rapidly replaced coal gas in the British energy system, and by 1981 the country was self-sufficient in oil. In the peak production year of 1986, the British sector of the North Sea produced 128.6 million tonnes of crude oil, accounting for over 20% of UK export earnings; in 1989, North Sea output amounted to 3% of total world production. In 1991, remaining reserves were estimated at 4 billion barrels – little more than four years' production at 1986 levels.

In taxes and royalties, North Sea oil gave an immense fillip to British government revenue, contributing more than £76 billion since 1979, and protecting the balance of payments despite severe industrial decline. There was much discussion as to the best use for this windfall money, which would taper away during the 1990s and vanish altogether in the next century; but it certainly helped finance substantial tax cuts during the controversial years of Mrs Thatcher's government. The sight of North Sea oil wealth flowing south to the Westminster treasury also provoked nationalist resentment in Scotland, off whose coast most of the oil rigs (and much of the gas) are located.

three canals over the Pennines by 1800) and many new roads.

From the 1840s town growth was rapid, and by the end of the 19th century 80% of the population was urban. While the working-class population was mainly housed in slums, the prosperity of the commercial and professional classes was reflected in the

Victorian 'villas' that, in varying degrees of splendour, appeared in select areas of the towns.

This phase of expansion continued until World War I. By the 1930s, however, there were signs that the prosperity of many older and industrial mining areas was threatened and efforts were made to bring new industries to areas of particularly high unemployment, such as the Northumberland and Durham coalfield, West Cumberland, and the South Wales coalfield. In all of these, whole areas had become virtually derelict because their coal was exhausted, or no longer in demand; one such casualty, especially in South Wales, was steam coal for ships, rapidly being replaced by oil.

The main areas of industrial growth since World War I have been around London and also in the West Midlands. A number of towns, for example Coventry, experienced extremely rapid growth. Conscious planning had the aim of controlling industrial expansion and preventing the indiscriminate growth of some towns, for example Oxford and Cambridge.

Today England is a significant steel producer and most of the steel produced is used in other British industries such as shipbuilding (Barrow, Merseyside, Tyneside, Teesside) and vehicle manufacture (West Midlands, Merseyside, London area) – although, as elsewhere in Western Europe, all three industries are currently facing considerable difficulties. Highly-skilled engineering industries are also important and centres include Birmingham, Wolverhampton and Manchester. Textiles are still a major industry, with cotton goods being produced mainly in Lancashire and woollens and worsteds in Yorkshire. Similarly, pottery is still important in the Midlands – though, like most manufacturing in Britain, it is losing out to service industries.

In an age when increased prosperity has spread leisure and the means of travel to millions of people, new emphasis has been placed on recreation. One result is the National Parks, another the many scenic areas under the control of the Countryside Commission and other national bodies. In these areas there are special provisions for conserving the beauty of the English countryside, and creating amenities that help people enjoy them.

Wales

United with England in 1535, Wales still preserves a sense of individuality – a separateness resting on history and sentiment rather than any clear boundary in the countryside. Although only 20% of the population speak Welsh, 75% of the inhabitants do so in the western counties of Gwynedd and Dyfed. The national sentiment is not only expressed through language, but also through literature, the arts (especially music), sport and political life. Cardiff, the capital, grew rapidly during the 19th century with the iron and steel industry and coal mining, but no Welsh town is centrally placed for the whole

COUNTRY: United Kingdom of Great Britain and Northern Ireland

AREA: 244,046 sq km [94,202 sq mls]

POPULATION: 57,237,000

CAPITAL (Population): London (6,378,000)

GOVERNMENT: Constitutional monarchy with a bicameral legislature

ETHNIC GROUPS: White 94%, Asian Indian 1%, West Indian 1%, Pakistani 1%

LANGUAGES: English (official), Welsh, Scots-Gaelic

RELIGIONS: Anglican 57%, Roman Catholic 13%, Presbyterian 7%, Methodist 4%, Baptist 1%, Muslim 1%, Jewish, Hindu, Sikh

NATIONAL DAY: 16 June (1990); HM Queen's Official Birthday

CURRENCY: £ sterling = 100 pence

ANNUAL INCOME PER PERSON: $16,070

SOURCE OF INCOME: Agriculture 2%, industry 25%, services 19%

MAIN PRIMARY PRODUCTS: Oil and natural gas, coal, wheat, fish, sugar

MAIN INDUSTRIES: Oil and gas, agriculture, machinery, iron and steel, vehicle manufacture, food processing, textiles, paper, clothing, chemicals, tourism, financial services

MAIN EXPORTS: Machinery and transport equipment 35%, rubber, paper, textile manufactures etc 15%, chemicals and related products 13%, manufactured items 12%, mineral fuels 11%, food, beverages and tobacco 7%

MAIN EXPORT PARTNERS: USA 14%, Germany 11%, France 10%, Netherlands 8%, Italy 5%, Belgium-Luxembourg 5%, Ireland 5%

MAIN IMPORTS: Machinery and transport equipment 35%, rubber, paper, textile manufactures etc 18%, manufactured items 14%, chemicals 9%, food and live animals 9%, mineral fuels 6%

MAIN IMPORT PARTNERS: Germany 17%, USA 10%, France 9%, New Zealand 7%, South Korea 5%, Japan 5%

EDUCATIONAL EXPENDITURE: 11.7% of national budget

DEFENCE: 12% of national budget

TOTAL ARMED FORCES: 311,650

TOURISM: 15,445,000 visitors per year

ROADS: 350,407 km [217,733 mls]

RAILWAYS: 38,053 km [23,645 mls]

POPULATION DENSITY: 235 per sq km [607 per sq ml]

URBAN POPULATION: 93%

POPULATION GROWTH: 0.1% per year

BIRTHS: 13.3 per 1,000 population

DEATHS: 11.6 per 1,000 population

INFANT MORTALITY: 8 per 1,000 live births

LIFE EXPECTANCY: Female 79 yrs, male 73 yrs

POPULATION PER DOCTOR: 611

ADULT LITERACY: 100%

PRINCIPAL CITIES (Population): Greater London 6,378,000 Manchester 1,669,000 Birmingham 1,400,000 Liverpool 1,060,000 Glasgow 730,000 Newcastle 617,000 Sheffield 445,000 Leeds 432,000 Edinburgh 404,000 Bristol 367,000 Teeside 363,000 Coventry 293,000 Belfast 281,000 Leicester 280,000 Bradford 274,000 Cardiff 273,000 Nottingham 262,000

country; meetings of the boards representing the colleges of the University of Wales – Cardiff, Swansea, Lampeter, Aberystwyth and Bangor – take place at Shrewsbury, an English border town.

Landscape: Wales is predominantly hilly and mountainous, although two-thirds of the rural area is farmland and one-third moorland. The most famous of the highland areas is Snowdonia, now a National Park covering 2,138 sq km [825 sq mls] from Snowdon to Cader Idris. But there are fine upland areas in central Wales, on both sides of the upper Severn Valley which cuts through them to the Dovey Valley and the coastal lowlands facing Cardigan Bay. South of the Severn, in the counties of Powys and Dyfed, the uplands dominate the landscape, and in the Brecon Beacons, south of the Usk Valley on which the old town of Brecon is situated, they provide another National Park, of 1,303 sq km [500 sq mls]. Many of the uplands and high lakes are sources of water for English towns, including Liverpool and Birmingham.

Mining and industry: Some writers on Wales regard the uplands as the country's real heartland, with their sheep pastures and forested valleys, interspersed by farming villages and small towns. But over half the population live in the industrialized area of South Wales, which includes the mining valleys of Gwent, Mid Glamorgan and West Glamorgan – all of which ceased to extract coal by the 1990s – and the towns of Newport, Cardiff and Swansea with their traditional heavy metal industries and newer factories for light industry. All are ports, and Cardiff now has many central buildings for the whole of Wales, including the National Museum and the Welsh Office.

No other area of Wales is so heavily dominated by mining and industry as Deeside. Flint and the Wrexham areas are also industrialized, with coalfields now in decline and modern light industries taking their place.

Tourism: Just as the railways stimulated economic growth in South Wales from the 1840s, so on the North Wales coast they stimulated the growth of holiday and residential towns, notably Rhyl, Colwyn Bay and Llandudno. These attracted English residents, many of them retired people from Lanca-

shire, and the holiday industry boomed. In the motoring age it developed further, so that almost every beach and coastal village had its guest houses, holiday cottages, caravan parks and camping sites. Now tourism has spread to virtually the whole of Wales. In Anglesey, many small places have devoted visitors who favour sailing as well as walking and sea bathing, while this is true also of many ports of the Welsh mainland coast. The south-west, formerly Pembrokeshire but now part of Dyfed, has fine scenery, forming the Pembrokeshire National Park with a coast path 268 km [167 mls] long.

Wales is rich in scenic attractions. The landscape is dominantly agricultural, with mixed farming, notably for dairying, cattle and sheep. Many upland farmers combine agriculture with the tourist trade, providing guest houses or camping centres. Forestry plantations exist in many upland valleys but the main characteristic is farmland, with country towns placed 20 km [12 mls] or so apart.

Scotland

Scotland is a generally cool, hilly and, in the west, wet country occupying about a third of Great Britain. Physically it can be divided into three parts: the Highlands and Islands, bounded by the edge of the mountains from Stonehaven to the mouth of the Clyde; Central Scotland – sometimes called the central lowland, though it is interspersed by hill ranges; and the Southern Uplands, defined in the north by a fault extending from Dunbar to Girvan, and in the south by the border with England.

The Highlands and Islands: More than half of Scotland's area is in the Highlands and Islands. These are divided by the Great Glen, from Fort William to Inverness, with its three lochs – Lochy, Oich and Ness (where the monster is prone to appear in the tourist season) – linked by the Caledonian Canal. Much of the whisky for which Scotland is famous is produced in the Highlands, notably near the River Spey.

The north-western part of the Highlands has splendid scenery – deep, glaciated valleys dominated by mountains, and only limited areas of farmland, much of it now abandoned.

The financial returns from crofting (small-scale

GLASGOW

Temperature

Precipitation
1109mm
44in

Like most of north-west Europe, Glasgow has a maritime climate with cool summers, mild winters and well-distributed rainfall with an autumn maximum. Variations to the general pattern occur with changes in altitude and proximity to the sea. The Clyde Valley, is more sheltered than the estuary where Greenock receives more than 1,500 mm [590 in] of rain annually. At Glasgow rain falls on about 200 days per year. It averages about 3–5 hours of sunshine per day compared to 4–5 hours in the south.

tenant farming) were meagre, and many old croft cottages have become holiday homes. Forests now cover many of the valleys; some of the mountains are deer parks, owned by landlords and let to visitors for seasonal shooting. Railways reach the western coast at Mallaig and Kyle of Lochalsh, from which there are boat services to Skye – to be augmented by a controversial bridge – and the Outer Hebrides. Roads are in part single track with passing places, although they are gradually being improved. At the various villages there are hotels, guest houses and other accommodation for visitors, and the main commercial occupations are fishing and home weaving.

The traditional weaving of Harris tweeds in the Hebrides is now industrially organized, with much of the work done in workshops. Skye has splendid climbing in the Cuillin Hills, and the numerous rivers and lakes are favoured by fishermen. Here, as in the rest of the Highlands, efforts to improve local industries have had some success.

The Highland area east of the Great Glen is a richer country, flanked on the east by the lowlands around Aberdeen, which extend into Buchan and then westwards to Moray Firth around Inverness. This is sound farming country, famous for pedigree cattle, and from these lowlands tongues of farmland extend into the valleys of the Dee, Don, Spey and others. Aberdeen and Fraserburgh are major fishing centres. Aberdeen has become increasingly prosperous with the oil extraction from the North Sea, as have many smaller places in the Highlands.

Ben Nevis at 1,343 m [4,406 ft] dominating the town of Fort William, is the highest summit in the British Isles (and one of the dullest to climb), and a number of peaks in the Cairngorms, including Ben Macdhui (1,311 m [4,300 ft]), are of almost equal height. Little known in the past, the Cairngorms have now been developed for winter skiing and summer climbing and fishing. There are still deer forests in the uplands but much of the country is used for sheep farming and tourism. Fort William and a few other centres have industry based on local hydro-electricity – aluminium smelting, for example – but Oban is the main holiday centre in the west.

In the north, the Orkney Islands are connected to Thurso (Scrabster) by boat and also to Aberdeen. Fishing and farming are the main support of the population, with a successful specialization in egg production. The Shetlands have a far harder environment, with craggy hills and limited areas suited to farming, though fishing is prominent, notably at Lerwick. The oil industry has brought great, if temporary, prosperity to some places in these islands.

The Central Lowlands: Scotland's economic heartland includes several ranges of rolling uplands – the Sidlaw Hills north of Dundee, the Ochils south of Perth, and the Pentlands extending in a southwesterly direction from the suburbs of Edinburgh. Most of Scotland's population and industrial activity occurs in this central area, and here too are its two largest cities – Glasgow on innumerable small

glacial hills (drumlins) in the Clyde Valley, and the capital Edinburgh on splendid volcanic ridges, dominated by Arthur's Seat.

Clydeside is still the greatest industrial area of Scotland. Textile industries, engineering and ship-building were the basis of the prosperity of Glasgow and its neighbouring towns, which in time grew into one another and held more than a third of Scotland's total population. There is now a wide range of industries in Central Scotland including electronics, printing, brewing and carpet-making.

Edinburgh, with its port of Leith, remained much smaller than Glasgow, with only half its population, but is still the administrative centre, and the seat of the main law courts and the National Museum and Library, as well as of many cultural organizations. A favoured centre for retirement in Scotland, it has an increasing tourist trade, particularly during the Edinburgh Festival in the summer. Much of the central area is rich farmland, especially to the east of Edinburgh where the soils have been upgraded by generations of enterprising farmers concentrating on both stock and crops.

The Southern Uplands: Though less spectacular than the Highlands, these include many fine hills, rolling moorlands and rich valleys. From the summit of Merrick (843 m [2,764 ft]) in Galloway can

be seen the Highlands to the north, the plateau of Northern Ireland to the west, and the Lake District, the Pennines and the Isle of Man to the south. The Tweed with its numerous tributaries and – further west – the Esk, Annan, Nith, Ken and Cree provide sheltered valleys for farming, and there is splendid agricultural country in Galloway, where dairying has been particularly successful. Cattle rearing with crop production is more general in the drier east, where many farms specialize in beasts for slaughter. The hills are used for sheep rearing. Some of the towns, notably Hawick and Galashiels, are prominent in the textile industry, especially exports.

Although tourism is relatively less important than in the Highlands, many people come to see the historic centres, such as Melrose and Dryburgh Abbey. To the west, in Galloway, there has been a policy of afforestation on the poorer soils, and several centres have been opened as small museums and educational sites. The coast attracts tourists and Forest Parks, such as that at Glen Trool close to Merrick, have been well laid out for visitors. In the west the towns are small, though there is heavy traffic to Stranraer, the packet station for the shortest sea crossing to Larne in Northern Ireland ■

[For geography of Northern Ireland see page 49.]

The districts of Northern Ireland have been numbered and can be identified by reference to this table

1. Londonderry
2. Limavady
3. Coleraine
4. Ballymoney
5. Moyle
6. Larne
7. Ballymena
8. Magherafelt
9. Cookstown
10. Strabane
11. Omagh
12. Fermanagh
13. Dungannon
14. Craigavon
15. Armagh
16. Newry & Mourne
17. Banbridge
18. Down
19. Lisburn
20. Antrim
21. Newtownabbey
22. Carrickfergus
23. North Down
24. Ards
25. Castlereagh
26. Belfast

● London   Capital
○ Truro   Administrative Centre

● Newcastle is also Admin. H.Q. for Northumberland
Cardiff is also Admin. H.Q. for Mid Glamorgan
Kingston is Admin. H.Q. for Surrey

IRELAND

The Irish flag was first used by nationalists in 1848 in the struggle for freedom from Britain and adopted in 1922 after independence. Green represents the Roman Catholics, Orange the Protestants and white stands for peace.

Geographically, Ireland is the whole island west of Britain; the Republic of Ireland (Eire, or the Irish Free State until 1949) comprises the 26 counties governed from Dublin, and Northern Ireland (Ulster) is the six counties that remained part of the United Kingdom from 1921, when the Free State was granted dominion status within the British Commonwealth. Today, the word 'Ireland' is used as political shorthand for the Republic – which occupies some 80% of the island of Ireland.

The original four provinces of Ireland gradually emerged as major divisions from Norman times. Three counties of the present Republic (Donegal, Cavan and Monaghan), together with the six counties which now make up Northern Ireland, formed the old province of Ulster; Connacht, in effect the land beyond the River Shannon, includes the five counties of Leitrim, Sligo, Roscommon, Galway and Mayo; Munster comprises Clare, Limerick, Tipperary, Kilkenny, Waterford, Cork and Kerry; and Leinster consists of the heart of the central lowland and the counties of the south-east (Wicklow, Wexford and Carlow) between Dublin and Waterford harbour.

Landscape

Physically the main outlines of Ireland are simple. In the western peninsulas of Donegal and Connacht ancient rocks were folded to form mountain chains running north-east to south-west; good examples are the fine Derryveagh range of Co. Donegal and the Ox Mountains of Co. Sligo. The highest peaks, for example Errigal, 752 m [2,466 ft], are generally of quartzite, a metamorphosed sandstone. The same trend is seen in the long range, including the Wicklow Mountains, between Dublin Bay and

Waterford harbour in the south-east, and in the Slieve Bloom of the central lowland. The fine east-west ranges of the south, extending from Waterford to the western peninsulas, and the islands of Kerry and West Cork, were formed at a later period. Much of lowland Ireland is floored by rocks contemporary with the coal-bearing measures in England, and these also form some uplands like those around Sligo. Unfortunately these rocks contain little coal; some is mined on a small scale in the Castlecomer area of Co. Kilkenny, and near Lough Allen in the upper Shannon Valley. The basalt lavas that poured out in the north-east of Ireland, forming the desolate Antrim Plateau with its fine scenic cliffs on the famous Coast Road, and the Giant's Causeway, are more recent.

Economy

Agriculture has been the traditional support of the Irish people, though fishing, home crafts and local labouring have been important extra sources of livelihood in the poorer western areas. There is a marked contrast between the richest and the poorest agricultural areas. In the eastern central lowland and the south-east, particularly the lowland areas of Wicklow and Wexford, there are splendid large farms, with pastures supporting fine-quality cattle, sheep and in some areas racehorses. From Wexford, too, rich farmlands extend through the valleys and lowlands westwards to the counties of Tipperary and Limerick, and from Waterford to Cork and Killarney.

North of the Shannon, in Clare and east Galway, there is intensive sheep and some cattle production; here the glacial deposits are thin and the soils derived from limestones. To the north farming is mixed,

Ireland, open to the Atlantic Ocean, has a mild, damp climate. Humidity is high with frequent fog and low cloud throughout the year. The declining influence of the ocean eastwards is most marked in winter, when temperatures in Dublin are several degrees colder than in the west; rainfall, which is very uniformly distributed throughout the year, is about half that of western coasts that face the prevailing winds off the ocean. Dublin has 762 mm [30 in] rainfall per year, falling on 140 days.

COUNTRY: Republic of Ireland

AREA: 70,280 sq km [27,135 sq mls]

POPULATION: 3,523,000

CAPITAL (Population): Dublin (921,000)

GOVERNMENT: Unitary multiparty republic with a bicameral legislature

ETHNIC GROUPS: Irish 94%

LANGUAGES: Irish and English (both official)

RELIGIONS: Roman Catholic 93%, Protestant 3%

NATIONAL DAY: 17 March; St Patrick's Day

CURRENCY: Irish pound = 100 new pence

ANNUAL INCOME PER PERSON: $9,550

MAIN PRIMARY PRODUCTS: Cereals, potatoes, vegetables, peat, fish, natural gas

MAIN INDUSTRIES: Agriculture, food processing, tourism, textiles, clothing, machinery

MAIN EXPORTS: Machinery and transport equipment 32%, food and live animals 24%, chemicals 12%

MAIN EXPORT PARTNERS: UK 35%, Germany 11%, France 9%, USA 7%, Netherlands 7%

MAIN IMPORTS: Machinery and transport equipment 34%, chemicals and related products 12%, foodstuffs 11%, petroleum 5%, clothing 4%

MAIN IMPORT PARTNERS: UK 42%, USA 18%, Germany 9%, France 5%, Japan 5%, Netherlands 3%

DEFENCE: 3.5% of national budget

TOURISM: 2,662,000 visitors per year

POPULATION DENSITY: 50 per sq km [130 per sq ml]

LIFE EXPECTANCY: Female 78 yrs, male 73 yrs

ADULT LITERACY: 99%

PRINCIPAL CITIES (Population): Dublin 921,000 Cork 174,000 Limerick 56,000 Galway 47,000

THE TROUBLES

The Anglo-Irish Treaty of 1921 established southern Ireland – Eire – as an independent state, with the six northern Irish counties, and their Protestant majority, remaining part of the United Kingdom (though Eire's constitution claimed authority over the whole island). Northern Ireland (Ulster) was granted local self-government from the Stormont parliament in Belfast. However, the Protestant majority (roughly two-thirds of the population) systematically excluded the Catholic minority from power and often from employment, despite occasional attacks from the near-moribund IRA – the Irish Republican Army, which had done most of the fighting that led to Eire's independence.

In 1968, inspired by the Civil Rights movement in the southern states of the USA, northern Catholics launched a civil rights movement of their own. But Protestant hostility threatened a bloodbath, and in August 1969 British Prime Minister Harold Wilson deployed army units to protect Catholics from Protestant attack.

Within a short period, the welcome given by Catholics to British troops turned to bitterness; the IRA and many of the Catholic minority came to see them as a hostile occupying force, and there were deaths on both sides. Protestant extremists were quick to form terrorist organizations of their own. In 1971, the British introduced internment without trial for suspected IRA terrorists, removing some of the main security risks from the streets but provoking violent protest demonstrations. In 1972, British troops killed 13 demonstrators in London-

derry, claiming to have been fired upon: the claims were vigorously denied by the demonstrators.

In an attempt to end the alienation of the Catholics, Britain negotiated an agreement with some Protestant politicians to share power in an executive composed of both communities, but the plan collapsed after dissatisfied Protestants staged a general strike. The British government responded by suspending the Stormont parliament and ruling Northern Ireland direct from Westminster. The failure of power-sharing encapsulated the British policy dilemma in Ulster: the Catholics, or most of them, wanted to join the Irish Republic; the Protestants, virtually without exception, did not. Each side bitterly distrusted the other, and long years of sectarian killing only increased the distrust.

The violence continued throughout the 1970s and 1980s, despite a series of political initiatives that included an Anglo-Irish agreement giving the Republic a modest say in Ulster's affairs. Among the conflict's victims over the following years were Earl Mountbatten and several senior British politicians, as well as soldiers, policemen, terrorists and thousands of ordinary men and women. A whole generation grew up accustomed to armed troops patrolling the streets, and almost daily reports of sectarian murders. Yet there was no sign of a compromise emerging. As the 1990s began, it seemed that only the increasing war-weariness of all Northern Ireland's people offered a prospect of peace – if not a resolution of the province's intractable political predicament.

---

with dairying, meat production, and in some cases specialization on crops such as potatoes and barley. Little wheat is grown; oats are better suited to the damp summer climate.

Farming in much of Ireland is now relatively prosperous, aided by EEC grants. The number of people working on the land continues to decline, but that is due to the introduction of machinery, the union of small farms into larger holdings, and the increased opportunities of finding employment in the towns, with overseas emigration still an alternative if not a choice for many Irish workers or families. The tradition of emigration dates back to the great famine of 1846–51, when over a million people fled to Britain and the USA.

Ireland is economically far more prosperous than it was in 1845, when the population of the island numbered 8.5 million. Industrialization only really happened in the north-east, especially Belfast, leaving the Free State an agrarian country from the 1920s. As a result, it has something of a 'Third World' profile: rural (though 25% of the population lives in Dublin and its suburbs), dependent on tourism and, increasingly, high-tech industries such as electronics and pharmaceuticals. Prosperity in the 1960s was followed by a slowdown in growth – when government spending was high – but with a new spirit of economic co-operation the 1980s appeared to have successfully reversed the trend ∎

NETHERLANDS

The Dutch national flag dates from 1630, during the long war of independence from Spain that began in 1568. The tricolour became a symbol of liberty and inspired many other revolutionary flags around the world.

Amsterdam has a climate typical of the coastal margins of north-west Europe. The range of temperature, both daily and annual, is small. Winters are mild with frequent wind and rain from Atlantic depressions. No monthly minimum temperature is below freezing. The prevailing westerly winds which once powered the Dutch windpumps keep summers cool. Rainfall increases from a spring minimum to a maximum in late summer and autumn, falling on about 130 days per year.

Often, and inaccurately, called Holland – this refers only to the two north-western provinces, where less than 40% of the population lives – the Netherlands is the most crowded country of any size in Europe. Yet the daunting figures for density are only an average: the east and south are relatively sparsely populated, while the figure for the province of Zuid-Holland is 1,080 people per sq km [2,800 per sq ml].

The greatest concentration of population is in the towns and cities of Randstad Holland, a 50 km [31 ml] diameter horseshoe of urban areas, with Dordecht at the centre of the loop. This area, dominant in the Dutch economy, includes most of the major cities, including (clockwise) Hilversum, Utrecht, Dordecht, Rotterdam, The Hague (home of the International Court of Justice), Leiden, Haarlem and Amsterdam, the last still the centre of Dutch cultural life despite being overtaken in size by Rotterdam. Nearly all of this crucial area, rich in history and culture, lies well below sea level.

To anyone travelling westwards from Germany,

the Netherlands' density of people is obvious in the landscape, for the fields are smaller, the villages more tightly concentrated with small neat houses, and the land is cultivated more intensively. Over much of the countryside rivers are at a higher level than the surrounding farmland, with villages sited above the flood level.

Seen from the air, most of the Netherlands is made up of richly cultivated fields, mainly rectangular, with water-filled ditches between them along which farmers travel by boat. Control of water is a major problem, for much of the best farmland lies at or below sea level.

Without the protection of dykes and sand dunes along the coast, more than two-fifths of the Netherlands (the 'Low Countries') would be flooded. Constant pumping – formerly by windpumps (as most picturesque 'windmills' were) and steam-pumps, but now by automated motor-pumps – lifts surplus water from ditches to canals at a higher level, and from canals to the rivers, particularly the Lek and Waal, which take the waters of the Rhine to the sea,

and the Maas (Meuse in France and Belgium).

The dunes that line much of the coast are carefully guarded against erosion by planting marram grass and, where possible, trees. There are massive dykes to guard the farmland and towns, but in 1953 the exceptionally high tides at the end of January broke through coastal dykes and sand dunes, causing widespread devastation.

For over a thousand years the Dutch have wrested land from the unforgiving North Sea and the process still continues; only in the last 60 years, however, has the balance between reclamation and flooding, between gain and loss of land, swung permanently and firmly in the people's favour. Since

COUNTRY: Kingdom of the Netherlands

AREA: 41,863 sq km [16,163 sq mls]

POPULATION: 15,019,000

CAPITAL (Population): Amsterdam (1,038,000); Seat of government: The Hague (684,000)

GOVERNMENT: Constitutional monarchy with a bicameral legislature

ETHNIC GROUPS: Netherlander 96%, Indonesian, Turkish, Moroccan, Surinamese

LANGUAGES: Dutch (official)

RELIGIONS: Roman Catholic 36%, Dutch Reformed Church 19%, Reformed Churches 8%

NATIONAL DAY: 30 April; Birthday of HM The Queen

CURRENCY: Netherlands guilder = 100 cents

ANNUAL INCOME PER PERSON: $17,330

SOURCE OF INCOME: Agriculture 4%, industry 22%, services 19%

MAIN PRIMARY PRODUCTS: Cereals, fruit, vegetables, sugar beet, livestock, fish, oil, gas, salt

MAIN INDUSTRIES: Agriculture, food processing, chemicals, iron and steel, clothing and textiles, shipbuilding, printing, diamond cutting, fish

MAIN EXPORTS: Machinery and transport equipment 21%, foodstuffs 20%, chemicals and chemical products

MAIN EXPORT PARTNERS: Germany 26%, Belgium-Luxembourg 15%, France 11%, UK 11%, Italy 6%

MAIN IMPORTS: Machinery and transport equipment 28%, foodstuffs 14%, chemicals 11%, mineral fuels 9%

MAIN IMPORT PARTNERS: Germany 26%, Belgium-Luxembourg 15%, UK 8%, France 8%

DEFENCE: 9.1% of national budget

TOTAL ARMED FORCES: 106,000

TOURISM: 3,189,000 visitors per year

ROADS: 111,891 km [69,528 mls]

RAILWAYS: 2,867 km [1,782 mls]

POPULATION DENSITY: 359 per sq km [929 per sq ml]

URBAN POPULATION: 89%

POPULATION GROWTH: 0.37% per year

BIRTHS: 11.8 per 1,000 population

DEATHS: 8.9 per 1,000 population

INFANT MORTALITY: 7 per 1,000 live births

LIFE EXPECTANCY: Female 81 yrs, male 74 yrs

POPULATION PER DOCTOR: 450

ADULT LITERACY: 99%

PRINCIPAL CITIES (Population): Rotterdam 1,040,000 Amsterdam 1,038,000 The Hague 684,000 Utrecht 526,000 Eindhoven 381,000 Arnhem 299,000

1900 almost 3,000 sq km [1,160 sq mls] have been added to the nation's territory.

The largest and most famous project has been the reclamation of the Zuiderzee, begun in 1920. The major sea barrage of 32 km [21 mls] was completed in 1932, and by 1967 four large 'island' areas were finished, providing some 1,814 sq km [700 sq mls] of former seabed not only for cultivation but also for planned towns and villages. A controversial fifth area, Markerwaard, is under way, leaving the IJsselmeer, a freshwater lake, the only remnant of the original inlet.

The use of land in the Netherlands varies. In the west the concentration on bulb farming is marked near Haarlem in soils of clay mixed with sand. There, too, glasshouse cultivation, combined on many holdings with the growing of flowers and vegetables out-of-doors, is widespread. The Dutch grow and sell more than 3 billion flowers every year.

Much of the produce is exported, some of it by air to London and other north European cities. Some soils are better suited to pastoral farming, with milk, cheese and butter production. In the areas above sea level, farming is varied, with a combination of cattle and crops, including fruit. Gouda has a famous cheese market, and the well-known round red-coated Edam cheeses come from northern areas.

Industry and commerce

Industry and commerce provide support for the greater part of the Dutch population. Mineral resources include china clay, which is abundant, natural gas from the North Sea, and coal, though commercial mining ceased in 1965. The emphasis of modern industry is on oil, steel, electrical engineering and chemicals.

In the area south of Rotterdam a vast port and industrial area, Europoort, has been developed since 1958. Together with Rotterdam's own facilities, the complex is the largest and busiest in the world. The Dutch are skilled at languages, to which a considerable part of the teaching time is given even in primary schools. This is essential to the country's prosperity, for now as in past centuries the Dutch control a main outlet for the commerce of Europe in the port of Rotterdam, with the Rhine Valley and a wider area as its hinterland. The main export markets are the EEC partners – Germany, Belgium, the UK and France – while strong trade links with Indonesia recall the Dutch colonial age ■

BELGIUM

The colours of Belgium's flag derive from the arms of the province of Brabant which rebelled against Austrian rule in 1787. It was adopted as the national flag in 1830 when Belgium gained independence from the Netherlands.

Belgium has a cool temperate maritime climate with the weather systems moving eastwards from the Atlantic. Rainfall is quite heavy in the higher Ardennes plateau with much snow from January to February. At Brussels, no month has a mean temperature below freezing and the summer is pleasantly warm. Temperatures well in excess of 30°C [86°F] have been recorded May–September. The temperatures are lower at all seasons in the higher land to the south of the country.

Throughout a chequered and stormy history as the 'cockpit of Europe', Belgium's fine cities, including Brussels, Ghent and Bruges, have maintained their churches and public buildings, though some have been rebuilt after wars. Following the Napoleonic Wars, from 1815, Belgium and the Netherlands were united as the 'Low Countries', but in 1830, a famous year of ferment in Europe, a National Congress proclaimed independence from the Dutch and in 1831 Prince Leopold of Saxe-Coburg was 'imported from Germany' to become king. At the Treaty of London in 1839 (which the Netherlands also signed), Britain, France and Russia guaranteed the independence of Belgium – and the famous 'scrap of paper' was upheld when Germany invaded Belgium in August 1914. For nearly four weary years the fields of Flanders became the battlefield of Europe.

The division between Belgium and the Netherlands rests on history and sentiment rather than on any physical features. Belgium is predominantly a Roman Catholic country, while the Netherlands is traditionally Protestant (though about 36% of the population are Roman Catholic). Both were neutral in foreign policy, but from 1940 until September 1944 they were occupied by the Nazis.

Since the end of World War II economic progress has been marked, for the geographical advantages Belgium possesses have given it a position of significance in Europe, especially in the EEC. The unity of the people, however, is less secure, and in the early 1990s there were growing signs that the fragile alliance which had preserved the nation for so long was beginning to crack.

Of the country's universities, Louvain (Catholic and Belgium's oldest, dating from 1426) provides courses in both Flemish and French; of the universities founded in the 19th century Ghent (1816) is Flemish and Liège (1817) French-speaking. At Brussels' Free University (founded in 1834) the courses are mainly in French, but provision is made for Flemish speakers. Gradually the grievances of the Flemish speakers have been removed and in 1974 regional councils were established for Flanders, Wallonia and the Brussels district.

Landscape and agriculture

Physically Belgium may be divided into the uplands of the Ardennes and the lowland plains, which are drained by the Meuse to the Rhine through the Netherlands, and by the Schelde through Antwerp to the North Sea. The Ardennes, rising in Belgium to about 700 m [2,296 ft] at the highest point, is largely moorland, peat bogs and woodland.

Lowland Belgium has varied soils, including some poor-quality sands in the Campine (Kempenland) area near the Dutch frontier, supporting only heaths and woodland. But careful cultivation, sound husbandry and attention to drainage have provided good soils; lowland farming is prosperous, with an emphasis on grain crops, potatoes and vegetables, hops, sugar and fodder beet.

Few hedges exist in the farmed landscape and the holdings are small with intensive cultivation.

THE GREAT DIVIDE

Belgium has always been an uneasy marriage of two peoples: the majority Flemings, speaking a very close relative of Dutch, and the Walloons, who speak French (rather than the old Walloon variation of French). The dividing line between the two communities runs east-west, just south of Brussels, with the capital itself officially bilingual.

Since the inception of the country the Flemings have caught up and overtaken the Walloons in cultural influence as well as in numbers. In 1932 the Belgian government was designated bilingual, and in 1970 the country was effectively splintered into four parts. In the far eastern frontier areas German is the official language; Brussels remained bilingual but its province of Brabant divided; and the other eight provinces were split into four Fleming and four Walloon – with only the dominant language being official.

Belgium has three governments: the national authority in Brussels, and regional assemblies for Flanders and Wallonia. During the 1980s, as power gradually devolved from the centre to the regions in crucial aspects of education, transport and the economy, the tension between the 'Germanic' Flemings and the 'Latin' Walloons increased in government. The various coalitions of Dutch- and French-speaking Christian Democrats and Socialists – which had held together for more than a decade under the astute stewardship of Prime Minister Wilfried Martens – was seriously undermined by the results of the emergency election of November 1991, with many experts predicting the break-up of the national state into two virtually independent nations before the end of the century – leaving Brussels (ironically the focal point of European integration) as a political island.

Traditionally many factory workers of the towns also had a smallholding. There is a small area of polders near the coast, in all less than 500 sq km [200 sq mls], which is rich agricultural land.

Industry and commerce

No minerals other than coal exist in significant quantities and the Belgian emphasis on manufacturing is based on the import of raw materials. The Ardennes includes the country's most productive coalfield (the Campine) in the Sambre-Meuse Valley, centred on the cities of Charleroi and Liège. Charleroi is a coal-mining and metallurgical city while Liège is the centre of the iron industry. The Campine coalfield continues into the Netherlands and Germany, but production has declined in recent years as uneconomic mines have been closed.

Still of major importance, however, is the textile industry, which has existed in the towns of Flanders from medieval times and in its modern form includes a wide range of products. It is associated particularly with Ghent and Bruges, which are equally renowned for their medieval architecture.

It is this part of the country that makes Belgium not only one of Europe's most crowded nations – 323 people per sq km [837 per sq ml] – but the most 'urban' of any reasonably sized independent state, with an official figure of 96.9%.

Belgium's main port is Antwerp, much modernized since 1956. The main industrial centres are served by ship canals, including one of 29 km [18 mls] from Ghent to Terneuzen. Constructed in 1825–7, it can take ships of as much as 61,000 tonnes in capacity. There are canals to Bruges from the North Sea at Zeebrugge, and also to Brussels, both completed in 1922. Barges of 1,372 tonnes capacity can use the 125 km [79 mls] Albert Canal to Liège, opened in 1939, and the Meuse and Sambre are being widened or deepened to take barges of similar capacity. Comparable improvements are being made in the River Schelde between Antwerp and Ghent, and in the Brussels-Charleroi Canal.

Now, as in past centuries, the lowlands of Belgium, and particularly the city of Brussels (headquarters of the EEC, of which Belgium was a founder member), remain a major focus of commercial and political life in Europe ■

COUNTRY: Kingdom of Belgium
AREA: 30,510 sq km [11,780 sq mls]
POPULATION: 9,845,000
CAPITAL (Population): Brussels (970,000)
GOVERNMENT: Constitutional monarchy with a bicameral legislature
ETHNIC GROUPS: Belgian 91% (Fleming 55%, Walloon 34%), Italian 3%, French, Dutch, Turkish, Moroccan
LANGUAGES: Flemish (Dutch) 57%, Walloon (French) 32%, German 1% – all official languages; 10% of population is legally bilingual
RELIGIONS: Roman Catholic 72%, Protestant, Muslim
NATIONAL DAY: 21 July; Independent kingdom (1839)
CURRENCY: Belgian franc = 100 centimes
ANNUAL INCOME PER PERSON: $15,440
MAIN PRIMARY PRODUCTS: Sugar beet, potatoes, livestock, timber, coal
MAIN INDUSTRIES: Engineering, iron and steel, petroleum refining, food processing, chemicals, coal, textiles, glassware, diamond cutting
MAIN EXPORTS: Vehicles 15%, chemicals 13%, foodstuffs 9%, iron and steel 7%, pearls, precious and semi-precious stones 6%, oil products 3%
MAIN EXPORT PARTNERS: France 20%, Germany 20%, Netherlands 15%, UK 8%, USA 5%
MAIN IMPORTS: Vehicles and parts 14%, chemicals 10%, foodstuffs 9%, petroleum and petroleum products 7%, non-industrial diamonds 6%
MAIN IMPORT PARTNERS: Germany 24%, Netherlands 17%, France 16%, UK 8%, USA 5%, Italy 4%
DEFENCE: 7.1% of national budget
TOURISM: 2,516,000 visitors per year
POPULATION DENSITY: 323 per sq km [837 per sq ml]
INFANT MORTALITY: 8 per 1,000 live births
LIFE EXPECTANCY: Female 79 yrs, male 72 yrs
ADULT LITERACY: 99%

LUXEMBOURG

Luxembourg's colours are taken from the Grand Duke's 14th-century coat of arms. The Grand Duchy's flag is almost identical to that of the Netherlands, but the blue stripe is a lighter shade and the flag itself is longer.

Europe's last independent duchy, Luxembourg formed an economic union with Belgium in 1922, extended in 1944 to include the Netherlands under the composite name of Benelux. Luxembourg is a founder member of NATO (1949) and the EEC (1957), and is perhaps best known to Europeans as the host for the Court of the European Communities, the Secretariat of the European Parliament, the European Investment Bank and the European Monetary Co-operation Fund.

Luxembourg consists partly of the picturesque Ardennes, well wooded and famed for its deer and wild boar, but the more prosperous agricultural areas are in the scarplands of Lorraine. Stock-rearing, especially of dairy cattle, is important, and crops include grains, potatoes, roots and fruit, and vines in the Moselle Valley. There is also a prosperous iron and steel industry based on rich iron-ore deposits.

Declaring itself a Grand Duchy in 1354, Luxembourg is the only one out of hundreds of independent duchies, which once comprised much of continental Europe, to survive and become a full member of the United Nations. Most Luxembourgers speak both German and French, but the main language is their own Germanic dialect.

With its suburbs, the capital accounts for nearly a third of the country's population. A similar proportion are foreign workers, attracted by opportunities in industry and the many international organizations. Though Luxembourg's population is barely a thousandth of the EEC total, it remains a relatively important player in Western European commerce and politics ■

COUNTRY: Grand Duchy of Luxembourg
AREA: 2,590 sq km [1,000 sq mls]
POPULATION: 384,000
CAPITAL (Population): Luxembourg (76,000)
GOVERNMENT: Constitutional monarchy with a bicameral legislature
ETHNIC GROUPS: Luxemburger 70%, Portuguese 8%, Italian 5%, French 4%, German 3%
LANGUAGES: Letzeburgish (Luxembourgian – official), French, German
RELIGIONS: Roman Catholic 93%
NATIONAL DAY: 23 June; Official birthday of the Grand Duke
CURRENCY: Luxembourg franc = 100 centimes
ANNUAL INCOME PER PERSON: $28,770
MAIN INDUSTRIES: Iron and steel, banking and financial services, chemicals, agriculture
MAIN EXPORTS: Base metals, plastic and rubber manufactures
MAIN IMPORTS: Mineral products, base metals and manufactures, machinery, transport equipment
DEFENCE: 3% of national budget
POPULATION DENSITY: 148 per sq km [384 per sq ml]
LIFE EXPECTANCY: Female 79 yrs, male 72 yrs
ADULT LITERACY: 99%

FRANCE

The colours of the French flag originated during the Revolution of 1789. The red and blue are said to represent Paris and the white the monarchy. The present design, adopted in 1794, is meant to symbolize republican principles.

The climate of France is formed from three influences: the Atlantic, the Mediterranean and the continent. With no mountain barriers to affect it the Atlantic regime extends far inland, giving mild weather with appreciable wind and rain, but little snow. To the east the climate gets warmer, but with colder winters. Towards the mountains and to the south the rainfall increases, snow lying permanently above 3,000 m [12,000 ft]. At Paris low rainfall is distributed evenly through the year.

Although replaced by the Ukraine as Europe's biggest 'country' in 1991, France remains a handsomely proportioned runner-up, well ahead of Spain and more than twice the area of the entire United Kingdom. Yet the nation possesses space as well as size, and while the growth of cities in the years since World War II has been spoken of in terms of crisis (*la crise urbaine*), urban expansion is a problem only in a few special areas, notably Paris and its immediate surroundings. In general, France has stayed predominantly rural.

Many French towns show traces of the country's long history. In the south, for example, at Arles and Carcassonne, there are famous Roman remains. Medieval churches are abundant with splendid cathedrals such as Reims, Amiens and Notre-Dame in Paris. Traces of the period before the 1789 Revolution include the famous châteaux, many of them built or rebuilt in the 18th century, when rich landlords were patrons of the arts.

Frontiers

Frontiers are a natural concern of continental European countries, but of France's 5,500 km [3,440 mls] almost half consists of sea coast and another 1,000 km [620 mls] winds through the mountains of the Pyrenees and the Alps. In general the Pyrenees frontier follows the crest line of the major hills, rather than the watershed between rivers flowing north into France or south into Spain. There are few easy crossings through the Pyrenees into Spain, but good coastal routes exist on the west from Bayonne into the Basque country, and on the east from Perpignan to Gerona.

In the south-east of France, Savoie and the county of Nice were ceded by Italy at the Treaty of Turin in 1860 and in the following year the Prince of Monaco gave Menton and a neighbouring area to France. The cession of Savoie meant that France's territory extended to the summit of Mont Blanc, the highest mountain in Europe outside the Caucasus.

It also gave France part of the shores of Lake Geneva. Geneva itself is Swiss, but French territory lies within walking distance, and special customs arrangements exist so that people from the French countryside may use the city's trading facilities. North of Geneva the frontier runs through the Jura Mountains to Basle on the Rhine where France, Germany and Switzerland meet. Though Basle itself is in Switzerland, its airport is in France.

North of Basle, for 160 km [100 mls] the border between France and Germany follows the Rhine. Alsace and Lorraine, west of the river, were sought by both countries for centuries, and after the Franco-Prussian War in 1870–1 the whole of Alsace and part of Lorraine were returned to Prussia. This frontier remained until the Treaty of Versailles following World War I, but in World War II it was violated again by the Germans – their third invasion of France in 70 years. The frontiers from the Rhine to the North Sea were defined in their present form during the 18th century.

Local government in France was reorganized during the French Revolution. In 1790 Turgot defined the *départements* as areas in which everyone could reach the central town within one day.

Landscape

Highland France: Most of France lies less than 300 m [1,000 ft] above sea level, but there are several distinctive upland areas. The most impressive are the Alps and the Pyrenees, but they also include the ancient massifs of Brittany and the Central Plateau, the Vosges and that part of the Ardennes which is within France.

The Alps are formed of complex folded rocks of intricate structure, with relief made even more complicated by the successive glaciations of the Ice Age. Areas of permanent snow exist on Mont Blanc and many other high peaks, and visitors to the upper Arve Valley at Chamonix, St Gervais and other holiday centres have easy access to glaciers. The Alps are visited by tourists throughout the year – in winter for skiing, and in summer for walking on the upland pastures (the original 'alps'). In the French Alps, as in the other alpine areas, hydroelectricity has become universal both for general home use and for industry. The Pyrenees, though comparable to the Alps, lack arterial routes.

The Breton massif includes part of Normandy and extends southwards to the neighbourhood of La Rochelle. In general physical character it is a much dissected hilly area. The Massif Central is more dramatic: it covers one-sixth of France between the Rhône-Saône Valley and the basin of Aquitaine, and its highest summits rise to more than 1,800 m [5,900 ft]; striking examples are Mont du Cantal (1,858 m [6,100 ft]) and Mont Dore (1,866 m [6,200 ft]). Volcanic activity of 10–30 million years ago appears in old volcanic plugs. Earlier rocks include limestones, providing poor soils for agriculture, and coal measures which have been mined for more than a century at St-Étienne and Le Creusot. The Vosges and the Ardennes are areas of poor soil, largely forested.

Lowland France: Although France has striking mountain areas, 60% of the country is less than 250 m [800 ft] above sea level. Fine rivers, including the Rhône, Garonne, Loire and Seine, along with their many tributaries, drain large lowland areas. From the Mediterranean there is a historic route

northwards through the Rhône-Saône Valley to Lyons and Dijon. North-westwards there is the famous route through the old towns of Carcassonne and Toulouse to Bordeaux on the Gironde estuary, into which the Garonne and the Dordogne flow. This is the basin of Aquitaine, bordered by the Massif Central to the north and the Pyrenees to the south. It is not a uniform lowland – there are several hilly areas and on the coast a belt of sand dunes, the Landes, extending for 200 km [125 mls] from Bayonne to the Gironde estuary.

From Aquitaine there is an easy route to the north, followed by the major railway from Bordeaux to Poitiers, Tours, Orléans and Paris. This lowland is called the Gate of Poitou, though in place of the word 'gate' the French say *seuil* or 'threshold', which is perhaps more appropriate. Crossing the threshold brings the traveller to the Paris basin, in the heart of which is the great city itself.

The ancient centre of Paris lies on the Île de la Cité, where the Seine was easily crossed. The Paris basin is a vast area floored by sedimentary rocks. Those that are resistant to erosion, including some limestones and chalks, form upland areas. The Loire, with its many tributaries in the south-west of the basin, and the Seine, with its numerous affluents (notably the Yonne, Aube, Marne, Aisne and Oise) offer easy routes between the upland areas.

Agriculture

The lowlands of France are warmer than those of England in summer; the cooler winters of the north, with more frost and snow than on the lowlands of England, have little adverse effect on agriculture. Rainfall is moderate, with a summer maximum in the north and a winter maximum in the areas of Mediterranean climate to the south.

Modern improvements in agriculture include the provision of irrigation during the summer in the south. This has transformed many areas in the Rhône and Durance valleys, and also the coastal lands such as the Crau, south-east of Arles. Without

THE VINEYARDS

While behind Italy in production of both grapes and wine, France remains the drink's spiritual home as well as its greatest per capita consumer. Vines are grown south of a line from Nantes to the Ardennes. In the northern areas they occur on sites with specially favourable climatic qualities, notably good southerly exposure to sunshine; in the southern areas the vine covers a high proportion of the agricultural land.

The threat of disease, the need to preserve the quality of particular named vines, and the necessity of maintaining the export trade, all involve government control. Different soils and varying types of grape, combined with local traditions of treating them, produce a wide range of wines, most of which are consumed locally. In the export market clarets from the Bordeaux area, burgundies from the Rhône Valley south of Dijon, and champagne, an aerated wine from the *pays* of the same name in the Paris basin, are all well known, but there are many other lesser-known wines of which smaller quantities are exported. The quality of the vintage varies each year according to climatic conditions.

irrigation this was a stony, steppe-like area; now it supports vast flocks of sheep and has fine hay crops, cut three times a year. Further west in the Camargue, on the Rhône delta, rice is grown with the help of irrigation and there are other areas of rice production close to the Mediterranean. Water comes either from canals, leading into ditches through the fields, or by sprinkler systems from a network of underground pumps; one water point can supply 4 hectares [10 acres].

France's agricultural revolution is far from complete. There are areas where modern technology has made large reclamation schemes possible, but there are still many independent peasant farmers, making a living that is a meagre reward for the labour expended, even with the generous terms of the EEC's Common Agricultural Policy (CAP). The younger generation tend to regard emigration to the towns as a more promising way of life.

Alpine areas: In the alpine areas of France, including the Pyrenees, farms are far more numerous on hillslopes having good exposure to sunlight (the *adret*) than on those less favoured (the *ubac*). There are fine upland pastures, apparently retaining their fertility through centuries of use, which provide summer feed for cattle. Although there is still traditional farming in these areas, many people have diversified or emigrated. Some find work in tourist resorts, and many of the old timber-built houses have been bought by people from the cities as holiday homes. The future of peasant farming in mountain areas is a problem that France shares with Switzerland, Austria and Spain.

Mediterranean France: From the French Riviera lowlands extend northwards through the Rhône and Saône valleys and westwards through Languedoc to the neighbourhood of Narbonne. This is the area of Mediterranean climate, having most rain in winter, with wheat, vines and olives as the traditional crops. Wheat is well suited to a Mediterranean climate, for it grows best with a cool, moist period followed by one that is warm and dry. Vines need summer warmth – with temperatures of at least 18° [64°F] for the greater part of the growing season, and dryness, but not to an excessive degree, during the 70 days from the opening of the buds to maturity. The olive is the traditional tree of the true Mediterranean climate. Originally a native of Egypt, through the

centuries it was planted first in the eastern and later in the western Mediterranean. The ripe, dark purple fruits contain oil, used for cooking; green, unripe olives are commonly used as appetizers.

These three crops are familiar in the south but with them are many more, including maize (the country is the world's fifth largest producer) and a wide range of vegetables. Mediterranean France is not everywhere a land of continuous agriculture, for in places it is interspersed with rocky outcrops unsuited to cultivation but covered with *maquis* or pines. Farmers have made fertile the patches of good soil and adequate moisture, and the general landscape is a mixture of rough hills and limestone pavements surrounding rich areas of cultivation.

Aquitaine: To the west, Aquitaine is not a uniform lowland; the agricultural land is interspersed by hills and plateaus that are generally wooded or left as heathland. It is nevertheless a richly productive area, with arable farming for cereal crops, maize and vegetables, and also pastures for cattle. Aquitaine is also a celebrated wine-producing area, with enormous fields laid out as vineyards. Many of the old farms have disappeared, and even whole villages have been abandoned, for example in the Dordogne, as vines have replaced other, less remunerative crops. Much of the wine is consumed on the home market as the normal *vin ordinaire*, mostly red but including some less favoured whites.

Around Bordeaux the famous claret-producing area includes the Medoc, between the Gironde estuary and the sea: here also are the districts that produce white table wines, such as graves and sauternes. Aquitaine can in fact boast a wide range of red and white wines; several of them, though well known locally, are not exported because the quantity produced is small, and possibly because they do not travel well. Cognac and Armagnac wines are suited to brandy distillation.

Northern France: Northwards from Aquitaine through the lowland Gate (*seuil*) of Poitou, the winters become cooler, with rain in the summer as well as the winter months. Though the summers are cooler in the Paris basin than in Aquitaine, vines flourish on favoured slopes facing south, and many fine French wines come from these northern areas.

As a whole the Paris basin is agriculturally rich, with varied soils. The last Ice Age has left many areas

BORDEAUX

The winters are quite mild and the summers warm; the average temperature for January is 5°C [41°F], and for June–September 18–21°C [64–70°F]. Reasonable rainfall falls fairly evenly throughout the year with a slight maximum in November–December. Rain falls on over 160 days in the year. Snow can fall and there can be 20–35 days with frost each year. The annual amount of sunshine exceeds 2,000 hours, with over seven hours daily April–October.

of drifts and wind-blown soils, here as elsewhere in Europe providing land of great fertility. Between the valleys of the Paris basin lie the *pays*, low plateaus, each with its own characteristic. Some, such as the Beauce, with fertile soils, are suited to crops; others, such as the Sologne, have poor, sandy soils, hard to cultivate and best suited to forest. Local farmers have for centuries adjusted their activity to the qualities of the soil, and now use their specialized production as a basis both for trade with other areas, and for sale in the towns. Despite all the profound changes in French life, the variety of agriculture and land use in the Paris basin remains clear – few areas of the world have so neat a division into units as the *pays* of France.

Finally, to the west of the Paris basin there is the area of ancient rocks covering Brittany and its margins. This area, regarded as archaic but picturesque, has small farms with fields divided by wooded hedges to give a sheltered *bocage* landscape. Rich in medieval churches, old customs and even costumes, it was never of great economic significance. Like Cornwall, in the far south-west of England, it had its own language (still used) and is part of the traditional Celtic west of Europe. There is now increasing pressure for local autonomy in Brittany, expressed particularly in efforts to improve agriculture by upgrading pastures, removing hedges to enlarge fields for animals and cultivation, developing market gardening, and encouraging industrial growth in the towns. Fishing remains a valued resource, while tourism (both from France and neighbouring Europe) brings additional prosperity to Brittany.

Agriculture remains a valued resource in the French economy – France accounts for almost 6% of the world's barley and wheat, for example (more of the latter than Canada), and agriculture contributes 17% of export earnings – and politicians make this clear both in Paris and outside France. But there are many changes. In general these appear to reflect the opinion of the American geographer, Isaiah Bowman, that 'man takes the best and lets the rest go'. Poor land is abandoned, perhaps for forest, but promising areas are made rich through investment. Improvements such as drainage, irrigation and

COUNTRY: French Republic
AREA: 551,500 sq km [212,934 sq mls]
POPULATION: 56,440,000
CAPITAL (Population): Paris (8,510,000)
GOVERNMENT: Republic with bicameral legislature
ETHNIC GROUPS: French 93%, Arab 3%, German 2%, Breton 1%, Catalan 1%
LANGUAGES: French (official), Arabic, Breton, Catalan, Basque
RELIGIONS: Roman Catholic 76%, other Christian 4%, Muslim 3%
NATIONAL DAY: 14 July; Fall of the Bastille (1789)
CURRENCY: Franc = 100 centimes
ANNUAL INCOME PER PERSON: $19,480
SOURCE OF INCOME: Agriculture 4%, industry 37%, services 59%
MAIN PRIMARY PRODUCTS: Crude petroleum, natural gas, bauxite, iron ore, agricultural products, lead, zinc, potash
MAIN INDUSTRIES: Aluminium, plastics, synthetic fibres and rubber, agriculture, wool, yarn, forestry, fishing, vehicles, steel, cement, paper, petroleum products
EXPORTS: $3,185 per person
MAIN EXPORTS: Machinery and transport equipment 35%, basic manufactures 18%, chemicals and related products 14%, food and live animals 11%
MAIN EXPORT PARTNERS: Germany 17%, Italy 12%, Belgium 9%, UK 9%, USA 7%, Netherlands 5%, Spain 5%

IMPORTS: $3,427 per person
MAIN IMPORTS: Machinery and transport equipment 32%, chemicals 11%, food and live animals 10%, petroleum and petroleum products 8%, textile yarns and fabrics 3%, iron and steel 3%
MAIN IMPORT PARTNERS: Germany 20%, Italy 12%, Belgium 9%, UK 7%, USA 7%, Netherlands 6%, Japan 4%
EDUCATIONAL EXPENDITURE: 23% of national budget
DEFENCE: 18.7% of national budget
TOTAL ARMED FORCES: 466,300
TOURISM: 36,818,000 visitors per year
ROADS: 804,765 km [500,055 mls]
RAILWAYS: 34,647 km [211,528 mls]
POPULATION DENSITY: 102 per sq km [263 per sq ml]
URBAN POPULATION: 74%
POPULATION GROWTH: 0.4% per year
BIRTHS: 13.6 per 1,000 population
DEATHS: 10.0 per 1,000 population
INFANT MORTALITY: 7 per 1,000 live births
LIFE EXPECTANCY: Female 81 yrs, male 73 yrs
POPULATION PER DOCTOR: 320
ADULT LITERACY: 98%
PRINCIPAL CITIES (Population): Paris 8,510,000 Lyons 1,170,000 Marseilles 1,080,000 Lille 935,000 Bordeaux 628,000 Toulouse 523,000 Nantes 465,000 Nice 449,000 Toulon 410,000 Grenoble 392,000 Rouen 380,000 Strasbourg 373,000

MARSEILLES

The Mediterranean climate extends over the south-east, pushes northwards into the Rhône Valley and into the mountain foothills, and over Corsica. The winters are very mild, with snow and frost a rarity. The summers are dry and the rain falls mainly September to March but on only around 75 days per year. One feature of the area is its peculiar winds, notably the Mistral, a cold, dry and strong wind which blows southwards during winter and spring, causing crop damage.

scientific fertilization in some areas counterbalance the decline in agriculture elsewhere, such as in the Alps and the Pyrenees. Loss of people from the land does not indicate a decline in agricultural production but rather an improvement in agricultural efficiency, and the freedom of people, no longer tied to the land, to seek, and generally to find, alternative and more satisfying employment.

Forests

Forests cover one-fifth of France. Most of them are on soils of poor quality, including the sands in parts of the Paris basin, the Vosges and the Landes between Bordeaux and the Spanish frontier, the poor limestones of Lorraine and the clay-with-flints of Normandy. Some of the great forests were planted by landowners as parts of their estates, like those of Fontainebleau and Rambouillet near Paris; others were planted as barriers between former kingdoms, such as those between Normandy and Picardy.

The greatest single forested area in France is the Landes, covering 10,000 sq km [3,860 sq mls]. This is mainly coniferous forest, interspersed only here and there by farms. Since 1956 attempts have been made to reclaim and replant the extensive areas devastated by fire, and to substitute a more varied rural economy for the exclusive exploitation of the pine forests. In the Alps and the Pyrenees about a quarter of the land is covered with forest.

In France two-thirds of all the woodlands are of deciduous trees, compared with less than a third in Germany, and about 60% of the country's timber, especially for paper pulp-making, has to be imported. Since World War II various laws have been passed to encourage softwood production.

Farms revert to waste when they are no longer cultivated, and become impenetrable thickets of vegetation. Through most of France this vegetation is known as *maquis*, from the shelter it gives to fugitives: the term *maquis* was given in World War II to the resistance forces in hiding. In dry summers the risk of fire is considerable, especially in the south.

Resources and industry

France is a declining but still significant producer of iron ore (mostly from Lorraine), and several other minerals are also mined, including bauxite, potash, salt and sulphur. There are old coalfields in the north-east, but the output of these does not meet the country's needs. France instead switched to new sources of energy, including experiments with solar power in the Pyrenees and the world's first major tidal power station on the Rance estuary in Brittany, but more significantly utilizing the water of the

[See page 264 for the list of département abbreviations.]

mountains for hydroelectric power (24% of output) and mined uranium – almost 10% of world production – to create the most nuclear-based output of any nation (approaching 70% by the end of the 1980s).

Since World War II the marked industrial expansion in France has been accompanied by a change in the distribution of population. Before the war France was regarded as a country with a fairly even distribution of population between town and country, but from the late 1940s there was a spectacular increase in the urban population. In the first postwar planning period, 1947–53, industrial production rose by 70%, agricultural production by 21% and the standard of living by 30%.

During the following three years there was further expansion, particularly in the chemical and electrical industries. In the period of the third plan, 1958–61, the success of export industries became notable, especially in such products as automobiles, aircraft and electrical goods. In this period, too, natural gas was discovered at Lacq, and such industries as chemicals and aluminium smelting prospered. However, traditional industries, such as textiles and porcelain, are still important, and despite technological innovation and success, France is still weak in 'high-tech' areas compared to Japan, the USA and several European rivals.

Nevertheless, the country's postwar transition to a prosperous, dynamic society with more relaxed attitudes has been rapid and pronounced. French life has been, and still is, focused to a remarkable degree on Paris, where traditional luxury industries, such as perfumes, thrive alongside commerce, light industry, heavy industry and services of all kinds. Virtually all the major commercial enterprises of France have their headquarters in Paris – and Paris and district now has almost a fifth of the total population.

The other important industrial centres are on and around the mining areas, and at or near the major ports where imported raw materials are used: Fos, west of Marseilles, for example, and the steel complex at Dunkerque. The aims of modern planning include the development of regional prosperity, based on such centres as Lyons, Marseilles, Toulouse, Nantes, Lille, Nancy and Strasbourg, home to the European parliament. While the industrial attraction of the Paris area remains powerful and population growth continues to exceed that of the second largest urban area, the district around Lyons, the traditional centralization of France is showing signs of weakening and governments of both complexions have sought to reduce state power both in local affairs and the economy.

Modern economic planning in France has been pursued at a time of great difficulty, which included the loss of the colonial territories in North Africa and South-east Asia, as well as the period of unrest in the 1960s, not only in the universities but throughout the country. Consumer industries have prospered, but some critics say that there is still inadequate provision for social services, including housing. Since World War II there has been agitation about the poor standard of housing throughout France, both rural and urban, much of it obsolete and without basic amenities. Rapid urban growth has resulted in overcrowding and even the growth of poor shanty towns to house immigrants, especially those from Spain and North Africa. The 4 million underprivileged workers from the Maghreb countries could prove to be one of the nation's most testing problems in the 1990s.

Achieving expansion and prosperity over the whole country has not been easy. In France, as in most other countries, there remains a disparity be-

Annexed by France from Genoa in 1768 – just months before the birth of Napoleon Bonaparte, its most famous son – Corsica is 168 km [105 mls] from France and just 11 km [7 mls] from Sardinia, which is Italian territory. Corsica is divided into two *départements* of France, with its administrative centre at Ajaccio on the west coast. Roughly oval in shape, it is 190 km [118 mls] long and half as wide.

Most of the island is formed of rugged mountains, some reaching over 2,900 m [9,500 ft]. Only a quarter of Corsica provides rough grazing for sheep and goats; another quarter is in forests with evergreen oak and cork oak to 650 m [2,000 ft], then chestnuts with beech followed by pines to the treeline, between 1,600 and 2,000 m [5,000–6,000 ft]. In winter there is heavy snow on the mountains, causing flooding in the numerous short rivers.

Only 2% of the island is cultivated, mainly in the valleys, on terraced hillsides or on the discontinuous fringe of alluvial lowland along the coasts. Fishing is a primary activity and industries include tunny and lobster canning, chiefly at Ajaccio and Bastia, the two main towns – though tourism is now the main earner. Separatist terrorist movements are still sporadically active in some areas.

tween the richer and poorer areas; for France this is between the east and the west, the richest of all being in closest touch with the great industrial complexes of Germany and the Benelux countries. Though often devastated in European wars, this always emerges in peacetime as one of the most prosperous corners of France ■

MONACO

An independent state since AD 980, Monaco has been ruled by the Grimaldi family since 1297. The colours of the flag, which was officially adopted in 1881, come from the Prince of Monaco's coat of arms.

COUNTRY: Principality of Monaco
AREA: 1.5 sq km [0.6 sq mls]
POPULATION: 29,000
CAPITAL: Monaco-Ville
LANGUAGES: French and Monégasque (official)

The world's smallest nation outside Rome, and by far its most crowded, the tiny principality of Monaco – comprising a rocky peninsula and a narrow stretch of coast – has increased in size by 20% since its land reclamation programme began in 1958. A densely populated modern city-state, it derives its considerable income almost entirely from services: banking, finance, and above all tourism; this is based not just on its Riviera climate but also on

the famous casino. Monégasques are not allowed to gamble there, but there is ample compensation in paying no state taxes.

Monaco has been ruled by the Grimaldi dynasty since 1297, though in 1815 (with the Treaty of Vienna) it came under the protection of the kingdom of Sardinia; the greater part, including Menton, was annexed by France in 1848 and the remainder came under its protection in 1861 – a

situation that essentially survives today within a customs union. The present monarch, Prince Rainier III (ascended 1949), drew up a new liberalizing constitution in 1962.

Monaco falls into four districts: vacation-oriented Monte Carlo; the old town of Monaco-Ville, with royal palace and cathedral; the shops, banks and smart houses of La Condamine; and the light industries and marinas of Fontvieille ■

GERMANY

The red, black and gold, dating back to the Holy Roman Empire, are associated with the struggle for a united Germany from the 1830s. The horizontal design was officially adopted for the FRG in 1949, and accepted by 'East Germany' on reunification.

The climate of northern Germany is due mainly to the weather coming in from the Atlantic. January and February are the only months with mean temperatures just below 0°C [32°F], and the summers are warm. Rainfall is moderate, 500 – 750 mm [20 – 30 in], falling in all months. Humidity is always high with fog in the autumn and winter can be overcast for long periods. Snow lies for long spells inland and in the hills. When the winds blow from Scandinavia very cold weather follows.

The German Empire that was created under Prussian dominance in 1871, comprising four kingdoms, six grand duchies, five duchies and seven principalities, and centred on the great imperial capital of Berlin, was to last for fewer than 75 years. Even at its greatest extent it left large areas of Europe's German-speaking population outside its boundaries, notably in Austria and large parts of Switzerland. Following the fall of Hitler in 1945, a defeated Germany was obliged to transfer to Poland and the Soviet Union 114,500 sq km [44,200 sq mls] situated east of the Oder and Neisse rivers, nearly a quarter of the country's pre-war area. The German-

speaking inhabitants were expelled – as were most German-speaking minorities in the countries of Eastern Europe – and the remainder of Germany was occupied by the four victorious Allied powers.

The dividing line between the zones occupied by the three Western Allies (USA, UK and France) and that occupied by the USSR rapidly hardened into a political boundary dividing the country. In 1948 West Germany was proclaimed as the independent Federal Republic of Germany (FRG), with a capital at Bonn (deemed 'provisional' pending hoped-for German reunification), and measuring 248,000 sq km [96,000 sq mls]. East Germany

became the German Democratic Republic (GDR), a Soviet satellite of 108,000 sq km [41,700 sq mls]. Berlin was similarly divided, the three western sectors of an enclave of occupation becoming 480 sq km [186 sq mls] embedded in the territory of the GDR, of which the Soviet-occupied East Berlin was deemed to be capital.

On reunification, West and East Germany moved from the ninth and 15th biggest countries in Europe to a combined fourth – still much smaller than France, Spain and Sweden – but with the independence of the Ukraine the following year dropped back to fifth. It is, nevertheless, 12th in the world in terms of population.

Landscape

Germany extends from the North Sea and Baltic coasts in the north to the flanks of the central Alps in the south. The country includes only a narrow fringe of Alpine mountains, with the Zugspitze (2,963m [9,721ft]) the country's highest peak. There is, however, a wide section of the associated Alpine foreland bordering Switzerland and Austria, stretching northwards from the foothills of the Alps to the Danube. The foreland is largely covered by moraines and outwash plains which, with many lakes, including the Bodensee (shared with Switzerland), are relics of the glacial age, and reminders of the many glaciers that once emerged from the Alpine valleys.

The central uplands of Europe are more amply represented, occupying a broad swathe of Germany. Four types of terrain are found. Block mountains are remnants of pre-Alpine fold mountains shattered and reshaped by the later earth movements. The Harz, Thüringer Wald and Erzgebirge (Ore Mountains) massifs rise above a varied scarpland terrain, notably the Thüringian Basin, which has the fertile Erfurt lowland at its heart.

Uplift was greatest in the south, close to the Alps, producing the Schwarzwald (Black Forest) and Böhmerwald. Between these great blocks of forested mountains are open basins of sedimentary rocks, their resistant bands picked out by erosion as in the magnificent scarp of the Schwäbische Alb, overlooking the Neckar Basin.

A third kind of country is provided by downfaulted basins filled with softer deposits of more recent age, notably the Upper Rhine plain between Basle and Mainz. Earth movement and eruptions produced a fourth element, such volcanic mountains as the Vogelsberg and the hot and mineral springs that gave rise to the famous spas. Here is Germany at its most picturesque, with baronial castles on wooded heights, looking down over vineyards to clustered villages of half-timbered houses, whose occupants still cultivate open-field strips as they have done for centuries.

The northern lowlands, part of the great North European Plain, owe their topography mainly to the retreat of the ice sheets. The most recent moraines, marked by forested ridges that may include good boulder-clay soils, are restricted to Schleswig-Holstein. The rest of the lowland is covered with leached older moraine and sandy outwash, so that in many places soils are poor. The glacial period also left behind loess, windblown dust deposited along the northern edge of the central uplands and in basins within them, providing some of the country's best soils for wheat, malting barley and sugar beet. This belt broadens in the lowland of Saxony around Halle and Leipzig.

The coast is also the product of glaciation and subsequent changes. The low Baltic shore is diversified by long, branching inlets, formed beneath the ice of the glacial period and now beloved by yachtsmen, while inland the most recent moraines have left behind a confused terrain of hills and lakes, but also areas of good soil developed on glacial till. The movement of water around the edge of the ice sheets carved stream trenches (*Urstromtäler*), south-east to north-west; these are now in part occupied by the present rivers, and have also proved convenient for canal construction. The North Sea is fringed by sandy offshore islands, the products of a beach bar now breached by the sea.

Agriculture

Over a quarter of Germany is forested, with particular concentration in the Alps, the massifs of the central uplands, and the poorer areas of the northern lowland. It is amazing that this economically most advanced country has some of Europe's smallest farms, particularly characteristic of southern Germany. Most are used for arable-based mixed farming, with minor livestock enterprises. In the warmer basins tobacco, vegetables and, increasingly, maize are grown. Vineyards and orchards clothe the slopes of the Rhine and its tributaries. Much larger wheat and sugar-beet farms with important livestock enterprises are characteristic of the loess soils on the northern edge of the central uplands. The Bavarian Alpine foreland in the south, and Schleswig-

Average temperatures, December–March, are low and frost is usual on over 50 days in this period. The spring is late. The summers are pleasantly warm, the highest recorded temperatures being 34–35°C [93–95°F] in July and August, the averages being 16–17°C [61–62°F]. Moderate rainfall is fairly evenly distributed through the year with a slight peak in July–August. Rain falls on nearly 200 days in the year. Fog is frequent and winter sunshine totals low.

Holstein in the north, are other areas of above-average farm size. The sandy northern lowland, which used to support a poor agriculture based on rye, potatoes and pigs, increasingly specializes in intensive meat and poultry production. Dairy specialization is typical of the milder north-west and the Alpine fringes.

Because of the generally small size of holdings many farmers seek a supplementary income outside agriculture – often a halfway stage to giving up agriculture altogether. Persons employed in agriculture, who were a quarter of the employed population of the FRG in 1950, accounted for well below 10% on reunification four decades later. With this movement out of agriculture, the average size of holding is steadily but all too slowly rising.

In the GDR, by contrast, all agricultural holdings were brought into 'co-operatives', many of over 500 hectares [1,236 acres] and some up to ten times that size. The East German government's version of the collective farm proved much more efficient than the equivalent in many other Communist states, however, and the economic outlook was quite promising prior to reunification.

As with industry, Germany's world rankings in agricultural production are impressive: second in sugar beet and barley (both over 8% of the total), third in rye (11%), cheese and butter (both 9%) and milk (7%), fourth in potatoes (6%) and pork (7%), and fifth in oats (nearly 5%).

Minerals and energy

Germany is the most important coal producer of continental Western Europe, though output from the Ruhr, Saar and Aachen fields has dropped since

THE REUNIFICATION OF GERMANY

In 1945, a devastated Germany was divided into four zones, each occupied by one of the victorious powers: Britain, France, the USA and the Soviet Union. The division was originally a temporary expedient (the Allies had formally agreed to maintain German unity), but the Russians published a constitution for the German Democratic Republic in 1946. The split solidified when the Russians rejected a currency reform common to all three Western zones. The German Federal Republic – 'West Germany' – was created in 1949.

Throughout the years of the Cold War, as NATO troops faced Warsaw Pact tanks across the barbed wire and minefields of the new frontier, the partition seemed irrevocable. Although both German constitutions maintained hopes of reunification, it seemed that nothing short of the total war both sides dreaded could bring it about. The West, with three-quarters of the population, rebuilt war damage and prospered. The East was hailed as the industrial jewel of the Soviet European empire, though some of its people were prepared to risk being shot to escape westwards.

By the late 1980s it was clear that the Soviet empire was crumbling. In the autumn of 1989, thousands of East Germans migrated illegally to the West across the newly open Hungarian border and mass demonstrations in East German cities followed. At first, the government issued a stream of threats, but when it became clear that there would be no Soviet tanks to enforce its rule, it simply packed up. With the frontiers open, it became clear that the 'successful' East German economy was a catastrophic shambles, a scrapyard poisoned by uncontrolled pollution, with bankruptcy imminent. The choice facing German leaders in 1990 was starkly simple: either unite East and West, or accept virtually the entire Eastern population as penniless refugees.

The West German government acted quickly, often bullying the weaker Easterners. The Western Deutschmark became the common currency and on 3 October 1990 – more than 45 years after Germany had lost the war – the country was formally reunited. The costs of bringing the East up to the standards of the West are high, and Germans will be paying them for years to come. But there had been no other possible choice.

desert' created by Parisian centralization is striking.

When industrial growth came in the 19th century, heavy industry naturally concentrated in the Ruhr and Saar coalfields, but thanks to the railways other production could disperse widely to these existing towns. Since 1945 the Ruhr and Saar coalfields have been undergoing a difficult period of conversion, owing to the problems of the now declining coal, steel and heavy engineering industries. Western Europe's largest industrial region, stretching from Duisburg to Dortmund, the Ruhr ('the forge of Germany') has seen its mines for top-grade coking coal cut from 145 to less than 20 and has been forced to diversify – the western end into petrochemicals based on the Rhine ports and pipelines, the east into lighter and computer-based industry.

By contrast, towns away from the coalfields, especially the great regional capitals of southern Germany, have flourished with the inauguration of modern industries (motor vehicles, electrical equipment, electronics), the growth of administrative and office work, and the division among a number of cities of capital functions formerly in Berlin.

As an advanced industrial country of western type, the role of East Germany within the Communist-bloc states was to provide technically advanced equipment, receiving in return supplies of raw materials and semi-finished products such as steel. Because of industrial inertia, the location of the important machine-building industry had not greatly changed since capitalist times, being heavily concentrated in and around the southern cities of Leipzig, Chemnitz (then Karl-Marx-Stadt) and Dresden. Other centres were Magdeburg and East Berlin, the leading producer of electrical equipment.

The GDR inherited a traditional strength in precision and optical industries, mostly located in Thüringia (such as the famous Zeiss works at Jena), the base for important developments in industrial instrumentation and electronics. The government tried to steer some major new developments into the rural north and east of the country, including shipbuilding at Rostock – also the site of a new ocean port, to avoid the use of facilities in the FRG – oil refining and chemicals at Schwedt, and iron smelting and steel rolling at Eisenhüttenstadt.

While the inner parts of the greatest cities have tended to lose population, their suburbs and satellites have exploded across the surrounding countrysides, forming vast urban areas of expanding population. In the west and south of the country, an axis of high population growth and high density stretches from the Rhine-Ruhr region (largest of all but checked in expansion by the problems of Ruhr industry) through the Rhine-Main (Frankfurt), Rhine-Neckar (Mannheim-Ludwigshafen) and Stuttgart regions to Munich. In the east and north the densely populated areas are more isolated, centred on Nuremberg, Hanover, Bremen, Hamburg, Dresden, Leipzig and of course Berlin.

the mid-1950s, owing mainly to competition from oil. Some oil and gas is home-produced, mainly extracted from fields beneath the northern lowland, but most of the oil consumed in Germany is delivered by pipeline from Wilhelmshaven, Europoort and the Mediterranean to refineries in the Rhineland and on the Danube.

Brown coal (lignite) is excavated between Cologne and Aachen, but the former GDR (East Germany) was unique in depending for energy supply on this source of low calorific value, economically mined in vast open pits. The older centre of mining was in the lowland of Saxony, between Halle and Leipzig, but the main area of expansion is now in Niederlausitz, south of Cottbus. Brown coal is increasingly reserved for electricity generation, although atomic plants built on the coast and principal rivers are expected to be of increasing importance (at present 34% of the total for the former FRG), with hydroelectric stations concentrated in the Bavarian Alps. Energy needs and feedstock for the important chemical industry around Halle are met by oil brought by pipeline from the former Soviet republics or by tanker through Rostock. The other mineral

resource of value is potash, mined south of the Harz; Germany is the world's third largest producer. The non-ferrous metallic ores of the Harz and other massifs of the central uplands are no longer of great significance, while high-grade imported iron ores have proved more economic than the home ores of the Siegen and Peine-Salzgitter districts.

Settlement and industry

From Neolithic times the core settlement areas of Germany were the fertile lowlands – areas like the northern edge of the central uplands in Lower Saxony and Westphalia, the Upper Rhine plain, the Main and Neckar basins, and the Alpine foreland. From these core areas land-hungry medieval peasants advanced to clear large areas of forest in the uplands, and also streamed eastwards to settle in lands beyond the Elbe and Saale.

The fragmentation of the Holy Roman Empire into a swarm of competing states had a positive side in the founding and fostering by local rulers, large and small, of a dense system of towns, among them future regional capitals like Hanover, Stuttgart or Munich (München). The contrast with the 'French

In the south the climate is a little warmer in the summer and a little colder in winter. It is also wetter, Munich receiving nearly twice as much rain as Berlin. Further south it is even wetter with more snow. The rainfall is much heavier in the summer months. The coming of spring is much earlier in the Rhine Valley and the south. The Föhn wind gets its name from this area. It is a dry warm wind that blows northwards from the Alps, mainly in the summer.

Since 1950 there has been a tendency for the West's population to drift towards the more attractive south. Urban population losses have in part been made up by immigrant workers (nearly 2.5 million at their peak in the early 1970s, with Turkey the principal source), increasingly joined by their families to supplement a German native population – which at the end of the 1960s entered a period of negative growth.

Germany's wary neighbours, fearing that a nation suddenly swollen to nearly 80 million through reunification could swamp Europe, could rest easy. According to a report from the Institute of German Economy, published in 1992, there will be 20 million fewer Germans alive than today by the year 2030, and on current trends the number of young people below the age of 15 will drop from 13.7 million in 1990 to 10 million in 2010. The findings suggested that, as a result, the country would need at least 300,000 new immigrants a year to fill the gap in its labour market.

Communications

Germany has the advantage of the superb Rhine waterway, which from its Alpine sources cuts right across the central uplands to the North Sea. A combination of summer snow-melt from the Alps and autumn-spring rainfall in the central uplands gives it a powerful and remarkably even flow – if increasingly polluted. Although traffic is at its most intensive between Rotterdam and the Rhine-Ruhr region, where Duisburg is the largest inland harbour of Europe, standard 1,250-tonne self-propelled barges can reach Basle. The Rhine-Main-Danube waterway has also opened a through route to Eastern Europe and the Black Sea, while for north German traffic the Mittelland Canal, following the northern edge of the central uplands, opens up links to the north German ports and Berlin. Unusually for Europe, Germany's rivers and canals carry as much freight as its roads.

Hamburg is Germany's biggest seaport, followed by Bremen with its outport, Bremerhaven. All German ports suffer by being too far from the main centre of European population and economic activity in the Rhinelands; the Belgian and Dutch ports are at a great advantage being closer.

Germany was the first European country to build motorways (Hitler's *Autobahns*, based on Berlin), and also enjoys an efficient if highly subsidized railway network. Both are crucial to a country which, on reunification, increased its land borders from nine to ten countries. Air travel, too, both internal and international, is increasingly important.

Administration

The system of powerful federal states (*Länder*) created in the FRG after World War II remained remarkably stable, though huge disparities of size have remained in spite of various reform proposals. Bavaria has by far the largest area, and North Rhine-Westphalia, with the Rhine-Ruhr region at its heart, has the largest population, over a fifth of the German total. At the other extreme are the 'city states' of Bremen and Hamburg, though Saarland is also small.

In 1990 the ten *Länder* of the FRG (excluding the enclave of West Berlin) were joined by the five rejuvenated old states of the GDR – Brandenburg, Mecklenburg-West Pomerania, Saxony, Saxony-Anhalt and Thüringia – plus the new 'united' Berlin. The East German organization had been very different, the country politically divided into 15 administrative districts (*Bezirke*) under the control of the central government in East Berlin.

The cost of unification

The stability of the federal system may well come under considerable strain in the early years of the reunited Germany. The phenomenal and sustained rise of the FRG from the ashes of World War II to become the world's third biggest economy and its largest exporter – the so-called *Wirtschaftswunder*, or 'economic miracle', accomplished with few natural resources – was already levelling out before the financial costs of reunification (such as the 'two-for-one' Deutschmark for Ostmark deal for GDR citizens) became apparent.

While East Germany had achieved the highest standard of living in the Soviet bloc, it was well short of the levels of advanced EC countries. Massive investment was needed to rebuild the East's industrial base and transport system, and that meant increased taxation. In addition, the new nation found itself funnelling aid into Eastern Europe (Germany led the EC drive for recognition of its old allies Slovenia and Croatia) and then into the former Soviet republics. All this took place against a background of continued downturn in world trade: in

BERLIN

Like defeated Germany itself, Berlin was formally divided between the four victorious powers – despite the fact that it was located in Prussia, 160 km [100 mls] inside Soviet-occupied eastern Germany. In June 1948, in an attempt to bring the whole city under their control, the Soviets closed all road and rail links with the West. The Western Allies supplied the city by a massive airlift; in October 1949 the blockade was abandoned, but Berlin's anomalous situation remained a potential flashpoint, and provoked a series of diplomatic crises – mainly because it offered an easy escape route to the West for discontented East Germans.

In August 1961, alarmed at the steady drain of some of its best-trained people, the East German authorities built a dividing wall across the city. Over the years, the original improvised structure – it was thrown up overnight – became a substantial barrier of concrete and barbed wire, with machine-gun towers and minefields; despite the hazards, many still risked the perilous crossing, and hundreds of would-be refugees – often youngsters – died in the attempt.

The Berlin Wall, with its few, heavily-guarded crossing points, became the most indelible symbol of the Cold War, the essential background to every spy thriller. When the East German government collapsed in 1989, the Wall's spontaneous demolition by jubilant Easterners and Westerners alike became the most unambiguous sign of the Cold War's ending.

When East Germany joined the West, Berlin became the formal capital of the unified state – though many Westerners worried over a possible revival of Prussian influence in their highly successful nation, and a few government ministries remained in the quiet, Rhineland city of Bonn.

February 1992 the German government officially announced the calculation of negative growth – it averaged 8% a year in the 1950s – and the German economy, on paper at least, was 'in recession'.

The costs could be social too. If Westerners resent added taxes and the burden of the GDR, and if the Easterners resent the overbearing, patronizing attitudes of the old FRG, there could be cultural as well as economic polarization. In 1992 there was the spectacle – not seen in 18 years – of several public sector strikes. More likely, however, are a revived German sense of identity bordering on hegemony, even a swing to the 'right', and a revival of Fascism.

Reunification soon appeared in the early 1990s to be the beginning rather than the end of a chapter in German history. At the very least, it would be a more complicated, expensive and lengthy undertaking than anyone was prepared to envisage as the Berlin Wall came crumbling down ∎

COUNTRY: Federal Republic of Germany
AREA: 356,910 sq km [137,803 sq mls]
POPULATION: 79,479,000
CAPITAL (Population): Berlin (3,301,000)
GOVERNMENT: Federal multiparty republic with bicameral legislature
ETHNIC GROUPS: German 92%, Turk 2%, Yugoslav 1%, Italian 1%, Greek
LANGUAGES: German (official)
RELIGIONS: Protestant 45% (predominantly Lutheran), Roman Catholic 37%, Muslim 2%
CURRENCY: Deutschmark = 100 Pfennige
ANNUAL INCOME PER PERSON: $17,000
SOURCE OF INCOME: Agriculture 2%, industry 51%, services 47%
MAIN PRIMARY PRODUCTS: Lignite, coal, timber, pigs, cattle, natural gas, salt, silver
MAIN INDUSTRIES: Motor vehicles, ship construction, iron, cotton yarn, forestry, aluminium, beer, synthetic fibres and rubber, petroleum products
MAIN EXPORTS: Machinery and transport equipment 48%, chemicals 13%, manufactured articles 11%, textiles 3%
MAIN EXPORT PARTNERS: France 12%, Italy 9%, Netherlands 9%, UK 9%, USA 9%, Belgium 7%, Switzerland 6%, Austria 5%, Japan 2%

MAIN IMPORTS: Machinery and transport equipment 28%, food and live animals 10%, chemicals 10%, petroleum and petroleum products 7%, clothing 6%, textile yarn
MAIN IMPORT PARTNERS: France 11%, Netherlands 11%, Italy 10%, Belgium 7%, UK 7%, USA 7%, Japan 6%, Switzerland 5%
EDUCATIONAL EXPENDITURE: 7.8% of national budget
DEFENCE: 22.6% of national budget
TOTAL ARMED FORCES: 494,300
TOURISM: 14,200,000 visitors per year
ROADS: 491,240 km [305,242 mls]
RAILWAYS: 67,536 km [41,965 mls]
POPULATION DENSITY: 223 per sq km [577 per sq ml]
URBAN POPULATION: 85%
BIRTHS: 11.1 per 1,000 population
DEATHS: 11.9 per 1,000 population
INFANT MORTALITY: 8 per 1,000 live births
LIFE EXPECTANCY: Female 78 yrs, male 72 yrs
POPULATION PER DOCTOR: 390
ADULT LITERACY: 99%
PRINCIPAL CITIES (Population): Berlin 3,301,000 Hamburg 1,594,000 Munich 1,189,000 Cologne 928,000 Essen 623,000 Frankfurt am Main 619,000 Dortmund 584,000 Düsseldorf 563,000 Stuttgart 552,000 Leipzig 545,000 Bremen 533,000 Duisburg 525,000 Dresden 518,000 Hanover 495,000 Nuremberg 472,000

SWITZERLAND

Switzerland's square flag was officially adopted in 1848, though the white cross on a red shield has been the Swiss emblem since the 14th century. The flag of the International Red Cross, based in Geneva, derives from this Swiss flag.

BERN

The Alpine foreland of northern Switzerland has a central European climate with a marked summer maximum of rainfall. In winter the region is often blanketed in low cloud resulting in a small diurnal range of temperature in contrast with the mountain resorts which lie above the cloud. Precipitation falls mainly as snow between December and March. Summers are warm with a daily average of eight hours of sunshine in July. December–February day temperatures at Davos are slightly colder than Bern.

Nearly 60% of Swiss territory is in the Alps, of which two notable peaks are on the Italian border: the Matterhorn (4,478 m [14,700 ft]) and the Monte Rosa (4,634 m [15,200 ft]). The Alps are drained by the upper Rhine tributaries and by the Rhône Valley via Lac Léman (Lake Geneva). Numerous lakes add to the scenic attraction of high mountains with permanent snow, and the Alps have become one of the great tourist attractions of the world. As a result, around 200,000 people work in the hotel and catering industries. Nationally, unemployment is very low by world standards.

Despite its lingering rural, pastoral image, Switzerland is a very advanced country, providing its citizens with a per capita income by far the highest of the reasonably sized economies and outstripped only by neighbouring Liechtenstein. The reasons for the high standard of living include neutrality in two World Wars, plentiful hydroelectric power, a central geographical position and rich mineral deposits, including uranium (37% of the electricity is now nuclear-derived) and iron ore. It would also be unfair, however – as in the case of Germany and Japan – not to include hard work, a sense of purpose and organizational ability in the list of attributes.

Agriculture is efficient, with both arable and pastoral farming; a wide range of produce is grown, including maize and other cereals, fruits, vegetables, and grapes for a local wine industry. The mountain pastures are still used for summer grazing, though most of the famous migrations of herds and herders up the mountains in summer no longer take place.

Industry is progressive and prosperous, in particular engineering, both mechanical and electrical, metallurgy, chemicals and textiles. Watch- and clock-making is perhaps the most famed of all Swiss industries, and is still very important for the national economy: along with precision instruments and jewellery it accounts for over 20% of exports.

In addition to agricultural and industrial strength Switzerland also has a world trade in banking and insurance, concentrated particularly in Zürich, while its revenues are boosted both by tourism and its position as the headquarters for numerous international bodies. Geneva alone hosts EFTA, GATT and the International Red Cross, as well as ten UN agencies that include WHO, ILO and the High Commission for Refugees, while there are over 140 others: Basle, for example, is home to the Bank for International Settlements (the central banks' bank). Ironically, Switzerland remains stubbornly outside the UN – a policy whose desirability to the Swiss was confirmed by a referendum held in 1986. However, as Europe moved towards greater economic and political union, Switzerland announced in May 1992 that it would be applying to join the EEC.

Switzerland is a multilingual patchwork of 2 cantons, each of which has control over housing and economic policy. Six of the cantons are French-speaking, one Italian-speaking, one with a significant Romansch-speaking community (Graubünden), and the rest speak German. It nevertheless remains a strongly united country – internationally recognized as a permanently neutral power, politically stable with an efficient reservist army (no navy!), active in good causes, and shrewdly trading with most of the countries of the world ■

COUNTRY: Swiss Confederation (Helvetica)
AREA: 41,290 sq km [15,942 sq mls]
POPULATION: 6,712,000
CAPITAL (Population): Bern (299,000)
GOVERNMENT: Federal state with a bicameral legislature
ETHNIC GROUPS: German 65%, French 18%, Italian 10%, Spanish 2%, Romansch 1%, Turkish 1%
LANGUAGES: French, German, Italian and Romansch (all official)
RELIGIONS: Roman Catholic 48%, Protestant 44%
NATIONAL DAY: 1 August
CURRENCY: Swiss franc = 100 centimes
ANNUAL INCOME PER PERSON: $32,790
MAIN PRIMARY PRODUCTS: Cereals, grapes, potatoes, cattle, timber
MAIN INDUSTRIES: Tourism, financial services, machinery, chemicals, clocks and watches

MAIN EXPORTS: Non-electrical machinery 20%, electrical machinery 12%, pharmaceuticals 8%, precision instruments 7%, jewellery 7%, watches 6%
MAIN EXPORT PARTNERS: Germany 21%, France 9%, USA 9%, Italy 8%, UK 8%, Japan 4%
MAIN IMPORTS: Machinery 20%, chemical products 11%, textiles and clothing 10%, precious metals and jewellery 7%
MAIN IMPORT PARTNERS: Germany 34%, France 11%, Italy 10%, UK 6%, USA 5%, Japan 5%
DEFENCE: 19.7% of national budget
TOURISM: 11,600,000 visitors per year
POPULATION DENSITY: 163 per sq km [421 per sq ml]
INFANT MORTALITY: 7 per 1,000 live births
LIFE EXPECTANCY: Female 81 yrs, male 75 yrs
ADULT LITERACY: 99%
PRINCIPAL CITIES (Population): Zürich 839,000 Geneva 389,000 Basle 359,000 Bern 299,000 Lausanne 263,000

THE ALPS

Thrust upwards by continental collision 25 or 30 million years ago, the Alps are Europe's principal mountain range: between north-eastern Italy and eastern Austria, they stretch for over 1,000 km [600 mls] and include Europe's highest mountain, Mont Blanc (4,807 m [15,771 ft]). The Alpine watershed is the source of many great European rivers, including the Rhine and the Po.

Despite the nine major passes that cross them, the mountains were seen by their pastoralist inhabitants and travellers alike as a troublesome obstacle until the 19th century, when interest in mountaineering, originally an English craze, gave puzzled locals new employment as guides. Six tunnels, including one under Mont Blanc, now make access very easy, and tourism (once confined to those eccentric mountaineers) has become a mass industry built around modern winter sports.

Alpine agriculture, once the mainstay of mountain life, is currently in decline, but skiing and summer tourism have brought new prosperity. Throughout the 1980s, the Alps attracted up to 50 million visitors a year, most intent on skiing some of the 40,000 runs that have been created for them. Unfortunately, the impact of mass skiing on the fragile Alpine environment is serious. Thousands of hectares of high forest have been bulldozed to create smooth *pistes*, denuding the slopes of scarce topsoil as well as creating perfect conditions for massive avalanches: in 1987, more than 60 people were killed by summer mudslides, and almost 50 towns and villages were damaged, some of them severely.

The remaining Alpine forests are also under threat from industrial air pollution. Acid rain, formed from dissolved sulphur dioxide, is destroying trees at an alarming rate: in some districts, two-thirds have been affected, and many of them will never recover

AUSTRIA

According to legend, the colours of the Austrian flag date from the battle of Ptolemais in 1191, when the only part of the Duke of Bebenberg's tunic not bloodstained was under his swordbelt. The design was officially adopted in 1918.

The western Alpine regions have an Atlantic-type climate, while the eastern lowlands are continental. The airflow is mainly from the west, which has twice the rainfall of the east at over 1,000 mm [40 in]. The winters are cold with snow (at Vienna over 60 days), and on the mountains there are glaciers and permanent snow in great depths. In Vienna the January temperature is below freezing and is around 20°C [68°F] in July. The wettest months, June–August, are also the warmest.

A federal republic comprising nine states (Länder) – including the capital, Vienna – Austria's present boundaries derive from the Versailles Treaty of 1919, which dissolved the Austro-Hungarian Empire. It was absorbed by the German Reich in 1938, occupied by the Allies in 1945 and recovered its full independence in 1955.

A mountainous country, Austria has two-thirds of its territory and rather less than a third of the population within the eastern Alps, which extend in a series of longitudinal ridges from the Swiss border in the west almost to Vienna in the east. The longitudinal valleys between the ridges accommodate much of the Alpine population.

Austria's lowlands include a section of the northern Alpine foreland, which narrows eastwards towards Vienna and contains the Danube basin. This is Austria's most important east-west route with rail, motorway and river navigation leading through Vienna to Budapest and beyond. Another important lowland is the Burgenland, a rich farming area bordering the eastern Alps and facing southeast towards Hungary.

Unlike Switzerland, Austria has important heavy industries based in large part on indigenous resources. The mountains are a major source of hydroelectric power. Oil and natural gas occur predominantly in the Vienna Basin and are supplemented by imports from the former Soviet republics and from German refineries. Minerals occur in the eastern Alps, notably iron ore in Steiermark (Styria); iron and steel production is located both at Donawitz (near Leoben) in the mountains, and also in the Alpine foreland which has become a major centre of metal, chemical engineering and vehicle manufacturing industries. Various industrial plants are also established around Vienna.

The capital stands at a major European crossroads where the Danube is joined by the Moravian Gate route from the northern lowlands of Europe, and by the Alpine route through the Semmering Pass. A city of political as well as cultural and artistic importance, Vienna is home to OPEC, the International Atomic Energy Agency and the UN Industrial Development Organization, among others, and contains one-fifth of Austria's population.

Like most European countries, Austria experienced low population growth or even a slight reduction in the 1960s and 1970s. Within the country, decline has been greatest in the east, while the west has gained from a higher birth rate, and also from the settlement of refugees and the industrialization of the Tirol since World War II.

Austria's neutrality was enshrined in the constitution in 1955, but unlike Switzerland it has not been frightened to take sides on certain issues. Though a member of EFTA since 1960, the government led the group of nations that applied for membership of the EEC with the approval of the single market by the end of 1993, hoping for admission the following year ∎

COUNTRY: Republic of Austria

AREA: 83,850 sq km [32,374 sq mls]

POPULATION: 7,712,000

CAPITAL (Population): Vienna (1,483,000)

GOVERNMENT: Federal multiparty republic

ETHNIC GROUPS: Austrian 96%, Yugoslav 2%, Turkish

LANGUAGES: German 94% (official), Slovene, Croat, Turkish, Slovak, Magyar

RELIGIONS: Roman Catholic 84%, Protestant 6%

NATIONAL DAY: 26 October; Proclamation of neutrality (1955)

CURRENCY: Schilling = 100 Groschen

ANNUAL INCOME PER PERSON: $19,240

MAIN PRIMARY PRODUCTS: Iron ore, lignite, oil and natural gas, graphite, timber, cattle, wheat

MAIN INDUSTRIES: Agriculture, tourism, iron and steel, wood products, wine, food processing

MAIN EXPORTS: Machinery and transport equipment 34%, iron and steel 7%, paper and board 6%, cork, wood and other crude materials 5%, foodstuffs 3%

MAIN EXPORT PARTNERS: Germany 35%, Italy 10%, Switzerland 7%, UK 5%, France 4%

MAIN IMPORTS: Machinery and transport equipment 35%, chemicals and pharmaceuticals 10%, mineral fuels and lubricants 7%, food stuffs 5%

MAIN IMPORT PARTNERS: Germany 44%, Italy 9%, Switzerland 5%, Japan 4%, France 4%

DEFENCE: 2.9% of national budget

TOURISM: 15,761,000 visitors per year

POPULATION DENSITY: 92 per sq km [238 per sq ml]

INFANT MORTALITY: 9 per 1,000 live births

LIFE EXPECTANCY: Female 79 yrs, male 72 yrs

ADULT LITERACY: 99%

PRINCIPAL CITIES (Population): Vienna 1,483,000 Graz 243,000 Linz 200,000 Salzburg 139,000 Innsbruck 117,000

LIECHTENSTEIN

The colours of Liechtenstein's flag originated in the early part of the 19th century. The gold crown, often turned 90° so that the flag can be hung vertically, was added in 1937 to avoid confusion with the flag then used by Haiti.

COUNTRY: Principality of Liechtenstein

AREA: 157 sq km [61 sq mls]

POPULATION: 29,000

CAPITAL (Population): Vaduz (4,919)

POPULATION DENSITY: 185 per sq km [475 per sq ml]

Standing at the end of the eastern Alps between Austria and Switzerland, where the Rhine cuts its way northwards out of the Alpine chains, tiny Liechtenstein became an independent principality within the Holy Roman Empire in 1719 and since then has always managed to escape incorporation into any of Europe's larger states.

Since 1923 Liechtenstein has been in customs and currency union with Switzerland, which also provides overseas representation; and although many Swiss regard it as their 27th canton, it retains full sovereignty in other spheres.

The capital, Vaduz, is situated on the Oberland plateau above the fields and meadows of the Rhine Valley, and rising numbers of tourists (there were as many as 72,000 overnight visitors in 1988) are arriving at its royal castle, intrigued by the notion of this miniature state. `

While Liechtenstein is best known abroad for its postage stamps – an important source of income – it is as a haven for international companies, attracted by extremely low taxation and the strictest (most secretive) banking codes in the world, that the state has generated the revenue to produce the highest GDP per capita figure on record.

Since World War II there has also been an impressive growth in specialized manufacturing – the product of a judicious mixture of Swiss engineers, Austrian technicians, Italian workers and international capital ∎

PORTUGAL

Portugal's colours, adopted in 1910 when it became a republic, represent Henry the Navigator (green) and the monarchy (red). The armillary shield – an early navigational instrument – reflects Portugal's leading role in world exploration.

The west coast of the Iberian Peninsula has the oceanic variety of a Mediterranean climate with cooler summers, milder winters and a smaller temperature range than in true Mediterranean lands. Sunshine at Lisbon is abundant, averaging 7.5 hours a day throughout the year. Frosts are virtually unknown, but temperatures over 30°C [86°F] have been recorded March-September, and over 40°C [104°F] in July and August. Most of the rain falls in the winter half of the year, with July and August virtually rainless.

The most westerly of Europe's 'mainland' countries, Portugal occupies an oblong coastland in the south-west of the Iberian peninsula, facing the Atlantic Ocean. Here the Meseta edge has splintered and in part foundered to leave upstanding mountain ranges, particularly in the Serra da Estrêla and its continuation just north of the River Tagus (Tejo), and in the Serra de Monchique.

Agriculture and fishing

The mild, moist airflow from the Atlantic encourages good tree growth. Forests reach a height of at least 1,300 m [4,260 ft] in the north and over a quarter of the country is forested. Pines form the most common species, especially on the sandy 'litorals' near the coast, where large plantations provide timber as well as resin and turpentine. Cork oaks abound in the Tagus Valley and farther south; Portugal is the world's leading producer of the cork that is derived from their bark.

A wide variety of fruits is cultivated, including olives, figs and grapes. Portugal is home to some of the world's greatest vineyards and once ranked fifth in wine production. However, harvests have fallen dramatically from a peak of over a million tonnes to just 368,000 in 1988.

Most of the grapes are grown north of the Tagus, where the most celebrated speciality is port wine from the Douro Valley near the Portuguese-Spanish frontier. The grape juice is transported by boat down the Douro to Vila Nova, where it is fortified and stored for export. The lower parts of the Douro and Minho basins produce famous sparkling *vinhos verdes*, while the vineyards near the Tagus estuary are noted for white table wines and brandy. In the south the Algarve, with its greater sunshine and aridity, specializes more in liqueurs and muscatels.

The Portuguese economy relies heavily on agriculture and fishing, which together employ over a quarter of the national workforce. These industries are mostly undercapitalized and still rather primitive by European standards, although they provide valuable exports. In the rainy north the pressure of overpopulation causes fragmented and tiny agricultural holdings (*minifundia*); in the drier south large holdings (*latifundia*) tend to create monoculture with below-average yields and seasonal unemployment. Recently there has been some investment in irrigation.

The main general crops are food cereals and vegetables, including a wide variety of the beans that form a frequent and favourite item of the Portuguese diet. Maize and rye predominate in the north, and wheat, barley and oats in the south. Of the many farm animals the pig deserves special mention as the forager of the heavy yield of acorns from the cork and evergreen oaks.

Portugal's long coastline provides an important supplementary source of livelihood and of foreign tourist currency. The shallow lagoons yield shellfish, especially oysters; the coastal waters supply sardines, anchovy and tunny; the deep-sea fisheries, long frequented by Portuguese sailors, bring hake, mackerel, halibut and, above all, cod.

Industry

While much of Portuguese industry is concerned with the products of farming, fishing and forestry, the manufacture of textiles and ceramics is also widespread. Modern engineering, associated with a complete iron and steel plant, has been established at Seixal near Lisbon. There is some small-scale mining for copper ores and wolfram (a tungstate of iron and manganese, from which tungsten is obtained), but a relative shortage of power resources is a problem. A small quantity of poor-quality coal is mined annually, and this is supplemented with foreign imports. Great efforts have been made to develop hydroelectric stations in the north, but Portugal remains the poorest member of the EEC since switching economic allegiance from EFTA on 1 January 1986.

Portugal has two conurbations with over a million inhabitants. Lisbon, the capital, is the chief centre of the country's financial, commercial and industrial concerns and has a fine sheltered harbour in the large Tagus estuary. Porto, the main centre for the densely-populated north, has an ocean outport. These two cities still dominate the nation, but during recent decades tourism and rapid residential growth have transformed the subtropical coastline of the Algarve, and have led to a substantial increase in its population ■

COUNTRY: Republic of Portugal
AREA: 92,390 sq km [35,672 sq mls]
POPULATION: 10,525,000
CAPITAL (Population): Lisbon (831,000)
GOVERNMENT: Parliamentary state with a unicameral legislature
ETHNIC GROUPS: Portuguese 99%, Cape Verdean, Brazilian, Spanish, British
LANGUAGES: Portuguese (official)
RELIGIONS: Roman Catholic 95%
NATIONAL DAY: 10 June; Portugal Day
CURRENCY: Escudo = 100 centavos
ANNUAL INCOME PER PERSON: $4,890
MAIN PRIMARY PRODUCTS: Cereals, olives, rice, timber, fruit, grapes, vegetables, cork, fish, copper, iron, tungsten, tin, salt
MAIN INDUSTRIES: Agriculture, textiles, food processing wine, chemicals, fishing, mining, machinery, tourism

EXPORTS: $1,210 per person
MAIN EXPORTS: Clothing 26%, machinery and transport equipment 20%, footwear 8%, paper and paper products 8%, agricultural products 7%
MAIN EXPORT PARTNERS: France 15%, Germany 15%, UK 14%, Spain 11%
IMPORTS: $1,803 per person
MAIN IMPORTS: Machinery 22%, road vehicles 15%, crude petroleum 9%, iron and steel products 4%, chemicals 4%
MAIN IMPORT PARTNERS: Germany 14%, Spain 14%, France 12%, Italy 9%, UK 8%
DEFENCE: 8.4% of national budget
TOURISM: 6,102,000 visitors per year
POPULATION DENSITY: 114 per sq km [295 per sq ml]
INFANT MORTALITY: 13 per 1,000 live births
LIFE EXPECTANCY: Female 78 yrs, male 71 yrs
ADULT LITERACY: 84%
PRINCIPAL CITIES (Population): Lisbon 831,000 Oporto 350,000

ANDORRA

Andorra is traditionally said to have been granted independence by Charlemagne in the 9th century, after the Moorish Wars. The flag, adopted in 1866, sometimes features the state coat of arms on the obverse in the central yellow band.

COUNTRY: Co-principality of Andorra
AREA: 453 sq km [175 sq mls]
POPULATION: 52,000
CAPITAL: Andorra la Vella
POPULATION DENSITY: 115 per sq km [297 per sq ml]

Perched near the eastern end of the high central Pyrenees, Andorra consists mainly of six valleys (the Valls) that drain to the River Valira. The population totals about 52,000, a third of whom are native born.

The rights of the *seigneurie* or co-principality have been shared since 1278 between the Spanish Bishop of Urgel and the French Comte de Foix. The latter's lordship rights passed to the French government, now represented by the prefect of the adjoining *département* of the Eastern Pyrenees. The people of Andorra pay a small annual sum to the bishop and the prefect, and each co-prince is represented in their Council by a *viguier*, but in most other respects the co-principality governs itself, and retains no armed forces.

Physically the country consists of deep glaciated valleys lying at altitudes of 1,000 to 2,900 m [3,280 to 9,500 ft]. On the north a lofty watershed forms the frontier with France and is crossed by a road over the Envalira Pass at 2,400 m [7,870 ft]; to the south the land falls away down the Valira Valley to the Segre Valley in Spain, again followed by the same vital highway. In the colder months the Envalira Pass often becomes snowbound and land communications are then only with Spain.

The climate is severe in winter and pleasantly cool in summer when, because the valleys lie in a rain-shadow, slopes above 1,400 m [4,600 ft] often suffer from drought and need irrigation. Some agriculture is possible on the slopes: sheep and cattle are grazed, and crops grow in terraced fields.

Andorra has five main sources of income: stock-rearing and agriculture, especially tobacco; the sale of water and hydroelectricity to Catalonia; fees from radio transmission services; tourism, based in winter on skiing; and the sale of duty-free goods and of postage stamps. Of these, tourism and duty-free sales are by far the most important – every year up to 10 million visitors come to Andorra to shop, and to witness this rare surviving example of a medieval principality ■

SPAIN

The colours of the Spanish flag date back to the old kingdom of Aragon in the 12th century. The present design, in which the central yellow stripe is twice as wide as each of the red stripes, was adopted during the Civil War in 1938.

A global position between coastal north-west Europe and Africa, and between the Mediterranean countries of the Old World and the Americas, made Spain a great crossroads. Yet the lofty Pyrenean barrier in the north weakened land contacts with the rest of Europe, while the narrow Strait of Gibraltar in the south encouraged African contacts, lending truth to the cliché that 'Africa begins at the Pyrenees'.

The chief physical feature of Spain is the vast central plateau, the Meseta, which tilts gently towards Portugal. A harsh and often barren area, the plateau is crossed by the Central Sierras, a mountain chain running north-west to south-east. This central divide separates two mountain basins: Old Castile in the north and New Castile in the south.

On the north-eastern and southern edges of the Meseta are large triangular lowlands. That on the north drains to the Ebro, that in the south to the Guadalquivir, the largest river wholly in Spain. Beyond the Ebro trough the land rises to the Pyrenees, which form the Franco-Spanish border, and continue westwards in the Cantabrian Mountains. Similarly, the Mediterranean flank of Andalusia rises to a lofty *cordillera* (mountain chain) that culminates in the snowy Sierra Nevada (peaking at

3,478 m [11,400 ft]). The Mediterranean side of the Meseta has summits of about 2,000 m [6,560 ft] and drops to narrow, discontinuous coastal plains.

Spain has perhaps the widest range of climate of any country in Western Europe. The most striking

The interior of Spain is a high plateau, isolated from the seas which surround the Iberian Peninsula. Summer days are very hot despite the altitude, above 25°C [77°F] June-September during the day, but at night temperatures fall sharply. Winters are much colder than in coastal districts and frost is not uncommon. Rain is fairly evenly distributed from September to May, but the summer drought is broken only by occasional storms. Madrid has an average of eight hours sunshine a day over the year.

GIBRALTAR

Local rock carvings demonstrate that Gibraltar has been inhabited since Neolithic times. Greeks and Romans also settled here, but the first sure date for colonization is AD 711 when Tariq ibn Zaid, a Berber chieftain, occupied it. Although taken over by Spaniards for a short while in the 14th century, it remained Moorish until 1462. An Anglo-Dutch naval force captured it in 1704 and it was formally recognized as a British possession at the Treaty of Utrecht in 1713. In spite of long sieges and assaults – not to mention pressure from Spain – it has remained British ever since, becoming a strategically vital naval dockyard and air base.

The Rock, as it is popularly known, guards the north-eastern end of the Strait of Gibraltar. It is 6.5 sq km [2.5 sq mls] in area, consisting largely of a narrow ridge thrusting south along the eastern side of Algeciras Bay, rising to 426 m [1,400 ft] at Europa Point. The topography prohibits cultivation and the Gibraltarians rely on the port, the ship-repairing yards, the military and air bases, and on tourism for their livelihood.

The 30,000 Gibraltarians are of British, Spanish, Maltese, Portuguese and Genoan descent. Though bilingual in Spanish and English, they remain staunchly pro-British. In 1966, following a long-standing claim, the Spanish government called on Britain to give 'substantial sovereignty' of Gibraltar to Spain and closed the border (1.2 km [0.74 mls]) to all but pedestrian traffic. In a 1967 referendum the residents voted overwhelmingly to remain under British control, and in 1969 they were granted the status of a self-governing dependency.

Spain closed the frontier completely, preventing thousands of Spaniards from reaching their daily work. The border was reopened fully by Spain in 1985 following British agreement that, for the first time, they would discuss the sovereignty of Gibraltar; but despite being fellow members of NATO (Spain joined in 1982) and the EEC (Spain joined on 1 January 1986), there has been no progress towards British compliance with the United Nations General Assembly's resolution for an end to Gibraltar's 'colonial status' by 1 October 1996.

---

contrast is between the humid north and north-west and the mainly arid remainder of the country. Large areas of the country are barren or steppeland, and about a fifth is covered by *matorral*, a Mediterranean scrub like the French *maquis*.

A large part of the farmland is used for pastoral purposes, but there are rich soils in some of the major river valleys, such as the Ebro and the Guadalquivir, and areas of very productive agriculture, especially where there are *huertas* (irrigated market gardens) and *vegas* (irrigated orchards).

Spain's vegetation falls into three broad categories: forest, *matorral* and steppe. Forests (almost 10% of the land surface) are today mainly confined to the rainier north and north-west, with beech and deciduous oak common. Towards the drier south and east, Mediterranean pines and evergreen oaks take over, and forests resemble open parkland. Widespread clearance for fuel and cultivation and grazing by sheep, goats and cattle have turned large areas into *matorral* or shrub.

This low bush growth, often of aromatic evergreen plants, may be dominated over large tracts by one species: thus *romillares* consist predominantly of rosemary, *tomillares* of thyme, *retamales* of broom. Where soils are thin and drought prevalent, *matorral* gives way to steppe, mainly of alfalfa and esparto.

Agriculture

Despite the problems of aridity and poor soils, agriculture occupies nearly a third of the national workforce. Irregular river regimes and deeply incised valleys make irrigation difficult and expensive and, on the higher and drier regions, tracts favourable for cultivation are often isolated by expanses of low fertility where only a meagre livelihood can be wrested from the soil. There are, too, problems connected with the size of farms. In semi-arid Spain large estates (*latifundios*) abound with much seasonal employment or share-cropping, while in the rainy north-west and north excessive fragmentation of small farms (*minifundios*) has proved uneconomic.

It is against this picture of difficulties that the great progress made since 1939 by the *Instituto Nacional de Colonización* (INC) must be viewed. The institute, by means of irrigation, co-operative farming schemes, concentration of landholdings, agricultural credit schemes and technical training, has resettled over a quarter of the land needing reorganization and reclamation. But, generally, crop yields are still comparatively modest and agricultural techniques remain backward.

Stock-rearing: Large areas of farmland are used solely or partly for pastoral purposes, which are of great economic importance. Spain has about 20 million sheep, mainly of the native merino type which produces a fine fleece. The Mesta, an old confederation of sheep-owners, controls the seasonal migrations on to the summer pastures on the high sierras. Areas too rocky and steep for sheep are given over to goats while cattle, apart from working oxen, are mostly restricted to regions with ample grass and

water – for example the north and north-west. Pigs are bred in the cattle districts of the north, and are also kept to forage the acorns in the large tracts of evergreen oaks in the south. Many working animals are kept, and fighting bulls are bred on the marshes (*marismas*) at the mouth of the Guadalquivir.

Arable crops: The typical arable crops are the classical Mediterranean trio of wheat, olive and vine, with maize important in rainier districts and vegetables and citrus fruits where there is irrigation water. Wheat occupies a third of the cropland and is usually followed in rotation by leguminous pulses or fallow, grazed and so manured by sheep.

In dry areas barley, oats and rye, grown for fodder, replace wheat, and in the wetter north maize dominates both for grain and feed. Rice is harvested in Murcia, Valencia and the Ebro Valley and Spain follows Italy for rice production in Europe.

Fruit-growing: Fruits occupy a high and honoured place in Spain's agricultural economy. The olive crop, mainly from large estates in Andalusia, makes Spain the world's chief producer of olive oil. Vines cover about 10% of the cultivated land and only Italy and France exceed the Spanish output of wine. Sherry (from Jérez) is renowned and among Spain's other fine wines are those of Rioja.

For citrus fruit Spain easily outstrips other European producers, the bulk of the crop being Seville oranges destined largely for Britain for making marmalade. Large quantities of other fruits, especially apricots and peaches, are grown with vegetables as a ground crop in market gardens and orchards.

Some of the *huertas* are devoted to industrial crops such as cotton, hemp, flax and sugar beet, while most richer soils in Andalusia are entirely given over to cotton. The poorer steppes yield *esparto* (a strong grass) for paper-making.

Maps of modern Spain clearly indicate the tremendous progress made recently in water reservation and river regulation on all the major rivers. Large new reservoirs have been constructed on the Miño, Duero, Tajo, Guadiana, Guadalquivir and other main rivers as well as numerous dams on the lesser water-courses. The INC, which directs this work, aims at bringing 70,000 hectares [173,000 acres] a year under irrigation as well as undertaking all kinds of land reclamation, drainage, reforestation, settlement schemes and farm co-operative planning.

Mining and industry

Spain is lamentably short of its own supplies of solid and liquid fuels and in an average year produces only small quantities of poor-quality coal (mainly from Asturias at Oviedo), and some lignite from a field south of Barcelona. Small deposits of petroleum found near Burgos and at the mouth of the Ebro have not yet proved economic to develop.

In contrast to fossil fuels, workable mineral ores are widespread. High-quality iron ores, with substantial reserves, occur in Vizcaya, Santander and

---

COUNTRY: Kingdom of Spain

AREA: 504,780 sq km [194,896 sq mls]

POPULATION: 38,959,000

CAPITAL (Population): Madrid (3,123,000)

GOVERNMENT: Constitutional monarchy

ETHNIC GROUPS: Castilian Spanish 73%, Catalan 16%, Galician 8%, Basque 2%

LANGUAGES: Castilian Spanish (official), Basque, Catalan, Galician

RELIGIONS: Roman Catholic 97%

NATIONAL DAY: 12 October; Discovery of America (1492)

CURRENCY: Peseta = 100 céntimos

ANNUAL INCOME PER PERSON: $10,920

MAIN PRIMARY PRODUCTS: Cereals, sugar cane, grapes, fruit, timber, olives, fish, cork, lignite, iron, coal, lead, copper, mercury, tungsten, zinc, tin

MAIN INDUSTRIES: Agriculture, wine, food processing, mining, iron and steel, textiles, chemicals, cement

MAIN EXPORTS: Transport equipment 17%, machinery and electrical equipment 13%, vegetables and fruit 9%, cast iron, iron and steel 9%, chemicals 7%, mineral fuels 6%

MAIN EXPORT PARTNERS: France 15%, USA 10%, Germany 10%, UK 9%, Benelux 8%, Italy 7%

MAIN IMPORTS: Machinery and electrical equipment 20%, mineral fuels and petroleum products 19%, chemicals 9%, transport equipment 8%

MAIN IMPORT PARTNERS: USA 11%, Germany 11%, France 9%, UK 7%, Mexico 6%, Italy 5%

DEFENCE: 9.5% of national budget

TOURISM: 32,900,000 visitors per year

POPULATION DENSITY: 77 per sq km [200 per sq ml]

LIFE EXPECTANCY: Female 80 yrs, male 74 yrs

ADULT LITERACY: 94%

PRINCIPAL CITIES (Population): Madrid 3,123,000 Barcelona 1,694,000 Valencia 739,000 Seville 668,000 Zaragoza 596,000 Malaga 595,000 Bilbao 378,000 Las Palmas 372,000 Valladolid 341,000

MALAGA

The narrow coastal plain of southern Spain, sheltered by the Sierra Nevada, is noted for its very hot and sunny summers. Rainfall at Malaga is sparse and, like much of the western Mediterranean region, evenly distributed throughout the winter half of the year – in contrast to the more prominent winter maximum further east. With an average of only 52 rainy days a year, Malaga is one of the most reliable holiday resorts. In winter it records over 5 hours of sunshine a day; 9–11 hours May–September.

Granada. Bilbao, the chief ore-exporting port, has an important integrated iron and steel plant; so have Oviedo, Gijón and other towns on the north coast..

Many localities yield non-ferrous ores in sufficient quantity to broaden the base of Spain's metallurgical industries. The chief workings are for copper at Río Tinto, lead and silver at Linares and Peñarroya (near Pueblonovo), and mercury at Almadén; in addition, manganese, titanium and sulphur are produced in small quantities and considerable amounts of potassium salts come from Catalonia. The country is also Europe's leading producer (and third in the world) of mercury.

But the major Spanish manufacturing industries are based on agriculture rather than minerals. Textiles, including cotton, wool, silk, jute and linen lead the industrial sector. Barcelona, Catalonia's great industrial, financial and commercial centre, is surrounded by textile towns, some specializing in spinning, as at Manresa and Ribas, and others in weaving, as at Sabadell and Granollers.

Cotton fabrics form the chief single product and supply a wide market, especially at home and in Latin America. However, Barcelona has a wide variety of light industries, including engineering, while the heavy metallurgical sectors are located mainly at Bilbao and other north-coast cities. Madrid has become an important centre for consumer goods, particularly electrical appliances.

Food-processing industries are concentrated in the north-east, the chief being flour-milling, sugar refining and oil-pressing. Fish canning and processing are widespread in the coastal towns and the Galicians and Basques of the Atlantic coastline are skilled fishermen.

Tourism and communications

The relative absence of closely-packed industrial plants and industrial pollution, the historical attractions of the relics of a long history dating from the Greeks and Arabs, and the dry warm sunny climate of the Mediterranean south and east have fostered tourism, the greatest of all Spain's non-agricultural industries. In recent years over 30 million tourists have visited Spain annually and the Costa Brava and Costa del Sol are internationally famous.

Equally significant is the great increase in the number of those who came to live permanently or for most of the year in these picturesque coastlands with warm winters and subtropical vegetation. However, the economic recession that affected Western Europe into the 1990s substantially reduced Spain's tourist trade, leaving many resorts on the Mediterranean coast uncertain about a future almost wholly dependent on visitors in search of sun and fun on 'package' holidays.

The prime communication routes in Spain focus on Madrid, which has radial links to the peripheral cities. First-class highways radiate to the main ports and good roads connect all the major towns; but

minor roads are seldom tarred and for so large a country relatively few vehicles are registered.

Railways likewise converge on Madrid with minor networks round the regional capitals and main ports. The tracks are not of standard European gauge, about 75% being broad gauge and the remainder narrow. The chief land communications with France run at either end of the Pyrenees and are supplemented by several high-level transmontane rail and road routes.

Air travel focuses on Madrid airport and, particularly for tourism, on 40 other civil airports, many of them with busy international services. The large coastal and ocean-going traffic involves 230 Spanish ports, but the bulk of the overseas trade passes through the modernized harbours – in particular Bilbao, Barcelona, Cartagena, Cádiz and Gijón.

Demography

The population of Spain is most dense on the coastlands and lowlands around the Meseta. Madrid, in the heart of the tableland, forms a grand exception. The capital stands on the small Manzanares River, a tributary of the Tagus, and has a long history dating

from early Roman times. The Moors first provided it with clean drinking water and Philip II made it the seat of the national government in 1561. A fine metropolis, it has flourished during the decades since the Civil War (1936–9) and now accommodates about 10% of the total population of continental Spain. The second Spanish city, Barcelona, is a great commercial and industrial centre; in all ways the core of Catalonia, it was given a huge boost by the staging of the summer Olympics in 1992.

The other major cities include Bilbao, the Basque capital and chief urban area of the north coast, long noted for its metallurgy; Cádiz, an important naval centre; Seville, the river port and regional capital of Andalusia; Valencia and Murcia, the largest of the Mediterranean *huerta* cities; Zaragoza, the expanding centre for the Ebro lowland, noted for food processing and engineering; and Málaga, the fast-growing nucleus of the Costa del Sol. Toledo, which was the national capital before Madrid, ranks for below these conurbations in size, but, protected as a national monument, is the finest medieval city that survives almost intact from the golden age of Spain ■

BALEARIC ISLANDS

The Islas Baleares group contains five larger islands (Majorca, Minorca, Ibiza, Formentera, Cabrera) and 11 rocky islets, together covering 5,014 sq km [1,936 sq mls] and spread over 350 km [218 mls].

Majorca (Mallorca), by far the largest island, has limestone ridges on the north-west and south-east with a plain covered with flat-bedded, very fertile marine sediments between them. Minorca (Menorca), the second largest, has limestone plains and small outcrops of crystalline rocks, but nowhere rises above 358 m [1,175 ft].

The typical sunny Mediterranean climate supports an equally typical vegetation. Shrub-growth (*matorral* or *garrigue*) still clothes the highest areas and is grazed by sheep and goats. The rainier upper slopes of the hills have been terraced for olives, carobs and vines, while the lower slopes are under market-garden crops. The level lowlands are planted with wheat and barley, usually in rotation with beans. Generally, almonds, apricots and carobs are more important here than vines and citrus fruits. The rural economy is essentially peasant with a high degree of self-sufficiency.

Population and industry

Like most Mediterranean islands the Balearics were settled early. Archaeological remains exist from 1,000 BC (Bronze Age) to the Roman period and include boat-shaped burial mounds (*navetas* or *naus*) and conical stone towers (*talayots*)

thought to be refuges from piratical raiding parties. Ibiza town and Port Mahon were originally settled from Carthage. During recent times the islands were repeatedly occupied by the British, French and Spanish and remained finally a province of Spain. Each different occupation has left its mark, and Port Mahon has fine buildings representing all these changes of ownership.

Today the population lives mainly either in agricultural villages some way inland or in small ports around the coast. Power resources and raw materials for manufacture are scarce, apart from agricultural products; textile manufacture (wool and cotton) and food processing are the only widespread factory occupations. Handicrafts flourish in response to the tourism that now dominates the whole economy.

Palma, the capital of Majorca and of the Balearic province, continues to grow rapidly. It has a fine harbour with regular sailings to Barcelona, Alicante and Valencia for passengers and the export of Balearic surpluses of almonds, grain, textiles and vegetables. It is also a regular port of call for Mediterranean cruise ships and its airport, one of the busiest in Spain, deals with well over a million visitors annually. Manacor, the only other large centre on Majorca, is an agricultural market town near limestone caves and subterranean lakes that attract numerous tourists. Port Mahon is the capital of Minorca, and Ibiza town the capital of that small island.

A Mediterranean-type climate of warm and dry summers with wet and cool winters. The coldest times of the year are the nights of December–March when the average temperature is 6–7°C [43–45°F]. July–August are the warmest months when the average daytime temperature is 29–30°C [84-86°F], with many days getting above 35°C [95°F]. Rainfall is low, being registered on only about 70 days in the year. June to August are almost rainless.

ITALY

When Napoleon invaded Italy in 1796, the French Republican National Guard carried a military standard of vertical green, white and red stripes. After many changes, it was finally adopted as the national flag after the unification of Italy in 1861.

Although the plains of Lombardy lie within the Mediterranean basin they have a climate more like that of central Europe, though with hotter summers and warmer winters. In Milan, January is the only month with average night temperatures just below freezing. Sunshine averages under five hours a day, far less than that of southern Italy. Winter is relatively dry and cold with occasional frost and snow. Rainfall is plentiful, with a double maximum in spring and autumn, and falling on 90 days per year.

In 1800 present-day Italy was made up of several political units, including the Papal States, and a substantial part of the north-east was occupied by Austria. The struggle for unification – the *Risorgimento* – began early in the century, but little progress was made until an alliance between France and Piedmont (then part of the kingdom of Sardinia) drove Austria from Lombardy in 1859. Tuscany, Parma and Modena joined Piedmont-Lombardy in 1860, and the Papal States, Sicily, Naples (including most of the southern peninsula) and Romagna were brought into the alliance. King Victor Emmanuel II was proclaimed ruler of a united Italy in Turin the following year, Venetia was acquired from Austria in 1866, and Rome was finally annexed in 1871. Since that time Italy has been a single state, becoming a republic following the abolition of the monarchy by popular referendum in 1946.

North and south

Since unification the population has doubled, and though the rate of increase is notoriously slow today, the rapid growth of population, in a poor country attempting to develop its resources, forced millions of Italians to emigrate during the first quarter of the 20th century. Italy's short-lived African Empire enabled some Italians to settle overseas, but it did not substantially relieve the population pressure. Now there are immigrant Italians to be found on all the inhabited continents. Particularly large numbers settled in the USA, South America and Australia, and more recently large numbers of Italians have moved for similar reasons into northern Europe.

Almost all Italians are brought up as Roman Catholics; since a 1985 agreement between Church and State, Catholic religious teaching is offered, but not compulsory, in schools. The Vatican, in theory an independent state, is in fact an enclave of Rome.

Despite more than a century of common language, religion and cultural traditions, great differences remain in the ways of life of people in different parts of Italy. These can partly be explained in terms of geography. The long, narrow boot-shaped peninsula, with coastal lowlands on either side of the central Apennines, extends so far south that its toe, and the neighbouring island of Sicily, are in the latitudes of North Africa. Southern Sicily is as far south (36°N) as Tunis and Algiers, while the northern industrial city of Milan (45½°N) is nearer to London than it is to Reggio in Calabria, the extreme south of peninsular Italy. Given their markedly disparate social and historical backgrounds, the long period of isolation that preceded the unification and widely differing climates, it is hardly surprising that northern and southern Italy retain their independence of character and culture.

The Alps and Apennines

Italy's topographical structure is determined mainly by the events of the Alpine period of mountain building, when the main ranges of the Alps and the Apennines were uplifted together. There are traces of earlier periods in the central Alps, between Mont Blanc (4,807 m [15,771 ft]) on the French border and Monte Rosa (4,634 m [15,203 ft]) on the Swiss border, and in the Carnic Alps in the north-east. Here ancient crystalline rocks predominate, although many of the higher peaks are formed from limestone. The Dolomite Alps, famous for their climbing and skiing resorts, have given their name to a particular form of magnesian limestone.

Generally lower than the Alps, the Apennines reach their highest peaks – almost 3,000 m [9,800 ft] – in the Gran Sasso range overlooking the central Adriatic Sea near Pescara. The most frequently occurring rocks are various types of limestone. The slopes are covered by thin soils and have been subjected to severe erosion, so that in many areas they are suitable only for poor pasture. Between the mountains, however, are long narrow basins, some of which contain lakes. Others have good soils and drainage and provide a basis for arable farming.

Italy is well known for volcanic activity and earthquakes. Three volcanoes are still active – Vesuvius, near Naples, renowned for its burial of Pompeii in AD 79, Etna in Sicily, and Stromboli on an island in the south Tyrrhenian Sea. Traces of earlier volcanism are to be found throughout the country. Ancient lava flows cover large areas, and where they have weathered they produce fertile soils. Mineral deposits, such as the iron ores of Elba and the tin ores of the Mt Annata area, are often associated with earlier volcanic intrusions. Italy is still subject to earthquakes and volcanic eruptions. During the 20th century disasters have occurred at Messina (1908 – the worst in Europe in recent times, with more than 80,000 deaths), Avezzano (1915), Irpinia (1930), Friuli (1976) and Naples (1980).

VENICE

The city of Venice originally grew up on a group of over 100 small islands, lying in a lagoon sheltered from the open Adriatic Sea by a sandbar. It now also includes the mainland industrial suburbs of Mestre and Marghera, where two-thirds of the city's population live. Causeways carry road and rail links to the mainland, but cars are not allowed in the old city. Boats of all types, from the traditional gondolas to the diesel-powered water-buses, use the canals which form the 'streets' of Venice.

Venice was once the capital of an imperial republic which, until overthrown by Napoleon in 1797, controlled much of the trade of the Adriatic and the eastern Mediterranean. The heart of the city is around St Mark's Square, where the cathedral and the Palace of the Doges (Dukes) who ruled the republic stand.

The unique site and the rich art treasures attract about 2 million tourists a year, providing a living for tens of thousands of Venetians who cater for them; tourists, too, help to support such craft industries as glass-blowing, for which the city is famous. For Expo 2000 the figure is expected to be over 250,000 a day, imposing a massive strain on a city already suffering from erosion, subsidence and pollution.

COUNTRY: Italian Republic

AREA: 301,270 sq km [116,320 sq mls]

POPULATION: 57,663,000

CAPITAL (Population): Rome (2,817,000)

GOVERNMENT: Democratic republic with bicameral legislature

ETHNIC GROUPS: Italian 94%, German, French, Greek, Albanian, Slovenian, Ladino

LANGUAGES: Italian (official) 94%, Sardinian

RELIGIONS: Roman Catholic 83%

NATIONAL DAY: 2 June; Republic (1946)

CURRENCY: Lira = 100 centesimi

ANNUAL INCOME PER PERSON: $16,850

SOURCE OF INCOME: Agriculture 4%, industry 40%, services 56%

MAIN PRIMARY PRODUCTS: Wheat, barley, vegetables, grapes, fruit, olives, fish oil, natural gas, iron ore, mercury, zinc, lignite, sulphur, marble

MAIN INDUSTRIES: Iron and steel, chemicals, food processing, oil refining, vehicles, textiles and clothing, wine, tourism

MAIN EXPORTS: Machinery 26%, textiles and clothing 13%, vehicles 9%, chemicals 7%, footwear 5%, petroleum products 3%, iron and steel 3%

MAIN EXPORT PARTNERS: Germany 19%, France 17%, USA 9%, UK 7%, Switzerland 5%, Belgium 3%, Spain 3%

MAIN IMPORTS: Machinery 17%, textiles and clothing 13%, vehicles 9%, chemicals 7%, footwear 5%, petroleum products 3%, iron and steel 3%

MAIN IMPORT PARTNERS: Germany 21%, France 15%, Saudi Arabia 6%, USA 16%, UK 6%, Belgium 5%

EDUCATIONAL EXPENDITURE: 8% of national budget

DEFENCE: 5.4% of national budget

TOTAL ARMED FORCES: 390,000

TOURISM: 25,749,000 visitors per year

ROADS: 300,292 [187,683 mls]

RAILWAYS: 15,983 km [9,989 mls]

POPULATION DENSITY: 191 per sq km [496 per sq ml]

URBAN POPULATION: 69%

POPULATION GROWTH: 0.1% per year

BIRTHS: 11.5 per 1,000 population

DEATHS: 10.5 per 1,000 population

INFANT MORTALITY: 9 per 1,000 live births

LIFE EXPECTANCY: Female 80 yrs, male 73 yrs

POPULATION PER DOCTOR: 234

ADULT LITERACY: 97%

PRINCIPAL CITIES (Population): Rome 2,817,000 Milan 1,464,000 Naples 1,203,000 Turin 1,012,000 Palermo 731,000 Genoa 715,000 Bologna 422,000 Florence 417,000 Catania 371,000 Bari 357,000 Venice 324,000 Messina 272,000 Verona 259,000 Taranto 245,000 Trieste 235,000

SARDINIA

Just a little smaller than Sicily, but with less than a third of its population, Sardinia's isolation from the mainstream of Italian life is due partly to its physical position, 480 km [300 mls] from the Italian coast, but the rugged, windswept terrain and lack of resources have also set it apart.

The chief crops on the lowlands are wheat, vines, olives and vegetables, and there are rough pastures for sheep and goats on the scrub-covered hills. Fishing for tuna provides an important source of income for the ports of the west coast. Sardinia is rich in minerals, including lead, zinc, iron ore and lignite, and the island is an increasingly popular tourist destination.

Lombardy

The great triangular plain of Lombardy, lying between the northern Alps and the Apennines, is drained by the River Po, which flows west to east, rising in the Ligurian Alps near the French frontier and flowing across a delta into the Gulf of Venice.

The Lombardy plains are the most productive area of Italy, both agriculturally and industrially. There is no shortage of water, as in the areas further south, although some places are served by irrigation canals. Crops include maize, wheat, potatoes, tomatoes, rice and mulberries – these associated with the development of the silk industry. In the Alpine valleys above the Lombardy plain vines are cultivated.

Industry and urban life in Lombardy is long established. Textiles – silk, cotton, flax and wool – metal-working and food processing all began long before the modern industrial period. Large-scale Italian industry was slower to develop than in Britain and Germany, partly because of the lack of coal, but in Lombardy this has been offset by the availability of hydroelectric power from the Alpine rivers, and by the development of a natural gas field in the area of the Po delta. Oil and gas are also imported by pipeline from Austria. Italy is more dependent on imported energy than any European country, nearly 60% of it oil, though Algeria remains a major

NAPLES

Naples lies in the north of the Mezzogiorno, the most typically Mediterranean region in Italy. Summers are hot and very sunny with occasional thunderstorms usually providing the only rain. From May to September sunshine is 8-10 hours per day, with day temperatures of 23-29°C [73-84°F]. Winters are mild and virtually free from frost with westerly winds bringing abundant rain to the western slopes of the Apennines. November is the wettest month throughout the region.

supplier of gas through the Transmed pipeline via Tunisia.

Engineering and metal-working are now the most important industries, centred on Milan and, in Piedmont, on Turin. Lombardy remains dominant, however: the most densely populated region, it accounts for a third of Italy's GDP and some 30% of export earnings, and in the 1992 election the separatist party made huge gains at the expense of established rivals.

Central Italy

Central Italy, between the Po Valley and the River Tiber, is a transitional zone between the industrially developed north and the poor, agrarian south. It contains Rome, which has survived as a capital city for over 2,000 years, Florence and Bologna.

The area has a glorious history of artistic and literary achievement, but with its limited resources, steep slopes and difficult communications it has been left behind in economic development by the more favoured lowlands of the north, and relies heavily on tourism for regional income.

Regions like Tuscany, Umbria and Lazio have considerable autonomy from Rome, with control over health and education, for example, and other devolved powers. Indeed five regions enjoy more autonomy than the rest: French-speaking Valle d'Aosta, in the north-west; Trentino-Alto Adige, the largely German-speaking area in the far north; Friuli-Venézia Giulia in the north-east; and the two island provinces of Sardinia and Sicily.

The Mezzogiorno

The south of Italy, known as the Mezzogiorno, is the least developed part of the country. It displays, in less severe form, many of the characteristics of the developing countries of the Third World. Its people depend for their livelihood on Mediterranean crops produced on small peasant farms too small to lend themselves to modern techniques, although there are some large estates.

Over a third of the people are still in agriculture, with unemployment three or more times that of the north. Though the eight regions of the Mezzogiorno cover some 40% of the land area (including Sicily and Sardinia) and contain more than a third of the country's population, they contribute only about a quarter of the GDP.

The birth rate is much higher than in the north, and there is a serious problem of overpopulation which is partly eased by large-scale, often temporary, migration to the cities of the north and to Italy's more developed partners in the EEC, as well as more permanent migration overseas. Migration often exacerbates the problems of the Mezzogiorno, however, as it tends to take away the younger, more active members of society, leaving behind an ageing population.

There are also serious urban problems, caused by the rapid growth of cities such as Naples and Reggio as young people leave the rural areas to live in the slums. As one of Italy's major ports, Naples imports oil, coal, iron ore, chemicals and cotton to provide the raw materials for manufacturing industries. In recent years great efforts have been made by a government-sponsored agency, the Cassa di Mezzogiorno, to found new factories in the Naples area, but they have had little effect on the mass poverty and unemployment of the region.

The problems of the Mezzogiorno, including especially those of the Naples area and Sicily, arise partly from geographical limitations and partly from historical circumstances. They are no longer a problem only for Italy, for the stability and prosperity of Italy is a matter of concern for the rest of Europe, and in particular for the countries of the EEC, of which Italy was a founder member. The continuing gulf between north and south has a disturbing effect on the economic and political health of Italy, a country whose people have contributed so much to the civilization of Europe.

Overall, however, Italy has made enormous progress since the devastation of World War II, particularly given its few natural resources and what outsiders have seen as a permanent state of near anarchy presided over by a succession of fragile coalition governments. In fact, Italy's government has always been more stable than it appeared: until the 1990s, coalitions were consistently dominated by the Christian Democrat Party.

Italian individualism continued to fuel the notorious black economy, which boosted offical GNP by at least 10% and probably much more while remaining free of government regulation and taxation. When black economy estimates were included in the official GNP in the 1980s, Italy overtook the United Kingdom in the world earning league. By then, the country was an important member of the G7 group. Once poor and agrarian, Italy had earned its place as one of the richest nations in the advanced, industrialized world ∎

VESUVIUS

Rising steeply from the Plain of Campania, behind the Bay of Naples, the massive cone of Vesuvius forms one of a family of southern Italian volcanoes, clustered in an area of crustal weakness. Others include the nearby island of Ischia, Stromboli and Vulcano of the Lipari Islands, and Etna in eastern Sicily. Ischia's volcanoes last erupted in the 14th century. Stromboli and Vulcano are currently active, emitting lava and gases, and Etna has a long record of eruptions from 475 BC to the present day. In April 1992 an eruption threatened to destroy a village on Etna's slopes.

Vesuvius, which probably arose from the waters of the bay some 200,000 years ago, has been intermittently active ever since; over 30 major eruptions have been recorded since Roman times. However, its slopes are forested or farmed, the fertile volcanic soils producing good crops during the quiescent periods between eruptive spells. There are many settlements on its flanks, and laboratories for volcanic and seismic studies.

The most famous eruption of Vesuvius occurred in AD 79, when the flourishing Roman port of Pompeii and nearby town of Stabiae were engulfed in a rain of ashes. Excavations begun in 1748 have revealed streets, shops, houses, frescoes, statues, and many other artefacts of Roman times – even the bread in the bakery.

---

map of Italy showing regions and neighbouring countries

⊚ National capital
⦿ Regional capital

SICILY

The triangular-shaped island of Sicily lies in a strategic position between the two basins of the Mediterranean, and has had a stormy history as successive powers wishing to dominate the Mediterranean have sought to conquer it. A beautiful island, with both natural and manmade attractions to interest the millions of tourists, it is nevertheless in a low state of economic development and its people are among the poorest in Europe.

There is some industrial development around the ports of Palermo, Catania, Messina and Syracuse, based on imported materials or on oil and natural gas found offshore during the 1960s. The only other local industrial materials are potash, sulphur and salt. However, a large proportion of the inhabitants still live by peasant farming, supplemented by fishing and work in the tourist industry.

There are few permanent streams on Sicily, as the island experiences an almost total drought in summer, and agriculture is restricted by the availability of water. Citrus fruits, vines and olives are among the chief crops. On coastal lowlands such as those around Catania, Marsala and Palermo, wheat and early vegetables are grown. The rapid growth in the population and the strong family ties which exist among Sicilians have, however, led to a situation in which too many people are trying to make a living from tiny parcels of land.

PALERMO

This is one of the hottest parts of Italy. The temperature averages are 20–26°C [68–79°F] May–October, with no month below 10°C [50°F]. Temperatures of just below freezing have been recorded January–March. Sunshine amounts are high with over ten hours per day June–August. Low rainfall comes mainly in the winter months, falling on about ten days each month November–February. The sirocco, a hot and humid wind from Africa, frequently affects Sicily.

SAN MARINO

The tiny republic of San Marino, enclosed completely within the territory of Italy, has been an independent state since AD 885. The flag's colours – white for the snowy mountains and blue for the sky – derive from the state coat of arms.

COUNTRY: Most Serene Republic of San Marino
AREA: 61 sq km [24 sq mls]
POPULATION: 24,000
CAPITAL: San Marino
POPULATION DENSITY: 393 per sq km [1,000 per sq ml]

Surrounded by Italy, the tiny independent state of San Marino – the world's smallest republic – lies 20 km [12 mls] south-west of the Adriatic port of Rimini. Most of the territory consists of the limestone mass of Monte Titano (725 m [2,382 ft]), around which are clustered wooded mountains, pastures, fortresses and medieval villages. The republic is named after St Marinus, the stonemason saint who is said to have first established a community here in the 4th century AD.

Nearly all the inhabitants live in the medieval fortified city of San Marino, which is visited by over 2 million tourists a year. The chief occupations are tourism (which accounts for 60% of total revenues), limestone quarrying and the making of wine, textiles and ceramics. San Marino has a friendship and co-operation treaty with Italy dating back to 1862; the ancient republic uses Italian currency, but issues its own stamps, which contribute a further 10% to state revenues. The *de facto* customs union with Italy makes San Marino an easy conduit for the illegal export of lira and certain kinds of tax evasion for Italians.

The state is governed by an elected council and has its own legal system. In 1957 a bloodless takeover replaced the Communist-Socialist regime that had been in power from 1945. It has no armed forces, and police are 'hired' from the Italian constabulary ■

VATICAN CITY

Since the 13th century, the emblem on the flag has represented the Vatican's role as the headquarters of the Roman Catholic Church. Consisting of the triple tiara of the Popes above the keys of heaven given to St Peter, it was adopted in 1929.

The world's smallest nation – a walled enclave on the west bank of the River Tiber in the city of Rome – the Vatican City State exists to provide an independent base for the Holy See, governing body of the Roman Catholic Church and its 950 million adherents round the world. Sustained by investment income and voluntary contribution, it is all that remains of the Papal States which, until 1870, occupied most of central Italy. In 1929 Mussolini recognized the independence of the Vatican City in return for papal recognition of the kingdom of Italy.

The Vatican consists of 44 hectares [109 acres], including St Peter's Square, with a resident population of about 1,000 – including the country's only armed force of 100 Swiss guards. The population is made up entirely of unmarried males.

The Commission appointed by the Pope to administer the affairs of the Vatican also has control over a radio station, the Pope's summer palace at Castel Gandolfo and several churches in Rome. The Vatican City has its own newspaper and radio station, police and railway station and issues its own stamps and coins, while the Papacy has since the 1960s played an important role in some areas of international diplomacy.

The popes have been prominent patrons of the arts, and the treasures of the Vatican, including Michelangelo's frescoes in the Sistine Chapel, attract tourists from all over the world. Similarly, the Vatican library contains a priceless collection of manuscripts from both pre-Christian and Christian eras. The popes have lived in the Vatican since the 5th century, apart from a brief period at Avignon in the 14th century ■

The summers are warm with June-September averages of over 20°C [68°F], but the winters can be cold, with averages in single figures for December–February, and with sub-zero temperatures having been recorded November–March. There are over 2,500 hours of sunshine per year ranging from only three in December, to 8–10 from May to September. Reasonable amounts of rain fall mainly in the winter and, in all, on only about 65 days per annum.

COUNTRY: Vatican City State
AREA: 0.44 sq km [0.17 sq mls]
POPULATION: 1,000
CAPITAL: Vatican City
GOVERNMENT: Papal Commission
LANGUAGES: Latin (official), Italian
RELIGIONS: Roman Catholic
CURRENCY: Italian lira = 100 centesimi

MALTA

The colours of Malta's flag, adopted on independence in 1964, are those of the Knights of Malta, who ruled the islands from 1530 to 1798. The George Cross was added in 1943 to commemorate the heroism of the Maltese people during World War II.

A former British colony and now an independent, non-aligned parliamentary republic within the Commonwealth, Malta lies in the centre of the Mediterranean, roughly halfway between Gibraltar and Suez, 93 km [58 mls] south of Sicily and 290 km [180 mls] from North Africa. Its strategic importance arises from its position, and from its possession of magnificent natural harbours – notable among them Grand Harbour and Marsamxett; these lie on either side of the rocky peninsula on which stands the capital, Valletta.

Malta and the neighbouring islands of Comino and Gozo have few natural resources (apart from splendid building stone), and with no rivers and sparse rainfall there are only limited possibilities for agriculture. Yet they constitute one of the world's most densely populated states, with two-thirds of the people living in the 'conurbation' of districts around Valletta. The native islanders are of mixed Arab, Sicilian, Norman, Spanish, English and Italian origin. Maltese and English are both spoken.

From the Napoleonic period until after World War II, the Maltese economy depended on agriculture (which still involves nearly half the workforce), and the existence of British military bases. Before the last garrison left in 1979 Malta had already obtained independence, and was developing export-oriented industries and 'offshore' business facilities that would replace the income from the military and naval connections. Germany became its chief trading partner ahead of the UK and Italy, though Libya supplies most of its oil.

Year-round tourism, taking advantage of the mild Mediterranean winters and the hot, dry summers, brings over 360,000 visitors annually, of whom two-thirds are British. The skill of the dockyard workers is still world-famous, however, and with help from overseas, Malta is developing a new port, wharf and storage facilities ■

The climate is Mediterranean with hot dry summers and cool wet winters. January–February average 12°C [54°F], while May–October are over 20°C [68°F], with 26°C [79°F] in July–August. The lowest temperature ever recorded is 5°C [41°F]. June–August have 11–12 hours of sunshine. Rainfall is low with little falling between April and September. It can be a windy island, and the winds bring cool, dry or hot and humid weather depending on its origin.

COUNTRY: Republic of Malta
AREA: 316 sq km [122 sq mls]
POPULATION: 354,000
CAPITAL (Population): Valletta (101,000)
GOVERNMENT: Multiparty republic
ETHNIC GROUPS: Maltese 95%, British 2%
LANGUAGES: Maltese and English (both official)
RELIGIONS: Roman Catholic 96%
NATIONAL DAY: 31 March; National Day
CURRENCY: Maltese lira = 100 cents = 1,000 mils
ANNUAL INCOME PER PERSON: $6,630
MAIN PRIMARY PRODUCTS: Stone and sand
MAIN INDUSTRIES: Tourism, light industry, agriculture
MAIN EXPORTS: Manufactured articles, clothing
MAIN IMPORTS: Food and live animals, mineral fuels
POPULATION DENSITY: 1,120 per sq km [2,901 per sq ml]
LIFE EXPECTANCY: Female 76 yrs, male 72 yrs
ADULT LITERACY: 84%

EUROPE

ALBANIA

The name of the country means 'land of the eagle' and the two-headed black eagle has been on the nation's flag since independence from centuries of Turkish rule in 1912. The Communist star above the eagle was added in 1945.

The Mediterranean-type climate in the west, with hot and dry summers and cooler winters, changes in the mountains and valleys of the east and north to become much wetter. November–April there is rain on about every other day. In the coastal lowlands, the temperature rarely drops below freezing. The lowest temperature recorded at Tirana is –8°C [18°F], and over 35°C [95°F] in July–September. In the mountainous interior, cold continental influences bring heavy snowfalls.

By far Europe's poorest country, Albania is also one of the most isolated, separated physically and culturally even from its closest neighbours, Greece and Yugoslavia. The Albanian language has no close affinities with other European languages, and until 1990 the political system, priding itself on being the last fortress of true Marxism-Leninism, emphasized the country's remoteness.

Albania declared independence in 1912, after five centuries under the rule of the Ottoman Turks. A legacy of this period is the fact that, until the government closed all religious establishments in 1967, some 70% of Albanians were Muslims. Today the figure is likely to be the same.

At the end of World War II, an Albanian People's Republic was formed under the Communist leadership who had led the partisans against the Germans. Pursuing a modernization programme on rigid Stalinist lines, the regime of Envar Hoxha has at various times associated politically and often

economically with Yugoslavia (up to 1948), the USSR (1948–61) and China (1961–77) before following a fiercely independent policy.

Geographical obstacles have reinforced Albania's linguistic and political isolation. The mountainous interior forms a barrier to penetration from the east. The main ranges, which rise to almost 2,000 m [6,500 ft] are continuations of the Dinaric Alps; these run from north-west to south-east, rising steeply from the coastal lowlands. Limestone is the most common type of rock, although in the central area there are igneous masses rich in mineral ores, including copper, iron, nickel and chrome. Albania relies heavily on exports of chrome for foreign exchange, and is the world's fifth largest producer, contributing 5.5% of the total in 1989.

Although the country has adequate energy resources – including petroleum, brown coal and hydroelectric potential – Albania remains one of the least industrialized countries in Europe, and transport is poorly developed. Horses and mules are widely used in rural areas, and there are no rail links with other countries. Most people still live by farming, with maize, wheat, barley, sugar beet and fruits predominant, though the country has always found it a difficult task feeding a population with a growth rate of 2.1% – the highest in Europe.

Hoxha's successor, Ramiz Alia, continued the dictator's austere policies after his death in 1985, but by the end of the decade even Albania was affected by the sweeping changes in Eastern Europe, and in 1990 the more progressive wing of the Communist Party (led by Alia) won the struggle for power. They instituted, somewhat reluctantly, a wide programme of reform, including the legalization of religion, the encouragement of foreign investment, the introduction of a free market for peasants' produce, and the establishment of pluralist democracy. In the elections of April 1991 the Communists comfortably retained their majority, but two months later the government was brought down by a general strike and an interim coalition 'national salvation' committee took over; this fragile 'government of stability' in turn collapsed after six months. Elections in the spring of 1992 brought to an end the last Communist regime in Europe.

Meanwhile, the country had descended into chaos and violence, triggered by food shortages.

COUNTRY: Republic of Albania
AREA: 28,750 sq km [11,100 sq mls]
POPULATION: 3,250,000
CAPITAL (Population): Tirana (226,000)
GOVERNMENT: Unitary republic with unicameral legislature
ETHNIC GROUPS: Albanian 96%, Greek 2%, Romanian, Macedonian, Montenegrin, Gypsy
LANGUAGES: Albanian (official)
RELIGIONS: Sunni Muslim 70%, Christian 5%
NATIONAL DAY: 28 November; Independence Day (1912)
CURRENCY: Lek = 100 qindars
ANNUAL INCOME PER PERSON: $1,000
MAIN PRIMARY PRODUCTS: Copper, chrome, petroleum and natural gas, cereals, fruit, timber, tobacco
MAIN INDUSTRIES: Agriculture, petroleum refining, mining, food and tobacco processing, textiles
DEFENCE: 11.5% of national budget
POPULATION DENSITY: 113 per sq km [293 per sq ml]
LIFE EXPECTANCY: Female 74 yrs, male 69 yrs
ADULT LITERACY: 63%
PRINCIPAL CITIES (Population): Tirana 226,000 Durrës 79,000 Elbasan 78,000 Shkoder 68,000 Vlorë 62,000

Tens of thousands of unwelcome refugees fled the civil unrest to Greece and Turkey, and in some places control rested with local bandits and brigands. In neighbouring Yugoslavia (itself in the throes of disintegration), the large Albanian population in the 'autonomous province' of Kosovo were in conflict with the Serbian authorities.

After a lifetime of Orwellian state control, a backward country was being catapulted without real government into modern industrialized Europe – and towards a Western world preoccupied with recession. At the end of 1991, a UN report put the annual income per capita figure for Albania at around $US400 – alongside many a struggling nation in what is still called the Third World ■

GREECE

Blue and white became Greece's national colours during the war of independence. Finally adopted in 1970, the flag's design represents the battle cry 'Freedom or Death' during the struggle against Ottoman (Turkish) domination in the war of 1821–9.

Athens has a climate typical of the eastern Mediterranean basin. A single maximum of rainfall occurs in winter and summers are dry, no rain falling in July or August on an average of one year in three. At Athens, snow can fall November–April, but on average on only two days January–February. On hot summer days the *calina*, a dusty heat haze, is common. The east coast of Greece is sunny with over 2,700 hours of sunshine a year and has only about half the rainfall of the west.

Mainland Greece consists of a mountainous peninsula which projects 500 km [312 mls] into the Mediterranean from the south-west corner of the Balkans, and an 80 km [50 ml] coastal belt along the northern shore of the Aegean Sea. Nearly a fifth of the total land area of Greece is made up of its 2,000 or so islands, mainly in the Aegean Sea to the east of the main peninsula but also in the Ionian Sea to the west; only 154 are inhabited, but they account for over 11% of the population. Some of the islands of the Dodecanese group in the eastern Aegean lie just 16 km [10 mls] off the coast of Turkey, and northern Corfu in the Ionian Islands is separated

from the Albanian coast by a narrow channel less than 3.2 km [2 mls] across.

The principal structural feature of Greece are the Pindos Mountains, which extend south-eastwards from the Albanian border to cover most of the peninsula. The island of Crete is also structurally related to the main Alpine fold mountain system to which the Pindos range belongs. Its highest peak, Mt Ida, is 2,456 m [8,057 ft] high. In these ranges limestone rocks predominate, though many of the Aegean Islands are of similar formation to the Rhodopi Massif in the north and made up of crystalline rocks.

With so much of Greece covered by rugged

mountains, only about a third of the area is suitable for cultivation, yet 40% of the population depend for their living on agriculture. The average farm size is under 4 hectares [10 acres], though on a few areas of flat land, mostly around the Aegean coasts in Macedonia and Thrace, large estates are found. Wheat, olives, vines, tobacco and citrus fruits are the chief crops. Most villagers keep a few domestic animals, particularly sheep and goats. The mountain pastures are poor, mainly consisting of scrubland, and many areas have been stripped of what tree cover they once had by goats (notoriously destructive of growing trees), and by the need for wood for ships, house building and charcoal burning.

Greece has been described as a land of mountains and of the sea. Nowhere in Greece is more than 80 km [50 mls] from the sea, and most of the towns are situated on the coast. Greater Athens, which consists of the capital city and its seaport, Piraeus, has a third of the total population and has grown sixfold since 1945. Thessaloniki (Salonica), the second city, is also a seaport, serving not only northern Greece but also southern Yugoslavia. Greece's mountainous terrain makes communications on land difficult, but the country has the world's largest merchant fleet (measured by ownership, not national registry), and shipbuilding and repairs are still important industries, while fishing provides a crucial supplement to the diet of a people who have difficulty wresting a living from their poor if beautiful homeland.

In the great days of classical Greece, during the thousand years before Christ, Greek colonies were established all round the shores of the Mediterranean and Black Seas. For a brief period in the 4th century BC, Alexander the Great built an empire which extended from the Danube, through Turkey and the Middle East to the Indus Valley of northern India. Even more important were the great contributions to philosophy, sculpture, architecture and literature made by the early Greeks.

The great epic poems of Greece – the *Iliad* and the *Odyssey* – speak of the exploits of ancient Greek seafarers who travelled around the Mediterranean. Today Greeks are still great seamen and wanderers, and large communities are to be found in the USA, Australia, Canada and Latin America. Since 1960 many Greek migrants have found work in Germany, and the admission of Greece to the European Community (on 1 January 1981) has given further opportunities for Greeks to find work in Western Europe.

COUNTRY: Hellenic Republic
AREA: 131,990 sq km [50,961 sq mls]
POPULATION: 10,269,000
CAPITAL (Population): Athens (3,072,000)
GOVERNMENT: Unitary multiparty republic
ETHNIC GROUPS: Greek 96%, Macedonian 2%, Turkish 1%, Albanian, Slav
LANGUAGES: Greek (official)
RELIGIONS: Greek Orthodox 97%, Muslim 1%
NATIONAL DAY: 25 March; Independence Day (1830)
CURRENCY: Drachma = 100 lepta
ANNUAL INCOME PER PERSON: $5,340
MAIN PRIMARY PRODUCTS: Wheat, tobacco, cotton, olives, grapes, bauxite, iron, chrome, crude oil
MAIN INDUSTRIES: Agriculture, tourism, chemicals, steel, aluminium, shipping, shipbuilding
MAIN EXPORTS: Foodstuffs, olive oil and tobacco 28%, textiles 23%, petroleum products 8%
MAIN EXPORT PARTNERS: Germany 25%, Italy 14%, France 9%, UK 9%, USA 6%
MAIN IMPORTS: Machinery and transport equipment 23%, foodstuffs and beverages 17%, oil 9%
MAIN IMPORT PARTNERS: Germany 20%, Italy 15%, France 8%, Netherlands 7%, Japan 6%, UK 5%
DEFENCE: 16.9% of national budget
TOURISM: 7,564,000 visitors per year
POPULATION DENSITY: 78 per sq km [202 per sq ml]
LIFE EXPECTANCY: Female 79 yrs, male 74 yrs
ADULT LITERACY: 92%

Greece is poorly endowed with industrial raw materials. There are deposits of iron ore, bauxite, nickel and manganese, but no coal and very small amounts of oil. The possibilities for hydroelectric development are severely limited because of the irregularity of the streams, many of which dry up entirely during the long summer drought. Thus Greece must import most of its sources of energy – mainly oil and coal. Industrial activity is largely concerned with the processing of agricultural produce – fruit and vegetables, canning, the production of wine and olive oil, cigarette manufacture, textiles and leather processing. Greece is one of the world's major producers of dried fruits; the word 'currant' is derived from the name of the Greek town of Corinth that lies on the narrow isthmus connecting the southern peninsula of the Pelopónnisos to the mainland. A 4.8 km [3 ml] canal, built in 1893, cuts through the isthmus, linking the Gulf of Corinth with the Aegean.

The tourist industry is vital. Overseas visitors are attracted by the warm climate, the beautiful scenery, especially on the islands, and also by the historical sites which survive from the days of classical Greece. However, a number of factors have combined to limit the importance of tourism in recent years, including the emergence of cheaper rivals like Turkey and Tunisia, the recession in Western countries and the appalling pollution in Athens – by some measures the most polluted city in Europe outside the former Eastern bloc, with 60% of the nation's manufacturing capacity.

The gap in economic strength and performance between Greece and most of its EEC partners remains wide, but the prospect of a single market may help to overcome the traditional obstacles of partisan, often volatile politics, an inflated, slow moving government bureaucracy, and a notorious 'black economy' ■

CRETE

The island of Crete was the home of the seafaring Minoan civilization, which flourished in the period 3500–1100 BC and left behind a wealth of archaeological sites and artefacts. Most southerly and by far the largest of the Greek islands, Crete has a milder, more maritime climate than the mainland. The rugged south coast, backed by steep limestone mountains, is the more inhospitable side, with winter gales adding to navigation hazards.

Most of the population of 502,000 live in the lowlands of the north, about a quarter of them in Iráklion (the capital) and Khania. Though Greek-speaking, Cretans differ in outlook from the mainlanders; they suffered long occupation by Venetians and then by Turks, remaining under Turkish rule until 1898, 70 years after mainland Greece had been liberated.

EUROPE

YUGOSLAVIA

Yugoslavia's colours date from 1918 when Serbia, Croatia and Slovenia united to form the new state. The Communist star was dropped from the flag in 1992 during the break-up of the federation.

The mountains running parallel with the Adriatic coast restrict the Mediterranean-type climate of warm winters and hot dry summers to the narrow coastal strip. The mountains themselves, with the Alps in the north, have cold winters with snow. They also have local fierce winds, such as the Bora. Further inland there is a continental climate of hot summers and very cold winters. There is a range of temperature of over 20°C [36°F].

In its original form the federation of Yugoslavia lasted 73 years, from its inception under Allied pressure after World War I – as the kingdom of Serbs, Croats and Slovenes from 1918, as Yugoslavia ('Land of the south Slavs') from 1929 – until the secession of Slovenia and Croatia as sovereign states in 1991. In that time the cohesion of this patchwork country was under constant threat from nationalist and ethnic tensions, primarily between the privileged Serbian majority (around 35%) and the other several minorities, notably the neighbouring Croats (around 20%).

In the interwar period the country was virtually a 'Greater Serbia', and after Hitler invaded in 1941 Yugoslavs fought both the Germans and each other. The Communist-led Partisans of 'Tito' (Josip Broz, a Croat) emerged victorious in 1945, re-forming Yugoslavia as a republic on the Soviet model. Failure to follow the Moscow line resulted in expulsion from the Communist bloc in 1948, but by 1961 Tito's position was enough to head up a new global non-alignment movement, and the country continued to make steady progress.

With Tito's death in 1980 the federation entered a decade of decline and ethnic unrest, with increasing clamour for political reform. In 1990 the first free elections since the war saw the Communists (restyled Socialists) ousted in four of the six republics – Serbia and Montenegro the exceptions – with nationalists taking power, while Serbia itself wrestled with the separatist aspirations of the predominantly Albanian population in the 'autonomous province' of Kosovo.

It was in the wealthier northern republics of Slovenia and Croatia that conflict worsened, especially between Croats and the minority Serb communities within their borders. Referenda in both republics favoured secession, and in June 1991 they declared independence from Belgrade; the Serb-dominated federal army then began a brutal campaign against Croatia – the most destructive conflict in Europe since 1945. After months of savage civil war, a 14th ceasefire finally took hold in January 1992 under UN auspices, with a view to deploying a peace-keeping force (the largest since the Congo in 1960).

Meanwhile, the European Community, with Germany firmly in the vanguard, recognized the two republics as independent nations; Bosnia-Herzegovina and Macedonia also sought recognition, but as relative peace returned to Croatia the conflict in Bosnia between Serbs, Croats and ethnic Muslims escalated into full-scale civil war by April 1992 – after the EC had recognized the republic and Serbia and Montenegro had reconstituted a new, far smaller Yugoslavia that had no international support. Macedonia, at that stage avoiding the bloodshed that blighted the rest of the old country, was still waiting for Brussels pressure on the Greek government to withdraw its veto on recognizing its neighbour's sovereignty.

Five natural and diverse regions formed the 'old' Yugoslavia, established at the end of World War I. In the north-west Slovenia adjoins Austria and Italy, its mountains continuing the main alpine system of central Europe and including Triglav (2,863 m [9,390 ft]) in the Julian Alps. The Dinaric region extends behind the coast from Slovenia to Albania: parallel ridges of bare limestone mountains, separated by narrow, marshy valleys, make a formidable barrier between the sea and the northern plains. The Adriatic coast, with its resort islands and Mediterranean climate, forms a third region. The Balkan Mountains are a fourth, lying between Bulgaria and Albania and covering parts of Bosnia, Serbia and Macedonia; this is a well-wooded region of ancient rounded crystalline rocks. The Pannonian lowlands in the north form a large and most populous fifth region, continuous with the central European plain and drained by the Danube and its tributaries ■

Until 1991 Yugoslavia comprised six republics and two 'autonomous provinces'. With the declaration of independence by Bosnia and Macedonia, the reconstituted Yugoslavia of 1992 comprised Serbia and Montenegro.

	Area sq km [sq mls]	Population
Bosnia-Herzegovina	51,129 [19,736]	4,440,000
Macedonia	25,713 [9,925]	2,090,000
Montenegro	13,812 [5,331]	632,000
Serbia	88,361 [34,107]	9,760,000*
Autonomous (Serbian) provinces:		
Vojvodina	21,506 [8,301]	2,050,000
Kosovo	10,877 [4,199]	1,850,000

*includes both autonomous provinces

SLOVENIA

The Slovene flag, based on the flag of Russia, was originally adopted in 1848. During the Communist period a red star appeared in the centre. The new emblem replaced this on 24 June 1991.

COUNTRY: Republic of Slovenia (Slovenija)
AREA: 20,251 sq km [7,817 sq mls]
POPULATION: 1,940,000
CAPITAL (Population): Ljubljana (305,000)
ETHNIC GROUPS: Slovene 94%

Part of the Austro-Hungarian Empire until 1918, Slovenia's Roman Catholic population found ready support from neighbours Italy and Austria (with Slovene populations of about 100,000 and 80,000 respectively) as well as Germany during its fight for recognition in 1991, when it stayed rela- tively free of the violence that plagued Croatia. A mountainous state with access to the Adriatic through Koper – giving it a flourishing transit trade from landlocked central Europe – it has both strong agricultural sectors (wheat, maize, root crops, live- stock) and industry (timber, textiles, steel, vehicles), with mineral resources that include coal, lead, zinc and mercury. Other important sources of income are wine-making and Alpine tourism. Along with Croatia, Slovenia went furthest in developing a mar- ket economy from 1988 before declaring indepen- dence from Belgrade in June 1991 ■

CROATIA

The red, white and blue flag was originally adopted in 1848. During the Communist period a red star appeared in the centre, but in 1990 this was replaced by the present arms, which symbolize the various parts of the country.

Formerly Yugoslavia's second largest and second most populous republic, Croatia bore the brunt of the Serbian-dominated Yugoslav Army's cam- paign to resist the break-up of the federation in the autumn war of 1991. Most of the 7,000 deaths and

COUNTRY: Republic of Croatia (Hrvatska)
AREA: 56,538 sq km [21,824 sq mls]
POPULATION: 4,680,000
CAPITAL (Population): Zagreb (1,175,000)
ETHNIC GROUPS: Croat 77%, Serb 12%

much of the destruction occurred in this 'U'-shaped state, and most of the 650,000 or more displaced persons were hapless Croats.

A massive reconstruction programme – funded by the West and particularly by the EC – would be needed to return many towns to anything like nor- mality; the vital tourist industry (Croatia accounted for 80% of the Yugoslav total in 1990) was also deci- mated, with the fine medieval city of Dubrovnik on the Dalmatian coast the prime casualty.

Rivalry between Croats and Serbs goes back cen- turies – Croatia was politically linked with Hungary, and therefore with Western Europe and the Cath- olic Church, from 1102 to 1918 – but were fuelled by the Croat position in World War II, when a pup- pet Fascist regime was set up (including much of Bosnia-Herzegovina) by Germany with the support of the Croatian Catholics. The split of 1991, however, left many questions unanswered, not least the positions of sizeable minorities in each country – pockets which would make peacekeeping a problem and render the existing federal frontiers far from a permanent solution.

Though mainly agricultural, using the fertile lowlands for cereals, potatoes, fruit, tobacco and livestock, Croatia also has significant industrial capacity centred on the main large towns, notably in metallurgy and textiles ■

BULGARIA

The Slav colours of white, green and red were used in the Bulgarian flag from 1878. The national emblem, incorporating a lion (a symbol of Bulgaria since the 14th century), was first added to the flag in 1947.

SOFIA
°C / °F
Temperature
Precipitation
661mm
26in
J F M A M J J A S O N D

The climate of Bulgaria is one of hot summers, cold but not severe winters and moderate rainfall, with a maximum April–August. This is changed by the influence of the nearby seas and the western mountains. The lowlands of the east and south have a much drier and warmer summer. Varna on the coast is usually 3–4°C [5–7°F] warmer than Sofia. The Danube lowlands are colder in winter with winds coming in from the continental interior. Temperatures are lower in the mountains.

The most subservient of the former Eastern bloc satellites, Bulgaria's links with Russia date back to 1878, when the Tsar's forces liberated the coun- try from five centuries of Ottoman (Turkish) rule. In the period after World War II, and especially under President Zhivkov from 1954, Bulgaria became all too dependent on its overseer; nearly two-thirds of its trade was conducted with the USSR – including most of its energy requirements.

Predictably, Bulgaria was the last and least pub- icized of the Eastern European countries to fall. In 1990 the Communist Party held on to power under increasing pressure by ousting Zhivkov, renouncing its leading role in the nation's affairs, making many promises of reform and changing its name to the Socialist Party before winning the first free elections since the war – unconvincingly and against confused opposition. With better organization the Union of Democratic Forces defeated the old guard the fol- lowing year and began the unenviable task of making the transition to a free market economy.

The new government inherited a host of prob- lems – inflation, food shortages, rising unemploy- ment, strikes, large foreign debt, limited Western interest, a declining traditional manufacturing

COUNTRY: Republic of Bulgaria
AREA: 110,910 sq km [42,822 sq mls]
POPULATION: 9,011,000
CAPITAL (Population): Sofia (1,129,000)
GOVERNMENT: Unitary socialist republic
ETHNIC GROUPS: Bulgarian 85%, Turkish 9%, Gypsy 3%, Macedonian 3%, Armenian, Romanian, Greek
LANGUAGES: Bulgarian (official), Turkish, Romany
RELIGIONS: Eastern Orthodox 80%, Sunni Muslim
NATIONAL DAY: 3 March; End of Ottoman rule (1878)
CURRENCY: Lev (leva) = 100 stotinki
ANNUAL INCOME PER PERSON: $2,210
MAIN PRIMARY PRODUCTS: Coal, oil and natural gas, lignite, cereals, fruit, cattle, sheep
MAIN INDUSTRIES: Agriculture, tobacco, iron and steel, textiles, chemicals, forestry, wine
MAIN EXPORTS: Machinery and equipment 57%, foodstuffs, wine and tobacco 14%
MAIN IMPORTS: Machinery and equipment 43%, fuels, mineral raw materials and metals 43%, chemicals
POPULATION DENSITY: 81 per sq km [210 per sq ml]
LIFE EXPECTANCY: Female 76 yrs, male 70 yrs
PRINCIPAL CITIES (Population): Sofia 1,129,000 Plovdiv 357,000 Varna 306,000 Burgas 198,000

industry, reduced demand at home and abroad, increased prices for vital raw materials, and a potential drop in the recently growing revenue from tourism. In addition there was the nagging worry of a sizeable Turkish minority disaffected with mismanaged attempts at forced assimilation.

With fertile soils but few natural resources, Bulgaria's economy has a distinct agricultural bias, with half the population still earning their living from the land. The most productive agriculture occurs in two lowland areas – the Danubian lowlands of the north, where wheat, barley and maize are the chief crops, and the warmer central valley of the River Maritsa, where grains, cotton, rice, tobacco, fruits and vines are grown.

Separating the two lowland areas are the Balkan Mountains (Stara Planina), which rise to heights of over 2,000 m [6,500 ft]. In the south-facing valleys overlooking the Maritsa plains, plums, vines and tobacco are grown. A particular feature of this area is the rose fields of Kazanluk, from which attar of roses is exported worldwide to the cosmetics industry.

South and west of the Maritsa Valley are the Rhodopi Mountains, containing lead, zinc and copper ores. There are also rich mineral veins of both iron and non-ferrous metals in the Stara Planina north of the capital and chief industrial city, Sofia ■

HUNGARY

The tricolour became popular in the revolution of 1848, though the colours had been in the Hungarian arms since the 15th century. Adopted in 1919, the design was amended in 1957 to remove the state emblem, which had been added in 1949.

The plains of Hungary have warm, sunny summers and cold winters with snow lying on between 30 and 40 days. At Budapest maximum temperatures exceed 20°C [68°F] from May to September, with the minimum below freezing December–February. There is a double maximum of rainfall, the first in early summer when convectional storms are most active. A second maximum in November becomes a marked feature of the climate towards the south-west.

As a large part of the Austro-Hungarian Empire, Hungary enjoyed an almost autonomous position within the Dual Monarchy from 1867, but defeat in World War I saw nearly 70% of its territory apportioned by the Treaty of Versailles to Czechoslovakia, Yugoslavia and Romania. Some 2.6 million Hungarians live in these countries today. The government hoped to regain lost land by siding with Hitler's Germany in World War II, but the result was the occupation of the Red Army and, in 1949, the establishment of a Communist state. The heroic Uprising of 1956 was put down by Soviet troops and its leader, Imre Nagy, was executed.

President János Kádár came to power in the wake of the suppression, but his was a relatively progressive leadership, introducing an element of political freedom and a measure of economic liberalism. Before the great upheavals of 1989 Hungary had gone further than any Eastern European Soviet satellite in decentralization and deregulation.

However, failure to tackle the underlying economic problems led in 1988 to some of his own Socialist Workers Party members exerting pressure for change. In 1989 the central committee agreed to a pluralist system and the parliament, previously little more than a rubber-stamp assembly, formally ended the party's 'leading role in society'. In 1990, in the first free elections since the war, Hungarians voted into office a centre-right coalition headed by the Democratic Forum.

Landscape and agriculture

Hungary has two large lowland areas – the aptly-named Great Plain (Nagyalföld) which occupies the south-eastern half of the country and is dissected by the country's two main rivers, the Danube and the Tisa, and the Little Plain (Kisalföld) in the north-west. Between them a line of hills runs south-west to north-west from Lake Balaton (72 km [45 mls] long) to the Czechoslovak border.

The Hungarian Plains have some of the most fertile agricultural land in Europe, especially in the areas covered by a mantle of loess (a windblown deposit dating from the Ice Age), but there are also infertile areas of marsh, sand and dry steppeland, where crop growing gives way to grazing.

Hungary has reserves of gas, but is poorly endowed with natural resources, bauxite being one of the few plentiful minerals. Industries have been built up on the basis of imported raw materials mainly from the former USSR. The main industrial centres are in the north, around Miskolc and Budapest (home to a fifth of the population) where iron and steel, engineering and chemicals predominate. Aluminium is manufactured north of Lake Balaton.

Unlike its more static neighbours, the new government of Prime Minister Jozsef Antall was able to press on with a rapid transition to a full market economy. The region's first stock market was set up, Budapest was chosen as the European Community's first regional office and Hungary – a founder member of the now defunct Warsaw Pact – applied to join NATO.

Hungary's move away from the classic Eastern European reliance on heavy industry and agriculture would be easier than, say, that of Poland, and many joint ventures with Western capital were inaugurated in the first months of the new democracy.

The lack of energy resources, however, remains a concern, and the government began pursuing an ambitious programme to increase its nuclear capacity from the 1988 figure of 49% of electricity generation. Even as a relative success, Hungary's progress has its cost, with inflation around 25–30% and unemployment doubling in 1991 alone to 700,000 – around 14% of the workforce ■

COUNTRY: Republic of Hungary
AREA: 93,030 sq km [35,919 sq mls]
POPULATION: 10,344,000
CAPITAL (Population): Budapest (2,115,000)
GOVERNMENT: Unitary republic
ETHNIC GROUPS: Magyar 97%, German, Slovak
LANGUAGES: Hungarian (official), Slovak, German
RELIGIONS: Roman Catholic 62%, Protestant 23%
NATIONAL DAY: 15 March
CURRENCY: Forint = 100 filler
ANNUAL INCOME PER PERSON: $2,780
DEFENCE: 7.0% of national budget
TOURISM: 11,826,000 visitors per year
POPULATION DENSITY: 111 per sq km [288 per sq ml]
LIFE EXPECTANCY: Female 75 yrs, male 68 yrs
ADULT LITERACY: 99%
PRINCIPAL CITIES (Population): Budapest 2,115,000 Debrecen 220,000 Miskolc 208,000 Szeged 189,000

THE DANUBE

With around 300 tributaries and a length of 2,850 km [1,750 mls], the Danube is Europe's second longest river. Rising from a source in the Black Forest in south-west Germany, it flows east and south through Austria, Czechoslovakia and Hungary, loops through Yugoslavia and forms a large part of the Romanian-Bulgarian frontier before entering the Black Sea through a wide, swampy delta on the border between Romania and the Ukraine.

Navigable as far upstream as Ulm in Bavaria, the Danube passes eight countries in all, and links the three capitals of Vienna, Budapest and Belgrade. It has long been one of Europe's main commercial waterways, and with the ending of the Cold War and the consequent divisions between East and West, it is likely to be of growing importance.

ROMANIA

Romania's colours come from the arms of the provinces that united to form the country in 1861, and the design was adopted in 1948. The central state coat of arms, added in 1965, was deleted in 1990 after the fall of the Ceausescu regime.

In general, central Europe has a large seasonal range of temperature and a summer rainfall maximum. Winter depressions which bring so much rain to north-west Europe are mostly prevented from reaching the east by persistent high pressure. Around Bucharest the heaviest rains fall as thundery showers in spring and early summer, when the air warms rapidly. With over 2,000 hours of sunshine annually, Romania is one of the sunniest parts of Europe.

On three sides Romania has clearly defined natural boundaries – the Danube in the south, the 200 km [125 ml] Black Sea coast in the east, and the River Prut in the north-east – but in the west the frontier with Hungary crosses the Hungarian Plain, cutting across several tributaries of the River Tisa. This area has a mixed population of Romanians and Hungarians – the western province of Transylvania once belonged to Hungary – and it was here, following the suppression of demonstrations in Timisoara by the secret police (the Securitate), that the army-backed revolt of 1989 began, culminating only days later in the execution of the dictator Nicolae Ceausescu and his wife on Christmas Day, on charges of genocide and corruption.

Landscape

Romania is dominated by a great arc of high fold mountains, the Carpathians, which curve round the plateaus of Transylvania in the heart of the country. South and east of the Carpathians are the plains of the lower Danube. The southern arm of the fold mountains, rising to 2,538 m [8,327 ft], is known as the Transylvanian Alps, the legendary home of Count Dracula. Where these meet the Danube, on the border with Yugoslavia, the river has cut a deep gorge – the Iron Gate (Portile de Fier) – whose rapids over 160 km [100 mls] long have been tamed by the construction of a huge barrage. In the east the Danube delta area has more than 3,000 glaciated lakes and some of Europe's finest wetland.

There is a great contrast between the fairy-tale landscape of wooded hills in Transylvania and the Carpathians, and the wheat and maize fields of the Danubian lowlands. Despite Ceausescu's manic programmes Romania is still a strong agricultural country, with an export surplus of cereals, timber, fruits and wine, though the agrarian workforce shrank from 75% in 1950 to less than 30% in 1984. In 1988 the country ranked fourth in maize production and seventh in wine.

Under Ceausescu there was a great drive to develop industries, based on the abundant oil and gas resources of areas on the flanks of the Transylvanian Alps; in 1988 Romania was the world's sixth biggest producer of natural gas. The copper, lead, zinc and aluminium industries use domestic supplies, mainly found in the Bihor Massif in Transylvania, but the iron and steel industry, especially the new plant at

Galati at the head of the Danubian delta, relies on imported ores.

Bucharest, the capital, lies between the Danube and the Carpathians. An important industrial centre, its manufactures include vehicles, textiles and foodstuffs.

Ceausescu's 24-year rule had been one of the Communist world's most odious. Corrupt and self-seeking, he had nevertheless won plaudits from the West for his independent stance against Soviet control – including a knighthood from Queen Elizabeth II. Coming to power in 1965, he accelerated the party policy of distancing the country from Moscow's foreign aims while pursuing a strict Stalinist approach on the domestic front.

The remorseless industrialization and urbanization programmes of the 1970s caused a severe debt problem, and in the 1980s he switched economic tack, cutting imports and diverting output to exports. But while Romania achieved the enviable status of a net creditor, its people – brainwashed by incessant propaganda – were reduced from sufficiency to subsidence to shortage, with food and energy both savagely rationed. Meanwhile, with many of his relatives in positions of power, Ceausescu built ghetto-like 'agro-industrial' housing complexes, desecrating some of the country's finest architecture and demolishing thousands of villages in the process.

After his death a provisional government of the National Salvation Front (founded only on 22 December) took control; much of the old administrative apparatus was dismantled, the Communist Party was dissolved and religion was re-legalized. In May 1990, under Ion Iliescu, the NSF won Romania's first free elections since the war by a huge majority – a result judged flawed but not fraudulent by international observers.

The NSF, however, contained many old-guard Communists, and its credibility sank further when Iliescu used miners to curb anti-government demonstrations. Strikes and protests continued, not only against the new authorities but also against the effects of a gradual but nevertheless marked switch to a market economy: food shortages, rampant inflation and rising unemployment. In addition, foreign investment was sluggish, deterred by the political instability. During 1991 the struggle between the two factions of the NSF – conservative President Iliescu (a former Ceausescu Politburo member) and reformist Prime Minister Petre Roman – personified the split that existed right across a country in desperate need of unity.

Another problem appeared with the new independent status of Moldavia. The republic has a vociferous Romanian minority in the large area of Bessarabia, handed over to the USSR as part of the Hitler-Stalin pact of 1940 and not returned by the Red Army in 1945. The new mood in the former Soviet Union rekindled the concept of *Romania Mare* ('Greater Romania').

In November 1991 the parliament in Bucharest overwhelmingly voted for a new constitution enshrining pluralist democracy, human rights and a market economy, with elections set for the spring of 1992. It was not special by the standards of contemporary Eastern European events – but it was a far cry from Ceausescu's hideous despotism ■

COUNTRY: Romania

AREA: 237,500 sq km [91,699 sq mls]

POPULATION: 23,200,000

CAPITAL (Population): Bucharest (2,014,400)

GOVERNMENT: Following 1989 revolution, Council of National Salvation (new constitution due end 1992)

ETHNIC GROUPS: Romanian 89%, Hungarian 8%

LANGUAGES: Romanian (official), Hungarian, German

RELIGIONS: Romanian Orthodox 70%, Greek Orthodox 10%, other Christian 4%

NATIONAL DAY: 23 August; Liberation Day (1945)

CURRENCY: Romanian leu = 100 bani

ANNUAL INCOME PER PERSON: $1,640

MAIN PRIMARY PRODUCTS: Cereals, sugar, fruit, vegetables, timber, livestock, fish, oil, natural gas

MAIN INDUSTRIES: Agriculture, mining, iron and steel, chemicals, forestry, textiles, food processing

LIFE EXPECTANCY: Female 74 yrs, male 69 yrs

ADULT LITERACY: 96%

CZECHOSLOVAKIA

Czechoslovakia's flag, officially adopted in 1920, features the red and white of Bohemia with the blue of Moravia and Slovakia, the colours of Pan-Slavic liberation. They were first used in a horizontal tricolour by Slovakia in 1848.

The mountains around the edges of Czechoslovakia cause the largest variations in the country's climate – lower temperatures, higher rainfall and snowfall. The winters in the lowlands are not very cold and the summers quite warm; Prague in January averages –1.6°C [29°F], and in July 19°C [66°F]. The lowlands have a relatively low rainfall with a maximum in the summer, from May to August, and with snow on about 30 days per year.

PRAGUE — Temperature — Precipitation 487mm 19in

Europe's largest landlocked country until Belo-russia achieved independence in 1991, Czechoslovakia came into existence at the end of World War I after the collapse of the Austro-Hungarian Empire. Since 1969 Czechoslovakia has been a federation of two nations, the Czechs occupying the western provinces of Bohemia and Moravia (61% of the land area), the Slovaks occupying the eastern part of the country (39%).

In the west, Bohemia is a diamond-shaped area, surrounded by ranges of mountains which enclose a basin drained by the River Elbe and its tributaries. In the centre lies Prague, the historic capital city. The mountains are rich in minerals, including iron ore, lead, zinc and uranium, while in western Bohemia there are also reserves of hard coal and lignite.

Moravia, in the middle of the country, is divided from Bohemia by plateau land known as the Moravian Heights. Central Moravia is a lowland, with Brno, home of the Bren gun, at its heart. Slovakia consists of a mountainous region in the north, part of the Carpathian system which divides Slovakia from Poland, and a southern lowland area with Bratislava, the country's second city, at its focus on the Danube, which forms the most southerly border with Hungary.

Though Czechoslovakia is the most highly industrialized of the East European countries, agriculture remains strong and well developed, with high yields of most crops suited to the continental climate. Food processing industries, including brewing, are important in the western provinces. The lowland area of Slovakia is extremely fertile with crops of wheat, barley, oats and sugar beet, and rye and potatoes on the higher ground. Dairying and pig breeding are also significant.

Politics and economy

Czechoslovakia's 'velvet revolution' of 1989 was Eastern Europe's smoothest transition, toppling the old Communist regime by 'people power' and soon replacing it with a multiparty system that elected a government headed by President Václav Havel, the country's best-known playwright and noted dissident (with Chapter 77, part of the coalition Civic Forum). It was all very different from 1968, when in the 'Prague Spring' Soviet forces suppressed an uprising supporting Alexander Dubcek's brave attempts at rekindling democracy and breaking the stranglehold of the party bosses.

As with all of Eastern Europe, the road to a free market economy was not going to be easy. The burdens that plagued the former Soviet satellites were all too obvious – large budget deficit, over-reliance on other Communist countries for trade, increasingly obsolete industrial capacity – and so were the immediate results: inflation, falling production, strikes, unemployment. There were signs, however, that the Czech experience would be better than, say, Poland; the foreign debt was serviceable and the country owned a skilled and adaptable workforce.

Politically, too, the future was uncertain. Pragmatic concerns soon dulled the euphoria of democratization and indeed Civic Forum split over the pace of economic reform. Principles of the new constitution were still the subject of controversy in 1992, with the threat of resurgent Slovak nationalism growing, fed in turn by economic factors ■

CZECHS AND SLOVAKS

As the election result of June 1992 illustrated, Czechoslovakia is an uneasy marriage of two peoples: the majority Czechs, stereotypically cultured, liberal (Protestant or agnostic), outgoing town-dwellers of the more industrial west; and the minority Slovaks, seen as reserved, conservative Roman Catholics of the rural agrarian east. Much in history divides them. Under Austrian rule in the 19th century the Czechs prospered and flourished, while under Hungarian rule for centuries, the Slovaks were subject to 'Magyarization' and kept backward. A further split derives from 1939, when after the proclamation of a pro-German Fascist regime in Slovakia, Hitler's troops invaded the Czech lands of Bohemia and Moravia.

COUNTRY: Czech and Slovak Federative Republic
AREA: 127,870 sq km [49,371 sq mls]
POPULATION: 15,678,000
CAPITAL (Population): Prague (1,194,000)
GOVERNMENT: Federal republic
ETHNIC GROUPS: Czech 63%, Slovak 32%, Hungarian 4%
LANGUAGES: Czech and Slovak (official), Hungarian
RELIGIONS: Roman Catholic 66%, other Christian 15%
NATIONAL DAY: 9 May; Liberation Day (1945)
CURRENCY: Koruna = 100 halura
ANNUAL INCOME PER PERSON: $3,140
MAIN PRIMARY PRODUCTS: Coal, iron ore, lignite, uranium, sugar beet, potatoes, cereals, livestock
MAIN INDUSTRIES: Transport equipment, iron and steel, machinery, chemicals, textiles

MAIN EXPORTS: Machinery 45%, road vehicles and parts 9%, iron and steel 7%, chemicals 6%
MAIN EXPORT PARTNERS: CIS nations 32%, Germany 16%, Poland 9%, Austria 5%, Hungary 5%
MAIN IMPORTS: Machinery and transport equipment 32%, mineral fuels and lubricants 30%
MAIN IMPORT PARTNERS: CIS nations 31%, Germany 16%, Poland 9%, Austria 5%
DEFENCE: 7.6% of national budget
TOURISM: 6,126,000 visitors per year
POPULATION DENSITY: 123 per sq km [318 per sq ml]
LIFE EXPECTANCY: Female 76 yrs, male 69 yrs
LITERACY: 99%
PRINCIPAL CITIES (Population): Prague 1,194,000 Bratislava 417,000 Brno 385,000 Ostrava 328,000 Kosice 222,000

POLAND

The colours of Poland's flag were derived from the 13th-century coat of arms of a white eagle on a red field, which still appears on the Polish merchant flag. The flag's simple design was adopted when Poland became a republic in 1919.

The weather and climate of Poland are transitional between maritime and continental. Warm, humid air masses come in from the west, cold Arctic air from the north and east, and warm air from the south. There is a cold snowy winter – becoming colder southwards and eastwards – and a warm summer with plenty of rain. The southern mountains have a high rainfall. The driest region is the central lowlands. Sunshine amounts exceed five hours per day April–September, with over eight hours in May and June.

The geographical location of Poland has had a strong influence on the country's stormy history. On many occasions powerful neighbours – notably Russia and Germany – have found it all too easy to invade and occupy the land. The most recent frontier changes came at the end of World War II – in which the country lost 6 million people, or a massive 17% of the total population – when Poland gave up territory to the USSR, and in compensation gained parts of Germany as far as the River Oder.

As a result of these changes Poland lost poor agricultural land in the east and gained an important industrial region in the west, including in the south-west Silesia and the former German city of Breslau (now called Wroclaw), in the north-west the Baltic port of Stettin (now Szczecin), and in the north the other port of Danzig (now Gdańsk). Acquisition of a length of Baltic coastline gave Poland a chance to develop maritime interests. Now a major fishing nation, Poland's fleets operate worldwide.

Before World War II Poland was primarily an agricultural country, with 65% of the population dependent on farming, but the postwar industrialization drive under Communism reduced this proportion to about 30%, most of them still on privately owned farms. Poland is still, however, a major supplier of agricultural produce: nearly two-thirds of the land surface is farmed, about half of this area

supporting crops of rye and potatoes. Oats, sugar beet, fodder crops, pigs and dairy produce are also important.

Poland's industrial development since World War II has been striking. Coal, lignite, sulphur, lead and zinc are the main mineral products, though Poland is also Europe's top producer of copper and silver. Underground salt deposits form the basis of important chemical industries. Most of Poland's industrial energy is derived from coal, but oil and natural gas are being developed, and hydroelectric power is being produced in increasing amounts from the Carpathians. Heavy industries include manufacture of steel and cement, and many secondary products. Many of Poland's newer industries are still almost wholly reliant on Russian gas and oil from various parts of the former Soviet Union – a difficult position in a changing world.

Poland's reliance on heavy industry, much of it state-controlled and unprofitable, proved to be a major obstacle in the country's 'fast-track' route from Communism to capitalism that followed the pioneering triumph of democratic forces in 1989. The old industries needed drastic measures – re-equipping, restructuring and diversifying – but this could be achieved only with huge assistance from the West; Poland received nearly 70% of all Western credits to Eastern Europe between 1989 and 1991,

COUNTRY: Republic of Poland

AREA: 312,680 sq km [120,726 sq mls]

POPULATION: 38,180

CAPITAL (Population): Warsaw (1,671,000)

GOVERNMENT: Republic with bicameral legislature

ETHNIC GROUPS: Polish 98%, Ukrainian 1%

LANGUAGES: Polish (official)

RELIGIONS: Roman Catholic 95%, other Christian 4%

NATIONAL DAY: 22 July

CURRENCY: Zloty = 100 groszy

ANNUAL INCOME PER PERSON: $1,700

MAIN PRIMARY PRODUCTS: Cereals, potatoes, sugar beet, fish, timber, copper, iron ore, sulphur, zinc

MAIN INDUSTRIES: Machinery, iron and steel, mining, shipbuilding, agriculture, food processing, oil refining

MAIN EXPORTS: Machinery and transport equipment 39%, chemicals 11%, fuel and power 10%, metal 10%, textiles and clothing 7%

MAIN EXPORT PARTNERS: CIS nations 25%, Germany 14%, Czechoslovakia 6%, UK 7%, Yugoslavia 3%

MAIN IMPORTS: Machinery and transport equipment 36%, chemicals 16%, fuel and power 15%, consumer products 9%, iron and steel products 8%

MAIN IMPORT PARTNERS: CIS nations 23%, Germany 21%, Czechoslovakia 6%, Austria 6%, Switzerland 5%

DEFENCE: 7.3% of national budget

TOURISM: 3,100,000 visitors per year

POPULATION DENSITY: 122 per sq km [316 per sq ml]

INFANT MORTALITY: 17 per 1,000 live births

LIFE EXPECTANCY: Female 76 yrs, male 68 yrs

ADULT LITERACY: 98%

PRINCIPAL CITIES (Population): Warsaw 1,671,000 Lódz 852,000 Kraków 744,000 Wroclaw 640,000 Poznan 586,000

adding to an already unserviceable foreign debt. Meanwhile, rising inflation (1,000% at one stage) and unemployment, coupled with a drastic drop in living standards (the economy shrank by 10% in 1991), led to a resurgence of militant unionism – the very movement that had set Poland on the path to democratization back in 1980.

Under the banner of the independent trade union Solidarity, based originally in the Gdańsk shipyards and led by Lech Walesa, Poland was the first of the Soviet satellites to challenge and bring down its Communist regime. The example set by the Poles (even though they were to be the last Eastern European country to implement full democratic processes, in October 1991), proved an inspiration not only to the other European Socialist states but also to the peoples of the Baltic republics.

Elected national president a year earlier, Lech Walesa found it a tough task to form a stable government after the 1991 elections, with the new constitution producing a parliament representing no less than 29 different parties. Solidarity itself had not lived up to its name, dividing in 1990 over personality clashes and the speed of political and economic reform. Poland's transition to a free market has proved more painful than that of more flexible societies such as Czechoslovakia and Hungary ∎

EUROPE

COMMONWEALTH OF INDEPENDENT STATES

After 74 years, the Union of Soviet Socialist Republics slipped into history a week ahead of schedule on Christmas Day 1991, when Mikhail Gorbachev resigned the leadership of what had become a nation only on paper. His offices in the Kremlin were occupied by Boris Yeltsin, first President of the Russian Federation and driving force behind the 'deconstruction' of the Soviet Union.

Though far from substituted, the USSR was in part replaced by the Commonwealth of Independent States, born in Minsk on 8 December 1991 when Russia, Ukraine and hosts Belorussia – between them responsible for 73% of the Soviet population, nearly 80% of its grain production and over 85% of its industrial output – signed a declaration effectively ending the former superpower's life both as a geopolitical entity and as a force in international relations. Two weeks later, in the Kazakhstan capital

of Alma Ata, they were joined by Moldavia, Armenia, Azerbaijan and the five Asian republics; missing were the three Baltic states (already *de facto* independent nations), and Georgia. The declaration from the 11 governments covered borders, human rights, ethnic minorities, non-interference and international law, while setting up committees on foreign affairs, defence, finance, transport and security.

These remarkable events, spread over less than three weeks, were traceable in 1985 and the appointment of Gorbachev as General Secretary of the Communist Party. His unprecedented policies of *glasnost* (openness) and *perestroika* (restructuring) were to have a devastating effect in a very short time. Through increased arms control, the withdrawal of troops from Afghanistan, the retreat from Eastern Europe, the acceptance of German unification and the dissolution of the Warsaw Pact, four decades of Cold War came to an end. The satellites of Eastern Europe and Mongolia abandoned Communist ideology and its Party's monopoly of power, introducing multiparty democracy and the market economy.

The domestic impact was equally dramatic, the republics of the USSR ridding themselves of doctrinaire Communism, adopting pluralism and declaring themselves independent of Moscow. In 1991, the entire system through which the Soviet Union had functioned for seven decades came crumbling down in the course of a calendar year.

The first signs of actual disintegration of the USSR came in January 1991 in Lithuania, and within weeks all three Baltic states had voted for independence, Georgia following in March. Over the next few months Gorbachev tried continually to establish consensus on a new Union treaty and economic reform, but when Yeltsin became directly elected President of Russia in June, his federation took the lead in opposing the Soviet president's increasingly personal and decree-based rule as he attempted to find a middle way between the old guard and the progressives.

While the new laws had produced far-reaching effects on the political and social lives of Soviet citi-

zens, the parallel restructuring of the economy patently failed – not least because the movement to a market economy was constantly hindered by party bureaucrats, factory managers, collective farm chairmen and many others who were unwilling to see the erosion of their positions.

In August hardline Communist leaders ousted Gorbachev – detaining him in his Crimean *dacha* – and a small emergency committee took control of the Soviet Union. Resistance, bravely led by Yeltsin, centred on Moscow, and after three days the coup collapsed. Gorbachev returned to his post in the Kremlin, but his already tenuous position, now undermined by events, was further weakened by the worst harvest for a decade, an energy crisis that included a coal miners' strike, and the collapse of the Soviet Central Bank.

On 21 December Gorbachev was told by the Alma Ata protocol that his services were no longer required; outmanoeuvred by Yeltsin and overtaken by events, he resigned on Christmas Day, and the tricolour flag of Russia replaced the hammer and sickle on the Kremlin. Two days later, the Chamber of Deputies of the Supreme Soviet, the USSR's parliament, formally voted itself out of existence, and the Soviet Union was clinically dead.

The CIS is not a sovereign state. It may well prove more than a useful temporary mechanism to disperse power from the Soviet centre to the republics, which in any case have great power in domestic policy. In the honeymoon period, early in 1992, it sorted out (at least on paper) the prickly issues of strategic nuclear weapons (owned by the three founder members, plus Kazakhstan) and the 3.7-million-strong Red Army; governed in the short to medium term by the interdependency created by the Soviet system, it will at least function as a common market. Its real political test, however, will come with disputes between its own members, notably and immediately the ancient problem of Nagorno-Karabakh. But there are others: of all the shared borders, for example, only one (Russia/Belorussia) is not contentious ∎

Commonwealth of Independent States
AREA: 22,023,900 sq km [8,503,472 sq mls]
POPULATION: 274,583,000
CAPITAL (Population): Minsk (1,589,000)
ETHNIC GROUPS: Russian 52%, Ukrainian 16%, Uzbek 5%, Belorussian 4%, Kazakh 3%, Tartar 2%, Azerbaijani 2%, Armenian 2%, Georgian 1%, Tajik 1%, Moldavian 1%
LANGUAGES: Russian (official), Ukrainian and over 100 others
RELIGIONS: Orthodox 32%, Muslim 11%, Protestant 3%, Roman Catholic 2%
CURRENCY: Ruble = 100 kopecks
MAIN PRIMARY PRODUCTS: Livestock, timber, fish, cereals, oil and natural gas, iron ore, coal, lignite, bauxite, copper, diamonds, uranium, zinc
MAIN INDUSTRIES: Iron and steel, engineering, vehicles, cement, electrical and electronic equipment, oil and gas, shipbuilding, fishing
MAIN EXPORTS: Machinery, iron and steel, crude oil, non-ferrous metals, timber, cotton, vehicles
MAIN IMPORTS: Machinery, clothing, ships, minerals, railway rolling stock, footwear

---

BELORUSSIA

On 19 September 1991 the old flag of Belorussia, previously adopted in 1917, was restored. The white and red derive from the ancient coat of arms, also used by Lithuania.

COUNTRY: Belorussia
AREA: 207,600 sq km [80,154 sq mls]
POPULATION: 10,300,000
CAPITAL (Population): Minsk (1,589,000)
ETHNIC GROUPS: Belorussian 80%, Russian 12%, Polish 4%, Ukrainian 2%, Jewish 1%
LANGUAGES: Belorussian 70%, Russian 25%
RELIGIONS: Belorussian Orthodox and Roman Catholic in west, Evangelicals in south-west

Landlocked and low-lying, a third forested and with 11,000 lakes, Belorussia ('White Russia') is not the most endowed of the republics. Though mainly agricultural – 46% of the land being used efficiently for flax, potatoes, cereals, dairying, pigs and peat-digging – it also has the largest petrochemical complex in Europe and the giant Belaz heavy-truck plants; these, however, like its many light industries, are heavily reliant on Russia for electricity and raw

materials, including steel. More integrated into the Soviet economy than any republic, Belorussia was also the most dependent on trade, at nearly 70%.

Most observers were surprised when this most conservative and Communist-dominated of parliaments declared independence on 25 August 1991, forcing the Party president to stand down. The quiet state of the European Soviet Union, it played a big supporting role in its deconstruction and the crea-

tion of the CIS; the latter's first meeting was in Minsk – subsequently chosen as its capital. Like the Ukraine, Belorussia has been a separate UN member since 1945, the end of World War II, during which one in four of its population died ∎

MOLDAVIA

The flag and the eagle are based on those of pre-Communist Romania, and the bull's head is the distinctive emblem of Moldavia. The flag was created on 12 May 1990.

COUNTRY: Moldavia
AREA: 33,700 sq km [13,000 sq mls]
POPULATION: 4,400,000
CAPITAL (Population): Kishinev (565,000)
ETHNIC GROUPS: Moldavian 64%, Ukrainian 14%, Russian 13%, Gagauz 4%, Jewish 2%, Bulgarian
LANGUAGES: Moldavian (Romanian) 61%, Russian
RELIGIONS: Russian Orthodox and Evangelical

The most densely populated of the former Soviet republics, Moldavia is also ethnically complex. Created by Stalin in his 1940 pact with Hitler by combining the Moldavian part of Ukraine with the larger Bessarabia – the section of Romania between the Prut and Dnestr rivers – its majority 'Moldavian' population is ethnically Romanian, and people on

both sides of the border favour reunification. This is opposed by Russians, Ukrainians, and, in the south, the Gagauz, the Christian Orthodox Turks. The last two groups both pronounced their sovereignty before the republic declared independence from Moscow on 27 August 1991.

Though barred from the Black Sea by an arm of

the Ukraine, Moldavia is well off. Fertile lands and a tolerant climate provide vines, tobacco and honey as well as more conventional produce, while light industry is expanding ∎

UKRAINE

The colours of the Ukraine flag were first adopted in 1848 and were heraldic in origin. The flag was first used in the period 1918-20 and was readopted on 4 September 1991.

Although on the same latitude as many European cities, Kiev is distant from maritime effects. Rainfall is fairly low and evenly distributed throughout the year with a slight summer peak. Snow may lie for over 80 days, and there is precipitation on over 160 days in the year. Winter temperatures are not too severe and only four months are sub-zero, though frosts can occur on over 180 days. Summers are warm: the months June–August are 20°C [36°F] warmer than January.

Although its name means 'Little Russia', the Ukraine nevertheless became the largest complete nation in Europe with its declaration of independence on 24 August 1991 and the subsequent disintegration of the Soviet Union. It is also a well-populated state: fourth in Europe, discounting Russia, and 22nd in the world.

The western Ukraine comprises the fertile uplands of Volhynia, with the Carpathians cutting across the far western corner of the country. The north is mostly lowlands, with the Dnepr River at its heart, which include marshes and the state capital of Kiev in addition to arable land. This area, however, suffered most from the Chernobyl nuclear disaster of 1986, with huge tracts of land contaminated by radioactivity. In the centre of the republic, south of Kiev and west of Kirovograd (Yelizavetgrad),

are the rich lands of *chernozem*, fertile black earth. In the south are dry lowlands bordering the Black Sea and the Sea of Azov, with Odessa the main port. Further south still is the Crimean peninsula, a favourite tourist area for Russians as well as Ukrainians. In the east are the main industrial cities, clustered round the coalfields and iron-ore mines of the vital Donets Basin.

Ukraine's main industries are coalmining, iron and steel, agricultural machinery, petrochemicals and plastics, but there are also numerous food-processing plants based on agricultural output.

Though traditionally 'the granary of the Soviet Union', the Ukraine is neither the largest nor the most efficient producer of grain; Russia accounted for more than 53% of the total in 1988 (Ukraine 24%), while Belorussia's agricultural output per capita was some 65% higher than that of its southern neighbour. Indeed the conventional image of the mutual dependency of Russia and the Ukraine is something of a myth, with the latter producing a quarter of all USSR coal and 35% of steel. Not blessed with huge reserves of oil, the Kiev government signed an agreement in February 1992 to secure future supplies from Iran. Even under the Soviet system, Ukraine's intrarepublican trade was less than a third of its total GNP.

The Ukraine's declaration of independence from Moscow was ratified by referendum on 1 December 1991, when Leonid Kravchuk, the former Communist Party ideological secretary, was voted president by direct poll over five rivals. A week later, in Minsk, Kravchuk helped Boris Yeltsin create the basis for the Commonwealth of Independent States, and in the early months of 1992 the Ukraine and Russia reached agreement on a number of potentially explosive issues, not least in the military field, with resolutions on nuclear weapons, the Red Army and the distribution of the Black Sea fleet.

The Ukraine, however, will not be seen as Russia's sidekick. While it suffered many of the economic agonies endured by its massive neighbour – notably chronic food shortages and the hyper-inflation that followed the abolition of price controls – it set out from the beginning to be a fully-fledged and large independent nation. While Russia assumed the diplomatic powers of the Soviet Union, the Ukraine already had a seat at the UN – a reward granted in 1945 for the appalling devastation caused by the German invasion in 1941 and its aftermath – and would seek separate representation on bodies such as the CSCE and OECD ■

COUNTRY: Ukraine

AREA: 603,700 sq km [233,100 sq mls]

POPULATION: 51,800,000

CAPITAL (Population): Kiev (2,587,000)

ETHNIC GROUPS: Ukrainian 74%, Russian 21%, Jewish 1%, Belorussian, Moldavian, Polish

LANGUAGES: Ukrainian 66%, Russian 32%

RELIGIONS: Ukrainian Orthodox Church (under Moscow Patriarchate) and Ukrainian Autocephalous Orthodox Church (under Kiev Patriarchate)

PRINCIPAL CITIES (Population): Kiev 2,587,000 Kharkov 1,611,000 Dnepropetrovsk 1,179,000

GEORGIA
1 Abkhazian Republic
2 Adjarian Republic
3 South Ossetian Region

AZERBAIJAN
4 Nagorno-Karabakh Region
5 Nakhichevan Republic

RUSSIA
6 Adygei Region
7 Karachaevo-Cherkess Republic
8 Kabardino-Balkar Republic
9 North Ossetian Republic
10 Checheno-Ingush Republic
11 Dagestan Republic
12 Mordovian Republic
13 Chuvash Republic
14 Mari Republic
15 Tatar Republic
16 Udmurt Republic

TAJIKISTAN
17 Gorno-Badakhshan Region

Autonomous Republic
Kray
Autonomous Oblast
National Okrug
o Capital

EUROPE

ESTONIA

Used for the independent republic of 1918–20, the Estonian flag was readopted in June 1988. The colours are said to symbolize the country's blue skies, its black earth and the snows of its long winter.

COUNTRY: Estonia
AREA: 44,700 sq km [17,300 sq mls]
POPULATION: 1,600,000
CAPITAL (Population): Tallinn (482,000)
ETHNIC GROUPS: Estonian 65%, Russian 28%, Ukrainian 3%, Belorussian 2%, Finnish 1%
LANGUAGES: Estonian (official) 64%, Russian 31%
RELIGIONS: Christian (Lutheran and Orthodox)
POPULATION DENSITY: 35 per sq km [92 per sq ml]

Smallest of the three Baltic states, and the least populous of any of the 15 former Soviet republics, Estonia is bounded on the north by the Gulf of Finland and on the west by the Baltic Sea. The country comprises mostly flat, rock-strewn, glaciated lowland, with over 1,500 lakes, and has more than 800 offshore islands, by far the biggest being Saaremaa and Hiiumaa. The largest lake, Chudskoye Ozero, forms much of the border with Russia in the east.

Over a third of the land is forested, and the timber industry is among the country's most important industries, alongside metal-working, shipbuilding, clothing, textiles, chemicals and food processing.

The last is based primarily on extremely efficient dairy farming and pig breeding, but oats, barley and potatoes suit the cool climate and average soils. Fishing is also a major occupation. Like the other two Baltic states, Estonia is not endowed with natural resources, though its shale is an important mineral deposit: enough gas is extracted by processing to supply St Petersburg, Russia's second largest city.

Related ethnically and linguistically to the Finns, the Estonians have managed to retain their cultural identity and now look to increasing their links with Europe, and with Scandinavia in particular. But despite having the highest standard of living of any of the 15 former Soviet republics, it has found the free market hard going. In January 1992 the combination of food shortages and an energy crisis forced the resignation of Prime Minister Edgar Savissar, who enjoyed wide popular and parliamentary support. A co-founder of the Popular Front, the country's pro-democracy movement, he was held responsible for a recession which appeared to have hit Estonia far harder than its two neighbours ■

LATVIA

The burgundy and white Latvian flag, revived after independence from the USSR in 1991, dates back to at least 1280; according to legend, it was first made from a white sheet stained with the blood of a Latvian hero who was wrapped in it.

Its Baltic coast heavily indented by the Gulf of Riga, Latvia is a small country of flat glaciated lowland, with natural vegetation and agriculture virtually mirroring that of Estonia. So, too, does much of its commerce; like its Baltic neighbours it contains much of the Soviet Union's less traditional, 'clever' industries, while Ventspils is an important conduit for the export of Russian oil and gas. Latvia is the

COUNTRY: Latvia
AREA: 63,100 sq km [24,400 sq mls]
POPULATION: 2,700,000
CAPITAL (Population): Riga (915,000)
ETHNIC GROUPS: Latvian 54%, Russian 33%, Belorussian 5%, Ukrainian 3%, Polish 3%
LANGUAGES: Latvian (official) 54%, Russian 40%
RELIGIONS: Christian (Lutheran, Catholic, Orthodox)
POPULATION DENSITY: 43 per sq km [111 per sq ml]

most urbanized of the Baltic states, with over 70% of the population living in cities and towns.

Although forming only a slender majority today, the native Latvians (Letts) have a highly developed folklore, their sense of identity honed during the nationalist drive in the late 19th century and re-kindled in the quest for separation from the Soviet Union more than 100 years later. Latvia declared independence in May 1990, two months after Lithuania, and despite a large 'foreign' population the subsequent referendum indicated a substantial majority in favour of a break with Moscow.

Strong ties remain, however. Like its neighbours, Latvia is (in the medium term at least) almost totally reliant on the network of Russian and Ukrainian energy supply, while Russia will not simply surrender the 'Soviet' investments in the country, most obviously in the ports ■

RIGA

Riga has warm summers and cold winters, with rain or snow in all months. June–August are the warmest months with temperatures over 15°C [59°F], and averages that are sub-zero, December–March. The temperature extremes are only just over 34°C [93°F] and –29°C [–20°F]. On average, rain will fall on a third of the days in the second half of the year, but the total is relatively light. The weather can be overcast for long periods. Snow cover is light, with many thaws.

LITHUANIA

The flag was created in 1918, at the birth of the independent republic; it was suppressed after the Soviet annexation in 1940, and restored in November 1988. The colours are reputed to represent Lithuania's rich forests and agricultural wealth.

Largest, most populous and in many ways the most important of the Baltic states, Lithuania is also the most homogeneous, some 80% of its population being staunch Catholics who speak the native language and are proud of their history and culture. From 1988 it was Lithuania which led the 'Balts' in their drive to shed Communism and regain their nationhood; in March 1990 it became the first of the 15 constituent Soviet republics to declare itself an independent, non-Communist country, resulting in the occupation of much of its capital by Soviet troops and a crippling economic blockade not suffered by the other states of the Union.

The successful crusade was led by the emotional president, Vytautas Landsbergis, whose crucial role in the process of 'deconstruction' – and that of his people – was somewhat overshadowed by the figure of Boris Yeltsin and the Russian Federation.

The country consists mostly of a low, glaciated but fairly fertile central lowland used primarily for cattle, pigs and poultry – livestock rearing having been highly intensified under the Soviet collective

system. Crops grown are very similar to those of Estonia, while there are also widespread forests and significant peat reserves, though Lithuania remains pitifully short of natural resources. In the east is an area of forested sandy ridges, dotted with lakes.

A range of industries, among them many of the most advanced programmes in the former Soviet Union, include timber, metal-working, textiles, building materials, fertilizers, fibres and plastics, computers and instruments, and food processing. Craftsmen still make jewellery from amber, a semi-precious fossilized resin found along the Baltic coast.

While Lithuania, in concert with the other Baltic states, seeks to establish closer ties with the rest of Europe – a US$2.5 billion highway is planned, linking the three capitals with Warsaw – it also has simmering ethnic problems of its own. Its significant Polish population, largely self-governing under the Soviets, now fear 'Lithuanization', while the majority who took on Moscow and won resent the pro-Union stance taken by Poles and Russians during their fight for freedom ■

THE BALTIC STATES

The three Baltic republics have always found it hard to establish their nationhood, though their cultures have proved resilient. Estonia and Latvia survived 1,000 years of rule by Danes, Swedes, Lithuanians and Poles before becoming part of the Russian Empire in 1721; Lithuania, once a powerful medieval empire, was united with Poland in 1385 but also came under Russian control in 1795.

Nationalist movements grew in all three countries in the late 19th century, and in 1920, following German occupation, the Soviet Union granted them the status of independent democratic republics. However, all had Fascist coups by the time Hitler assigned them to Stalin in the notorious secret pact of 1939 – operative in 1940, with the establishment of a government acceptable to Moscow.

After three years of occupation by (Nazi) Germany, incorporation into the USSR was confirmed by plebiscite in 1944. On declaring independence in 1990, the Baltic states claimed this was fraudulent and that their countries were never legally part of the Soviet Union. Referenda supported this view, and on 6 September 1991 the transitional State Council of the Soviet Union recognized them as independent sovereign states. All three were United Nations members by the end of the year.

COUNTRY: Lithuania
AREA: 65,200 sq km [25,200 sq mls]
POPULATION: 3,751,000
CAPITAL (Population): Vilnius (582,000)
ETHNIC GROUPS: Lithuanian 80%, Russian 9%, Polish 7%, Belorussian 2%
LANGUAGES: Lithuanian (official) 70%, Russian 30%
RELIGIONS: Christian (predominantly Roman Catholic)
POPULATION DENSITY: 56 per sq km [149 per sq ml]

GEORGIA

The flag was first adopted in 1917 and lasted until 1921. The colours represent the good times of the past and the future (wine-red), the period of Russian rule (black) and the hope for peace (white). It was readopted on independence in 1990.

Nestling between the Caucasus and the mountains of Armenia, Tbilisi is sheltered both from the winter cold of central Asia and the heavy rain of the Black Sea coast. The rather sparse rainfall is effective in spring but evaporates quickly in the heat of summer when conditions resemble those of the Mediterranean region. It rains on only about 70 days per year. Winters are less severe than might be expected in a continental location, temperatures rarely falling below freezing in December and January.

Positioned between Russia and Turkey, Georgia comprises four main areas: the Caucasus Mountains in the north, including Mt Elbrus (5,633 m [18,841 ft]) on the Russian border; the Black Sea coastal plain in the west; the eastern end of the mountains of Asia Minor to the south; and a low plateau in the east, protruding into Azerbaijan. Separating the two mountain sections is the crucial Kura Valley, in which the capital Tbilisi stands.

The largest of the three Transcaucasian republics, Georgia is rich in citrus fruits and wine (notably in the Kakhetia region), tea (the main crop), tobacco, wheat, barley and vegetables, while perfumes are made from flowers and herbs and, in Imeretia, silk is a flourishing industry. Almost 40% forested, it also has a significant stake in timber. Georgia has large deposits of manganese ore, but despite reserves of coal and huge hydroelectric potential, most of its electricity is generated in Russia and the Ukraine.

Always a maverick among the Soviet republics, Georgia was the first to declare independence after the Baltic states (April 1991), and the only one not to join the Commonwealth of Independent States. When Gorbachev resigned, the democratically elected leader of Georgia, Zviad Gamsakhurdia, found himself holed up in Tbilisi's KGB headquarters, under siege from rebel forces representing widespread disapproval of his policies, from the economy to the imprisonment of opponents. In January he fled the country (now ruled by a military council), returning to lead resistance from his home territory in the west, though to little effect. Gamsakhurdia had also been in conflict with the Ossetian

EUROPE

minority in one of the republic's three autonomous regions, who feared being swamped in a new independent nation. In March 1992 former Soviet foreign minister Eduard Shevardnadze agreed to become chairman of the ruling council.

Mostly Orthodox Christians, Georgians have a strong national culture and a long literary tradition based on their own language and alphabet. Land of the legendary Golden Fleece of Greek mythology, the area was conquered by the Romans, Persians and Arabs before establishing autonomy in the 10th century, but Tartars, Persians and Turks invaded before it came under Russian domination around 1800. Renowned for their longevity, the population's most famous product was Josef Stalin, born in Gori, 65 km [40 mls] north-west of Tbilisi ■

COUNTRY: Georgia
AREA: 69,700 sq km [26,900 sq mls]
POPULATION: 5,500,000
CAPITAL (Population): Tbilisi (1,194,000)
ETHNIC GROUPS: Georgian 70%, Russian
LANGUAGES: Georgian 69%, Armenian 9%, Russian 7%, Azerbaijani 5%, Ossetian 3%

ARMENIA

The flag first used in the period 1918-22 was readopted on 24 August 1990. The colours represent the blood shed in the past (red), the land of Armenia (blue) and the courage of the people (orange).

COUNTRY: Armenia
AREA: 29,800 sq km [11,506 sq mls]
POPULATION: 3,283,000
CAPITAL (Population): Yerevan (1,199,000)
ETHNIC GROUPS: Armenian 90%, Azerbaijani 6%, Russian 2%, Kurd 2%
LANGUAGES: Armenian 89%, Azerbaijani, Russian

The smallest of the 15 republics of the former Soviet Union, Armenia was also one of the weakest. A rugged, mountainous country landlocked between traditionally hostile neighbours, it has few natural resources (though lead, copper and zinc are mined), limited industry, and registered the poorest agricultural output per head in the Union; the main products are wine, tobacco, olives and rice, the main occupation the raising of livestock. Much of the west is recovering from the earthquake of 1988, in which some 55,000 people died. Its vulnerability is heightened by the lack of support for its conflict with Azerbaijan over Nagorno-Karabakh, and its heavy reliance for energy on other republics.

Originally a much larger independent kingdom centred on Mt Ararat, the legendary resting place of Noah's Ark, Armenia had already been established for more than 1,000 years when it became the first country in the world to make Christianity (Armenian Apostolic) the official state religion in the 4th century. Ever since, its people have been subject to war, occupation and massacre – the most documented example being the genocide by Turks in World War I, when 600,000 Armenians were killed and 1.75 million deported to Syria and Palestine. Today, some 1.5 million live in north-east Turkey, Europe and the USA, with minorities in Azerbaijan (notably Nagorno-Karabakh) and Georgia ■

AZERBAIJAN

This flag was instituted on 5 February 1991. The blue stands for the sky, the red for freedom and the green for the land; the crescent and star symbolize Islam, and the points of the star represent the eight races of Azerbaijan.

COUNTRY: Azerbaijan
AREA: 86,600 sq km [33,436 sq mls]
POPULATION: 7,100,000
CAPITAL (Population): Baku (1,757,000)
ETHNIC GROUPS: Azerbaijani 78%, Russian 8%, Armenian 8%, Daghestani 3%
LANGUAGES: Azerbaijani 78%, Russian

Now in relative decline (3% of the Soviet total in 1989), oil is still the mainstay of Azerbaijan's revenue. It was being collected by the Caspian Sea near Baku over 1,000 years ago, and burning natural gas leaking from the ground gave the area its name: 'Land of eternal fire'. Today, along with industries both traditional (carpets, timber, iron) and modern (cement, aluminium, chemicals), it makes the country's economy a viable one. Though much of Azerbaijan is semi-arid – there is also a large tract below sea level – it nevertheless grows crops such as cotton, grains, rice and grapes, with fishing also important.

As the Azerbaijanis look to their fellow Shiite Muslims in Iran after independence (declared in August 1991), their biggest problem remains that of their western neighbour, Armenia, and the intractable problem of Nagorno-Karabakh, the predominantly Armenian *oblast* enclave of 177,000 people in the south-west, scene of bitter fighting and appalling atrocities since 1988. Soviet troops went in early in 1990, and two years later it became a real test for the new Commonwealth. Ironically, Azerbaijan has itself an enclave, the autonomous republic of Nakhichevan (pop. 270,000), completely isolated from the main part of the country on the border of Armenia and Turkey. Nearly three times the size of Armenia, with more than twice the population, more wealthy and with help from its fellow Muslims, Azerbaijan is well equipped to defend Nagorno-Karabakh – though in 1992 the Armenians opened up a wide corridor to the enclave ■

ASIA

ASIA

The largest continent, accounting for a third of the world's land surface – and well over half its population – Asia extends from the Mediterranean Sea to the Pacific Ocean and from the tropical islands of the East Indies to the frozen shores of the Arctic. Most of its boundary is shoreline, but the boundary with Europe is the subject of some debate.

Geologically, Asia is made up of two vast sets of rock platforms – the Russian and Siberian in the north, and the Arabian, Indian and Chinese platforms in the south, which for eons have converged on each other, squashing between them an enormous extent of sedimentary rocks that were laid down in ancient seas. The platforms provide the great, stable plateaus on the periphery; the sediments have been squeezed and folded into the massive mountain ranges that spread across the continent from Turkey ('Asia Minor') in the west to the Pacific seaboard in the east.

Climatically Asia includes almost every known combination of temperature, precipitation and wind, from the searing heat of Arabia in summer to the biting chill of north-eastern Siberia in winter. Similarly, almost every pattern of vegetation from polar desert and tundra to tropical rainforest can be found within the bounds of this vast continent.

Asia comprises a 'heartland' centred on Siberia, and a series of peripheral areas of widely different character. The heartland includes the tundra wastes of the north, the coniferous forests ('taiga'), and the vast, thinly-populated interior deserts of Mongolia, north-west China and Tibet. Not entirely desert, some of the heartland was traditionally pastoral and is now responding to new agricultural techniques, while the wealth of its minerals is slowly being developed. To the west lie the plains of Russia, homeland of the 16th- and 17th-century invaders who, unlike their many predecessors, finally came to settle in the heartland and organize its massive resources. To the south-west lies the 'fertile crescent' of the Tigris and Euphrates valleys, possibly the world's first centre of agriculture, and beyond it the Mediterranean coastlands of Turkey, Syria, Lebanon and Israel.

From Iran eastwards, right around the shores of the continent and its off-lying islands as far as eastern Siberia, lie the coastlands that contain and support the main masses of Asia's populations. Isolated by the northern mountain barrier, India has traditionally formed a subcontinent in its own right. China, the second great civilization of Asia, centred on the 'Middle Kingdom' of 18 historic provinces, has expanded steadily over the centuries and is a great influence on neighbouring states. Beyond the mainland coasts lie the mountainous but mostly highly fertile islands of the volcanic arcs that skirt the eastern edge of the continental shelf. The populations of

these islands, already high, are among the fastest growing in the world – though only Japan provides a standard of living comparable to those of the West.

The Indian subcontinent, though a relatively small part of Asia as a whole, is almost continental in its impact on the traveller and in its share (nearly one-fifth) of the world's population. It extends from subequatorial coral beaches in the south to icy mountains overlooking the Vale of Kashmir in the north – approximately in the latitude of Greece.

South Asia is a subcontinent of unity and diversity. Binding it in unity is the annually occurring rhythm of human activities caused by the seasonal reversal of winds in the monsoon. Yet diversity arises from the same cause – the annual vagaries of the monsoon – that bring drought and near-famine to one region, flood and disease to another, in apparently random patterns. There is a cultural unity, too, to which the sensitive traveller reacts, from Kashmir to Cape Comorin (Kanya Kumari). Yet here again is the paradox of extraordinary diversity. Variety of race, language and religion all contribute, often related to invasions, trading connections or a colonial past. At the root of the culture of this subcontinent lies South Asia's millennial role as the cradle of Hinduism and Buddhism.

East Asia comprises the lands to the east of the

great mountain barrier which runs from south-western China, through the Himalayas, the Karak-oram and the Tian Shan, to the Altai range on the borders of Mongolia, China and Russia. It occupies roughly 9% of the land area of the globe, and exhibits a very great diversity of relief and climate. Altitudes vary from the high Tibetan plateau, where the average elevation is over 4,500 m [14,760 ft], to the floor of the Turfan (Turpan Hami) depression to the north, 154 m [505 ft] below sea level. East Asian climates range from the cold continental of northern Mongolia to the warm humid tropical of southern China and Hainan.

The area contains well over a quarter of mankind. This population is unevenly distributed with the main concentrations in lowland areas open to the influence of the summer monsoon in eastern China, Korea, and Japan. Until recent times the whole area has been strongly dominated by the Chinese civilization.

Only since World War II has the term 'Southeast Asia' become widely used to describe the series of peninsulas and islands which lie east of India and south of China. The name was first employed around 1900 to designate a particular trade and shipping area, but the concept of a South-east Asian region goes back a long way. This was recognized by both the Chinese and the Japanese, who respectively

called it the Nan Yang and the Nanyo, both meaning the 'southern seas'. Today the region includes Burma, Thailand, Laos, Vietnam, Cambodia, Malaysia, Singapore, Brunei and the islands of Indonesia and the Philippines.

South-east Asia, which lies almost wholly in the humid tropics, is an area of rivers and seas. Each of the mainland states is focused on one major river, with the Irrawaddy in Burma, the Chao Phraya in Thailand, the Mekong in Cambodia and South Vietnam, and the Hongha in North Vietnam. The maritime states, however, revolve around a series of seas and straits, from the highly strategic Strait of Malacca in the west to the Sulu, Celebes and Banda Seas in the east.

The tropical rainforests of South-east Asia are estimated to cover about 250 million hectares [618 million acres]. They are the richest in species of all forest areas in the world. The region is thought to possess some 25,000 species of flowering plants, around 10% of the world's flora.

The evergreen rainforest of the ever-wet, ever-hot tropics is a very complex community. In 20 hectares [49 acres] there can be as many as 350 different species of trees. In the forest, climbing and strangling plants are abundant. Many of the trunks are buttressed, and certain trees bear their flowers and fruits directly on the trunks and branches. The

canopy is the home of a wide range of birds, bats and other mammals, including the orang-utan.

Much of the rainforest has now been destroyed by shifting cultivators or felled for timber by extracting companies, and the remaining tracts are also under pressure from mining concerns, rubber companies, hydroelectric developments and tourism.

The peaks and high plateaus of the Himalayas and central Asia are forested up to about 4,000 m [13,000 ft] with an open woodland of pines, cedars, cypresses, bamboos and rhododendrons. Above lies a zone of dwarf shrubs – willows, birches and junipers that spend half their year among swirling snow. This grades into a rough, semi-frozen tundra of coarse sedges and grasses, dotted with cushions of intensely-coloured alpine flowers; primulas, edelweiss and gentians become prominent as the snow retreats in early summer. Insects are surprisingly plentiful in the thin, cool air at 4,500 to 5,500 m [15,000 to 18,000 ft]. At 6,000 m [19,500 ft] tundra turns to dry desert and both plants and animals become rare.

Larger grazing animals – yaks, hangul deer and blue sheep, for example – emerge from the forest to feed on the high plateaus in summer, and mountain goats and ibex find a living among the high, snow-encrusted crags. Wolves, snow leopards and high-flying eagles are their main predators ∎

ASIA

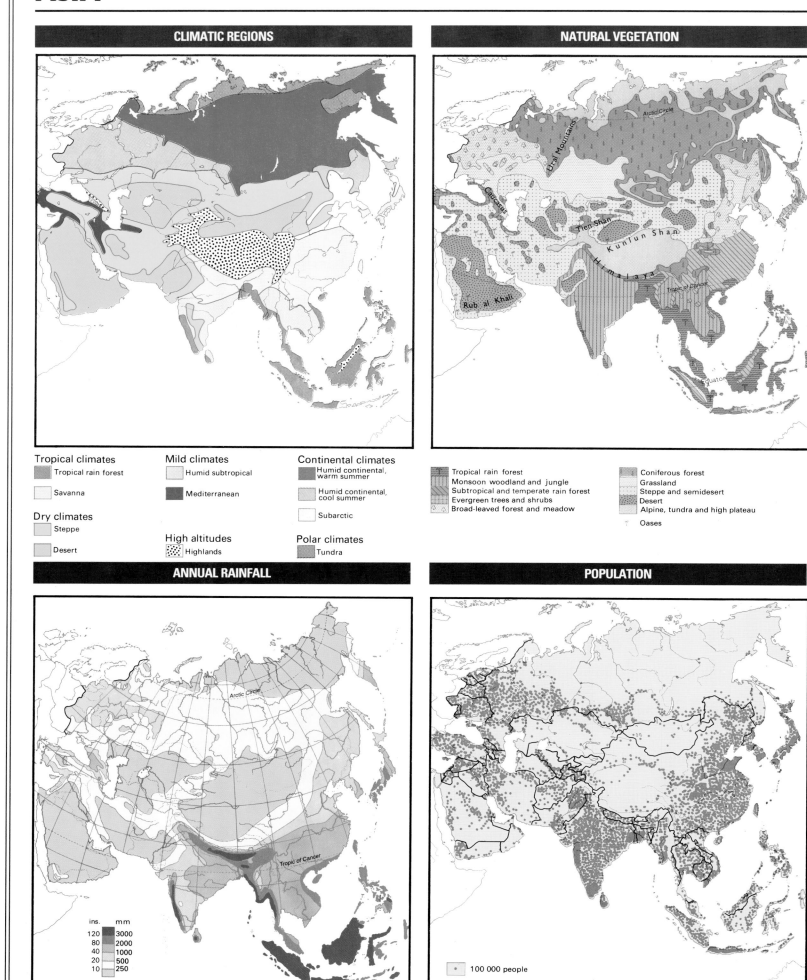

CLIMATIC REGIONS

Tropical climates
- Tropical rain forest
- Savanna

Dry climates
- Steppe
- Desert

Mild climates
- Humid subtropical
- Mediterranean

High altitudes
- Highlands

Continental climates
- Humid continental, warm summer
- Humid continental, cool summer
- Subarctic

Polar climates
- Tundra

NATURAL VEGETATION

- Tropical rain forest
- Monsoon woodland and jungle
- Subtropical and temperate rain forest
- Evergreen trees and shrubs
- Broad-leaved forest and meadow
- Coniferous forest
- Grassland
- Steppe and semidesert
- Desert
- Alpine, tundra and high plateau
- Oases

ANNUAL RAINFALL

ins.	mm
120	3000
80	2000
40	1000
20	500
10	250

POPULATION

• 100 000 people

86

LAND USE

LAND USE

- Arable land
- Arable land with permanent pasture
- Fruit trees, vineyards and plantations
- Permanent pasture
- Woods and forests
- Rough grazing
- Rough grazing with trees
- Non-productive land

LIVESTOCK

- Cattle
- Sheep

MINERALS

Asbestos	**Co**	Cobalt	
Bauxite	**Mg**	Magnesium	
Copper	**Mn**	Manganese	
Diamonds	**Hg**	Mercury	
Gold	**Ni**	Nickel	
Iron ore	**Ti**	Titanium	
Lead			
Lead and zinc	**POWER**		
Mica		Coalfields	
Silver		Gasfields	
Tin		Oilfields	
Zinc		Hydroelectric power	
Sb Antimony			
Cr Chrome			

CROPS

Bananas		Soya beans	
Barley		Sugar beet	
Citrus fruits		Sugar cane	
Coffee		Tea	
Cotton		Tobacco	
Date palms		Vines	
Groundnuts		Wheat	
Maize			
Millet			
Potatoes		Principal fishing areas	
Rice			
Rubber			

LAND USE

Other land 35·8%

Arable land and permanent crops 14·5%

Permanent pasture 18·6%

Woods and forests 31·1%

Total land area 4 903.8 million hectares
(12 117·3 million acres)

Projection Bonne

East from Greenwich

COPYRIGHT GEORGE PHILIP LTD.

ASIA

RUSSIA

Distinctive Russian flags were first instituted by Peter the Great, based on those of the Netherlands. This flag became the official national flag in 1799 but was suppressed in the Bolshevik Revolution. It was restored on 22 August 1991.

Despite a large temperature range and cold winters (temperatures rarely rise above freezing, December–February), Moscow has a less extreme continental climate than more easterly parts of Russia. Prevailing westerly winds and absence of mountains allow the Atlantic Ocean to extend its influence deep into the continent. Rainfall is well distributed with a slight summer maximum. Winters are cloudy with frequent snow and a very small daily variation in temperature.

It is an indication of the sheer size of the former Soviet Union that, having shed very nearly a quarter of its area with the departure of the 14 republics in 1991, its Russian Federation remains by far the largest country in the world, still getting on for twice the size of Canada, China or the USA.

Diversity certainly characterizes Russia's landforms, for within the country's borders are to be found rugged peaks and salt flats, glaciers and deserts, marshes and rolling hills as well as broad level plains. In the west the North European Plain, underlain by the ancient peneplained rocks of the Russian platform, occupies the greater part of European Russia as well as much of Ukraine and all of Belorussia and the Baltic nations. On the eastern side of the plain are the Ural Mountains: popularly seen as the divide between Europe and Asia, the Urals are low and rounded with few peaks rising above 1,600 m [5,248 ft]. The eastern slopes of the Urals merge into the West Siberian lowland, the largest plain in the world, with extensive low-lying marshes. Still further to the east the Siberian platform, similar in origin to the Russian platform, underlies the Central Siberian Plateau.

The plains of Russia are surrounded on the south and east by mountain ranges of geologically recent origin: the Caucasus, on the borders of Georgia and Azerbaijan; the Altai and Sayan, extending into Mongolia; and, beyond Lake Baykal and the Lena River, the East Siberian ranges at the easternmost tip of the Asian land mass. The Kamchatka peninsula is still geologically unstable – part of the 'Pacific Rim' – and volcanic eruptions and earthquakes occur fairly often.

Much of Russia's landscape bears the imprint of

LAKE BAYKAL

With a lowest point of 1,620 m [5,315 ft], Oz Baykal in southern Siberia is the world's deepest lake. Also the largest in Eurasia – at 636 km [395 mls] long by an average width of 48 km [30 mls] it measures some 31,500 sq km [12,160 sq mls], more than the area of Belgium – it is so deep that it is the world's largest body of fresh water and indeed contains no less than a fifth of the fresh water contained in all the world's lakes. Its volume of 23,000 cu km [5,520 cu mls] is as much as the five Great Lakes of North America combined.

Situated in a deep tectonic basin, and fed by 336 rivers and streams, it acts as a reservoir for only one river: the Angara, which flows north to join the Yenisey. Though renowned for its purity and its endemic lifeforms (65% of its 1,500 animal species and 35% of its plant species are unique to Baykal), industrial plants have caused increasing pollution since the 1960s.

The *graben* fault that hosts the arc-shaped lake was caused by gigantic upheavals in the Earth's crust some 80 million years ago; when the climate turned wetter, about 25 million years ago, the lake began to fill – and it is still getting larger. When the *sarma* wind blows from the north-west, it generates waves more than 5 m [16.5 ft] high. Located 80 km [50 mls] from the Mongolian border, Baykal drains an area of 540,000 sq km [208,500 sq mls] – 13% more than the area drained by all five of North America's Great Lakes.

the last Ice Age in the form of chaotic drainage systems, extensive marshlands, lakes and moraines in the lowland areas and cirques and 'U'-shaped valleys in the mountains. More than half the total area has permafrost – permanently frozen ground which may extend hundreds of metres in depth.

The rivers that flow across the Russian plains are among the longest and most languid in the world. Drainage in European Russia forms a radial pattern with the hub in the Central Uplands west of Moscow. The Volga flows from this area for 3,700 km [2,300 mls] south to the landlocked Caspian Sea, the world's largest inland body of water. In Siberia the main rivers flow north to the Arctic – among them the Yenisey-Angara, the Ob-Irtysh and the Lena, respectively the fifth, sixth and 11th longest in the world.

Natural regions

Extending latitudinally across Russia, and corresponding to the major climatic belts, are a series of sharply differentiated natural zones – from north to south the tundra, the taiga, the mixed forests and the steppe. The dominant natural zones can also be seen as vertical bands in the mountainous regions.

Tundra: This zone forms a continuous strip north of the Arctic Circle from the Norwegian border to Kamchatka. Climatic conditions here restrict plant growth and soil formation so that the region well deserves its name 'bald mountain top', the meaning of the word 'tundra' in Lapp. Stunted shrubs, mosses, lichens and berry-bearing bushes growing in thin, infertile soils form the vegetation cover, supporting the herds of reindeer which for centuries have formed the basis of the local tribes' economy.

Taiga: Extending south from the boundary with the tundra and occupying about 60% of the country are the coniferous forests that make up the taiga – larger than the Amazonian rainforest. Soils under the forest are acidic and usually unsuitable for cultivation unless fertilized. A major source of wealth in the taiga has always been its large population of fur-bearing animals such as ermine, sable and beaver.

Mixed forest: In the west and east the coniferous forests merge into zones of mixed forest containing both coniferous species and broadleaves such as oak, beech, ash, hornbeam and maple. Today much of the natural vegetation has been cleared for farming, despite the fact that the soils require heavy application of fertilizers to be productive.

Steppe: Sandwiched between the forests to the north and the semi-deserts and deserts of the Central Asian republics to the south is the steppe zone. Hardly any natural vegetation remains in the steppe today as vast expanses have been brought under the plough. The soils of the steppe are *chernozems*, black-earths, and they are among the most fertile in the world. Before conversion into farmland the steppe consisted of extensive grasslands which in the north were interspersed with trees.

Natural resources

Russia's physical environment offers varied opportunities for exploitation. The vast stretches of forest make it the world's largest possessor of softwoods.

The rivers, lakes and seas have yielded marine and freshwater products from early days. In the 11th century fishing villages were already established on the northern coast of European Russia for whaling,

sealing and fishing. Today fish catches are large on the Pacific coast, while in fresh water the sturgeon continues to be valued for its caviare.

Because of the widespread occurrence of poor soils and harsh climatic conditions, agriculture is confined to a relatively small area. Most of the arable is in the steppe and forest-steppe and from the time this was first ploughed it has been used for grains. On the Black Sea coast, subtropical conditions allow the cultivation of wines, tea and citrus fruits.

While agriculture is limited, mineral and energy resources are abundant and have formed the basis of the former USSR's powerful industrial economy. The most notable mineral deposits are found on the Kola peninsula by the Barents Sea, in eastern Siberia and the far east where spectacular discoveries of gold, lead, zinc, copper and diamonds have been made. Iron ore is found in most regions – the Soviet Union produced a quarter of the world total.

Energy resources are varied. Estimates show Russia to have sufficient coal to last several hundred years, while oil and natural gas deposits are projected to last for several decades, with the main fields in the Volga–Urals region and western Siberia. Large hydro-power complexes have also been built on many rivers, though the development of nuclear energy was under review following the disaster of Chernobyl (in the Ukraine) in 1986.

History

The present size of Russia is the product of a long period of evolution. In early medieval times the first Slavic state, Kievan Rus, was formed at the junction of the forest and steppe in what is now the Ukraine. As the centuries wore on other states were formed further to the north. All were eventually united under the principality of Muscovy. In the 13th century Mongol hordes from the east penetrated the forests and held sway over the Slavic people there.

It was only in the 16th century that the Mongol yoke was thrown off as the Slavs, under Ivan the Terrible, began to advance across the steppes. This signalled the beginning of a period of expansion from the core area of Slavic settlement to the south, east and west. Expansion across Siberia was rapid and the first Russian settlement on the Pacific, Okhotsk, was established in 1649. Progress across the open steppe was slower but by 1696 Azov, the

COUNTRY: Russia

AREA: 17,068,000 sq km [6,590,000 sq mls]

POPULATION: 147,400,000

CAPITAL (Population): Moscow (8,967,000)

ETHNIC GROUPS: Russian 83%, Tatar 4%, Ukrainian 3%, Chuvash 2%, over 100 other nationalities

LANGUAGES: Russian 87%

RELIGIONS: Christian, Muslim, Buddhist

POPULATION DENSITY: 9 per sq km [22 per sq ml]

PRINCIPAL CITIES (Population): Moscow 8,967,000
St Petersburg 5,020,000 Nizhniy Novgorod 1,438,000
Novosibirsk 1,436,000

key to the Black Sea, was secured. A series of struggles in the 17th and 18th centuries against the Swedes and Poles resulted in the addition of the Gulf of Finland, the Baltic coast and part of Poland to the growing Russian Empire, and in the 19th century the Caucasus, Central Asia and new territories in the Far East were added.

Russia has been a centralized state throughout its history. A major landmark in the country's history, and indeed in the history of the world, was the 1917 Revolution, when the Tsarist order was overthrown and a Communist government established under Lenin – replacing one form of totalitarianism with another. The years from 1917 witnessed colossal changes, the most dramatic and far-reaching of which took place from the 1930s when Stalin instituted central planning of the economy, collectivized agriculture and began a period of rapid industrialization. After Stalin's death in 1953, Soviet leaders modified some policies but they remained true to the general principles of Communism until the radical approach of Mikhail Gorbachev changed the face of Russia – and the Communist world.

The state that the Communists inherited in 1917 was not merely large; it was also made up of peoples of very diverse ethnic, religious and cultural backgrounds. Among the varied peoples – speaking over 100 languages – the Slavs, consisting of the Russians, Ukrainians and Belorussians, were the most numerous. Other groups include the Turkik and Persian people of Central Asia, the Caucasians, the Baltic peoples, Finno-Ugrians, Mongols and many others. Under Soviet rule the ethnic diversity of the state was recognized in the existence of federal republics (of very disparate size), and in addition autonomous republics and regions were set up to recognize smaller ethnic groups.

Although all parts of Russia are inhabited, even the most remote, the greatest concentration of people has traditionally been in the European part of the country. It was here that in the centuries before the Revolution the first Russian towns with their fortresses (*kremlins*) and onion-domed churches were founded. Outside this settled core there were town and cities which the Russians acquired during their expansion or themselves established on the frontiers. In central Asia the Russians took over what had once been a flourishing urban civilization, gaining towns such as Samarkand, Khiva and Bukhara.

After the Revolution, changes took place in the distribution of population so that the former pattern of a small highly populated core and 'empty' periphery began to break down. Today the settled area extends into Siberia and, in a narrow band, across to the Pacific Ocean. As a result, a far higher proportion of the Russian population is to be found east of the Urals than before the Revolution, even before World War II. This redistribution has been actively encouraged by a regime committed to a policy of developing the east.

Though not the most severe climate in Russia, that of Krasnoyarsk is harsh. There are sub-zero temperature averages for seven months, October–April, with low records exceeding –30°C [–22°F]. Summers are not too warm, though a temperature of over 40°C [104°F] has been measured in July. The annual range of temperature is 36°C [65°F]. Snow lies on the ground for over six months of the year, but the amounts are not great. The rainfall total is low.

THE TRANS-SIBERIAN RAILWAY

The world's longest line, the Trans-Siberian Railway runs for 9,310 km [5,785 mls] from Moscow to Vladivostok and Nakhodka on the Sea of Japan. The Siberian section, beginning at Chelyabinsk in the southern Urals, was built between 1881 and 1905, with an extension round Lake Baykal in 1917, and the line has played a crucial role in opening up Siberia for settlement and industrialization. Today the journey from capital to coast (involving 92 stops in eight time zones) takes over seven days.

Migration to the towns and cities has also been marked since 1917 so that the greater part of the Russian population is now urban. The most famous city is the capital Moscow (Moskva); like the other cities of the North European Plain, it is a mixture of the old and the new, but it is also a mixture of European and Asian styles and cultures.

Economic development

The Soviet government transformed the USSR from an underdeveloped country into the second most powerful industrial nation of the world. At the time of the Revolution (1917) most industrial development was concentrated in a few centres in the European part of the country: Moscow, St Petersburg and, in the Ukraine, the Donbas.

As in many other parts of the world, Soviet industrialization was initially based on the iron and steel industry. In Stalin's drive of the 1930s, heavy national investment went into expanding production in the already existing industrial areas of European Russia and establishing the industry in central and eastern Russia; new large integrated steel mills were built in the southern Urals and on the Kuzbas coalfield in western Siberia. Later the industry was introduced into the Kazakh republic on the Karaganda coalfield. Most recently a new plant has been established at Kursk in European Russia.

The shift away from coal as a basis for industrial development to alternative energy sources has taken place later in the Soviet Union than in many other countries. Since the 1960s, however, petroleum and natural gas industries have begun to develop rapidly and the same is true of industries based on hydroelectricity; HEP has been especially important in building up industry in eastern Siberia, where massive installations on the River Angara provide the energy for aluminium production.

Although the introduction of large-scale industry into formerly backward parts of the country has helped to even out levels of development, regional imbalances in production in the territories of the old Soviet Union remain large. The pre-revolutionary foci of development continued to attract a large proportion of available investment and retained their leading position in Soviet industry. This means, effectively, Russia – and of the regions developed since the Revolution only western Siberia can be said today to have a well-developed mature industrial structure. Other parts of the country, and especially the non-Russian republics in the south, still have relatively weak industrial economies.

While overall industrial production forged ahead, agriculture was the 'Achilles' heel' of the Soviet economy, and in several years from the middle 1960s foreign grain had to be imported. Since 1965 there has been an improvement in yields but even so output and consumption per capita can only just keep ahead of increases in population.

Soviet farms were of two types, collective (*kolkhozi*) and state (*sovkhozi*). The former were,

The prevailing winds in winter from the bitter north-west give low temperatures to this coastal town at latitude 43°N. Temperatures below –20°C [–4°F] have been recorded in all months, November–March. Snow lies usually from mid-December to mid-February. There are many foggy days in May–July making the sunshine totals lower in the summer than the winter. Rainfall is quite low, with the monthly total exceeding 100 mm [4 in] in only July–September.

according to the official definition, democratically-run producers' co-operatives which, in return for a grant of land, delivered some of their produce to the state. In theory free to run their affairs, they were always subject to considerable government interference. The equally large state farms were state owned and managed. Until the 1950s they were relatively uncommon because they were expensive to run, but in the last two decades their number increased. While the greater part of total Soviet agricultural output came from collective and state farms, a large share of market garden produce and some livestock products originated on so-called personal plots.

In the drive for economic development, the Soviet government at first neglected the consumer sector. Growth rates in textiles, food industries and wood processing, for example, lagged behind those for iron and steel production. The paucity of consumer goods, often compounded by gross inefficiencies in the state distribution system, was obvious in the size of the queues that formed whenever scarce products came on sale. Another indication is the existence of a flourishing black market.

During Stalin's rule a conscious policy to restrict foreign trade and maximize self-sufficiency was pursued. With the formation of COMECON, the

THE KURIL ISLANDS

A chain of 56 windswept volcanically active islands extending 1,200 km [750 mls] between the end of Russia's Kamchatka Peninsula and the tip of Japan's northern island of Hokkaido, the Kurils separate the Sea of Okhotsk from the Pacific Ocean. Totalling 15,600 sq km [6,000 sq mls] but sparsely peopled, they were discovered by the Dutch in 1634, divided between Russia and Japan in the 18th century and ceded to Japan in 1875. At the end of World War II they were seized by Stalin, giving his fleets ice-free northern access to the Pacific. The Japanese, however, still regard the southern section – Etorofu, Kunashir, Shikotan and the Habomai islets – as theirs, referring to them as the 'northern territories' and allotting 7 February as a national day in their honour.

Though there are rich fishing grounds in the territorial waters and the possibility of mineral wealth, it is indeed a matter of honour rather than economics for Tokyo. The Soviets offered to return Shikotan and the Habomai islands in 1956, but the Japanese held out for all four, and the offer was withdrawn. While the advent of Gorbachev and *glasnost* made little difference, the deconstruction of the Soviet Union certainly has: Boris Yeltsin's Russia, desperate for substantial Japanese aid and co-operation, found the islands a stumbling block to assistance. However, more than half of the population who have moved there since 1945 are Russian, and in a 1991 poll the islanders voted 4–1 to remain under Moscow's control.

ASIA

Eastern trading block, after World War II and the realization that much of Western technology would be useful to its own continued development, the USSR revised trade policy. By the 1980s the Soviet Union was trading with most countries of the world, although the Soviet share of total turnover was small. Again, Russia had the lion's share: while only 15% of its output went to other Soviet republics in 1989, the nearest rivals were Ukraine and Kazakhstan (32%), while six republics recorded a dependency of more than 60% and another four a figure of more than 50%.

With this apparent status it may be thought that Russia would not need the Commonwealth of Independent States, its economic strength (properly managed) making it more than viable as a major nation and a natural successor internationally to the Soviet Union; indeed it inherited the USSR's mantle on the UN Security Council and its diplomatic missions worldwide, while applying for membership of CSCE and even NATO.

But Russia, despite its size, fears isolation. With the Eastern European countries and the Baltic states fully independent, the three Caucasus republics unstable, the Asian republics looking increasingly to

their Islamic neighbours, and even Mongolia converting to democracy and the free market, Russia has little control of the former 'buffer zones'.

Despite Gorbachev's best and at times brave efforts, the Russian President Boris Yeltsin inherited an economy in crisis, bogged down by lumbering and often obstructive bureaucracy, inept use of resources and an inefficient transport system.

After the abolition of price controls sent the cost of basic commodities rocketing, the first months of

1992 saw food shortages worsen and unemployment rise, hastening the possibility of a Communist backlash.

Neither is the nation homogenous. Several autonomous regions – including Karelia, Komi, North Ossetia, Tartarstan, Bashkiria, Gorny-Altay, Buryatia and the vast Yakutia – declared independence in the last months of Soviet control. They could well pursue their policy, seeing Russia shrink further in size and influence in the region ■

KAZAKHSTAN

Although a modest second in size behind Russia among the former Soviet republics, Kazakhstan is a colossal country – more than two and a half times the combined area of the other four Central Asian states, over four times the size of Ukraine (Europe's largest 'whole' state), bigger than any nation in Africa and indeed ninth in the world.

This massive new nation, stretching from near the Volga River in the west to the Altai Mountains in the east, comprises mainly vast plains with a (mineral-rich) central plateau. North to south, the steppe gradually gives way to desert, though irrigation schemes have led to the fertilization of large areas between the Aral Sea and Lake Balkhash, a rich fishing ground. Though its agriculture is traditionally associated with livestock rearing, Kazakhstan accounted for 20% of the cultivated area of the Soviet Union and some 12% of its grain output in 1989.

The first extension of the Russian Empire in Central Asia, the area's 'khanates' were gradually subdued or bought off from the 18th century, though rural resistance persisted well into the Soviet era. It was Kazakhstan that gave Mikhail Gorbachev his first ethnic problem, when in 1986 nationalist riots erupted after a Russian replaced a Kazakh as the republic's Party leader, and in 1991 it led the Central Asian states into the new Commonwealth; indeed, the meeting that finally buried the Soviet Union was held in Alma Ata, testimony to Kazakhstan's rank as number three in the hierarchy – an estimate helped by its 1,800 nuclear warheads.

It was not always so. Successive Soviet regimes used the huge republic as a dumping-ground and test-bed. Stalin exiled Germans and other 'undesirables' there, and Khrushchev experimented with his (largely catastrophic) Virgin Lands Programme; the Soviet missile- and rocket-launching site was located at Baykonur, north-east of the Aral Sea (shrunk by 70% after disastrous Soviet irrigation projects dried up its two feeder rivers), and the USSR's first fast-breeder nuclear reactor was built at Mangyshlak, on the Caspian Sea.

Kazakhstan has nevertheless emerged as a powerful entity, wealthier and more diversified than the other Asian republics. Well endowed with oil

Kazakhstan is a large country in the centre of Asia and its climate is markedly continental. The summers are warm and the winters cold, the annual temperature range being 30°C [54°F]. Half the year will experience frost (at Alma Ata) and snow lies for about 100 days. Rainfall is low with only around 250mm [10in] in the north and twice this amount in the south, with desert and semi-desert conditions covering large areas.

and gas, it also has good deposits of coal, iron ore, bauxite, copper, nickel, tungsten, zinc, silver, and gold (70% of the Soviet total). Though not industrialized by Western standards, it is growing in oil refining (notably for aviation fuel), metallurgy, engineering, chemicals, footwear, food processing and textiles, the last mostly dependent on home-grown cotton and, increasingly, high-quality native wool.

Kazakhstan could provide the 'new order' with a valuable bridge between East and West, between Islam and Christianity; it is the only former Soviet republic where its ethnic population is actually outnumbered by another group (the Russians), and its (Sunni) Muslim revival is relatively muted. Such divisions can of course have the opposite effect, leading to ethnic tensions and cruelties ■

COUNTRY: Kazakhstan

AREA: 2,717,300 sq km [1,049,200 sq mls]

POPULATION: 16,700,000

CAPITAL (Population): Alma Ata (1,128,000)

ETHNIC GROUPS: Russian 41%, Kazakh 36%, Ukrainian 6%, Tatar 2%

RELIGIONS: Christian, Sunni Muslim

UZBEKISTAN

Only a fraction of Kazakhstan's size, but with a larger population, Uzbekistan stretches from the shores of the shrinking Aral Sea, through desert and increasingly fertile semi-arid lands, to the peaks

COUNTRY: Uzbekistan

AREA: 447,000 sq km [172,600 sq mls]

POPULATION: 20,300,000

CAPITAL (Population): Tashkent (2,073,000)

ETHNIC GROUPS: Uzbek 69%, Russian 11%, Tatar 4%, Kazakh 4%, Tajik 4%, Kara-Kalpak 2%

of the Western Pamirs and the mountainous border with Afghanistan, with a populous eastern spur jutting into Kirghizia.

The fertile sections comprise an intensely irrigated zone that made Uzbekistan the world's third largest cotton producer, contributing 67% of the Soviet total; the republic was also responsible in 1989 for half the rice, a third of astrakhan and 85% of the hemp. However, oil and gas (especially in the desert of Kyzylkum), coal and copper are important, while other industries are slowly gaining ground.

The Uzbeks were the ruling race in southern Central Asia before the Russians took over in the 19th century. Today the Russians are a vulnerable minority in the republic noted for ethnic violence, most dangerously between Uzbeks, a Turkic people speaking Jagatai Turkish, and the Tajiks, a Persian people who speak an Iranian dialect. This problem,

Most of the country is extremely dry with less than 200mm [8in] of rain a year. This increases in the mountains to over 500mm [20in], but is nowhere excessive. There is a winter maximum but near-drought conditions in the summer. The summer is hot and dry; over 40°C [104°F] has been recorded, May–October, and the winters are not too severe, though the range from January to July is approaching 30°C [54°F].

added to a suspect economy overdependent on one commodity and a deserved, enduring reputation for government corruption, could well see Uzbekistan struggle as an independent nation ■

TURKMENISTAN

More than 90% of Turkmenistan is arid, with over half the country covered by the Karakum, Asia's largest sand desert. As much Middle Eastern as Central Asian, its population is found mainly around oases, growing cereals, cotton and

fruit, and rearing karakul lambs. Apart from astrakhan rugs and food processing, industry is largely confined to mining sulphur and salt and the production of natural gas, its biggest export.

Dependent on trade with other former Soviet republics for more than 75% of its GDP – and much of that subsidized – Turkmenistan is still a one-party state. Since declaring independence in October 1991 it has looked south to the Muslim countries rather than to the CIS for support – like its Turkic associates, Azerbaijan and Uzbekistan, it has joined

the Economic Co-operation Organization formed by Turkey, Iran and Pakistan in 1985 – and its future links with Iran would appear strong ■

COUNTRY: Turkmenistan

AREA: 488,100 sq km [188,500 sq mls]

POPULATION: 3,600,000

CAPITAL (Population): Ashkhabad (398,000)

ETHNIC GROUPS: Turkmen 68%, Russian 13%, Jewish 1%

RELIGIONS: Shiite Muslim, some Christian

KIRGHIZIA

COUNTRY: Kirghizia
AREA: 199,000 sq km [76,800 sq mls]
POPULATION: 4,400,000
CAPITAL (Population): Bishkek (616,000)
ETHNIC GROUPS: Kirghiz 41%, Russian 22%, Uzbek 10%, Ukrainian 3%, Tatar 2%
RELIGIONS: Sunni Muslim, Christian

Despite its geographical isolation on the borders of China's Xinjiang province, its mainly mountainous terrain and its conventionally strong links with Moscow, Kirghizia has pursued very aggressive, 'European' policies towards Western-style capitalist democracy in the period since independence was declared in August 1991. Its young president, Askar Akayev, has introduced rapid privatization, nurtured pluralism, and encouraged trade and investment links with OECD countries. In addition, he has established good relations with China, a suspicious neighbour and potential foe. However, the large Russian minority (in positions of power under the Soviet regime), disenchanted Uzbeks and an influx of Chinese Muslim immigrants have the potential for an ethnic tinderbox.

Although dominated by the western end of the Tian Shan, with peaks rising to the 7,439m [24,000ft] of Pik Pobedy on the Chinese border, Kirghizia has a strong agricultural economy. Much of the lower land is pasture for sheep, pigs, cattle, goats, horses and yaks – pastoralism is the traditional livelihood of the Mongoloid Kirghiz, though few nomads remain – while irrigated land produces a wide range of crops from sugar beet and vegetables to rice, cotton, tobacco, grapes and mulberry trees (for silkworms). The main manufacturing industry is textiles ■

TAJIKISTAN

The smallest of the five Central Asian CIS republics, Tajikistan lies on the borders of Afghanistan and China. Only 7% of the country is below 1,000m [3,280ft] and the eastern half is almost all above 3,000m [9,840ft]. In the north-west the land is irrigated for wheat, cotton, fruit, vegetables and mulberry trees (for silkworms), and there is a thriving electro-chemical industry.

Tajikistan, however, was the poorest of the Soviet republics, and independence (declared in September 1991) brought huge economic problems. The Tajiks are a Persian people, and with a population that is 95% Muslim – albeit Sunnis – the country was the most likely of the Central Asian republics to follow the Islamic fundamentalism of Iran rather than the secular, pro-Western model of Turkey. Judged by the ethnic violence of 1990, the large Uzbek and Russian minorities are unlikely to agree, and the state faces an uncertain future ■

COUNTRY: Tajikistan
AREA: 143,100 sq km [55,250 sq mls]
POPULATION: 5,300,000
CAPITAL (Population): Dushanbe (595,000)
ETHNIC GROUPS: Tajik 59%, Uzbek 23%, Russian 10%
RELIGIONS: Sunni Muslim, some Christian

TURKEY

Although the crescent moon and the five-pointed star are symbols of Islam, their presence on Turkey's flag dates from long before the country became a Muslim state. The flag was officially adopted when the republic was founded in 1923.

ANKARA

Temperature

Precipitation
346mm
14in

J F M A M J J A S O N D

The plateau of Anatolia is a region of continental extremes and scanty precipitation. Ankara lies just to the north of the driest part of the plateau which is situated around the large saltwater Lake Tuz. Summer days are hot and sunny and nights pleasantly cool; over 11 hours of sunshine and 15–30°C [59–86°F]. Winters are cold with the mean temperature in January close to freezing. Snow falls on average on 20 to 30 days a year. Annual rainfall is low, in some years failing July–October.

The most populous country in south-west Asia, Turkey comprises the broad peninsula of Asia Minor, together with its 'roots' around Lake Van, and in Europe that part of Thrace (Thraki) which lies to the east of the lower Maritsa River. The straits separating the European (5%) and Asiatic parts of Turkey have been of strategic importance for thousands of years. The Dardanelles, joining the Aegean Sea to the Sea of Marmara, are 1.6 km [1 ml] wide at their narrowest point; the Bosphorus, linking the Sea of Marmara to the Black Sea, measures just 640 m [2,100 ft] at one point and is spanned by two suspension bridges at Istanbul.

The heart of the country is the high karst plateau of Anatolia, semi-desert around the central salt lake, but mainly sheep country. The Taurus ranges afford summer grazing for the plateau flocks, and also timber. The northern Pontic ranges are better wooded, with fertile plains. The valleys of the Gediz and Cürüksu, which open westwards from the plateau to the Aegean, export tobacco and figs, while the deltaic plain around Adana grows abundant cotton. The very high and thinly-peopled plateaus and ranges to the east of the Euphrates produce chrome, copper and oil.

Istanbul, the former imperial capital of Byzantium and Constantinople, which controls the straits between the Black Sea and the Mediterranean, is the country's chief port and commercial city, but the function of capital has been transferred to the more centrally-placed town of Ankara. Turkey, with a rapidly growing population, now has one of the best railway networks in the Middle East, and though lacking in large resources of mineral oil has built up a thriving industrial economy based on imported oil, on coal (from Zonguldak), and above all on hydro-electric power. Though still important, agriculture has been overtaken by manufacturing, particularly textiles and clothing.

Constantinople's huge Ottoman Empire had been in decline for centuries when alliance with Germany in World War I ended in the loss of all non-Turkish areas. Nationalists led by Mustafa Kemal – known later as Atatürk ('father of the Turks') – rejected peace proposals favouring Greece and after a civil war set up a republic. Turkey's present frontiers were established in 1923, when Atatürk became president, and until 1938 he ruled as a virtual dictator, secularizing and modernizing the traditional Islamic state.

Between 1960 and 1970 the government was overthrown three times by military coups; civilian rule returned in 1983 and since then democracy has been relatively stable, though the country's human rights record remained more Third World than Western European.

The economic progress that partnered political stability in the mid-1980s – growth averaged more than 7% a year – encouraged Turkey to apply for EEC membership in 1987, but the response from Brussels was unenthusiastic. Turkey's disputes with Greece – notably over Ankara's invasion of northern Cyprus in 1974, but also over claims to territory and mineral rights in the Aegean – plus the country's poor human rights record and still-low standard of living were all factors. While Turkey has been a NATO member since 1952, this was likely to remain the EEC's position for some time – while the emergence of Islamic fundamentalism raised new doubts about Turkey's 'European' stance.

Situated at one of the world's great geopolitical crossroads, the nation seemed destined to remain sandwiched between Europe and the Middle East. Turkey nevertheless has a two-way traffic in people with Western Europe: while tourism was a boom industry in the late 1980s (often at the expense of Greece), with 2.5 million visitors a year visiting the country, these were outnumbered by Turkish men working (or seeking work) in EEC cities, the majority of them in Germany ∎

COUNTRY: Republic of Turkey

AREA: 779,450 sq km [300,946 sq mls]

POPULATION: 57,326,000

CAPITAL (Population): Ankara (2,252,000)

GOVERNMENT: Multiparty republic with a unicameral legislature

ETHNIC GROUPS: Turkish 86%, Kurdish 11%, Arab 2%

LANGUAGES: Turkish (official), Kurdish

RELIGIONS: Sunni Muslim 99%, Eastern Orthodox

NATIONAL DAY: 29 October; Republic Day (1923)

CURRENCY: Turkish lira = 100 kurual

ANNUAL INCOME PER PERSON: $1,630

MAIN PRIMARY PRODUCTS: Cereals, cotton, pulses, sugar beet, cattle, sheep, tobacco, fruit, vegetables, coal, lignite, crude oil, iron, boron, copper, chrome

MAIN INDUSTRIES: Agriculture, steel, food processing, textiles, oil, chemicals, fishing, mining

MAIN EXPORTS: Textiles 24%, agricultural products 20%, metals 14%, foodstuffs 7%

MAIN EXPORT PARTNERS: Germany 18%, Iraq 8%, Italy 7%, USA 7%, UK 5%, France 4%, Saudi Arabia 3%

MAIN IMPORTS: Fuels 19%, machinery 17%, chemicals 14%, iron and steel 12%, pharmaceuticals 7%

MAIN IMPORT PARTNERS: Germany 14%, USA 11%, Iraq 10%, Italy 7%, UK 6%, France 5%

DEFENCE: 17.5% of national budget

TOURISM: 2,468,000 visitors per year

POPULATION DENSITY: 74 per sq km [190 per sq ml]

INFANT MORTALITY: 62 per 1,000 live births

LIFE EXPECTANCY: Female 68 yrs, male 65 yrs

ADULT LITERACY: 74%

PRINCIPAL CITIES (Population): Istanbul 5,495,000 Ankara 2,252,000 Izmir 1,490,000 Adana 776,000 Bursa 614,000

CYPRUS

The design, featuring a map of the island with two olive branches, has been the official state flag since independence from Britain in 1960. However, Cyprus is now divided and the separate communities fly the Greek and Turkish flags.

The highest rainfall on the island is in the Troodos Mountains and is under 1,000 mm [40 in]. The rest of the island is very dry with rain on about 60 days per year, and virtually no summer rain. The summers are hot and the winters warm, although the winters are cold in the mountains. The daily temperature in July–August can be very hot – the highest recorded April–October are all over 40°C [104°F]. May to September has over ten hours of sunshine per day.

A small but strategically situated Mediterranean island, Cyprus is a detached fragment of the mainland mountains to the east. In the south, the broad massif of Troödos, rich in minerals, is a classic example of an ophiolite, or intrusive dome of ancient sub-oceanic rocks. The northern coast is backed by the long limestone range of Kyrenia. The fertile central plain between Morphou and Famagusta grows fruits, flowers and early vegetables. The former forests were cut mainly in classical times to fuel the copper smelteries; 'Kypros' is the Greek for copper. Turks settled in the north of the island during Ottoman rule, from 1571 to 1878, when Cyprus came under British administration. In the 1950s Greek Cypriots, led by Archbishop Makarios (later President), campaigned for union with Greece (Enosis), while the Turks favoured partition. After a guerrilla campaign by EOKA a power-sharing compromise was reached and in 1960 the island became a republic. This fragile arrangement broke down in 1963 and the following year the UN sent in forces to prevent more intercommunal fighting.

In 1968 the Turkish Cypriots set up an 'autonomous administration' in the north, but in 1974, following a coup by Greek-born army officers that deposed Makarios, Turkey invaded the mainland and took control of the northern 40% of the country, displacing 200,000 Greek Cypriots. The UN has since supervised an uneasy partition of the island.

The Greek Cypriot sector has prospered from tourism, British bases, invisible earnings and agriculture, as well as manufacturing. The more agriculturally based north has done less well: the 'Turkish Republic of Northern Cyprus' is recognized only by Ankara and relies heavily on aid from Turkey ■

COUNTRY: Cyprus
AREA: 9,250 sq km [3,571 sq mls]
POPULATION: 702,000
CAPITAL (Population): Nicosia (167,000)
GOVERNMENT: Multiparty republic
ETHNIC GROUPS: Greek Cyp. 81%; Turkish Cyp.19%
LANGUAGES: Greek and Turkish
RELIGIONS: Greek Orthodox and Muslim
NATIONAL DAY: 1 October; Independence Day (1960)
CURRENCY: Cyprus £ = 1,000 mils
ANNUAL INCOME PER PERSON: $8,040
MAIN INDUSTRIES: Cement, mosaic tiles, wine making, footwear, cigarettes
MAIN PRIMARY PRODUCTS: Asbestos, pyrites, copper
MAIN EXPORTS: Wine, vegetables, fruit, clothing, shoes
MAIN IMPORTS: Food, petroleum, chemicals
DEFENCE: 1% of national budget
POPULATION DENSITY: 76 per sq km [197 per sq ml]
LIFE EXPECTANCY: Female 80 yrs, male 74 yrs
ADULT LITERACY: 93%

LEBANON

Adopted in 1943, Lebanon's colours are those of the Lebanese Legion in World War I. The cedar tree, many of which grow in the country's mountains, has been a Lebanese symbol since biblical times.

For three decades after its independence from the French mandate in 1944 Lebanon was a relatively peaceful and prosperous country by Middle East standards. An association with France going back a century – before that the country was part of the Ottoman Empire – had bequeathed a distinct Gallic flavour, though with so many racial and religious groups the population was truly cosmopolitan; Beirut, the dominant city, was both a centre of international commerce (the Lebanese are descendants of the Phoenicians, legendary traders and businessmen) and an elegant playground of the wealthy.

All that changed suddenly after March 1975 when this beautiful country saw sporadic conflict spiral into violent civil war between Christians, Muslims and Druses. The complex politics of the next 14 years proved almost unfathomable as Lebanon sank into a seemingly permanent state of ungovernable chaos. Bombing, assassination and kidnapping became routine as numerous factions and private militias – Maronite, Druse, Sunni and Shia groups (including fundamentalists backed by Iran) – fought for control. The situation was complicated by a succession of interventions by Palestinian liberation organizations, Israeli troops, the Syrian Army, Western and then UN forces, as the country became a patchwork of occupied zones and 'no-go' areas.

The core religious confrontation has deep roots: in 1860 thousands of Maronites (aligned to the Catholic Church) were murdered by Druses (so tangential to other Islamic sects that they are now not regarded as Muslims), and Muslim tolerance of Christian power after independence lasted only until 1958. Though not directly involved, Lebanon was destablized by the Arab-Israeli War of 1967, and the exile of PLO leadership to Beirut in 1970. By 1990 the Syrian Army had crushed the two-year revolt of Christian rebels against the Lebanese government, but peace proved fragile and a solution elusive: at the start of 1992 Israel still occupied the south of the country (claimed to be a base for Palestinian terrorists), while the fundamentalist Hezbollah still controlled much of the Beqaa Valley in the north ■

COUNTRY: Republic of Lebanon
AREA: 10,400 sq km [4,015 sq mls]
POPULATION: 2,701,000
CAPITAL (Population): Beirut (702,000)
GOVERNMENT: Multiparty republic
ETHNIC GROUPS: Arab 93% (Lebanese 83%, Palestinian 10%), Armenian 5%
LANGUAGES: Arabic and French (official), English, Armenian
RELIGIONS: Muslim 57%, Christian 40%, Druse 3%
NATIONAL DAY: 22 November; Independence Day
CURRENCY: Lebanese £ = 100 piastres
ANNUAL INCOME PER PERSON: $2,000
MAIN PRIMARY PRODUCTS: Salt, gypsum, tin
MAIN EXPORTS: Clothing, jewellery, aluminium and pharmaceutical products, food production
MAIN IMPORTS: Cereals, petroleum products, machinery
DEFENCE: 21% of national budget
POPULATION DENSITY: 260 per sq km [673 per sq ml]

The coast of Lebanon has the hot, dry summers and mild, wet winters characteristic of much of the Mediterranean basin. The four months from June to September are almost completely dry. In winter, onshore winds rise against the steep western edge of the Lebanon mountains bringing heavy rain at sea level with snow at high altitude, raining on every other day between December and February. Close to the sea, there is a small daily range of temperature.

ISRAEL

The blue and white stripes on Israel's flag are based on a Hebrew prayer shawl. In the centre is the ancient six-pointed Star of David. The flag was designed in America in 1891 and officially adopted by the new Jewish state in 1948.

East of the Mediterranean Sea the annual rainfall decreases inland and the length of the summer dry season increases to more than five months. At over 700 m [2,250 ft], Jerusalem has lower temperatures and a greater range than coastal regions of Israel. To the south, rainfall decreases rapidly to only 70 mm [2.5 in] in the rocky desert around the Dead Sea. There is an average daily sunshine total of over 9 hours, ranging from 6–12 hours.

In 1948 the new Jewish state of Israel comprised the coastal plain, the vale of Esdraelon (Jezreel) behind Haifa, the foothills in the south, most of the hill country of Samaria, and half of Jerusalem with a corridor to the west. It was also the intention of the UN that Israel should acquire either Galilee in the north or the Negev Desert in the south, but in the event both these regions were included.

The rest of Palestine, mainly Judaea and the rift valley west of the river, was added to Jordan, but as a result of the Six-Day War in 1967, its administration as the 'West Bank' was taken over by Israel along with East Jerusalem. At the same time the Israelis also occupied the Gaza Strip (Egypt) and the Golan Heights (Syria).

In general, the country is most fertile in the north, and becomes progressively more desert-like towards the south. The object of the Jordan-Western Negev scheme, the most ambitious of Israel's irrigation enterprises, has been to direct through canals and culverts all the water that can be spared from the Upper Jordan and the streams and drainage channels of the coastal plain southwards to the deserts of the Negev.

In the north of Israel, Galilee is rolling hill country with good rainfall and a rich black soil weathered from basalt. Both here and in the hills of Judaea, new pine-woods have been established to fix the soil and hold the water. The Upper Jordan Valley is excellent farmland, reclaimed from the swamps of Lake Huleh.

The valley of Jezreel, with a deep alluvial soil washed down from Galilee, is intensively tilled with market gardens. South of the promontory of Carmel, the coastal plain of Sharon is excellent fruit-growing country, but needs irrigation, especially in its southern stretches. Here dunes have been fixed with grass and tamarisk and reclaimed for pasture.

The Negev Desert

Between Sinai and the rift valley, the great wedge of desert plateau known as the Negev accounts for about half the total territory of Israel. Its bedrock is widely covered with blown sand and loess, which will grow tomatoes and grapes in profusion if supplied with fresh water.

The Negev south of Be'er Sheva is pioneer territory, with new towns mining oil, copper and phosphates, factories using the potash and salt of the Dead Sea, and farms experimenting with solar power and artificial dew. Carob trees have been planted for fodder, and dairy farms and plantations of bananas and dates have been established with the aid of the artesian springs of the rift valley or Araba. Elat on the Gulf of Aqaba is an increasingly successful tourist town and Israel's sea outlet to Africa and most of Asia. From here, a pipeline takes imported oil to the refinery at Haifa.

Industry

To supplement the facilities of Haifa, Israel built a deep-sea port at Ashdod to replace the old anchorage at Jaffa (Yafo).

Israel has become the most industrialized country in the Near East. Iron is smelted at Haifa and converted to steel at the foundries of Acre. Chemicals are manufactured at Haifa and at plants by the Dead Sea. With the aid of a national electricity grid, factories for textiles, ceramics and other products have been widely established in country towns, including the new foundations of Dimona and Mizpe Ramon in the Negev. Some railways were inherited from the British, but most commercial movement is now along the road network.

Despite its expansion, Israel remains vulnerable on many fronts: reliance on huge US aid (the world's biggest per capita movement); terrorism and international pressure over Palestine; hostile neighbours and huge defence spending; massive influx of immigrants, often overqualified and notably now from the former Soviet republics; and a lack of natural resources forcing dependence on imported raw materials. For the Jewish state, however, little of this is anything new ∎

COUNTRY: State of Israel
AREA: 26,650 sq km [10,290 sq mls]
POPULATION: 4,659,000
CAPITAL (Population): Jerusalem (483,000)
GOVERNMENT: Multiparty republic
ETHNIC GROUPS: Jewish 83%, Arab 16%
LANGUAGES: Hebrew and Arabic (official)
RELIGIONS: Jewish 82%, Muslim 14%, Christian 2%
NATIONAL DAY: 10 May (variable each year); Independence Day (1948)
CURRENCY: Israeli sheqel = 100 agorat
ANNUAL INCOME PER PERSON: $10,970
MAIN PRIMARY PRODUCTS: Livestock, natural gas, fruit
MAIN INDUSTRIES: Agriculture, mining, food processing, textiles, clothing, fertilizers, cement
MAIN EXPORTS: Machinery 29%, diamonds 29%, chemicals 22%, textiles 8%, foodstuffs 5%
MAIN EXPORT PARTNERS: USA 31%, UK 8%, Japan 7%, Germany 5%, Hong Kong 5%, Netherlands 5%
MAIN IMPORTS: Diamonds 20%, capital goods 15%, consumer goods 11%, fuels and lubricants 8%
MAIN IMPORT PARTNERS: USA 16%, Belgium-Luxembourg 15%, Germany 11%, UK 9%, Switzerland 9%, Ireland 6%, France 4%
DEFENCE: 18.2% of national budget
TOURISM: 1,379,000 visitors per year
POPULATION DENSITY: 175 per sq km [453 per sq ml]
LIFE EXPECTANCY: Female 78 yrs, male 74 yrs
ADULT LITERACY: 92%

JERUSALEM

Though held sacred by all of the world's three great monotheisms, Jerusalem's religious importance has brought the city little peace. King David's capital in the 11th century BC, with the building of the great Temple of Solomon, it became the cult centre of Judaism. The Temple was destroyed by the Assyrians and rebuilt in the 6th century, reassuming its importance until AD 70, when Jerusalem, Temple and all, was destroyed by Roman legions during the great Jewish Revolt against the Empire. Later, a rebuilt Jerusalem became a great centre of Christian pilgrimage. In the 7th century, the city was captured by the expanding armies of Islam, and for Muslims, too, Jerusalem (al-Quds in Arabic) is also a holy place: it was visited by the Prophet Mohammed during the 'Night Journey' recounted in the Koran, and Muslims also believe that it was from Jerusalem that the Prophet ascended to paradise. The great mosque known as the Dome of the Rock was built on the site of the Jewish Temple.

During the Israeli War of Independence, Arab and Jew fought bitterly for possession of the city: neither could oust the other and until 1967 it was divided by bristling fortifications, with the Wailing Wall, the only surviving part of the old Temple, firmly under Arab control. In the Six-Day War, Israeli soldiers at last captured all of the city, to universal Jewish rejoicing and Arab lamentation.

SYRIA

The flag of Syria is the one adopted in 1958 by the former United Arab Republic (which included Syria, Egypt and Yemen). At various times in their history Egypt and Syria have shared the same flag, but since 1980 Syria has used this design.

Damascus is isolated from the maritime influence of the Mediterranean by the Lebanon Mountains. Rainfall, confined to winter, is less than on the coast and more variable. The Syrian winter becomes colder further to the east, and frost and snow are not uncommon. Frosts can occur at Damascus between November and March. On the higher mountains, patches of snow persist throughout the year. Summers are very hot and dry with a large diurnal range of temperature of up to 20°C [36°F].

The northern part of the former Ottoman province of the same name, Syria stretches from the Mediterranean to the Tigris, and from the southern edge of the Kurdish plateau in the north to the heart of the Hamad or stony desert in the south. The northern border for most of its length follows the railway from Aleppo to Mosul. Syria has only one large harbour, at Latakia, though the country usually enjoys privileged access to the ports of Lebanon.

The Orontes River flows northwards along the great rift valley, through alternating gorges and wide valleys which have been reclaimed by drainage and irrigation. Near Hamah and Hims the ranges of Lebanon and Anti-Lebanon, which flank the valley to west and east, are relatively low, but further south the Anti-Lebanon rises to the Heights of Hermon, whose snows water the gardens of the capital, Damascus, on the eastern or desert side. In the far

south, by the frontier with Jordan, the volcanic mass of Mount Hauran supports a group of oases around the town of Suwayda. The Golan Heights, in the south-west, are occupied by Israel.

Aleppo, the second city of Syria, is set in a well-watered agricultural area. Further east the steppe becomes progressively drier. This was traditionally winter pasture for the nomads who moved in from their summer homes in the mountains of Lebanon, but in recent years, thanks to techniques of dry-farming with machinery, it has become a prosperous farming zone, devoted almost exclusively to cotton and cereals. The water from the Euphrates barrage, which produces 70% of the country's electricity, will extend agriculture in this region.

Syria has struck oil in the 'panhandle' by the Tigris in the far north-east, and a pipeline has been laid from there to the Mediterranean. Another pipeline crosses the desert further south from the Kirkuk fields in Iraq to the sea-terminal at Baniyas.

President Assad's repressive but stable regime, in power since 1970, was heavily reliant on Arab aid, but Syria's anti-Iraq stance in the 1991 Gulf War will almost certainly result in greater Western assistance to the improving economy. Though small compared to Egypt or Saudi Arabia, Syria's position (both historical and geographical) makes the country a key player in the complicated power game of Middle East politics ■

COUNTRY: Syrian Arab Republic

AREA: 185,180 sq km [71,498 sq mls]

POPULATION: 12,116,000

CAPITAL (Population): Damascus (1,361,000)

GOVERNMENT: Unitary multiparty republic with a unicameral legislature

ETHNIC GROUPS: Arab 89%, Kurdish 6%

LANGUAGES: Arabic (official), Kurdish, Armenian

RELIGIONS: Muslim (mostly Sunni) 90%, Christian 9%

NATIONAL DAY: 17 April

CURRENCY: Syrian £ = 100 piastres

ANNUAL INCOME PER PERSON: $990

MAIN PRIMARY PRODUCTS: Sheep, goats, cattle, cotton, sugar, fruit, cereals, crude oil, natural gas, phosphates, manganese, salt

MAIN INDUSTRIES: Agriculture, oil and gas, cotton, wool, metal goods, glass, flour, soap

MAIN EXPORTS: Crude petroleum and natural gas 33%, chemicals 29%, textiles and clothing 26%, foodstuffs

MAIN EXPORT PARTNERS: Italy 31%, CIS nations 21%, France 10%, Romania 9%, Iran 5%, Germany 5%

MAIN IMPORTS: Machinery and equipment 30%, chemicals 21%, foodstuffs 12%, basic metal products 8%, textiles 3%

MAIN IMPORT PARTNERS: France 10%, CIS nations 8%, Iran 8%, Germany 8%, Italy 7%, Libya 6%, USA 5%

DEFENCE: 34.9% of national budget

POPULATION DENSITY: 65 per sq km [169 per sq ml]

LIFE EXPECTANCY: Female 69 yrs, male 65 yrs

ADULT LITERACY: 61%

PRINCIPAL CITIES (Population): Damascus 1,361,000 Aleppo 1,308,000 Homs 464,000 Latakia 258,000

THE MIDDLE EAST CONFLICT

Arab-Jewish hostility in the Middle East dates from the so-called Balfour Declaration of 1917, when an embattled British government proposed a 'Jewish national home' in the then Turkish imperial province of Palestine without prejudicing the 'existing rights' of the overwhelmingly Arab (Christian and Muslim) population. After World War I, Palestine became a League of Nations mandate under British control; throughout the 1920s, a trickle of Jewish immigrants inspired rioting without noticeably affecting the population balance. But the rise of Nazism in Europe brought floods of Jewish refugees, and Arab-Jewish violence became endemic.

In 1947 the recently formed United Nations proposed a formal partition of the land, accepted by the Jews and rejected by the Palestinians. Even before the British announced they would withdraw in May 1948, 150,000 Arab refugees had fled. On 14 May, the day the British quit, the independence of a new State of Israel was declared. Egypt, Lebanon, Syria, Transjordan and Iraq at once launched an invasion, later joined by Yemen and Saudi Arabia. By the 1949 ceasefire, though, Israel had beaten them off and controlled more territory than the UN partition plan had allocated the Jews. Jerusalem remained a divided city, half controlled by Israel, half by the armies of Transjordan, later the kingdom of Jordan.

An uneasy peace descended, with sporadic border clashes; hundreds of thousands of Palestinians lost their homes. In 1956, full-scale war

erupted once more when Israel joined with Britain and France in an attack on Egypt. Egypt's armies were badly mauled, but Israel's borders remained unchanged. In 1967, Israel responded to an Egyptian maritime blockade – and public threats from Syria and Egypt – with a pre-emptive strike that left it in control of the Sinai peninsula, the Gaza Strip and the 'West Bank' of the Jordan, as well as all of Jerusalem. But Israeli battle skills brought real peace no nearer: instead, Israel had acquired (along with the newly occupied territories) an Arab population of several million. Palestinian freedom fighters – 'terrorists' to their enemies – began a worldwide campaign, including aircraft hijacking, to broadcast their people's plight.

A 1973 Egyptian attack across the Suez Canal, backed by Syria, came close to over-running Sinai, but Israeli counter-attacks recovered much of the lost territory. Egypt's partial victory eventually led to the Camp David accord of 1979, by which Israel returned Sinai in exchange for Egyptian recognition of Israel's right to exist. Egypt was excoriated by its former Arab allies, and Palestinian terrorism continued. Between 1982 and 1985 Israeli forces were heavily engaged in Lebanon, seeking to destroy Palestinian bases at heavy cost to the Lebanese people. Israeli settlements began to proliferate in the occupied territories, provoking, from 1987 onwards, a low-intensity Palestinian uprising – the *intifada* – which Israel repressed by increasingly brutal methods.

ASIA

JORDAN

Green, white and black are the colours of the three tribes who led the Arab Revolt against the Turks in 1917, while red is the colour of the Hussein dynasty. The points of the star represent the first seven verses of the Koran.

The Jordan Valley marks the eastern limit of the true Mediterranean region, and although Amman lies only a short distance east of Jerusalem, it has a much lower rainfall and a longer dry season. Rain is almost unknown May–September. Its semi-arid climate is transitional between the Mediterranean type and the true desert to the east. Temperatures are similar on average to those of Jerusalem but summer days are hotter.

After World War I the Arab territories of the Ottoman Empire were divided by the League of Nations and the area east of the River Jordan ('Transjordan') was awarded to Britain as part of Palestine, becoming a separate emirate in 1923. When the mandate ended in 1946 the kingdom became independent, as Jordan, and two years later (in the first Arab-Israeli War) it acquired the West Bank, which was officially incorporated into the state in 1950.

This crucial area, including Arab Jerusalem, was lost to Israel in the 1967 war, and Jordan has since carried the burden of Palestinian refugees on its own limited territory. In the 1970s the guerrillas using Jordan as a base became a challenge to the authority of King Hussein's government, and after a short civil war the Palestinian leadership fled the country. In 1988 Hussein suddenly renounced all responsibility for the West Bank – a recognition that the PLO and not long-suffering Jordan was the legitimate representative of the Palestinian people.

Palestinians nevertheless still formed a majority of the population; Jordan sustains some 900,000 refugees (nearly half the total), a figure which puts an intolerable burden on an already weak economy. Jordan is not blessed with the natural resources enjoyed by some Middle East countries – whether oil or water – and a limited agricultural base is supported by mining of phosphates and potash, the main exports.

The country's position was further undermined by the 1991 Gulf War, when despite official neutrality the pro-Iraq, anti-Western stance of the Palestinians did nothing to improve prospects of trade and aid deals with Europe and the US, Jordan's vital economic links with Iraq having already been severed. Another factor was the expulsion and return of large numbers of Palestinians and Jordanians from crucial jobs in Kuwait, Saudi Arabia and other wealthy Gulf states.

There were, however, signs of political progress: in 1991 the ban on political parties was removed and martial law was lifted after a period of 21 years ■

THE PALESTINIANS

The sorrowful modern history of the Palestinians began in 1948, when the birth of Israel transformed most of their former territory into a foreign state; some 700,000 fled, most finding no better homes than refugee camps in Jordan, Lebanon and Egypt's Gaza Strip. After the 'Six-Day War' in 1967, most Palestinians not already refugees found themselves living under enemy occupation. Since 1964, the Palestine Liberation Organization has existed to free them by 'armed struggle', but the PLO's adoption of international terrorism as a tactic alienated many potential allies, as did their alliance with Saddam Hussein during the 1991 Gulf War. The 1987 *intifada* brought much world support, but by late 1991, when desultory peace talks with Israel at last began, almost half the Palestinian population were still classified as refugees – 16% of the world's total. No matter what the change in the diplomatic climate, it seems unlikely that the long-suffering Palestinians will realize their dream of statehood in the foreseeable future.

COUNTRY: Hashemite Kingdom of Jordan
AREA: 89,210 sq km [34,444 sq mls]
POPULATION: 4,009,000
CAPITAL (Population): Amman (1,160,000)
ETHNIC GROUPS: Arab 99% (Palestinian 60%)
GOVERNMENT: Constitutional monarchy
LANGUAGES: Arabic (official)
RELIGIONS: Sunni Muslim 93%, Christian 5%
NATIONAL DAY: 25 May; Independence Day (1948)
CURRENCY: Jordan dinar = 1,000 fils
ANNUAL INCOME PER PERSON: $1,240
POPULATION DENSITY: 45 per sq km [116 per sq ml]
LIFE EXPECTANCY: Female 70 yrs, male 66 yrs
ADULT LITERACY: 75%

SAUDI ARABIA

The inscription on the Saudi flag above the sword means 'There is no God but Allah, and Mohammed is the Prophet of Allah'. The only national flag with an inscription as its main feature, the design was adopted in 1938.

In the interior of Saudi Arabia the diurnal temperature range is much greater than in coastal regions. In the glaring heat of summer, daytime temperatures frequently exceed 40°C [100°F], but fall sharply at night. At over 400 m [1,300 ft] above sea level Riyadh has unusually cold winters for its latitude, with no rain at all between June and October. Frosts have been recorded in January and February. Most of the rain falls as short but heavy showers in spring, with no rain between June and October.

During and shortly after World War I, the Saudis of Najd (central Arabia) extended their territory at the expense of the Rashidis and Hashemites, and consolidated their control over the greater part of the Arabian peninsula, including the holy cities of Mecca (Makkah) and Medina (Al Madinah). The frontiers with neighbours to the south and east remained ill-defined, but this mattered little until its vast reserves of oil (the world's largest) were tapped after World War II; since then some disputes have been settled, notably the division of the Gulf-shore Neutral Zone with Kuwait.

The heart of the state – the largest in the Middle East but over 95% desert – consists of the province of Najd, within which are three main groups of oases. Najd is enclosed on its east side by a vast arc of sandy desert which broadens out into the two great dune-seas of Arabia, the Nafud in the north, and in the south the Rub 'al Khali, or 'Empty Quarter', the largest expanse of sand in the world. Here are found most of the country's Bedouin nomads, still deriving a living as traders and herdsmen.

To the west, Najd is separated from the border hills of the Red Sea by fields of rough basaltic lava. Particularly in its southern section towards the border with Yemen, this coastal strip is quite well supplied with water, and a high storage dam has been built inland from Jizan. The hills of Asir which back the plain here benefit from the summer monsoon, and are extensively terraced to grow grain and orchard trees.

For the most part, however, lack of water is a big problem. Saudi Arabia relies heavily on desalination plants and has the world's biggest on the shores of the Gulf – vulnerable to the oil pollution resulting from the 1991 war against Iraq.

The eastern province, by the shores of the Gulf, is known as the Hasa. Near its chief city of Hufuf in particular, the long underground seepage of water from the Hijaz, the western mountains, breaks out in the artesian springs of the oases. This region contains the country's great oilfields including Ghawar, the world's largest. The oil port of Az Zahran is linked with Riyadh by the only railway; asphalt roads and, increasingly, air travel are the country's main means of transport.

The world's third largest producer and biggest exporter of oil – a position extended by the limits on Kuwait and Iraq from 1991 – Saudi Arabia used the enormous revenues (peaking at more than $100 billion a year after the 400% price hikes of 1973) to launch a colossal industrial and domestic development programme: some $250 billion was spent on the plan for 1980–5, requiring over a million foreign workers. A strictly Muslim society suddenly boasted some of the most advanced architecture and facilities in the world, as well as introducing an array of social and educational benefits.

Progress has not always been smooth. In the mid-1980s world oil prices slumped dramatically, disrupting many of the projects begun in the boom years. Meanwhile, expenditure on defence is high even by the profligate standards of the region. The country's position as the West's staunchest Middle East ally has often conflicted with its role as the guardian of Islam's holy places – hundreds of thousands make the pilgrimage to Mecca every year – and despite large donations to poorer Arab nations (Saudi Arabia is by far the world's biggest donor by percentage of GNP), its commitment to their cherished cause of a Palestinian state has at times appeared relatively weak.

While supporting Iraq against Shiite Iran in the First Gulf War, Saudi Arabia then invited Western forces in to protect it against possible Iraqi aggression following the invasion of Kuwait in 1990, playing a significant role in the quick victory of the Allies over Saddam Hussein ■

MECCA

The holiest city of Islam, Mecca was an important centre of pilgrimage long before the birth of the Prophet Mohammed. Its chief sanctuary, then as now, was the Ka'ba, a square building housing a remarkable and much venerated black stone of probable meteoric origin, said to have been given to the patriarch Abraham by the Archangel Gabriel.

In 632, shortly before his death, the Prophet undertook his own final pilgrimage to the city; the pilgrimage to Mecca – the Hajj – remains the fifth of the Five Pillars of Islam, and every Muslim is expected to make it at least once in a lifetime.

Mecca is also part of the Second Pillar, the duty of prayer, for it is towards the Ka'ba (now enclosed by Mecca's Great Mosque) that the world's Muslims face five times daily when they pray.

At the beginning of the 20th century, Mecca was a provincial town in the Ottoman Empire; now, with a population of over 600,000, it is the administrative capital of the Western Province of Saudi Arabia. Its chief business remains, as ever, the Hajj, with upwards of 1.5 million pilgrims visiting annually. Non-Muslims (infidels) are to this day excluded from the city.

COUNTRY: Kingdom of Saudi Arabia
AREA: 2,149,690 sq km [829,995 sq mls]
POPULATION: 14,870,000
CAPITAL (Population): Riyadh (2,000,000)
GOVERNMENT: Absolute monarchy with advisory councils
ETHNIC GROUPS: Arab 92% (Saudi 82%, Yemeni 10%)
LANGUAGES: Arabic (official)
RELIGIONS: Muslim (mainly Sunni) 98%, Christian 1%
NATIONAL DAY: 23 September; Unification of the Kingdom (1932)
CURRENCY: Saudi riyal = 100 malalah
ANNUAL INCOME PER PERSON: $6,230
MAIN EXPORTS: Crude oil 83%, petrochemicals 11%
MAIN EXPORT PARTNERS: Japan 22%, USA 19%
MAIN IMPORTS: Machinery 19%, foodstuffs 17%, transport equipment 14%, textiles 13%, metals 8%
MAIN IMPORT PARTNERS: Japan 17%, USA 15%, UK 8%
DEFENCE: 36% of national budget
POPULATION DENSITY: 7 per sq km [18 per sq ml]
INFANT MORTALITY: 58 per 1,000 live births
LIFE EXPECTANCY: Female 68 yrs, male 64 yrs
ADULT LITERACY: 57%
PRINCIPAL CITIES (Population): Riyadh 2,000,000 Jedda (Jiddah) 1,400,000 Mecca 618,000 Medina 500,000

ASIA

KUWAIT

Kuwait's national flag dates from 1961, when the country ceased to be a British protectorate and gained its independence. The flag features the four Pan-Arab colours, the black portion having an unusual trapezium shape.

In winter the northern end of the Gulf comes under the influence of low-pressure systems moving eastwards from the Mediterranean and rainfall is more reliable than that further down the Gulf. In the wake of low pressure, winds blowing from the north-west bring cooler air to the region. Summers are hot and dry. The frequent *shamal* winds which blow steadily by day give way to calm, sultry nights.

The impressive if unevenly distributed prosperity built by the ruling Sabah family in Kuwait since oil was first commercially produced in 1946 was suddenly and brutally undermined by the Iraqi invasion of 1990. Occupying troops were soon expelled by a US-led multinational force – but not before they had set fire to more than 500 oil-wells (causing unprecedented pollution) and destroyed almost all industrial and commercial installations.

Kuwait's revenge over the devastation was directed mainly at the huge contingent of Palestinian, Jordanian and Yemeni immigrant workers (seen as pro-Iraq) on whom the economic progress of the country had been founded for more than two decades. Reconstruction was expected to cost hundreds of billions of dollars, but foreign investments made during the good years had produced massive funds to get it under way, using chiefly American rather than European companies ■

COUNTRY: State of Kuwait
AREA: 17,820 sq km [6,880 sq mls]
POPULATION: 2,143,000
CAPITAL (Population): Kuwait City (189,000)
GOVERNMENT: Constitutional monarchy
ETHNIC GROUPS: Kuwaiti Arab 40%, non-Kuwaiti Arab 38%, various Asian 21%
LANGUAGES: Arabic 78%, Kurdish 10%, Farsi 4%
RELIGIONS: Muslim 92% (Sunni 80%), Christian 6%
NATIONAL DAY: 25 February
CURRENCY: Kuwaiti dinar = 1,000 fils
ANNUAL INCOME PER PERSON: $16,380
MAIN EXPORTS: Petroleum and petroleum products 87%
MAIN IMPORTS: Electrical machinery, transport equipment, chemicals, iron and steel
DEFENCE: 21% of national budget
POPULATION DENSITY: 120 per sq km [311 per sq ml]
LIFE EXPECTANCY: Female 76 yrs, male 72 yrs
ADULT LITERACY: 75%

QATAR

The maroon colour of the Qatari flag is said to result from the natural effect of the sun on the traditional red banner. The proportions of the flag, which dates back to the mid-19th century (though it was not adopted until 1971), are unique.

Occupying a low, barren peninsula on the Persian Gulf, the former British protectorate of Qatar derives its high standard of living from oil and gas. Despite diversification into cement, steel and fertilizers, these still account for over 80% of revenues, and gas reserves are enormous.

The economy of the country (and many institutions) is heavily dependent on the immigrant workforce, notably from the Indian subcontinent and poorer Middle East states ■

COUNTRY: State of Qatar
AREA: 11,000 sq km [4,247 sq mls]
POPULATION: 368,000
CAPITAL (Population): Doha (217,000)
GOVERNMENT: Constitutional absolute monarchy
ETHNIC GROUPS: Southern Asian 34%, Qatari 20%
LANGUAGES: Arabic (official)
RELIGIONS: Sunni Muslim 92%, Christian, Hindu
CURRENCY: Riyal = 100 dirhams

YEMEN

The new straightforward design of Yemen's flag, incorporating the Pan-Arab colours, dates from 1990 when the Yemen Arab Republic (in the north and west) united with the People's Democratic Republic of Yemen (in the south and east).

Sana lies at over 2,000 m [6,500 ft], on the eastern side of the Yemen highlands. Temperatures are much lower than at sea level and the diurnal range is very large (over 20°C [36°F] in winter), frost occurring in winter. In August the south-west monsoon brings heavy thunderstorms. As in Ethiopia, across the Red Sea, minor rains occur in spring. The western side of the mountains, famous for its coffee plantations, is wetter and cloudier. The yearly average for sunshine hours per day is 9.5.

The optimism that greeted unification of the two Yemeni countries in May 1990 proved short-lived; support for Iraq in the Gulf War, publicized by a vote on the UN Security Council, wrought swift revenge from Iraq's Arab enemies on the ending of hostilities, with Kuwait and Saudi Arabia expelling vast numbers of Yemeni workers. This not only removed the main source of earnings for a homeland already struggling with a weak economy, but it also jeopardized hopes of much-needed foreign aid from rich Gulf nations and the West. Saudi Arabia alone forced the repatriation of some 800,000 immigrants.

It was scant reward for the successful process of marrying the disparate needs of a traditional state (an independent kingdom since 1918 and backed by the Saudis) and the failed Marxist regime based in the South Yemen capital of Aden, formerly a vital British staging post on the journey to India. Though a good deal smaller than the South, the North provided over 65% of the population.

The new nation may do well (oil was discovered on the borders only in 1984), but many observers predicted disaster for a poor rural country united more by chronic need than political wisdom ■

COUNTRY: Republic of Yemen
AREA: 527,970 sq km [203,849 sq mls]
POPULATION: 11,282,000
CAPITAL (Population): Sana (500,000)
GOVERNMENT: Multiparty democracy
ETHNIC GROUPS: Arab 96%, Somali 1%
LANGUAGES: Arabic (official)
RELIGIONS: Muslim (Sunni 53%, Zaidist Shiite 47%)
CURRENCY: Northern riyal = 100 fils and Southern dinar = 1,000 fils (co-existing during transitional period)
ANNUAL INCOME PER PERSON: $500
MAIN EXPORTS: Cotton, coffee, fish
MAIN IMPORTS: Foodstuffs, live animals, machinery
POPULATION DENSITY: 21 per sq km [55 per sq ml]
LIFE EXPECTANCY: Female 55 yrs, male 52 yrs
ADULT LITERACY: 20%

BAHRAIN

The white on Bahrain's flag is a result of the British request in 1820 that it be included in the flags of all friendly Arab states around the Persian Gulf. Red is the traditional colour of Kharijite Muslims. The flag dates from about 1932.

Bahrain island is more humid and has a smaller diurnal range of temperature than other parts of the southern Gulf. The island is noted for extreme heat and humidity in summer, particularly at Muharraq in the north-east. A hot, dry wind, the shamal, sometimes blows from the north. Winter nights are relatively chilly and heavy dew may occur. Rainfall occurs mainly as winter thunderstorms. Sunshine levels are high; November-April have 6-9 hours daily, the rest of the year having over 10 hours.

Comprising 35 small islands, by far the largest of them called Bahrain, this relatively liberal state led the region in developing oil production after discovery in 1932. When production waned in the 1970s it diversified into other sectors: its aluminium-smelting plant is the Gulf's largest non-oil industrial complex, and the moves into banking, communications and leisure came when the cosmopolitan centre of Beirut was plunging into chaos. Banking now accounts for some 15% of GDP, while oil takes as much as 20% – though far more of government revenues. Most of the land is barren, but soil imports have created some fertile areas.

Bahrain does have problems, however. Tension between the Sunni and majority Shiite population (the latter favouring an Islamic republic) has been apparent since before independence, and during the First Gulf War Iran responded to Bahrain's support for Iraq by reiterating its claims to the territory. In 1986 a rumbling dispute began with Qatar over claims to a cluster of oil-rich islands, reefs and sand-bars; the disagreement was taken by Qatar to the International Court of Justice in 1991 ■

COUNTRY: Emirate of Bahrain
AREA: 678 sq km [262 sq mls]
POPULATION: 503,000
CAPITAL (Population): Manama (152,000)
GOVERNMENT: Monarchy (emirate) with a cabinet appointed by the Emir
ETHNIC GROUPS: Bahraini Arab 68%, Persian, Indian and Pakistani 25%, other Arab 4%, European 3%
LANGUAGES: Arabic (official)
RELIGIONS: Muslim (Shiite majority) 85%, Christian 7%
NATIONAL DAY: 16 December
CURRENCY: Bahrain dinar = 1,000 fils
ANNUAL INCOME PER PERSON: $6,500
LIFE EXPECTANCY: Female 74 yrs, male 70 yrs
ADULT LITERACY: 75%

UNITED ARAB EMIRATES

When seven small states around the Persian Gulf combined to form the United Arab Emirates in 1971, this flag was agreed for the new nation. It features the Pan-Arab colours, first used in the Arab revolt against the Turks from 1916.

In 1971 six of the seven British-run Trucial States of the Gulf – Abu Dhabi, Ajman, Dubai, Fujairah, Sharjah and Umm al-Qaiwain – opted to form the United Arab Emirates (UAE), with Ras al-Khaimah joining in 1972. It could have been a federation of nine, but Bahrain and Qatar chose independence. Abu Dhabi is more than six times the size of the other countries put together, has the largest population and is easily the biggest oil producer. Nevertheless, the capitals of Dubai and Sharjah also contain over 250,000 people.

Though mainly low-lying desert, the UAE's oil and gas have provided the highest GNP per capita figure in Asia after Japan. However, only 20% of the population are citizens – the rest are expatriate workers – and traditional values, sustained by the control of the emirs, remain strong ■

COUNTRY: United Arab Emirates
AREA: 83,600 sq km [32,278 sq mls]
POPULATION: 1,589,000
CAPITAL (Population): Abu Dhabi (293,000)
GOVERNMENT: Monarchy with an advisory council
ETHNIC GROUPS: Arab 87%, Indo-Pakistani 9%, Iranian 2%
LANGUAGES: Arabic (official), English
RELIGIONS: Muslim 96% (Sunni 80%, Shiite 16%)
NATIONAL DAY: 2 December; National Day (1971)
CURRENCY: UAE dirham = 100 fils
ANNUAL INCOME PER PERSON: $19,860
DEFENCE: 37% of national budget
POPULATION DENSITY: 19 per sq km [49 per sq ml]
LIFE EXPECTANCY: Female 74 yrs, male 70 yrs
ADULT LITERACY: 73%

OMAN

Formerly Muscat and Oman, the state's flag was plain red – the traditional colour of the people who lived in the area. When Oman was established in 1970, the state arms of sword and dagger were added with stripes of white and green.

Backward compared to its oil-rich Persian Gulf neighbours to the west until 1970 – when with British collusion Sultan Said was deposed by his son Qaboos – Oman has since made substantial strides, seeing an end to the civil war against Yemen-backed left-wing separatist guerrillas in the southern province of Dhofar (Zufar) and enjoying an expanding economy based on oil reserves far larger than expected when production began modestly in 1967. Petroleum now accounts for more than 90% of government revenues – and because of Oman's detached situation the industry was not hit by the lack of confidence that afflicted the Gulf states in the 1991 war. In addition, huge natural gas reserves were discovered in 1991 that were equal in size to all the finds of the previous 20 years. There are also some copper deposits.

An absolute ruler – as his family heads have been since 1749 – Qaboos has tended to forego the usual prestigious projects so favoured by wealthy Arab leaders, in favour of social programmes. Even so, by 1989 only one in five adults of this arid, inhospitable country were literate (less than 1% of the land is cultivated) and defence and internal security were taking more than 40% of the annual budget ■

COUNTRY: Sultanate of Oman
AREA: 212,460 sq km [82,031 sq mls]
POPULATION: 1,502,000
CAPITAL (Population): Muscat (250,000)
GOVERNMENT: Monarchy with a consultative council
ETHNIC GROUPS: Omani Arab 77% other Asian 25%
LANGUAGES: Arabic (official), Baluchi, English
RELIGIONS: Muslim 86% (Ibadi 75%)
NATIONAL DAY: 18 November
CURRENCY: Omani rial = 1,000 baizas
DEFENCE: 33% of national budget
POPULATION DENSITY: 7 per sq km [18 per sq ml]
LIFE EXPECTANCY: Female 60 yrs, male 57 yrs

IRAQ

Using the four Pan-Arab colours, Iraq's flag was adopted in 1963 at the time of the proposed federation with Egypt and Syria. Iraq retained the three green stars, symbolizing the three countries, even though the union failed to materialize.

The central plains of Iraq experience the extremes of temperature typical of continental interiors. Winters are cool with occasional frost; temperatures below 10°C [50°F] can be expected at night November–March. Rain falls between November and April when low-pressure systems invade from the west. In summer it is dry and hot. Shamal winds from the north-west raise dust and sand storms by day. Heat and humidity increase southwards towards the Gulf.

A bsorbed into the Ottoman (Turkish) Empire in the 16th century, Iraq was captured by British forces in 1916 and after World War I became a virtual colony as a League of Nations mandated territory run by Britain. The Hashemite dynasty ruled an independent kingdom from 1932 (British occupation 1941–5), but in 1958 the royal family and premier were murdered in a military coup that set up a republic. Ten years later, after struggles between Communists and Pan-Arab Baathists, officers for the latter seized control. From 1969 the vice-president of this single-party government was Saddam Hussein, who in a peaceful transfer of power became president in 1979. The next year he invaded neighbouring Iran.

The country includes a hilly district in the north-east, and in the west a large slice of the Hamad or Syrian Desert; but essentially it comprises the lower valleys and deltas of the Tigris and Euphrates. Rainfall is meagre, but the alluvium is fertile.

The north-east of Iraq includes part of the Zagros Mountains, where fruits and grains grow without the help of irrigation. The Kirkuk oilfield is the country's oldest and largest, and nearby the Lesser Zab River has been impounded behind a high dam. The population here includes many Turks, and Kurdish tribes akin to those in Iran.

In addition to the Kirkuk oilfield, which exports by pipeline through Syria and Lebanon, there are reserves of oil near Mosul, Khanaqin and Basra. Basra is connected to the Gulf by the crucial Shatt-al-Arab Waterway, shared with Iran and the ostensible cause of the First Gulf War (Iran-Iraq War).

The Gulf Wars

Supplied with financial help and arms by the West, the Soviets and conservative Arab countries, all of whom shared a fear of the new Islamic fundamentalism in Iran, Saddam amassed the fourth largest army in the world by 1980. His attack on Iran was meant to be a quick, land-grabbing, morale-boosting victory. Instead it led to an eight-year modern version of Flanders which drained Iraqi resolve (over a million men were killed or wounded, many of them fighting fellow Shiites), and nearly crippled a healthy if oil-dependent economy that had, despite colossal defence spending, financed a huge development programme in the 1970s. Even then, Iraq was still the world's sixth biggest oil producer in 1988, and Saddam's regime continued to enjoy support from Western countries.

If Iraq was hit by this long war, it was decimated by the Second Gulf War. In August 1990 Saddam, having accused Kuwait of wrecking Baghdad's

COUNTRY: Republic of Iraq
AREA: 438,320 sq km [169,235 sq mls]
POPULATION: 18,920,000
CAPITAL (Population): Baghdad (4,649,000)
GOVERNMENT: Unitary single-party republic
ETHNIC GROUPS: Arab 79%, Kurd 16%, Turkmen 2%, Persian 2%
NATIONAL DAY: 17 July; Military revolution (1958)
LANGUAGES: Arabic (official), Kurdish, Turkish
RELIGIONS: Shiite Muslim 54%, Sunni Muslim 42%
CURRENCY: Iraqi dinar = 20 dirhams = 1,000 fils
ANNUAL INCOME PER PERSON: $2,000
MAIN PRIMARY PRODUCTS: Crude oil, natural gas, dates, cattle, sheep, cereals, goats, camels
MAIN INDUSTRIES: Oil and gas production, food processing, textiles
MAIN EXPORTS: Fuels and other energy 98%
MAIN IMPORTS: Machinery and transport equipment 40%, manufactured goods 27%, foodstuffs 16%, chemicals 8%
POPULATION DENSITY: 43 per sq km [112 per sq ml]
LIFE EXPECTANCY: Female 67 yrs, male 65 yrs
ADULT LITERACY: 60%
PRINCIPAL CITIES (Population): Baghdad 4,649,000 Basra 617,000 Mosul 571,000

economy by exceeding its oil quota and forcing prices down, ordered the invasion of Kuwait, then annexed it as an Iraqi province. It gave him more oil and far better access to the Gulf. Unlike a decade before, the international community were almost unanimous in their condemnation of the invasion and following the imposition of sanctions a multinational force – led by the USA but backed primarily by Britain, France and Saudi Arabia – was dispatched to the Gulf to head off possible Iraqi move on to Saudi oilfields.

After Saddam failed to accede to repeated UN demands to withdraw his troops, the Second Gulf War began on 16 January 1991 with an Anglo-American air attack on Baghdad, and in late February a land-sea-air campaign freed Kuwait after just 100 hours, Iraq accepting all the terms of the UN ceasefire and coalition troops occupying much of southern Iraq. This did not prevent the brutal suppression of West-inspired revolts by Shiites in the south and Kurds in the north, millions of whom fled their homes. International efforts were made to help these refugees, some of whom had fled to Iran and, less successfully, Turkey.

Saddam Hussein, though surviving in power, was left an international leper in charge of a pitiful country. Much of the infrastructure had been destroyed in the war, disease was rife and food scarce, trade had virtually ceased and oil production was near a standstill. Sanctions, war damage and mismanagement have combined to cause economic chaos and personal hardship, and normal life is unlikely to return until the establishment of a regime acceptable to the rest of the international community; that, in turn, means the end of Saddam ■

IRAN

Iran's flag has been in use since July 1980 after the fall of the Shah and the rise of Ayatollah Khomeini. Along the edges of the stripes is the legend 'Allah Akbar' (God is Great) repeated 22 times; in the centre is the new national emblem.

Tehran lies at over 1,200 m [4,000 ft] on the high Iranian plateau, enclosed on all sides by mountains, and experiences the dryness and extreme temperatures of a continental climate. Rain falls on only about 30 days in the year. Summers are hot, sunny and dry with low humidity. Most of the rain falls in winter and spring. Winters are cold with strong north-west winds. Snow and frost occur in most years. The annual range of temperature is over 25°C [45°F].

The most populous and productive parts of Iran lie at the four extremities – the fisheries, rice fields and tea gardens of the Caspian shore in the foothills of the earthquake zone to the north, the sugar plantations and oilfields of Khuzestan to the south (target of the Iraqi invasion in 1980), the wheat fields of Azarbayjan in the west, and the fruit groves of the oases of Khorasan and Seistan in the east. In between are the deserts of Kavir and Lut, and the border ranges which broaden in the west into the high plateaus of the Zagros, the summer retreats of the tribes of Bakhtiars and Kurds.

The cities of the interior depend on ingenious arrangements of tunnels and channels for tapping underground water, and these have been supplemented by high dams, notably at Dezful. The burgeoning capital of Tehran is the crossing-point of the country's two great railways, the Trans-Iranian from the Gulf to the Caspian and the east-west track from Mashhad to Tabriz.

The Islamic Revolution

Called Persia until 1935, the country retained its Shah – thanks first to British and later American support – until 1979, when the emperor's extravagantly corrupt regime (a single-party affair from 1975) was toppled by a combination of students, middle-class professionals and, above, all, clerics offended by the style and pace of Westernization.

The despotism was replaced with another: that of a radical fundamentalist Islamic republic inspired by the return of exiled leader Ayatollah Khomeini. The revolution created a new threat to the conservative Arabs of the Gulf and beyond, who saw it as a dangerous call to challenge the flimsy legitimacy of their own oil-rich governments. The effect would rumble round the Muslim world: 12 years later, in far-off Algeria, the Islamic Salvation Front won the democratic elections.

Many Arab states were less hostile, however, and despite Iranian backing of a series of international terrorist attacks and hostage takings linked to the Palestinian issue, their regime won respect for the steadfast way they fought the Iraqis from 1980–8, when hundreds of thousands of zealous young Shiite men died defending their homeland.

The war left Iran's vital oil production at less than half the level of 1979 (though still seventh highest in the world and supported by the largest known gas reserves outside Russia), and the government began to court the Western powers. Iran's stance during the Second Gulf War (albeit predictable) and a tempering of the militant position to one of peace-broker on international issues – led by President Rafsanjani – encouraged many powers to re-establish closer links with a country whose role took on even greater significance with the Muslim republics of the former Soviet Union to the north gaining independence from Moscow in 1991 ■

COUNTRY: Islamic Republic of Iran

AREA: 1,648,000 sq km [636,293 sq mls]

POPULATION: 58,031,000

CAPITAL (Population): Tehran (6,043,000)

GOVERNMENT: Unitary Islamic republic, religious leader (elected by Council of Experts) exercises supreme authority

ETHNIC GROUPS: Persian 46%, Azerbaijani 17%, Kurdish 9%, Gilaki 5%, Luri, Mazandarani, Baluchi, Arab

LANGUAGES: Farsi (Persian) 48% (official), Kurdish, Baluchi, Turkic, Arabic, French

RELIGIONS: Shiite Muslim 91%, Sunni Muslim 8%

NATIONAL DAY: 1 April; Islamic Republic Day (1979)

CURRENCY: Rial = 100 dinars

ANNUAL INCOME PER PERSON: $2,450

MAIN PRIMARY PRODUCTS: Crude oil, natural gas, lead, chrome, copper, iron, sheep, cattle, cereals, timber

MAIN INDUSTRIES: Oil refining, gas, steel, textiles, electrical goods, fishing, sugar, flour milling

MAIN EXPORTS: Petroleum products 98%

MAIN IMPORTS: Machinery and transport equipment 33%, iron and steel 15%, foodstuffs 13%

DEFENCE: 12% of national budget

TOURISM: 69,000 visitors per year

POPULATION DENSITY: 35 per sq km [91 per sq ml]

INFANT MORTALITY: 53 per 1,000 live births

LIFE EXPECTANCY: Female 68 yrs, male 67 yrs

ADULT LITERACY: 51%

PRINCIPAL CITIES (Population): Tehran 6,043,000 Mashhad 1,464,000 Esfahan 987,000 Tabriz 971,000 Shiraz 848,000

THE KURDS

With between 15 and 17 million people dispersed across the territories of five countries – Turkey (8 million), Iran, Iraq, Syria and Armenia – the Kurds form the world's largest stateless nation, and they are likely to remain so. The 1920 Treaty of Sävres, a postwar settlement designed to dismember the old Ottoman Empire, proposed a scheme for Kurdish independence, but it was never implemented.

Neither Arab nor Turk, the Kurds are predominantly Sunni Muslims, and in the past have provided more than their fair share of Islam's leaders: indeed, Saladin, the near-legendary nemesis of the Crusaders, was a Kurd. Now, as in the past, the Kurds are an agricultural people; many earn their living by pastoralism, a way of life that pays little attention to borders or the governments that attempt to control them. Since World War II, they have suffered consistent repression by most of their titular overlords. Turkey has regularly used armed force against Kurdish nationalists; an uprising in Iran was put down in 1979–80, and during the Iran-Iraq war of the 1980s, Iraqi forces used chemical weapons – as well as more orthodox brutality – against Kurdish settlements.

The defeat of Iraqi dictator Saddam Hussein by Coalition forces in 1991 inspired another massive uprising, but Saddam's badly weakened army still proved quite capable of murdering Kurdish women and children on a scale that provoked a limited Western intervention. The outcome, though, was upwards of 1.5 million Kurds living in refugee camps, with the dream of Kurdistan no nearer realization.

AFGHANISTAN

After many design changes in the late 1970s, Afghanistan readopted its traditional colours in 1980 and added the new state emblem. This includes a pulpit, sheaves of wheat, a rising sun and red star, and a copy of the Koran.

The climate of Afghanistan is governed more by its high altitude and being cut off by mountain ranges than by its latitude. From December to March the air masses come from the cold continental north and bring very cold weather and snow on the mountains. June to September is very hot and dry, with the east getting some rain from a weakened monsoon. Kabul, at 2,000 m [6,000 ft], has a range of temperature from -5°C to 25°C [23–77°F]. There are over ten hours of sunshine daily, May–August.

Nearly three-quarters of Afghanistan is mountainous, comprising most of the Hindu Kush and its foothills, with several peaks over 6,400 m [21,000 ft], and much of the rest is desert or semi-desert. However, the restoration of the Helmand canals has brought fertility to the far south-west, and the sweet waters of the Hamun support fish and cattle; the plains of the north, near the borders with Turkmenistan, Uzbekistan and Tajikistan, yield most of the country's limited agriculture.

The most profitable crop may well be opium, from poppies grown in the hills of the Pathans adjoining Pakistan's North-West Frontier province. With the Islamic Revolution in Iran and the crackdown in the 'Golden Triangle' of Laos, Burma and Thailand, Pakistan became the world's biggest source of heroin (the derivative drug); but while US pressure saw the Pakistani government start to control production on its side of the border, it could do little to stem the flow from Afghanistan – a prime source of revenue for the Mujaheddin's fight against occupying Soviet forces in the 1980s.

History and politics

Landlocked Afghanistan has always been in a critical position in Asia: the Khyber Pass was both the gateway to India and the back door to Russia. Since earliest times it has been invaded by Persians, Greeks, Arabs, Mongols, Tartars and the British, who finally failed in their attempts to create a buffer state between India and Russia and bowed to Afghan independence after the Third Afghan War in 1921. The latest invaders, entering the country on Christmas Day 1979, were 80,000 men of the Soviet army.

The Russian forces were sent in support of a Kremlin-inspired coup that removed a revolutionary council set up after the ousting of the pro-Soviet government of Mohammed Daud Khan. Killed in that 1978 coup – the Saur Revolution – Daud Khan had been in power since 1953, first as prime minister and then, after he toppled the monarchy in 1972, as founder, president and prime minister of a fiercely pro-Soviet single-party republic.

The Saur Revolution and subsequent Soviet occupation led to a bitter and protracted civil war, the disparate Muslim tribes uniting behind the banner of the Mujaheddin ('holy warriors') to wage an unrelenting guerrilla war financed by the US and oiled with the co-operation of Pakistan. Despite their vastly superior weaponry and resources, the Soviet forces found it impossible to control the mountain-based rebels in a country the size of Texas, and Afghanistan quickly threatened to turn into an unwinnable war – Moscow's 'Vietnam'.

President Gorbachev began moves to end the conflict soon after coming to power in 1985, and in 1988 a ceasefire was agreed involving both Afghanistan and Pakistan, its main overt ally. In February 1989 the Soviet troops withdrew, leaving the cities in the hands of the pro-Moscow government and the countryside under the control of the Mujaheddin; the civil war intensified, however, fuelled by internecine and traditional feuds.

The war, which cost over a million Afghanis their lives, left what was an already impoverished state almost totally crippled. Before the Soviet invasion Afghanistan had one of the world's poorest records for infant mortality, literacy, women's rights and a host of other measurements, but the occupation also reduced the economy to ruins. Before the 1978 Marxist revolution Afghanis abroad sent home remittances worth some $125 million, and tourism brought in about $50 million; now all that had gone. Based on natural gas, exports were not helped by the decision of the USSR to cap the wells in 1989.

The greatest problem, however, was the one of refugees. Some 2 million people had moved into crowded cities and towns to avoid the Russian shelling, but far more – somewhere between 3 million and 5 million by most accounts, but nearer 6 million according to the UN Commissioner – fled the country altogether, predominantly to Pakistan. This latter estimate, the UN stated in 1990, was around 42% of the entire world total of displaced persons.

In the spring of 1992, after a prolonged onslaught by the Mujaheddin, the government in Kabul finally surrendered, bequeathing an uncertain future to the country ■

COUNTRY: Republic of Afghanistan

AREA: 652,090 sq km [251,772 sq mls]

POPULATION: 16,433,000

CAPITAL (Population): Kabul (1,127,000)

GOVERNMENT: Unitary single-party People's Republic

ETHNIC GROUPS: Pashtun ('Pathan') 52%, Tajik 20%, Uzbek 9%, Hazara 9%, Chahar, Turkmen, Baluchi

LANGUAGES: Pashto (50%), Dari Persian

RELIGIONS: Sunni Muslim 74%, Shiite Muslim 25%

NATIONAL DAY: 27 April; Anniversary of Saur Revolution

CURRENCY: Afghani = 100 puls

ANNUAL INCOME PER PERSON: $450

MAIN INDUSTRIES: Agriculture, carpets, textiles

MAIN EXPORTS: Natural gas 42%, dried fruit 26%, fresh fruit 9%, carpets and rugs 7%

MAIN EXPORT PARTNERS: CIS nations 55%, Pakistan 16%, India 12%

MAIN IMPORTS: Wheat 5%, vegetable oil 4%, sugar 3%

MAIN IMPORT PARTNERS: CIS nations 62%, Japan 13%

POPULATION DENSITY: 25 per sq km [65 per sq ml]

INFANT MORTALITY: 162 per 1,000 live births

LIFE EXPECTANCY: Female 44 yrs, male 43 yrs

ADULT LITERACY: 20%

PAKISTAN

Pakistan's flag was adopted when the country gained independence from Britain in 1947. The green, the crescent moon and five-pointed star are traditionally associated with Islam. The white stripe represents Pakistan's other religions.

Lahore, situated to the south-west of the Himalayas, has a higher rainfall than Karachi, but still with a marked July–August maxima. Temperatures in the summer are very high with over 40°C [104°F] having been recorded in every month March–October, and averages of over 20–30°C [68–86°F]. Night temperatures in winter are very chilly. The annual variation of temperature in Lahore is about 20°C [36°F], while at Karachi it is only 11°C [20°F].

As Egypt is the gift of the Nile, so Pakistan is the gift of the Indus and its tributaries. Despite modern industrialization, irrigated farming is vital to this Islamic state, both in Punjab, the 'land of the five rivers' – Indus, Jhelum, Beas, Ravi and Sutlej – and on the dry plains flanking the Indus between Khairpur and Hyderabad. The stations at Tarbela (on the Indus) and Mangla (on the Jhelum) are among the world's biggest earth- and rock-filled dams.

West of the Indus delta the arid coastal plain of Makran rises first to the Coast Range, then in successive ridges to the north – stark, arid, deforested and eroded. Between the ridges lie desert basins like that containing the saltmarsh of Hamun-i-Mashkel on the Iranian border. Ridge and basin alternate through Baluchistan and the earthquake zone round Quetta, the *daman-i-koh* ('skirts of the hills') still irrigated by the ancient tunnels called *karez* or *qanats*, for growing cereals and fruit.

North again stretches the famous North-West Frontier province, pushing up between the towering Hindu Kush and Karakoram, with K2 on the border with China the world's second highest mountain at 8,611 m [28,251 ft]. East of Peshawar lies Kashmir, which Pakistan controls to the west of the 1947 ceasefire line, and India to the east. The ceasefire ended war and appalling internecine slaughter that followed the grant of independence from Britain, when the old Indian Empire was divided between India and Pakistan – Hindu and Muslim states. The Kashmir problem was partly religious – a mainly Muslim population ruled by a Hindu maharaja who acceded to India – but there was also an underlying strategic issue: five rivers rising in or passing through Kashmir or the neighbouring Indian state of Himachal Pradesh are vital to Pakistan's economy, and could not be left in the hands of possible enemies.

Like most developing countries, Pakistan has increased both mineral exploitation and manufacturing industry. To the small oil and coal field near Rawalpindi has now been added a major resource of natural gas between Sukkur and Multan. Karachi, formerly the capital and developed in the colonial period as a wheat port, is now a considerable manufacturing centre, principally textiles; so is the cultural centre, Lahore, in the north. The well-planned national capital of Islamabad, begun in the 1960s, is still growing to the north-east of Rawalpindi, with the outline of the Murree Hills – refuge for the wealthier citizens on weekends – as a backdrop to the architecture of the new city.

The world's ninth most populous country, Pakistan is likely to be overtaken by Bangladesh – its former partner separated by 1,600 km [1,000 mls] of India – by the end of the century. Then East Pakistan, Bangladesh broke away from the western wing of the nation in 1971, following a bitter civil war and Indian military intervention, but neither country state has enjoyed political stability or sound government.

Pakistan has been subject to military rule and martial law for much of its short life, interspersed with periods of fragile democracy resting on army consent. During one such, in 1988, Benazir Bhutto – daughter of the president executed after his government (the country's first elected civilian administration) was overthrown by the army in 1977 – was freely elected prime minister, the first female premier in the Muslim world. Two years later she was dismissed by the president following accusations of nepotism and corruption.

'West' Pakistan's economy has also done better than poor Bangladesh, while reserves of some minerals (notably bauxite, copper, phosphates and manganese) have yet to be exploited. Yet there are huge problems: dependence on textiles, an increasingly competitive area, and on remittances from Pakistani workers abroad, especially in the Middle East (the main source of foreign income); a chronic trade deficit and debt burden; massive spending on defence and security; growing drug traffic through the North-West Frontier; and the added pressure of some 5 million Afghan refugees who fled the civil war in their homeland. However, the fall of Kabul to Afghan Mujaheddin rebels in the spring of 1992 brought the prospect of an improvement in Pakistan's refugee problem – though it also raised the prospect of renewed Pathan nationalism ■

COUNTRY: Islamic Republic of Pakistan

AREA: 796,100 sq km [307,374 sq mls]

POPULATION: 112,050,000

CAPITAL: (Population): Islamabad (204,000)

GOVERNMENT: Federal republic

ETHNIC GROUPS: Punjabi 60%, Sindhi 12%, Pushtun 13%, Baluch, Muhajir

LANGUAGES: Urdu 8% (official), Punjabi 60%, Pashto 13%, Sindhi 12%, Baluchi, Brahvi, English (official)

RELIGIONS: Muslim 96% (predominantly Sunni), Hindu, Christian, Buddhist

NATIONAL DAY: 23 March; Republic Day (1956)

CURRENCY: Pakistan rupee = 100 paisa

ANNUAL INCOME PER PERSON: $380

MAIN PRIMARY PRODUCTS: Cotton, rice, sugar cane, cereals, dates, tobacco, natural gas, iron ore

MAIN INDUSTRIES: Agriculture, cotton, oil refining

MAIN EXPORTS: Raw cotton 14%, cotton yarn 12%, cotton fabrics 11%, rice 8%, leather 6%, carpets 6%

MAIN EXPORT PARTNERS: Japan 11%, USA 11%, Germany 7%, UK 7%, Italy 6%, Saudi Arabia 5%

MAIN IMPORTS: Machinery 18%, mineral oils 16%, chemicals 9%, transport equipment 9%

MAIN IMPORT PARTNERS: Japan 15%, USA 11%, Germany 8%, Kuwait 7%, UK 7%, Saudi Arabia 5%

DEFENCE: 35% of national budget

POPULATION DENSITY: 137 per sq km [354 per sq ml]

LIFE EXPECTANCY: Female 59 yrs, male 59 yrs

ADULT LITERACY: 30%

The summer monsoon rains decrease rapidly in intensity from the Indian penisula westwards into Pakistan, leaving much of the Indus lowland arid. Rain falls on only about 20 days in the year, half of these in July and August. Karachi is hot throughout the year but, being on the coast, has a smaller range of temperature than inland. The summer rains are thundery and vary greatly in intensity from year to year. Small amounts of winter rain are brought by low-pressure systems from the west.

INDIA

India's flag evolved during the struggle for freedom from British rule. The orange represents the Hindu majority, green the country's many Muslims and white peace. The Buddhist wheel symbol was added on independence in 1947.

The summer rains, typical of the Indian monsoon, arrive later and are less intense at Delhi than in the lower parts of the Ganges Valley. From November to May, the dry season, there is abundant sunshine and temperature increases rapidly until the arrival of the rains in June. During the rainy season the temperature is uniformly hot, with little diurnal variation. The latter part of the year is sunny, dry and much cooler. Night temperatures December–February are usually below 10°C [50°F].

A diamond-shaped country – the world's seventh largest – India extends from high in the Himalayas through the Tropic of Cancer to the warm waters of the Indian Ocean at 8°N. More than 800 million people live here in the world's second most populous state – and its largest democracy.

Landscape and agriculture

The mountainous north: The Himalayan foothills make a stunning backdrop for northern India, rising abruptly from the plains in towering ranks. Harsh dry highlands, sparsely occupied by herdsmen, stretch northwards to the everlasting snows of the Karakoram. Below lie alpine meadows, lakes and woodlands, often grazed in summer by seasonally migrant flocks from lower villages. The fertile Vale of Kashmir has emerald-green rice-terraces, walnut and plane trees, and apple and apricot orchards around half-timbered villages.

The wet, forested eastern Himalayas of Assam are ablaze with rhododendrons and magnolias, and terraced for buckwheat, barley and rice-growing. The high plateau of Meghalaya ('abode of the clouds') is damp and cool; nearby Cherrapunji has one of the highest rainfalls in the world. Tropical oaks and teaks on the forest ridges of Nagaland, Manipur and Mizoram, bordering Burma, alternate with rice-patches and small towns; on the hilltops dry cultivation of rice is practised.

The plains: The great plains form a continuous strip from the Punjab eastwards. Heavily irrigated by canals engineered in the late 19th century, the rich alluvial soils have provided prosperity for Sikh and Jat farmers of the Punjab and Haryana. Here are grown winter wheat and summer rice, cotton and sugar cane with sorghum in the drier areas, the successful agriculture forming a foundation for linked industrial development.

Somewhat similar landscapes extend east to the plains surrounding Delhi, India's third largest city on the west bank of the Jumna (Yamuna) River. An ancient site, occupied for over 3,000 years, it now includes the Indian capital New Delhi, designed by Sir Edwin Lutyens and built from 1912. Old city and new lie at a focal point of road and rail links, and like many Indian cities rapidly became overcrowded. To the east again are the lowlands of Uttar Pradesh, criss-crossed by the Ganges and Jumna rivers and their many tributaries. Slightly wetter, but less irrigated, these plains are farmed less for wheat and rice than for spiked millet and sorghum.

Among the most densely populated areas of India (the state of Uttar Pradesh has a population larger than Nigeria, Pakistan or Bangladesh), these lowlands support dozens of cities and smaller settlements – notably Agra, with its Red Fort and Taj Mahal, and the sacred cities of Allahabad and Varanasi (Benares). Along the Nepal border the *terai* or hillfoot plains, formerly malaria-infested swamp forest, have now been cleared and made healthy for prosperous farming settlements.

Downstream from Tinpahar ('three hills'), near the Bangladeshi border, the Ganges begins its deltaic splitting into distributary streams, while still receiving tributaries from the north and west. West Bengal consists largely of the rice- and jute-growing lands flanking the distributary streams that flow south to become the Hooghly, on which Calcutta is built. The Ganges-Kobadak barrage now provides irrigation for the north of this tract, while improving both water supply and navigation lower down the Hooghly. The Sundarbans – mangrove and swamp forests at the seaward margin of the Ganges delta – extend eastwards into Bangladesh.

South-west from the Punjab plains lies the Thar or Great Indian Desert, its western fringes in Pakistan but with a broad tract of dunes in the northeastern lowlands in Rajasthan, India's largest state. The desert ranges from perenially dry wastelands of shifting sand to areas capable of cultivation in wet years. As the name Rajasthan implies, this state was once (until 1950) a land of rajahs and princes, palaces and temples. Rajasthan rises in a series of steps to a jagged, bare range of brightly-coloured

Calcutta has a tropical monsoon climate with wind flow in winter the reverse of that in summer. In winter, north-westerlies bring dry, sunny weather with a large daily range of temperature of about 14°C [25°F]. By May, the increasing intensity of the sun gives rise to thunderstorms which precede the northwards sweep of the summer monsoon across the Bay of Bengal, bringing four months of heavy rain and constant high temperature and humidity.

sandstone ridges, the Aravallis, that extend north-eastwards and end at Delhi.

South and west of the Aravallis lie the cotton-growing lands of tropical Gujarat; Ahmadabad is its chief city. Between the Gulfs of Khambhat and Kachchh is the low peninsular plateau of Kathiawar, whose declining deciduous forests still harbour small groups of tribal peoples, and indeed the last of India's native lions. Between this and the Pakistan border stretches the desert saltmarsh of the Rann of Kachchh, once an arm of the Arabian Sea and still occasionally flooded by exceptionally heavy rains.

South-east of the Aravallis is an area of transition between the great plains of the north and the uplands and plateaus of peninsular India. First come the Chambal badlands (wastelands south of Agra, now partly reclaimed), then rough hill country extending south-eastwards to Rewa. The River Sone provides a lowland corridor through the hills south of Rewa, and an irrigation barrage provides water for previously arid lands west of Gaya. Eastwards again the hills are forested around Ambikapur and Lohardaga. Industrial development becomes important around the coalfields of the Damodar Valley, centred on Asansol and the developing steel town of Jamshedpur.

Peninsular India: South of the Chambal River and of Indore (a princely capital until 1950) the sandy plateau of the north gives way to forested hills, split by the broad corridors of the Narmada and Tapi rivers. Tribal lands persist in the Satpura Range, and the Ajanta Range to the south is noted for primitive cave paintings near Aurangabad. From here to the south volcanic soils predominate.

Bombay, India's second largest city, lies on the coastal lowlands by a broad estuary, among rice-fields dotted with low lava ridges. Fishing villages with coconut palms line the shore, while inland rise the stepped, forested slopes and pinnacles of peninsular India's longest mountain chain, the Western Ghats (Sahyadri).

East of the Ghats stretch seemingly endless expanses of cotton and sorghum cultivation. Arid in late winter and spring, and parched by May, they spring to life when the rains break in late May or June. The sleepy market towns follow a similar rhythm, full of activity when the agricultural cycle demands, and then relaxing under the broiling sun.

South from the holiday beaches of Goa (formerly a Portuguese enclave, still Portuguese in flavour), past busy Mangalore, Calicut and Cochin to the state capital of Kerala, Trivandrum, the coast becomes a kaleidoscope of coconut groves and fishing villages, ricefields, scrublands, cashew orchards and tapioca plantations. Here the Ghats are edged with granite, gneiss, sandstone and schist, and clad in heavy rainforest. To the east the peninsula is drier, with rolling plateaus given over to the production of millet, pulses and other dry crops. Sugar, rice and spices are grown where simple engineering provides tanks, stopped with earth or masonry dams, to save

the summer rains; now canals peform the same task. Bangalore and Hyderabad, once sleepy capitals of princely states, are now bustling cities, respectively capitals of Karnataka and Andhra Pradesh.

History

India's earliest settlers were widely scattered across the subcontinent in Stone Age times. The first of its many civilizations developed in the Indus Valley about 2600 BC, and in the Ganges Valley from about 1500 BC. By the 4th and 3rd centuries BC Pataliputra (modern Patna) formed the centre of a loosely-held empire that extended across the peninsula and beyond into Afghanistan. This first Indian empire broke up after the death of the Emperor Asoka in 232 BC, to be replaced by many others. The Portuguese who crossed the Indian Ocean in the late 15th century, and the British, Danes, French and Dutch who soon followed, found a subcontinent divided and ripe for plundering.

As a result of battles fought both in Europe and in India itself, Britain gradually gained ascendancy over both European rivals and local factions within the subcontinent; by 1805 the British East India

THE HIMALAYAS

The Earth's highest mountain range, with an average height of 6,100 m [20,000 ft], the Himalayas are structurally part of the high plateau of Central Asia. The range stretches over 2,400 km [1,500 mls] from the Pamirs in the north-west to the Chinese border in the east. There are three main ranges: Outer, Middle and Inner; in Kashmir, the Inner Himalayas divide into five more ranges, including the Ladakh Range and the Karakorams. The world's highest mountain, Mt Everest (8,848 m [29,029 ft]) is on the Tibet-Nepal border; next highest is K2 (8,611 m [28,251 ft]) in the Karakorams, and there are a further six peaks over 8,000 m [26,250 ft].

The name comes from the Nepalese words *him* ('snows') and *alya* ('home of'), and the mountains are much revered in Hindu mythology, as the abode of gods. Recently, the hydroelectric potential of the range has inspired more secular reverence: enormous quantities of energy could be tapped, although certainly at some cost to one of the world's most pristine environments.

COUNTRY: Republic of India

AREA: 3,287,590 sq km [1,269,338 sq mls]

POPULATION: 843,931,000

CAPITAL: New Delhi (part of Delhi)

GOVERNMENT: Multiparty federal republic with bicameral legislature

ETHNIC GROUPS: Indo-Aryan (Caucasoid) 72%, Dravidian (Aboriginal) 25%, others (mainly Mongoloid) 3%

LANGUAGES: Hindi 30% and English (both official), Telugu 8%, Bengali 8%, Marati 8%, Urdu 5%, and over 70 others

RELIGIONS: Hindu 83%, Sunni Muslim 11%, Christian 2%, Sikh 2%, Buddhist 1%

NATIONAL DAY: 26 January; Republic Day (1950)

CURRENCY: Indian rupee = 100 paisa

ANNUAL INCOME PER PERSON: $350

SOURCE OF INCOME: Agriculture 32%, industry 30%, services 38%

MAIN PRIMARY PRODUCTS: Wheat, sugar cane, rice, millet, sorghum, jute, barley, tea, cattle, coal, iron ore, lead, zinc, diamonds, oil and natural gas, bauxite, chromite, copper, manganese

MAIN INDUSTRIES: Textiles, chemicals, petroleum products, oil refining, jute, cement, fertilizers, food processing, diesel engines, beverages, iron and steel

EXPORTS: $19 per person

MAIN EXPORTS: Gems and jewellery 17%, clothing 9%, leather and leather manufactures 6%, machinery and transport equipment 6%, cotton fabrics 5%, tea and maté 4%

MAIN EXPORT PARTNERS: USA 19%, CIS nations 15%, Japan 10%, Germany 6%, UK 6%

IMPORTS: $24 per person

MAIN IMPORTS: Non-electrical machinery 18%, mineral fuels 13%, iron and steel 7%, pearls, precious and semi-precious stones 7%, electrical machinery 4%, transport equipment 3%, edible vegetable oil 3%

MAIN IMPORT PARTNERS: Japan 13%, USA 10%, Germany 9%, UK 8%, CIS nations 5%

EDUCATIONAL EXPENDITURE: 14% of national budget

DEFENCE: 27.6% of national budget

TOTAL ARMED FORCES: 1,260,000

TOURISM: 1,164,000 visitors per year

ROADS: 1,772,000 km [1,101,000 mls]

RAILWAYS: 61,810 km [38,407 mls]

POPULATION DENSITY: 257 per sq km [665 per sq ml]

URBAN POPULATION: 28%

POPULATION GROWTH: 1.9% per year

BIRTHS: 30 per 1,000 population

DEATHS: 10 per 1,000 population

INFANT MORTALITY: 88 per 1,000 live births

LIFE EXPECTANCY: Female 61 yrs, male 60 yrs

POPULATION PER DOCTOR: 2,521

ADULT LITERACY: 43%

PRINCIPAL CITIES (Population): Calcutta 9,194,000 Bombay 8,243,000 Delhi 5,729,000 Madras 4,289,000 Bangalore 2,922,000 Ahmadabad 2,548,000 Hyderabad 2,546,000 Poona 1,686,000 Kanpur 1,639,000 Nagpur 1,302,000

KASHMIR

Until Indian independence in August 1947, Kashmir's mainly Muslim population was ruled, under British supervision, by a Hindu maharaja. Independence obliged the maharaja to choose between Pakistan or India; hoping to preserve his own independence, he refused to make a decision. In October, a ragtag army of Pathan tribesmen invaded from newly created Pakistan. Looting industriously, the Pathans advanced slowly, and India had time to rush troops to the region. The first Indo-Pakistan war resulted in a partition that satisfied neither side, with Pakistan holding one-third and India the remainder, with a 60% Muslim population. Despite promises, India has refused to allow a plebiscite to decide the province's fate. Two subsequent wars, in 1965 and 1972, failed to alter significantly the 1948 ceasefire lines.

In the late 1980s, Kashmiri nationalists in the Indian-controlled area began a violent campaign in favour of either secession to Pakistan or local independence. India responded by flooding Kashmir with troops and accusing Pakistan of intervention. By 1992, at least 3,000 Kashmiris had died. India stood accused of torture and repression, and there was little sign of a peaceful end to the conflict.

Company was virtually in control, and the British Indian Empire (which included, however, many autonomous states) was gradually consolidated throughout the 19th and early 20th centuries. Organized opposition to Britain's rule began before World War I and reached a climax after the end of World War II. In August 1947 the Indian subcontinent became independent, but divided into the separate states of India, a mainly Hindu community, and Pakistan, where Muslims formed the vast majority. In the boundary disputes and reshuffling of minority populations that followed perhaps a million lives were lost – and events since then have done little to promote good relations between the two states.

India is a vast country with enormous problems of organization. It has over a dozen major languages, each with a rich literature, and many minor languages. Hindi, the national language, and the Dravidian languages of the south (Tamil, Telugu and Malayalam) are Indo-European; in the north and east occur Sino-Tibetan tongues, and in forested hill refuges are found residual Austric languages. Racial stocks too are mixed, with dark tribal folk in forest remnants, Mongoloids in the north and east, and lighter-coloured skins and eyes in the north-west.

The mosaic of religion also adds variety – and potential conflict. Hinduism is all-pervasive (though the state is officially secular), and Buddhism is slowly reviving in its country of origin (the Buddha was born on the border of India and Nepal about 563 BC). Buddhism's near-contemporary Mahavira

and Jainism are strong in the merchant towns around Mt Abu in the Aravalli hills north of Ahmadabad. Islam contributes many mosques and tombs to the Indian scene; the Taj Mahal being the most famous. The forts of Delhi, Agra and many other northern cities, and the ghost city of Fatehpur Sikri, near Agra, are also Islamic relics of the Mogul period (1556–1707). Despite the formation of Pakistan, India retains a large Muslim minority of about 76 million. Now it is the turn of the Punjab's militant Sikhs, claiming to represent their population of 13 million, who seek separation.

Christian influences range from the elaborate Catholic churches and shrines remaining from Portuguese and French settlement, to the many schools and colleges set up by Christian denominations and still actively teaching; there are also notable church unions in both south and north India. The British period of rule left its own monuments; Bombay and Calcutta both have some notable Victoriana, and New Delhi is a planned Edwardian city.

Communications and development

A more vital memorial is the railway network – a strategic broad-gauge system fed by metre-gauge subsidiaries, with additional light railways, for example to the hill-stations of Simla (in Himachal Pradesh), Darjeeling (between Nepal and Bhutan) and Ootacamund (in Tamil Nadu). Among developments since independence are the fast and comfortable inter-city diesel-electric trains, but steam-engines remain the main workhorses in a country that is the world's fifth largest coal producer.

The road system also has strategic elements from the Mogul and British past, now part of a national network. Main roads are passable all the year round, and feeder-roads are largely all-weather dirt roads taking traffic close to most of India's 650,000 villages. The well-served international airports are linked with good, cheap internal services.

At independence India was already established as a partly industrialized country, and has made great strides during a succession of five-year plans that provided explicitly for both nationalized and private industry. The Damodar coalfield around Asansol has been developed, and new fields opened.

The Tata family's steel city of Jamshedpur, itself now diversified by other industries, has been complemented by new state plants and planned towns at Durgapur and other places, in collaboration with Britain, Germany and the former Soviet Union. Major engineering factories have been built at Bangalore, Vishakhapatnam and elsewhere (including the ill-fated Bhopal), and oil refineries set up at Barauni in the north-east, and near Bombay for new fields recently developed in the north-west. Several nuclear power stations are in operation, and the massive potential of hydroelectric power is being exploited. Small-scale industry is also being encouraged. Industrial estates have had mixed success, but do well in places like Bangalore where there are enough related industries to utilize interactions.

In the countryside a generation of effort in community and rural development is starting to achieve results, most obviously where the Green Revolution of improved seeds and fertilizers has been successful, for example in the wheatlands of the Punjab and Haryana, or where irrigation has been newly applied and brought success. In such areas it can be argued that the gap between landless labourers and prosperous farmers widens when new methods bring greater yields; but this is one of many social problems that beset a complex, diverse society which appears to be always on the verge of collapse into chaos, but despite its size, burgeoning population and potential for division manages to remain intact.

Sikkim, after Goa the smallest of India's 25 self-governing states, was a Buddhist kingdom before being ruled by Britain from 1866 and protected by India from 1950 to 1975, when following a plebiscite it joined the Union. On the border with Nepal is Mt Kanchenjunga, at 8,598 m [28,028 ft] the world's third highest peak.

Indian islands. The Andaman and Nicobar Islands, in the Bay of Bengal, became an Indian state in 1950 and now form one of the country's seven Union territories (population 180,000); a similar status is held by the Lakshadweep (Laccadive) Islands, off the Malabar Coast, where 27 of the coral atolls are inhabited (population 40,000) ■

Bombay's climate is hot and humid. January and February are the coldest months, with night temperatures just below 20°C [68°F] – the only time in the year that they go below that figure. March–May is hot and then the monsoon rains come, lasting from June to September. Over 2,000 mm [79 in] fall and from July to August rain falls on 45–50 days; more than 500 mm [20 in] has been recorded in one day. For the rest of the year, the heat returns.

NEPAL

This Himalayan kingdom's uniquely shaped flag was adopted in 1962. It came from the joining together in the 19th century of two triangular pennants – the royal family's crescent moon emblem and the powerful Rana family's sun symbol.

The high altitude of the Himalayan parts of the country give temperatures throughout the year that are sub-zero with the resultant snow, ice and high winds. In the lower regions, the temperatures are subtropical and the rainfall quite high, though it tends to be drier in the west. At Katmandu, the day temperatures for most of the year are 25–30°C [77–86°F], but dropping at night to 10–20°C [50–68°F]. The lowest recorded is only just below freezing. Rainfall is quite high, mainly May–September.

Over three-quarters of Nepal lies in a mountain heartland located between the towering Himalayas, the subject of an inconclusive boundary negotiation with China in 1961, and the far lower Siwalik Range overlooking the Ganges plain. Its innumerable valleys are home to a mosaic of peoples, of Indo-European and Tibetan stock, with a wide range of cultures and religions, and exercising fierce clan loyalties.

This heartland, some 800 km [500 mls] from west to east, is divided between the basins of Nepal's three main rivers – the Ghaghara, Gandak and Kosi. Between the last two, on a smaller river flanked by lake deposits, stands Katmandu, the royal and parliamentary capital, surrounded by emerald rice-fields and orchards. The provincial centre of Pokhara is in a similar valley tributary to the Gandak, north of Nuwakot.

South of the Siwalik Range, the formerly swampy and malarious *terai*, or hillfoot plain, is now an economic mainstay, with new farming settlements growing rice, wheat, maize, jute and sugar. Development is encouraged by the *terai* section of the Asian Highway. There are two short railways from India, Jaynagar-Janakpur and Raxaul-Amlekganj, where the railhead from the south meets the road that takes goods up to Katmandu. As well as general development aid from the West, China has built a road from Tibet to Katmandu, India one from near Nautanwa to Pokhara. Nepal's most

famous assets are the mountains, now an increasing tourist attraction bringing vital revenue to the country. Everest (8,848 m [29,029 ft]) and Kanchenjunga (8,598 m [28,208 ft]) are the tallest peaks of a magnificent range, giving a backdrop that dominates every vista in Nepal.

The authorities now hope for more than increased tourism. Today's plan is for the Himalayas to be tapped for their colossal hydroelectric potential, to supply the factories of India; Nepal's goal is to become the powerhouse of the region. If the scheme envisaged by the government and the World Bank gets under way, the first stage would be under way by the mid-1990s at Chisapani Gorge.

Financing such schemes – at $6 billion Chisapani alone is nearly twice the total gross national product – is a huge problem for a country which ranks alongside Laos as the poorest in Asia. With Chinese Tibet to the north and India to the south, the nation is already heavily reliant on Indian trade and cooperation – a fact emphasized when border restrictions operated in the late 1980s. Devoid of coast, independent trade links and mineral resources, Nepal has remained an undeveloped rural country, with more than 90% of the adult population (only one in four of whom can read) working as subsistence farmers. In addition, indiscriminate farming techniques have led to deforestation – in turn resulting in the erosion of precious soils.

While tourism is now encouraged, it was only in

1951 that Nepal was opened up to foreigners. Before that it had been a patchwork of feudal valley kingdoms, and though these were conquered by the Gurkhas in the 18th century – forming the present country – local leaders always displayed more allegiance to their clans than to the state. From the mid 19th century these families (notably the powerful Rana) reduced the power of the central king, but in 1951 the monarchy was re-established. A brief period of democracy ended with the return of autocratic royal rule in 1960 under King Mahendra, but after mass demonstrations and riots his son Birendra, despite attempts at stalling, was forced to concede a new constitution incorporating pluralism and basic human rights in 1990 and the hierarchical system of *panchayats* (rubber-stamping local councils) was over. In May 1991 the first democratic elections for 32 years took place with 10 million voters, and were won by the left-of-centre Nepali Congress Party. Though the birthplace of Buddha (Prince Siddhartha Gautama, c. 563 BC), Nepal remains a predominantly Hindu country ■

COUNTRY: Kingdom of Nepal

AREA: 140,800 sq km [54,363 sq mls]

POPULATION: 18,916,000

CAPITAL (Population): Katmandu (235,000)

GOVERNMENT: Constitutional monarchy

ETHNIC GROUPS: Nepalese 58%, Bihari 19%, Tharu 4%, Tamang 4%, Newar 3%

LANGUAGES: Nepali 58% (official), and 20 others

RELIGIONS: Hindu 90%, Buddhist 5%, Muslim 3%

NATIONAL DAY: 28 December; Birthday of the King

CURRENCY: Nepalese rupee = 100 paisa

ANNUAL INCOME PER PERSON: $170

MAIN PRIMARY PRODUCTS: Rice, cereals, timber, sugar

MAIN EXPORTS: Basic manufactures 35%, foodstuffs 23%, machinery and transport equipment 22%

MAIN IMPORTS: Basic manufactured goods 30%, machinery and transport equipment 23%, chemicals 13%, mineral fuels 11%, foodstuffs 10%

POPULATION DENSITY: 134 per sq km [348 per sq ml]

LIFE EXPECTANCY: Female 53 yrs, male 54 yrs

BHUTAN

The striking image on Bhutan's flag is explained by the name of this Himalayan kingdom in the local language, which means 'land of the dragon'. The saffron colour stands for royal power and the orange-red for Buddhist spiritual power.

COUNTRY: Kingdom of Bhutan

AREA: 47,000 sq km [18,147 sq mls]

POPULATION: 1,517,000

CAPITAL (Population): Thimphu (60,000)

POPULATION DENSITY: 32 per sq km [84 per sq ml]

Geographically a smaller and even more isolated version of Nepal, the remote mountain kingdom of Bhutan faces many of the same problems and hopes for many of the same solutions – notably the harnessing of hydroelectric power from the Himalayas: India has already built one plant and commissioned two more from King Jigme Singye Wangchuk. The monarch is head of both state and government, though foreign affairs are under Indian guidance following a treaty of 1949.

The world's most 'rural' country (less than 6% of the population live in towns and over 90% are dependent on agriculture), Bhutan produces mainly rice and maize as staple crops and fruit and cardamom as cash crops. Timber is important, too, though outweighed by cement (25% of exports) and talcum (10%) in earning foreign exchange. Despite these activities, plus tourism and stamps, the World Bank in 1989 ranked Bhutan the world's ninth poorest country, ahead only of Laos, Nepal and

Bangladesh in Asia. Aircraft and diesel fuels are its main imports, supplying crucial contacts.

Like Nepal, Bhutan was subject to a series of pro-democracy demonstrations in 1990, but because the protesters were mainly Hindus there has been little political progress in this predominantly Buddhist country. The Hindu minority, mostly Nepali-speakers, maintain that they are the victims of discrimination, denied basic rights such as religious freedom and the ownership of property ■

SRI LANKA

This unusual flag was adopted in 1951, three years after 'Ceylon' gained independence from Britain. The lion banner represents the ancient Buddhist kingdom and the stripes the island's minorities – Muslims (green) and Hindus (orange).

The western side of Sri Lanka has an equatorial climate with a double maximum of rainfall in May and October and very uniform high temperatures throughout the year. The periods of heaviest rain at Colombo mark the advance and retreat of the summer monsoon, which gives a single wet season over the Indian subcontinent to the north. The eastern side of the island, sheltered from the south-west winds, is drier; Trincomalee has an annual rainfall of 1,646 mm [65 in].

Known as Ceylon until 1972, when it became a Socialist republic, Sri Lanka has been described as 'the pearl of the Indian Ocean'; the island is also its crossroads. First inhabited by forest-dwelling negroid Veddas, it was settled later by brown-skinned Aryans from India. These are now dominant in the population, though diluted by successive waves of incomers. Long-resident Tamils farm in the northern limestone peninsula of Jaffna, and Arab dhow sailors and merchants settled in the ports. After Vasco da Gama's contact with India in the 15th century came new traders and colonists – first Portuguese, then Dutch, then British (in control from 1796 to 1948) – and new immigrant Tamils were brought in from south-east India to farm the plantations.

From mountain core to coral strand stretches the 'wet zone' of south-western Sri Lanka, supporting cool, grassy downs, rainforests and tea-gardens near the ancient religious centre of Kandy, and evergreen forest and palm-fringed beaches in the lowlands from Colombo to east of Galle. White Buddhist shrines and peasant cottages dot the cultivated land among coconut palms, rice-paddies, sugar-cane plantations and spice gardens. In contrast are the much drier zones of the north and east.

While light industry has gone some way to diversifying an agricultural base dependent on tea (third producer in the world after China and India), rubber (fourth) and coconuts (fifth), Sri Lanka's economic progress since independence – when it was a relatively prosperous state – has been plagued by civil war and communal violence. The main conflict, between the Sinhalese Buddhist majority and the Tamil Hindu minority, led to disorders in 1958, 1971 and 1977; since 1983 the conflict has been virtually continuous as Tamil guerrillas have fought for an independent homeland in the north (Eelam), with Jaffna the capital.

An Indian-brokered ceasefire in 1987 allowed an Indian peace-keeping force in, but it failed to subdue the main terrorist group, the Tamil Tigers, and withdrew in March 1990. Between then and the start of 1992 more than 12,000 people died in renewed clashes between the predominantly Sinhalese government forces and the rebels, despite an agreement on Tamil autonomy. Many civilians, too, have lost their lives, and the conflicts have stemmed the potential flow of tourists to this lush, beautiful island. In addition, the authorities were dogged by a rumbling rebellion of the left-wing Sinhalese nationalist movement (JVP) in the south. Banned in 1983, the JVP escalated their campaign after the Indo-Sri Lankan pact of 1987, but their guerrillas were virtually broken by an offensive initiated by the new government – elected democratically after a delay of some six years in 1988 ■

COUNTRY: Democratic Socialist Republic of Sri Lanka

AREA: 65,610 sq km [25,332 sq mls]

POPULATION: 16,993,000

CAPITAL (Population): Colombo (1,412,000)

GOVERNMENT: Unitary multiparty republic with a unicameral legislature

ETHNIC GROUPS: Sinhalese 74%, Tamil 18%, Sri Lankan Moor 7%

LANGUAGES: Sinhala (official), Tamil, English

RELIGIONS: Buddhist 69%, Hindu 16%, Muslim 8%, Christian 7%

NATIONAL DAY: 4 February; Independence and National Day (1948)

CURRENCY: Sri Lanka rupee = 100 cents

ANNUAL INCOME PER PERSON: $470

MAIN PRIMARY PRODUCTS: Rice, coconuts, rubber, tea, fish, timber, iron ore, precious and semi-precious stones, graphite

MAIN INDUSTRIES: Agriculture, mining, forestry, fishing, textiles, oil refining, cement, food processing

MAIN EXPORTS: Tea 27%, rubber 7%, precious and semi-precious stones 6%, coconuts 3%

MAIN EXPORT PARTNERS: USA 27%, Germany 8%, UK 6%, Japan 5%, Pakistan 2%

MAIN IMPORTS: Petroleum 15%, machinery and transport equipment 13%, sugar 4%, vehicles

MAIN IMPORT PARTNERS: Japan 15%, UK 7%, USA 6%, Iran 5%, India 4%, China 3%

DEFENCE: 26.6% of national budget

TOURISM: 183,000 visitors per year

POPULATION DENSITY: 259 per sq km [671 per sq ml]

INFANT MORTALITY: 28 per 1,000 live births

LIFE EXPECTANCY: Female 74 yrs, male 70 yrs

ADULT LITERACY: 87%

PRINCIPAL CITIES: (Population): Colombo 1,412,000 Dehiwala-Mt Lavinia 191,000 Moratuwa 143,000

MALDIVES

The Maldives used to fly a plain red flag until the Islamic green panel with white crescent was added early this century. The present design was officially adopted in 1965, after the British left the islands.

Surrounded by the warm waters of the Indian Ocean, the islands are hot throughout the year, with monthly temperature averages of 26–29°C [79-84°F], and even night temperatures going no lower than 23–27°C [73–81°F]. The temperature record is only 37°C [99°F]. Monsoon rainfall is heavy with an annual total of over 1,500 mm [59 in], most of this falling June–November, though there is rain in all months, and December–March are the driest.

The archipelago of the Maldives comprises over 1,190 small low-lying islands and atolls (202 of them inhabited), scattered along a broad north-south line starting 650 km (400 mls) west-south-west of Cape Comorin.

The islands were settled from Sri Lanka about 500 BC. For a time under Portuguese and later Dutch rule, they became a British protectorate in 1887, administered from Ceylon but retaining local sultanates. They achieved independence in 1965, and the last sultan was deposed three years later.

Adequately watered and covered with tropical vegetation, the islands' crops are coconuts, bananas, mangoes, sweet potatoes and spices, but much food is imported – as are nearly all capital and consumer goods. Fish are plentiful in lagoons and open sea; bonito and tuna are leading exports (45%) together with copra and coir. Tourism, however, has now displaced fishing as the mainstay of the economy, though its future depends much on political stability; the 1988 coup against the authoritarian nationalist government was put down with Indian troops ■

COUNTRY: Republic of the Maldives

AREA: 298 sq km [115 sq mls]

POPULATION: 215,000

CAPITAL (Population): Malé (46,000)

BANGLADESH

Bangladesh adopted this flag in 1971 following the break from Pakistan. The green is said to represent the fertility of the land, while the red disc commemorates the blood shed in the struggle for freedom.

The Ganges delta has a classic monsoon climate. From June–September the winds blow from the south over the Bay of Bengal, bringing very heavy rain, over 240 mm [10 in] per month. On occasions, the winds are so strong they pile the sea water up against the outflowing river, bringing flood devastation. April is the hottest month and temperatures remain high throughout the monsoon season, though with little bright sunshine. January, with winds from the north, is the coldest month.

Battered by a relentless cycle of flood and famine, and plagued by political corruption and a succession of military coups, Bangladesh is perhaps Asia's most pitiful country, once known as Golden Bengal (Sonar Bangla) for its treasures but gradually plundered and now pushed near to the bottom of the Third World pile. It is – apart from statistically irrelevant city-states and small island countries – the most crowded nation on Earth: the 1990 figure was a density of some 803 people per sq km [2,080 per sq ml], well ahead of the next realistic rival Taiwan (554 per sq km [1,435 per sq ml]) and far greater than Europe's contender Belgium (323 per sq km [837 per sq ml]), which in any case has a much larger urban proportion. The world's tenth biggest population – a figure expected to increase by another 36 million or more between 1988 and 2000 – lives on an area of precarious flat lowlands smaller than the US states of Illinois or Iowa.

Landscape

Apart from a south-eastern fringe of forested ridges east of Chittagong, Bangladesh consists almost entirely of lowlands – mainly the (greater) eastern part of the large delta formed jointly by the Ganges and Brahmaputra. The western part (now West Bengal, in India) is largely the 'dying delta' – its land a little higher and less often flooded, its deltaic channels seldom flushed by flood-waters. In contrast, the heart of Bangladesh, following the main Ganges channel and the wide Brahmaputra, is the 'active delta'. Frequently flooded, with changing channels that are hazardous to life, health and property, the rivers also renew soil fertility with silt washed down from as far away as the mountains of Nepal and Tibet. Indeed, while deforestation in the Himalayan

foothills has caused enough silt to form new 'islands' for the burgeoning Bangladeshi population, it has also led to the blocking of some waterways – 60% of the country's internal trade is carried by boat – and danger to fish stocks, as well as increased risk of flooding.

The alluvial silts of the 'active delta' yield up to three rice crops a year as well as the world's best jute, and though Bangladesh is now only the third largest producer in a declining market, high-quality fibre is exported to India; jute and cotton are processed also in post-independence mills, for example at Narayanganj.

There is a large hydroelectric plant at Karnaphuli reservoir, and a modern paper industry using bamboo from the hills. Substantial reserves of coal await exploitation, but a more realistic development may be the construction of a 320 km [200 ml] canal to transfer water from the flooding Brahmaputra to the Ganges, in order to increase supplies to India's drought-affected areas. The scheme, like so many others, has run into the political problems and mutual suspicion that dog the area.

History and politics

Bangladesh was until 1971 East Pakistan, the oriental wing of the Muslim state set up by the partition of British India in 1947. Separated by 1,600 km [1,000 mls] of India from the politically-dominant, Urdu- and Punjabi-speaking western province, the easterners felt the victims of ethnic and economic discrimination. In 1971 resentment turned to war when Bengali irregulars, considerably aided and abetted by Indian troops, convened the independent state of 'Free Bengal', with Sheikh Mujibur Rahman as head of state.

THE DELTA CYCLONES

Most of Bangladesh is almost unbelievably low and flat, and the people of the coastal fringes are all too familiar with the cyclones from the Bay of Bengal. Even so, 1991 brought the worst in memory: the official death toll was a staggering 132,000 (it may well be higher), and more than 5 million people, almost all of them poor peasants already living around or below the poverty line, were made homeless.

The cyclone caused inestimable damage to the area around Chittagong: crops and fields were inundated with sea water; herds of cattle and goats and flocks of poultry were decimated; dykes were breached and trees ripped up; wells filled up with salt water. The struggling survivors were victims of dysentery and cholera, dehydration and malnutrition. However generous, aid rarely reached the most needy, as it was sifted and filtered down the line despite the efforts of charity administrators. Corrupt practices, like cyclones, are endemic to Bangladesh; funds allocated for concrete cyclone-proof shelters, for example, were appropriated by individuals and government officials. As with most natural disasters – earthquakes, volcanic eruptions, tidal waves, landslips – the cyclones usually affect countries least equipped to deal with them and least able to withstand the losses.

COUNTRY: People's Republic of Bangladesh

AREA: 144,000 sq km [55,598 sq mls]

POPULATION: 115,594,000

CAPITAL (Population): Dacca (4,770,000)

GOVERNMENT: Unitary multiparty republic

ETHNIC GROUPS: Bengali 98%, Bihari, tribal

LANGUAGES: Bengali (official), English (legal/commercial), nearly 100 tribal dialects

RELIGIONS: Sunni Muslim 87%, Hindu 12%, Buddhist, Christian

NATIONAL DAY: 26 March; Independence Day (1971)

CURRENCY: Taka = 100 paisa

ANNUAL INCOME PER PERSON: $200

MAIN PRIMARY PRODUCTS: Rice, jute, natural gas, sugar cane, cattle, fish, timber, tea, wheat, glass, sand, tobacco

MAIN INDUSTRIES: Jute spinning, textiles, sugar, fishing

EXPORTS: $12 per person

MAIN EXPORTS: Jute goods and raw jute 33%, fish and fish preparations 12%, hides and skins 12%

MAIN EXPORT PARTNERS: USA 30%, Italy 9%, Japan 6%, Singapore 6%, UK 6%

IMPORTS: $33 per person

MAIN IMPORTS: Machinery and basic manufactures 24%, food 16%, petroleum products 15%

MAIN IMPORT PARTNERS: Japan 13%, Canada 10%, Singapore 9%, USA 7%, Germany 6%

DEFENCE: 14% of national budget

POPULATION DENSITY: 803 per sq km [2,080 per sq ml]

LIFE EXPECTANCY: Female 53 yrs, male 53 yrs

ADULT LITERACY: 29%

PRINCIPAL CITIES (Population): Dacca (Dhaka) 4,770,000 Chittagong 1,840,000 Khulna 860,000

The Sheikh's assassination in 1975 – during one of four military coups in the first 11 years of independence – led finally to a takeover by General Zia Rahman, who created an Islamic state before himself being murdered in 1981. General Ershad took over in a coup the following year and resigned as army chief in 1986 to take up the civilian presidency, lifting martial law; but by 1990 protests from supporters of his two predecessors toppled him from power and, after the first free parliamentary elections since independence, a coalition government was formed in 1991.

The new authority faced not only the long-term problems of a debt-ridden, aid-reliant country where corruption is a way of life: it also had to deal with the consequences of the worst cyclone in living memory and, from 1992, the increasing prospect of war with Burma, triggered by Rangoon's treatment of the Rohingyas, its Muslim minority. As far back as 1978 Bangladesh took in some 300,000 Rohingyas fleeing persecution, and while most went back, the emigrants of the 1990s are unlikely to follow suit.

Meanwhile, both nations amassed troops on a border that snakes its way through misty hills, mahogany forests and rubber plantations. Defence spending is already too high, and funds should go on other areas: for example, Bangladesh's hospital capacity (one bed for each 5,000 population) is the world's worst. As in West Bengal, an urban educated élite holds the real power, and corruption is widespread. However, Bangladesh's biggest problem remains a single one: it has far too many people ■

ASIA

MONGOLIA

On Mongolia's flag the red for Communism appears with blue, the country's national colour. The gold star stands for endurance and the Communist Party and the traditional Mongolian soyonbo symbol under the star represents freedom.

COUNTRY: State of Mongolia
AREA: 1,566,500 sq km [604,826 sq mls]
POPULATION: 2,190,000
CAPITAL (Population): Ulan Bator (500,000)
GOVERNMENT: Multiparty republic
ETHNIC GROUPS: Khalkha Mongol 77%, Kazakh 5%
LANGUAGES: Khalkha Mongolian (official), Chinese, Russian
RELIGIONS: Shamanist 31%, Muslim 4%, Buddhist
NATIONAL DAY: 11 July; Independence Day (1921)
CURRENCY: Tugrik = 100 möngös

Worthy of its harsh, isolated reputation, Mongolia is the world's largest landlocked country and the most sparsely populated. Despite its traditional nomads, more than half the population live in towns, a quarter of them in Ulan Bator, a modern city built in the postwar Soviet mould. Geographically Mongolia divides into two contrasting regions, north and south of a line joining the mountains of the Altai, Hangayn and Hentiyn ranges.

In the north, high mountains alternate with river valleys and lake basins. Pastures are watered enough to support herds of cattle and wheat is grown, especially where black earth soils occur. In the far north-west, where the Altai rise to over 4,000 m [13,120 ft], boreal forests blanket the slopes.

The southern half of the country, still averaging 1,500 m [4,900 ft], has a strong continental climate with meagre, variable rainfall. In these semi-desert steppelands, salt lakes and pans occupy shallow depressions, poor scrub eventually giving way to the arid wastes of the Gobi Desert.

Mongolia is still a land of nomadic pastoralists – less than 1% of the land is cultivated – and huge herds of sheep, goats, yaks, camels and horses form the mainstay of the traditional economy. Herdsmen's families inhabit *gers* (*yurts*), circular tents covered in felt, and subsist on a diet of milk, cheese and mutton.

Politics and economy

Outer Mongolia broke away from China following the collapse of the Ch'ing dynasty in 1911, but full independence was not gained until 1921 – with Soviet support in what was the world's second Socialist revolution. In 1924 a Communist People's Republic was proclaimed and the country fell increasingly under Soviet influence, the last example being a 20-year friendship and mutual assistance pact signed in 1966.

Textiles and food processing were developed, with aid from the USSR and Comecon also helping to open up mineral deposits such as copper, molybdenum and coking coal: in addition, Mongolia is the world's third biggest fluorspar producer. In the late 1980s minerals overtook the agricultural sector as the country's main source of income.

In recent years Mongolia has followed the path of other less remote Soviet satellites, reducing the presence of Soviet troops (1987–9), introducing pluralism (the country's first multiparty elections were held in 1990), launching into privatization and a free market economy (1991), and early in 1992 adopting a new constitution eschewing Communism and enshrining democracy.

The pace of change was frantic after seven decades of authoritarian rule – Mongolia still owes Moscow $15 billion – and like the newly independent republics of the former Soviet empire the Mongolians will not find the transition easy ∎

Ulan Bator lies on the northern edge of a vast desert plateau in the heart of Asia. Winters are extremely dry and cold and six months have a mean temperature below freezing. The extreme heat of summer is moderated by altitude. A large diurnal temperature range of over 15°C [27°F] occurs throughout the year. Rain falls almost entirely in the summer, the amount varying greatly from year to year.

CHINA

Red, the traditional colour of both China and Communism, was chosen for the People's Republic flag in 1949. The large star represents the Communist Party programme, the small stars represent the four principal social classes.

By far the most populous country in the world – one in every five people is a citizen – the People's Republic of China also ranks as the third largest country after Russia and Canada, being marginally bigger than the USA. Before the development of modern forms of transport, the vast size of China often hampered communication between the centre of the country and the peripheries. Distances are huge. By rail, the distance from Peking (Beijing) to Canton (Guangzhou) is 2,324 km [1,450 mls].

One of the main determining influences on the evolution of Chinese civilization had been the geographical isolation of China from the rest of the world. Surrounded to the north, west and south by forests, deserts and formidable mountain ranges, and separated from the Americas by the Pacific Ocean, China until modern times was insulated from frequent contact with other civilizations, and its culture and society developed along highly individual lines. In the 1990s China again finds itself an enigma – the great giant of Communism in an era when the creed is experiencing a global collapse.

Landscape and relief

The Chinese landscape is like a chequerboard in which mountains and plateaus alternate with basins and alluvial plains. There are two intersecting systems of mountain chains, one trending from north-north-east to south-south-west, the other from east to west. Many mountain areas have been devastated by soil erosion through indiscriminate tree-felling. The agricultural wealth of China is all in the lowlands of the east – where most of its people live.

Manchuria, in the far north, comprises a wide area of gently undulating country, originally grassland, but now an important agricultural area. The loess lands of the north-west occupy a broad belt from the great loop of the Hwang Ho (Huang He) into Shanxi and Henan provinces. Here, valley sides, hills and mountains are blanketed in loess – a fine-grained unstratified soil deposited by wind during the last glaciation. Within this region, loess deposits occur widely in the form of plateaus which are deeply incised by spectacular gorges and ravines.

By contrast with the loess lands, the landscape of the densely populated North China Plain is flat and monotonous. Settlement is concentrated in walled villages while large fields are the product of post-1949 land consolidation schemes. Further south the Yangtze delta is a land of large lakes. Water is a predominant element – the low-lying alluvial land with its irrigated rice-fields is traversed by intricate networks of canals and other manmade works, many of which date back several centuries.

Far inland in the Yangtze basin, and separated from the middle Yangtze valley by precipitous river gorges, lies the Red Basin of Szechwan (Sichuan). To the north, west and south, the basin is surrounded by high mountain ranges. The mountains of the Qin Ling ranges, in particular, protect the basin from cold winter winds. With its mild climate and fertile soils, the Red Basin is one of the most productive and densely populated regions of China. Rice-fields, often arranged in elaborate terraces, dominate the landscape.

Other distinctive landscapes of southern China include those of north-eastern Guizhou province, where limestone spires and pinnacles rise vertically

The climate of China is controlled by the air masses of Asia and the Pacific, and the mountains in the west. In the winter the cold, dry Siberian air blows southwards. In the summer the tropical Pacific air dominates, bringing high temperatures and rain. In summer the temperature in eastern China is high with little difference between north and south; in winter there is over 20°C [36°F] difference. Annual rain decreases from over 2,000 mm [80 in] in the south to the desert conditions of the north-west.

TIBET

With an average elevation of 4,500 m [14,750 ft] – almost as high as Europe's Mont Blanc – and an area of 1.2 million sq km [460,000 sq mls], Tibet is the highest and most extensive plateau in the world. It is a harsh and hostile place, and most of its population of just over 2 million people live in the relatively sheltered south of the country.

For much of its history Tibet has been ruled by Buddhist priests – lamas – as a theocracy. The Dalai Lama, a title passed on in successive incarnations from a dying elder to a newborn junior,

usually dominated from Lhasa. Between 1720 and 1911 Tibet was under Chinese control, and in 1950 Tibet was reabsorbed by a resurgent Red China; after an unsuccessful uprising in 1959, the Dalai Lama fled to Delhi and a brutal process of forced Chinese acculturation began: in 1961, a report of the International Commission of Jurists accused China of genocide. An 'Autonomous Region of Tibet' was proclaimed in 1965, but during the 1966-76 Cultural Revolution, many Tibetan shrines and monasteries were destroyed.

Tibetans call their country 'The Land of Snows', but the Himalayas act as a barrier to rain-bearing winds and the amount of precipitation is low, Lhasa in the south getting 400 mm [16 in], this decreasing northwards to desert conditions. There is always snow at altitudes higher than about 5,000 m [16,000 ft]. In Lhasa night temperatures will be below freezing on nearly every night from late October to early April, the constant wind making this feel much colder.

above small, intensively cultivated plains, and the Guangdong coastal lowlands, with their villages in groves of citrus, bananas, mangoes and palms.

The Hwang Ho and the Yangtze

The two major rivers of China are the Hwang Ho (Huang He) and the Yangtze (Chang Jiang), the world's seventh and third longest. The Hwang Ho, or Yellow River (so called from the large quantities of silt which it transports), is 4,840 km [3,005 mls] long. Also known as 'China's Sorrow', it has throughout history been the source of frequent and disastrous floods. In 1938, dykes along the Hwang Ho were demolished in order to hamper the advance of the Japanese army into northern China, and the river was diverted so as to enter the sea to the south of the Shandong peninsula. In the catastrophic floods which followed, nearly 900,000 lives were lost and 54,000 sq km [21,000 sq mls] of land was inundated. Since 1949, the incidence of flooding has declined sharply, largely as a result of state investment in flood prevention schemes.

The Yangtze, China's largest and most important river, is 6,380 km [3,960 mls] long, and its catchment basin is over twice as extensive as that of the Hwang Ho. Unlike the Hwang Ho, the Yangtze is navigable. During the summer months, ocean-going vessels of 10,000 tonnes may reach Wuhan, and 1,000-tonne barges can go as far upstream as Chongqing. Despite the post-1949 improvement of roads and railways, the Yangtze remains an important transport artery.

Climate and agriculture

Although the Chinese subcontinent includes a wide variety of relief and climate, it can be divided into three broad regions.

Northern China: Throughout northern China, rainfall is light and variable, and is generally insufficient for irrigated agriculture. In winter, temperatures fall to between –1°C and –8°C [30°F and 18°F] and bitterly cold winds blow eastwards across the North China Plain from the steppes of Mongolia. Summer temperatures, by contrast, are little different from those of southern China, and may reach a daily average of 28°C [82°F]. The growing season diminishes northwards and in nothern Manchuria only 90 days a year are free of frost. Despite advances in water conservation since World War II, aridity and unreliability of rainfall restrict the range of crops that can be grown. Millet, maize and winter wheat are the staple crops of the North China Plain, while coarse grains and soya beans are cultivated in Manchuria.

Southern China: The area to the south of the Qin Ling ranges receives heavier and more reliable rainfall than the north, and winter temperatures are generally above freezing point. Summer weather, especially in the central Yangtze Valley, is hot and humid. At Nanjing, temperatures as high as 44°C [111°F] have been recorded. Inland, the mild climate and fertile soils of the Red Basin make this an important agricultural region. Rice production is dominant but at lower altitudes the climate is warm enough to allow the cultivation of citrus fruits, cotton, sugar cane and tobacco, of which China is the world's biggest producer.

The far south of China, including Guangdong province and the island of Hainan, lies within the tropics and enjoys a year-round growing season. Irrigated rice cultivation is the economic mainstay of southern China. Double cropping (rice as a main crop followed by winter wheat) is characteristic of the Yangtze Valley; along the coast of Guangdong

province two crops of rice can be grown each year, and in parts of Hainan Island the annual cultivation of three crops of rice is possible; the country produces more than 35% of the world total. Crops such as tea, mulberry and sweet potato are also cultivated, and in the far south sugar cane, bananas, and other tropical crops are grown.

The interior: While the Qin Ling ranges are an important boundary between the relatively harsh environments of the north and the more productive lands of the south, a second major line, which follows the Da Hinggan Ling mountains and the eastern edge of the high Tibetan plateau, divides the intensively cultivated lands of eastern China from the mountains and arid steppes of the interior. In the north, this boundary line is marked by the Great Wall of China. Western China includes the Dzungarian basin, the Turfan depression, the arid Takla Makan desert, and the high plateau of Tibet.

Although aridity of climate has hampered the development of agriculture throughout most of western China, oasis crops are grown around the rim of the Takla Makan desert, and farming settlements also exist in the Gansu corridor to the north of the Qilian mountains.

Early history

Early Chinese civilization arose along the inland margins of the North China Plain, in a physical setting markedly harsher (especially in terms of winter temperatures) than the environments of the other great civilizations of the Old World. The Shang dynasty, noted for its fine craftsmanship in bronze, flourished in northern China from 1630 to 1122 BC. Shang civilization was followed by many centuries of political fragmentation, and it was not until the 3rd century BC that China was unified into a centrally administered empire. Under the Ch'in dynasty (221 to 206 BC) the Great Wall of China was completed, while Chinese armies pushed southwards beyond the Yangtze, reaching the southern Chinese coast in the vicinity of Canton.

In succeeding centuries there was a gradual movement of population from the north to the warmer, moister, and more productive lands of the south. This slow migration was greatly accelerated by incursions of barbarian nomads into north China, especially during the Sung dynasty (AD 960 to 1279). By the late 13th century the southern lands, including the Yangtze Valley, probably contained somewhere between 70% and 80% of the Chinese population.

During the Han, T'ang and Sung dynasties, a remarkably stable political and social order evolved within China. The major distinguishing features of Chinese civilization came to include Confucianism, whereby the individual was subordinated to family obligations and to state service, the state bureaucracy, members of which were recruited by public examination, and the benign rule of the emperor – the 'Son of Heaven'. Great advances were made in

COUNTRY: People's Republic of China

AREA: 9,596,960 sq km [3,705,386 sq mls]

POPULATION: 1,139,060,000

CAPITAL (Population): Peking (9,750,000)

GOVERNMENT: Single-party Communist republic

ETHNIC GROUPS: Han (Chinese) 93%, 55 others

LANGUAGES: Mandarin Chinese (official); in the south and west, local dialects are spoken

RELIGIONS: Confucian (officially atheist) 20%, Buddhist 6%, Taoist 2%, Muslim 2%, Christian

NATIONAL DAY: 1 October; Proclamation of People's Republic (1949)

CURRENCY: Renminbi (yuan) = 10 jiao = 100 fen

ANNUAL INCOME PER PERSON: $370

MAIN PRIMARY PRODUCTS: Antimony, coal, fish, gold, iron ore, manganese, natural gas, petroleum, phosphates, pigs, rice, salt, sheep, timber, tobacco, tungsten

MAIN INDUSTRIES: Agriculture, cement, forestry, textiles, steel, bicycles, petroleum, newsprint, fertilizers

MAIN EXPORTS: Manufactured goods 19%, food and live animals 16%, mineral fuels 13%, chemicals 6%

MAIN EXPORT PARTNERS: Hong Kong 32%, Japan 16%, USA 10%, Singapore 1%, UK 1%

MAIN IMPORTS: Machinery and transport equipment 40%, chemicals 9%, raw materials 7%, food and live animals 5%

MAIN IMPORT PARTNERS: Japan 28%, Hong Kong 14%, USA 12%, Germany 4%

DEFENCE: 7.7% of national budget

TOTAL ARMED FORCES: 3,030,000

TOURISM: 10,760,000 visitors per year

ROADS: 942,000 km [588,750 mls]

RAILWAYS: 52,487 km [32,804 mls]

POPULATION DENSITY: 119 per sq km [307 per sq ml]

BIRTHS: 21 per 1,000 population

DEATHS: 7 per 1,000 population

INFANT MORTALITY: 27 per 1,000 live births

LIFE EXPECTANCY: Female 73 yrs, male 69 yrs

POPULATION PER DOCTOR: 1,000

ADULT LITERACY: 69%

PRINCIPAL CITIES (Population): Shanghai 12,320,000 Peking 9,750,000 Tianjin 5,459,000 Shenyang 4,285,000 Wuhan 3,493,000 Guangzhou 3,359,000 Chongqing 2,832,000 Harbin 2,668,000 Chengdu 2,642,000 Xi'an 2,387,000 Zibo 2,329,000 Nanjing 2,290,000 Nanchang 2,289,000 the manufacture of porcelain, silk, metals and lacquerware, while gunpowder, the compass, and printing were among several Chinese inventions which found their way to the West in medieval times. Nevertheless, the economy of pre-modern China was overwhelmingly agricultural, and the peasant class accounted for most of the population.

Despite the geographical diversity and great size of its territory, China during pre-modern times experienced long periods of unity and cohesion rarely disturbed by invasion from outside. Two important dynasties, the Yuan (1279–1368) and the Ch'ing (1644–1912), were established by the Mongols and Manchus respectively, but, almost invariably, alien rulers found it necessary to adopt Chinese methods of government, and the Chinese cultural tradition was preserved intact.

The birth of the Republic

In the 18th century, China experienced a rapid acceleration in the rate of population growth, and living standards began to fall. By the early 19th century, the government was weak and corrupt, and the country suffered frequent famines and political unrest. British victory in the Opium War (1839–42) was followed by the division of China into spheres of influence for the major Western imperialist powers,

and by the establishment of treaty ports, controlled by Western countries, along the Chinese coast and the Yangtze.

Meanwhile, the disintegration of imperial China was hastened by peasant uprisings such as the Taiping rebellion (1850–64), and by the defeat of China in the Sino-Japanese War of 1894–5. Belated attempts were made to arrest the decline of the Chinese empire, but in 1912, and following an uprising in Wuhan, the last of the Chinese emperors abdicated and a republic was proclaimed.

Although the republican administration in Peking was regarded as the legitimate government, real power rested with army generals and provincial governors. Rival generals, or warlords, raised private armies and plunged China into a long and disastrous period of internal disorder. Alternative solutions were offered by two political parties – the Kuomintang (or Chinese Nationalist Party) formed by Sun Yat-sen and later led by Chiang Kai-shek, and the Communist Party. In 1931, Japan seized Manchuria, and in 1937 full-scale war broke out between the two countries. In the bitter fighting which followed, the Communists, under Mao Tse-tung, gained the support of the peasantry and proved adept practitioners of guerrilla warfare.

The defeat of Japan in 1945 was followed by a

The annual rainfall total decreases from over 2,000 mm [80 in] in the south to the desert conditions of the north-west. Most of this rain falls in the summer months. Summer is also the typhoon season. Northwards the winters get drier and the rain becomes more variable from one year to the next. At Shanghai it rains on average ten days per month. Daily sunshine levels are not high; 4–5 hours, November–March with only 7.5 hours in August.

civil war which cost 12 million lives: the Communists routed the Xuomintang armies, forcing them to take refuge on the island of Taiwan, and the People's Republic of China was officially proclaimed on 1 October 1949.

Communist China

Under Communist rule the mass starvation, malnutrition and disease which afflicted China before World War II were virtually eliminated, and living standards greatly improved, especially in the countryside.

One of the salient features of the centrally

- ▣ National capital
- ● Autonomous region capitals
- ◉ Province capitals

100 200 300 400 500 600 700 800km
100 200 300 400 500

planned economy was the organization of the rur
population into 50,000 communes – self-sufficien
units of varying size which farm the land collectivel
Communes also ran rural industries, and are re
sponsible for the administration of schools and clin
ics. Labour has been organized on a vast scale t
tackle public works such as water conservatio
flood control and land reclamation.

Living standards improved markedly, with li
expectancy doubling and education improvin
though the GNP per capita figure remained that of
poor Third World nation – some 1.5% that of Japa
The agricultural communes were not notably su
cessful, and since peasants have been freed fro
petty bureaucracy, harvests of the major grain crop
went up by over 40% in the decade from 1976.

Although food supply has generally kept abrea
of population growth, the size and growth rate of th
Chinese population has always given cause for con
cern. By the early 1980s, the population was grov
ing at 1.3% per year, a net annual increase of abo
13 million people; penalties and incentives have me
with some success, but between 1988 and 2000
was expected to grow by 187 million – slightly le
than the prediction for India, but more than th
1988 totals for Indonesia or Brazil.

Only 10% of the land area of China is cultivabl
but environmental constraints are such that there
little prospect of meeting increased food demand k
reclaiming land for agriculture. Future growth
food supply must come from continued intensif
cation of land use and gains in yields.

Although China is an agricultural countr
government planners, especially since the death
Mao Tse-tung in 1976, have emphasized the nee
to industrialize. China has sufficient resources
coal, iron ore and oil to support an industrial eco
omy, but it is deficient in capital and industrial tecl
nology. While refusing to bow to the wave
political reform sweeping through world socialism
1990 and 1991 – the country's record on huma
rights is appalling – the Chinese leadership ha
loosened the reins on the economy, allowing certa
market forces to operate, encouraging furth
foreign investment and promoting the enormo
potential of tourism.

Peking, the capital city of China, is a gover
mental and administrative centre of prime impor
ance. Several buildings of outstanding architectur
interest, such as the former imperial palace comple
(once known as the Forbidden City) and the Ten
ple and Altar of Heaven, have been carefully pr
served and are now open to the public. In the 19
and early 20th centuries, with a large community
foreign merchants, Shanghai grew rapidly as a maj
banking and trading centre. Since 1949, the city ha
lost its former commercial importance, but
remained China's largest and has emerged as
major centre for iron and steel, ships, textiles and
wide range of engineering products ■

MACAU

Portugal declared Macau independent from China in 1849, and a century later proclaimed it an Overseas Province. China's influence has grown steadily since the mid-1960s, and in 1976 Portugal granted Macau greater autonomy.

COUNTRY: Chinese territory under Portuguese administration
AREA: 16 sq km [6 sq mls]
POPULATION: 479,000
CURRENCY: Pataca = 100 avos

A Portuguese colony from 1557 and for 200 years one of the great trading centres for silk, gold, spices and opium, Macau was overtaken in importance by Hong Kong in the 19th century. When China re-established diplomatic relations with the colonial power in 1979, the coastal enclave was redefined as 'Chinese territory under Portu-

guese administration', and in 1987 the powers agreed that the territory will return to China in 1999 as a Special Administrative Region of that country – an agreement based on the 'one country, two systems' principle used by China and Britain to settle the future of Hong Kong in 1984.

Macau is a peninsula at the head of the Canton

(Pearl) River, 64 km [40 mls] west of Hong Kon and connected to China by a narrow isthmus. Th main industries are textiles and tourism, but there no airport – most visitors arrive via Hong Kong and the territory, with a population that is 98° Chinese, is heavily reliant on the Chinese mainlar for food, water and raw materials ■

TAIWAN

In 1928 the Nationalists adopted this design as China's national flag and used it in the long struggle against Mao Tse-tung's Communist army. When they were forced to retreat to Taiwan (then Formosa) in 1949, the flag went with them.

Taiwan is on the tropic line, but as the central island range reaches over 3,000 m [10,000 ft] at many points, it bears snow in the winter. Taipei has night temperatures below 20°C [68°F] from October–March, but over 30°C [86°F] in the daytime, June–September. There is heavy rainfall, heavier in the east than in the west of the island, falling mainly in the summer. Sunshine levels in the north are quite low – under three hours per day December–March and only over seven hours in July and August.

Ceded by the Chinese Empire to Japan in 1895, Taiwan was surrendered by the Japanese Army to General Chiang Kai-shek's Nationalist Chinese government in 1945. Beaten by Mao Tse-tung's Communists, some 2 million Nationalists and their leader fled the mainland to the island in the two years before 1949. The influx was met with hostility by the 8 million Taiwanese, and the new regime was imposed with force.

Boosted by US help, Chiang's government set about ambitious programmes for land reform and industrial expansion, the latter taking Taiwan into the world's top 20 nations by 1980 and providing high living standards. The island nevertheless remained politically isolated, losing its UN seat to Communist China in 1971, and being diplomatically abandoned by the US in 1979, when Washington switched recognition to Peking. Though few countries take seriously Taipei's claim to be the sole legitimate government of China, the country administers a number of islands (dao) off the mainland, notably Quemoy (Jinmen) and Matsu (Mazu).

High mountain ranges, which extend for the entire length of the island, occupy the central and eastern parts of Taiwan, and only a quarter of the island's surface area is cultivated. The central ranges rise to altitudes of over 3,000 m [10,000 ft], and carry dense forests of broadleaved evergreen trees such as camphor and Chinese cork oak. Above 1,500 m [5,000 ft], conifers such as pine, larch and cedar dominate.

With its warm, moist climate, Taiwan provides a highly favourable environment for agriculture, and the well-watered lands of the western coastal plain produce heavy rice crops. Sugar cane, sweet potatoes, tea, bananas and pineapples are also grown. Recently, however, agriculture has declined as industrial output has risen.

COUNTRY: Taiwan (Republic of China)
AREA: 36,000 sq km [13,900 sq mls]
POPULATION: 20,300,000
CAPITAL (Population): Taipei (2,680,000)
GOVERNMENT: Unitary republic with a unicameral legislature
ETHNIC GROUPS: Taiwanese (Han Chinese) 84%, mainland Chinese 14%
LANGUAGES: Mandarin Chinese (official)
RELIGIONS: Buddhist 43%, Taoist 21%, Christian 7%, Confucian
NATIONAL DAY: 10 October; Republic proclaimed (1911)
CURRENCY: New Taiwan $ = 100 cents
ANNUAL INCOME PER PERSON: $6,600
MAIN INDUSTRIES: Textiles, electrical and electronic goods, chemicals and fertilizers, plastics, agriculture, fishing
MAIN EXPORTS: Textiles and clothing 16%, electronic products 12%, information technology 7%, plastic and rubber 6%, footwear 6%, toys and games 5%
MAIN IMPORTS: Machinery and electrical equipment 29%, base metals 13%, chemicals 11%, transport equipment 8%, crude oil 5%, foodstuffs 5%
DEFENCE: 7.7% of national budget
POPULATION DENSITY: 554 per sq km [1,435 per sq ml]
INFANT MORTALITY: 7 per 1,000 live births
LIFE EXPECTANCY: Female 76 yrs, male 71 yrs
ADULT LITERACY: 91%
PRINCIPAL CITIES Population: Taipei 2,680,000 Kaohsiung 1,343,000 Tai-chung 715,000 Tainan 657,000 Chilung 349,000

Taiwan produces a wide range of manufactured goods, including colour television sets, electronic calculators, footwear and ready-made clothing, and is the world's leading shipbreaker. Taipei, the capital, is a modern and affluent city, and an important administrative and cultural centre.

Less than half the size of Ireland or Tasmania, but supporting 20 million people, Taiwan has been a remarkable success story, averaging nearly 9% growth every year from 1953 to the 1990s. The authoritarian regime lifted martial law after nearly 40 years in 1987, a native Taiwanese became president in 1988, and in 1991 came the country's first full general election. Technically still at war with Peking, there were signs – as in nearby Korea – that the thaw of the Cold War might reach the island ■

HONG KONG

Hong Kong has flown the Blue Ensign since 1841 when it became a British dependent territory. The coat of arms dates from 1959, and includes the British lion and the Chinese dragon. In 1997 Hong Kong will revert to Chinese government control.

Situated on the south coast of China and within the tropics, Hong Kong experiences the full power of the South-east Asian monsoon. Winter is mild and has enough rain to keep the land green; rain falls on only about 30 days between October and February. The summer is hot and humid with heavy rain, particularly between May and September. Typhoons (cyclones) occur mainly between June and October. Many swing northwards towards Japan but those which cross the coast can do great damage.

COUNTRY: Crown Colony of Hong Kong
AREA: 1,071 sq km [413 sq mls]
POPULATION: 5,801,000
GOVERNMENT: UK appointed governor with bicameral legislative assembly
ETHNIC GROUPS: Chinese 98%, others 2% (including European)
LANGUAGES: English and Chinese (official)
RELIGIONS: Buddhist majority, Confucian, Taoist, Christian, Muslim, Hindu, Sikh, Jewish
NATIONAL DAY: Christian and Chinese festivals, Queen's official birthday; 29 August – Liberation Day
CURRENCY: Hong Kong $ = 100 cents
ANNUAL INCOME PER PERSON: $11,540
MAIN INDUSTRIES: Textiles, electronics, watches, plastic goods, engineering, agriculture and fishing
MAIN EXPORTS: Textiles, clothing, plastic and light metal products, electronic goods
MAIN IMPORTS: Machinery, manufactures, chemicals
POPULATION DENSITY: 5,416 per sq km [14,029 per sq ml]
LIFE EXPECTANCY: Female 80 yrs, male 74 yrs
ADULT LITERACY: 85%

On 1 July 1997 the British Crown Colony of Hong Kong will pass into the hands of the Chinese government. What Peking will receive is Hong Kong Island, 235 smaller islands, the Kowloon peninsula on their province of Guangdong and the 'New Territories' adjoining it.

More important, they will inherit the world's biggest container port, its biggest exporter of clothes and its tenth biggest trader. Hong Kong's economy has been so successful since World War II that its huge neighbour will be increasing its export earnings by more than a quarter; in return, under a 1984 accord, China agrees to allow the territory to enjoy full economic autonomy and pursue its capitalist path for at least another 50 years.

Certainly the entrepreneurial spirit was still abroad as time ticked away to the changeover: in 1992 Hong Kong embarked on its scheme for a controversial new airport to replace the dangerous Kai Tak – the world's largest civil engineering project and due for opening in 1997, with final completion in 2040. Nevertheless, in the early 1990s, with the future uncertain and the spectre of Tiananmen Square still fresh, the economy began to slow as some businessmen drifted elsewhere and some services shifted to rivals such as Singapore.

The fortunes of this dynamic, densely populated community are based on manufacturing, banking and commerce, with the sheltered waters between Kowloon and Victoria providing one of the world's finest natural deep-water harbours. Yet the colony has little else, and most of its food, water and raw materials have to be brought in, principally from China. Its prosperity rests on the ingenuity, acumen and hard work of the people – and only time will tell if these attributes will be permitted to flourish ■

ASIA

NORTH KOREA

The Korean Democratic People's Republic has flown this flag since the country was split into two separate states in 1948. The colours are those of the traditional Korean standard, but in a new Communist design with a red star.

The eastern margins of Eurasia have much more extreme climates than those of the west, as can be seen by comparing Pyongyang with Lisbon at the same latitude. In winter, winds from central Asia give three months of bitter cold with some snow, particularly on the mountains to the east; the winter low records are around −28°C [−18°F]. In summer the wind blows from the ocean, bringing rain and increasing the average temperature by more than 30°C [54°F].

Mountains and rugged hills occupy most of the Korean peninsula, and only 20% of the surface area is suitable for cultivation. The interior of North Korea is a harsh environment, characterized by long and severe winters during which lakes and rivers regularly freeze over. High forested mountains, cut by river gorges, lie along the borders of North Korea and Manchuria. Further south, a chain of bare, eroded mountains runs for almost the entire length of the peninsula, parallel with and close to the eastern coast.

The most productive land in the peninsula occurs along the southern coast, where winters are relatively mild. While South Korea contains the best rice lands in the peninsula, most mineral resources, including coal – which supplies 70% of the country's energy needs – and iron ore, are concentrated in North Korea. Though the North has nearly 55% of the land area, it has only just over a third of the total Korean population.

The Stalinist regime of North Korea installed by the Soviet Union after World War II – and supported by China during the Korean War of 1950–3 – has been a total dictatorship revolving around the extraordinary and dynastic personality cult of Kim Il Sung and his nominated heir, Kim Jung Il, whom the president has also designated his successor as supreme commander of the army. The world's most durable Communist ruler, Kim Il Sung has imposed on North Korea his own unique brand of Marxism-Leninism which rests on the principles of self-reliance and party supremacy.

Since taking power, the 'Great Leader' has presided over the creation of a forbidding society virtually closed to foreigners and with few international friends. As the Cold War ended and the Soviet satellites strived for a new age, North Korea remained isolated from the momentous events taking place outside. In 1991, however, there were quite sudden signs of progress (*see South Korea*), with various and unexpected breakthroughs appearing to end confrontation on the peninsula.

While the Communist regime's collectivist agriculture programme has been reasonably successful – around 90% of cultivated land is under the control of co-operative farms – most of its effort went into the development of heavy industry, a decision which, after initial success, left the economy lagging well behind the 'sunrise' countries of the region, which moved quickly into electronics and computers. Defence, too, continues to be a significant drag on the economy, accounting for a quarter of state expenditure – another reason for healing the rift with South Korea and taking on a more open stance in international relations ∎

COUNTRY: Democratic People's Republic of Korea
AREA: 120,540 sq km [46,540 sq mls]
POPULATION: 21,773,000
CAPITAL (Population): Pyongyang (2,639,000)
GOVERNMENT: Single-party People's Republic
ETHNIC GROUPS: Korean 99%
LANGUAGES: Korean (official), Chinese
RELIGIONS: Traditional beliefs 16%, Chondogyo 14%, Buddhist 2%, Christian 1%
NATIONAL DAY: 15 August; Independence Day (1945)
CURRENCY: North Korean won = 100 chon
ANNUAL INCOME PER PERSON: $900
MAIN PRIMARY PRODUCTS: Coal, rice, iron ore
MAIN INDUSTRIES: Agriculture, iron and steel, chemicals, engineering, cement
MAIN EXPORTS: Iron and other metals, agricultural products, textiles
MAIN EXPORT PARTNERS: CIS nations 44%, Japan 15%, China 13%
MAIN IMPORTS: Crude petroleum, coal, machinery, transport equipment, chemicals, grain
MAIN IMPORT PARTNERS: CIS nations 35%, China 19%, Japan 13%
DEFENCE: 24% of national budget
POPULATION DENSITY: 181 per sq km [468 per sq ml]
LIFE EXPECTANCY: Female 74 yrs, male 68 yrs
ADULT LITERACY: 90%
PRINCIPAL CITIES (Population): Pyongyang 2,639,000 Hamhung 775,000 Chongjin 754,000

SOUTH KOREA

Adopted in 1950, South Korea's flag is the traditional white of peace. The central emblem signifies nature's opposing forces: the black symbols stand for the four seasons, the points of the compass and the sun, moon, Earth and heaven.

Strong north-westerly winds from central Asia give cold, dry weather in winter. Night temperatures, December–March, are usually well below freezing. Snow occurs on the western slopes of the mountains to the east of Seoul. Summer is hot and wet, the rapid transition giving rise to sea fog around the coasts in spring as warmer air from the south moves over the cold water surface. In July and August it rains on average every other day; from September to May it usually rains on under five days in a month.

For centuries the Koreans were very much a united people, an independent kingdom – 'Land of the Morning Calm' – knitted together by race, language and culture. Then, in 1910, came annexation by Japan and its harsh colonial rule, followed after World War II with division by the Allied powers into the Soviet (North) and American (South) zones of occupation each side of the 38th parallel. In 1948 the Soviets established a Communist regime in the North, the Americans a republic in the South, and the country – especially after the civil war of 1950–3 – seemed permanently partitioned. With a handful of interruptions, the two govern-

ments retained their hostile positions on the artificial frontier for nearly four decades; then, in 1991, the sides began to talk.

They first came together over a combined table-tennis team, yet only ten months later they had signed a full-blown non-aggression pact. In January 1992, following New Year messages from both presidents talking of unification, they signed a nuclear weapons agreement, setting up a joint control committee. While German-style reunification still seems a remote possibility in the near future – deep suspicion remains on both sides, and much depends on the events in North Korea after Kim Il Sung's departure – it was a remarkable breakthrough from such institutionalized positions.

The story of South Korea since the civil war had been a very different one from the North, though it was hardly a Far Eastern oasis of liberalism. While land reform based on smallholdings worked well enough to produce some of the world's highest rice yields (and self-sufficiency in food grains), the real economic miracle came in industrial expansion from the early 1960s. Initiated by a military government – one of several bouts of army rule since the inauguration of the republic – and based on slender natural resources, the schemes utilized cheap, plentiful but well-educated labour to transform the economy and make South Korea one of the strongest countries in Asia. The original manufacturing base of textiles remains important, but South Korea is now a world leader in footwear (first), shipbuilding (second), consumer electronics, toys and vehicles.

Seoul, hiding its pollution and housing shortages as best it could, celebrated the country's growth by hosting the 1988 Olympic Games: from a population of 1.4 million in 1950, it had reached 10.5 million by 1985. The dynamism of the country must now be linked to more liberal policies – and less spending on defence.

The economy was growing, too: at nearly 9% a year from 1960 to 1990. South Korea has now opened up the possibility of trade links with China, which, though Communist, is desperate to broaden its economic possibilities, while approaches are

being made to bodies to recognize the country's achievements and net status. Membership of the OECD for example, seems only a matter of time, though neither the South nor the North is a member of the United Nations ■

THE KOREAN WAR

Hastily divided in 1945 between a Soviet-occupied North and an American-occupied South, Korea was considered by most Western strategists an irrelevance to the developing Cold War. But when the heavily-armed North invaded the South in June 1950, US President Truman decided to make a stand against what he saw (mistakenly) as Moscow-organized aggression. A Soviet boycott of the UN allowed American troops – assisted by contingents from Britain, Canada, France and other allies – to fight under the UN flag, and under General Douglas MacArthur they went on the offensive. American seapower permitted a landing far behind North Korean lines, and soon the Northerners were in retreat.

With some misgivings, Truman ordered his forces north of the 38th parallel, the former partition line. But as US troops neared the Chinese frontier in November 1950, hundreds of thousands of Chinese 'volunteers' surged across the Yalu River and threatened to overwhelm them. They retreated far southwards in disarray, until a 1951 counter-attack slowly pushed back up the country and the combatants became entrenched along the 38th parallel in a bitter war of attrition that endured until an armistice was negotiated in 1953. Not until 1991, almost 40 years later, were North and South able to agree to a tentative non-aggression pact.

COUNTRY: Republic of Korea
AREA: 99,020 sq km [38,232 sq mls]
POPULATION: 43,302,000
CAPITAL (Population): Seoul (10,513,000)
GOVERNMENT: Unitary multiparty republic
ETHNIC GROUPS: Korean 99%
LANGUAGES: Korean (official)
RELIGIONS: Buddhist 20%, Protestant 16%, Roman Catholic 5%, Confucian 1%
NATIONAL DAY: 15 August; Independence Day (1945)
CURRENCY: South Korean won = 100 chon
ANNUAL INCOME PER PERSON: $5,400
MAIN PRIMARY PRODUCTS: Tungsten, rice, fish
MAIN INDUSTRIES: Agriculture, chemicals, electronic and electrical goods, shipbuilding, iron and steel
MAIN EXPORTS: Transport equipment 11%, electrical machinery 9%, footwear 6%, textile fabrics 5%
MAIN EXPORT PARTNERS: USA 39%, Japan 18%, Hong Kong 5%, Germany 4%, UK 3%, Canada 3%
MAIN IMPORTS: Petroleum and petroleum products 11%, electronic components 6%, chemicals 5%
MAIN IMPORT PARTNERS: Japan 33%, USA 21%, Germany 4%, Australia 3%
DEFENCE: 32.5% of national budget
TOURISM: 1,875,000 visitors per year
POPULATION DENSITY: 437 per sq km [1,133 per sq ml]
LIFE EXPECTANCY: Female 73 yrs, male 66 yrs
ADULT LITERACY: 93%
PRINCIPAL CITIES (Population): Seoul 10,513,000 Pusan 3,754,000 Taegu 2,206,000 Inchon 1,604,000

JAPAN

The geographical position of Japan in the East is expressed in the name of the country, Nihon-Koku (Land of the Rising Sun) and in the flag. Officially adopted in 1870, the simple design had already been used by Japanese emperors for many centuries.

Despite its maritime location, Tokyo has a large annual range of temperature (23°C [41°F]) due to the seasonal reversal of wind, blowing from the cold heart of Asia in winter and from the warm Pacific in summer. Winter weather is usually fine and sunny, but cold dry north-westerly winds often blow and frost may occur as late as April. Summer in Tokyo is hot and humid with abundant rainfall. The day temperature in August is usually over 30°C [86°F].

The Japanese archipelago lies off the Asian mainland in an arc extending from 45°N to 30°N, occupying a latitudinal range comparable to the Atlantic seaboard of the USA from Maine to Florida. Four large and closely grouped islands (Hokkaido, Honshu, Shikoku and Kyushu) constitute 98% of the nation's territory, the remainder being made up of some 4,000 smaller islands, including the Ryukyus, which lie between Kyushu and Taiwan. Japan is a medium-sized country, smaller than France but slightly larger than Italy.

Japan is a predominantly mountainous country and only 16% of the land is cultivable. Although Japan lacks extensive habitable areas, the population is nevertheless the seventh largest in the world. Limited land must therefore support many people, and Japan is now one of the most densely populated

countries in the world – with an ever-ageing profile.

The Japanese islands occupy a zone of instability in the Earth's crust, and earthquakes and volcanic eruptions are frequent. Throughout Japan, complex folding and faulting has produced an intricate mosaic of landforms, in which mountains and forested hills alternate with small inland basins and coastal plains. The pattern of landforms is further complicated by the presence of several volcanic cones and calderas. The highest mountain in Japan, the majestic cone of Fuji-san (3,776 m [12,388 ft]) is a long-dormant volcano which last erupted in 1707.

In the mountains, fast-flowing torrents, fed by snow-melt in the spring and by heavy rainfall during the summer, have carved out a landscape of deep valleys and sharp ridges. In central Japan, dense mixed forests of oak, beech and maple blanket

mountain slopes to an altitude of 1,800 m [5,900 ft]; further north in Hokkaido, boreal forests of fir and spruce predominate. In central Honshu, the Japan Alps with their snow-capped ridges provide spectacular mountain scenery.

Small intensively cultivated coastal plains, separated from one another by rugged mountain spurs, make up most of Japan's lowlands. None of the plains is extensive: the Kanto plain, which is the largest, covers an area of only 13,000 sq km [5,000 sq mls]. Most of the coastal plains are formed of material deposited by rivers, and their soils have been improved by centuries of careful cultivation.

Early Japan was peopled by immigrants arriving in successive waves from Korea and elsewhere on the Asian mainland. The earliest zone of settlement included northern Kyushu and the coastlands of the Setonaikai (Inland Sea). By the 5th century AD, Japan was divided amongst numerous clans, of which the largest and most powerful was the Yamato. Shinto, a polytheistic religion based on nature worship, had already emerged, as had the Japanese imperial dynasty.

During the next three centuries Chinese cultural and political influences entered Japan. These included Buddhism, the Chinese script, and Chinese methods of government and administration. At a later stage, Confucianism was also imported. Early cities, modelled on the capital of T'ang-dynasty China, were built at Nara (710) and at Kyoto (794); the latter city remained the seat of the imperial court until 1868.

The adoption of the Chinese system of centralized, bureaucratic government was relatively short-lived. From the early 12th century onwards, political power passed increasingly to military aristocrats, and government was conducted in the name of the emperor by warrior leaders known as *shoguns*. Civil warfare between rival groups of feudal lords was endemic over long periods, but under the rule of the Tokugawa *shoguns* (1603–1867), Japan enjoyed a great period of peace and prosperity; society was feudal and rigidly stratified, with military families (the feudal lords and their retainers, or *samurai*, forming a powerful élite. In the 1630s, Japan embarked on a lengthy phase of enforced isolation from the rest of the world.

This policy of seclusion could not be maintained indefinitely. In 1853, Commodore Perry of the US Navy arrived in Japan and demanded that ports be opened to Western trade. The capitulation of the *shogun* to Perry's demands prepared the way for the overthrow of the Tokugawa government, and the Meiji Restoration (1868) resumed imperial rule.

Under Western-style government, a programme of modernization was set in train. Industrialization proceeded swiftly, and after victories in the Sino-Japanese War (1894–5) and the Russo-Japanese War (1904–5), Japan began to build up an overseas empire which included the colonies of Taiwan and Korea. The growing strength of the Japanese military was demonstrated by the army's seizure of Manchuria in 1931. During the 1930s, and especially after the outbreak of war between Japan and China in 1937, militarist control of the government of Japan grew steadily. In 1941, the launching of a surprise attack on the American naval base of Pearl Harbor took Japan – and drew the USA – into World War II.

From its defeat in 1945 to 1952, Japan was administered by US forces. Many liberal and democratic reforms were enacted, and under the new constitution the power of the emperor was much reduced, with sovereignty vested in the people.

The main centres of population and industry are concentrated within a narrow corridor stretching from the Kanto plain, through the coastlands of the Setonaikai, to northern Kyushu. This heavily urbanized zone contains nine cities with populations of over a million and three great industrial regions centring respectively on Tokyo, Osaka and Nagoya. The capital Tokyo, almost certain to be overtaken by Mexico City and São Paulo as the world's most populous metropolis, forms the nucleus of a large and congested conurbation ■

COUNTRY: Japan (Nippon)

AREA: 377,800 sq km [145,869 sq mls]

POPULATION: 123,537,000

CAPITAL (Population): Tokyo (11,829,000)

GOVERNMENT: Constitutional monarchy with a bicameral legislature

ETHNIC GROUPS: Japanese 99%, Korean, Chinese

LANGUAGES: Japanese (official), Korean, Chinese

RELIGIONS: Shinto 93%, Buddhism 74%, Christian 1% (Most Japanese consider themselves to be both Shinto and Buddhist)

NATIONAL DAY: 23 December; the Emperor's birthday

CURRENCY: Yen = 100 sen

ANNUAL INCOME PER PERSON: $25,430

SOURCE OF INCOME: Agriculture 3%, industry 41%, services 56%

MAIN PRIMARY PRODUCTS: Rice, vegetables, timber, fish, copper, gold, sulphur, natural gas, coal, lead

MAIN INDUSTRIES: Iron and steel, electrical and electronic equipment, cars, ships, textiles, chemicals, food processing, forestry, petroleum refining

EXPORTS: $2,235 per person

MAIN EXPORTS: Machinery, electrical, electronic equipment 36%, vehicles and transport equipment 20%, iron and steel 6%, chemicals 6%, textiles 3%, ships 2%

MAIN EXPORT PARTNERS: USA 84%, South Korea 6%, Germany 6%, Taiwan 5%, Hong Kong 4%, UK 3%, China 3%

IMPORTS: $1,713 per person

MAIN IMPORTS: Petrol and petroleum products 18%, food and live animals 14%, machinery and transport equipment 11%, metals 10%, chemicals 8%, timber and cork 4%, textile fibres 2%

MAIN IMPORT PARTNERS: USA 21%, Indonesia 5%, South Korea 5%, Australia 5%, China 4%, Saudi Arabia 4%, Taiwan 4%

EDUCATIONAL EXPENDITURE: 9% of national budget

DEFENCE: 6.6% of national budget

TOTAL ARMED FORCES: 247,000

TOURISM: 1,939,000 visitors per year

ROADS: 1,127,500 km [700,600 mls]

RAILWAYS: 25,776 km [16,016 mls]

POPULATION DENSITY: 327 per sq km [847 per sq ml]

URBAN POPULATION: 77%

POPULATION GROWTH: 0.4% per year

BIRTHS: 10 per 1,000 population

DEATHS: 6 per 1,000 population

INFANT MORTALITY: 5 per 1,000 live births

LIFE EXPECTANCY: Female 82 yrs, male 76 yrs

POPULATION PER DOCTOR: 663

ADULT LITERACY: 99%

PRINCIPAL CITIES (Population): Tokyo 11,829,000 Yokohama 2,993,000 Osaka 2,636,000 Nagoya 2,116,000 Fukuoka 1,160,000 Sapporo 1,543,000 Kyoto 1,479,000 Kobe 1,411,000 Kawasaki 1,089,000

THE JAPANESE BOOM

In 1945 Japan lay in ruins, with its major cities in ashes – two of them dangerously radioactive. Its smouldering ports were choked with the sunken remnants of its merchant marine, and its people were demoralized. Less than two generations later, the Japanese economy was second only to that of the United States. Its high-technology products dominated world markets, while Japanese banks and private investors owned huge slices of industry and real estate on every continent.

The far-sighted American Occupation authorities deserve some of the credit. Realizing that industrial recovery could only go hand in hand with political development, they wrote Japan a new constitution. As a link with the past, the Emperor kept his place, but as a constitutional monarch answerable to a democratically elected Diet, with women given full voting rights for the first time. Trade unions, with the right to strike, were established, and land reform eliminated politically subservient tenants: by 1950, 90% of farmland was owner-cultivated. Great industrial conglomerates were broken into smaller units, and education was enormously expanded. Most ordinary Japanese accepted the reforms: they remembered the pain the old ways had brought.

The Korean War in 1950 gave the slowly recovering Japanese economy a tremendous boost. Japanese factories, well paid in American dollars, provided much of the steel, vehicles and other equipment the war demanded. When the Occupation formally ended in 1952, Japan was clearly on the way up. The American military presence, guaranteed by treaty, continued, but caused no resentment: on the contrary, safe beneath the US defence umbrella, Japan could devote its resources to productive industry, not armaments.

The Japanese owed the first stage of their transformation to the Americans; the rest, they did themselves. Carefully planned economic policies, directed by the Ministry of Trade and Industry –

nicknamed 'Japan Inc.'s Corporate Headquarters' – directed investment to key industries. First, the metal, engineering and chemical industries were rationalized and modernized. With the education system producing a steady stream of graduates, already trained in the industrial disciplines their future employers required, results were soon appearing. In the 1950s and 1960s efficient Japanese steelmakers consistently undersold European and American rivals, while producing better-quality steel. 'Made in Japan', once a sneering joke to describe shoddy goods, was taking on an entirely new commercial meaning.

Japan's major weakness was its near-total lack of natural resources; but foresight and planning made up for them. After the 1970s oil crisis, it was clear that the costs of heavy industry were going to rise unprofitably high; besides, the pollution they had brought was reaching dangerous levels. MITI switched resources to automobiles and electronics. Soon, Japan began to capture and dominate these markets, too.

By the 1980s, Japan's trading partners were becoming seriously alarmed. Noting that trade with Japan was largely a one-way traffic – Japan's home market is still notoriously hard to penetrate – they built protective walls of tariffs and duties. Japan responded with its usual flexibility: it bought factories within its rivals' walls, and traded from them. The Tokyo stock market even survived a serious 'crash' in the spring of 1992 – testament to the strength of the national economy. Even so, Japan's colossal trade surpluses in the early 1990s were causing not only resentment but also real danger to the world economic system.

President Bush secured some trading assurances from the Tokyo government, but these were largely cosmetic – and many economic experts continued to predict that the Japanese GNP figure would indeed be greater than that of the USA by the end of the century.

The winters of the north are cold with much snow. At Sapporo temperatures below -20°C [4°F] have been recorded between December and March, and frosts can occur from October–April. The temperature averages from November–May are all below 10°C [50°F]. Rain falls throughout the year, but it is drier February–June. Rainfall is just over 1,000 mm [39 in], but Hokkaido is one of the driest parts of Japan. The summers are warm with temperatures often exceeding 30°C [86°F].

BURMA

The colours were adopted following independence from Britain in 1948. The Socialist symbol, added in 1974, includes a ring of 14 stars for the country's states. The gearwheel represents industry and the rice plant symbolizes agriculture.

Once a green and gentle land, rich in agriculture and timber and blessed with many natural resources from precious stones to oil, Burma has become one of the three poorest countries in Asia and run by a regime whose record on human rights is among the world's worst. A change of name – the title Union of Myanmar was officially adopted in 1989 – has not changed the political complexion of a desperate nation.

Geographically, the country has three main regions. The core area is a great structural depression, largely drained by the Chindwin and Irrawaddy rivers. Its coastal zone has a wet climate, but the inner region between Prome and Mandalay constitutes a 'dry zone', sheltered from the south-west monsoon and with an annual rainfall of less than 1,000 mm [40 in]. In this dry zone, which was the original nucleus of the Burmese state, small-scale irrigation has long been practised in the narrow valleys, and rice, cotton, jute and sugar cane are important crops. Until 1964 Burma was the world's leading exporter of rice, and the crop still accounts for more than 40% of Burma's meagre export earnings. This central area was also the base of Burmah Oil, hosting the small fields that once made the country the British Empire's second largest producer. Even today it has sufficient oil and gas to meet most of Burma's needs.

To the west lie the fold mountains of the Arakan Yoma, while to the east rises the great Shan Plateau. In the south-east, running down the isthmus that takes Burma on to the Malay Peninsula, are the uplands of the Tenasserim, with hundreds of islands dotted along the coast of the Andaman Sea. More than 60% of the country is forested, rubber plantations augmenting the indigenous teak.

British since 1895, Burma was separate from

The rain associated with the south-east monsoon affects all the Burmese coastlands (4,000 mm [160 in]), but the rainfall is less in the shadows of the mountain ranges, with a dry zone in the middle Irrawaddy (400 mm [16 in]). The rainy season is May–October, and a very dry period is centred on December–January. Snow falls on the mountains of the north and east, but they also act as a barrier to the colder northern winter winds. Temperatures are high with little annual variation.

India as a crown colony in 1937. A battleground for Japanese and British troops in World War II, it became an independent republic in 1948 and left the Commonwealth. Military dictatorship came in 1962 and a one-party state in 1974, both headed by General Ne Win, leader of the Burma Socialist Programme Party.

'The Burmese Way to Socialism'

The party's rigid combination of state control, Buddhism and isolation, under the banner 'The Burmese Way to Socialism', had disastrous results, the country plunging quickly from prosperity to poverty. Politically, too, Burma was in a perilous state, with over a third of the country in rebel hands.

In the south-east the guerrillas of two Karen liberation movements control large tracts of mountains near the Thai border; in the north and east the Burmese Communist Party holds sway in most of Kachin and a good deal of Shan; here also, at the western end of the 'Golden Triangle', the authorities try to contain the local warlords' trafficking in opium. Another flashpoint is in the west, where Rohinya, the Muslim minority, have been persecuted by the army and repeatedly pushed over the border with Bangladesh in tens of thousands.

Burma spends more than 35% of its budget on 'defence' – much of it on the brutal suppression of political opposition and of human rights. In 1990, the coalition NLD won over 80% of the votes in a multiparty election conceded by the regime following violent demonstrations, but the ruling junta simply refused to accept the result – keeping its leader, Nobel Peace Prize winner Aung San Suu Kyi, under house arrest. The powerless opposition were forced to renounce the result and agree to a new and no doubt again ineffective agenda for a return to democracy.

Meanwhile, the country continued to crumble, if with great charm; despite the hideous regime a black market flourishes behind the crumbling colonial façade of Rangoon, once a rival to Bangkok and Singapore. Though some visitors make the trips round the attractions of Rangoon, Mandalay and Pagan, tourism is hardly encouraged by the suspicious government, and most of the country is still closed to foreigners.

Tenth biggest nation in Asia in both area and population, Burma remains an anomaly, holding out almost friendless against the tide of democratic and diplomatic change that swept the world in the late 1980s and early 1990s. It seems that, even with some form of conciliation, it will not long survive as a geopolitical entity ■

COUNTRY: Union of Myanmar (Socialist Republic of the Union of Burma)

AREA: 676,550 sq km [261,216 sq mls]

POPULATION: 41,675,000

CAPITAL (Population): Rangoon (2,459,000)

GOVERNMENT: Military regime

ETHNIC GROUPS: Burman 69%, Shan 9%, Karen 6%, Rakhine 5%, Mon 2%, Chin 2%, Kachin 1%

LANGUAGES: Burmese (official), English

RELIGIONS: Buddhist 85%, Christian 5%, Muslim 4%

NATIONAL DAY: 4 January; Independence Day (1948)

CURRENCY: Burmese kyat = 100 pyas

ANNUAL INCOME PER PERSON: $500

MAIN PRIMARY PRODUCTS: Zinc, tungsten, nickel, natural gas, oil, rubber, timber, cotton, groundnuts

MAIN INDUSTRIES: Forestry, mining, fishing, oil production

MAIN EXPORTS: Rice 41%, teak 24%, metals and ores 9%

MAIN EXPORT PARTNERS: India 12%, EC countries 12%, African countries 9%, Japan 6%, Middle East 6%

MAIN IMPORTS: Machinery 18%, base metals 10%, transport equipment 8%

MAIN IMPORT PARTNERS: Japan 33%, EC countries 13%, Eastern Europe 16%

DEFENCE: 35.5% of national budget

TOURISM: 47,000 visitors per year

POPULATION DENSITY: 62 per sq km [160 per sq ml]

INFANT MORTALITY: 59 per 1,000 live births

LIFE EXPECTANCY: Female 64 yrs, male 61 yrs

ADULT LITERACY: 79%

PRINCIPAL CITIES (Population): Rangoon 2,459,000 Mandalay 533,000 Moulmein 220,000 Pegu 150,000 Bassein 144,000

THAILAND

The two red and white stripes are all that remain of Thailand's traditional red-on-white elephant emblem, removed from the flag in 1916. The blue stripe was added in 1917 to show solidarity with the Allies in World War I.

BANGKOK

Temperature

Precipitation
1397mm
55in

Mountains shelter Bangkok from the rain-bearing south-westerly winds in summer, and although the distribution of rainfall is similar to much of South-east Asia, the total is relatively small, being less than half that of the other side of the mountains, a short distance to the west. Sometimes there can be near-drought conditions in November–April. The warm waters of the Gulf of Thailand to the south sustain uniformly high temperatures throughout the year. March to May are the hottest months.

Meaning 'Land of the Free' (*Muang Thai*), and known as Siam until 1939, Thailand is the only South-east Asian country that has not been colonized, or occupied by foreign powers, except in war. Comparable in size to France or Spain, Thailand is centred on the valley of the Chao Phraya River that flows across the central plain extending from the Gulf of Siam to the foothills of the northern mountains. Bounded in the west by the narrow mountain range that borders Burma, and in the east by lower hills separating the plain from the higher Khorat Plateau (Cao Nguyen Khorat), the central plain is Thailand's rice-bowl; it presents long vistas, with extensive rice-fields, canals and rivers that provide the main routeways, with villages on stilts.

The capital city Bangkok stands at the southern edge of the plain, near the mouth of the Chao Phraya; with a seaport and international airport it is the transport centre of the country. Ornate Buddhist temples stand side by side with modern concrete buildings, and the growing population is already over a tenth of the total. Extraordinarily, the country's next largest city is less than 200,000.

Northern Thailand is a region of fold mountains, with agriculturally rich intermontane basins. The hill forests produce teak and other valuable timbers. Thailand's highest mountain, Doi Inthanon (2,576m [8,451ft]) and the high hills surrounding it are the home of many hill tribes who live by shifting cultivation of dry rice and opium poppies; Chiengmai, the beautiful northern capital, lies in this area. The Khorat Plateau to the east is a sandstone region of poor soils supporting savanna woodlands; glutinous rice and cassava (the country has overtaken Brazil as the world's leading producer) are its main crops. The long southern part of Thailand, linked to the Malay Peninsula by the Isthmus of Kra, is a forested region of rolling hills, producing tin ore and plantation rubber.

Economy and politics

Thailand has long been famous for rice production; though fifth in the world league, it is the biggest exporter and it is still the country's best agricultural earner, despite the increasing importance of several other commodities including rubber, tapioca products and sugar. Wolfram, forest products and fisheries are also being exploited. Industries remain largely underdeveloped, but manufacturing based on cheap labour is expanding rapidly in textiles, clothing, electrical goods and food processing, contributing more to GDP than agriculture since 1984, while local crafts in the villages help to provide overseas income, as does tourism. In 1987 Thailand received nearly 3.5 million visitors – compared with Burma's 47,000.

An absolute monarchy until 1932, when the king graciously surrendered to a bloodless coup that set up a provisional constitution, Thailand has seen a more stable recent history than most of its unfortunate neighbours, though for most of the next 40 years it was dominated by military rulers. Forced into alliance with Japan in World War II, the Thais aligned themselves firmly to the USA after 1945 – a policy that has brought much military, technical and financial aid.

Despite continuing army involvements and interventions – the bloodless coup of 1991, claimed to be protecting King Rama IX and promising a swift return to civilian democracy, was the 17th takeover in half a century – and despite the presence of Cambodian refugees and its use by various camps as a political conduit and military springboard for intentions in South-east Asia, Thailand's subtle and pragmatic approach to life has seen the country prosper. In a system often referred to as 'semi-democracy', constitutional rule propped up by the pillars of military, monarch, bureaucracy and religion, Thailand has managed (not without criticism) to avoid the dreadful events that have afflicted the rest of mainland South-east Asia since the end of World War II – though in May 1992 the unelected leadership found itself under serious pressure. Hundreds died in protests against the takeover as prime minister by the head of the army, and an uneasy peace was restored only after his removal and an appeal for order from the King.

Situated about 30km [20mls] from the Gulf of Thailand, Bangkok is perhaps more dominant in its country's life than any Asian capital. A chaotic city of over 5 million people, it is a remarkable mixture of ancient and modern, subtle and gauche. The old city is a place of more than 300 temples and monasteries (*wats*) dotted near canals (*klongs*). Founded as a royal capital in 1782, this 'Venice of the East' is rich in examples of Thai culture, including fantastic statues of Buddha.

The name Bangkok is in fact incorrect: it means 'village of the wild plum' and refers only to the Thon Buri side of the Chao Praya River; the proper term is Krung Thep ('city of angels' – like Los Angeles). Today, however, it is a sprawling metropolis hopelessly ill-equipped to absorb the waves of migrants who pour in from the rural areas in search of work; while many of the girls find themselves not angels but prostitutes in what has become notorious as 'the sex capital of the world' ∎

COUNTRY: Kingdom of Thailand

AREA: 513,120 sq km [198,116 sq mls]

POPULATION: 57,196,000

CAPITAL (Population): Bangkok (5,609,000)

GOVERNMENT: Constitutional monarchy with a multiparty bicameral legislature

ETHNIC GROUPS: Thai 80%, Chinese 12%, Malay 4%, Khmer 3%

LANGUAGES: Thai (official), Chinese, Malay

RELIGIONS: Buddhist 95%, Muslim 4%, Christian 1%

NATIONAL DAY: 5 December; Birthday of HM the King

CURRENCY: Thai Baht = 100 stangs

ANNUAL INCOME PER PERSON: $1,420

MAIN PRIMARY PRODUCTS: Rice, rubber, maize, sugar cane, cassava, timber, fish, fruit, tin, iron, tungsten

MAIN INDUSTRIES: Agriculture, food processing, paper, cement, clothing, mining, forestry

MAIN EXPORTS: Textiles and clothing 15%, rice 9%, rubber 7%, tapioca products 5%, canned fish products 4%

MAIN EXPORT PARTNERS: USA 19%, Japan 15%, Singapore 9%, Netherlands 7%, Germany 5%, Hong Kong 4%

MAIN IMPORTS: Machinery and transport equipment 34%, basic manufactures 20%, chemicals 15%, fuels and lubricants 13%, crude materials 8%, foodstuffs 4%

MAIN IMPORT PARTNERS: Japan 26%, USA 12%, Singapore 8%, Germany 6%, Malaysia 4%, China 4%, Taiwan 4%, UK 3%

DEFENCE: 19.0% of national budget

TOURISM: 3,483,000 visitors per year

POPULATION DENSITY: 111 persq km [289 persq ml]

INFANT MORTALITY: 32 per 1,000 live births

LIFE EXPECTANCY: Female 69 yrs, male 65 yrs

ADULT LITERACY: 91%

PRINCIPAL CITIES (Population): Bangkok 5,609,000 Nakhon Ratchasima 191,000 Chiang Mai 151,000

ASIA

LAOS

Since 1975 Laos has flown the flag of the Pathet Lao, the Communist movement which won the long struggle for control of the country. The blue stands for the Mekong, the white disc the moon, the red the unity and purpose of the people.

Like much of South-east Asia, Laos experiences the seasonal reversal of winds associated with the monsoon. In winter Vientiane is sheltered from the north-east winds by mountains and the weather is sunny and dry. Rain falls often on only 1–5 days per month, October–April. The temperature increases steadily until April, when south-westerly winds mark the beginning of the wet season. There is great variation in daily sunshine, with 1–3 hours June–September, and 6–7 hours November–March.

Designated Asia's poorest country by the World Bank in 1989, Laos is a narrow, landlocked, largely mountainous country with no railways – the Mekong River is the main artery – where 85% of the sparse population work on collective farms at subsistence level, growing mainly rice. The hilly terrain broadens in the north to a wide plateau, 2,000 m [6,500 ft] above sea level, which includes the Plain of Jars, named after prehistoric stone funerary jars found by early French colonialists.

The Communists took power in 1975 after two decades of chaotic civil war following the departure of the colonial French, their policies bringing isolation and stagnation under the dominance of the Vietnamese government in Hanoi, who had used the country as a great supply line during their war with the US.

In 1986 the politburo embarked on their own version of *perestroika*, opening up trade links with neighbours (notably China and Japan), but most

crucially developing the export of hydroelectric power from the Mekong to Thailand. Most enterprises are now outside state control, while alternative crops to opium (Laos was estimated the world's third biggest source in the late 1980s) are being tried. Political reform towards a multiparty democracy, however, remains a forlorn hope ■

COUNTRY: Lao People's Democratic Republic
AREA: 236,800 sq km [91,428 sq mls]
POPULATION: 4,139,000
CAPITAL (Population): Vientiane (377,000)
GOVERNMENT: Single-party republic with a unicameral legislature
ETHNIC GROUPS: Lao 67%, Palaung-Wa 12%, Thai 8%, Man 5%
LANGUAGES: Laotian (official), French
RELIGIONS: Buddhist 58%, tribal religionist 34%, Christian 2%, Muslim 1%

NATIONAL DAY: 2 December
CURRENCY: New Kip = 100 cents
ANNUAL INCOME PER PERSON: $200
MAIN PRIMARY PRODUCTS: Rice, tin, gypsum
MAIN INDUSTRIES: Subsistence farming
MAIN EXPORTS: Electricity 50%, wood 29%, coffee
MAIN IMPORTS: Machinery and vehicles, petroleum, woven cotton fabrics
POPULATION DENSITY: 17 per sq km [45 per sq ml]
LIFE EXPECTANCY: Female 53 yrs, male 50 yrs
ADULT LITERACY: 45%

CAMBODIA

As well as being associated with Communism and revolution, red is the traditional colour of Cambodia. The silhouette is the historic temple of Angkor Wat. The blue symbolizes the water resources which are so vital to the people of Cambodia.

The heartland of Cambodia is a wide basin drained by the Mekong River, in the centre of which lies the Tonlé Sap ('Great Lake'), a former arm of the sea surrounded by a broad plain. From November to June, when rains are meagre and the Mekong low, the lake drains to the south and away to the sea. During the rainy season and period of high river water in June to October the flow reverses, and the lake more than doubles its area to become the largest freshwater lake in Asia.

The Tonlé Sap lowlands were the cradle of the great Khmer Empire, which lasted from 802 to 1432; its zenith came in the reign of Suryavarman II (1113–50), who built the great funerary temple of Angkor Wat: together with Angkor Thom, the 600 Hindu temples form the world's largest group of religious buildings. The wealth of 'the gentle kingdom' rested on abundant fish from the lake and rice from the flooded lowlands, for which an extensive system of irrigation channels and storage reservoirs was developed.

To the south-west stand low mountain chains, while the northern rim of the country is bounded by the Phanom Dangrek uplands, with a prominent sandstone escarpment. Three-quarters of the country is forested, and 90% of the population live on the fertile plains, mostly in small village settlements;

Phnom Penh, the capital, is the only major city.

Cambodia was under French rule from 1863 as part of French Indo-China, achieving independence in 1954. In a short period of stability during the late 1950s and 1960s the country developed its small-scale agricultural resources and rubber plantations – it has few workable minerals or sources of power – remaining predominantly rural but achieving self-sufficiency in food, with some exports. However, following years of internal political struggles, involvement in the Vietnam War, a destructive civil war and a four-year period of ruthless Khmer Rouge dictatorship – under which Pol Pot ordered the genocide of somewhere between 1 million and 2.5 million people – Cambodia was left devastated.

After the overthrow of Pol Pot in 1979 by Viet-

nam there was civil war between their puppet government of the People's Republic of Kampuchea (Cambodia) and the government of Democratic Kampuchea, a coalition of Prince Sihanouk – deposed by a US-backed coup in 1970 – Son Sann's Khmer People's Liberation Front and the Khmer Rouge, who from 1982 claimed to have abandoned their Communist ideology. It was this strange tripartite government in exile that was recognized by the United Nations.

Denied almost any aid, Cambodia continued to decline, but it was only the withdrawal of Vietnamese troops in 1989, sparking a fear of a Khmer Rouge revival, that forced a settlement. In October 1991, following numerous failures, a UN-brokered peace plan for elections by 1993 was accepted by all parties concerned, and a glimmer of real hope returned to the beleaguered people of Cambodia. However, peace was fragile and there was the massive problem of hundreds of thousands of refugees camped over the border in Thailand – itself plunged into turmoil in the spring of 1992 ■

COUNTRY: State of Cambodia
AREA: 181,040 sq km [69,900 sq mls]
POPULATION: 8,246,000
CAPITAL (Population): Phnom Penh (500,000)
GOVERNMENT: Single-party republic with one legislative assembly
ETHNIC GROUPS: Khmer 93%, Vietnamese, Chinese
LANGUAGES: Khmer (official), French
RELIGIONS: Buddhist 88%, Muslim 2%

CURRENCY: 1 riel = 100 sen
ANNUAL INCOME PER PERSON: $300
MAIN PRIMARY PRODUCTS: Salt, iron ore, phosphates
MAIN INDUSTRIES: Agriculture
MAIN EXPORTS: Iron and steel, rubber manufactures
MAIN IMPORTS: Machinery and transport equipment
POPULATION DENSITY: 46 per sq km [118 per sq ml]
LIFE EXPECTANCY: Female 52 yrs, male 50 yrs
ADULT LITERACY: 48%

VIETNAM

First used by the forces of Ho Chi Minh in the liberation struggle against Japan in World War II, the design was adopted as the national flag of North Vietnam in 1945. It was retained when the two parts of the country were reunited in 1975.

Temperature variation throughout the year is not great. April–May are the hottest months, November–January the coolest, but never falling below 25°C [77°F]. Night temperatures rarely fall below 20°C [68°F]. There are lower temperatures in the inland mountains. There is heavy rainfall throughout the year, except January–March which are drier, with some years having no rain in these months. Typhoons (cyclones) can hit the coastal areas.

A land of mountains, coastal plains and deltas, Vietnam is perhaps Asia's most strangely shaped country. In the north the coastal lands widen into the valley and delta of the Hongha (Red) River and the valley of the Da. This region has long been the main cultural focus of the country, and it was the original core of the Annamite Empire which came

into being with the revolt against Chinese rule in AD 939. In the south of the country, the coastal plains open out into the great delta of the Mekong, the world's tenth longest river.

For most of their length the coastal lowlands are backed in the west by the mountains of the Annamite Chain, and to the north the country is dominated by the plateaus of Laos and Tongking, often characterized by an intensely craggy, inhospitable karstic (limestone) landscape. The mountain areas are the home of many different hill peoples.

Vietnam already had a long and turbulent history before the French, following decades of missionary involvement and a military campaign lasting 25 years, made it a French protectorate in 1883, later joined by Laos and Cambodia in the French Indo-Chinese Union. Freedom movements starting early in the 20th century made little headway until the end of World War II, when Communist-led guerrillas under Ho Chi Minh, having fought the Japanese occupation, declared Vietnam once again united and free. There followed a war against the French (1946–54), which produced Communist North Vietnam and non-Communist South Vietnam, and then the cataclysm of over a decade of war against the USA, before reunificaiton as a Communist state.

Vietnam was left exhausted – 2 million of its people died in the American war alone and the countryside was devastated – and the problems facing the new Communist government in 1976 were enormous. Doctrinaire policies and further aggravation of the Western powers in Cambodia did not help its economic and political isolation, and in 1978

there started the sad saga of the 'Boat People' – peasants fleeing hardship and perhaps persecution in Vietnam to find a new life in Hong Kong and elsewhere; after being put into camps, many were forcibly repatriated years later.

The Hanoi regime softened its position in many ways from the late 1980s, efforts being made to establish diplomatic and trading ties with important international clients and aid donors, Soviet assis-

tance having dwindled with the events in the USSR. However, Vietnam's huge standing army of 1.2 million (plus reserves of 3 million) remained a great drain on a desperately poor nation subsisting on agriculture: rice, cassava, maize, sweet potatoes and the world's largest population of ducks. Despite the industries of the north, based on natural resources, the economy needed to diversify along the pattern of the 'sunrise' countries of eastern Asia ■

COUNTRY: Socialic Republic of Vietnam
AREA: 331,689 sq km [128,065 sq mls]
POPULATION: 66,200,000
CAPITAL (Population): Hanoi (3,100,000)
GOVERNMENT: Unitary single-party socialist republic
ETHNIC GROUPS: Vietnamese 87%, Chinese (Hoa) 2%, Tai 2%, Thai 2%, Khmer 1%, Muong 1%, Nung 1%
LANGUAGES: Vietnamese (official), Chinese, Tho (Tay), Khmer, Muong, Thai, Nung, Miao, Jarai, Rhadé, Hre, Bahnar
RELIGIONS: Buddhist 55%, Roman Catholic 7%
NATIONAL DAY: 2–3 September
CURRENCY: Dong = 10 hao = 100 xu
ANNUAL INCOME PER PERSON: $300
MAIN PRIMARY PRODUCTS: Coal, anthracite, lignite, cereals, timber

MAIN INDUSTRIES: Mining, food processing, textiles, agriculture
MAIN EXPORTS: Raw materials 46%, handicrafts 24%, agricultural products 10%
MAIN EXPORT PARTNERS: CIS nations 51%, Hong Kong 14%, Japan 9%, Singapore 9%, Czechoslovakia 5%, EC countries 3%, Poland 2%, Hungary 2%
MAIN IMPORTS: Fuel and raw materials 45%, machinery 23%, wheat flour and food products 17%
MAIN IMPORT PARTNERS: CIS nations 69%, Japan 8%, Singapore 7%, Hong Kong 3%, EC countries 3%
POPULATION DENSITY: 200 per sq km [517 per sq ml]
INFANT MORTALITY: 54 per 1,000 live births
LIFE EXPECTANCY: Female 66 yrs, male 62 yrs
ADULT LITERACY: 94%
PRINCIPAL CITIES (Population): Ho Chi Minh City 3,900,000 Hanoi 3,100,000 Haiphong 1,279,000 Da Nang 319,000

CONFLICT IN INDO-CHINA

Vietnamese conflict dates back at least to 1939, when the Viet Minh coalition of nationalists, including Communists, began agitating for independence from France; by 1945, with experience in anti-Japanese resistance behind them, they would not accept a quiet return to colonial administration after the Japanese collapse. Proclaiming the Democratic Republic of Vietnam, within months they were fighting French troops sent from Europe. Gradually, the Viet Minh, increasingly dominated by a well-organized Communist leadership under Ho Chi Minh, began to overwhelm the French. The US, alarmed by the Viet Minh's Communism, provided weaponry and logistical support, but Presidents Truman and Eisenhower both refused to allow American military aid. The climax came in May 1954, when a besieged French army surrendered at Dien Bien Phu. At a subsequent peace conference at Geneva, the French abandoned their colony. The country was partitioned between a Communist north, its capital in Hanoi, and a non-Communist south, administered from Saigon. The Geneva accord assumed Vietnamese elections would follow, and included an explicit proviso: the division was 'provisional, and should not in any way be interpreted as constituting a political or territorial boundary'.

Still anxious to avoid military engagement, the US poured aid into the South, the supposedly Democratic Republic of Vietnam. In fact, as US intelligence reports repeatedly explained to the White House, the republic was far from democratic, and its ruling élite was quite incapable of running the country, far less inspiring its people's loyalty; most of them would vote Communist if the elections were ever held. The elections were postponed, on the grounds that Communist violence would prevent a fair outcome – probably true, but giving Hanoi justification for a guerrilla campaign in the South, spearheaded by the Viet Cong, heirs to the Viet Minh tradition.

The newly elected President Kennedy decided to make a stand against Communism in Vietnam, despite the cautious counsel of his most experienced diplomats. American aid was backed up by military advisers, then combat units. The Viet Cong continued to make headway. After Kennedy's assassination in 1963, President Johnson increased the military commitment. US aircraft blasted Vietnam with more explosives than had been used in all of World War II; American casualties began to rise – more than 50,000 would die – and with them the tide of anti-war sentiment back home. By 1968, Johnson was convinced that the war could not be won; he stood down from power. Under his successor, Richard Nixon, the war continued, drawing neighbouring Cambodia into the cauldron. Yet real military progress remained as elusive as ever.

Finally, in 1972, a peace was signed. The Americans withdrew; in 1975 North Vietnamese troops rolled across the 'provisional' border, and the country was reunited. To delay a Communist victory by less than 20 years, the Americans had paid a high price in prestige abroad and political discord at home. The Vietnamese had paid vastly higher in lives. And although Vietnam triumphed in a subsequent 1979 war against its former Chinese allies, political repression and economic disaster caused its people to risk their lives by the thousand in seaborne escapes – the refugee 'Boat People' – during the 1980s.

MALAYSIA

The red and white bands date back to a revolt in the 13th century. The star and crescent are symbols of Islam; the blue represents Malaysia's role in the Commonwealth. This version of the flag was first flown after federation in 1963.

In common with many coastal places close to the Equator, Kuala Lumpur has very uniform temperature throughout the year. The length of daylight and the intensity of the noonday sun varies little from one season to another and the sea is always very warm. The daytime temperature is about 32°C [90°F]. Rainfall is abundant at all seasons, but with a double maximum around the equinoxes, when the tropical rainbelt lies close to the Equator. Rain falls on over 200 days in the year.

The new country of Malaysia was born in 1963 by the joining of the Federation of Malaya (independent from Britain since 1957), the island state of Singapore and the colonies of Sarawak and North Borneo (renamed Sabah). In 1965 Singapore seceded to become an independent nation, and the present federation comprises 11 states and a federal territory (Kuala Lumpur) on the Malay Peninsula, and two states and a federal territory (Labuan) in northern Borneo. The regions are separated by some 650 km [400 mls] of the South China Sea.

The Malay Peninsula is dominated by fold mountains with a north-south axis. There are seven or eight ranges, with frequently exposed granite cores. The most important is the so-called Main Range, which runs from the Thai border to the south-east of Kuala Lumpur, attaining 2,182 m [7,159 ft] at its highest point, Gunong Kerbau. South of the Main Range lies the flat and poorly drained lowland of Johor, which is punctuated by isolated hills, often rising over 1,060 m [3,500 ft]. The small rivers of Malaya have built up a margin of lowland around the coasts.

Northern Borneo has a mangrove-fringed coastal plain, up to 65 km [40 mls] wide, backed by hill country averaging 300 m [1,000 ft] in height. This is dominated by the east-west fold mountains of the interior, which rise from 1,400 m to 2,300 m [4,500 to 7,500 ft]; the most striking is the granite peak of Mt Kinabalu (4,101 m [13,455 ft]) in Sabah, Malaysia's highest mountain.

The natural vegetation of most of Malaysia is lowland rainforest and its montane variants. The Malaysian forests, which are dominated by the dip-terocarp family of trees, are the richest in species of all the world's forests. Unfortunately, few undisturbed areas remain, mostly in such national parks as the Gunong Mulu in Sarawak and the Kinabalu in Sabah.

An early golden age of Malay political power came in the 15th century with the rise of the kingdom of Malacca, which controlled the important sea routes and trade of the region. In 1414, the ruler of Malacca accepted the Islamic faith, which remains the official religion of Malaysia today. The country is, however, characterized by great ethnic, religious and cultural diversity, with Malays of many different origins, Chinese and Indians (mainly brought in by the British to work the tin mines and rubber plantations), Eurasians, Europeans and a number of aboriginal peoples, notably in Sabah and Sarawak.

This patchwork has, understandably, caused tensions, particularly between the politically dominant Muslim Malays and the economically dominant, mainly Buddhist, Chinese, but while riots did break out in 1969, it has never escalated into serious armed conflict; nor has it prevented remarkable economic growth that has, according to the World Bank ratings, made Malaysia an upper middle income country.

The traditional mainstays of the economy – rice plus exports of rubber, palm oil and tin (Malaysia is the world's biggest producer of all three) – have been supplemented by exploitation of other natural resources, notably oil and timber, though the pace of the latter is causing widespread unrest among environmentalists. Exports are now safely diverse, from Sarawak's pepper to the new Proton 'national car', and with a growing tourist industry in support Malaysia seems set to join Japan and the four 'little dragons' as a success story of postwar eastern Asia ▶

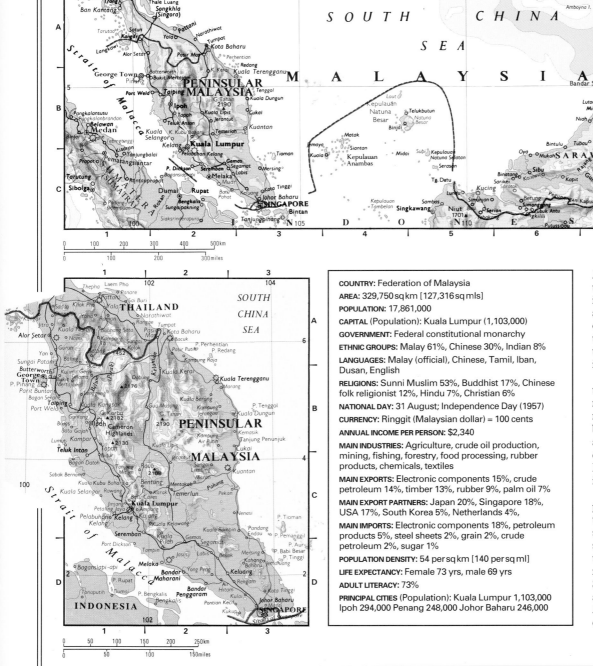

COUNTRY: Federation of Malaysia

AREA: 329,750 sq km [127,316 sq mls]

POPULATION: 17,861,000

CAPITAL (Population): Kuala Lumpur (1,103,000)

GOVERNMENT: Federal constitutional monarchy

ETHNIC GROUPS: Malay 61%, Chinese 30%, Indian 8%

LANGUAGES: Malay (official), Chinese, Tamil, Iban, Dusan, English

RELIGIONS: Sunni Muslim 53%, Buddhist 17%, Chinese folk religionist 12%, Hindu 7%, Christian 6%

NATIONAL DAY: 31 August; Independence Day (1957)

CURRENCY: Ringgit (Malaysian dollar) = 100 cents

ANNUAL INCOME PER PERSON: $2,340

MAIN INDUSTRIES: Agriculture, crude oil production, mining, fishing, forestry, food processing, rubber products, chemicals, textiles

MAIN EXPORTS: Electronic components 15%, crude petroleum 14%, timber 13%, rubber 9%, palm oil 7%

MAIN EXPORT PARTNERS: Japan 20%, Singapore 18%, USA 17%, South Korea 5%, Netherlands 4%,

MAIN IMPORTS: Electronic components 18%, petroleum products 5%, steel sheets 2%, grain 2%, crude petroleum 2%, sugar 1%

POPULATION DENSITY: 54 per sq km [140 per sq ml]

LIFE EXPECTANCY: Female 73 yrs, male 69 yrs

ADULT LITERACY: 73%

PRINCIPAL CITIES (Population): Kuala Lumpur 1,103,000 Ipoh 294,000 Penang 248,000 Johor Baharu 246,000

BRUNEI

The yellow background represents the Sultan, with the black and white stripes standing for his two main advisers (wazirs). The arms contain the inscription in Arabic 'Brunei, Gate of Peace' and a crescent, the symbol of Islam.

The climate is hot and humid, the temperatures varying little over the year from a minimum of 24°C [75°F] to a maximum of 30°C [86°F]. Rainfall is heaviest in November and March, when the equatorial monsoon blows onshore. When the monsoon is offshore, June–August, the weather is a little drier and brighter. Rainfall can exceed 5,000 mm [200 in] well up in the mountainous interior. The amount of sunshine varies between 6.5–8.5 hours a day.

Comprising two small enclaves on the coast of northern Borneo, Brunei rises from humid plains to forested mountains over 1,800 m [6,000 ft] high along the Malaysian border. Formerly a British protectorate, and still a close ally of the UK, the country was already rich from oil (discovered by Shell in 1929) when it became independent in 1983. Today oil and gas account for 70% of GDP and even more of export earnings – oil 41%, gas 53% – though income from the resultant investments overseas exceeds both. Imports are dominated by machinery, transport equipment, manufactures and foodstuffs. Brunei is, however, currently undergoing a drive towards agricultural self-sufficiency.

The revenues have made Sultan Hassanal Bolkiah (crowned 1968) allegedly the world's richest man, and given his people the second highest income per capita in Asia after Japan. There is no income tax system in Brunei and citizens enjoy free cradle-to-the-grave welfare. All government employees (two-thirds of the workforce) are banned from political activity, and the Sultan and his family retain firm control ∎

COUNTRY: The Islamic Sultanate of Brunei
AREA: 5,770 sq km [2,228 sq mls]
POPULATION: 266,000
CAPITAL (Population): Bandar Seri Begawan 58,000
GOVERNMENT: Absolute monarchy with an advisory legislative body and councils
ETHNIC GROUPS: Malay 69%, Chinese 18%, Indian
LANGUAGES: Malay and English (official), Chinese
RELIGIONS: Muslim 63%, Buddhist 14%, Christian 10%
NATIONAL DAY: 23 February
CURRENCY: Brunei $ = 100 cents
ANNUAL INCOME PER PERSON: $6,000
POPULATION DENSITY: 46 per sq km [119 per sq ml]
LIFE EXPECTANCY: Female 73 yrs, male 70 yrs
ADULT LITERACY: 80%

SINGAPORE

Adopted in 1959, this flag was retained when Singapore broke away from the Federation of Malaysia in 1963. The crescent stands for the nation's ascent and the stars for its aims of democracy, peace, progress, justice and equality.

Uniformly high temperature, averaging 27°C [80°F], high humidity and heavy rain in all months of the year are typical of a place situated very close to the Equator and surrounded by water. The daytime temperature is usually always above 30°C [86°F]. Rain is usually intense and thunder occurs on an average of 40 days a year. As in much of the tropics, rainfall varies greatly from year to year, the highest recorded being more than twice the lowest. Rain falls on over 180 days per year.

When Sir Stamford Raffles established British influence in 1819, leasing the island and its muddy Malay fishing village for the East India Company, there were only 150 inhabitants. This had not always been so; 'Singapura' (the city of the lion) was an important settlement in the 14th century, but had been destroyed in the rivalry between the great kingdoms of Madjapahit (Java) and Siam. The modern city, originally planned by Raffles, remained under British rule until self-government in 1959. In 1963, Singapore became part of the Federation of Malaysia, but seceded in 1965 to become a fully independent nation.

The republic comprises the main island itself and an additional 54 much smaller islands lying within its territorial waters. The highest point on the main island is Bukit Tiamah (177 m [581 ft]). The position of Singapore at the southernmost point of the Malay Peninsula, controlling the Strait of Malacca, has throughout history been one of enormous strategic importance.

Singapore is one of the world's most remarkable commercial and industrial experiments. It is, in effect, a city-state, its downtown thick with skyscrapers, the most densely populated country in South-east Asia and an economy based on its vast port, manufacturing and commerical and financial services.

The port began its modern expansion as a conduit for shipping out tin and rubber from Malaya. Today, easily the world's busiest, it handles nearly 70 million tonnes a year, much of it entrepôt (re-export) trade but also involving significant amounts of materials for and from its own thriving industries.

The success of Singapore owes much to the vision and dynamism of Lee Kuan Yew, prime minister from independence in 1959 to 1990, who despite having a predominantly Chinese population in a Malay region made his ambitious policies work. The strategy of industrialization, first labour- and later skill-intensive, gave Singapore an average growth of 7% a year and made it the richest of Asia's four 'little dragons'.

The cost, however, was a lack of genuine democracy, his regime increasingly bordering on a one-party dictatorship; his attitude, essentially, was that Singapore could not afford the luxury – or danger – of political debate. Impressive though the new city may be, most Singaporeans live in massive apartment blocks reminiscent of postwar Eastern Europe, with most aspects of their lives rigidly controlled and much of their former culture buried forever beneath a Western façade.

Lee's groomed successor, Goh Chok Tong, seemed set to continue his policies with equal vigour, turning Singapore into the hub of an expanding region. Despite its political stance, it was in the vanguard of nations opening up links with the reticent Communist countries of Laos, Vietnam and North Korea in the post-*perestroika* era.

The future of his party's wealthy establishment appeared secure, with the island state setting its sights on replacing Hong Kong as eastern Asia's second financial and commercial centre after Tokyo. The feeling nevertheless persisted that Singapore's crucial tertiary activity would give it little to fall back on in the face of a really deep and lasting world recession ∎

COUNTRY: Republic of Singapore
AREA: 618 sq km [239 sq mls]
POPULATION: 3,003,000
CAPITAL (Population): Singapore (2,680,000)
GOVERNMENT: Unitary multiparty republic with a unicameral legislature
ETHNIC GROUPS: Chinese 76%, Malay 15%, Indian 7%
LANGUAGES: Chinese, Malay, Tamil, English (all official)
RELIGIONS: Buddhist 28%, Christian 19%, Muslim 16%, Taoist 13%, Hindu 5%
NATIONAL DAY: 9 August; Independence Day (1965)
CURRENCY: Singapore dollar = 100 cents
ANNUAL INCOME PER PERSON: $12,310
MAIN PRIMARY PRODUCTS: Rubber, coconuts, vegetables, fruit, fish
MAIN INDUSTRIES: Oil refining, oil drilling equipment, chemicals, textiles, shipbuilding, electronic goods

EXPORTS: $16,671 per person
MAIN EXPORTS: Machinery and transport equipment 50%, mineral fuels 15%, manufactured goods 8%, chemicals 6%, crude materials 4%, foodstuffs 4%
MAIN EXPORT PARTNERS: USA 24%, Malaysia 14%, Japan 9%, Hong Kong 6%, Thailand 6%, Germany 4%
IMPORTS: $18,536 per person
MAIN IMPORTS: Machinery and transport equipment 44%, mineral fuels 14%, manufactured goods 9%, chemicals 8%, foodstuffs 5%
MAIN IMPORT PARTNERS: Japan 22%, USA 16%, Malaysia 15%, Taiwan 5%, Saudi Arabia 4%
DEFENCE: 20.7% of national budget
TOURISM: 3,373,000 visitors per year
POPULATION DENSITY: 4,859 per sq km [12,585 per sq ml]
INFANT MORTALITY: 8 per 1,000 live births
LIFE EXPECTANCY: Female 77 yrs, male 71 yrs
ADULT LITERACY: 86%

ASIA

INDONESIA

While the colours date back to the Middle Ages, they were adopted by political groups in the struggle against the Dutch in the 1920s and became the national flag in 1945, when Indonesia finally proclaimed its independence from the Netherlands.

The most remarkable feature of Jakarta's climate is the almost constant high temperature throughout the year. Daytime temperatures reach 29–31°C [84–88°F], only cooling to around 23°C [73°F] at night. This is due to its location on the shores of the hot Java Sea and the uniform intensity of the midday sun and duration of daylight, with an average of over six hours of sunshine a day. Rainfall is heaviest in summer, most of it falling in thunderstorms which occur on average 136 days a year.

With the break-up of the Soviet Union in 1991, Indonesia moved up from the fifth to the fourth most populous nation on Earth. It is also the world's largest archipelago, with 13,677 islands (less than 6,000 of which are inhabited) scattered over an enormous area of tropical sea. However, three-quarters of the area is included in the five main centres of Sumatra, Java, Kalimantan (southern Borneo), Sulawesi (Celebes) and Irian Jaya (the western end of New Guinea), which also include over 80% of the people; more than half the population live on Java alone, despite its being only 7% of the land area.

Most of the big islands stand on continental shelves and have extensive coastal lowlands, though Sulawesi and the chain of islands between Java and Irian Jaya rise from deep water. All are mountainous, for this is an area of great crustal activity. Along the arc formed by Sumatra, Java and the Lesser Sunda Islands stand over 200 volcanoes – including Krakatoa (Pulau Rakata).

The natural vegetation of the tropical lowlands is rainforest, which also spreads up into the hills. Much of this has now been cleared by shifting cultivators and replaced by secondary growth, though forest is still the dominant vegetation on most of the less populated islands. About a tenth of the land area is under permanent cultivation, mostly rice, maize, cassava and sweet potato, and Indonesia remains essentially an agricultural nation. There are also large plantations of rubber (second in the world), sugar cane, coffee (first in Asia) and tea. Accessible parts of the rainforest are being exploited at an alarming rate for their valuable timber; native forest in Sumatra is now virtually restricted to reserves and national parks, though mountain forests, less vulnerable because they are more isolated, still remain over wide areas. Many of the coasts are lined with mangrove swamps, and several accessible islands are stunningly beautiful; tourism is one of the country's fastest growing sectors.

The population of Indonesia is complex and varied. There is a wide range of indigenous peoples, speaking some 25 different languages and over 250 dialects. Four of the world's major religions – Islam, Hinduism, Christianity and Buddhism – are well represented, though followers of Islam are in the great majority and Indonesia is the world's most populous Muslim nation.

The first important empire in the region was centred at Palembang in south-eastern Sumatra. This was the great maritime power of Sri Vijaya, which held sway from the 8th to 13th centuries over the important trade routes of the Malacca and Sunda Straits. During the 14th century it was replaced by the kingdom of Madjapahit, centred on the fertile lands of east-central Java. From the 16th century onwards, European influences grew, the area coming progressively under the domination and ruthless exploitation of the Dutch East India Company. Freedom movements starting in the early 20th century found their full expression under Japanese occupation in World War II, and Indonesia declared its independence on the surrender of Japan in 1945. After four years in intermittent but brutal fighting, the Dutch finally recognized the country as a sovereign state in 1949 under Achmed Sukarno, leader of the nationalist party since 1927.

Sukarno's anti-Western stance and repressive policies plunged his sprawling country into chaos and poverty, while costly military adventures drained the treasury. In 1962 he invaded Dutch New Guinea (Irian Jaya) and between 1963 and

1966 he attempted to destabilize the fledgling Federation of Malaysia by incursions into northern Borneo. Throughout his dictatorship Indonesia seemed to be permanently on the edge of disintegration, government forces fighting separatist movements in various parts of the island chain.

In 1967 Sukarno was toppled by General Suharto, following the latter's suppression of a two-year allegedly Communist-inspired uprising that cost 80,000 lives. However, his military regime, with US technical and financial assistance, brought a period of relatively rapid economic growth, supported by an oil boom that by 1970 accounted for 70% of export earnings – a figure that shrank to less than 50% by 1990. Self-sufficiency in rice and a degree of population control also helped raise living standards, though Java's overcrowding remained a problem, and in 1986 a 'transmigration programme' was initiated to settle large numbers of Javanese on sparsely populated islands, notably (and notoriously) on Irian Jaya.

While the Javanese dominate Indonesian affairs, most of the country's wealth – oil, timber, minerals and plantation crops – comes from other islands. Establishing better relations with the West and its ASEAN (Association of South-east Asian Nations) neighbours, the government has now deregulated much of the economy, but corruption and nepotism remain rife and power is firmly in the hands of Golkar, the military-backed coalition which thwarts the aspirations of the two permitted political parties. The army, perhaps correctly, continues to regard itself as the only protector of stability in a country that has proved almost impossible to govern ■

EAST TIMOR

Invaded by Indonesian troops in 1975, East Timor has effectively remained its 21st state despite numerous UN condemnatory resolutions. The end of the Cold War has done little to ease the people's plight; Australia still does not recognize their right to self-determination, while the Western powers leave the problem to the ineffectual UN.

East Timor was a neglected, coffee-growing Portuguese colony for 300 years before Lisbon promised independence in 1974. The 1975 free elections were won by Fretilin, the left-wing nationalists who had fought the empire for years, but the following month Indonesia occupied the territory. Their policies of deportation, resettle-ment, harassment, torture, bombings, summary executions and massacres – including one filmed by a British film crew in 1991 – have resulted in the deaths of a third of the population (still officially 630,000) and the encampment of 150,000 or more, according to Amnesty International. At the same time, 100,000 Indonesians have been settled in a country rich in sandalwood, marble and coffee, with oil reserves of 5 billion barrels.

Fretilin's fighters, who returned to the hills in 1975, have since kept up a sporadic and dispersed campaign, while the population – mostly Catholic – await international help. In practice, however, East Timor stays closed to the world.

COUNTRY: Republic of Indonesia

AREA: 1,904,570 sq km [735,354 sq mls]

POPULATION: 179,300,000

CAPITAL (Population): Jakarta (7,348,000)

GOVERNMENT: Unitary multiparty republic with bicameral legislature

ETHNIC GROUPS: Javanese 40%, Sundanese 15%, Bahasa Indonesian 12%, Madurese 5%, over 300 others

LANGUAGES: Bahasa Indonesia (official), Javanese, Sundanese, Dutch, over 20 others

RELIGIONS: Sunni Muslim 87%, Christian 10% (Roman Catholic 6%), Hindu 2%, Buddhist 1%

NATIONAL DAY: 17 August; Anniversary of the Proclamation of Independence (1945)

CURRENCY: Indonesian rupiah = 100 sen

ANNUAL INCOME PER PERSON: $560

MAIN PRIMARY PRODUCTS: Rice, cassava, sweet potatoes, sugar cane, soya beans, coffee, tobacco, tea, rubber, fish, timber, oil and natural gas, bauxite

MAIN INDUSTRIES: Agriculture, mining, oil refining, fishing, textiles, cement, fertilizers, chemicals

MAIN EXPORTS: Crude petroleum 35%, natural gas 14%, wood and cork manufacture 11%, coffee, tea

MAIN IMPORTS: Machinery 30%, chemicals 19%, iron and steel 15%, petroleum and petroleum products 9%

TOURISM: 900,000 visitors per year

POPULATION DENSITY: 94 per sq km [244 per sq ml]

LIFE EXPECTANCY: Female 60 yrs, male 57 yrs

ADULT LITERACY: 74%

PRINCIPAL CITIES (Population): Jakarta 7,348,000 Surabaya 2,224,000 Medan 1,806,000 Bandung 1,567,000 Semarang 1,206,000

PHILIPPINES

The eight rays of the large sun represent the eight provinces that led the revolt against Spanish rule in 1896, and the three smaller stars stand for the three main island groups. The flag was adopted on independence from the USA in 1946.

The climate of the Philippines is tropical, the temperature, except in the mountains, rarely dropping below 20°C [68°F]. There is a dry season between about December–April, but there is very high rainfall often associated with typhoons in the rest of the year, especially July and August. The latter is particularly true in the eastern Pacific-facing islands and coastlands. The cooler and drier seasons usually coincide. February to May are the sunniest months, with an average of 7–8 hours per day.

The Republic of the Philippines consists of 7,107 islands, of which, 2,770 are named and about 1,000 permanently inhabited, with the two largest, Luzon and Mindanao, taking up over two-thirds of the total area. The country lacks extensive areas of lowland and most of the islands are characterized by rugged interior mountains, the highest of which are Mt Apo (2,954m [9,691ft]) in Mindanao and Mt Pulog (2,929m [9,610ft]) in Luzon. There are over 20 active volcanoes in the islands, including Mt Apo and Mt Pinatubo, which erupted violently in 1991. The most important lowland region is the central plain of Luzon, a key rice-producing area and a major zone of population concentration, including the Manila Bay area.

The most impressive man-made sight, however, is the spectacular series of irrigated rice terraces that contour the mountain slopes in the northern interior of Luzon. These have been constructed by Igorot tribesmen, descendants of some of the earliest people to colonize the Philippines. Elsewhere in the islands, and especially on Cebu, Leyte and Negros, maize is the staple foodstuff, reflecting the Philippines' former contacts with Spanish America. Another link is Roman Catholicism; over 80% Catholic, and named after King Philip II of Spain, the country is the only predominantly Christian nation of any size in Asia.

Following three centuries of harsh Spanish rule the islands were ceded to the US in 1898 after the Spanish-American War. Ties with the USA have remained strong, notably during the corrupt regime of President Ferdinand Marcos (1965–86), though in 1991 the Philippines government announced the closure of Subic Bay naval base, the largest in Asia, by the end of 1992.

Marcos was overthrown by the 'people power' revolution that brought to office Cory Aquino, wife of the opposition leader assassinated in 1983, but the political situation remained volatile, with Communist and Muslim Nationalist rebels undermining stability. The economy, lacking any real natural resources, is weak, and levels of unemployment and emigration among Filipinos are high ∎

COUNTRY: Republic of the Philippines

AREA: 300,000 sq km [115,300 sq mls]

POPULATION: 61,480,000

CAPITAL (Population): Manila (1,728,000)

GOVERNMENT: Unitary republic with a bicameral legislature

ETHNIC GROUPS: Tagalog 30%, Cebuano 24%, Ilocano 10%, Hiligaynon Ilongo 9%, Bicol 6%, Samar-Leyte 4%

LANGUAGES: Pilipino (Tagalog) and English (official), Spanish, Cebuano, Ilocano, over 80 others

RELIGIONS: Roman Catholic 84%, Aglipayan 6%, Sunni Muslim 4%, Protestant 4%

NATIONAL DAY: 12 June; Independence Day (1946)

CURRENCY: Philippine peso = 100 centavos

ANNUAL INCOME PER PERSON: $730

MAIN PRIMARY PRODUCTS: Copper, coal, iron, nickel, chrome, rice, maize, sugar cane, coconuts, abaca, tobacco, rubber, coffee, pineapples, bananas

MAIN INDUSTRIES: Agriculture, food processing, textiles, chemicals, mining, timber, fishing

MAIN EXPORTS: Electrical and electronic equipment 20%, clothing 19%, coconut oil and products 8%, minerals 5%, fish 3%, timber 3%

MAIN EXPORT PARTNERS: USA 35%, Japan 17%, Netherlands 5%, Germany 5%, Hong Kong 5%, UK 5%

MAIN IMPORTS: Mineral fuels 19%, chemicals 13%, parts for electrical equipment 11%, machinery 8%, electrical machinery 7%, base metals 6%

MAIN IMPORT PARTNERS: USA 22%, Japan 17%, Taiwan 6%, Kuwait 5%, Hong Kong 5%, Germany 4%

DEFENCE: 14.7% of national budget

POPULATION DENSITY: 205 per sq km [531 per sq ml]

LIFE EXPECTANCY: Female 67 yrs, male 63 yrs

ADULT LITERACY: 86%

PRINCIPAL CITIES (Population): Manila 1,728,000 Quezon City 1,326,000 Cebu 552,000 Caloocan 525,000

AFRICA

AFRICA

Extending to some 35° north and south of the Equator, the vast continent of Africa covers a wide range of environments. Mediterranean Africa, lying north of the Sahara, includes the sharply folded and eroded Atlas Mountains; the coastal and Nile Valley lands were the home of the ancient civilization of Egypt, with rich evidence of early Phoenician, Greek, Roman and Muslim contacts. The Sahara Desert stretches across northern Africa from west to east, containing the mountain massifs of Hoggar and Tibesti; lowlands to the east are threaded from south to north by the Nile Valley.

South of the Sahara, Africa may be divided by the 1,000 m [3,000 ft] contour line running from south-west (Angola) to north-east (Ethiopia). North of this line the low plateaus of Central and West Africa surround the great basins of the Congo and Niger rivers and the inland basin of Lake Chad. Here are Africa's major areas of tropical rainforest, with savanna dominant on the inner and higher ground. East and south of this contour lie Africa's highest plateaus and mountains, and the complex rift valley systems of north-eastern and East Africa.

The rift valleys of East Africa are part of the most extensive fissure in the Earth's crust, extending south from the Dead Sea, down the Red Sea, across the Ethiopian Highlands, through Kenya to reach the sea again near the mouth of the Zambezi. Both this main rift and its principal branch to the west of Lake Victoria contain deep, long lakes of which Tanganyika, Turkana (formerly Rudolf) and Nyasa are the largest. Here also are the high, open and grassy savanna plains with most of Africa's famous

West from Greenwich   East from Greenwich

0   400   800   1200   1600km
0   200   400   600   800   1000miles

wildlife game parks and great snow-capped peaks, notably Kilimanjaro. South and west of the Zambezi River system lie the arid uplands of the Kalahari and Namib deserts, and the dry highlands of Namibia. In the far south a damper climate brings Mediterranean conditions to the plains of South Africa, and to the Drakensberg and Cape Ranges.

The Sahara Desert formed a barrier that was at least partly responsible for delaying European penetration; Africa south of the Sahara remained the 'Dark Continent' for Europeans until well into the 19th century. The last 15 years of the century saw the final stages of the European 'scramble for Africa', that resulted in most of the continent being partitioned between and colonized by Britain, France, Germany, Belgium, Portugal and Spain. Today almost all the states of Africa are independent, though traces of their recent colonial history are still evident in their official languages, administrative institutions, legal and educational systems, architecture, transport networks and economics.

The colonial pattern, and the current political pattern succeeding it, were superimposed on a very complex and fluid system of indigenous tribal states and cultures, many of which have proved to be remarkably resilient. There are many hundreds of ethnic groups, languages and religions; indeed the peoples of Africa themselves are of many physical types, at many different levels of economic, social and political development, and they have reacted in differing ways to European colonial rule: the continent's peoples are culturally just as heterogeneous as the indigenous peoples of any continent ■

AFRICA

CLIMATIC REGIONS

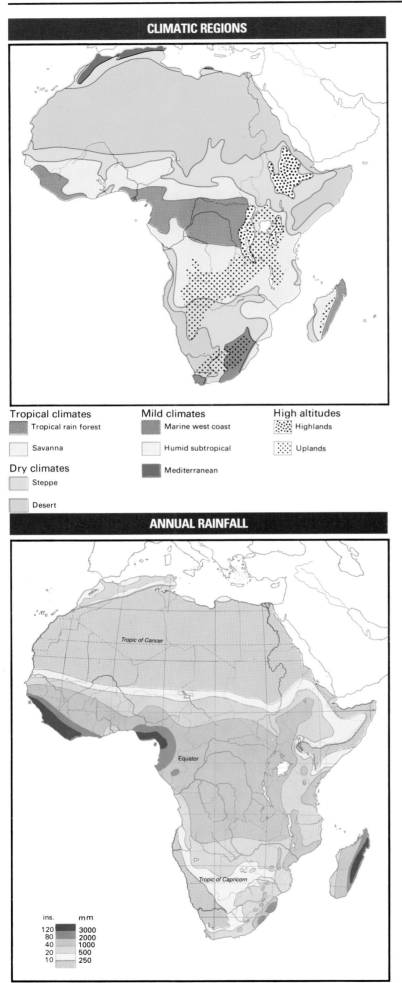

Tropical climates
- Tropical rain forest
- Savanna

Dry climates
- Steppe
- Desert

Mild climates
- Marine west coast
- Humid subtropical
- Mediterranean

High altitudes
- Highlands
- Uplands

ANNUAL RAINFALL

ins.	mm
120	3000
80	2000
40	1000
20	500
10	250

NATURAL VEGETATION

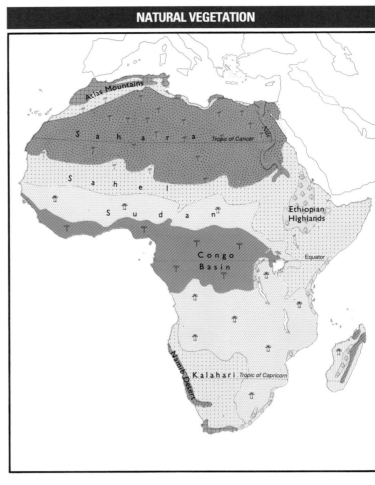

Atlas Mountains

Sahara

Sahel

Sudan

Tropic of Cancer

Nile

Ethiopian Highlands

Congo Basin

Equator

Namib Desert

Kalahari

Tropic of Capricorn

- Equatorial rain forest
- Temperate forest
- Evergreen trees and shrubs
- Grassland and savanna
- Oases and Nile valley
- Steppe and semidesert
- Desert

POPULATION

- · 100 000 people

AFRICA

LAND USE

LAND USE	
Arable land	Woods and forests
Arable land with permanent pasture	Rough grazing
Fruit trees, vineyards and plantations	Rough grazing with trees
Permanent pasture	Non-productive land

LIVESTOCK

Cattle   Sheep

CROPS

Bananas		Olives
Barley		Palm oil
Cacao		Rice
Citrus fruits		Rubber
Cloves		Sisal
Coconut palms		Sugar beet
Coffee		Sugar cane
Cotton		Tea
Date palms		Tobacco
Groundnuts		Vines
Maize		Wheat
Millet		Principal fishing areas

MINERALS

Asbestos		Uranium
Bauxite		Zinc
Copper	Sb	Antimony
Diamonds	Cr	Chrome
Gold	Co	Cobalt
Graphite	Mn	Manganese
Iron ore	Ni	Nickel
Lead		
Lead and zinc		**POWER**
Phosphate		Coalfields
Silver		Gasfields
Tin		Oilfields
		Hydroelectric power

0 200 400 600 800 1000km

0 200 400 600miles

LAND USE

Arable land and permanent crops 7%

Permanent pasture 27%

Other land 44·4%

Woods and forests 21·6%

Total land area 2 964.6 million hectares (7 325·5 million acres)

Projection: Zenithal Equidistant   West from Greenwich   East from Greenwich

COPYRIGHT GEORGE PHILIP LTD.

AFRICA

MOROCCO

A red flag had been flown in Morocco since the 16th century and the star-shaped green pentagram, the Seal of Solomon, was added in 1915. This design was retained when Morocco gained independence from French and Spanish rule in 1956.

The Atlantic coast of Morocco is washed by the cool Canaries Current which keeps summers notably cool for the latitude, the highest recorded temperatures being only just over 40°C [100°F]. Inland, summers are hot and dry with bright sunshine, but near the coast low cloud and fog are not infrequent. In winter the prevailing winds are westerly, bringing rain from the Atlantic and often heavy snow over the High Atlas Mountains of the interior. Frosts have been recorded at Casablanca.

the home of the University of Kairaouin – founded in 859 and the oldest educational institution in the world. Morocco is Africa's biggest tourist destination, the only one attracting more than 2 million visitors a year (1987 figures). Tunisia and Egypt are its nearest rivals.

Western Sahara is a former Spanish possession (and the province of Spanish Sahara from 1960) occupying the desert lands between Mauritania and the Atlantic coast; with an area of 266,000 sq km [102,700 sq mls] it is more than half the size of Morocco. Most of the indigenous population are Sahrawis, a mixture of Berber and Arab, almost all of whom are Muslims. The capital is El Aaiún which has 97,000 of the country's 173,000 inhabitants. Many of these are desert nomads.

Rich in phosphates – it has the world's largest known deposits of phosphate rock – the country has since the mid-1970s been the subject of considerable conflict, with the Rabat government claiming the northern two-thirds as historically part of 'Greater Morocco'. While Morocco has invested heavily in the two-thirds or so of Western Sahara it controls the rich earnings from the phosphate exports could finance more economic, social and educational programmes. In 1991, more than 170,000 Sahrawi refugees were living in camps around Tindouf, in western Algeria.

A ceasefire was agreed in 1991 between the Rabat government and the Polisario Front, the Sahrawi liberation movement, which are still in dispute over the territory. In 1992 the peace, overseen by the UN, remained fragile ∎

The name Morocco is derived from the Arabic *Maghreb-el-Aksa* ('the Farthest West'). Over the centuries the country's high mountains have acted as a barrier to penetration, so that Morocco has been much less affected by outside influences than Algeria and Tunisia. Morocco was the last North African territory to succumb to European colonialism; not until 1912 did the Sultan of Morocco accept the French protectorate, in a settlement that gave Spain control of the Rif Mountains and several enclaves along the coast (of which Ceuta and Melilla remain under Spanish administration).

In 1956 France and Spain gave up their protectorate as Morocco became independent, and in 1958 the international zone of Tangier was incorporated in a unified Morocco, which became an independent kingdom. Ruled since 1961 by the authoritarian and nationalistic regime of King Hassan II, Morocco is today one of only three kingdoms left on the continent of Africa, though the king's grip was showing signs of slipping during the 1980s.

Since independence a large proportion of the once-important European and Jewish communities have departed. To the difficulties accompanying reunification were added the burdens of a fast-growing population – nearly half the people are under 15 – high unemployment and lack of trained personnel and capital. Yet Morocco has considerable potential for economic development: the country possesses large cultivable areas, abundant water

supplies for irrigation and hydroelectric power, and diverse mineral resources including deposits of iron ore, lead and zinc.

Agriculture and industry

More than a third of Morocco is mountainous. The main uplands are the High, Middle and Anti 'arms' of the Atlas Mountains in the west and north, and a plateau in the east. Two principal ways of life exist in the mountains – peasant cultivation and semi-nomadic pastoralism.

In contrast to these, modern economic development is found in the Atlantic plains and plateaus. The major irrigation schemes created during the colonial period are situated here, and the majority of Morocco's agricultural production – citrus fruits, grapes (for wine), vegetables, wheat and barley.

Phosphates, of which Morocco is the world's leading exporter and third largest producer, are mined around Khouribga as well as in Western Sahara. These are the vital raw material for fertilizers. But the country's modern industry is concentrated in the Atlantic ports, particularly in Casablanca, which is the largest city, chief port and major manufacturing centre.

The biggest growth industry, however, is tourism, based on the Atlantic beaches, the Atlas Mountains and the rich, international history of cities like Casablanca, Tangier, Agadir, Marrakech, Rabat and Fès (Fez), famed not only for its hat but also as

COUNTRY: Kingdom of Morocco
AREA: 446,550 sq km [172,413 sq mls]
POPULATION: 25,061,000
CAPITAL (Population): Rabat (893,000)
GOVERNMENT: Constitutional monarchy
ETHNIC GROUPS: Arab-Berber 99%
LANGUAGES: Arabic (official), Berber
RELIGIONS: Muslim (mainly Sunni) 99%
NATIONAL DAY: 3 March; Accession of Hassan II (1961)
CURRENCY: Moroccan dirham = 100 Moroccan francs
ANNUAL INCOME PER PERSON: $950
MAIN INDUSTRIES: Agriculture, wine, food processing, textiles, leather goods, fertilizers, mining, forestry
MAIN EXPORTS: Food and beverages 27%, phosphoric acid 15%, phosphates 13%, clothing 10%
MAIN IMPORTS: Capital goods 21%, crude oil 15%, consumer goods 12%, foodstuffs 11%, sulphur 6%
DEFENCE: 14% of national budget
TOURISM: 2,248,000 visitors per year
POPULATION DENSITY: 56 per sq km [145 per sq ml]
INFANT MORTALITY: 68 per 1,000 live births
LIFE EXPECTANCY: Female 65 yrs, male 62 yrs
ADULT LITERACY: 70%
PRINCIPAL CITIES (Population): Casablanca 2,158,000 Rabat-Salé 893,000 Fès 548,000 Marrakech 482,000

ALGERIA

Algeria's flag features traditional Islamic symbols and colours, and the design dates back to the early 19th century. Used by the liberation movement that fought against French rule after 1954, it was adopted on independence in 1962.

ALGIERS

Algiers is exposed to the maritime influences of the Mediterranean Sea but is sheltered from the Sahara to the south by the Atlas Mountains. The temperature range, both annual and diurnal, is remarkably small – annual 13°C [23°F], diurnal 6°C [11°F]. Frosts have not been recorded. Rainfall has a winter maximum typical of the Mediterranean region and amounts vary greatly from year to year. The mountains to the south are often snow-covered in winter.

COUNTRY: Democratic and Popular Republic of Algeria

AREA: 24,960,000 sq km [919,590 sq mls]

POPULATION: 24,960,000

CAPITAL (Population): Algiers (1,722,000)

GOVERNMENT: Socialist republic with unicameral legislature

ETHNIC GROUPS: Arab 83%, Berber 16%, French

LANGUAGES: Arabic (official), Berber

RELIGIONS: Sunni Muslim 98%, Roman Catholic

NATIONAL DAY: 1 November; Anniversary of the Revolution (1954)

CURRENCY: Algerian dinar = 100 centimes

ANNUAL INCOME PER PERSON: $2,060

MAIN PRIMARY PRODUCTS: Oil and natural gas, phosphates, iron ore, lead, copper, cereals, fruit, olives, timber, livestock

MAIN INDUSTRIES: Oil refining, gas, petrochemicals, mining, agriculture, wine, food processing

MAIN EXPORTS: Crude oil, petroleum products, natural gas 97%, wine, vegetables and fruit

MAIN IMPORTS: Machinery and transport equipment 29%, semi-finished products 29%, foodstuffs 18%

DEFENCE: 9.6% of national budget

TOURISM: 800,000 visitors per year

POPULATION DENSITY: 10 per sq km [27 per sq ml]

LIFE EXPECTANCY: Female 67 yrs, male 63 yrs

ADULT LITERACY: 50%

PRINCIPAL CITIES (Population): Algiers 1,722,000 Oran 664,000 Constantine 449,000 Annaba 348,000 Blida 191,000

THE ATLAS MOUNTAINS

Extending from Morocco into northern Algeria and Tunisia, the Atlas is a prominent range of fold mountains. Its highest peak and the highest in North Africa, Jebel Toubkal (4,165 m [13,670 ft]), is one of a jagged row – the High Atlas – in central Morocco; the lesser ranges cluster on either side and to the east, generally with a north-east to south-west trend.

In Morocco there are the Anti-Atlas in the south-west, the Middle Atlas in the centre of the country and the Er Rif mountains near the Mediterranean coast. In Algeria the range includes the Saharan Atlas and, further north, the Tell or Maritime Atlas. Heavily glaciated during the Ice Age, the highest Atlas ranges are now capped with alpine tundra and patches of permanent snow. North-facing slopes receive good winter rainfall, and are forested with pines, cedars, and evergreen and cork oaks. Tablelands between the ranges provide high pastures and rich soils for farming. The southern and eastern ranges are drier and covered with semi-desert scrub.

After Sudan, Algeria is the biggest political unit in the Middle East and Africa, and the world's 10th largest nation. However, over 90% of the country's 24.9 million inhabitants live in the Mediterranean coastlands. The vast Saharan territories, covering over 2 million sq km [772,200 sq mls], or about 85% of the total area, are very sparsely populated; most of the inhabitants are concentrated in the oases, which form densely-populated 'islands'. The majority of the population speak Arabic, but there is a significant Berber-speaking indigenous minority in the mountainous north-east.

Like its neighbours Morocco and Tunisia, Algeria experienced French colonial rule and settler colonization. Algeria was the first Maghreb country to be conquered by France and the last to receive independence, following years of bitter warfare between nationalist guerrillas and the French armed forces. European settlers acquired over a quarter of the cultivated land, mainly in north-western Algeria, and rural colonization transformed the plains, producing cash crops.

Oil was discovered in the Algerian Sahara in 1956 and Algeria's natural gas reserves are among the largest in the world. The country's crude-oil refining capacity is the biggest in Africa. Since independence in 1962 revenues from oil and gas, which provide 65% of all revenue and account for over 90% of exports, have enabled the government to embark on an ambitious economic development programme, with rapid industrialization.

Industrial developments include iron and steel plants, food processing, chemicals and textiles, while Algeria is one of the few African nations to have its own car-manufacturing facility, producing about a third of its commercial vehicles. In addition there is an array of production allied to the oil and gas reserves: oil refineries, petrochemical plants and gas liquefication units. While most of the larger industries are nationalized, much of the light industry remains under private control.

Though agriculture has suffered by comparison, about 30% of Algerians are farmers. Arable land accounts for only 3% of Algeria's total land area, but the rich northern coastlands produce wheat, barley, vines and olives – as well as early fruit and vegetables for the European markets, notably France and Italy. Further south, dates are important, but in the mountains the primary occupation of the Berber population is the rearing of sheep, cattle and goats.

In January 1992, with the Islamic fundamentalist FIS on course for electoral victory, the government cancelled the second round and declared a state of emergency, effectively ending Algeria's four-year flirtation with Western-style democracy ∎

TUNISIA

The Tunisian flag features the crescent and the star, traditional symbols of Islam. It originated in about 1835 when the country was still officially under Turkish rule and was adopted after independence from France in 1956.

Although most of the rain in Tunisia falls in winter when the region is affected by low pressure, prevailing north-easterly winds from the sea in summer result in a shorter dry season than is found in many parts of the Mediterranean basin. Rain falls on a few days throughout the summer. The influence of the sea also helps to moderate extremes of temperature and although they are mostly sunny, summer days are seldom oppressive, humidity being quite low.

Smallest of the three Maghreb countries that comprise north-west Africa, Tunisia has a long and rich history. It was the first part of the region to be conquered by the Phoenicians, Romans (Carthage is now a suburb of Tunis) and later the Arabs and Turks, and each successive civilization has left a marked impression on the country. Consequently Tunisia has acquired a distinct national identity, with a long tradition of urban life. Close contacts with Europe have always existed – France established a protectorate in 1881 – and the majority of today's 1.8 million tourists a year are European.

Tunisia consists of the eastern end of the Atlas Mountains together with the central steppelands to the south, which are separated from the country's Saharan sector by the vast low-lying saltpans of Chott Djerid. In the north the lower Medjerda Valley and the low-lying plains of Bizerte and Tunis were densely colonized. Major irrigation schemes have been carried out in recent years and these lowlands, which produce cereals, vines, citrus fruits, olives and vegetables, represent the country's most important agricultural area. New industries, sometimes coupled with tourism, have transformed a number of coastal towns, including Sfax, Monastir and Sousse. By comparison the interior has been neglected. Although Tunisia has introduced the elements of democracy since the removal of Habib Bourguiba in 1987, it remains effectively a one-party (RCD) dictatorship. In 1992 the government also clamped down heavily on the already outlawed Islamic fundamentalist movement, latest threat to its supremacy ■

COUNTRY: Republic of Tunisia
AREA: 163,610 sq km [63,170 sq mls]
POPULATION: 8,180,000
CAPITAL (Population): Tunis (774,000)
GOVERNMENT: Multiparty republic
ETHNIC GROUPS: Arab 98%, Berber 1%, French
LANGUAGES: Arabic (official), French
RELIGIONS: Sunni Muslim 99%
NATIONAL DAY: 20 March; Independence Day (1956)
CURRENCY: Dinar = 1,000 millimes
ANNUAL INCOME PER PERSON: $1,420
MAIN PRIMARY PRODUCTS: Crude oil and natural gas, phosphates, salt, lead, iron, timber, fruit, wheat
MAIN INDUSTRIES: Tourism, mining, oil refining, food processing, phosphate processing, textiles
MAIN EXPORTS: Petroleum and derivatives 24%, clothing 20%, fertilizers 12%
MAIN EXPORT PARTNERS: France 22%, Germany 20%, Italy 17%, Belgium 7%
MAIN IMPORTS: Machinery 17%, petroleum and derivatives 8%, raw cotton, cotton yarn and fabrics
MAIN IMPORT PARTNERS: France 27%, Germany 13%, Italy 11%, USA 6%
TOURISM: 1,875,000 visitors per year
POPULATION DENSITY: 50 per sq km [129 per sq ml]
LIFE EXPECTANCY: Female 68 yrs, male 67 yrs

LIBYA

The simplest of all world flags, Libya's represents the nation's quest for a green revolution in agriculture. Libya flew the flag of the Federation of Arab Republics until 1977, when it left the organization.

When the kingdom of Libya gained independence from British and French military administration in 1951, the former Turkish possession and Italian colony was one of the poorest countries in the world, with a predominantly desert environment, few known natural resources and a largely nomadic, poor and backward population. This bleak picture changed dramatically after 1959 with the discovery of vast reserves of oil and gas.

With growing revenues from petroleum and gas exports, important highways were built to link the different regions across the desert, and considerable investment was made in housing, education and health provision. Today the country's income per head is twice that of its nearest rivals on the African continent – Algeria, Gabon and South Africa. But despite a high population growth rate (6.5%), the process of agricultural development and industrialization still relies heavily on immigrant specialists and workers.

In 1969 a group of 12 army officers overthrew King Idris in a coup and control of all matters has since been in the hands of the Revolutionary Command Council, chaired in dictatorial style by Colonel Muammar Gaddafi. While this includes a violently pro-Palestinian and anti-Western stance, Gaddafi also has long-running disputes with his neighbours, notably Chad and Sudan ■

COUNTRY: Socialist People's Libyan Arab Jamahiriya
AREA: 1,759,540 sq km [679,358 sq mls]
POPULATION: 4,545,000
CAPITAL (Population): Tripoli (980,000)

EGYPT

Egypt has flown a flag of red, white and black (the Pan-Arab colours) since 1958 but with various emblems in the centre. The present design, with the gold eagle emblem symbolizing the Arab hero Saladin, was introduced in 1984.

The rainfall of Egypt is very low, falling, if at all, in the winter months from November to February. The Nile, carrying tropical rainfall northwards to the Mediterranean, is the lifeline of the land. In the south and on the Red Sea coast no rain may fall for many years. The winters are cool but the summers very hot, getting hotter north to south. Hot dusty winds can blow into the Nile from the surrounding deserts from March–July. Daily sunshine hours range from seven in December to over 11 in June–August.

But for the River Nile, which brings the waters of the East African and Ethiopian Highlands to the Mediterranean, Egypt would scarcely be populated, for 96% of the present population lives in the Nile Valley and its rich delta.

The vast majority of the country, away from the Nile, is desert and semi-desert. Egypt's deserts offer varied landscapes. Beyond the Gulf of Suez and the Suez Canal the Sinai Peninsula in the south is mountainous and rugged; it contains the highest of Egypt's mountains – Gebel Katherina (2,637 m [8,650 ft]) – and is almost entirely uninhabited. The Eastern Desert, between the Nile and the Red Sea, is a much dissected area and parts of the Red Sea Hills are over 2,000 m [6,560 ft].

The Western Desert includes almost three-quarters of Egypt and consists of low vales and scarps, mainly of limestones. Over its stony and sandy surfaces great tank battles were fought in World War II. A number of depressions in the desert surface fall below sea level. There are a number of oases, the most important being Khârga, Dakhla, Farâfra, Baharîya and Siwa. By drawing on deep-seated artesian waters it is hoped to expand the farming area of the first four of these as a contribution to the solution of Egypt's population problem.

The Nile

The Nile Valley was one of the cradles of civilization. The dependable annual flooding of the great river each summer and the discovery of the art of cultivating wheat and barley fostered simple irrigation techniques and favoured co-operation between the farmers. Stability and leisure developed arts and crafts, city life began and the foundations were laid of writing, arithmetic, geometry and astronomy. Great temples and pyramid tombs within the valley remain as memorials to this early civilization – and a magnet for tourists.

Today, even more than in the past, the Egyptian people depend almost entirely on the waters of the Nile. These are extremely seasonal, and control and storage have become essential during this century. For seasonal storage the Aswan Dam (1902) and the Jebel Awliya Dam in Sudan (1936) were built. The Aswan High Dam (1970), sited 6.4 km [4 mls] above the Aswan Dam, is the greatest of all. Built with massive Soviet aid, it holds back 25 times as much as the older dam and permits year-round storage. Through this dam the Egyptian Nile is now regulated to an even flow throughout the year. The water that has accumulated behind the dam in Lake Nasser (about 5,000 sq km [1,930 sq mls]) is making possible the reclamation of more desert land. The dam is also a source of hydroelectric power and aids the expansion of industry.

Most of Egypt's industrial development has come about since World War II. Textiles, including the spinning, weaving, dyeing and printing of cotton, wool, silk and artificial fibres, form by far the largest industry. Other manufactures derive from local agricultural and mineral raw materials, and include sugar refining, milling, oil-seed pressing, and the manufacture of chemicals, glass and cement. There are also iron-and-steel, oil-refining and car-assembly industries, and many consumer goods such as radios, TV sets and refrigerators are made. The main cities of Cairo, the capital, and Alexandria are also the major industrial centres.

The Suez Canal, opened in 1869 and 173 km [107 mls] long, is still an important trading route. Though it cannot take the large modern cargo-vessels, oil-tankers and liners, it still carries more than 20,000 vessels a year between the Mediterranean and the Red Sea. The British-built canal was nationalized in 1956 by the Egyptian president, Gamal Abdel Nasser, who from 1954 until his death in 1970 was the leader of Arab nationalism. In 1952 the army had toppled the corrupt regime of King Farouk, the last ruler of a dynasty dating back to 1841. Egypt had previously been part of the Ottoman Empire (from 1517), though British influence was paramount after 1882 and the country was a British protectorate from 1914 to 1922, when it acquired limited independence ■

COUNTRY: Arab Republic of Egypt

AREA: 1,001,450 sq km [386,660 sq mls]

POPULATION: 53,153,000

CAPITAL (Population): Cairo (6,325,000)

GOVERNMENT: Republic with a unicameral legislature

ETHNIC GROUPS: Egyptian 99%

LANGUAGES: Arabic (official), French, English

RELIGIONS: Sunni Muslim 94%, Christian

NATIONAL DAY: 23 July; Anniversary of the Revolution (1952)

CURRENCY: Egyptian pound = 100 piastres = 1,000 millièmes

ANNUAL INCOME PER PERSON: $600

MAIN PRIMARY PRODUCTS: Cotton, rice, maize, sugar, sheep, goats, phosphates, oil and natural gas

MAIN INDUSTRIES: Oil refining, cement, textiles, fertilizers, iron and steel, tourism

MAIN EXPORTS: Mineral products including crude petroleum 65%, textiles 19%

MAIN IMPORTS: Foodstuffs 30%, machinery and electrical equipment 20%

DEFENCE: 14% of national budget

TOURISM: 1,795,000 visitors per year

POPULATION DENSITY: 53 per sq km [138 per sq ml]

LIFE EXPECTANCY: Female 65 yrs, male 62 yrs

ADULT LITERACY: 45%

PRINCIPAL CITIES (Population): Cairo 6,325,000 Alexandria 2,893,000 Giza 1,858,000 Shubra el Kheima 711,000

AFRICA

MAURITANIA

The Mauritanian Islamic Republic's flag features the star and the crescent, traditional symbols of the Muslim religion. It was adopted in 1959, the year before the country gained its independence from France.

The amount of rain and the length of the wet season increases from north to south. Much of the country receives less than 250 mm [10 in] of rain, due to the dry north-east and easterly winds throughout the year in the north, but the reverse occurs in the south, when south-westerlies bring rain in the summer. Sunshine hours and temperatures are very high, every month having recorded over 40°C [104°F]. The monthly temperature ranges from 30°C [86°F], August–October, to 20°C [68°F] in January.

Over two-thirds of Mauritania – twice the size of France but with just over 2 million people – consists of desert wastes, much of it in the Sahara. Apart from the main north-south highway and routes associated with mineral developments, land communications consist of rough tracks.

Only in the southern third of the country and along the Atlantic coast is precipitation sufficient to support Sahelian thorn-bush and grassland. Apart from oasis settlements such as Atar and Tidjikdja, the only permanent arable agriculture is in the south, concentrated in a narrow strip along the Senegal River. Crops of millet, sorghum, beans, peanuts and rice are grown, often using the natural late-summer floods for irrigation. When the Senegal River Project is complete, large areas should be developed for irrigated crops of rice, cotton and sugar cane.

Many people are still cattle-herders who drive their herds from the Senegal River through the Sahel steppelands in tandem with the seasonal rains. In good years the country's livestock outnumber the human population by about five to one, but the ravages of drought and the development of the mining industries in the 1980s – allied to overgrazing – have reduced the nomadic population from three-quarters to less than a third of the national total.

Off the Atlantic coast the cold Canaries Current is associated with some of the richest fishing grounds in the world. The national fishing industry is still evolving and over 100,000 tonnes of fish are landed and processed each year, mainly at the major fishing port of Nouadhibou (Port Etienne); the potential catch is estimated at 600,000 tonnes.

As the Atlantic coast in the south of the country lacks good harbours, a port and capital city have been constructed at Nouakchott. This now handles a growing proportion of the country's trade, including exports of copper mined near Akjoujt. Exported minerals, particularly high-grade iron ores, worked from the vast reserves around Fdérik, provide the country with most of its foreign revenue, though animal products, gum arabic and dates are also among the exports.

The rulers in Nouakchott surrendered their claims to the southern part of the Western Sahara in 1979. The following year slavery was formally abolished – though some estimates put the number of 'Haratines' (descendants of black slaves) still in bondage as high as 100,000. Unlike several of the former colonial territories of West and Central Africa, Mauritania was not affected by the wave of democratization that toppled military and single-party regimes from the late 1980s, though multiparty elections and an amnesty for political prisoners were announced in 1991 ∎

COUNTRY:	Islamic Republic of Mauritania
AREA:	1,025,520 sq km [395,953 sq mls]
POPULATION:	2,025,000
CAPITAL (Population):	Nouakchott (500,000)
GOVERNMENT:	Military-controlled republic
ETHNIC GROUPS:	Moor (Arab-Berber) 81%, Wolof 7%, Tukulor 5%
LANGUAGES:	Arabic and French (official), Fulfulde, Fulani
RELIGIONS:	Sunni Muslim 99%
NATIONAL DAY:	28 November; Independence Day
CURRENCY:	Ouguiya = 5 khoums
ANNUAL INCOME PER PERSON:	$500
DEFENCE:	14% of national budget
POPULATION DENSITY:	2 per sq km [5 per sq ml]
LIFE EXPECTANCY:	Female 50 yrs, male 46 yrs
ADULT LITERACY:	28%

MALI

Mali's flag uses the Pan-African colours employed by the African Democratic Rally before the French colony (then called French Sudan) won independence from France in 1960. It was federated with Senegal, 1959–60.

In the 14th century the centre of a huge West African Malinka empire based on the legendary city of Timbuktu (Tombouctou), Mali is today a poor, landlocked, butterfly-shaped country consisting mainly of lifeless Saharan desert plains.

Water (or the lack of it) dominates the life of the people and most of the country's population is concentrated along the Senegal and Niger rivers, which provide water for stock and irrigation and serve as much-needed communication routes. The Niger and its tributaries support a fishing industry that exports dried fish to neighbouring Ivory Coast, Burkina Faso and Ghana.

With the exception of small areas in the south of the country, irrigation is necessary for all arable crops. The savanna grasslands and highland areas in the Sahelian south-east are free of tsetse fly (carrier of sleeping sickness), and large numbers of sheep and cattle are traditionally kept in the area, though grazing lands have been decimated by a series of catastrophic droughts. Northern Mali is entirely poor desert, inhabited only by Tuareg and Fulani nomads.

Millet, cotton and groundnuts are important crops on the unirrigated lands of the south, while rice is intensively grown with irrigation. A large irrigation scheme has been developed near Ségou which produces rice, cotton and sugar cane, and there are many other smaller schemes. Industry is confined mainly to one commercial gold mine, salt production and embryonic manufacturing – shoes, textiles, beer and matches.

Mali – a French colony between 1893 and 1960 – was governed by a radical Socialist government for the first eight years of independence, before this was overthrown by a bloodless coup under General Moussa Traoré. His repressive military, single-party regime did little for the country – despite successful pressure from aid donor nations to liberalize the planned economy – and in 1987 the World Bank

classified Mali as the world's fourth poorest country; they were still in the bottom 20 in 1989.

In 1985 the government had been involved in a border dispute with neighbouring Burkina Faso; the International Court of Justice finally granted Mali 40% of its claimed land.

Student-led protests finally ended Traoré's 23-year reign in 1991, and the new president, Colonel Amadou Touré, promised to implement free and democratic elections with a multiparty system. He also faced the problem of Tuaregs demanding a separate homeland ∎

COUNTRY: Republic of Mali	**RELIGIONS:** Muslim 90%, traditional animist beliefs 9%, Christian 1%
AREA: 1,240,190 sq km [478,837 sq mls]	**NATIONAL DAY:** 22 September; Independence Day (1960)
POPULATION: 8,156,000	**CURRENCY:** CFA franc = 100 centimes
CAPITAL (Population): Bamako (646,000)	**ANNUAL INCOME PER PERSON:** $270
GOVERNMENT: Multiparty republic with a unicameral legislature	**DEFENCE:** 11% of national budget
ETHNIC GROUPS: Bambara 31%, Fulani 13%, Senufo 12%, Soninké 8%	**POPULATION DENSITY:** 7 per sq km [17 per sq ml]
LANGUAGES: French (official), languages of the Mande group 60%, including Bambara, Soninké, Malinké	**LIFE EXPECTANCY:** Female 48 yrs, male 44 yrs
	ADULT LITERACY: 17%

NIGER

Niger's flag was adopted shortly before independence from France in 1960. The circle represents the sun, the orange stripe the Sahara Desert in the north, the green stripe the grasslands of the south and the white goodness and purity.

The climate of southern Niger is very similar to other places within the vast tropical grassland belt of northern Africa – the Sahel. From November to April the hot, dry Harmattan wind blows from the Sahara, skies are clear and there is no rain. From March to May is the hot season, when the intensity of the sun increases rapidly. In June the inter-tropical rainbelt reaches the region and increasing cloud and rain give cooler conditions.

The title Niger, derived from the Tuareg word *n'eghirren* ('flowing water'), is something of a misnomer for the country that bears the river's name. West Africa's great waterway runs through only the extreme south-west of what is, apart from its fertile southern strip, a desolate territory of hot, arid sandy and stony basins.

The monotony of the northern 60% of the country is broken by the jagged peaks of the Aïr Mountains, rising to 1,900 m [6,230 ft] from the desert plains; here rainfall is sometimes sufficient to permit the growth of thorny scrub. However, severe droughts since the 1970s have crippled the traditional life style of the nomads in the area, grazing their camels, horses, cattle and goats, and whole clans have been wiped out as the Sahara slowly makes its way south.

The same period has seen the growth of uranium mining in the mountains by the government in con-

junction with the French Atomic Energy Commission, and this has now overtaken groundnuts as Niger's chief export, despite the drop in world demand during the 1980s. Tin and tungsten are also mined here, but the country's reserves of other minerals, including iron ore, manganese and molybdenum, remain largely untouched. Over 95% of Niger's population still derive their living from agriculture and trading.

The southern part of the country, including the most fertile areas of the Niger basin and around Lake Chad, have also been affected by drought; but here desertification, linked to overgrazing, climbing temperatures as well as water shortage, is a wider problem. The crucial millet and sorghum crops – often grown by slash-and-burn techniques – have repeatedly failed, and migration to the already crowded market towns and neighbouring countries is widespread. The capital of Niamey, a mixture of

traditional African, European colonial and modern Third World, is the prime destination for migrants travelling in search of food and work. South of Niamey is the impressive 'W' national park, shared with Burkina Faso and Benin. The wooded savanna – protecting elephants, buffaloes, crocodiles, cheetahs, lions and antelopes – is intended to attract growing numbers of tourists in the 1990s.

Niger comes close to the bottom of all the world tables measuring aspects of poverty, along with its Sahara/Sahel neighbours Mali and Chad. French colonial rule came to an end in 1960, and the original post-independence government was overthrown in 1974, in the wake of a prolonged drought, and military rule followed. Civilian control was reinstated in 1989 (with army backing) and in 1990, after student protests, a route to democracy was mapped out; after a 90-day conference in the autumn of 1991, the last pillars of military dictatorship were abolished, with multiparty elections to be held early in 1993 ∎

COUNTRY: Republic of Niger	
AREA: 1,267,000 sq km [489,189 sq mls]	
POPULATION: 7,732,000	
CAPITAL (Population): Niamey (399,000)	
GOVERNMENT: Single-party republic	
ETHNIC GROUPS: Hausa 52%, Djerma 14%, Fulani 10%	
LANGUAGES: French (official) and Hausa	
RELIGIONS: Sunni Muslim 97%	
NATIONAL DAY: 18 December; Republic Day (1958)	
CURRENCY: CFA franc = 100 centimes	
ANNUAL INCOME PER PERSON: $310	
MAIN PRIMARY PRODUCTS: Uranium, tin, gypsum, salt	
MAIN EXPORTS: Uranium ore, live animals, vegetables	
MAIN IMPORTS: Cereals, machinery, vehicles, fuels	
DEFENCE: 5% of national budget	
POPULATION DENSITY: 6 per sq km [16 per sq ml]	
LIFE EXPECTANCY: Female 48 yrs, male 45 yrs	
ADULT LITERACY: 14%	

AFRICA

CHAD

Adopted in 1959, Chad's colours are a compromise between the French and Pan-African flags. Blue represents the sky, the streams of the south and hope, yellow the sun and the Sahara Desert in the north, and red national sacrifice.

The central regions of Chad lie within the tropical grassland belt traditionally known as the Sudan, which extends across North Africa. The climate is markedly seasonal. A dry season with north-easterly winds extends from November to April. The sky is clear and the daily range of temperature is large. The heat increases until the beginning of the rainy season in June, when cloud and rain bring cooler but more humid conditions.

Africa's largest landlocked country, and twice the size of France, its former ruler, Chad is a sprawling, strife-torn, desperately poor state with no industries except for the processing of agricultural products. Over 90% of the population make a living from crop cultivation, notably cotton, or by herding. In the Saharan northern third of the country, a sparse nomadic Arabic population lives in a harsh, hot desert containing extensive tracts of mobile dunes and the volcanic Tibesti Mountains.

The wetter southern portions of the country are covered by wooded savanna and crops of cotton, groundnuts, millet and sorghum are grown – drought permitting – by settled black cultivators. A central bank of thorn bush (Sahel) provides pasturage for migratory cattle and herds of game, though drought and desertification have combined to wreak havoc here in recent years.

Lake Chad is the focal point of much of the country's drainage, affecting two-thirds of the country. However, most water feeding the lake comes from the rivers Chari and Logone, the only large perennial water courses in the country and now only streams. Agriculture and population are concentrated along their valleys and in the vicinity of Lake Chad, now shrinking fast – some estimates state that the water area is only 20% of its size in 1970, and the levels much lower; and while fishing is locally important, catches are less each year.

Since independence Chad has been plagued by almost continuous civil wars, primarily between the Muslim Arab north and the Christian and animist black south, but also with many subsidiary ethnic conflicts. In 1973 Colonel Gaddafi's Libya, supporters of the Arab faction, occupied the mineral-rich Aozou Strip in the far north.

Libya tried incursions further south in 1983 – to back the forces of the previously separate state of Bourkou-Ennedi-Tibesti – and in 1987, to support one of many abortive coups against a succession of repressive governments in Ndjamena; the former ended in agreement on 'joint withdrawal', the latter in crushing victory for French and Chadian forces.

Diplomatic relations were restored with Libya in 1988, but Chad's massive commitments in maintaining control in the drought-afflicted country as well as on several of its borders – in addition to an impossible foreign debt – make it one of the terminally ill nations of Africa ■

COUNTRY: Republic of Chad (Tchad)
AREA: 1,284,000 sq km [495,752 sq mls]
POPULATION: 5,679,000
CAPITAL (Population): Ndjamena (512,000)
GOVERNMENT: Single-party republic
ETHNIC GROUPS: Bagirmi, Sara and Kreish 31%, Sudanic Arab 26%, Teda 7%
LANGUAGES: French and Arabic (official), but more than 100 languages and dialects spoken
RELIGIONS: Sunni Muslim 44%, Animist 38%, various Christian 17%
NATIONAL DAY: 11 August; Independence Day (1960)
CURRENCY: CFA franc = 100 centimes
ANNUAL INCOME PER PERSON: $190
MAIN PRIMARY PRODUCTS: Cotton, salt, uranium, fish, sugar, cattle
MAIN INDUSTRIES: Cotton ginning, sugar refining
MAIN EXPORTS: Cotton, live cattle, animal products
MAIN IMPORTS: Cereals, petroleum products, chemicals
DEFENCE: 40% of national budget
POPULATION DENSITY: 5 per sq km [12 per sq ml]
LIFE EXPECTANCY: Female 44 yrs, male 42 yrs
ADULT LITERACY: 25%

CENTRAL AFRICAN REPUBLIC

The national flag of the Central African Republic, adopted in 1958, combines the green, yellow and red of Pan-African unity with the blue, white and red of the flag of the country's former colonial ruler, France.

The climate of this landlocked country is tropical. Day temperatures rarely fall below 30°C [86°F] during the day, and below 20°C [68°F] at night. The north-east trade winds blow from November to February from the Sahara, causing a dry season with high temperatures. There are no real mountains to affect this airflow. The south-west winds bring a slightly cooler regime and a wet season from July– October. Annual rainfall is high with some rain in all months and little variation in the total figure.

Declared independent in 1960, this former colony of French Equatorial Africa hit the headlines briefly in 1976 when the ex-French Army sergeant Jean-Bedel Bokassa crowned himself head of the 'Central African Empire' in an outrageously lavish ceremony. His extravagance and repressive methods were ended in 1979 with the help of French paratroops, and the self-styled emperor went into exile. He returned in 1986 expecting to regain power, but was sentenced to death – later commuted to life imprisonment. The army continued in power, but moves towards pluralism, approved by voters a decade before, were initiated in 1991.

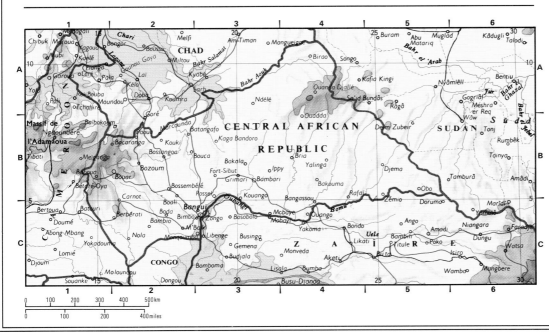

This poor, landlocked country lies on an undulating plateau between the Chad and Congo basins; the numerous rivers drain to both, and natural erosion has been accentuated by the planting of trees in rows on foreign plantations.

The rest of the country is savanna, much depopulated for the European and Arab slave trades and later for forced labour. Most farming is for subsistence, but coffee, cotton and groundnuts are exported, as well as significant amounts of timber and uranium. The main earner is gem diamonds ■

COUNTRY: Central African Republic
AREA: 622,980 sq km [240,533 sq mls]
POPULATION: 3,039,000
CAPITAL (Population): Bangui (597,000)
GOVERNMENT: Single-party republic
ETHNIC GROUPS: Banda 29%, Baya 25%, Ngbandi 11%, Azande 10%
LANGUAGES: French (official), Sango (linguafranca)
RELIGIONS: Traditional beliefs 57%, Christian 35%, Sunni Muslim 8%

NATIONAL DAY: 1 December
CURRENCY: CFA franc = 100 centimes
ANNUAL INCOME PER PERSON: $390
MAIN EXPORTS: Coffee, cotton, cork, wood and diamonds
MAIN IMPORTS: Cereals, machinery and transport equipment, medicines
DEFENCE: 6.6% of national budget
POPULATION DENSITY: 5 per sq km [13 per sq ml]
LIFE EXPECTANCY: Female 49 yrs, male 46 yrs
ADULT LITERACY: 40%

SUDAN

The design of Sudan's flag is based on the flag of the Arab revolt used in Syria, Iraq and Jordan after 1918. Adopted in 1969, it features the Pan-Arab colours and an Islamic green triangle symbolizing material prosperity and spiritual wealth.

The Sudan, formerly an Anglo-Egyptian Condominium, is the largest state of Africa. It consists essentially of vast clay plains and sandy areas, parts of the Nile basin and the Sahara, but it presents two very different landscapes. The extreme north is virtually uninhabited desert; to the south, nomads move over age-old tribal areas of semi-desert.

The belt across the centre of the country holds most of the population. Here low rainfall, supplemented by wells and small reservoirs for irrigation, allows subsistence farming, but the bulk of the population lives by or near the Blue and White Niles. This is the predominantly Arab part of the Sudan, where 70% of the population live. Cotton and oilseed are grown for export, sugar cane and sorghum for local consumption.

Southern Sudan presents a very different landscape. Much of it is a great clay plain, fringed by uplands and experiencing a heavy annual rainfall.

The Sudan suffers from an awesome amalgam of ills: ethnic, religious and ideological division; political repression and instability; intermittent civil war, with high spending on 'defence'; economic crisis and massive foreign debt which, to service, would cost three times as much as export earnings; prolonged drought (punctuated by flash floods such as those in 1988, which left 1.5 million homeless); and

an influx of famine-stricken refugees from Ethiopia since the 1980s.

The 17-year-old civil war that ended in 1972 was rekindled in 1983 by the (largely effective) pressure from extremists for the reinstatement of fundamental Sharic law. The renewed rivalries of the Arab north and the non-Muslim south have caused the deaths of hundreds of thousands of people and the decimation of a traditional way of life in an area already prone to drought and severe food shortages.

While the power in the land rests in the north with the military council in Khartoum – a city laid

Sudan extends from the Sahara almost to the Equator and the climate changes from desert to equatorial as the influence of the inter-tropical rainbelt increases southwards. At Khartoum rain falls during three summer months when the rainbelt is at its most northerly extent. The rain may be squally and accompanied by dust storms called haboobs. There is a large daily range of temperature and summer days are particularly hot.

out in the pattern of the British flag at the confluence of the White Nile and Blue Nile – there seems little hope of a return to democracy, and the possibility of the south seceding remains a distinct if distant one ■

COUNTRY: Republic of the Sudan
AREA: 2,505,810 sq km [967,493 sq mls]
POPULATION: 25,204,000
CAPITAL (Population): Khartoum (476,000)
GOVERNMENT: Multiparty republic with a unicameral legislature, suspended by military regime
ETHNIC GROUPS: Sudanese Arab 49%, Dinka 12%, Nuba 8%, Beja 6%, Nuer 5%, Azande 3%
LANGUAGES: Arabic (official), Nubian and other local languages, English
RELIGIONS: Sunni Muslim 73%, traditional beliefs 17%, Roman Catholic 6%, Protestant 2%
NATIONAL DAY: 1 January; Independence Day (1956)
CURRENCY: Sudanese pound = 100 piastres
ANNUAL INCOME PER PERSON: $450
MAIN PRIMARY PRODUCTS: Cotton, dates, livestock, gum arabic, wheat, beans, chromium, crude oil, natural gas
MAIN INDUSTRIES: Agriculture, oil, food processing
MAIN EXPORTS: Cotton 30%, gum arabic 18%, sesame seeds 9%
MAIN IMPORTS: Machinery and transport equipment 33%, manufactured goods 19%, oil products 19%, food and tobacco 16%, chemicals 10%, textiles 3%
DEFENCE: 32% of national budget
POPULATION DENSITY: 10 per sq km [26 per sq ml]
LIFE EXPECTANCY: Female 53 yrs, male 51 yrs
ADULT LITERACY: 22%
PRINCIPAL CITIES (Population): Omdurman 526,000 Khartoum 476,000 Khartoum North 341,000

ETHIOPIA

Ethiopia's tricolour was first flown as three separate pennants, one above the other. The combination of red, yellow and green dates from the late 19th century and appeared in flag form in 1897. The present sequence was adopted in 1941.

Located at the centre of the Shewan plateau, at an altitude of 2,450 m [8,000 ft], Addis Ababa experiences an average annual temperature of 20°C [68°F], the altitude lowering the expected temperatures for these latitudes. The highest temperatures are recorded in October (22°C [72°F]), with June and July the coolest months at about 18°C [64°F]. As much as 1,151 mm [45 in] of rain falls throughout the year, with December–March the wettest months. The rainy season tends to lower temperatures.

Previously known as Abyssinia, Ethiopia was thrust before the attention of the world late in 1984 by unprecedented television pictures of starving millions – victims not only of famine but also of more than two decades of civil war and a Marxist government determined to enforce hardline economic and social policies. While that regime was finally toppled in 1991, and aid continued to pour in from the richer nations, the accumulative effects of drought combined with administrative mismanagement had left the nation destitute. By 1989, Ethiopia was at or near the bottom of any table of standards of living.

Ethiopia's main feature is a massive block of volcanic mountains, rising to 4,620 m [15,150 ft] and divided into Eastern and Western Highlands by the Great Rift Valley. Steep escarpments face each other across the rift, opening northwards to form the southern and eastern boundaries of the high Welo plateau. The Eastern Highlands fall away gently to the south and east. The Western Highlands, generally higher and far more extensive and deeply trenched, are the sources of the Blue Nile and its tributaries. Off their north-eastern flank, close to the Red Sea, lies the Danakil Depression, an extensive desert that falls to 116 m [380 ft] below sea level.

Coptic Christianity reached the northern kingdom of Aksum in the 4th century, surviving there and in the mountains to the south when Islam spread through the rest of north-east Africa. These core areas also survived colonial conquest; indeed Ethiopia (Abyssinia) itself became a colonial power between 1897 and 1908, taking Somali and other peoples into its feudal Empire. Invaded by Italy in 1935, Ethiopia became independent again six years later when British troops forced the Italians out.

Emperor Haile Selassie ('the Lion of Judah'), despite promising economic and social reforms following a two-year drought, was deposed after his 44-year rule by a revolutionary military government in 1974. A month later Ethiopia was declared a socialist state: foreign investments and most industries were nationalized and a programme of land collectivization was started, sweeping away the feudal aristocracy. Though the ideology changed, it was still centralized, bureaucratic despotism.

By 1977 President Mengistu had assumed control, and with massive Soviet military and financial aid pursued interlocking policies of eliminating rival left-wing groups, suppressing secessionist movements (in Eritrea, Tigre, Wollo, Gondar and Ogaden) and instituting land reform, including the forced resettlement of millions from their drought-afflicted homelands. His period of 'Red Terror' killed tens of thousands of innocent people. Collectivist agriculture failed miserably to cope with deforestation, overgrazing and the effects of drought, while for 14 years more than 60% of the national budget was spent on defence and 'security'.

The dogmatic Marxist government, plagued by incursions by Somalia (into Ogaden in 1978, and lasting for ten years), as well as internal rebellions, drained vital resources from the economy. After a decade of unparalleled disaster driven by drought, Mengistu was finally put to flight in 1991 as Addis Ababa was taken by forces of the EPRDF (Ethiopian People's Revolutionary Democratic Front). The EPRDF announced a caretaker coalition government and plans for multiparty elections, but

COUNTRY: People's Democratic Republic of Ethiopia

AREA: 1,221,900 sq km [471,776 sq mls]

POPULATION: 50,974,000

CAPITAL (Population): Addis Ababa (1,686,000)

GOVERNMENT: Republic with a unicameral legislature under provisional control until 1993 election

ETHNIC GROUPS: Amharic 38%, Galla 35%, Tigre 9%, Gurage 3%

LANGUAGES: Amhara (official), Galla, Tigre

RELIGIONS: Ethiopian Orthodox 53%, Muslim 31%, traditional beliefs 11%

NATIONAL DAY: 12 September; People's Revolution Day (1974)

CURRENCY: Ethiopian Birr = 100 cents

ANNUAL INCOME PER PERSON: $120

MAIN PRIMARY PRODUCTS: Cattle, cereals, sorghum, coffee, cotton, timber, sugar cane, salt

MAIN INDUSTRIES: Agriculture, textiles, food processing

MAIN EXPORTS: Coffee 56%, hides and skins 11%

MAIN EXPORT PARTNERS: Germany 18%, Netherlands 13%, Japan 11%, USA 10%

MAIN IMPORTS: Machinery and transport equipment 39%, petroleum 17%, textile yarn 17%, chemicals

MAIN IMPORT PARTNERS: CIS nations 20%, USA 15%, Germany 10%, UK 10%, Japan 1%

DEFENCE: 18% of national budget

POPULATION DENSITY: 42 per sq km [108 per sq ml]

INFANT MORTALITY: 143 per 1,000 live births

LIFE EXPECTANCY: Female 45 yrs, male 41 yrs

ADULT LITERACY: 28%

the administration faced one of the most daunting tasks in the Third World. Relief organizations estimated that of the 25 million people facing starvation in Africa, some 6 million were Ethiopians.

Eritrea, the far northern province of Ethiopia, was an Italian colony until 1941, when it passed to British military administration. In 1952 it became an autonomous region within the Federation of Ethiopia and Eritrea; ten years later the region was effectively annexed by Haile Selassie.

The Eritrean People's Liberation Front (EPLF) then pressed for independence with an unrelenting guerrilla campaign. They held large tracts of the countryside for years while government forces occupied the towns. With the fall of the Mengistu regime in 1991 the EPLF gained agreement on independence for Eritrea.

Eritrea was Ethiopia's third largest province but, with 2.6 million, only seventh in terms of population. However, the capital, Asmara, was easily the country's second city (319,000) after Addis Ababa ∎

DJIBOUTI

Djibouti's flag was adopted on independence from France in 1977, though its use by the independence movement had begun five years earlier. The colours represent the two principal peoples in the country: the Issas (blue) and the Afars (green).

DJIBOUTI

°C / °F
Temperature
Precipitation
129mm
5in

JFMAMJJASOND

Along the western shores of the Gulf of Aden is a narrow strip of hot, arid lowland between the Gulf and the Ethiopian highlands. The temperature is high throughout the year and summer days are cloudless and exceptionally hot, regularly exceeding 40°C [100°F]. Night temperatures rarely fall below 20°C [68°F]. The sparse and variable rainfall occurs in winter, when northerly winds bring moisture from the Red Sea and the Gulf of Aden. On average it rains on only 26 days per year.

This small state lies in the Afro-Asian rift valley system, forming a hinterland to the Gulf of Tadjoura. Part of Djibouti lies below sea level; much of the low ground is hot, arid and unproductive basalt plain. Mt Goudah, the principal mountain, rises to 1,783m [5,848ft], and is covered with juniper and box forest.

Djibouti is important because of the railway link with Addis Ababa, which forms Ethiopia's main artery for overseas trade and was vital to an Ethiopian government whose only other access to the sea was through rebel-held Eritrea. Its town grew from 1862 around a French naval base, which is being redeveloped as a container port, thanks to its important position as a staging post between the Indian Ocean and Red Sea. The French still maintain a garrison there and offer support of various kinds to the authoritarian one-party regime of Hassan Ghouled Aptidon.

Djibouti was previously the French territory of the Afars and Issas. The majority of Afars, most of whom are nomadic, live in Ethiopia and are better

known by the Arabic word 'Danakil' while the Issas (or Ishaak) are Somali. This majority dominate the struggling economy, and there is periodic unrest among the underprivileged Afars ■

COUNTRY: Republic of Djibouti
AREA: 23,200 sq km [8,958 sq mls]
POPULATION: 409,000
CAPITAL (Population): Djibouti (290,000)
GOVERNMENT: Unitary single-party republic
ETHNIC GROUPS: Issa 47%, Afar 38%, Arab 6%
LANGUAGES: Arabic and French (official), Cushitic
RELIGIONS: Sunni Muslim 94%, Roman Catholic 4%
NATIONAL DAY: 4 July; Independence Day (1977)
CURRENCY: Djibouti franc = 100 centimes
ANNUAL INCOME PER PERSON: $1,000
POPULATION DENSITY: 18 per sq km [46 per sq ml]
LIFE EXPECTANCY: Female 51 yrs, male 47 yrs
ADULT LITERACY: 18%

SOMALIA

In 1960 British Somaliland (in the north) united with Italian Somalia (in the south) to form present-day Somalia and the flag of the southern region was adopted. The points of the star represent the five regions of East Africa where Somalis live.

MOGADISHU

°C / °F
Temperature
Precipitation
371mm
15in

JFMAMJJASOND

Nowhere is rainfall heavy, few places receiving more than 500mm [20in] per year. The wettest regions are in the south and in the mountains of the interior. The rains come from March–November with a slight dry season in the middle. At Mogadishu there is only a monthly temperature variation of a few degrees. The temperatures on the Gulf of Aden coast during June–August can exceed 40°C [104°F]. Frosts can occur in the mountains, which exceed 2,000m [6,500ft].

More than twice as large as Italy (which formerly ruled the southern part), the Somali Republic became independent in 1960. The northern section, formerly British Somaliland and the literal 'Horn of Africa', is the highest and most arid, rising to 2,408m [7,900ft]; the mountains are an easterly projection of the Ethiopian Highlands, wooded with box and cedar. The east and south have some 500mm [20in] rainfall on the coast. Dunes have diverted one of the country's two rivers, the Scebeli, to the south, making it available for irrigation, and bananas are a major export from this area, especially to Italy. Inland is low plain or plateau, an arid landscape with grass and thorn bush.

The Somali, though belonging to separate tribes or clans, are conscious of being one people and members of one of Africa's rare nation states. Expatriate Somali living in southern Djibouti, Ogaden (eastern Ethiopia) and north-east Kenya are mostly pastoralists, who move across borders in an increasingly desperate search for pasture and water. The quest for a reunification of all the Somali peoples led to conflict with neighbouring countries, notably Ethiopia and the Ogaden war of 1978, which has continued intermittently since and caused thousands of Somali refugees to flee across the border.

Somalia relied heavily on Soviet aid until Ethiopia went Marxist and sought massive help from Moscow; the revolutionary socialist government of President Siyad Barre, which had seized power and suspended the constitution in 1969, then became increasingly reliant on Italian support and, most important, US aid.

Grievances against the repressive regime, spearheaded by secessionist guerrillas in the north, reached their peak in 1991 with the capture of Mogadishu. Free elections and the independence of the north-east part of the country, as the Somaliland

COUNTRY: Somali Democratic Republic
AREA: 637,660 sq km [246,201 sq mls]
POPULATION: 7,497,000
CAPITAL (Population): Mogadishu (1,000,000)
GOVERNMENT: Single-party republic, military dominated with a unicameral legislature
ETHNIC GROUPS: Somali 98%, Arab 1%
LANGUAGES: Somali and Arabic (official), English, Italian
RELIGIONS: Sunni Muslim 99%
NATIONAL DAY: 21 October; Anniversary of coup (1969)
CURRENCY: Somali shilling = 100 cents
ANNUAL INCOME PER PERSON: $150
MAIN PRIMARY PRODUCTS: Livestock, bananas, sugar cane, maize, millet
MAIN INDUSTRIES: Raising livestock and subsistence agriculture, sugar refining
MAIN EXPORTS: Livestock, bananas, myrrh, hides
MAIN IMPORTS: Petroleum, foodstuffs, construction materials, machinery and parts
DEFENCE: 40% of national budget
POPULATION DENSITY: 12 per sq km [30 per sq ml]
LIFE EXPECTANCY: Female 49 yrs, male 45 yrs
ADULT LITERACY: 12%

Republic, were promised after the ceasefire and Barre's fall from power, but vicious factional fighting continued not only in the capital but also in many parts of the countryside. The Western nations virtually abandoned Somalia to its fate, with thousands dying every week in inter-clan bloodletting. One of the world's poorest countries – it has the worst recorded rate of adult literacy, for example – was plunged into anarchy. The situation deteriorated further into 1992, despite UN attempts at mediation and several ceasefires. Much of Mogadishu was reduced to rubble, violence spread to country areas, and tens of thousands of refugees fled to northern Kenya and eastern Ethiopia ■

AFRICA

SENEGAL

Apart from the green five-pointed star, which symbolizes the Muslim faith of the majority of the population, Senegal's flag is identical to that of Mali. It was adopted in 1960 when the country gained its independence from France.

COUNTRY: Republic of Senegal
AREA: 196,720 sq km [75,954 sq mls]
POPULATION: 7,327,000
CAPITAL (Population): Dakar (1,382,000)
GOVERNMENT: Republic with unicameral legislature
ETHNIC GROUPS: Wolof 36%, Fulani 18%, Serer 17%
LANGUAGES: French (official), African dialects
RELIGIONS: Sunni Muslim 91%, Christian, Animist beliefs
NATIONAL DAY: 4 April
CURRENCY: CFA franc = 100 centimes
ANNUAL INCOME PER PERSON: $710
MAIN PRIMARY PRODUCTS: Groundnuts, phosphates, fish
MAIN INDUSTRIES: Agriculture, fishing, seed cotton, cement, textiles
MAIN EXPORTS: Groundnuts, phosphates and textiles
MAIN IMPORTS: Crude petroleum, cereals, vehicles
DEFENCE: 6% of national budget
POPULATION DENSITY: 37 per sq km [97 per sq ml]
LIFE EXPECTANCY: Female 50 yrs, male 46 yrs
ADULT LITERACY: 35%

On gaining independence in 1960 Senegal had a well-planned capital, a good road network and a top-heavy administration, all legacies from its role as the administrative centre for French West Africa. One-fifth of the country's population lives in Dakar and the area around volcanic Cape Verde (Cap Vert), the most westerly point on mainland Africa. The name derives from the Zenega Berbers, who invaded from Mauritania in the 14th century, bringing Islam with them.

Dakar, once the administrative centre for France's federation of West African colonies, has large modern docks with bunkering and ship-repair facilities and is the nation's major industrial centre. In the north-east of the country Fulani tribesmen eke out a spartan existence by keeping herds of cattle on the scrub and semi-desert vegetation. In contrast, in the wetter and more fertile south the savanna bushlands are cultivated and cassava, sorghum and rice are grown. About half of the cultivated land produces groundnuts, a crop that still dominates the country's economy and exports. The only other major exports are phosphates.

In an attempt to diversify and stabilize the economy the government is encouraging fishing and tourism, and is involved with Mali and Mauritania in a major scheme to increase irrigated crop production. One of the few African countries to remain stable and democratic through the 1980s, Senegal nevertheless struggles economically, is prone to drought and reliant on aid. Federations with Mali (1959–60) and Gambia (1981–9) were unsuccessful, and since 1989 there have been violent, though sporadic, clashes with Mauritania.

Senegal was the only African colony where French citizenship was granted to the people, and indeed the Senegalese were encouraged to become 'black Frenchmen'. As a result many of the Wolof – the largest tribe group and traditionally savanna farmers – are now city-dwellers in Dakar, dominating the political, economic and cultural life of the country. Strangely, today's quality of life is for most Senegalese little better than their neighbours ■

THE GAMBIA

The blue stripe in the Republic of The Gambia's flag represents the Gambia River that flows through the country, while the red stands for the sun overhead and the green for the land. The design was adopted on independence from Britain in 1965.

Winds along the West African coast alternate seasonally between dry north-easterlies in winter and moist south-westerlies in summer. The proportion of the year for which the south-westerlies blow – and hence the length of the rainy season – decreases northwards. At Banjul it lasts from June to October during which period the temperature is very uniform, with warmer nights. In the dry season skies are clear, with over ten hours of sunshine per day, and the temperature range is much greater.

Britain's first (1765) and last colony in Africa, this small low-lying state forms a narrow strip on either side of the River Gambia, almost an enclave of the French-oriented Senegal. Except for the capital Banjul, which is also the major port, no town has a population of more than 10,000, and all the large settlements are on the river, which provides the principal means of communication.

Rice is grown in swamps and on the floodplains of the river (though not enough to feed the country's modest population), with millet, sorghum and cassava on the higher ground. Groundnuts still dominate the economy and provide nine-tenths of export earnings, but a successful tourist industry has now been developed: whether northern Europeans looking for sunshine or black Americans tracing their ancestry, the number of visitors rose from a few hundred at independence to more than 90,000 a year in 1990. Though much poorer than its larger neighbour, The Gambia is determined to go it alone and continues to reject suggestions of unification with francophone Senegal ■

COUNTRY: Republic of The Gambia
AREA: 11,300 sq km [4,363 sq mls]
POPULATION: 861,000
CAPITAL (Population): Banjul (146,000)
GOVERNMENT: Multiparty republic
ETHNIC GROUPS: Malinke 40%, Fulani 19%, Wolof 15%, Dyolo 10%, Soninke 8%

LANGUAGES: English (official), Mandinka, Fula, Wolof
RELIGIONS: Sunni Muslim 95%, Christian 4%
NATIONAL DAY: 18 February; Independence Day
CURRENCY: Dalisi = 100 butut
ANNUAL INCOME PER PERSON: $260
LIFE EXPECTANCY: Female 47 yrs, male 43 yrs
ADULT LITERACY: 75%

GUINEA-BISSAU

The Republic of Guinea-Bissau adopted this flag, using the Pan-African colours, on gaining independence from Portugal in 1973. The five-pointed black star represents the PAIGC political party that led the struggle from 1962.

COUNTRY: Republic of Guinea-Bissau
AREA: 36,120 sq km [13,946 sq mls]
POPULATION: 965,000
CAPITAL (Population): Bissau (125,000)
GOVERNMENT: Single-party republic
ETHNIC GROUPS: Balante 39% Malinke 23% Mandyako 11% Pepel 10%
LANGUAGES: Portuguese (official), Crioulo
RELIGIONS: Traditional beliefs 65%, Muslim 30%
NATIONAL DAY: 24 September; National Day
CURRENCY: Peso = 100 centavos
ANNUAL INCOME PER PERSON: $180
POPULATION DENSITY: 27 per sq km [77 per sq ml]
LIFE EXPECTANCY: Female 49 yrs, male 45 yrs
ADULT LITERACY: 31%

Guinea-Bissau is largely composed of swamps and estuaries. On independence in 1974 the country possessed few basic services and agriculture had been severely dislocated by the guerrilla war.

About 85% of the active population are subsistence farmers. Large numbers of livestock are kept on the grasslands in the east, and there is considerable potential for growing irrigated rice and sugar cane. A fishing industry and cash crops such as tropical fruits, cotton and tobacco are being developed, and there are untapped reserves of bauxite and phosphates as well as offshore oil – hampered by disputes with Guinea and Senegal.

In December 1991 the Supreme Court ended 17 years of Socialist one-party rule by legalizing the opposition Democratic Front. However, rivalry between black Guineans (especially predominant Balante) and the mestizo élite remained strong ■

GUINEA

Guinea's Pan-African colours, adopted on independence from France in 1958, represent the three words of the national motto: work (red), justice (yellow) and solidarity (green). The design is based on the French tricolour.

Along the coastlands rainfall exceeds 4,000 mm [157 in], declining inland to below 1,500 mm [59 in]. The wet season lasts from April–October with rain falling almost every day at its height. The sunshine levels are also at their lowest and so this is the coolest period. The highest temperatures coincide with the dry season, when the hot and dry harmattan wind blows south-westwards from the Sahara. Temperatures are cooler along the coast and in the highlands.

The first independent state of French-speaking Africa, Guinea is a country of varied landscapes, ranging from the grasslands and scattered woodland of the interior highlands and Upper Niger plains, to the swampy mangrove-fringed plains of the Atlantic coast. Dense forests occupy the western foothills of the Fouta Djalon.

Two-thirds of the population are employed in agriculture and food processing. Bananas, palm oil, pineapples and rice are important crops on the wet Atlantic coastal plain, where swamps and forests have been cleared for agriculture, while in the drier interior cattle are kept by nomadic herdsmen.

France granted the troublesome territory independence after a referendum in 1958, and for more than a quarter of a century Guinea was ruled by the repressive regime of President Ahmed Sékou Touré, who isolated Guinea from the West and leaned towards the Eastern bloc for support. Though reconciled with France in 1978, it was not until after the military coup following Touré's death in 1984 that economic reforms began to work.

Guinea's natural resources are considerable: it has some of the world's largest reserves of high-grade bauxite, and the three large mines account for some 80% of export earnings. The Aredor diamond mine has also been very profitable since opening in 1984, and there is great potential for iron-ore mining and hydroelectric power ■

COUNTRY: Republic of Guinea
AREA: 245,860 sq km [94,927 sq mls]
POPULATION: 5,756,000
CAPITAL (Population): Conakry (705,000)
GOVERNMENT: Military state
ETHNIC GROUPS: Fulani 39%, Malinke 23%, Susu 11%
LANGUAGES: French (official), Soussou and Manika
RELIGIONS: Muslim 69%, traditional beliefs 30%
NATIONAL DAY: 3 April; Independence Day (1958)
CURRENCY: Guinean franc = 100 cauris
ANNUAL INCOME PER PERSON: $480
LIFE EXPECTANCY: Female 46 yrs, male 43 yrs
ADULT LITERACY: 28%

SIERRA LEONE

The colours of Sierra Leone's flag, adopted on independence from Britain in 1961, come from the coat of arms. Green represents the country's agriculture, white stands for peace and blue for the Atlantic Ocean.

Freetown, the capital of Sierra Leone ('lion mountain'), has the best natural harbour in West Africa, and was established as a settlement for freed slaves at the end of the 18th century.

At independence in 1961 three-quarters of the population were employed in subsistence agriculture, yet rice had to be imported, and only small surpluses of palm kernel, coffee and ginger were produced.

Revenues from diamond and iron-ore mining, of major importance since the 1930s, plus other minerals, provide the country with funds for education and agricultural developments. Sierra Leone is also one of the few producers of rutile (titanium ore), now its most important export, and is also expanding production of bauxite.

The main centres for the production of coffee, cocoa, and timber products are in the south-east of the country near Kenema. Rice and palm oil are produced throughout Sierra Leone, except in the drier north, where groundnuts and cattle herding are more important. The government has established large-scale mechanized rice cultivation in the bolilands of the north-west, the seasonally-flooded

COUNTRY: Republic of Sierra Leone
AREA: 71,740 sq km [27,699 sq mls]
POPULATION: 4,151,000
CAPITAL (Population): Freetown (470,000)
GOVERNMENT: Single-party republic
ETHNIC GROUPS: Mende 34%, Temne 31%, Limba 8%
LANGUAGES: English (official), Creole, Mende, Limba and Temne
RELIGIONS: Traditional beliefs 51%, Sunni Muslim 39%, Christian
NATIONAL DAY: 27 April; Independence Day (1961)
CURRENCY: Leone = 100 cents
ANNUAL INCOME PER PERSON: $240
MAIN PRIMARY PRODUCTS: Iron ore, bauxite, diamonds, rutile concentrates
MAIN INDUSTRIES: Mining
MAIN EXPORTS: Rutile, diamonds, coffee, bauxite, cocoa beans
MAIN IMPORTS: Food and live animals, mineral fuels, machinery and transport equipment
DEFENCE: 4% of national budget
POPULATION DENSITY: 58 per sq km [150 per sq ml]
LIFE EXPECTANCY: Female 45 yrs, male 41 yrs
ADULT LITERACY: 29%

The coast of Sierra Leone faces directly into the rain-bearing south-west monsoon and is backed by the high Fouta Djalon plateau, which forces the air to ascend and release moisture. For seven months of the year, April–October, rainfall is heavy, reaching a maximum in July of nearly 1,200 mm [47 in]. Temperature and humidity along the coast are uniformly high. In winter the wind is offshore and there is little rain for four months. Day temperatures are around 27–30°C [81–86°F].

riverine grasslands of the south-east and the mangrove swamps near Port Loko, in an effort to boost rice production.

Apart from mills processing palm oil and rice, most factories are in or near Freetown. The government is aiding Sierra Leone's growing tourist industry and modern hotels have been established on the coast near Freetown, where it is hoped that the beautiful palm-fringed beaches will prove attractive to foreign visitors.

A military government ruled a one-party state after the coup of 1968, but in 1991 the regime claimed to 'welcome' multiparty democracy. Any progress appeared difficult, however, after the invasion by Liberian forces in April 1991, which disrupted the south of the country and threatened the regime ■

AFRICA

LIBERIA

Liberia was founded in the early 19th century as an American colony for freed black slaves wanting to return to Africa from the United States. The flag, based on the American 'Stars and Stripes', was adopted on independence in 1847.

West Africa's oldest independent state, Liberia lacks a legacy of colonial administration. A sparsely populated country with large tracts of inaccessible tropical rainforest, Liberia is popularly known for its 'flag of convenience' (used by about one-sixth of the world's commercial shipping), and for large American-owned rubber plantations.

There has been an open-door policy towards foreign entrepreneurs, and the economy has developed rapidly following the exploitation of large iron-ore deposits by foreign companies, mainly American. Though diamonds and gold have long been worked, iron ore accounts for about half the value of all exports. The economy is a mixture of large foreign-owned corporations operating mines and plantations, and of various indigenous peoples who still exist largely as shifting subsistence cultivators.

In 1989 Liberia was plunged into vicious civil war when a force led by Charles Taylor invaded from the Ivory Coast. The president, Samuel Doe, who had seized power in a coup in 1980, was later assassinated and a jigsaw of conflicts developed between his successor, Amos Sawyer, Taylor and other rebel forces, including those led by Prince Johnson. Peace-keeping troops from five West African countries arrived in October 1990 but despite several agreements fighting continued into 1991. Estimates put the number of civilian deaths at more than 13,000, and some 800,000 people – nearly a third of the population – have fled to neighbouring countries, leaving the nation and its devastated capital in poverty and chaos ■

COUNTRY: Republic of Liberia
AREA: 111,370 sq km [43,000 sq mls]
POPULATION: 2,607,000
CAPITAL (Population): Monrovia (425,000)
GOVERNMENT: Multiparty republic .
ETHNIC GROUPS: Kpelle 19%, Bassa 14%, Grebo 9%, Gio 8%, Kru 7%, Mano 7%
LANGUAGES: English (official), Mande, West Atlantic and Kwa
RELIGIONS: Christian 68%, Muslim 14%, traditional 18%
NATIONAL DAY: 26 July; Independence Day (1847)
CURRENCY: Liberian $ = 100 cents
ANNUAL INCOME PER PERSON: $500
MAIN PRIMARY PRODUCTS: Iron ore, diamonds, gold
MAIN INDUSTRIES: Rubber, agriculture, forestry, fishing
MAIN EXPORTS: Iron ore and concentrates, natural rubber, coffee, timber, cocoa
MAIN IMPORTS: Foodstuffs, machinery and transport equipment, mineral fuels, chemicals
POPULATION DENSITY: 23 per sq km [61 per sq ml]
LIFE EXPECTANCY: Female 58 yrs, male 55 yrs
ADULT LITERACY: 35%

IVORY COAST

On independence from France in 1960 this former colony adopted a compromise between the French tricolour and the colours of the Pan-African movement. Orange represents the northern savannas, white peace and unity and green the forests.

The uniform high temperature and humidity and the double rainfall maxima are a distinctive feature of the climate of the West African coast as far west as Liberia. The total rainfall increases steadily westwards as the south-west monsoon winds of summer have a longer sea track. The heaviest and most prolonged rainfall is in May and June, when the inter-tropical rainbelt moves northwards ahead of the monsoon. Nearly half the annual rainfall falls in these two months and on about 40 days.

Except for Nigeria, the Ivory Coast is the largest Guinea coastal land – a little larger than Italy. Formally known as Côte d'Ivoire since 1986, it has substantial forests in the south where the basic resources of coffee, cocoa and timber are produced, as well as the lesser crops of bananas and pineapple. The depletion of the rainforest, as in much of West Africa, is rapid.

In terms of such indices as GNP and international trade figures, the relatively stable Ivory Coast is one of Africa's most prosperous countries. This show of prosperity was initiated by the Vridi Canal, opened in 1950, which made Abidjan a spacious and sheltered deep-water port – a rarity in an area of Africa renowned for barrier reefs. The Ivory Coast's free market economy has proved attractive to foreign investors, especially French firms, and France has given much aid, particularly for basic services and education. It has also attracted millions of migrant West African workers. On achieving independence, the Ivory Coast freed itself economically from support of seven other countries in the French West African Federation. The country is the world's largest exporter of cocoa and Africa's biggest producer of coffee. It has few worked minerals, but its manufacturing industries are developing.

Outward prosperity is visually expressed in Abidjan, whose skyline is a minor Manhattan, and where most of the 44,000 French live. However, the cost of living for Ivoriens is high; almost everything is centralized in Abidjan – which is due to be replaced as the country's capital by Yamoussoukro (120,000) site of the world's biggest church (consecrated by Pope John Paul II in 1990) – and there are great social and regional inequalities. Nevertheless, a second port has been developed since 1971 at San Pedro, and efforts are being made to develop other towns and the relatively backward north.

In 1990 the country's first multiparty presidential election returned to power Felix Houphouët Boigny, leader since 1960 and already Africa's longest-ruling head of state ■

COUNTRY: Republic of Côte d'Ivoire
AREA: 322,460 sq km [124,502 sq mls]
POPULATION: 11,998,000
CAPITAL (Population): Abidjan (1,850,000)
GOVERNMENT: Single-party republic
ETHNIC GROUPS: Akan 41%, Kru 18%, Voltaic 16%, Malinke 15%, Southern Mande 10%
LANGUAGES: French (official), African languages
RELIGIONS: Traditional beliefs 44%, Christian 32%, Muslim 24%
NATIONAL DAY: 7 December; Independence Day
CURRENCY: CFA franc = 100 centimes
ANNUAL INCOME PER PERSON: $730
MAIN PRIMARY PRODUCTS: Petroleum, timber
MAIN INDUSTRIES: Agriculture, timber, petroleum
MAIN EXPORTS: Cocoa, coffee, timber, canned fish, fruit
MAIN IMPORTS: Crude petroleum, machinery and transport equipment, chemicals, vehicles
POPULATION DENSITY: 37 per sq km [96 per sq ml]
LIFE EXPECTANCY: Female 56 yrs, male 53 yrs
ADULT LITERACY: 43%

BURKINA FASO

Formerly Upper Volta, this country adopted a new name and flag in 1984, replacing those used since independence from France in 1960. The colours are the Pan-African shades of Burkina Faso's neighbours.

COUNTRY: Burkina Faso

AREA: 274,200 sq km [105,869 sq mls]

POPULATION: 9,001,000

CAPITAL (Population): Ouagadougou (422,000)

GOVERNMENT: Military-dominated republic

ETHNIC GROUPS: Mossi 48%, Mande 8%, Fulani 8%

LANGUAGES: French (official)

RELIGIONS: Traditional beliefs 45%, Sunni Muslim 43%, Christian 12%

NATIONAL DAY: 4 August; Independence Day (1960)

CURRENCY: CFA franc = 100 centimes

ANNUAL INCOME PER PERSON: $330

MAIN PRIMARY PRODUCTS: Sorghum, millet, maize

MAIN INDUSTRIES: Agriculture, mining, food processing

MAIN EXPORTS: Ginned cotton, livestock

MAIN IMPORTS: Transport equipment, non-electrical machinery, petroleum products and cereals

DEFENCE: 17% of national budget

POPULATION DENSITY: 33 per sq km [85 per sq ml]

LIFE EXPECTANCY: Female 51 yrs, male 48 yrs

ADULT LITERACY: 13%

Landlocked Burkina Faso ('land of upright men') is the successor to Mossi, an early West African state dating from 1100. As large as Italy, and with just over 9 million inhabitants, it is nevertheless over-populated: low, seasonal and erratic rainfall, thin, eroded soils, desertification and a dearth of other natural resources combine to keep Burkina Faso one of the poorest and most agrarian states in the world, heavily reliant on aid.

The Mossi people, who are the majority tribe, live around Ouagadougou, the capital; another major group, the Bobo, dwell around the second city of Bobo Dioulasso. Both grow cotton and millet, guinea corn (sorghum) and groundnuts for food, and collect shea nuts for cooking oil. Nomadic Fulani keep cattle. Though small surpluses of all these products are sold overseas and to the better-off countries to the south, especially the Ivory Coast, re-mittances sent home by migrants working in those countries probably provide most of Burkina Faso's foreign income. Manganese mining could be de-veloped in the far north-east, though this would necessitate a 340 km [210 ml] extension to the rail-way from Abidjan already 1,145 km [715 mls] long.

Another hope lies in eliminating the simulium fly, whose bite causes blindness. This would permit set-tlement and farming of the valleys, which have the most fertile and best watered lands. Among these are the 'W' national park, shared with Niger and Benin.

Plagued by numerous coups and political assassinations, Burkina Faso tasted democracy in December 1991 for the first time in more than a decade when the military regime of Blaise Com-paore granted elections. However, 20 opposition parties combined to produce a boycott involving 76% of the electorate (claiming that it was a ploy to legitimize the military rule), and the government registered a hollow victory ∎

GHANA

Adopted on independence from Britain in 1957, Ghana's flag features the colours first used by Ethiopia, Africa's oldest independent nation. Following Ghana's lead, other ex-colonies adopted them as a symbol of black Pan-African unity.

The climate of the coastal regions of Ghana is similar to much of the Guinea coast, with uniformly high temperatures, high humidity and a marked double maximum of rainfall associated with the two passages of the inter-tropical rainbelt. However, the total rainfall is less than that of coastal regions to the east and west of Ghana, a feature which is attributed to the presence of a local upwell of cooler water offshore. The total rainfall in some years can be as low as 300 mm [12 in].

Formerly known appropriately as the Gold Coast, Ghana's post-colonial name recalls the state which lay north of the upper Niger from the 8th to the 13th centuries, and from whose population some of today's Ghanaians may be descended.

In 1957 Ghana was the first tropical African country to become independent of colonial rule, and until 1966 was led by Dr Kwame Nkrumah, a prominent Third World spokesman and pioneer of Pan-African Socialism. Under him the Akosombo Dam was completed below Lake Volta (one of the world's largest artificial lakes), providing power to smelt imported alumina into aluminium, and for the main towns, mines and industries in the Takoradi-Kumasi-Tema triangle, the most developed part of the country. To build the dam, a second deep-water port was built at Tema, east of Accra, the capital. Tema is now Ghana's main port for imports and for cocoa export.

Cocoa has been the leading export since 1924, and until the late 1970s Ghana was the world's lead-ing producer. However, neighbouring Ivory Coast has now overtaken Ghana both in this and in for-estry production. In turn, Ghana has attempted to expand fishing, tourism and agriculture.

Unlike the Ivory Coast, Ghana has long been a producer of minerals – gold has been exploited for a thousand years. However, production of most min-erals is currently static or declining. The few remain-ing gold mines, with the notable exception of Obuasi, are now scarcely economic. Manganese production was recently revived to meet a new demand in battery manufacture, but the country's substantial reserves of bauxite remain undeveloped while imported alumina is used in the Tema alu-minium smelter. Industrial diamonds contribute modestly to Ghana's economy.

Nkrumah's overthrow in 1966 was followed by a succession of coups and military governments, with Flight-Lieutenant Jerry Rawlings establishing him-self as undoubted leader in 1981. While his hardline regime has steadied the economy, political progress has been token: an agreement to set up a consulta-tive assembly (in place of his ruling Provisional National Defence Council) was set for a referendum in March 1992, but was seen by opponents as merely window-dressing ∎

COUNTRY: Republic of Ghana

AREA: 238,540 sq km [92,100 sq mls]

POPULATION: 15,028,000

CAPITAL (Population): Accra (965,000)

GOVERNMENT: Republic with military–civilian council

ETHNIC GROUPS: Akan, Mossi, Ewe

LANGUAGES: English (official), Akan 52%, Mossi 16%, Ewe 12%, Ga-Adangme 8%, Gurma 3%, Yoruba 1%

RELIGIONS: Protestant 28%, traditional beliefs 21%, Roman Catholic 19%, Muslim 16%

NATIONAL DAY: 6 March; Independence Day (1957)

CURRENCY: Cedi = 100 pesewas

ANNUAL INCOME PER PERSON: $390

MAIN PRIMARY PRODUCTS: Maize, cassava, cocoa, bananas, sorghum, timber, diamonds, gold

MAIN INDUSTRIES: Agriculture, mining, bauxite and oil refining, food processing, forestry

MAIN EXPORTS: Cocoa 59%, gold 15%, timber 4%, manganese ore 2%, industrial diamonds 1%

MAIN IMPORTS: Mineral fuels and lubricants 29%, machinery and transport equipment 26%

POPULATION DENSITY: 63 per sq km [163 per sq ml]

LIFE EXPECTANCY: Female 58 yrs, male 54 yrs

ADULT LITERACY: 53%

TOGO

Togo's Pan-African colours stand for agriculture and the future (green), mineral wealth and the value of hard work (yellow), and the blood shed in the struggle for independence from France in 1960 (red), with the white star for national purity.

LOME

Togo has a tropical climate of high temperatures with little variation throughout the year, and high rainfall, except on the coast and in the north. Temperatures are lower in the central highlands and higher in the north. The wet season is from March–July, and in the south a minor wet season is October–November. In the south rain falls on less than 100 days per year and on average there are over six hours of sunshine per day from October to May.

COUNTRY: Republic of Togo
AREA: 56,790 sq km [21,927 sq mls]
POPULATION: 3,531,000
CAPITAL (Population): Lomé (366,000)
GOVERNMENT: Multiparty republic
ETHNIC GROUPS: Ewe-Adja 43%, Tem-Kabre 26%, Gurma 16%
LANGUAGES: French (official), Ewe and Kabiye
RELIGIONS: Traditional beliefs 58%, Christian 27%, Sunni Muslim 12%
NATIONAL DAY: 27 April; Independence Day (1960)
CURRENCY: CFA franc = 100 centimes
ANNUAL INCOME PER PERSON: $410
MAIN PRIMARY PRODUCTS: Natural phosphates
MAIN INDUSTRIES: Agriculture, phosphate extraction
MAIN EXPORTS: Phosphates, cotton, coffee, cocoa
MAIN IMPORTS: Foodstuffs, fuels, machinery
DEFENCE: 7% of national budget
POPULATION DENSITY: 62 per sq km [161 per sq ml]
LIFE EXPECTANCY: Female 57 yrs, male 53 yrs
ADULT LITERACY: 40%

A small country nowhere more than 120 km [75 mls] wide, Togo stretches inland from the Gulf of Guinea for some 500 km [312 mls] between Ghana to the west and Benin to the east. The Togo-Atacora Mountains cross the country from south-west to north-east, and the major forests and cash crops are in the south-west.

The railway inland from the coast stops at Blitta, in central Togo, and the road is the only means of keeping the poorer, drier northern parts of this awkwardly shaped country in touch with the more developed areas of the south, including the capital and main port of Lomé and the important phosphate mining area, with its port of Kpémé. Phosphates, coffee and cocoa are the important exports, but major food crops are cassava, yams, maize and sorghum-millets.

As Togoland the country was colonized by Germany in 1884 and then occupied by Franco-British troops during World War I. It was partitioned between the two powers under a League of Nations mandate in 1922, with British Togoland later becoming part of Ghana and the larger eastern French section eventually gaining independence as Togo in 1960.

From 1967 Togo was ruled by the military regime of General Gnassingbé Eyadéma, whose government took a pro-Western stance and pioneered privatization in Africa. Following strikes and protests, the principle of multiparty elections was conceded in March 1991, but by the end of the year there were violent clashes between the army and the new civilian government, with old rivalries between Eyadéma's northern Kabye people and the dominant Ewe tribe re-emerging to block the path to stable democratization ■

BENIN

On independence from France in 1960 the country (then called Dahomey) flew the red, yellow and green Pan-African colours, but on becoming the People's Republic of Benin in 1975, the yellow was dropped and the present design adopted.

Previously called Dahomey (the name of an old cultured kingdom centred on Abomey), Benin, one of Africa's smallest countries, extends some 620 km [390 mls] north to south, although the coastline is a mere 100 km [62 mls] long.

After the Dutch expelled the Portuguese from the Gold Coast in 1642, they established their West African headquarters at Ouidah where, until 1961, there was a tiny Portuguese enclave. Several million slaves were shipped from here, mainly to Brazil, where Dahomean customs survive among blacks there. Because of early European contact, and through returned ex-slaves, coastal Benin early acquired an educated élite, as did Senegal, Sierra Leone and Gabon.

Rival tribal kingdoms flourished in this part of Africa for centuries until the French began establishing their presence from around 1850, creating a colony (Dahomey) in 1892 and formally making the country part of French West Africa in 1904.

Before that, from the 13th century, the area had been the western part of the Kingdom (or Empire) of Benin, centred on the Nigerian city of that name and famous for its life-size brass heads and plaques for its ruler, the Oba, from the 15th century. Situated east of Lagos, Benin City is now capital of the Nigerian state of Bendel.

Today's dominant tribe in Benin is the Fon, who (with the Yoruba) occupy the more populous equatorial and fertile south, mostly as subsistence farmers, growing yams, cassava, sweet potatoes and vegetables. In the central parts and some of the north are the Bariba, renowned for their horsemanship, and the Somba, while some Fulani still follow the increasingly precarious nomadic lifestyle in the far north, the least populated of the regions.

In the north, too, are two of West Africa's most beautiful wildlife parks—the Pendjari and the much larger 'W', shared with both Burkina Faso and Niger. Like many neighbouring countries, Benin's government hopes that in the long term these will encourage expansion of tourism, which in the 1980s was still under 100,000 a year.

Benin has little to sell, its main exports being palm-oil produce, cotton and groundnuts, with the timber from the central rainforest belt depleting rapidly. Fees from Niger's transit trade through Cotonou are an important additional source of revenue, but illegal trade with Nigeria is also rife. Offshore oil began production in 1982, but output peaked three years later and the industry has since been hampered by low prices.

Following independence from France in 1960, the country experienced a series of coups and power struggles, going through 11 changes of government in 12 years. Then, during the military single-party regime of General Mathieu Kerekou, who in 1974 introduced 'scientific socialism' (and the following year dropped the name Dahomey), Benin found itself sitting awkwardly as a Marxist state between the market-oriented economies of Togo and Nigeria. Kerekou officially abandoned his path in 1989, and in 1990 he was forced to concede multiparty elections in a referendum. He was roundly beaten in March 1991, when the country enjoyed a relatively peaceful return to democracy for the first time in nearly two decades ■

COUNTRY: People's Republic of Benin
AREA: 112,620 sq km [43,483 sq mls]
POPULATION: 4,736,000
CAPITAL (Population): Porto-Novo (208,000)
GOVERNMENT: Multiparty republic with unicameral legislature
ETHNIC GROUPS: Fon 66%, Bariba 10%, Yoruba 9%, Somba 5%
LANGUAGES: French (official), Fon 47%
RELIGIONS: Traditional beliefs 61%, Christian 23%, Sunni Muslim 15%
NATIONAL DAY: 30 November; Independence Day (1960)
CURRENCY: Franc = 100 centimes
ANNUAL INCOME PER PERSON: $360
MAIN PRIMARY PRODUCTS: Palm oil and kernel oil
MAIN INDUSTRIES: Agriculture
MAIN EXPORTS: Fuels, raw cotton, palm products
MAIN IMPORTS: Manufactured goods, textiles
DEFENCE: 18% of national budget
POPULATION DENSITY: 42 per sq km [109 per sq ml]
LIFE EXPECTANCY: Female 50 yrs, male 47 yrs
ADULT LITERACY: 26%

NIGERIA

The design of Nigeria's flag was selected after a competition to find a new national flag in time for independence from Britain in 1960. The green represents the country's forests and the white is for peace.

LAGOS

Temperature

Precipitation
1464mm
58in

The coastal belt of Nigeria has uniform temperature and humidity through most of the year. The coolest months are July and August when the monsoon brings oceanic air from beyond the Equator, but even then the lowest recorded temperature is 16°C [61°F]. There are two periods of heaviest rain: the long rains with a maximum in June, and the short rains with a maximum in October, with rain on about every other day in the month. Humidity is high and sunshine levels relatively low.

Four times the size of the United Kingdom, whose influence dates from 1861, Nigeria is tropical Africa's most important country. Ranking seventh as a world producer of oil, there are many other resources (albeit dwarfed in exports by oil), including cocoa in the south-west, timber, rubber and palm oil in the south-centre and east, and cotton and groundnuts in the north. The variety of these resources reflects the latitudinal (4–14°N) and altitudinal extent of the country: highlands rise to over 1,830 m [6,000 ft].

There are nearly 109 million Nigerians, making it by far the most populous African state; one in every six Africans is Nigerian. It is also the second most populated country of the Commonwealth, and eighth in the world. Natural wealth and substantial armed forces give Nigeria a commanding position in Africa, and its oil and gas reserves are a focus of worldwide interest.

Nigeria's landscape varies from the savanna of the north – much of it under threat of desertification – through mountains and tropical rainforests to the coastal lands on the Gulf of Guinea. The coast has huge expanses of fine sandy beaches, interspersed with mangrove swamps where rivers join the ocean. Much of the country's coast is formed by the Niger delta, behind which lie thousands of creeks and lagoons.

Before roads were constructed, these inland waterways provided crucial transport, and boats and canoes still carry both people and cargoes between towns and villages in the area. Here the heavy rains produce yams, cassava, maize and vegetables, with rice grown on the patches of land beside rivers and creeks and on large stretches of irrigated land where streams do not flood in the wet seasons.

Farther north, in the forest belt, the hills rise towards the Jos Plateau – famous for its holiday resorts – and in the east towards the steep valleys and wooded slopes of the Cameroon Highlands. These areas produce Nigeria's important tree crops – cocoa, rubber, hardwoods and palm oil. North of the Jos Plateau, parkland gives way to grassland, but the savanna becomes increasingly dry and some areas are now little more than semi-arid scrub.

Northern Nigeria is reliant on one precarious wet season, while the south enjoys two. Poor-quality millet and sorghum are the staples, with cotton and groundnuts the main cash crops. Where desertification has not taken hold, livestock are still important – enjoying the absence of the tsetse fly that afflicts the area of moist vegetation in the south.

Nigeria is unique in Africa south of the Sahara for the numerous pre-colonial towns of the south-west (such as Ibadan) and the north (such as Kano). Domestic trade between these and Nigeria's very varied regions was developed in pre-colonial days, and is now intense. European contact dates back to the 15th century.

A federation of 30 states, many of which are larger than most independent African states, Nigeria includes many tribal groups, the largest being the Yoruba of the south-west, the Ibo of the east, and the Hausa, Fulani and Kanuri of the north. The north is predominantly Muslim, and the Islamic influence is increasing in the south, where most people are pagan or Christian. With so many diversities, including those of religion and a developing social system, Nigeria suffers internal stresses and national unity is often strained.

DEMOCRACY IN AFRICA

The great flush of liberty that followed decolonization in the 1950s and 1960s did not bring the rewards of peace, prosperity and self-government that many early African nationalists had envisaged. Instead, within a few years, most of the newly-independent African nations had been transformed into corrupt and incompetent dictatorships, at best authoritarian one-party states, usually heavily reliant on Western or Soviet subsidies and often plagued by guerrilla fighting and banditry. Governments were changed, if at all, by means of a *coup d'état*.

In the late 1980s, however, new hope reached the world's poorest continent. Everywhere, it seemed, dictators were succumbing quite peacefully to popular demands for multiparty elections and many long-running civil wars were coming to an end. By the early 1990s, some form of democracy was in place in 80% of African nations.

But democracy has no easy answer to Africa's chronic problem: its poverty, and the continuing collapse in world prices for most African commodities. In some instances Western-style democracy may even prove to be impossible, as in Algeria, where in 1992 the military intervened to prevent power passing to elected Islamic fundamentalists, who had sworn to destroy the system that would have given them their victory.

AFRICA

DESERTIFICATION OF THE SAHEL

The Sahel is a wide band of scrub and savanna grassland stretching from Mauritania and northern Senegal in the west through parts of Mali, Burkina Faso, Benin and Niger to southern Chad in the east, and including much of northern Nigeria. To the north is the vast Sahara, the world's largest desert; to the south are the rainforests of tropical West and Central Africa. Though used mainly for pasture, the whole area has irregular and unpredictable rainfall and suffers frequently from drought. Attention was first drawn to the desperate plight of the region by the Sahelian famine of 1973, when hundreds of thousands died, and the problem has since became virtually permanent.

Over the past 30 years, the Sahara has gradually encroached southwards in the world's most blatant example of 'desertification'. The causes are many and interwoven. As well as declining rainfall (possibly as a result of global warming), there are the pressures of a growing population; herdsmen overgrazing the land with their cattle, sheep and goats; overcultivation by uneducated farmers; cutting of ground cover, mainly for fuelwood; and poor or faulty irrigation techniques, where limited water supplies are wasted and the land left too saline or alkaline to support crops.

Ironically, the problem was aggravated in the previous two decades, when above-average rainfall encouraged the expansion of settlement and the cultivation of cash crops into marginal land. Experts estimate that as much as two-thirds of the world's pasture and grazing lands are now in danger from desertification. Africa, and notably the Sahel, is the worst affected: in places the Sahara has advanced more than 350km [200 mls] in just two decades. The process is containable – even reversible – if the land is allowed to recover and the soil rejuvenated through tree planting, terracing and proper irrigation under careful and consistent management with sufficient funds. But these conditions are rarely found: pressures of population, lack of finance and changing policies all mean that such techniques have not been applied anywhere in the Sahel on a substantial scale.

The north of Nigeria extends into the great belt of tropical grassland known as the Sudan which extends across North Africa from the Red Sea to the Atlantic. The climate is markedly seasonal with hot, dry winters and hot, wet summers. In winter the hot, dry Harmattan blows from the Sahara. With clear skies and no rain, the daily range of temperature is large, in January dropping from 30°C [86°F] in the day to 13°C [55°F] at night. In June, rain approaches from the south, often preceded by tornadoes.

Though blessed with many natural resources, Nigeria has had an uneasy path since independence in 1960 (becoming a full republic in 1963). Democratically elected governments have found it an impossible task to unify and stabilize an unruly jigsaw of more than 250 ethnic and linguistic groups, and civilian administrations have held sway for only ten years since the departure of the British.

An unwieldy tripartite federal structure first introduced in 1954 proved unable to contain rivalries after independence and in 1966 the first Prime Minister, Abubaka Tafawa Balewa, and many other leaders were assassinated in a military coup. A counter-coup brought General Yakubu Gowon to power, but a vicious civil war ensued from 1967 when the Eastern Region, dominated by the Christian Ibo and known as Biafra, attempted to secede from the union after the slaughter of thousands of members of their tribe in the north by Muslim Hausa – and wrangles over increasing oil revenues.

Hundreds of thousands died (most from starvation) before Biafra admitted defeat early in 1971. The federation was gradually splintered from three to 21 full states (now 30) to try to prevent one area becoming dominant. Gowon was overthrown in 1975, but another attempt at civilian rule (1979–83) also ended in a military takeover. The latest coup, a bloodless affair in 1985, brought General Ibrahim Babangida to office, and he immediately faced the crucial problems of falling oil prices and mounting foreign debts.

Nigeria's foreign exchange earnings from oil, the country's prime source of income (accounting for over 90% of exports), were halved in a year. Oil production had begun in the 1950s and risen steadily to a peak of 2.4 million barrels a day in the early 1980s. Foreign exchange earnings peaked in 1980 at $26 billion, but by the end of the decade this figure had shrunk to $9 billion.

At the same time the foreign debt, constantly shuffled and rescheduled, had blossomed to some $36 billion, easily Africa's largest. In seven years the annual income of the average Nigerian has shrunk from $1,120 (among the top three on the continent) to a meagre $270, a figure below even that of some poor neighbours. In 1991 the World Bank officially reclassified Nigeria as a low-income rather than middle-income country.

In the early 1990s there were, nevertheless, signs of a recovery, with agriculture (50% of the population still rely on farming) and some areas of manufacturing growing quickly. The political scene was changing too, with Babangida's promise of civilian rule by October 1992 (made in 1989) beginning to take shape – though the two permitted parties were both created by his Armed Forces Ruling Council, and genuine pluralism seems a long way off. Whatever the regime, Nigeria's biggest worry could simply be numbers: already nearly half the population is under 15 years of age, and on the trends of the 1980s the total could be more than 300 million by the year 2025 ■

COUNTRY: Federal Republic of Nigeria

AREA: 923,770 sq km [356,668 sq mls]

POPULATION: 108,542,000

CAPITAL (Population): Lagos (1,097,000)

GOVERNMENT: Federal republic

ETHNIC GROUPS: Hausa 21%, Yoruba 20%, Ibo 17%, Fulani 9%

LANGUAGES: English (official), Hausa, Yoruba, Ibo

RELIGIONS: Sunni Muslim 45%, Protestant 26%, Roman Catholic 12%, African indigenous 11%

NATIONAL DAY: 1 October; Republic Day (1963)

CURRENCY: Nigerian Naira = 100 kobo

ANNUAL INCOME PER PERSON: $270

SOURCE OF INCOME: Agriculture 34%, industry 36%, services 29%

MAIN PRIMARY PRODUCTS: Groundnuts, maize, cocoa, cotton, millet, cassava, livestock, rice, timber, iron ore, oil and natural gas, tin, coal

MAIN INDUSTRIES: Mining, oil and natural gas, agriculture, fertilizers, vehicles, food processing

MAIN EXPORTS: Mineral fuels and lubricants 96%, foodstuffs 2%

MAIN EXPORT PARTNERS: USA 18%, Italy 16%, France 16%, Netherlands 12%, Germany 7%, UK 4%

MAIN IMPORTS: Machinery and transport equipment 35%, basic manufactures 24%, foodstuffs

MAIN IMPORT PARTNERS: UK 20%, USA 13%, Germany 13%, France 9%, Japan 7%

EDUCATIONAL EXPENDITURE: 2.4% of national budget

DEFENCE: 5.2% of national budget

TOTAL ARMED FORCES: 94,500

TOURISM: 340,000 visitors per year

ROADS: 124,000 km [77,500 mls]

RAILWAYS: 3,505 km [2,191 mls]

POPULATION DENSITY: 117 per sq km [304 per sq ml]

URBAN POPULATION: 35%

POPULATION GROWTH: 3.43% per year

LIFE EXPECTANCY: Female 54 yrs, male 51 yrs

ADULT LITERACY: 42%

PRINCIPAL CITIES (Population): Lagos 1,097,000 Ibadan 1,060,000 Ogbomosho 527,000 Kano 487,000 Oshogbo 345,000 Ilorin 344,000

SÃO TOMÉ AND PRÍNCIPE

Adopted on independence from Portugal in 1975, this variation of the familiar Pan-African colours had previously been the emblem of the national liberation movement. The black stars represent the two islands that comprise the country.

These mountainous, volcanic and heavily forested Atlantic islands some 145 km [90 mls] apart, comprise little more than twice the area of Andorra, with São Tomé the larger and more developed of the two. A Portuguese colony since 1522, the islands were suddenly granted independence in 1975, and the cocoa plantations that formed the platform for the economy quickly deteriorated under a one-party hardline Socialist state. Reliance on the Soviet Union was lessened from the mid-1980s and the cocoa industry revived – as well as diversification into palm oil, pepper and coffee and the encouragement of tourism. In 1990 Marxism was abandoned altogether and, following the lead from many mainland African nations and

The seasonal change in the wind systems brings to the islands greatly varied monthly rainfall totals. There is a dry season, June–September, with practically no rain, July–August, and a lesser dry spell, January–February. Rainfall is not high – below 1,000 mm [39 in]. There are also less than half the amounts of possible sunshine. Temperatures are not excessive, 34°C [93°F] being the upper record, and the warmest month is March and the coolest July.

COUNTRY: The Democratic Republic of São Tomé and Príncipe

AREA: 964 sq km [372 sq mls]

POPULATION: 121,000

CAPITAL (Population): São Tomé (35,000)

GOVERNMENT: Single-party republic

LANGUAGES: Portuguese

CURRENCY: Dobra = 100 centimos

pressure from Portugal (the main trading partner) and France (the major aid donor), São Tomé held multiparty elections in 1991 – won by the opposition ■

CAMEROON

Cameroon's flag employs the Pan-African colours, as used by many former African colonies. The design, with the yellow liberty star, dates from 1975 and is based on the tricolour adopted in 1957 before independence from France in 1960.

The north-east corner of the Gulf of Guinea is a region of very high rainfall and uniformly high temperatures and humidity. The rain is at its heaviest during July, August and September when the south-west monsoon is at its strongest and steadiest and the temperature hardly varies. Sunshine levels are low, averaging only three hours per day. The rainfall on the seaward slopes of Cameroon Peak is even heavier and exceeds 9,000 mm [350 in] in places.

Half the size of neighbouring Nigeria, Cameroon has only a tenth of the population. It is, nevertheless, a remarkably diverse country, stemming from more than 160 ethnic groups (each with their own language) and a colonial past involving several European countries. The mountainous borderlands between Nigeria and Cameroon lie on a line of crustal weakness dating from the break-up of the supercontinent, Gondwanaland. Mostly volcanic, the mountains include Mt Cameroon (4,070 m [13,350 ft]) which is occasionally active. There is desert to the north, dense tropical rainforest in the south and dry savanna in the intermediate area.

The word Cameroon is derived from the Portuguese *camarões* – prawns fished by Portuguese explorers' seamen in coastal estuaries – but European contact dates mainly from German rule as a protectorate after 1884. After World War I the country was divided according to League of Nations mandates between France (mainly) and Britain. The French Cameroons became independent in 1960, while following a 1961 plebiscite the north of the British Cameroons voted to merge with Nigeria and the south federated with the new independent state; this became unitary in 1972 and a republic in 1984. Though Cameroon is officially bilingual, the government and public sector are dominated by French-speakers – a fact that continues to upset the rest of the population.

Despite oil production passing its peak in the 1980s and likely to stop before the end of the century, and despite patchy industrial development, Cameroon is one of tropical Africa's better-off nations, with an annual income per person of $940 and rare self-sufficiency in food. This relative prosperity rests partly on diverse but well-managed agriculture, with extensive plantations of palm, rubber, bananas and other crops in the south-west dating from colonial times. Douala is Cameroon's main port for exports of cocoa, coffee (the chief cash

COUNTRY: Republic of Cameroon
AREA: 475,440 sq km [183,567 sq mls]
POPULATION: 11,834,000
CAPITAL (Population): Yaoundé (654,000)
GOVERNMENT: Republic with a unicameral legislative assembly
ETHNIC GROUPS: Fang 20%, Bamileke and Mamum 19%, Duala, Luanda and Basa 15%, Fulani 10%
LANGUAGES: French and English (both official), Sudanic and Bantu
RELIGIONS: Animist 25%, Sunni Muslim 22%, Roman Catholic 21%, Protestant 18%
NATIONAL DAY: 20 May; National Day
CURRENCY: CFA franc = 100 centimes
ANNUAL INCOME PER PERSON: $940
MAIN INDUSTRIES: Aluminium, cement, rubber, palm oil
MAIN EXPORTS: Aluminium products, coffee, cocoa, cotton fibre, logs
MAIN IMPORTS: Transport equipment, iron and steel, medicine, textiles
DEFENCE: 7% of national budget
POPULATION DENSITY: 25 per sq km [64 per sq ml]
LIFE EXPECTANCY: Female 55 yrs, male 51 yrs
ADULT LITERACY: 56%

crops) and aluminium, and for the transit trade of neighbours, while Kribi exports timber. Aluminium is produced at Edéa, using hydroelectric power generated from the Sanaga River, and a railway is being built to the north.

The austerity programme of President Paul Buja, initiated in 1987, appeared to reap rewards by the end of the decade, but there was widespread unrest at the repressive regime (one-party politics was introduced in 1966 by Buja's mentor and predecessor Ahmadou Ahidjo, who had been president since independence), and in 1991 Buja agreed to an amnesty for political prisoners and promised multi-party elections ■

EQUATORIAL GUINEA

Equatorial Guinea's flag dates from independence from Spain in 1968. Green represents the country's natural resources, blue the sea, red the nation's struggle for independence and the white stands for peace.

At the turn of the 15th century the Papacy awarded Africa and Asia to Portugal, and the Americas west of 50°W to Spain. The latter sought a source of slaves in Africa, and in 1778 the Portuguese ceded the islands of Fernando Poó (Bioko) and Annobon (Pagalu), together with rights on the mainland, Mbini (Rio Muni), against Spanish agreement to Portuguese advance west of 50°W in Brazil. Plantations of coffee and cocoa were established on these mountainous and volcanic islands, similar to many Caribbean islands.

Mainland Mbini, which accounts for over 90% of the country's land area, is very different, lower and thinly peopled, less developed, and with fewer foreign enterprises, except in forestry (especially okoume and mahogany production) and palm oil. Coffee and cocoa are also grown, though the economy relies heavily on foreign aid.

Guinea, a name which derives from an ancient African kingdom, was once used to describe the whole coastal region of West Africa. Equatorial

COUNTRY: Republic of Equatorial Guinea
AREA: 28,050 sq km [10,830 sq mls]
POPULATION: 348,000
CAPITAL (Population): Malabo (37,000)
GOVERNMENT: Military single-party republic
ETHNIC GROUPS: Fang 82%, Bubi 15%, Duala 3%
LANGUAGES: Spanish, Fang, Bubi
RELIGIONS: Christian (mainly Roman Catholic) 89%, though banned in 1978
NATIONAL DAY: 12 October; Independence Day (1968)
CURRENCY: CFA franc = 100 centimes
ANNUAL INCOME PER PERSON: $330
POPULATION DENSITY: 12 per sq km [32 per sq ml]
LIFE EXPECTANCY: Female 50 yrs, male 47 yrs
ADULT LITERACY: 37%

Guinea was granted partial autonomy from Spain in 1963, and gained full independence in 1968. Thanks to its cocoa plantations, Equatorial Guinea once boasted the highest per capita income in West Africa. But after independence, the bloody 11-year dictatorship of President Macías Nguema left the economy in ruins, and the one-party rule of his nephew Obiang has since survived several coup attempts. Many have fled both regimes, and some 100,000 Equatorial Guineans now live outside the country ■

153

AFRICA

GABON

Gabon's tricolour was adopted on independence from France in 1960. The yellow, now representing the sun, used to be thinner to symbolize the Equator on which the country lies. The green stands for Gabon's forests and the blue for the sea.

The climate of Gabon is mainly equatorial with uniform heat and humidity throughout the year and very high rainfall. At Libreville the rains last from September to May, with maxima in November and April following the passage of the sun across the Equator at the equinoxes. In these months it rains on over 20 days per month. From June to August winds blow offshore and it is almost rainless. Sunshine levels average only 4–5 hours a day, with monthly totals ranging from 3–6 hours.

The name Gabon derives from that given by a 16th-century Portuguese explorer. In the 19th century the French Navy suppressed the local slave trade, and landed freed slaves at Libreville.

Figures for GNP suggest that Gabon is one of Africa's richest states, but this is misleading: though rich in resources, the country has a low population (just over a million in an area larger than the UK), to whom the wealth has not yet spread.

Most of the country is densely forested, and valuable timbers were the main export until 1962. Since then minerals have been developed, as so often in Africa, by foreign companies whose profits leave the country. First came oil and gas from near Port Gentil (oil still provides over 65% of export earnings). Then the world's largest deposit of manganese was mined at Mouanda, near Franceville, although originally the ore had to be exported through the Congo by a branch of the Congo-Ocean railway. Gabon is the world's fourth biggest producer of manganese and has about a quarter of the world's known reserves. Lastly, there is uranium from nearby Mounana; Gabon, Niger and the Central African Republic are France's main sources of uranium.

Gabon became a one-party state in 1968 and though multiparty elections were held in 1990, there were allegations of government fraud ∎

COUNTRY: Gabonese Republic
AREA: 267,670 sq km [103,347 sq mls]
POPULATION: 1,172,000
CAPITAL (Population): Libreville (350,000)
GOVERNMENT: Single-party republic
ETHNIC GROUPS: Fang 36%, Mpongwe 15%, Mbete 14%
LANGUAGES: French (official), Bantu languages
RELIGIONS: Christian 96% (Roman Catholic 65%)
NATIONAL DAY: 17 August; Independence Day (1960)
CURRENCY: CFA franc = 100 cents
ANNUAL INCOME PER PERSON: $3,220
MAIN INDUSTRIES: Agriculture, forestry, petroleum
MAIN EXPORTS: Petroleum and petroleum products, manganese, timber, uranium
MAIN IMPORTS: Machinery, transport equipment, food products, metal and metal products
DEFENCE: 12% of national budget
POPULATION DENSITY: 4 per sq km [11 per sq ml]
LIFE EXPECTANCY: Female 55 yrs, male 52 yrs
ADULT LITERACY: 62%

CONGO

The People's Republic of the Congo was created ten years after independence in 1960 and adopted this new flag, which shows the country's Socialist beliefs. The hammer and hoe represent industry and agriculture, and the palm branches stand for peace.

A former French colony and half the area of France, the Congo has just over 2 million inhabitants. Although astride the Equator, only the near-coastal Mayombe ridges and the east-central and northern parts of the Congo Basin have truly equatorial climate and vegetation, and these are the sources of valuable exports of timber and palm-oil produce.

In 1970 the Congo became Africa's first declared Communist state, but Marxist-Leninist ideology did not prevent the government seeking Western help in exploiting the vast deposits of offshore oil, soon by far the country's main source of income (as Africa's fifth largest producer). The timber industry, in relative decline, has always been hampered by poor transport – despite the spectacular Congo-Ocean railway from Brazzaville (formerly capital of French Equatorial Africa) to Pointe Noire, the nation's only significant port. Marxism was officially abandoned in 1990 and the regime announced the planned introduction of a multiparty system; in 1992 Prime Minister André Milongo submitted to army pressure for changes to his interim government.

Because of the huge areas of dense forest more than half the population live in towns – a high proportion for Africa – though subsistence agriculture, mainly for cassava, occupies a third of the fast-growing workforce ∎

COUNTRY: People's Republic of the Congo
AREA: 342,000 sq km [132,046 sq mls]
POPULATION: 2,271,000
CAPITAL (Population): Brazzaville (596,000)
GOVERNMENT: Republic with a unicameral legislature
ETHNIC GROUPS: Kongo 52%, Teke 17%, Mboshi 12%, Mbete 5%
LANGUAGES: French (official), Kongo, Teke, Ubangi
RELIGIONS: Roman Catholic 54%, Protestant 24%
NATIONAL DAY: 15 August; Independence Day (1960)
CURRENCY: CFA franc = 100 centimes
ANNUAL INCOME PER PERSON: $1,010
MAIN INDUSTRIES: Petroleum and forestry
MAIN EXPORTS: Petroleum, timber, diamonds
MAIN IMPORTS: Machinery, iron, steel, transport equipment, food
DEFENCE: 15% of national budget
POPULATION DENSITY: 7 per sq km [17 per sq ml]
LIFE EXPECTANCY: Female 52 yrs, male 49 yrs
ADULT LITERACY: 63%

BURUNDI

The three stars in Burundi's flag symbolize the nation's motto 'Unity, Work, Progress'. Green represents hope, red the struggle for independence, and white peace. Burundi adopted this unusual design when it became a republic in 1966.

From the capital of Bujumbura on Lake Tanganyika a great escarpment rises to the rift highlands – reaching 2,670 m [8,760 ft] – which make up most of Burundi. Cool and healthy, the highlands support a dense but dispersed farming population, the Hutu, and a minority of the unusually tall cattle-owning Tutsi. This is similar to Rwanda and being also a small country and overpopulated, employment is sought in neighbouring countries. Coffee is widely grown for export throughout the uplands (80% of total earnings), and cotton is grown on the rift valley floor in the Ruzizi Valley, which forms part of the frontier with Zaïre and links Lake Kivu in the north with Lake Tanganyika in the south.

The enmity between the Hutu and Tutsi is (as in neighbouring Rwanda) centuries old. The worst recent manifestation was in 1972, when the murder of the deposed king in an attempted coup led to the massacre of more than 100,000 Hutu, but some 20,000 were also killed in 1988. As in Rwanda, the indigenous pygmoid Twa people now comprise a tiny proportion of a burgeoning population ∎

COUNTRY: Republic of Burundi
AREA: 27,830 sq km [10,745 sq mls]
POPULATION: 5,458,000
CAPITAL (Population): Bujumbura (273,000)
GOVERNMENT: Military state
ETHNIC GROUPS: Hutu 85%, Tutsi 14%, Twa 1%
LANGUAGES: French and Kirundi (both official)
RELIGIONS: Roman Catholic 62%, traditional beliefs 30%, Protestant 5%
NATIONAL DAY: 1 July; Independence Day (1962)
CURRENCY: Burundi franc = 100 centimes
ANNUAL INCOME PER PERSON: $210
POPULATION DENSITY: 196 per sq km [508 per sq ml]
LIFE EXPECTANCY: Female 53 yrs, male 49 yrs
ADULT LITERACY: 34%

[For map of Burundi see Rwanda, page 156.]

ZAÏRE

The Pan-African colours of red, yellow and green were adopted for Zaïre's flag in 1971. The central emblem symbolizes the revolutionary spirit of the nation and was used by the Popular Movement of the Revolution, formed in 1967.

The Equator passes through the northern half of Zaïre, and in this zone the rainfall and temperature are high throughout the year. To the north and south is a subtropical zone with slightly lower temperatures and a marked wet and dry season. The climate near the coast, because of a cold ocean current, is cooler and drier. In the east there is a mountain climate. At Lubumbashi there is practically no rain from May to September, but December–February rain falls on 25 days each month.

Formerly made up of several African kingdoms, more recently a Belgian colony, Zaïre and her peoples suffered successively from the slave trade and then the brutal methods and corruption of the Congo Free State (1884–1908), the personal possession of King Leopold II, before Belgium assumed administration until independence was granted in 1960. The country's huge size and small population stretched Belgium's modest resources. Africa's third biggest and the world's 11th biggest country, Zaïre is no less than 77 times the size of its former master.

In colonial days, palm and rubber plantations were developed in the equatorial Congo Basin (the world's second largest river drainage system), with mining on the Congo-Zambezi watershed and coffee-growing on the Congo-Nile watershed in the north-east. The Congo (Zaïre) River was developed as a major artery, its rapids and falls by-passed by the railways – including the Boyoma (Stanley), the world's most voluminous, and an important railway built from the river port of Kinshasa to the coastal port of Matadi. Despite its vast size, Zaïre's Atlantic coastline consists of only 27 km [17 mls].

Minerals from the 'Copperbelt' in the far southeastern province of Shaba (formerly Katanga), refined on the spot, provide much of Zaïre's export income. Most outstanding of many minerals are copper (world's fifth producer) and cobalt (by far the world's leading producer, as much as 30% of the total), with copper accounting for more than half the country's export earnings, but manganese, tin, gold and diamonds (world's second producer) are also important. 'Strategic minerals', including cadmium, also emanate from Shaba. Industry was already substantial at independence, and the massive hydro-electric developments at Inga, below Kinshasa, which supplies power to the mining town of Kolwezi in Shaba, some 1,725 km [1,800 mls] to the southeast, should provide for further expansion under new government policies.

Belgium left the country politically unprepared for its sudden withdrawal, and within days of independence the army mutinied and the richest province, Katanga (Shaba), tried to secede. Then called the Congo, the country invited the UN to intervene, but the appallingly violent civil war lasted three years. In 1965 General Mobutu seized control in a period of sustained confusion and remained in power into the 1990s, declaring a one-party state in 1967 and renaming the nation Zaïre in 1971 as part of a wide-ranging Africanization policy.

His long, chaotic dictatorship was a catalogue of repression, inefficiency and corruption in government and unrest, rebellion and poverty among the people, with impenetrably inconsistent policies wreaking havoc in the economy even during the various mineral booms of the 1970s and 1980s.

On the whole, he was supported by the West, notably France, Belgium and the USA, who valued his strategic minerals and his support to the UNITA rebels in Angola and wanted Zaïre outside the Soviet sphere of influence. But with the end of the Cold War that support evaporated: indeed, the US soon pushed hard for reform. This, combined with increasing protests, finally forced Mobutu in 1990 to concede limited multiparty elections for the summer of 1991. But the new elected leaders faced complete chaos in Kinshasa as thousands rioted against inflation spiralling towards 2,000% a year. French and Belgian troops were sent in to restore order and evacuate European nationals while Mobutu – who, according to the US State Department, enjoyed a personal wealth of about $5 billion, around the same figure as the nation's debts – clung to power ■

COUNTRY: Republic of Zaïre

AREA: 2,345,095 sq km [905,441 sq mls]

POPULATION: 35,562,000

CAPITAL (Population): Kinshasa (2,654,000)

GOVERNMENT: Single-party republic with a unicameral legislature

ETHNIC GROUPS: Luba 18%, Kongo 16%, Mongo 14%, Rwanda 10%, Azandi 6%, Bangi and Ngale 6%

LANGUAGES: French (official), Lingala (linguafranca), Swahili, Kikongo, Tshiluba

RELIGIONS: Roman Catholic 48%, Protestant 29%, indigenous Christian 17%, traditional beliefs 3%,

NATIONAL DAY: 24 November; Anniversary of the Second Republic (1965)

CURRENCY: Zaïre = 100 makuta = 10,000 sengi

ANNUAL INCOME PER PERSON: $230

MAIN PRIMARY PRODUCTS: Cassava, plantains and bananas, groundnuts, sugar cane, coffee, rubber, cotton, palm oil, cocoa, tea, timber, oil, gas, copper

MAIN INDUSTRIES: Agriculture, food processing, oil refining, textiles and clothing, mining, forestry

MAIN EXPORTS: Copper 52%, coffee 16%, diamonds 11%, crude petroleum 8%, cobalt 5%, zinc 1%

MAIN IMPORTS: Mining equipment 32%, foodstuffs 15%, energy 14%, transport equipment 8%, consumer goods 7%

DEFENCE: 3.9% of national budget

POPULATION DENSITY: 15 per sq km [39 per sq ml]

INFANT MORTALITY: 90 per 1,000 live births

LIFE EXPECTANCY: Female 56 yrs, male 53 yrs

ADULT LITERACY: 61%

PRINCIPAL CITIES (Population): Kinshasa 2,654,000 Lubumbashi 543,000 Mbuji Mayi 423,000

AFRICA

UGANDA

Adopted on independence from Britain in 1962, Uganda's flag is that of the party which won the first national election. The colours represent the people (black), the sun (yellow), and brotherhood (red); the country's emblem is a crested crane.

The north shores of Lake Victoria are the rainiest tract of East Africa due to moisture provided by the lake. Temperatures show the uniformity associated with the equatorial region but are moderated by altitude. There is a double maximum of rainfall, the heaviest rains occurring after the noonday sun is at its hottest around the equinoxes. Much of the rain falls in thunderstorms which move northwards from the lake by day.

large extinct volcano of Mt Elgon.

In the south rainfall is abundant in two seasons, and patches of the original rainforest (25% of land area) remain. However, most of the forest has been cleared from the densely settled areas, notably in the historic kingdoms of Buganda and Busoga. Here the banana is a staple of diet, and coffee, tea and sugar are cash crops; Uganda is the world's sixth largest coffee producer. Here, too, are the capital Kampala, and the industrial centre of Jinja, adjacent to the huge Owen Falls hydroelectric plant. The western areas, the former kingdoms of Bunyoro, Toro and Ankole, depend more on cattle-rearing.

To the north, one rainy season each year supports a savanna of trees and grassland. Population is generally less dense, and farmers grow finger-millet and sorghum, with cotton and tobacco as cash crops. Tsetse fly inhibits cattle-keeping in some areas, which have become game parks, but the dry north-east (Karamoja) supports nomadic pastoralists.

Blessed with an equable climate, fertile soils and varied resources, from freshwater fish to copper, Uganda could have lived up to Churchill's colonial description as 'the pearl of Africa'. Instead, independence soon brought two decades of disaster with almost ceaseless internal conflict and a shattered economy.

Between the break from Britain in 1962 and the takeover by Yoweri Museveni in 1986 the country suffered a succession of linked civil wars, violent coups, armed invasions and tribal massacres. The worst of several bad periods was the sordid regime of Idi Amin, who in 1971 ousted the first Prime Minister Milton Obote – then president of a one-party state – and in an eight-year reign of terror killed up to 300,000 people as all political and human rights

were suspended. Amin was finally removed when he tried to annex part of Tanzania and President Nyerere ordered his troops to carry on into Uganda after they had repelled the invaders.

Obote returned to power but the bloodshed continued and he was ousted again in 1985. The following year brought in Museveni, who achieved some success in stabilizing the situation as a prelude to a return to democracy though soaring inflation remained a constant problem ■

COUNTRY: Republic of Uganda
AREA: 235,880 sq km [91,073 sq mls]
POPULATION: 18,795,000
CAPITAL (Population): Kampala (459,000)
GOVERNMENT: Military regime
ETHNIC GROUPS: Baganda 18%, Banyoro 14%, Teso 9%, Banyan 8%, Basoga 8%, Bagisu 7%, Bachiga 7%, Lango 6%, Acholi 5%
LANGUAGES: English and Swahili (official)
RELIGIONS: Roman Catholic 40%, Protestant 29%, Animist 18%, Sunni Muslim 7%
NATIONAL DAY: 9 October; Independence Day (1962)
CURRENCY: Uganda shilling = 100 cents
ANNUAL INCOME PER PERSON: $220
DEFENCE: 13% of national budget
POPULATION DENSITY: 80 per sq km [206 per sq ml]
LIFE EXPECTANCY: Female 55 yrs, male 51 yrs
ADULT LITERACY: 57%

Extending from Lake Victoria to the western arm of the Great Rift Valley and beyond, Uganda is a land of lakes (sources of the White Nile) originating from the tilting and faulting associated with the rift valley system. On the western side of the country the Ruwenzori block has been uplifted to 5,109 m [16,762 ft], while the eastern frontier bisects the

RWANDA

Adopted in 1961, Rwanda's tricolour in the Pan-African colours features the letter 'R' to distinguish it from Guinea's flag. Red represents the blood shed in the 1959 revolution, yellow for victory over tyranny and green for hope.

Uplift on the flank of the western arm of the Great Rift Valley has raised much of Rwanda to well over 2,000 m [6,000 ft]. On the northern border are the perfectly shaped but extinct volcanoes of the Mufumbiro Range, rising to 4,507 m [14,786 ft] and a last reserve of the mountain gorilla.

A small, landlocked and poor rural country, Rwanda is by far Africa's most densely populated state and the steep slopes are intensively cultivated, with contour ploughing to prevent erosion. Exports include coffee (70%), tea, pyrethrum and tungsten, but when conditions permit there is a large movement into neighbouring countries for employment.

As in Burundi, there are deep social and cultural divisons between the farming majority and the traditional, nomadic owners of cattle. Several decades of ethnic strife climaxed in 1990 when a rebel force of Tutsi 'refugees' invaded from Uganda and occupied much of the north before being repulsed by French, British and Zaïrian troops brought in by the Hutu-dominated Rwanda government. The problems stem from the revolution of 1959, when the Hutu overthrew the aristocratic Tutsi minority rulers in one of the most violent clashes in modern

African history. In February 1991, in return for its neighbours granting Tutsi refugees citizenship, Rwandan leaders agreed to the principle of a return to democracy, but the violence continued into 1992. The original people, the pygmy Twa, today form around only 1% of a fast-rising population.

Rwanda was merged with Burundi by German colonialism in 1899, making Ruanda-Urundi part of German East Africa. Belgium occupied it during World War I, and then administered the territory under a League of Nations mandate, later (1946) a UN trusteeship. In 1959 it was again divided into two, Rwanda finally achieving full independence in 1962, the same year as Burundi ■

COUNTRY: Republic of Rwanda
AREA: 26,340 sq km [10,170 sq mls]
POPULATION: 7,181,000
CAPITAL (Population): Kigali (157,000)
GOVERNMENT: Single-party republic
ETHNIC GROUPS: Hutu 90%, Tutsi 9%, Twa 1%
LANGUAGES: French and Kinyarwanda (official)
RELIGIONS: Roman Catholic 65%, Protestant 12%, Muslim and traditional beliefs
NATIONAL DAY: 1 July; Independence Day (1962)
CURRENCY: Rwanda franc
ANNUAL INCOME PER PERSON: $310
LIFE EXPECTANCY: Female 52 yrs, male 49 yrs
ADULT LITERACY: 47%

KENYA

The Kenyan flag, which dates from independence from Britain in 1963, is based on the flag of the Kenya African National Union, which led the colonial struggle. The Masai warrior's shield and crossed spears represent the defence of freedom.

NAIROBI

Temperature

Precipitation
1130mm
44in

J F M A M J J A S O N D

The Equator passes through the centre of Kenya, and while the climate is tropical, it is very much affected by altitude, the western half of the country being over 1,000 m [3,250 ft]. In summer, Nairobi is 10°C [18°F] cooler than Mombasa on the coast. There are two temperature maxima associated with the passage of the sun. Nights can be cool with temperatures around 10°C [50°F], but it never falls below freezing. The rains fall April to May with a lesser period from November to December.

Bisected by the Great Rift Valley, the Kenya Highlands were formed by volcanoes and lava flows rising from 1,500 m [4,900 ft] to the snow-capped peak of Mt Kenya at 5,199 m [17,000 ft].

Some 80% of the people crowd into about 15% of the plains in the south-west of the country, where average rainfalls of over 750 mm [30 in] a year support dense farming populations. Corn meal is the staple diet.

The western Highlands descend to the equally populous Lake Victoria basin around Kakamega and Kisii, focusing on Kisumu. Nakuru and Eldoret are farming centres originally settled by Europeans. The modern capital city of Nairobi is within this core area of Kenya, from which derive most of the exports of tea (Kenya is the world's fourth largest producer), coffee, pyrethrum and sisal, with soda ash from the Magadi alkaline lake.

By the standards of tropical Africa, Kenya has a stable and safe economy, even allowing for the tra-ditionally thriving black market and usual reliance on aid. The country could nevertheless be in danger from two explosions, one in AIDS and the other, by contrast, in sheer numbers of people. Though relatively sparse in terms of density, Kenya's extra-ordinarily high birth rate of 4.2% is expected to pro-duce an increase of 82% in its population between 1988 and 2000 – a figure exceeded only by Haiti. By 1990 it was already registering the world's 'youngest' profile, with more than 52% of the total under 15 years of age.

The 1990s brought signs, too, of increasing pol-itical problems as Daniel arap Moi, president since 1978 and successor to the moderate Jomo Kenyatta, found his authoritarian one-party regime under threat. In December 1991, after months of pressure and government defections, he was forced to con-cede the principle of pluralist democracy – not seen since 1969. The president (a Kalenjin in a country whose affairs have always been dominated by the Kikuyu) had always maintained throughout his campaign of repression that a multiparty system would lead to chaos based on tribal rivalries ∎

COUNTRY: Republic of Kenya

AREA: 580,370 sq km [224,081 sq mls]

POPULATION: 24,032,000

CAPITAL (Population): Nairobi (1,429,000)

GOVERNMENT: Single-party republic with a unicameral legislature

ETHNIC GROUPS: Kikuyu 21%, Luhya 14%, Luo 13%, Kamba 11%, Kalenjin 11%

LANGUAGES: Swahili and English (both official), Kikuyu, over 200 tribal languages

RELIGIONS: Christian 72% (Roman Catholic 27%, Protestant 19%, others 26%), African indigenous 18%, Muslim 6%

NATIONAL DAY: 12 December; Independence Day

CURRENCY: Kenyan shilling = 100 cents

ANNUAL INCOME PER PERSON: $370

MAIN PRIMARY PRODUCTS: Maize, millet, cassava, beans, pyrethrum, tea, coffee, sugar, cattle, sisal

MAIN INDUSTRIES: Agriculture, oil refining, food processing, tourism, cement

MAIN EXPORTS: Coffee 26%, tea 22%, petroleum products 13%, vegetables and fruit 10%

MAIN IMPORTS: Machinery and transport equipment 34%, crude petroleum 20%, chemicals 18%

TOURISM: 662,000 visitors per year

POPULATION DENSITY: 41 per sq km [107 per sq ml]

LIFE EXPECTANCY: Female 63 yrs, male 59 yrs

ADULT LITERACY: 69%

AIDS AND POVERTY IN AFRICA

The Acquired Immune Deficiency Syndrome was first identified in 1981, when American doctors found otherwise healthy young men suc-cumbing to rare infections. By 1984, the cause had been traced to the Human Immunodeficiency Virus (HIV), which can remain dormant for many years and perhaps indefinitely; only half of those known to carry the virus in 1981 had developed AIDS ten years later. By the early 1990s, AIDS was still largely restricted to male homosexuals or needle-sharing drug users in the affluent West. However, here the disease is spreading fastest among heterosexual men and women, its usual vector in the Third World, where most of its victims live, and where most of them will die.

Africa is the most severely hit. In 1991, a World Health Organization conference in Dakar, Senegal, was told that AIDS would kill more than 6 million Africans in the coming decade. In the same period, 4 million children would be born with the dis-ease, and millions more would be orphaned by it. In Uganda, an esti-mated million people are thought to be carrying the virus. The conference heard that Africa's educated élites were among those most at risk – trained people desperately needed to help the continent's development in the 21st century.

Africans are also more than usually vulnerable to HIV and AIDS infection, partly because of urban-ization and sexual freedom. But most are poor, many are undernourished; many more suffer from various, debilitating, non-fatal diseases: para-site infestations, for example. Their immune systems are already weak, making them less likely to shrug off exposure to the virus, and more likely to develop full-blown AIDS.

Thus in Africa, a pregnant mother with HIV has a one-in-two chance of passing the virus to her child; in the West, the child of a similarly afflicted mother has only one chance in eight of contracting the infection. African poverty also means that victims have virtually no chance of receiving any of the expensive drugs developed to prolong the lives of AIDS sufferers. Even if researchers succeed in deve-loping an AIDS vaccine, it is likely to be well beyond the reach of countries whose health budget is seldom much more than $2 a year for each citizen; there are few refrigerators to store such a vaccine, and few needles to administer it safely.

Africa faces millions of individual human tragedies. Yet even so, AIDS-related deaths are unlikely to im-pinge significantly on continental population growth, despite the claims of some authorities. At its cur-rent rate of increase – 2.97% per annum – Africa by the year 2000 will have acquired more than 243 million extra people – more than 40 times the number of predicted deaths from AIDS. And AIDS is only the newest scourge Africa must suffer – not the greatest. Malaria, measles, a host of water-borne infections and simple malnutrition will kill far more Afri-cans, especially African children, dur-ing the same period.

AFRICA

MALAWI

The colours in Malawi's flag come from the flag adopted by the Malawi Congress Party in 1953. The rising sun symbol, representing the beginning of a new era for Africa, was added when the country gained independence from Britain in 1964.

A small, hilly if not mountainous country, Malawi's strange shape (nowhere is it more than 160km [100mls] wide) derived from a 19th-century missionaries' and traders' route up the Zambezi, Shire and Lake Nyasa (Malawi). The country is relatively poor in natural resources, and compared with its neighbours has a high population density, placing excessive pressure on the land. This problem was inflamed during the 1980s, when Malawi became the main host to nearly a million refugees from neighbouring Mozambique, putting an intolerable burden on an already weak economy, despite massive aid packages.

Industrial and urban development are extremely limited. Most of the commercial activity centres on agriculture, which provides over 90% of Malawi's domestic exports. Tea and tobacco, mostly from large estates, are the principal export crops while basic foodstuffs such as maize are largely derived from small, quasisubsistence peasant holdings which occupy most of the farmland. Malawi has a long history as an exporter of labour migrants, and large numbers of Malawians still work or seek work abroad, notably in South Africa.

Malawi's recent history has been dominated by one man: Dr Hastings Kumuzu Banda. Already 62 years old, he led the country (formerly Nyasaland) to independence in 1964, and two years later declared a one-party republic with himself as president – for life from 1971. His autocratic regime was different from most of black Africa in being conservative and pragmatic, hostile to socialist neighbours but friendly with South Africa.

At first his austerity programme and agricultural policies seemed to have wrought an economic miracle, but the 1980s sealed a swift decline and a return to poverty. As well as a million refugees Malawi faced another immediate problem – the world's worst recorded national incidence of Aids. Malawi means 'the land lake where the sun is reflected in the water like fire', but the reality for most of the people is a good deal less romantic ■

COUNTRY: Republic of Malawi
AREA: 118,480 sq km [45,745 sq mls]
POPULATION: 8,556,000
CAPITAL (Population): Lilongwe (187,000)
GOVERNMENT: Single-party republic
ETHNIC GROUPS: Maravi (Chewa, Nyanja, Tonga, Tumbuka) 58%, Lomwe 18%, Yao 13%, Ngoni 7%
LANGUAGES: Chichewa and English (both official)
RELIGIONS: Christian (mostly Roman Catholic) 64%, Muslim 12%, widespread animism
NATIONAL DAY: 6 July; Independence Day (1966)
CURRENCY: Kwacha = 100 tambala
ANNUAL INCOME PER PERSON: $200
MAIN PRIMARY PRODUCTS: Limestone and timber
MAIN INDUSTRIES: Agriculture, fishing
MAIN EXPORTS: Tobacco, tea and sugar
MAIN IMPORTS: Fuel, vehicles and clothing
DEFENCE: 5% of national budget
POPULATION DENSITY: 72 per sq km [187 per sq ml]
LIFE EXPECTANCY: Female 50 yrs, male 48 yrs
ADULT LITERACY: 41%

TANZANIA

In 1964 Tanganyika united with the island of Zanzibar to form the United Republic of Tanzania and a new flag was adopted. The colours represent agriculture (green), minerals (yellow), the people (black), water and Zanzibar (blue).

From the islands of Zanzibar and Pemba, Tanzania extends across the high plateau of eastern Africa, mostly above 1,000m [3,000ft], to the rift valleys filled by lakes Tanganyika and Nyasa (Malawi), whose deepest waters reach below sea level. The Northern Highlands flank branches of the eastern rift valley, containing the strongly alkaline Lake Natron and lakes Eyasi and Manyara, and dominated by the ice-capped extinct volcano of Kilimanjaro which, at 5,895m [19,340ft], is the highest mountain in Africa. The Southern Highlands overlook Lake Nyasa at the southern end of the rift system.

Tanzania's population is dispersed into several concentrations mostly on the margins of the country, separated by sparsely inhabited savanna woodland (*miombo*). Attempts to develop the *miombo* woodlands have been hindered by sleeping sickness, drought and poor soils, and traditional settlement is based on shifting cultivation.

Along the coast and on self-governing Zanzibar and other islands are old cities and ruins of the historic Swahili-Arab culture, and the major ports and railway termini of Dar es Salaam and

In East Africa the winds blow mainly parallel to the coast throughout the year and rainfall is less than in many equatorial regions. The heaviest rain occurs in April and May, when the inter-tropical rain belt moves northwards. It is followed by the south-east trade winds, which have lost much of their moisture over the mountains of Madagascar before reaching East Africa. The temperature is uniformly high throughout the year.

Tanga. Rail connections enable Dar es Salaam to act as a port for Zambia and, by ferry across Lake Tanganyika, for eastern Zaïre. Local products include sisal and cashew nuts with cloves from Zanzibar and Pemba, and there are some good beach resorts for the tourist industry.

The Northern Highlands centre on Moshi and support intensive agriculture, exporting coffee, tea and tobacco. This contrasts with the nomadic Masai pastoralists of the surrounding plains. Tea also comes from the Southern Highlands. South of Lake Victoria is an important cotton-growing and cattle-rearing area, focusing on Mwanza.

Tanzania was formed in 1964 when mainland Tanganyika – which had become independent from Britain in 1961 – was joined by the small island state of Zanzibar. For 20 years after independence Tanzania was run under the widely admired policies of self-help (*ujamaa*) and egalitarian socialism pioneered by President Julius Nyerere. While his schemes produced relatively high levels of education and welfare for Africa, economic progress was stifled not only by lack of resources and falling world commodity prices but also by inefficient state corporations and corrupt bureaucracies. As a result the country ranks little better than war-torn states like Ethiopia and the Somali Republic in terms of income, and is almost as dependent on foreign financial aid.

Nyerere stepped down as president in 1985, but retained the (only) party leadership and considerable influence for another five years. In the meantime his successor, Ali Hassan Mwinyi, was attempting to liberalize the economy – if not the political system. Another target was tourism: Tanzania received 103,000 visitors in 1987; this is less than a sixth of Kenya's total, but there are hopes of a rise.

COUNTRY: United Republic of Tanzania
AREA: 945,090 sq km [364,899 sq mls]
POPULATION: 25,635,000
CAPITAL (Population): Dar es Salaam (1,100,000)
GOVERNMENT: Single-party republic
ETHNIC GROUPS: Nyamwezi and Sukama 21%, Swahili 9%, Hehet and Bena 7%, Makonde 6%, Haya 6%
LANGUAGES: English and Swahili (both official)
RELIGIONS: Christian (mostly Roman Catholic) 34%, Sunni Muslim 33% (in Zanzibar 99%), traditional beliefs
NATIONAL DAY: 26 April; Union Day (1964)

CURRENCY: Tanzanian shilling = 100 cents
ANNUAL INCOME PER PERSON: $120
MAIN PRIMARY PRODUCTS: Agricultural and diamonds
MAIN INDUSTRIES: Agriculture, food processing
MAIN EXPORTS: Coffee 26%, cotton 24%, sisal 1%
MAIN IMPORTS: Machinery and industrial goods 73%
DEFENCE: 20% of national budget
POPULATION DENSITY: 27 per sq km [70 per sq ml]
INFANT MORTALITY: 97 per 1,000 live births
LIFE EXPECTANCY: Female 57 yrs, male 53 yrs
ADULT LITERACY: 85%

Certainly it has many of the prerequisites for a successful tourist industry. There are 17 national parks and reserves – among them the Selous, the largest game reserve in the world; the celebrated Serengeti; and the Ngorongoro crater, renowned for its wildlife. In addition, there are important archaeological sites such as Olduvai Gorge, west of the Serengeti, where in 1964 Louis Leakey, the British archaeologist and anthropoligist, discovered the remains of humans some million years old ■

MOZAMBIQUE

The green stripe represents the fertile land, the black stripe Africa and the yellow stripe mineral wealth. The badge on the red triangle contains a rifle, hoe, cogwheel and book, which are all Marxist symbols of the struggle against colonialism.

Maputo is located on the coast of Mozambique at the southern end of an extensive lowland. The range of temperature is less than that of the interior plateaus, and summers are hot and humid – partly due to the warm Agulhas Current which flows southwards along the coast. Day temperatures reach 30°C [86°F], rarely dropping below 18°C [64°F] at night. Most of the rain falls in summer, when the inter-tropical rainbelt is at its furthest south. There is a not entirely rainless dry season in winter.

Like other former ex-Portuguese African countries, Mozambique arose from the search for a route round Africa to the riches of Asia; Vasco da Gama and his successors established forts at Beira (Sofala), Quelimane and Moçambique Island. Dutch conquest of Portuguese Asia in the 17th century, and subsequent concentration by the Portuguese on the slave trade from West Africa to the Americas, resulted in decay of Mozambique settlements. However, being so little affected by the slave trade, and acting as a refuge in wars, Mozambique was never depopulated to the extent of Angola, and still maintains a higher population on a smaller area.

Because of the warm Mozambique (Agulhas) Current, all the country is tropical. Coral reefs lie offshore, and the only real natural harbour is Maputo (Lourenço Marques). Here is southern Africa's widest coastal plain, with plantations of coconut, sisal and sugar on the alluvial flats. As in the northern foothills, farmers grow maize, groundnuts, cotton and cashew. Only the inner borderlands are high; because of this and its remoteness from Portugal,

Mozambique attracted few European settlers. At the limit of navigation on the Zambezi is Africa's largest dam, Cabora Bassa, whose power goes largely to South Africa. Large deposits of coal, copper, bauxite and offshore gas have yet to be exploited.

Despite the relentless civil war Mozambique forms a transit route for much of the overseas trade of Swaziland, the Transvaal, Zimbabwe and Zambia, involving mainly the ports of Maputo, Beira and Nacala-Velha, just north of Moçambique. Rail, port and handling services provide employment and substantial revenues.

Mozambique has been plagued by civil war since well before Portugal abruptly relinquished control in 1975. Combined with frequent droughts and floods, this has caused tens of thousands of deaths and, by 1989, had reduced the country to the status of the world's poorest.

When the Portuguese rulers and settlers abandoned Mozambique they left behind a country totally unprepared for organizing itself – the literacy rate, for example, was less than 1%. The Marxist-Leninist government of Samora Machel's Frelimo movement, which had been fighting the colonial regime for more than a decade, tried to implement ambitious social policies, but erratic administration, along with a series of natural disasters, reduced the economy to ruins by the mid-1980s.

From the 1970s the progress was also severely hampered by the widespread activities of the Mozambique National Resistance (MNR, or Renamo), backed first by Rhodesia and later by South Africa. Renamo soon controlled huge areas of the countryside – convoys could only cross the 'Tete Corridor' escorted by Zimbabwean and Malawian forces – forcing more than a million refugees to flee their land, the vast majority of them going to poor Malawi; by 1988 almost half of all Mozambique's population was reliant on external aid.

Well before Machel was mysteriously killed in a plane crash inside South Africa in 1986, his government had been opening up the country to Western investment and influence – a policy continued by his successor, President Joaquim Chissano. In 1989 Frelimo formally abandoned its Marxist ideology, and the following year agreed to end one-party rule and hold talks with the rebels. Despite South Africa's withdrawal of official assistance, the talks dragged on without a permanent ceasefire and hostilities continued to dog the country. Relief agencies estimated in 1991 that up to 3 million people had been displaced by the war – and that as many again faced starvation ■

COUNTRY: People's Republic of Mozambique
AREA: 801,590 sq km [309,494 sq mls]
POPULATION: 15,656,000
CAPITAL (Population): Maputo (1,070,000)
GOVERNMENT: Single-party republic
ETHNIC GROUPS: Makua/Lomwe 47%, Tsonga 23%, Malawi 12%, Shona 11%, Yao 4%, Swahili 1%, Makonde 1%
LANGUAGES: Portuguese (official), other Bantu languages approximately as ethnic groups
RELIGIONS: Traditional beliefs 60%, Roman Catholic 18%, Muslim 13%
NATIONAL DAY: 25 June; Independence Day (1975)
CURRENCY: Metical = 100 centavos
ANNUAL INCOME PER PERSON: $80
MAIN PRIMARY PRODUCTS: Cotton, cereals, cashew nuts, sugar, tea, fruit, sisal, groundnuts, coal
MAIN INDUSTRIES: Agriculture, textiles, chemicals, mining, food processing, fishing
MAIN EXPORTS: Shrimps 39%, cashew nuts 32%, cotton 7%, sugar 3%, copra 3%
MAIN IMPORTS: Foodstuffs 38%, capital equipment 19%, machinery and spare parts 15%, petroleum 10%
DEFENCE: 38% of national budget
POPULATION DENSITY: 20 per sq km [51 per sq ml]
LIFE EXPECTANCY: Female 50 yrs, male 47 yrs
ADULT LITERACY: 38%

AFRICA

ANGOLA

The flag is based on that of the Popular Movement for the Liberation of Angola during the struggle for independence from Portugal (1975). The emblem, with a half gearwheel and a machete, symbolizes Angola's Socialist ideology.

Angola has a tropical climate with temperatures above 20°C [68°F], slightly lower on the plateau to the east. The rainfall is low on the coast, especially in the south, because the winds are blowing over the cold Benguela Current or from the dry, hot interior. At Luanda, rain falls on only about 50 days per year. The wettest parts are in the north and east, and the rainy season is from about November to April.

COUNTRY: People's Republic of Angola

AREA: 1,246,700 sq km [481,351 sq mls]

POPULATION: 10,020,000

CAPITAL (Population): Luanda (1,200,000)

GOVERNMENT: One-party socialist republic with a unicameral House of Assembly; pluralism planned

ETHNIC GROUPS: Ovimbundu 37%, Mbundu 23%, Kongo, Luimbe, Humbe, Chokwe

LANGUAGES: Portuguese (official), but Ovimbundu, Kimbundu, Bakango and Chokwe in common use

RELIGIONS: Christian (mainly Roman Catholic) 64%, Animist 34%

NATIONAL DAY: 11 November; Independence Day (1975)

CURRENCY: Kwanza = 100 lwei

ANNUAL INCOME PER PERSON: $620

MAIN PRIMARY PRODUCTS: Coffee, cassava, crude petroleum, diamonds, cotton, sisal

MAIN INDUSTRIES: Agriculture, oil-related products

MAIN EXPORTS: Mineral products, pearls, gemstones, precious metals

MAIN IMPORTS: Base metals, electrical and transport equipment

DEFENCE: 38% of national budget

POPULATION DENSITY: 8 per sq km [21 per sq ml]

LIFE EXPECTANCY: Female 48 yrs, male 45 yrs

ADULT LITERACY: 28%

More than 13 times the size of its colonial ruler, Portugal, Angola is southern Africa's largest state, extending through 13° of latitude. There is a strong cooling effect from the cold offshore Benguela Current, and climate and vegetation vary from desert on the south coast to equatorial and montane conditions in the centre and north. Thus Angola has exceptionally varied agricultural output, while the coastal waters are rich in fish.

Portugal established Luanda in 1575, and Angola's capital is the oldest European-founded city in Africa south of the Sahara. As a centre of the slave trade, some 3 million captives from Angola passed through it to the Americas, and the depopulation dislocated local life for many generations. As a Portuguese colony and then overseas province, Angola's development was hampered by the small population, by Portugal's economic weakness, centralized rule and mercantilist theories, and more recently by years of persistent guerrilla warfare between several rival nationalist groups.

Potentially, Angola is one of Africa's richest countries. Oil reserves are important both on the coast and offshore near Luanda in the enclave of Cabinda, and hydroelectric power and irrigation developments are substantial. Diamonds, a major export (Angola is the world's sixth largest producer) come from the north-east, and there are unexploited reserves of copper, manganese and phosphates.

Economic progress has been hampered by austere Marxist policies and vast spending on defence and security, but in 1991 the crippling 16-year war between the MPLA government and UNITA rebels – the former supported by Cuba and the Soviet Union, the latter by South Africa and the USA – appeared finally to end in a peace accord. The MPLA, already liberalizing the economy, formally renounced Marxism-Leninism and agreed to introduce a multiparty system ∎

ZAMBIA

The colours of Zambia's distinctive national flag are those of the United Nationalist Independence Party, which led the struggle against Britain. The flying eagle represents freedom. The design was adopted on independence in 1964.

COUNTRY: Republic of Zambia

AREA: 752,614 sq km [290,586 sq mls]

POPULATION: 8,073,000

CAPITAL (Population): Lusaka (900,000)

GOVERNMENT: Republic with a unicameral legislature

ETHNIC GROUPS: Bemba 34%, Tonga 16%, Malawi 14%, Lozi 9%

LANGUAGES: English (official), Bemba, Tonga, Nyanja, Lozi, Lunda, Luvale and Kaonde

RELIGIONS: Christian 54%, Animist 40%

CURRENCY: Kwacha = 100 negwee

ANNUAL INCOME PER PERSON: $420

MAIN PRIMARY PRODUCTS: Copper, coal, zinc, lead

MAIN INDUSTRIES: Mining, agriculture

MAIN EXPORTS: Copper, cobalt, zinc, tobacco

MAIN IMPORTS: Machinery, transport equipment

DEFENCE: 2% of national budget

POPULATION DENSITY: 11 per sq km [28 per sq ml]

LIFE EXPECTANCY: Female 57 yrs, male 54 yrs

ADULT LITERACY: 76%

A vast expanse of high plateaus in the interior of south-central Africa, most of Zambia (formerly Northern Rhodesia) is drained by the Zambezi and two of its major tributaries, the Kafue and the Luangwa. The latter and the central section of the Zambezi occupy a low-lying rift valley bounded by rugged escarpments. Lake Kariba, formed by damming in 1961 and the second largest artificial lake in Africa, occupies part of the floor of this valley; like the hydroelectric power it generates, the lake is shared with Zimbabwe, though power from the Kafue River now supplements supplies from Kariba. The magnificent Victoria Falls are similarly shared between the two countries. Much of northern Zambia is drained to the Atlantic Ocean by headwaters of the Zaïre (Congo), including the Chambeshi, which loses itself within the vast swamps of the Bangweulu Depression.

Zambia is the world's fifth biggest producer of copper, but despite efforts to diversify, the economy remains stubbornly dependent (95% of export earnings in 1989) on this one mineral, with Japan (35%), Italy and France between them accounting for more than half of the trade. The Copperbelt, centred on Kitwe, is the dominant urban region while the capital, Lusaka, provides the other major growth pole. Rural-urban migration has increased markedly since independence in 1964 – Zambia has 'black'

southern Africa's highest proportion of town-dwellers – but work is scarce.

Commercial farming, concentrated in central regions astride the railway, and mostly maize, frequently fails to meet the needs of the growing urban population, but as a landlocked country heavily dependent on international trade, Zambia relies on its neighbours for access to ports via Zimbabwe, Mozambique and South Africa. Alternatives, notably a railway, highway and oil pipeline to Dar es Salaam, have been developed, but Zambia continues to have serious transport problems compounded by lack of finance.

President Kenneth Kaunda's government enjoyed reasonable income until the copper crash of the mid-1970s, but his collectivist policies failed to diversify the economy (before or after) and neglected agriculture. In 1972 he declared UNIP the only legal party, and it was nearly 20 years before democracy returned: then, in the 1991 elections (conceded by Kaunda after intense pressure in 1990), he was trounced by union leader Frederick Chiluba of the Movement for Multiparty Democracy – Kaunda's first challenger in 27 years of post-colonial rule. Chiluba inherited a foreign debt of $4.6 billion – one of the world's biggest per capita figures ■

ZIMBABWE

Adopted when legal independence was secured in 1980, Zimbabwe's flag is based on the colours of the ruling Patriotic Front. Within the white triangle is the soapstone bird national emblem and a red star, symbolizing the party's Socialist policy.

Formerly Rhodesia (and Southern Rhodesia before 1965), Zimbabwe is a compact country lying astride the high plateaus between the Zambezi and Limpopo rivers. It was nurtured by Britain as a 'white man's country', and there were some 280,000 Europeans there when Ian Smith declared UDI in 1965. Guerrilla action against the Smith regime soon escalated into a full-scale civil war, eventually forcing a move to black majority rule in 1980. The rift that followed independence, between

Robert Mugabe's ruling ZANU and Joshua Nkomo's ZAPU, was healed in 1989 when they finally merged after nearly three decades and Mugabe renounced his shallow Marxist-Leninist ideology. In 1990 the state of emergency that had lasted since 1965 was allowed to lapse – three months after Mugabe had secured a landslide election victory.

Zimbabwe's relatively strong economy – founded on gold and tobacco but now far more diverse – evolved its virtual self-sufficiency during the

In common with other places on the high interior plateau of southern Africa, Harare has a large diurnal range of temperature, particularly in the dry, sunny winter, and is much cooler than lowlands at the same latitude. Frosts have been recorded in June–August. The main rains of summer are brought by south-easterly winds from the Indian Ocean. They are usually preceded by isolated thundery outbreaks which extend the rainy season from late October–March, when it usually rains over 15 days per month.

days of international sanctions against Smith's white minority regime. After 1980 there was a surge in most sectors, with successful agrarian policies enabling the nation to supply less endowed well-off neighbours with food in good years and the exploitation of the country's rich and varied mineral resources. However, a fast-growing population will exert pressure on both land and resources of all kinds in the 1990s ■

COUNTRY: Republic of Zimbabwe
AREA: 390,579 sq km [150,873 sq mls]
POPULATION: 9,369,000
CAPITAL (Population): Harare (681,100)
GOVERNMENT: Republic with bicameral legislature
ETHNIC GROUPS: Shona 71%, Ndebele 16%
LANGUAGES: English (official), Shona and Ndebele
RELIGIONS: Christian 44%, Animist 40%
CURRENCY: Zimbabwe $ = 100 cents
NATIONAL DAY: 18 April; Independence Day (1980)
ANNUAL INCOME PER PERSON: $640
MAIN PRIMARY PRODUCTS: Nickel, copper, coal, cobalt, asbestos, gold, iron ore, silver, tin
MAIN INDUSTRIES: Agriculture, mining, manufacturing
MAIN EXPORTS: Food, tobacco, cotton lint, asbestos, copper, nickel, iron and steel bars
MAIN IMPORTS: Chemicals, mineral fuels, machinery, transport equipment, foodstuffs
DEFENCE: 8% of national budget
POPULATION DENSITY: 24 per sq km [62 per sq ml]
LIFE EXPECTANCY: Female 63 yrs, male 59 yrs
ADULT LITERACY: 74%

AFRICA

NAMIBIA

One of the world's newest states, Namibia adopted its flag after independence in 1990. The red and white colours symbolize the country's human resources while the green, blue and the gold sun represent the natural resources, mostly minerals.

Windhoek lies at 1,700 m [5,500 ft] on the Namibian Plateau and is isolated from the effects of the cold Benguela Current which washes the coast to the west. With little cloud and clear, dry air the daily range of temperature is much larger than on the coast. Summer days are hot and frost may occur on winter nights. Thundery rain in summer provides enough water to support vegetation, contrasting with the deserts to the east and west. For most of the year there is about ten hours of sunshine per day.

Born out of the late 19th-century scramble for Africa, Namibia is a country of enormous diversity, physically and socially. Fringing Namibia's southern Atlantic coastline is the arid Namib Desert, virtually uninhabited, separated by a major escarpment from a north-south spine of mountains which culminate in the Khomas Highlands near Windhoek. This rugged spine, built of thick schists and quartzites, rises to 2,483 m [8,150 ft] in the peak of Moltkeblik. To the east the country occupies the fringes of the Kalahari Desert.

Apart from the British enclave of Walvis Bay, Namibia was (as South West Africa) a German protectorate from 1884 before being occupied by the Union of South Africa at the request of the Allied powers in 1915. Granted a League of Nations mandate in 1920, South Africa refused to place the territory under UN trusteeship after World War II, and in 1966 the mandate was cancelled. However, South Africa continued to exploit Namibia, even though in 1971 the International Court of Justice ruled that its occupation of the country was illegal; the main nationalist movement, SWAPO, began a guerrilla campaign supported by Cuba and Angola, but it was not until 1990, following increasing international pressure, that the country eventually won its independence.

In African terms it was well worth fighting over. Though 60% of the population is engaged in agriculture, and offshore the Benguela Current feeds some of the Atlantic's richest fishing grounds, 90% of Namibia's income comes from exports of minerals – notably uranium (nearly 10% of the world total) and diamonds. There are also large gasfields and good prospects for oil.

The status of Walvis Bay, the crucial deep-water port and military base, was in doubt at independence, but in 1991 South Africa and Namibia agreed to set up joint administration there ∎

COUNTRY: Namibia
AREA: 824,290 sq km [318,258 sq mls]
POPULATION: 1,781,000
CAPITAL (Population): Windhoek (115,000)
GOVERNMENT: Democratic republic
ETHNIC GROUPS: Ovambo 50%, Kavango 9%, Herero 7%, Damara 7%, White 6%
LANGUAGES: Afrikaans and English (both official)
RELIGIONS: Christian 90% (Lutheran 51%), Animist
NATIONAL DAY: 21 March; Independence Day
CURRENCY: South African Rand = 100 cents
ANNUAL INCOME PER PERSON: $1,000
MAIN PRIMARY PRODUCTS: Uranium, tin, copper, lead, zinc, silver and diamonds
MAIN INDUSTRIES: Mining and agriculture
DEFENCE: 19% of national budget
POPULATION DENSITY: 2 per sq km [6 per sq ml]
LIFE EXPECTANCY: Female 60 yrs, male 58 yrs
ADULT LITERACY: 73%

BOTSWANA

Botswana's flag dates from independence from Britain in 1966. The black and white zebra stripe represents the racial harmony of the people, and blue symbolizes the country's most vital need – rainwater.

The British protectorate of Bechuanaland from 1885, Botswana became an independent state after a peaceful six-year transition in 1966. It was then one of the world's poorest countries, with cattle as the only significant export, and its physical environment hardly induced optimism: more than half of the country's land area is occupied by the Kalahari Desert, with much of the rest taken up by salt-pans and swamps. Although the Kalahari extends into Namibia and South Africa, Botswana accounts for the greater part of this vast dry upland. It is, however, not a uniform desert: occasional rainfall allows growth of grasses and thorny scrub, enabling the area's sparse human population of about 100,000 – mostly nomadic Bantu herdsmen – to graze their cattle.

Botswana was transformed by the mining of vast diamond resources, starting at Orapa in 1971, and, despite a protracted drought, expanding output in the 1980s made the economy the fastest growing in sub-Saharan Africa, paving the way for wide-ranging social programmes. By the end of the decade Botswana was producing some 16% of the world's total, behind Australia and Zaïre.

Politically stable under Seretse Khama, the country's main target became diversification, not only to reduce dependence on diamonds (85% of export earnings) and on South African imports, but also to create jobs for a rapidly expanding – though still relatively sparse – population. Copper has been mined at Selebi-Pikwe since 1974, but the emphasis in the 1980s was put on tourism: 17% of Botswana's huge area (the world's highest figure) is assigned to wildlife conservation and game reserves, and more than half a million visitors a year are drawn to them, mostly from South Africa ∎

COUNTRY: Botswana
AREA: 581,730 sq km [224,606 sq mls]
POPULATION: 1,291,000
CAPITAL (Population): Gaborone (120,000)
GOVERNMENT: Multiparty republic
ETHNIC GROUPS: Tswana 76%, Shana 12%, San (Bushmen) 3%
LANGUAGES: English (official), Setswana (Siswana, Tswana – national language)
RELIGIONS: Traditional beliefs (over 50%), Christian (mainly Anglican) 30%
NATIONAL DAY: 30 September; Independence Day
CURRENCY: Pula = 100 thebe
ANNUAL INCOME PER PERSON: $2,040
MAIN PRIMARY PRODUCTS: Diamonds, copper, nickel, coal, cobalt, sorghum and pulses
MAIN INDUSTRIES: Agricultural and mining
MAIN EXPORTS: Diamonds, copper-nickel matte, meat and meat products
MAIN IMPORTS: Food, beverages, tobacco, machinery, electrical goods and transport
DEFENCE: 4% of national budget
POPULATION DENSITY: 2 per sq km [6 per sq ml]
LIFE EXPECTANCY: Female 64 yrs, male 58 yrs
ADULT LITERACY: 71%

SOUTH AFRICA

The design of South Africa's flag, adopted in 1928, is based on one brought by the first Dutch settlers in the 17th century. On the central stripe are the British union flag and the flags of the Orange Free State and the Transvaal.

Geologically very ancient, South Africa has only scant superficial deposits of sediments less than 500 million years old. Geological history has had a great effect on all aspects of its development.

The country is divisible into two major natural zones – the interior and the coastal fringe – the interior in turn consisting of two major parts. Most of Cape Province, the Transvaal and the Orange Free State are drained by the Orange River and its important right-bank tributaries which flow with gentle gradients over level plateaus, varying in height from 1,200–2,000 m [4,000–6,000 ft]. The northern Transvaal is occupied by the Bushveld, an area of granites and igneous intrusions.

The coastal fringe is divided from the interior by the Fringing Escarpment, a feature that makes communication within the country very difficult. In the east the massive basalt-capped rock wall of the Drakensberg, at its most majestic near Mont-aux-Sources and rising to over 3,000 m [over 10,000 ft],

overlooks the Natal and Transkei coastlands. In the west there is a similar divide between the interior plateau and the coastlands, though this is less well developed. The Fringing Escarpment also runs along the south coast, where it is fronted by many independent mountain ranges.

South Africa's economic and political development is closely related to these physical components. The country was first peopled by negroids from the north, who introduced a cattle-keeping, grain-growing culture. Entering by the plateaus of the north-east, they continued southwards into the well-watered zones below the Fringing Escarpment of present-day Natal and Transkei. Moving into country occupied by Bushmanoid peoples they absorbed some of the latter's cultural features, especially the 'clicks' so characteristic of the modern Zulu and Xhosa languages. By the 18th century these Bantu-speaking groups had penetrated to the south-east.

Simultaneously with this advance, a group of

In winter the air is very dry and the sky almost cloudless on the High Veld. The large diurnal range of temperature resembles that of other places on the high plateaus of southern Africa; it often exceeds 15°C [27°F]. Summer is the rainy season, when north-easterly winds bring moist air from the Indian Ocean. Rainfall is more abundant and the winter dry season shorter than in western areas at the same latitude. From May to September it usually rains on 1–3 days per month.

Europeans was establishing a victualling point for the Dutch East India Company on the site of modern Cape Town. These Company employees, augmented by Huguenot refugees, eventually spread out from Cape Town, beginning a movement of European farmers throughout southern Africa and bringing about the development of the Afrikaners. Their advance was channelled in the south by the parallel coastal ranges, so that eventually black and white met near the Kei River. To the north, once the Fringing Escarpment had been overcome, the level surface of the plateaus allowed a rapid spread

AFRICA

CAPE TOWN

°C / °F — Temperature

Precipitation
508mm
20in

J F M A M J J A S O N D

The south-western corner of South Africa has a very different climate from the rest of the country. It lies far enough south to be affected by westerly winds which blow across the Southern Ocean in winter, bringing cloud and rain. The dry, sunny summers and wet winters resemble those of the Mediterranean region, but it is less hot in summer due to the cold Benguela Current flowing northwards along the coast. There are over ten hours of sunshine per day, October–February.

COUNTRY: Republic of South Africa
AREA: 1,221,040 sq km [471,444 sq mls]
POPULATION: 35,282,000
CAPITAL (Population): Pretoria (823,000)
GOVERNMENT: Multiparty republic with tricameral legislature
ETHNIC GROUPS: Black 68%, White 18%, Coloured 11%, Asian 3%
LANGUAGES: Afrikaans and English (official), Xhosa, Zulu
RELIGIONS: Black Christian churches 31%, Dutch Reform 23%, Roman Catholic 15%, Hindu 3%
NATIONAL DAY: 31 May; Republic Day (1961)
CURRENCY: Rand = 100 cents

ANNUAL INCOME PER PERSON: $2,520
MAIN PRIMARY PRODUCTS: Gold, iron ore, copper, uranium, diamonds, coal, zinc, tin, phosphates
MAIN INDUSTRIES: Mining, iron and steel, vehicles, food processing, oil refining, agriculture, clothing
MAIN EXPORTS: Gold 39%, base metals 14%, mineral products 10%, pearls, chemical products
MAIN IMPORTS: Mechanical equipment 31%, transport equipment 14%, chemical products 11%
TOURISM: 703,000 visitors per year
ADULT LITERACY: White 98%, Asian 69%, Black 32%
PRINCIPAL CITIES (Population): Cape Town 1,912,000 Johannesburg 1,726,000 East Rand 1,038,000

northwards. From this colonizing process, aided by an implanting of British people in the south-east and near Durban, the present disposition of black-dominated and white-dominated lands arose.

Stretching from the Transvaal's western border with Botswana, running in a horseshoe to the north of Pretoria and then southwards through Natal and the Transkei, are the so-called Homelands – territories occupied almost exclusively by Africans. From the outset the Africans operated a form of mixed agriculture, giving them subsistence but little more. The men were cattle-keepers and warriors, the women tilled the plots, in a culture based on extensive holdings of communal land. European farming was also based on extensive holdings but incorporated individual land rights. Not surprisingly, conflict arose from the juxtapositioning of the two groups, and with the discovery of valuable minerals – gold in the Banket deposits of the Witwatersrand, diamonds in the Kimberlite pipes of the Cape, platinum in the Bushveld and coal in the Transvaal and Natal – both were drastically affected. South Africa still produces 30% of the world's gold, and today we can add chrome (34%), uranium (9%), nickel (3.7%) and many others to the list.

Exploitation of southern Africa's minerals led to trade with overseas markets and the development of major urban complexes. Johannesburg grew fastest; its growth encouraged the expansion of Durban and to a large extent caused Cape Town and Port Elizabeth to flourish. The appearance of a capitalist, market-oriented economy caused even greater divergence between white and black. The politically-dominant whites reproduced a European-style

economy and, after the transfer of political power, developed strong links with Britain.

The African farmers gained little from the mineral boom. With their constant needs for new grazing grounds frustrated by the white farmers, and with taxes to pay, they had little alternative but to seek employment in the cities and mines, and on European-owned farms; the African areas became labour pools. Migrant labour became the normal way of life for many men, agriculture in the Native Reserves (so designated early in the 20th century), stagnated and even regressed, with yields decreasing and soil erosion becoming rampant.

Small groups of Africans took up urban life in 'locations' which became a typical feature of all towns whatever their size. Separated by a *cordon sanitaire* of industry, a river or the railway line from the white settlement, these townships with their rudimentary housing, often supplemented by shanty dwellings and without any real services, mushroomed during World War II and left South Africa with a major housing problem in the late 1940s. Nowhere was this problem greater than in the Johannesburg area, where it was solved by the building of a vast complex of brick boxes, the South-Western Townships (SOWETO).

The contrast in prosperity between South African whites and blacks, which increased steadily, is nowhere more visibly expressed than in their respective urban areas. The white areas could be Anytown in North America; skyscrapers, multitrack roads and well-tended suburbs. The black towns could only be South African: though rudimentary in what they offer, they are rigidly planned ∎

THE RISE AND FALL OF APARTHEID

From its 1948 institution, apartheid – 'separate development' – meant not only racial segregation but also massive racial discrimination. Over the next generation, a whole body of apartheid law was created. Key measures deprived blacks of political rights except in 'homelands' – modest tracts of poor land. Whites were guaranteed exclusive ownership of most of the country's best land, and most blacks, with no right of residence outside homelands few had ever seen, found themselves foreigners in their own country, obliged to carry passes at all times in a police state.

The African National Congress, the main black political organization, was banned, and black opposition was brutally suppressed. South Africa's racial policies led to increasing isolation from the rest of the world.

Changing demographic patterns – the blacks were outnumbering whites by more and more every year – combined with international sanctions made apartheid increasingly unsupportable. The 1989 election of liberal Nationalist President F.W. de Klerk brought dramatic change. Veteran ANC leader Nelson Mandela was released from jail to the negotiating table, and in 1991 de Klerk announced his intention to dismantle the entire structure of apartheid. In 1992, an all-white referendum gave him a mandate to move quickly towards a multiracial democratic system. But violence between rival black groups – 5,000 have died in inter-tribal fighting since 1986 – was becoming dangerously endemic.

LESOTHO

In 1987 this succeeded the flag adopted on independence from Britain in 1966. The white, blue and green represent peace, rain and prosperity – the words of the national motto. The emblem comprises shield, knobkerrie and ostrich feather sceptre.

COUNTRY: Kingdom of Lesotho
AREA: 30,350 sq km [11,718 sq mls]
POPULATION: 1,774,000
CAPITAL (Population): Maseru (109,000)
GOVERNMENT: Military-dominated monarchy
ETHNIC GROUPS: Sotho 99%
LANGUAGES: Sesotho and English (both official)
RELIGIONS: Christian 93% (Roman Catholic 44%)
NATIONAL DAY: 4 October; Independence Day (1966)
CURRENCY: Loti = 100 lisente
ANNUAL INCOME PER PERSON: $470
MAIN PRIMARY PRODUCTS: Diamonds
MAIN INDUSTRIES: Agriculture, mining
MAIN IMPORTS: Food, vehicles, clothing, oil products
MAIN EXPORTS: Diamonds, mohair, wool
POPULATION DENSITY: 58 per sq km [151 per sq ml]
LIFE EXPECTANCY: Female 63 yrs, male 54 yrs
ADULT LITERACY: 74%

Consisting mainly of a high mountainous plateau deeply fretted by the headwaters of the Orange (Oranje) River, Lesotho declines altitudinally from east to west, with the highest ridges, over 3,000 m [9–10,000 ft], developed on basaltic lavas. This treeless zone with its steep valleys has an excess of water, making it boggy in summer, frozen in winter. It is nevertheless overpopulated. All of this contrasts with the lower narrow western belts of the foothills and lowlands, stretching southwards from Butha-Buthe to Mohale's Hoek. Here the dominant rock is sandstone.

The physical environment and being surrounded on all sides by South Africa provide major economic and political problems for the country. Most of the population are involved in subsistence agriculture, battling for a living against steep slopes and thin soils. The only urban and industrial development lies at Maseru, but the trend is still for people to drift to the small towns or to find employment in the gold and coal mines of South Africa. The country's scenery is conducive to tourism and the altitude allows winter sports; however, massive capital investment, especially in roads, would be necessary to develop this potential ∎

SWAZILAND

The kingdom has flown this distinctive flag, which is based on that of the Swazi Pioneer Corps of World War II, since independence from Britain in 1968. The emblem has the weapons of a warrior – ox-hide shield, two assegai and a fighting stick.

COUNTRY: Kingdom of Swaziland
AREA: 17,360 sq km [6,703 sq mls]
POPULATION: 768,000
CAPITAL (Population): Mbabane (38,000)
GOVERNMENT: Monarchy with bicameral legislature

Although the smallest country in sub-Saharan Africa, Swaziland nevertheless reveals strong scenic contrasts. From west to east the country descends in three altitudinal steps: the Highveld, average altitude 1,200 m [4,000 ft], and the Middleveld, lying between 350 and 1,000 m [1,000 and 3,500 ft] are made of old, hard rocks; the Lowveld, average height 270 m [900 ft] is of softer shales and sandstones in the west, and basalts in the east. Shutting the country in on the east are the Lebombo Mountains (800 m [2,600 ft]). Rivers rising in South Africa completely traverse these belts; their valleys provide communication lines and are sources of perennial water, important for irrigation.

In the late 19th century European colonists settled and today the main economic features result from basic differences in occupational structures between 'black' and 'white' Swazi. Those derived from European stock are involved in commerce, industry and, predominantly, production of exports such as sugar, citrus fruits and wood pulp as well as farming cereals and cattle. The majority indigenous Swazi are still mostly engaged in subsistence farming based on maize, with fragmented landholdings and a dispersed settlement pattern. As a result there are few large towns, but the population remains far better off than in Lesotho, with which it is often compared, somewhat unrealistically.

Swaziland, which gained independence from Britain in 1968, is part of a customs union which includes South Africa, but for overseas trade the country relies largely on the port of Maputo, to which it is linked by the only railway. During the 1980s this was frequently inoperative because of the war in Mozambique – while Swaziland was also burdened with a flow of refugees. The kingdom would no doubt rather have tourists: there are already more than 270,000 a year ■

MADAGASCAR

Madagascar's colours are those of historical flags of South-east Asia, from where the island's first inhabitants came before AD1000. The present flag was adopted in 1958 when the country first became a republic after French rule.

Apart from the east coast, which has rain at all seasons, Madagascar has a summer rainy season and a marked dry season. Antananarivo lies in the central highlands and temperatures are considerably moderated by its altitude. The island, especially the north-west, is reputed to be one of the world's most thundery regions. In February tropical cyclones from the Indian Ocean may affect the island. Only on a few occasions have temperatures exceeded 30°C [86°F].

The world's fourth largest island, Madagascar is virtually a semi-continent, bigger than France and immensely varied, physically, ecologically and culturally. Almost all geological eras are represented, and made more vivid by steep faulting, volcanic outpourings and deeply-trenched valleys. There are extensive rugged areas, so that soils are often poor and farming unrewarding, and the coasts are hostile, with little natural shelter. The north and east are hot and wet, and subject to cyclones. The west is drier, and the south and south-west are arid.

Separated from the African mainland for more than 50 million years, Madagascar developed a distinct flora and fauna – over 150,000 plant and animal species are unique to the island. Before the coming of people some 3,000 years ago, nearly all the island was variously forested, and though much of it was cleared for agriculture a strange collection of animals survived in the remnants – among them 40 species of chameleons, pygmy hippos, elephant birds and the renowned lemurs.

Also unique to the island is its mixture of peoples, derived from several continents. Those on the west side are of Bantu origin, drawn from southern Africa via the Comoros Islands 'bridge'. Those of the centre and east (the Merina or Hova people) came first from Indonesia, as early as 2,000 years ago, with later waves arriving during the 7th to 15th centuries. Other Asians followed, all rice-growers, reverent to cattle, with language and funeral rites similar to those in South-east Asia. They had a monarchy until French occupation in 1895. In the south, the Betsileo are more mixed Bantu-Indonesian, as are other groups, yet all feel 'Malagasy' rather than African or Asian. Many other immigrant groups, including Europeans, Chinese and Indians, have also settled.

Both landscapes and agriculture (dominantly rice with cattle and pigs) in the central highlands are south Asian in character; the east coast and northern highlands are more African, with fallow-farming of food crops and cultivation of coffee, sugar, essential oil plants and spices for export – the country produces two-thirds of the world's vanilla. In the dry west and south nomadic pastoralism is important, and rice is grown by irrigation. Significant minerals are graphite, chromite and mica. Because of the rough terrain, wet season and size of the country, air transport is important, with a network of over 60 airports and airstrips.

The government which took power on independence in 1960 continued Madagascar's links with France, but a resurgence of nationalism in the 1970s was followed by the emergence of Didier Ratsiraka, who seized power in 1975 and established a dictatorial one-party socialist state. In 1991 there were widespread riots against the Ratsiraka regime, whose incompetence over 16 years had seen the country plunge into poverty. With 90% of the forest gone, Madagascar today is one of the most eroded places in the world, its coasts clogged with red lateritic soils. Free-market policies had served only to plunder resources further, and despite electoral reform the island seemed destined for a decade of despair as its population burgeoned ■

COUNTRY: Democratic Republic of Madagascar
AREA: 587,040 sq km [226,656 sq mls]
POPULATION: 11,197,000
CAPITAL (Population): Antananarivo (703,000)
GOVERNMENT: Republic with unicameral legislature
ETHNIC GROUPS: Merina 26%, Betsimisaraka 15%, Betsileo 12%
LANGUAGES: Malagasy (official), French, English
RELIGIONS: Christian 50% (Roman Catholic 28%) traditional beliefs 47%, Muslim 3%
NATIONAL DAY: 26 June; Independence Day (1960)
CURRENCY: Franc (FMG) = 100 centimes
ANNUAL INCOME PER PERSON: $230
MAIN INDUSTRIES: Agriculture, fishing, mining
MAIN EXPORTS: Coffee, vanilla, sugar and cloves
MAIN IMPORTS: Petroleum, chemicals, machinery and vehicles
POPULATION DENSITY: 19 per sq km [49 per sq ml]
LIFE EXPECTANCY: Female 57 yrs, male 54 yrs
ADULT LITERACY: 53%

INDIAN OCEAN

SEYCHELLES

The Seychelles are a compact group of four large and 36 small granitic islands, plus a wide scattering of coralline islands (14 of them inhabited) lying mainly to the south and west; 82% of the land area is composed of the four main islands which host 98% of the population, the vast majority on lush and mountainous Mahé.

With a beautiful tropical oceanic climate the Seychelles produce copra, cinnamon and tea, though rice is imported. Fishing and luxury tourism (50% of revenue and growing) are the two main industries. French from 1756 and British from 1814, the islands gained independence in 1976. A year later a political coup set up a one-party Socialist state that several attempts have failed to remove, though in 1991 President France Albert René promised a return to multiparty democracy.

Formerly part of the British Indian Ocean Territory, Farquhar, Desroches and Aldabra (famous for its unique wildlife) were returned to the Seychelles in 1976. BIOT now includes only the Chagos Archipelago, with Diego Garcia, the largest island, supporting a US naval base ■

COUNTRY: Republic of Seychelles
AREA: 455 sq km [176 sq mls]
POPULATION: 67,000
CAPITAL (Population): Victoria (23,000)

COMOROS

The Comoros are three large mountainous islands and several smaller coral islands, lying at the northern end of the Mozambique Channel. Njazidja (formerly Grande Comoro) rises to an active volcano; Nzwami (Anjouan) is a heavily eroded volcanic massif; Mwali (Mohéli) is a forested plateau. With fertile soils, the islands were originally forested; now they are mostly under subsistence agriculture and produce coconuts, coffee, cocoa and spices, vanilla accounting for 78% of exports. Formerly French, the Comoros became independent (without the agreement of France) following a referendum in 1974. One of the world's poorest countries, it is plagued by lack of resources and political turmoil.

Mayotte, the easternmost of the large islands (population 77,000), voted to remain French in the 1974 referendum, and in 1976 became a Territorial Collectivity ■

COUNTRY: French Islamic Republic of the Comoros
AREA: 2,230 sq km [861 sq mls]
POPULATION: 551,000
CAPITAL (Population): Moroni (21,000)

MAURITIUS

Mauritius consists of the main island, situated 800 km [500 mls] to the east of Madagascar, Rodruigues (formerly a dependency), 20 nearby islets and the dependencies of the Agalega Islands and the tiny Cargados Carajas shoals (St Brandon). French from 1715 and British from 1810, the colony gained independence within the Commonwealth in 1968.

The beautiful main island, fringed with coral reefs, rises to a high lava plateau. Good rainfall (up to 5,000 mm [200 in] a year) and steep slopes have combined to give fast-flowing rivers, now harnessed for limited hydroelectric power. Similar to Réunion in climate and soils, its vast plantations produce sugar cane (now declining but with derivatives like molasses still accounting for over 40% of exports), tea and tobacco, while home consumption centres around livestock and vegetables. To some extent the decline in sugar has been offset by the growth in tourism (239,000 visitors in 1988) and the expansion of textiles and clothing (nearly half of exports), though Mauritius remains badly in debt – having been a Third World success story in the 1970s.

The islands also suffer from increasing tensions between the Indian majority – descended from contract workers brought in to tend the plantations after the end of slavery in 1834 – and the Creole minority. Attempts to create a republic failed in 1990 ■

COUNTRY: Mauritius
AREA: 1,860 sq km [718 sq mls]
POPULATION: 1,075,000
CAPITAL (Population): Port Louis (139,000)
GOVERNMENT: Constitutional monarchy
ETHNIC GROUPS: Creole 56%, Indian 40%, European 4%

RÉUNION

Réunion is the largest of the Mascarene islands, lying east of Madagascar and south-west of Mauritius and composed of a rugged, mountainous forested centre surrounded by a fertile coastal plain. The volcanic mountains rise in spectacular scenery to the peak of Piton des Neiges (3,070 m [10,076 ft]), which is sporadically active. Réunion receives heavy rainfall from the cool south-east trade winds in winter, while the summers can be oppressively hot and humid. The lowlands are intensely cultivated with huge plantations of sugar cane; providing 75% of exports (plus rum 3%), this remains the island's only significant industry, though vanilla, perfume oils and tea also produce revenue. Local consumption revolves round vegetables, maize and livestock.

Tourism is a big hope for the future, following the success of Mauritius, but unemployment is high and France still subsidizes the islands heavily in return for its use as its main military base in the area. The people of the island – which has a very varied and potentially explosive ethnic mix – are divided on its status; as in the other Overseas Departments (Guadeloupe, Martinique and French Guiana) there is increasing pressure on Paris for independence. In 1991 several people were killed in outbreaks of civil unrest ■

COUNTRY: French overseas department
AREA: 2,510 sq km [969 sq mls]
POPULATION: 599,000
CAPITAL (Population): St-Denis (109,000)
ETHNIC GROUPS: Mixed 64%, East Indian 28%, Chinese 2%, East African 1%
RELIGIONS: Roman Catholic 90%, Muslim 1%

AUSTRALIA AND OCEANIA

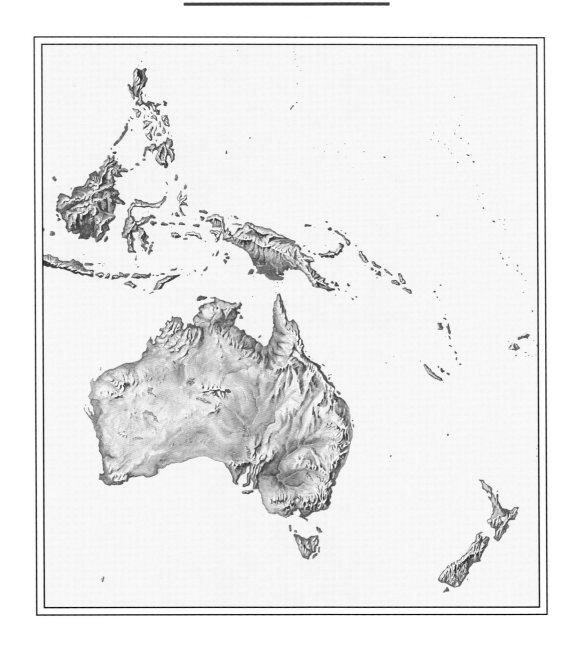

AUSTRALIA AND OCEANIA

A somewhat awkward geographical label, 'Oceania' is a collective term for Australia, New Zealand, most of the Pacific islands and the eastern part of New Guinea. It is characterized by a seemingly bewildering array of islands, of varying origins; some are coral islands, others volcanic and yet others, such as New Guinea, 'continental' islands. Only about 3,000 of the tens of thousands scattered from Belau to Easter Island and from Midway to Macquarie are large enough even to merit names. The Pacific is the largest expanse of water in the world, occupying more than a third of the Earth's surface; Magellan's first crossing in 1520-1 took no less than four months. However, its islands are nearly all tiny, and even with Australia 'Oceania' is still far smaller than Europe.

The islands of the south and western Pacific divide into three groups, based as much on ethnic differences as on geography. Melanesia ('black islands') comprises New Guinea and the larger groups close to Australia. The name refers to the dark complexion of the fine-featured people with black, frizzy hair who are today the main indigenous coasta dwellers of the South-west Pacific. Polynesia ('many islands') includes numerous islands in the centra Pacific. The basically Caucasoid Polynesians, skilled in navigation, are sometimes termed 'the supreme navigators of history'. Micronesia ('small islands') includes the many minute coral atolls north of Mela nesia and a narrow Polynesian 'corridor' linking the Society Islands with South-east Asia. Micronesians today are often markedly Polynesian, but in the wes are more Malay or Mongoloid ∎

LAND USE

LAND USE
- Arable land
- Market gardening
- Permanent pasture
- Woods and forests
- Rough grazing
- Non-productive land
- Industrial

CROPS
- Oats
- Maize
- Barley
- Rice
- Wheat
- Sugar cane
- Bananas
- Fruit
- Citrus fruits

- Vines
- Cacao
- Coffee
- Tobacco
- Coconut palms
- Principal fishing areas

LIVESTOCK
- Beef cattle
- Dairy cattle
- Sheep

POWER
- Coalfields
- Lignite
- Oilfields
- Gasfields
- Hydroelectric power

MINERALS

Non-ferrous metals
- Silver
- Bauxite
- Gold
- Copper

- Lead and zinc
- Antimony
- Tin
- Uranium

Iron ore and ferro-alloys
- Iron ore
- Manganese
- Nickel
- Tungsten

LAND USE

Other land 16·2%

Arable land and permanent crops 6%

Woods and forests 18%

Permanent pasture 59·8%

Total land area 761.8 million hectares
(1 882·4 million acres)

CLIMATIC REGIONS

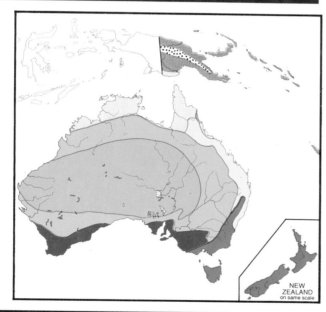

Tropical climates
- Tropical rain forest
- Savanna

Mild climates
- Marine west coast
- Humid subtropical
- Mediterranean

Dry climates
- Steppe
- Desert

High altitudes
- Highlands

ANNUAL RAINFALL

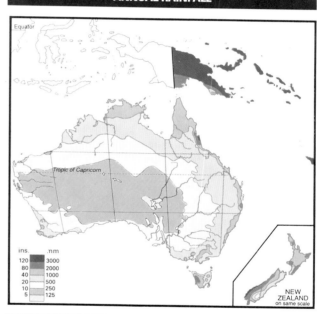

ins.	.mm
120	3000
80	2000
40	1000
20	500
10	250
5	125

NATURAL VEGETATION

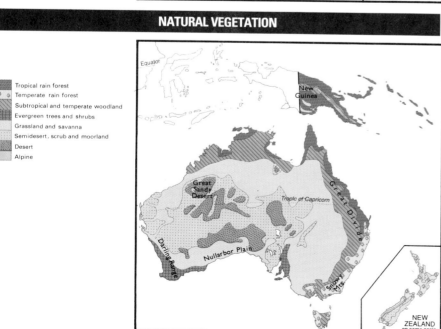

- Tropical rain forest
- Temperate rain forest
- Subtropical and temperate woodland
- Evergreen trees and shrubs
- Grassland and savanna
- Semidesert, scrub and moorland
- Desert
- Alpine

POPULATION

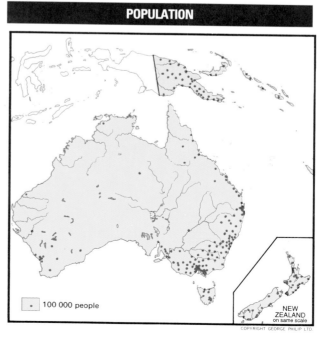

- 100 000 people

AUSTRALIA AND OCEANIA

AUSTRALIA

Showing its historical link with Britain, Australia's flag, adopted in 1901, features the British Blue Ensign. The five stars represent the Southern Cross constellation and the larger star symbolizes the Federal Commonwealth.

SYDNEY

Temperature / Precipitation 1181mm 46in

In the south-east, the annual rainfall total is reasonably high and distributed throughout the year, with maxima April–June. Rain falls on 12–13 days each month. The vast valleys inland of the Great Divide, in the lee of the rain-bearing winds, are drier. The temperatures are moderate, with winter night frosts throughout the south and the interior. Snow falls on the uplands of the south-east and Tasmania. Frosts are unknown in Sydney, the lowest temperatures being 2–4°C [36–39°F].

Whether Australia is the world's largest island or its smallest continental land mass – or both, or neither, depending on the school of geography – it is primarily a land of low to medium altitude plateaus that form monotonous landscapes extending for hundreds of kilometres. The edges of the plateaus are more diverse, particularly in the east where deep gorges and waterfalls create rugged relief between the Great Divide and the coast. In the north-west, impressive gorge scenery is found in the Hammersley Range and Kimberley area.

The western half of Australia is formed of ancient rocks. Essentially an arid landscape of worn-down ridges and plateaus, with depressions occupied by sandy deserts and occasional salt lakes, this area has little surface water.

The eastern sixth of the continent, including Tasmania, forms the Eastern Highlands, the zone of greatest relief, greatest rainfall, most abundant vegetation and greatest population. Peaks in this region include Mt Kosciusko, at 2,230 m [7,316 ft] Australia's highest. Much of this area shows signs of volcanic activity in the relatively recent geological past, and these young basalts support nutrient-rich soils in contrast to the generally well-weathered, nutrient-poor soils of nearly all the remainder of Australia.

Between the western plateaus and Eastern Highlands lie the Carpentaria, central and Murray lowlands. The central lowlands drain to the great internal river systems supplying Lake Eyre, or to the

Bulloo system, or through great inland deltas to the Darling River. The parallel dune ridges of this area form part of a great continent-wide set of dune ridges extending in a huge anti-clockwise arc, eastwards through the Great Victoria Desert, northwards through the Simpson Desert and westwards in the Great Sandy Desert. All these, though inhospitable, are only moderately arid, allowing widespread if sparse vegetation cover.

Vegetation

On the humid margins of the continent are luxuriant forests. These include the great jarrah forests of tall eucalyptus hardwoods in the extreme south-west of Western Australia; the temperate rainforests with the Antarctic beech found in Tasmania and on humid upland sites north through New South Wales to the Queensland border; and the tropical and subtropical rainforests found in the wetter areas along the east coast, from the McIllwraith Range in the north to the vicinity of Mallacoota Inlet in the south. Some of these rainforest areas are maintained as managed forests, others are in national parks, but most of the original cover has been cleared for agriculture, particularly for dairying and cattle-fattening, and for sugar and banana cultivation north of Port Macquarie.

The most adaptable tree genus in Australia is the *Eucalyptus*, which ranges from the tall flooded gum trees found on the edges of the rainforest to the dry-living mallee species found on sand-plains and interdune areas. Acacia species, especially the bright-yellow flowered wattles, are also adapted to a wide range of environments. Associated with this adaptation of plants is the wide variety of animal adaptations, with 277 different mammals, about 400 species of reptiles and some 700 species of birds. Aborigines arriving from Asia over 40,000 years ago brought the dingo, which rapidly replaced the Tasmanian wolf, the largest marsupial predator, and preyed on smaller animals. Fires, lit for hunting and allowed to burn uncontrolled, altered much of the vegetation, probably allowing eucalyptus forests to expand at the expense of the rainforest. However, the Aborigines understood their environment, carefully protecting vital areas of natural food supply,

restricting the use of certain desert waterholes which tradition taught would be reliable in a drought, and developing a resource-use policy which was aimed at living with nature.

European settlement after 1788 upset this ecological balance, through widespread clearing of coastal forests, overgrazing of inland pastures and introduction of exotic species, especially the destructive rabbit. But Europeans also brought the technology which enabled the mineral, water and soil resources of Australia to be developed.

Mineral resources

Much of Australia's growth since the beginning of European settlement has been closely related to the exploitation of mineral resources, which has led directly to the founding, growth and often eventual decline of the majority of inland towns. Broken Hill and Mount Isa are copper, lead, zinc and silver producing centres, while Kalgoorlie, Bendigo, Ballarat and Charters Towers all grew in the 19th-century gold rushes. Today, less glamorous minerals support the Australian economy. In Western Australia, the great iron-ore mines of Mount Tom Price, Mount Newman and Mount Goldsworthy are linked by new railways to special ports at Dampier and Port Hedland. Offshore are the oil and gas fields of the north-west shelf.

In the east, the coal mines of central Queensland and eastern New South Wales are linked by rail to bulk loading facilities at Sarina, Gladstone, Brisbane, Newcastle, Sydney and Port Kemble, which enable this high-grade coking coal to be shipped to worldwide markets and by 1986 had made Australia the biggest exporter (15% of export earnings). Bauxite mining has led to new settlements at Nhulunbuy and Weipa on the Gulf of Carpentaria, with associ-

PERTH

Temperature / Precipitation 881mm 35in

The vast interior of Australia is very dry, and with high temperatures much of the rain that does fall evaporates quickly. There are no great areas of high land that could form a barrier to the rain-bearing winds or a relief to the high temperatures. Along the southern coast the rainfall is slightly higher than in the interior. There is higher rainfall in the extreme south-west around Perth, which experiences a Mediterranean-type climate of hot, dry summers and warm, wet winters.

COUNTRY: Commonwealth of Australia

AREA: 7,686,850 sq km [2,967,893 sq mls]

POPULATION: 17,086,000

CAPITAL (Population): Canberra (289,000)

GOVERNMENT: Federal constitutional monarchy with bicameral legislature

ETHNIC GROUPS: White 94%, Asian 2%, Aboriginal 1%

LANGUAGES: English (official)

RELIGIONS: Roman Catholic 26%, Anglican 24%, other Christian 16%, Muslim, Jewish, Buddhist

NATIONAL DAY: 26 January; Australia Day

CURRENCY: Australian $ = 100 cents

ANNUAL INCOME PER PERSON: $17,080

SOURCE OF INCOME: Agriculture 4%, industry 34%, services 61%

MAIN PRIMARY PRODUCTS: Coal, crude petroleum, bauxite, sheep, cattle, timber, zircon, natural gas, gold, silver

MAIN INDUSTRIES: Metal fabrication, mining, construction of vehicles and aircraft, agriculture, petrol refining, chemicals, electronics

MAIN EXPORTS: Food and live animals 22%, coal, oil and gas 19%, metallic ores 14%, textile fibres 11%, machinery 6%, transport equipment 3%

MAIN EXPORT PARTNERS: Japan 25%, USA 12%, New Zealand 5%, South Korea 4%, UK 4%, Germany 3%, Hong Kong 3%, Taiwan 3%

MAIN IMPORTS: Machinery and transport equipment 40%, basic manufactures 16%, chemicals 8%, petroleum products 5%, food and live animals 5%

MAIN IMPORT PARTNERS: USA 22%, Japan 21%, Germany 8%, UK 7%, New Zealand 4%, Taiwan 4%

EDUCATIONAL EXPENDITURE: 6.4% of national budget

DEFENCE: 9.3% of national budget

TOTAL ARMED FORCES: 69,600

TOURISM: 1,785,000 visitors per year

ROADS: 840,000 km [525,000 mls]

RAILWAYS: 39,251 km [22,657 mls]

POPULATION DENSITY: 2 per sq km [6 per sq ml]

URBAN POPULATION: 86%

POPULATION GROWTH: 1.2% per year

INFANT MORTALITY: 7 per 1,000 live births

LIFE EXPECTANCY: Female 80 yrs, male 74 yrs

ADULT LITERACY: 99%

PRINCIPAL CITIES (Population): Sydney 3,531,000 Melbourne 2,965,000 Brisbane 1,215,000 Perth 1,083,000 Adelaide 1,013,000 ated refineries at Kwinana, Gladstone and Bell Bay.

Rum Jungle, south of Darwin, became well known as one of the first uranium mines, but now deposits further east in Arnhem Land are being developed. Meanwhile, new discoveries of ore bodies continue to be made in the ancient rocks of the western half of Australia. Natural gas from the Cooper Basin, just south of Innamincka on Cooper Creek, is piped to Adelaide and Sydney, while oil and gas from the Bass Strait and brown coal from the Yallourn-Morwell area have been vital to the industrial growth of Victoria. Fossil fuels are supplemented by hydroelectric power from major schemes in western Tasmania and the Snowy Mountains and smaller projects near Cairns and Tully in north Queensland.

Australia's mineral wealth is phenomenal. In 1989 it produced over a third of the world's diamonds and bauxite, 14% of lead, 11% of iron ore, uranium and zinc, 10% of gold, 9% of manganese, 7% of nickel and silver, and was the biggest exporter of mineral sands. Even this impressive array could not help Australia resist slumps in world demand, however, and by 1991 the country was experiencing its worst recession since the 1920s.

Agriculture

Apart from the empty and largely unusable desert areas in Western Australia and the Simpson Desert, extensive cattle or sheep production dominates all of Australia north and west of a line from Penong in South Australia, through Broken Hill in New South Wales to Bundaberg in Queensland, and east of a line from Geraldton to Esperance in Western Australia. Cattle and sheep populations in this zone are sparse, individual pastoral holdings are large, some over 400,000 hectares [1 million acres], and towns are both small and far apart.

Some Aborigines retain limited tracts of land in Arnhem Land and on the fringes of the deserts where they live by hunting and gathering, but nearly all Aborigines now live close to government settlements or mission stations. Many are employed as stockmen and seasonal agricultural workers, while thousands of others have migrated to country towns and the major cities.

AUSTRALIAN TERRITORIES

Australia is responsible for a number of other territories. In the Indian Ocean Britain transferred sovereignty of Heard Island and McDonald Island (both 1947), and further north the Cocos (Keeling) Islands (1955) and Christmas Island (1958). Australia also has jurisdiction over the Ashmore and Cartier Islands in the Timor Sea, the Coral Sea Islands Territory, and Norfolk Island in the south-west Pacific – while Lord Howe Island and Macquarie Island are administered by New South Wales and Tasmania respectively. Of all these, only the Cocos Islands (690), Christmas Island (1,300), Norfolk Island (1,980) and Lord Howe Island (300) have permanent populations.

The country is also in charge of the largest sector of Antarctica, a continent protected from military and nuclear pollution under international agreement since 1991. A member of ANZUS since 1951, Australia has reviewed its own defence position since New Zealand banned US Navy nuclear warships in 1985.

AUSTRALIA AND OCEANIA

Only 10% of Australia receives more than 1,000 mm [39 in] of rain and these areas are in the north, the east coast and the south-west tip of the continent. Much of the centre receives less than 250 mm [10 in], which fails in many years. The northern half of Australia lies within the tropics and the monsoon brings a lot of rain from December to March. Typhoons can hit the northern Queensland coast. Day temperatures in all months are over 30°C [68°F], with night temperatures above 20°C [68°F].

The intensive pastoral and agricultural zones support the bulk of the sheep and cattle of Australia, and wool, mutton and beef production is still the basic industry. The country is the world's largest producer of wool and third in lamb and mutton. Wheat is cultivated in combination with sheep raising over large tracts of the gentle inland slopes of the coastal ranges.

Along the east coast are important cattle-fattening, dairy and sugar-cane industries, the latter significant on the east coast from Brisbane to Cairns. Irrigated areas also support cotton, rice, fruit and vegetable crops, largely for consumption within Australia. Wine production around Perth, Adelaide, central Victoria and eastern New South Wales has expanded in recent decades, producing vintages of international renown.

Development

European settlement in Australia began in 1788 as a penal colony in New South Wales, spreading quickly to Queensland and Tasmania. During the 19th century the continent became divided into the states of New South Wales, Queensland (1859), South Australia (1836), Tasmania (1825), Victoria (1851) and Western Australia (1829), with the area now forming the Northern Territory being under the control of South Australia. During this colonial period the state seaport capitals of Sydney, Brisbane, Adelaide, Hobart, Melbourne and Perth became established as the dominant manufacturing, commercial, administrative and legislative centres of their respective states – a position none of them have since relinquished.

In 1901, the states came together to create the Commonwealth of Australia with a federal constitution. Trade between the states became free, and external affairs, defence and immigration policy became federal responsibilities, though health, education, transport, mineral, agricultural and indus-

trial development remained firmly in the hands of each state. Only gradually did powers of taxation give the federal government the opportunity to develop national policies.

The federal capital established at Canberra, in the new Australian Capital Territory, grew from a tiny settlement in 1911 to become a great seat of administration and learning, and the largest inland regional commercial centre. The federal government's territorial responsibilities also include the Northern Territory, self governing since 1978.

Immigration has changed the ethnic character of Australia since about 1960. Australian society now has Greek, Italian, Yugoslav, Turkish, Lebanese and South-east Asian communities alongside the longer-established Aboriginal, British, Irish, Chinese, Dutch and German communities, though the culture remains strongly British in flavour. Almost 60% of the total Australian population live in Sydney, Melbourne, Adelaide, Brisbane, Perth and Hobart. Migration within the states from inland rural areas to capital cities or coastal towns leaves many rural communities with an ageing population, while the new mining centres have young populations. The most rapid growth outside new mining centres is occurring in coastal towns through migration on retirement and attempts to establish an alternative lifestyle by leaving the big cities.

Soon after 1788, small-scale manufacturing began to supply domestic goods and machinery to the colonial community. Inevitably manufacturing grew in the colonial seaport capitals, especially Sydney and Melbourne, which now have over 60% of all manufacturing industry (though only 40% or so of the total population).

Under the Australian Constitution, the federal government has control over interstate and overseas transport, with the state governments responsible for regulation within their own borders. Seven railway systems thus exist, each state system focusing on its capital city, with the Commonwealth Railways responsible for the Trans-Australian, Central Australian and Northern Territory routes. The notorious differences in gauges between the states have been partially overcome by the construction of the standard-gauge links from Brisbane to Sydney, Sydney to Melbourne, and Sydney to Perth via Broken Hill. The completion of the Tarcoola-Alice Springs route will provide the basic strategic standard-gauge rail network for Australia.

Railways are vital for bulk freight, especially mineral ores, coal and wheat. Among the busiest of the railways are the iron-ore lines in the north-west of Western Australia. Most cattle and sheep, however, are carried by 'road trains' – a powerful unit pulling several trailers.

A rapidly improving highway system links all major cities and towns, providing easy mobility for a largely car-owning population. Some journeys are still difficult, especially when floods wash away sections of road or sand-drifts bury highways. Although 90% of all passenger transport is by road, air services cope with much interstate travel.

Australia is also well served by local broadcasting and television. The radio remains a lifeline for remote settlements dependent on the flying doctor or aerial ambulance, and for many others when floods or bush fires threaten isolated communities.

The worldwide economic depression of the late 1980s was mirrored in Australia by a deterioration of the country's hitherto buoyant export of agricultural products and its worst unemployment for 60 years. It was against this background that the Labour Prime Minister, Bob Hawke, was elected for an unprecedented fourth term, but in 1991 the worsening economic situation forced his replacement by Paul Keating. Under Keating's administration the key issue of Australia's trade relations, following the extension of the European Community and the success of the Pacific Rim economies, came to the fore, as did the associated question of the country's national identity.

With Britain joining the EEC, Australia had looked increasingly to the Pacific Rim countries, and especially to Japan, for its trade, However, fears of a flood of Japanese investment cloaked deeper concerns for many ordinary 'Aussies' ■

PAPUA NEW GUINEA

When Papua New Guinea became independent from Australia in 1975 it adopted a flag which had been used for the country since 1971. The design includes a bird of paradise in flight and the stars of the Southern Cross constellation.

Close to the Equator and surrounded by a warm ocean, Port Moresby has a very small temperature range both diurnally (about 7°C [13°F]) and seasonally (about 3°C [5°F]). Rainfall is far more variable, with a wet season when the humid north-west monsoon blows, and a dry season associated with the south-east trade winds. The total rainfall is small compared with most of New Guinea. Over 3,000 mm [130 in] falls on the north coast, with even higher amounts in the mountains.

Forming part of Melanesia, Papua New Guinea is the eastern section of the island of New Guinea, plus the Bismarck Archipelago and the copper-rich island of Bougainville – geographically, though not politically, part of the Solomons. The backbone of the main island is a high cordillera of rugged fold mountains, averaging between 2,500 to 4,600 m [8,000 to 15,000 ft] in height and covered with tropical montane 'cloud' forest. Isolated valleys and intermontane basins run parallel with the main ranges. Fertile with alluvium and volcanic materials, these are the sites of isolated settlements, even today linked only by light aircraft. The capital city, Port Moresby, is not linked by road to any other major centre, and communication with the highlands depends on the country's 400 airports and airstrips.

The traditional garden crops of the 'highlanders' include kaukau (sweet potato), sugar cane, bananas, maize, cassava and nut-bearing pandans. Pigs are kept mainly for status and ritual purposes. In the lowlands, taro is the staple food, although yams and sago are also important. The main cash crops are coconuts, coffee, cocoa and rubber.

Although the first European contact came as early as 1526, it was only in the late 19th century that permanent German and British settlements were established. After World War II, the UN Trust Territory of New Guinea and the Territory of Papua were administered by Australia. Self-government came in 1973, with full independence in 1975.

While 80% of the population still live by agriculture, minerals (notably copper, gold and silver) have provided an increasingly important share of exports, encouraging 'PNG' to reduce its dependence on Australian aid. Most of the copper, however, comes from the world's biggest mine at Panguna on Bougainville, where demands by the islanders for a greater share of the earnings spiralled into a separatist struggle by 1989 – followed by the closure of the mine, a declaration of independence by the secessionists and a total blockade of the island by the government in Moresby. Despite a peace accord of 1991, the position was still unchanged after three years – with the 'revolution' passing into the hands of criminal gangs ■

COUNTRY: Independent State of Papua New Guinea
AREA: 462,840 sq km [178,703 sq mls]
POPULATION: 3,699,000
CAPITAL (Population): Port Moresby (152,000)
GOVERNMENT: Parliamentary monarchy with a unicameral legislature
ETHNIC GROUPS: Papuan 84%, Melanesian 15%
LANGUAGES: Motu and English (official)
RELIGIONS: Christian and traditional beliefs
NATIONAL DAY: 16 September; Independence Day
CURRENCY: Kina = 100 toea
ANNUAL INCOME PER PERSON: $860
MAIN EXPORTS: Gold 39%, copper ore and concentrates, coffee, timber, cocoa beans, copra
MAIN IMPORTS: Machinery and vehicles 34%, manufactured goods, mineral fuels, foodstuffs
POPULATION DENSITY: 8 per sq km [21 per sq ml]
LIFE EXPECTANCY: Female 57 yrs, male 55 yrs
ADULT LITERACY: 45%

SOLOMON ISLANDS

The double chain of islands forming the Solomons and Vanuatu extends for some 2,250 km [1,400 mls] and represents the drowned outermost crustal fold on the borders of the ancient Australian continent. New Caledonia lies on an inner fold, nearer the mainland. The main islands, all of volcanic origin, are Guadalcanal, Malaita, New Georgia, San Cristóbal, Santa Isabel and Choiseul.

The northern Solomons have a true hot and wet tropical oceanic climate, but further south there tends to be an increasingly long cool season. The coastal plains are used for the subsistence farming that sustains about 90% of the population. While coconuts (giving copra and palm oil) and cocoa are important exports, tuna fish is the biggest earner and lumbering the main industry, with Japan the main market for both. Significant phosphate deposits are also mined on Bellona Island. Plagued by a population growth of 3.5% – half the total is under 20 – the Solomons' progress is faltering, with development hampered by the mountainous and densely forested environment of the six main islands; transport is often impossible between scattered settlements. The economy was also hit by a devastating cyclone in 1986.

Occupied by the Japanese during World War II,

COUNTRY: Solomon Islands
AREA: 28,900 sq km [11,158 sq mls]
POPULATION: 321,000
CAPITAL (Population): Honiara (34,000)
GOVERNMENT: Constitutional monarchy with a unicameral legislature
ETHNIC GROUPS: Melanesian 94%, Polynesian 4%
LANGUAGES: English (official), over 80 vernacular languages
RELIGIONS: Protestant and Roman Catholic
CURRENCY: Solomon Islands $ = 100 cents
POPULATION DENSITY: 11 per sq km [29 per sq ml]

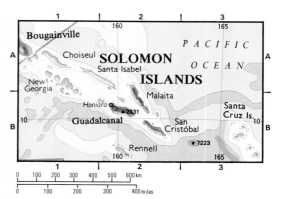

the islands were the scene of fierce fighting, notably the battle for Guadalcanal, on which the capital Honiara lies. Known as the British Solomons, the islands won full independence in 1978. Though a stable parliamentary monarchy, political activity is turbulent, and it is likely that a federal republican structure will be introduced during the 1990s ■

NEW CALEDONIA

Most southerly of the Melanesian countries, New Caledonia comprises the main island of Grande Terre and the dependencies of the Loyalty Islands (Îles Loyauté), Île des Pins and the Bélep archipelago. The remaining islands (many of them coral atolls) are all small and uninhabited.

New Caledonia's economy is dominated by a single commodity, nickel, which accounts for over 83% of export earnings. The world's largest producer in the 1960s, it has slipped to third place – though still with a healthy 10% of the share and with reserves estimated at more than a third of the known world total. Other exports are copra and coffee.

A French possession since 1853 and Overseas Territory from 1958, New Caledonia today has a fundamental split on the question of independence from Paris. The Kanaks, the indigenous Melanesian people (but numbering under half the total), on the whole support it; the less numerous French settlers (many of whom fled Algeria after it gained independence) are passionately against it. An agreement for increased autonomy – supposedly leading to independence before the end of the 1990s – helped to ease tension but the future looks cloudy. Much may depend on finance: France provides a third of the government budget, but separatists have purchased the islands' largest nickel mine ■

COUNTRY: French Overseas Territory
AREA: 19,000 sq km [7,334 sq mls]
POPULATION: 168,000
CAPITAL: Nouméa (60,000)

AUSTRALIA AND OCEANIA

FIJI

The Fijian flag, based on the Blue Ensign, was adopted in 1970 after independence from Britain. The state coat of arms shows a British lion, sugar cane, a coconut palm, bananas and a dove of peace.

By far the most populous of the Pacific nations, Fiji comprises more than 800 Melanesian islands, the larger ones volcanic, mountainous and surrounded by coral reefs, the rest being low coral atolls. Easily the biggest are Viti (10,430 sq km [4,027 sq mls]), with the capital of Suva on its south coast, and Vanua Levu, just over half the size of the main island, though a very different shape. The islands' economy is basically agricultural, with sugar cane (45% of exports), copra and ginger the main cash crops, and fish and timber also exported. However, nearly 20% of revenues are generated by sales of gold. The main trading partners are the UK and Australia for exports, and the US, New Zealand and Australia for imports.

Fiji suffers today from its colonial past. The Indian workers brought in by the British for the sugar plantations in the late 19th century now outnumber the native Fijians, but have been until recently second-class citizens in terms of electoral representation, economic opportunity and, crucially, land ownership. The constitution adopted on independence in 1970 was intended to ease racial tension, but two military coups in 1987 overthrew the recently elected (and first) Indian-majority government, suspended the constitution and set up a Fijian-dominated republic outside the British Commonwealth.

The country finally returned to full civilian rule in 1990; but with a new constitution guaranteeing Melanesian political supremacy, many Indians had already emigrated before the elections of 1992, taking with them their valuable skills. The turmoil

COUNTRY: Republic of Fiji

AREA: 18,270 sq km [7,054 sq mls]

POPULATION: 765,000

CAPITAL (Population): Suva (141,000)

GOVERNMENT: Republic with a constitution still being drafted

ETHNIC GROUPS: Indian 49%, Fijian 46%

LANGUAGES: English, Bauan, Hindustani

RELIGIONS: Christian 53%, Hindu 38%, Muslim 8%

NATIONAL DAY: 10 October

CURRENCY: Fiji $ = 100 cents

MAIN PRIMARY PRODUCTS: Sugar cane, copra, ginger

MAIN INDUSTRIES: Agriculture (sugar cane dominating), tourism, mining

MAIN EXPORTS: Sugar, gold, food products

MAIN IMPORTS: Petroleum products, machinery and electrical goods, transport equipment, textile yarn and fibres, iron and steel

POPULATION DENSITY: 42 per sq km [108 per sq ml]

LIFE EXPECTANCY: Female 71 yrs, male 71 yrs

ADULT LITERACY: 85%

The south-east trades blow all year round, producing local contrasts; windward slopes are cloudier and wetter with rainfall exceeding 3,000 mm [120 in]. Rainfall varies greatly from year to year, but usually falls on 200 days per year. Typhoons can cause great damage from December to April. Temperatures are uniformly high throughout the year, rising to 32°C [90°F] in the hot season (December–April), dropping by only a few degrees at night to 23°C [73°F].

of the late 1980s also had a disastrous effect on the growing tourist industry – and by the time the situation stabilized most of the Western countries that provide the foreign visitors were already in deep recession ■

NEW ZEALAND

Like Australia, New Zealand flies a flag based on the design of the British Blue Ensign. Designed in 1869 and adopted in 1907 on acquiring Dominion status, it displays four of the five stars of the Southern Cross constellation.

Geologically part of the Circum-Pacific Mobile Belt of tectonic activity, New Zealand is mountainous and partly volcanic. Many of the highest mountains – the Southern Alps and Kaikoura Range of the South Island, for example – were thrust up from the seabed in the past 10 to 15 million years, representing only the latest in a long series of orogenies. Much of the North Island was formed by volcanic action even more recently, mainly in the past 1 to 4 million years. Minor earthquakes are common, and there are several areas of volcanic and geothermal activity, especially in the North Island.

Its youth makes New Zealand a rugged country with mountains always in sight and about 75% of the total land area above the 200 m [650 ft] contour. The North Island has many spectacular but low ranges with peaks of 1,200 to 1,500 m [4,000 to 5,000 ft], made up of folded sedimentary rocks that form good soils. Folding and faulting give the eastern half of the island a strong north-east to south-west 'grain', especially in the south-east where the rivers have cut broad, fertile valleys between the ranges. The Coromandel Range and hilly Northland peninsula are softer and more worn, with few peaks over 800 m [12,600 ft].

Overlying these older rocks in the centre and north are massive spreads of lava, pumice and volcanic tuffs, formed during the past 1 to 3 million years. The great central plateau is dominated by three slumbering volcanoes – Ruapehu (2,797 m [9,176 ft], the North Island's highest peak), Ngauruhoe and Tongariro. Further north extensive fields of lava and ash cones lies across the base of the Northland peninsula, forming a firm, rolling site for the suburbs of Auckland, New Zealand's largest city.

The far larger South Island is also mainly mountainous, with an alpine backbone extending obliquely from north-east to south-west. The highest peaks form a central massif, the Southern Alps, clustered around Mt Cook, at 3,753 m [12,313 ft], New Zealand's highest mountain. From this massif, which is permanently ice-capped, glaciers descend on either flank, and on the east the outwash fans of glacier-fed rivers form the Canterbury Plains – South Island's only extensive lowland. The north end of the island has many high, rolling ranges rising to the steeply-folded and faulted Kaikoura Ranges of the north-east. In the far south-west (Fjordland), the coast is indented by deep, steeply-walled sounds that wind far into the forested mountains.

New Zealand was discovered by Abel Tasman in 1642 and charted thoroughly by James Cook in 1769–70. Both explorers recorded the presence of Maoris-Polynesians who hunted and farmed from well-defended coastal settlements, who were themselves relatively recent arrivals on the islands. Sealing gangs and whalers were New Zealand's first European inhabitants, closely followed by missionaries and farmers from Britain and Australia. By the early 1830s about 2,000 Europeans had settled there.

In 1840 Britain took possession, in a treaty which gave rights and privileges of British subjects to the Maori people. The following decades saw the arrival of thousands of new settlers from Britain, and by mid-century there were over 30,000. Though their relationships with the Maoris (who at this stage outnumbered them two to one) were generally good, difficulties over land ownership led to warfare in the 1860s. Thereafter the Maori population declined while European numbers continued to increase.

THE MAORIS

'Strong, raw-boned, well-made, active people, rather above than under the common size ... of a very dark brown colour, with black hair, thin black beards, and ... in general very good features.' So Captain James Cook described the Maoris he met in New Zealand in 1770. Of Polynesian stock, the Maoris settled (mainly in North Island) from about AD 800 to 1350. A warlike people, living in small fortified settlements, they cultivated kumaras (sweet potatoes) and other crops, hunted seals and moas (large flightless birds, now extinct) and gathered seafoods.

The Maoris befriended the early European settlers; readily accepting British sovereignty, Christianity and pacification, they rebelled only as more and more of their communal land was bought for the settlers' use. Given parliamentary representation from 1876, they eventually integrated fully. Now Maoris form about 9% of New Zealand's population, still living mostly in North Island. Though socially and politically equal in every way to whites, they are still over-represented in the poorer, unskilled sections of the population, separated more by poverty and lack of opportunity than by colour from the mainstream of national life.

COUNTRY: New Zealand

AREA: 268,680 sq km [103,737 sq mls]

POPULATION: 3,429,000

CAPITAL (Population): Wellington (325,000)

GOVERNMENT: Constitutional monarchy with a unicameral legislature

ETHNIC GROUPS: White 81%, Maori 9%, Polynesian 3%

LANGUAGES: English (official) and Maori

RELIGIONS: Anglican 24%, Presbyterian 18%, Roman Catholic 15%, Methodist 5%

NATIONAL DAY: 6 February; Treaty of Waitangi (1840)

CURRENCY: New Zealand $ = 100 cents

ANNUAL INCOME PER PERSON: $12,680

MAIN PRIMARY PRODUCTS: Sheep, cereals, fruit and vegetables, cattle, fish, coal, natural gas, iron

MAIN EXPORTS: Meat and meat preparations 20%, wool 14%, fruit and vegetables 7%, forest products 7%, hides, skins and pelts 4%, butter 4%, fish 3%

MAIN EXPORT PARTNERS: USA 17%, Japan 15%, Australia 15%, UK 9%

MAIN IMPORTS: Machinery and electrical goods 26%, transport equipment 15%, chemicals 12%, textiles, clothing and footwear 7%, fuels and oils 5%

MAIN IMPORT PARTNERS: Japan 20%, Australia 18%, USA 16%, UK 10%

DEFENCE: 4.3% of national budget

TOURISM: 901,000 visitors per year

POPULATION DENSITY: 13 per sq km [33 per sq ml]

LIFE EXPECTANCY: Female 79 yrs, male 73 yrs

ADULT LITERACY: 99%

PRINCIPAL CITIES (Population): Auckland 885,377 Wellington 325,000 Hamilton 148,000 Napier-Hastings 110,000 Dunedin 109,000

British settlers found a climate slightly warmer than their own, with longer growing seasons but variable rainfall, sometimes with crippling drought in the dry areas. From 1844, when the first Merinos were introduced from Australia, New Zealand became predominantly a land of sheep, the grassy lowlands (especially in the South Island) providing year-round forage. Huge flocks were built up, mainly for wool and tallow production. From the lowlands they expanded into the hills – the 'high country' which was cleared of native bush and sown with European grasses for pasture. More than half the country is still covered with evergreen forest. The North Island proved more difficult to turn into farmland, later proving its value for dairying.

New Zealand's early prosperity was finally established when the export of frozen mutton and lamb carcasses began in 1882. Soon a steady stream of chilled meat and dairy products – and later of fruit – was crossing the oceans to established markets in Britain, and the country is still the world's second

NEW ZEALAND TERRITORIES

New Zealand comprises not just the two main islands, Stewart Island, Chatham Island and a number of uninhabited outlying islands, but also territories further out in the Pacific, including the Kermadec Islands (with an isolated meteorological station) and Tokelau (population 1,690); formerly part of the Gilbert and Ellice Islands – now called Kiribati – and transferred from Britain to New Zealand in 1926, the group became part of the country in 1949.

The Cook Islands (population 17,200) became an internally self-governing state in 'free association' with New Zealand in 1965; Niue (population 2,530) has had the same status since 1974. These Polynesian islanders have full citizenship, while Wellington controls defence and foreign affairs. The main exports are citrus fruits and juices, copra (coconut), bananas and honey.

biggest producer of lamb. Wheat and other cereals were also grown. High productivity was maintained by applications of fertilizers, mainly based on rock-phosphate mined on Nauru.

New Zealand is a prosperous country, with a high standard of living for a refreshingly harmonious multiracial population. Since 1907 a self-governing Dominion, it long relied on British markets for the export of agricultural produce, and has generally strong ties and affinities with Britain. Though agricultural products are still the main exports, the economy has diversified considerably since World War II, including fish, timber and wood pulp. Iron ores, coal and small amounts of gold are among the few valuable minerals, recently boosted by natural gas and petroleum. Geothermal and hydroelectric power are well developed, and timber and forest products are finding valuable overseas markets. Despite the country's isolation, a promising tourist industry is also developing, based on the scenic beauty, abundance of game animals, and relatively peaceful and unhurried way of life.

However, the idyll was showing signs of cracking from the 1970s, beginning when the UK joined the EEC and New Zealand's exports to Britain shrank from 70% to 10%. Along with a re-evaluation of its defence position, the country has had to rethink its previous 'safe' economic strategy – cutting subsidies to farmers, privatization, seeking new markets in Asia – and, like Australia and most fellow members of the OECD, find a way to survive the recession of the late 1980s and early 1990s ■

WELLINGTON

The islands are set in a vast ocean which moderates temperatures, and although Wellington is at the same latitude as Rome (41°), summers are 8°C [14°F] cooler. In the lowlands, no monthly temperature is below freezing. Auckland has briefly registered zero temperatures and sub-zero temperatures have been recorded in every month in Invercargill. Temperatures above 25°C [77°F] are rare.

Precipitation 1124mm 44in

DUNEDIN

New Zealand lies within the influence of westerly winds throughout the year and has a well-distributed rainfall, varying from over 6,000mm [236in] on the west coast of the South Island to below 300mm [12in] in the lee of the Southern Alps. There is a slight winter maximum and rain usually falls on over half the days in the year. In spite of this, sunshine levels are high, with over 2,000 hours over most of the area.

Precipitation 937mm 37in

AUSTRALIA AND OCEANIA

NORTHERN MARIANAS

The Northern Marianas comprise all 17 Mariana Islands except Guam, the most southerly, with a total land area of 477 sq km [184 sq mls]. Part of the US Trust Territory of the Pacific from 1947, its people voted in a 1975 UN plebiscite for Commonwealth status in union with the USA. Washington approved the change in 1976, granting US citizenship, and internal self-government followed in 1978.

The population of 22,000 is concentrated on three of the six inhabited islands, with Saipan and the capital town of Susupe accounting for 19,000. Tourism appears to be the key to the future: the number of foreign visitors rose from 130,000 in 1984 to over 300,000 in 1989 ■

GUAM

Largest of the Marianas, measuring 541 sq km [209 sq mls], Guam is composed mainly of a coralline limestone plateau, with mountains in the south, hills in the centre and narrow coastal lowlands in the north. Populated for over 3,000 years, charted by Magellan in 1521, colonized by Spain from 1668 but ceded to the US after the 1896–8 war and occupied by the Japanese 1941–4, it is today – as a 'self-governing unincorporated territory' – of huge strategic importance to Washington, and a third of its usable land is occupied by American naval and airforce establishments.

Though parts are highly developed along American lines, there are also traditional villages, beautiful beaches and dense jungles. Textiles, beverages, tobacco and copra are the main exports, but most food is imported. As a Pacific tourist destination, it is second only to Hawaii. All this helps to give Guamanians a relatively high standard of living, with an annual per capita income of over $7,000.

Almost half the population of 128,000 are Chamorro – of mixed Indonesian, Spanish and Filipino descent – and another quarter Filipino, but 20% of the total is composed of US military personnel and their families. In 1979 a referendum backed a return of much of the military land to civilian use, and a 1982 vote showed support for the Commonwealth status enjoyed by the Northern Marianas ■

BELAU

The last remaining member of the four states that comprised the US Trust Territory of the Pacific, established under UN mandate in 1947 – thanks to sustained American skulduggery, Belau (Palau) voted to break away from the Federated States of Micronesia in 1978, and a new self-governing constitution became effective in 1981. The territory then entered into 'free association with the USA', providing sovereign-state status, but in 1983 a referendum rejected the proposal, since Washington refused to accede to a 92% vote in a 1979 referendum that declared the nation a nuclear-free zone. The result is stalemate, with the UN Trusteeship still technically in force.

The republic comprises an archipelago of six Caroline groups, totalling 26 islands and over 300 islets varying in terrain from mountain to reef and measuring 458 sq km [177 sq mls]. The country relies heavily on US aid – indeed Washington has a policy of deliberate indebtedness – and the US government is the largest employer.

Eight of the islands are permanently inhabited, including Beleliu (Peleliu) and Angaur. Most of the largely Catholic population speak the official Belauan (Palauan), but English is widely used. The present capital is Koror (population 8,000 – over half the national total); a new capital is being built in the east of Babelthuap, the largest island, where coastal plains surround a high jungle interior ■

MARSHALL ISLANDS

The Marshall Islands became a republic 'in free association with the USA' in 1986, moving from Trust Territory status to a sovereign state responsible for its own foreign policy but not (until 2001) for its defence and security. Self-governing since 1979, the country comprises over 1,250 islands and atolls – including the former US nuclear testing sites of Bikini and Enewetak – totalling just 181 sq km [70 sq mls]. The population, mainly Micronesian, Protestant and English-speaking, is 43,000, with nearly half living in the capital of Majuro. The economy, based on agriculture and tourism, is very heavily supported by aid from the US, which still retains a missile site on the largest island, Kwajalein ■

FEDERATED STATES OF MICRONESIA

The Federated States of Micronesia became a sovereign state in 1986, when after 17 years of negotiation they entered into 'free association with the USA', which had run them as a US Trust Territory since 1947 and will continue to control defence and security until 2001.

Comprising the bulk of the Carolines, the Federation – despite a land area of just 705 sq mls [272 sq mls] – stretches across more than 3,200 km [2,000 mls] of Pacific, with the Equator as the southern boundary; the 607 islands divide into four groups and range from mountains to low atolls. Over half the area is contributed by the main island, Pohnpei, on which the capital of Kolonia stands; Pohnpei, also accounts for 52,000 out of a total population of 111,000 (Kolonia 7,000).

The cultures of the 'FSM', both Micronesian and Polynesian, are diverse, and four main languages are spoken in line with the four states of Yap, Truk, Pohnpei and Kosrae – though English is official. While some areas are highly Americanized, the traditional way of life has survived in others, based on subsistence farming and fishing. Copra is the main crop and phosphate is also exported, while tuna-fishing brings in revenue from American, Japanese and Korean fleets ■

NAURU

A low-lying coral atoll of just 21 sq km [8 sq mls] located halfway between Australia and Hawaii, 40 km [25 mls] south of the Equator, Nauru is the world's smallest republic. The climate is hot and wet, though the rains can fail. Discovered by Britain in 1798, the island was under the control of Germany (1888), Australia (1914), Japan (1942) and Australia again (with a UN trusteeship from 1946) before it gained independence in 1968.

A plateau rising to over 60 m [200 ft], surrounded by a belt of fertile, cultivated land, has provided the island with rich deposits of high-grade phosphate rock, exported to the Pacific Rim countries for fertilizer. The industry, nationalized in 1970, accounts for over 98% of exports, and though Nauru is only the 12th largest world producer this is enough to furnish the population with an average national income of US$20,000 – a similar figure to Canada or Denmark – giving them exemption from taxes and free education and welfare. The 6,000 native people – of mixed Micronesian and Polynesian origin, speaking a hybrid Nauruan language and predominantly Christian (mainly Protestant) – are supplemented by more than 2,500 migrants.

Nauru's future is nevertheless uncertain, since the phosphates are likely to be exhausted by the end of the century. The government is planning to derive new revenues from shipping and air services ■

KIRIBATI

Known as the Gilbert Islands until independence in 1979, the republic of Kiribati comprises three groups of coral atolls – 16 Gilbert Islands, eight Phoenix Islands and 11 of the Line Islands – plus the higher and volcanic Banaba. Though amounting to only 728 sq km [281 sq mls], they are scattered over 5 million sq km [2 million sq mls] of the Pacific, straddling both the Equator and the International Date Line.

Together with the Ellice Islands (which broke away as Tuvalu in 1975), the Gilberts were a British protectorate from 1892 and a colony from 1916; they were occupied by the Japanese in World War II, and recaptured after the battle for Tarawa in 1943. Today the capital has 24,000 residents, out of a total population of 70,000. The people of the islands are almost exclusively Christian, with a slight Roman Catholic majority.

Little of the coral islands rises above 4 m [13 ft], though coconuts, bananas, papayas, and breadfruits are harvested, with taro (babai) laboriously cultivated in deep pits to provide the staple vegetable. Following the exhaustion of Banaba's phosphate deposits in 1980, the main exports are copra (63%), and fish and fish preparations (24%), but Kiribati remains heavily dependent on foreign aid. The future, both medium-term economic and long-term environmental (due to possible rising sea levels from global warming) is bleak, compounded by an overcrowding problem that has forced the resettlement of some 4,700 people in the 1990s ■

TUVALU

Tuvalu became an independent constitutional monarchy within the Commonwealth in 1978, three years after separation from the Gilbert Islands – a decision supported by a large majority in a referendum held in 1974. None of its nine coral atolls – total area 24 sq km [9 sq mls] – rises more than 4.6 m [15 ft] out of the Pacific, and poor soils restrict vegetation to coconut palms, breadfruit trees and bush. The population of 9,000 (a third of which lives on the main island of Funafuti) survive by subsistence farming, raising pigs and poultry, and by fishing. Copra is the only significant export crop, but most foreign exchange comes from the sale of elaborate postage stamps to the world's philatelists. The people are almost all Protestant, speaking both Tuvaluan, a Polynesian-Samoan dialect, and usually English. The population, once far higher, was reduced from about 20,000 to just 3,000 in the three decades after 1850 by Europeans abducting workers for other Pacific plantations ■

VANUATU

An archipelago of 13 large islands and 70 islets, the majority of them mountainous and volcanic in origin, with coral beaches, reefs, forest cover and very limited coastal cultivation, Vanuatu totals 12,190 sq km [4,707 sq mls] in land area. Nearly two-thirds of the population of 160,000 lives on four islands, 19,000 of them in the capital of Port Vila, on Efate.

Formerly the New Hebrides and governed jointly by France and Britain from 1906, the islands became independent as a parliamentary republic in 1980. The francophone island of Espiritu Santo attempted separation from the anglophone government, and politics have remained unstable. The Melanesian, Bislama-speaking people live largely by subsistence farming and fishing, with copra (45%) and beef and veal (14%) the main exports ∎

TONGA

Tonga is an absolute monarchy. Since 1965 the ruler has been Taufa'ahau Tupou IV, latest in a line going back a thousand years, who presided over the islands' transition from British protectorate to independent Commonwealth state in 1970. His brother is prime minister on a council that has hereditary chiefs as well as elected representatives; there are no parties.

The archipelago comprises more than 170 islands, 36 of which are inhabited, covering 750 sq km [290 sq mls] in a mixture of low coralline and higher volcanic outcrops. Nearly two-thirds of the Polynesian population – over 100,000 and growing fast – live on the largest island of Tongatapu, 30,000 of them in the capital of Nuku'alofa, site of the royal palace. Vava'u (15,000) in the north is the next most populous. Predominantly Christian, the people speak Tongan, though English is also official.

Most Tongans live off their own produce, including yams, tapioca and fish. While the government owns all land, men are entitled to rent areas to grow food – a policy now under pressure with a burgeoning young population. The main exports are coconut oil products and bananas, with New Zealand the main trading partner. Tourism is starting, with 45,000 visitors to the islands in 1988 ∎

WALLIS AND FUTUNA ISLANDS

The smallest, least populous and poorest of France's three Pacific Overseas Territories, the Wallis and Futuna Islands comprise three main islands and numerous islets, totalling 200 sq km [77 sq mls]. Futuna and uninhabited Alofi, main constituents of the Hoorn group, are mountainous; the much larger Uvea, the chief island of the Wallis group, is hilly with coral reefs. Uvea contains 60% of the 12,000 population, 800 of them in the capital of Mata-Utu.

In a 1959 referendum the Polynesian islanders voted overwhelmingly in favour of change from a dependency to an Overseas Territory, and French aid remains crucial to an economy based mainly on tropical subsistence agriculture. The territory shares the currency of the Pacific franc with French Polynesia and New Caledonia ∎

WESTERN SAMOA

Western Samoa comprises two large islands, seven small islands and a number of islets, forming a land area of 2,840 sq km [1,097 sq mls]. The main islands of Upolu and Savai'i both have a central mountainous region, surrounded by coastal lowlands and coral reefs. Upolu contains two-thirds of the population of 185,000.

The cradle of Polynesian civilization, Western Samoa first gained independence in 1889, but ten years later became a German protectorate. Administered by New Zealand from 1920 – first under a League of Nations mandate and later a UN trusteeship – the island achieved independence as a parliamentary monarchy in 1962, following a plebiscite. Under a friendship treaty New Zealand handles relations with governments and organizations outside the Pacific islands zone. The first elections using universal suffrage were held in 1991.

The population remains mainly Polynesian, with a Maori majority, and almost exclusively Christian (70% Protestant); Samoan and English are both official languages. The traditional lifestyle still thrives, with over 60% of the workforce engaged in agriculture, chiefly tropical fruits and vegetables, and in fishing. The main exports are coconut oil (43%), taro and cocoa, with New Zealand the main partner. Many of the 50,000 tourists a year visit the home of Robert Louis Stevenson – now the official residence of King Malietoa Tanumafili II ∎

AMERICAN SAMOA

A self-governing 'unincorporated territory of the US', American Samoa is a group of five volcanic islands and two atolls covering a land area of 197 sq km [76 sq mls] in the South Pacific, with Tutuila the largest. Swain Island to the north also comes under its administration, taking the total population to about 38,000. More than twice that number of American Samoans live in the US.

The Samoan Islands were divided in 1899, with British consent, between Germany and the US along a line 171° west of Greenwich. Though the US naval base at Pago Pago closed in 1951, the American influence in the territory is still vital, giving substantial grants and taking 90% of exports.

While Pago Pago – the recipient of about 5,000 mm [200 in] of rain a year – is the capital, the seat of government is to the east at Fagatogo. There is little prospect of Samoan reunification: the American islands enjoy a standard of living some ten times as high as their neighbours in Western Samoa ∎

FRENCH POLYNESIA

French Polynesia consists of 130 islands, totalling only 4,000 sq km [1,540 sq mls] but scattered over 4 million sq km [1.5 million sq mls] of ocean half-way between Australia and South America. Tahiti is the largest island and home to the capital of Papeete.

The tribal chiefs of Tahiti eventually agreed to a French protectorate in 1843, and by the end of the century France controlled all the present islands. They formed an overseas territory from 1958, sending two deputies and a senator to Paris, and in 1984 gained increased autonomy with a territorial assembly. There are calls for independence, but the high standard of living (the annual per capita income is US$8,000) comes largely from the links with France, including a substantial military presence. France began stationing personnel there in 1962, including nuclear testing at Mururoa.

The other factor which changed the islands' economy from subsistence agriculture and fishing was tourism; in 1988 this earned about half as much as all visible exports. After petroleum re-exports (45%), the main earners are cultured pearls, vanilla and citrus fruits. Almost half the territory's trade is with France, and it shares a currency (the Pacific franc) with New Caledonia and Wallis and Futuna.

The population is 196,000, of which nearly half live on Tahiti – 65,000 in Papeete. Nearly 70% of the people are Polynesian, the rest being French (10%), descendants of Chinese labourers brought in by a British-owned plantation in the 1860s (7%), or

The climate is warm and humid with nearly continuous cloud cover over the mountain peaks. Temperatures remain high throughout the year with a slight maximum in March, during the warm rainy season. Rainfall is abundant and heaviest on the windward slopes (north-facing and east-facing). There are long periods of calm between April and June, when the weather is brighter and drier.

of mixed descent. Overwhelmingly Christian (Protestant 47%, Roman Catholic 40%), they speak French, the official language, and Tahitian ∎

PITCAIRN is a British dependent territory of four islands (48 sq km [18.5 sq mls]), situated half-way between New Zealand and Panama. Uninhabited until 1790, it was occupied by nine mutineers from HMS *Bounty* and some men and women from Tahiti. The present population of 49, all living in Adamstown on Pitcairn, come under the administration of the British High Commission in Wellington and use the New Zealand dollar ∎

NORTH AND CENTRAL AMERICA

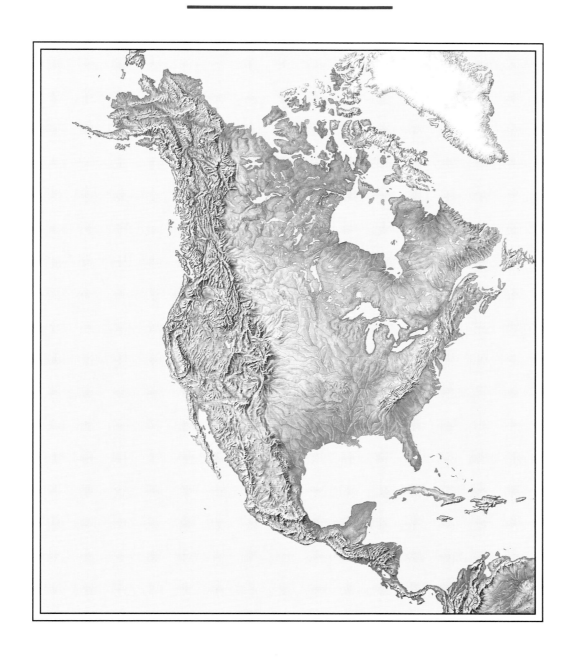

NORTH AND CENTRAL AMERICA

Third largest of the world's continents, North America spans 116° of longitude from Newfoundland to Bering Strait – almost a third of the northern hemisphere; in latitude it extends from the tropical Gulf of Mexico in the south to the Arctic.

With a reputation for containing the biggest and best of everything, North America tends towards superlatives and extremes. Its highest peaks fall short of the highest in Asia and South America, but it includes the world's largest freshwater lake (Lake Superior) and greatest canyon (Grand Canyon, Arizona). Climatic extremes are common, though some of its world records reflect little more than good coverage by an unusually complete network of well-equipped weather stations.

Topography and climate combine to provide an immense range of natural habitats across North America, from mangrove swamps and tropical forests in the south, through hot deserts, prairie, temperate and boreal forests, taiga and tundra to polar deserts in the far north. North America can claim both the largest and oldest known living organism (giant redwood cedars and bristlecone pines), both found in the western USA.

Standing at the edge of one of the world's six great crustal plates, North America has been subject to pressure and uplift from its neighbouring Pacific plate, with results that show clearly on a physical map. Roughly a third of the continent, including the whole of the western flank, has been thrown into a

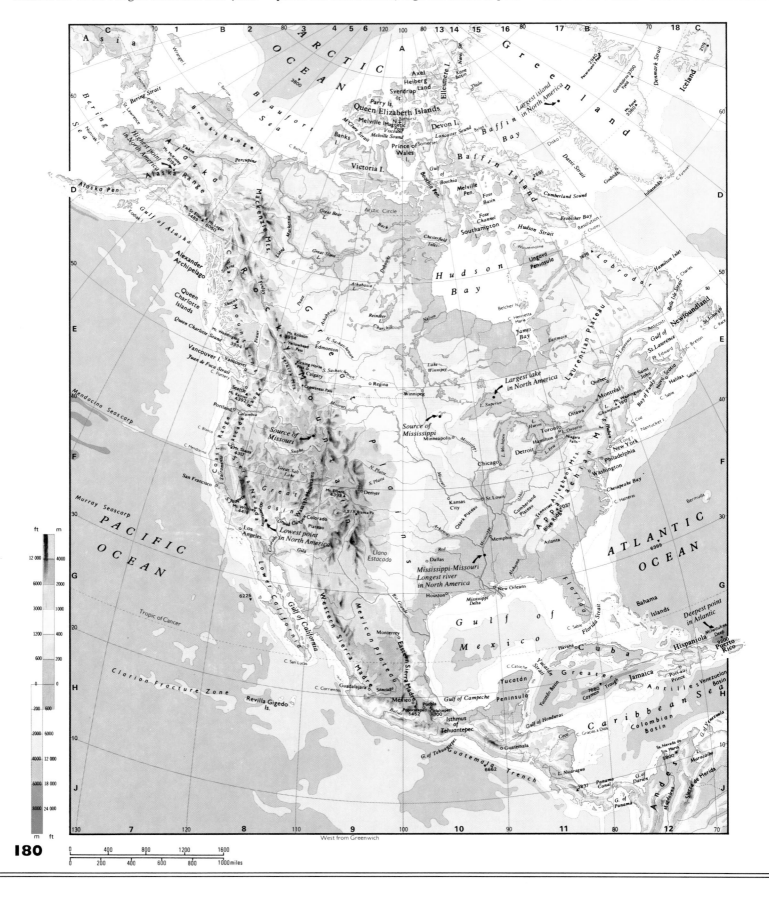

West from Greenwich

spectacular complex of young mountains, valleys and plateaus – the Western Cordilleras. To the east lie much older mountains, longer-weathered and lower – the Appalachians in the south and the Laurentian Highlands in the north; these are separated from the western ranges by broad interior lowlands drained by the Mississippi-Missouri system.

The bleak northern plains, centred about Hudson Bay, rest on a shield or platform of ancient rocks that underlies most of central and eastern Canada.

This Laurentian Shield, though warped and split by crustal movements, was massive enough to resist folding through the successive periods of mountain building that raised the Western Cordilleras. Planed by more than a million years of glaciation throughout the Ice Age, it is now free of permanent ice except on a few of the northern islands. Its surface remains littered with glacial debris that forms thin, waterlogged tundra or forest soils, and the once glaciated region is fringed by a crescent of interlinked

lakes and waterways, including the Great Bear Lake and the five Great Lakes.

Central America is the narrow waistline of the Americas, known to the world for the canal that links the two great oceans in Panama. The backbone of the isthmus is mountainous, many of the volcanic vertebrae reaching heights of over 4,000m [13,000ft]. It is the most tectonically active zone in the Americas with over 100 large volcanoes and frequent earthquakes ■

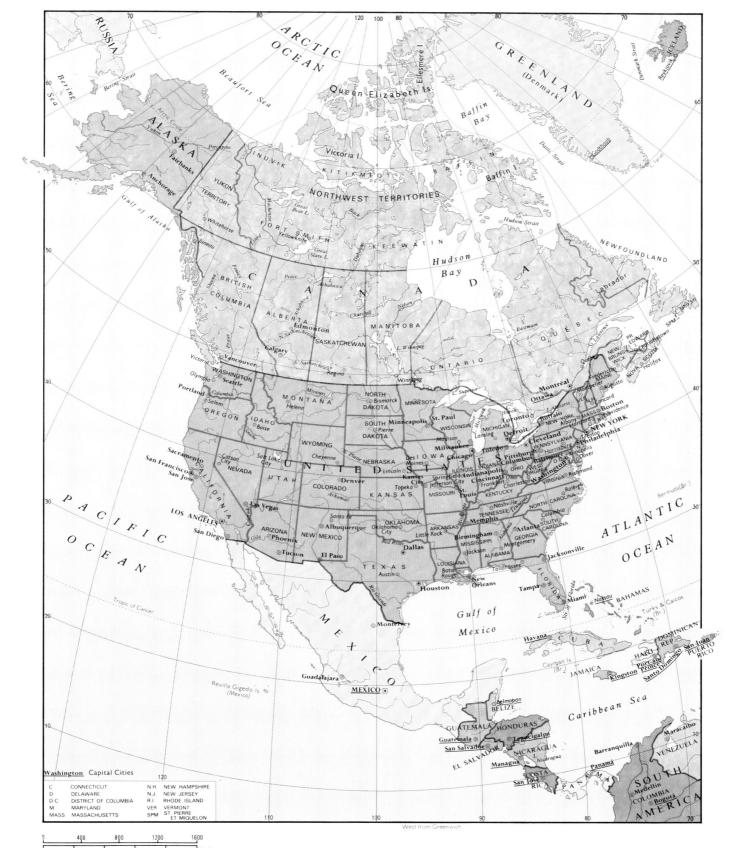

NORTH AND CENTRAL AMERICA

CLIMATIC REGIONS

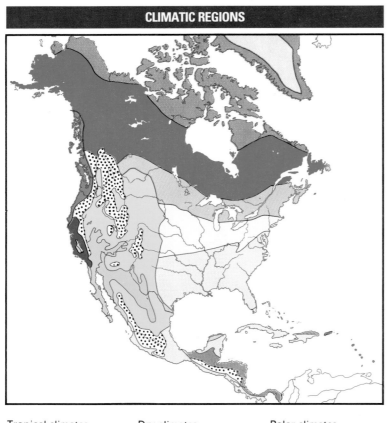

Tropical climates
Tropical rain forest

Savanna

Dry climates
Steppe

Desert

Polar climates
Tundra

Ice cap

Mild climates
Marine west coast

Humid subtropical

Mediterranean

Continental climates
Humid continental, warm summer

Humid continental, cool summer

Subarctic

High altitudes
Highlands

NATURAL VEGETATION

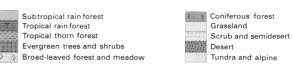

Subtropical rain forest
Tropical rain forest
Tropical thorn forest
Evergreen trees and shrubs
Broad-leaved forest and meadow

Coniferous forest
Grassland
Scrub and semidesert
Desert
Tundra and alpine

ANNUAL RAINFALL

ins.	mm
120	3000
80	2000
40	1000
20	500
10	250

POPULATION

· 100 000 people

LAND USE

LAND USE

- Arable land
- Arable land with grazing
- Market gardening, fruit trees, bushes and orchard land
- Permanent pasture
- Woods and forests
- Woods and forests with grazing land
- Rough grazing
- Non-productive land

LIVESTOCK
- Beef cattle
- Sheep
- Dairy cattle

CROPS
- ꠸ Bananas
- ◆ Citrus fruits
- ◠ Coffee
- ◔ Cotton
- • Fruit
- ◟ Groundnuts
- ꠸ Maize
- • Olives
- ○ Rice
- ⌄ Sisal
- ◇ Sugar cane
- ⊤ Tobacco
- ▼ Vegetables
- ꠸ Wheat
- ⇀ Principal fishing areas

MINERALS
- ● Asbestos
- ○ Bauxite
- ▲ Copper
- △ Gold
- ◆ Iron ore
- ◇ Lead
- ◇ Lead and zinc
- ● Mica
- ▼ Phosphate
- ▽ Silver
- ◆ Uranium
- △ Zinc
- Sb Antimony
- Co Cobalt
- Mg Magnesium
- Hg Mercury
- Mo Molybdenum
- Ni Nickel
- Ti Titanium

POWER
- ▲ Coalfields
- ■ Gasfields
- ▪ Oilfields
- ▪ HEP

LAND USE

Other land 37·5%

Arable land and permanent crops 12·7%

Permanent pasture 16·2%

Woods and forests 33·6%

Total land area 2 140.5 million hectares (5 289·2 million acres)

Projection: Polyconic

West from Greenwich

COPYRIGHT GEORGE PHILIP LTD.

NORTH AND CENTRAL AMERICA

CANADA

The British Red Ensign was used from 1892 but became unpopular with Canada's French community. After many attempts to find a more acceptable design, the present flag – featuring the simple maple leaf emblem – was finally adopted in 1965.

The effect of the Great Lakes is felt in the Ontario Peninsula with slightly warmer winters than in Québec. The temperatures in northern Canada are violent; along the Arctic Circle the mean monthly temperatures for over seven months are below freezing. Rainfall is moderate throughout the year with no marked peak and a reasonable amount of snow. In the mid-west the July temperature is about 17°C [63°F], but the cold of December is nearly -14°C [6°F], an annual range of over 30°C [54°F].

A vast confederation of ten provinces and two territories, Canada is the world's second largest country after Russia, and with an even longer coastline (250,000 km [155,000 mls]). Sparsely populated, it has huge areas of virtually unoccupied mountains, forests, tundra and polar desert in the north and west.

To the east lie the Maritime provinces of Newfoundland, Nova Scotia, New Brunswick and Prince Edward Island, and the predominantly French-speaking province of Québec; clustered about the Gulf of St Lawrence, they are based on ancient worn-down mountains – the northern extension of the Appalachians – and the eastern uptilted edge of the even older Canadian Shield. The central province of Ontario borders the Great Lakes, extending north across the Shield to Hudson Bay. Further to the west come the prairie provinces of Manitoba, Saskatchewan and Alberta; like Québec and Ontario, these include fertile farmlands in the south, where most of the population is to be found, and lake-strewn forest on the subarctic wastelands to the north.

South-western Alberta includes a substantial block of the Rocky Mountains, with peaks rising to over 4,000 m [13,120 ft] in Banff, Yoho and Kootenay National Parks. The westernmost province of British Columbia is mountainous, a land of spectacular forests, lakes and fjords, with sheltered valleys harbouring rich farmland. The huge northern area includes the relatively small and mountainous Yukon Territory in the west, bordering Alaska, and the much more extensive Northwest Territories stretching from the 60th parallel to the northern tip of Ellesmere Island.

Exploration and settlement

Norse voyagers and fishermen were probably the first Europeans briefly to visit Canada, but John Cabot's later discovery of North America, in 1497, began the race to annex lands and wealth, with France and Britain the main contenders.

Jacques Cartier's discovery of the St Lawrence River in 1534 gave France a head start; from their settlements near Québec explorers, trappers and missionaries pioneered routes deeply penetrating the northern half of North America. With possible routes to China and the Indies in mind, Frenchmen followed the St Lawrence and Niagara rivers deep into the heartland of the continent, hoping for the riches of another Eldorado.

Discovering the Great Lakes, they then moved north, west and south in their search for trade. From the fertile valley of the upper St Lawrence, French influence spread north beyond the coniferous forests and over the tundra. To the west and south they reached the prairies – potentially fertile farming country – exploring further to the Rockies and down the Ohio and Mississippi rivers.

By 1763, after the series of wars that gave Britain brief control of the whole of North America, French-speaking communities were already scattered widely across the interior. Many of the southern settlements became American after 1776, when the USA declared independence from Britain, and the northern ones became a British colony.

British settlers had long been established on the Atlantic coast, farming where possible, with supplementary fishing. In the 1780s a new wave of English-speaking settlers – the United Empire Loyalists – moved north from the USA into Nova Scotia, New Brunswick and Lower Canada. With further waves of immigration direct from Britain, English speakers came to dominate the fertile lands between Lakes Huron and Erie. From there they gradually spread westwards.

The birth of Canada

Restricted to the north by intractable coniferous forests and tundra, and to the south by the USA, the settlers spread through Québec into Upper Canada – now Ontario, the only province along the Canadian shores of the Great Lakes. Mostly English-speaking and retaining British traditions, they continued westwards to establish settlements across the narrow wedge of the northern prairie, finally crossing the Rockies to link with embryo settlements along the Pacific coast. So the fertile lowlands of the St Lawrence basin and the pockets of settlement on the Shield alone remained French in language and culture. The bulk of Canada, to east and west, became predominantly British.

Canada's varied topography and immense scale inhibited the development of a single nation; to promote Canadian unity across so wide a continent has been the aim of successive governments for more than two centuries. The union of British Upper Canada and French Lower Canada was sealed by the Confederation of 1867, when as the newly-named Provinces of Ontario and Québec they were united with the Maritime core of Nova Scotia and New Brunswick. Three years later the settlement on the Red River entered the Confederation as Manitoba, and in the following year the Pacific colonies of Vancouver Island and British Columbia, now united as a single province, completed the link from sea to sea. Prince Edward Island joined in 1873, the prairie provinces of Alberta and Saskatchewan in 1905, and Newfoundland in 1949.

Though self-governing in most respects from the time of the Confederation, Canada remained technically subject to the British Imperial parliament until 1931, when the creation of the British Commonwealth made the country a sovereign nation under the crown.

With so much of the population spread out along a southern ribbon of settlement, 4,000 km [2,500 mls] long but rarely more than 480 km [300 mls] wide, Canada has struggled constantly to achieve unity. Trans-continental communications have played a critical role. From the eastern provinces the Canadian Pacific Railway crossed the Rockies to reach Vancouver in 1885. Later a second rail route, the Canadian National, was pieced together, and the Trans-Canada Highway links the extreme east and west of the country symbolically as well as in fact. Trans-continental air routes link the major centres, and local air traffic is especially important over trackless forests, mountains and tundra. With radio and telephone communications, all parts of the confederation – even the most remote corners of the Arctic territories – are now firmly linked, though the vastness is intimidating and the country spans six time zones: at noon in Vancouver it is already 3 pm in Toronto, and 4.30 pm in St Johns, Newfoundland.

A constant hazard to Canadian nationhood is the proximity of the USA. Though benign, with shared if dwindling British traditions, the prosperous giant to the south has often seemed to threaten the very survival of Canada through economic dominance and cultural annexation. The two countries have the largest bilateral trade flow in the world.

A real and growing threat to unity is the persistence of French culture in Québec province – a last-

West of the Rockies, and to a lesser extent on the eastern coast, the nearby ocean changes the expected climate. At Vancouver, rainfall is high with maximum October–March. There is little snow, with only just over 50 frost-days. No month has an average minimum below freezing. Summers are cool, with no mean temperatures above 18°C [64°F], the record being 34°C [93°F] in August. Winter temperatures decline a little to the north along this coastal fringe.

SAINT-PIERRE ET MIQUELON

The last remaining fragment of once-extensive French possessions in North America, Saint-Pierre et Miquelon comprises eight islands (total area 242 sq km [93 sq mls]) off the south coast of Newfoundland. Settled by Frenchmen in the 17th century and a colony from 1816, it became an overseas department in 1976, thus enjoying – like Martinique, Guadeloupe, Guiana and Réunion – the same status as the departments in Metropolitan France. In 1985, however, it became a 'territorial collectivity' (a status already held by Mayotte), sending one representative to the National Assembly in Paris and one to the Senate. The population of 6,300 (the vast majority of whom live on Saint-Pierre, the rest on Miquelon) depend mainly on fishing – the cause of disputes with Canada. The French-speaking population of Canada occasionally voices separatist claims, but most Québecois seem content with the status quo and the benefits it brings to their 'distinct society', the term used in the Meech Lake accord of 1987.

The July temperature is about 17°C [63°F], but the cold of December is nearly -14°C [6°F], an annual range of over 30°C [54°F], almost as great as in Arctic Canada. But high summer temperatures are recorded in these areas, over 30 having been recorded in all months, April–September. Rainfall is low with a maximum June–August, and there is little snowfall. On average there are over 210 frost-days. Westwards into the Rockies, the snow can reach great depths.

THE TUNDRA

Beyond their habitable southern rim, the north-lands of Canada and Alaska are bleak and bare; in the subarctic zone conifers stretch across the continent, but northwards the boreal forest thins and dies out, replaced with tundra. Glaciation has scoured the rocks bare, and soils have had insufficient time to form; the surface thaws in summer, but subsoils remain frozen. Winters are long and bitterly cold, summers brief and cool. Even in the south the season of plant growth is only 70–80 days. Precipitation is light – usually less than 25cm [10in] a year, and most of it snow; except where it drifts, the snow seldom lies deep, but it provides cover for vegetation and burrowing animals.

The tundra is covered with low grasses, lichens, mosses and spindly shrubs, providing food for migrating reindeer and resident hares, voles, lemmings and other small browsers and grazers. Their numbers are augmented each summer by hosts of migrant birds – ducks, geese, swans, waders, and many others – that fly in from temperate latitudes to feed on the vegetation and insects.

COUNTRY: Canada

AREA: 9,976,140 sq km [3,851,788 sq mls]

POPULATION: 26,522,000

CAPITAL (Population): Ottawa (819,000)

GOVERNMENT: Federal multiparty parliamentary state

ETHNIC GROUPS: British 40%, French 27%, other European 20%, Asiatic 2%, Amerindian/Inuit (Eskimo) 2%

LANGUAGES: English 63% and French 25% (both official)

RELIGIONS: Roman Catholic 47%, Protestant 41%, Eastern Orthodox, Jewish, Muslim, Hindu

NATIONAL DAY: 1 July

CURRENCY: Canadian $ = 100 cents

ANNUAL INCOME PER PERSON: $20,450

SOURCE OF INCOME: Agriculture 49%, industry 40%, services 56%

MAIN PRIMARY PRODUCTS: Coal, cobalt, copper, fish, furs, gold, iron ore, lead, molybdenum, natural gas, nickel, platinum, petroleum, silver, timber, wheat

MAIN INDUSTRIES: Transport equipment, food, paper and allied products, primary metal, fabricated metal, electrical and electronics equipment, wood and timber, rubber and plastics

MAIN EXPORTS: Passenger vehicles, trucks and parts 26%, food, feed, beverages and tobacco 6%, timber 5%, newspaper print 5%, wood pulp 4%, petroleum 4%, natural gas 3%, industrial machinery 3%

MAIN EXPORT PARTNERS: USA 75%, Japan 6%, UK 2%

MAIN IMPORTS: Vehicles and parts 26%, machinery 9%, food, feed, beverages and tobacco 6%, chemicals 5%, computers 4%, petroleum 3%, iron and steel 2%

MAIN IMPORT PARTNERS: USA 68%, Japan 7%, Germany 4%

EDUCATIONAL EXPENDITURE: Controlled by provinces

DEFENCE: 10% of national budget

TOTAL ARMED FORCES: 89,000

TOURISM: 39,253,000 visitors per year [36,147,000 from USA]

ROADS: 280,251 km [175,157 mls]

RAILWAYS: 93,544 km [58,465 mls]

POPULATION DENSITY: 3 per sq km [7 per sq ml]

URBAN POPULATION: 76%

POPULATION GROWTH: 0.9% per year

BIRTHS: 15 per 1,000 population

DEATHS: 7 per 1,000 population

INFANT MORTALITY: 8 per 1,000 live births

LIFE EXPECTANCY: Female 81 yrs, male 74 yrs

POPULATION PER DOCTOR: 515

ADULT LITERACY: 96%

PRINCIPAL CITIES (Population): Toronto 3,427,000 Montréal 2,921,000 Vancouver 1,381,000 Ottawa-Hull 819,000 Edmonton 785,000 Calgary 631,000 Winnipeg 623,000 Québec 603,000 Hamilton 557,000

---

ing political wedge between the western prairie and mountain provinces and the eastern Maritimes. Urbanization and 'Americanization' have fuelled a separatist movement that seeks to turn the province into an independent French-speaking republic. This issue may obscure a wider and more fundamental division in Canadian politics, with the development of a Montréal-Toronto axis in the east, and a Vancouver-Winnipeg axis in the west.

Population and urbanization

Though the population of Canada expanded rapidly from Confederation onwards, it remained predominantly rural for many generations; only in recent decades have Canada's cities grown to match those of the USA. At Confederation in 1867 about 80% was rural, and only Montréal had passed the 100,000 population mark, with but six towns over 25,000. Not until the end of World War II did the rural and urban elements stand in balance, and today the situation is reversed: 76% of Canada's population is urban.

The metropolitan areas of Toronto and Montréal jointly contain a quarter of the total, and together with Vancouver account for over 30% of the entire population. By contrast the urban centres of Newfoundland and the Maritimes have been relatively stable.

Agriculture and industry

Although farming settlements still dominate the landscape, if not the economy, abandonment of farmland is a serious problem in the eastern provinces, where the agrarian economy – except in such favoured areas as the Annapolis Valley, Nova Scotia - has always been marginal. Through the St Lawrence lowlands and Ontario peninsula farms are more prosperous and rural populations are denser, thinning again along the north shores of the Great Lakes. On the prairies mechanization of grain farming long ago minimized the need for labour, so population densities remain low; the mixed farming communities on the forest margins are often denser. The Pacific coast population is generally concentrated in such rich farming areas as the Okanagan and lower Frazer River basins.

Industry, often dependent on local development of power resources, has transformed many remote and empty areas of Canada. Newfoundland's

Labrador iron-ore workings around Schefferville are powered by the huge hydroelectric plant at Churchill Falls, one of the largest of its kind in the world. Cheap hydroelectric power throughout Québec and Ontario, coupled with improved transmission technology, has encouraged the further development of wood pulp and paper industries, even in distant parts of the northern forests, and stimulated industry and commerce in the south. Canada is by far the world's leading producer and exporter of paper and board. Mining, too, has helped in the development of these provinces; Sudbury, Ontario, supplies about 20% of the western world's nickel, while Canada is the world leader in both zinc (16%) and uranium (33%).

Tourism is also an important industry; Canada's spectacular open spaces attract visitors from around the world. In the prairie provinces, small marketing, distribution and service centres have been transformed by the enormous expansion of the petrochemical industry; the mineral-rich province of Alberta produces 90% of the country's oil output, and the boom towns of Alberta, Edmonton and Calgary have far outpaced the growth of the eastern cities during recent decades. By contrast – lacking

hydrocarbons, depending mainly on farming, logging and pulping for their prosperity – the settlements of Pacific Canada have on the whole grown slowly, with the notable exception of Vancouver.

The northlands

Canada's northlands, virtually uninhabited apart from small Inuit communities, have an immense though localized potential for development. Though the soils are poor and the climate is unyielding, mineral wealth is abundant under the permanently frozen subsoils. Already a major producer of uranium, zinc and nickel, the North also holds vast reserves of copper, molybdenum, iron, cadmium, and other metals of strategic importance; sulphur, potash and asbestos are currently being exploited, and natural gas and petroleum await development beyond the Mackenzie River delta.

Much of this immense mineral wealth will remain in the ground until the high costs of extraction and transportation can be justified. Also, pressure for legislation to protect the boreal forest and tundra against unnecessary or casual damage is rapidly growing – a trend which one day may also curb the massive timber industry ∎

NORTH AND CENTRAL AMERICA

NORTH AND CENTRAL AMERICA

UNITED STATES OF AMERICA

The 'Stars and Stripes' has used the same basic design since 1777, during the War of Independence. The 13 stripes represent the original colonies that rebelled against British rule, the 50 stars the present states of the Union.

The USA east of the Rockies is isolated from the maritime influences of the Pacific and experiences similar extremes to the heart of Eurasia, though the margins of the Great Lakes are warmer in winter and cooler in summer than elsewhere. Temperatures of –20°C [–4°F] have been recorded between December and February. Rainfall is well distributed, with a summer maximum, and the average winter snowfall at Chicago is almost 1,000 mm [40 in].

The world's fourth largest country – and third most populous – the United States of America fills the North American continent between Canada and Mexico and also includes Alaska and the archipelago of Hawaii. Geographically, the main part (of 48 states) falls readily into an eastern section, including the Appalachian Mountains and eastern coastal plain; a central section, including the Mississippi basin and the broad prairie plains from the Dakotas to Texas; and a western section, including the Rocky Mountains and Pacific coastlands.

The East

Eastern North America is crossed by a band of low, folded mountains: though nowhere much above 2,000 m [6,500 ft], they long formed a barrier to settlers. In the north are the Adirondacks, a southern extension of the ancient granite shield of Canada, rising to 1,629 m [5,344 ft]. From Maine to Alabama runs a broad range of sedimentary mountains, the Appalachians. Younger than the Adirondacks (though much older than the Rockies) the Appalachians separate the Atlantic coastlands of the east from the Great Lakes and low plateaus of Ohio, Kentucky and Tennessee.

North-east of New York City lie the six New England states – the fertile wooded country that, at least in summer, made the early settlers feel at home. To the south the coastal plain widens, to be split by the drowned estuaries of the Susquehanna and Potomac rivers, draining into Chesapeake Bay. From Virginia south to Florida smaller rivers drain eastwards, across a much broader plain, many of them entering coastal sounds with offshore sandbars and islands.

In New York state a major spillway cuts through the mountains between the Adirondacks and Appalachians, linking the Great Lakes with the Hudson Valley and the Atlantic Ocean. This is the line of the famous Erie Canal route, the most used of several that gave the early settlers access to the Ohio country beyond the mountains. Other routes led to Pittsburgh and, through the southern Appalachians, into Tennessee. Central Ohio, Indiana and Illinois, which once formed America's North-west Territory, are rolling uplands and plains, smoothed by

glaciation in the north but more rugged in the south, and drained by the rambling Ohio River.

Vegetation: The original vegetation of eastern America, on either flank of the mountains, was broadleaf deciduous forest of oak, ash, beech and maple, merging northwards into yellow birch, hemlock and pine. In the drier Mid-West these immense woodlands turned to open country. Patchy grasslands covered northern Indiana and southern Illinois; central Illinois was forested along most watercourses, with prairie blue-stem grasses on the drier interfluves. Around the southern Appalachians mixed oak, pine and tulip-tree dominated; pines covered the coastal plains to the south and east with bald cypress in northern Florida. Spruce blanketed the highlands from northern Maine to the Adirondacks; spruce, tamarack and balsam fir covered the high Appalachians.

Most of this original forest is now gone, but there is still enough left – and some regenerating on abandoned farmland – to leave the mountains a blaze of colour each autumn. Despite more than 300 years of European settlement, the overall impression of eastern America, seen from the air, is still one of dense semi-continuous forests, except in the extensive farmlands north of the Ohio.

Settlement and development: The eastern USA is the heartland of many of America's rural and urban traditions. In the 19th century European immigrants poured through the ports of Boston, New York, Philadelphia and Baltimore. Many stayed to swell the cities, which grew enormously. Others moved across the mountains to populate the interior and start the farms that fed the city masses. As raw materials of industry – coal and iron ore especially – were discovered and exploited, new cities grew up in the interior. Some were based on old frontier forts: Fort Duquesne became Pittsburgh and Fort Dearborn became Chicago.

Railways spread over the booming farmlands, linking producer and consumer. Huge manufacturing cities, vast markets in their own right, developed along the Great Lakes as people continued to arrive – firstly from abroad, but latterly from the countryside, where mechanization threw people off the land into the cities and factories. In less than a hundred

years between the late 18th and 19th centuries the Ohio country passed from Indian-occupied forests and plains to mechanized farmlands of unparalleled efficiency, becoming virtually the granary of the Western world and spawning some of its greatest and wealthiest industrial centres.

While the north boomed, the warmer southern states slipped into rural lethargy; becoming over-dependent on cotton cultivation, they remained backward and outside the mainstream of American prosperity. Though fortunes were made on the rich cotton estates of the south-east, Tennessee and the southern Appalachians spelled rural poverty for many generations of settlers.

Today the pattern is much the same, though prosperity has increased throughout the east. The densest concentrations of industry and population lie in the north-east, especially in central New England. New York remains an important financial hub, while Washington D.C., now part of a vast, sprawling megalopolis, loses none of its significance as the centre of federal government. The south-eastern states remain relatively rural and thinly populated, though they are increasingly popular with the retired, notably Florida.

The Central States

Within the 1,400 km [875 mls] from the Mississippi to the foothills of the Rockies, the land rises almost 3,000 m [9,850 ft], though the slope is often imperceptible to the traveller. From the Gulf of Mexico northwards to Minnesota and the Dakotas the rise is even less noticeable, though the flatness is occasionally relieved by the outcrops of uplands – the Ozarks of northern Arkansas, for example. In summer nothing bars the northwards movement of hot moist air from the Gulf of Mexico, nor in winter the southwards movement of dry, cold air from the Arctic. These air masses produce great seasonal contrasts of climate, exacerbated by storms, blizzards and tornadoes. Westwards from the Mississippi the climate grows progressively drier.

The plains are crossed by a series of long, wide rivers, often of irregular flow, that drain off the Rockies: the Missouri, the Platte, the Arkansas, the Canadian and the Red. In contrast to the Ohio, which

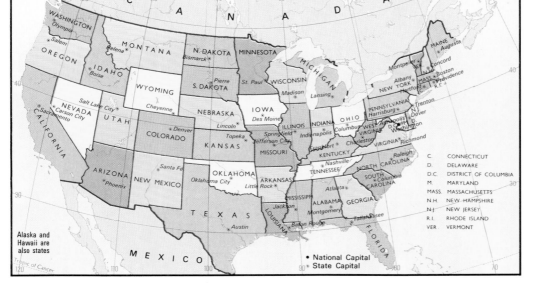

Alaska and Hawaii are also states

C.	CONNECTICUT
D.	DELAWARE
D.C.	DISTRICT OF COLUMBIA
M.	MARYLAND
MASS.	MASSACHUSETTS
N.H.	NEW HAMPSHIRE
N.J.	NEW JERSEY
R.I.	RHODE ISLAND
VER.	VERMONT

• National Capital
★ State Capital

0 200 400 600 800 1000 km
0 200 400 600 miles

Southern Texas has a Gulf-type of climate with abundant rain at all seasons to contrast to the Great Plains with their winter dry season. In summer the prevailing winds are from the south-east and in winter from the north-east. In winter, very cold air from Canada may penetrate as far south as the Gulf, causing a sharp fall in temperature, and in autumn the region may be affected by hurricanes. Several degrees of frost can be recorded November–March.

New York is 40°N, but its average temperature December–February is only just above freezing. Temperatures lower than -20°C [-4°F] have been recorded, December–February, while the daily high from May to August is above 20°C [68°F], with records of 35–40°C [95–104°F]. Rain and snow are more or less evenly distributed through the year, with rain falling on about a third of the days. Sunshine totals are high, averaging 6–9 hours daily from March to October.

enabled travellers to pass downstream and so westwards to the Mississippi, these rivers of the plains provided little help to settlers moving westwards, due to their seasonal variations in flow and the effort which was needed to move upstream when floods gave them depth.

Vegetation: West of the margins of the Mississippi tall blue-stem prairie grasses once extended from the Canadian border to southern Texas. Only along the watercourses were there trees – cottonwood and willow in the north, merging into oak and hickory further south. Westwards the prairie grasslands thinned to the bunch grass and needle grass of the Great Plains in a belt from central North Dakota to western Oklahoma; locally-favoured areas such as western Nebraska had patches of broadleaf evergreens amidst shrubs and grasses.

West of about meridian 100°W a variety of short grasses stretched from Montana and the Dakotas southwards to north-west Texas: in the far south on the Mexican border low xerophytic shrubs indicated increasing aridity. Higher ground, for example the Black Hills of south-western South Dakota, supported stands of pine.

Settlement and development: Over 30 major tribes of native Indians used these vast and varied plains. Some – the Mandan, the Omaha and the Kansa along the Missouri River, for example – were settled farmers, while on the drier western plains the Blackfoot, Crow, Arapaho, Kiowa and Comanche were nomadic, following the buffalo, the game and the pasture.

European influences revolutionized their lives. By 1800 the horse, introduced from the south by the Spanish, made the Indian population of about 100,000 mobile as never before. Then English- and French-speaking trappers and traders from the east brought firearms: the mounted Indian with a gun became too efficient a hunter, and rapidly depleted his food supply. Behind the traders came white settlers, killing off the buffalo and crowding in other native peoples that they had driven from homelands in the south-east. As railways, cattle trails and fences of the ranchers crossed the old hunting grounds, Indian farmers and hunters alike lost their traditional lands and livelihoods to the European intruders, and the plains settlement was virtually completed by the late 19th century.

The coming of the railways after the Civil War of the 1860s not only doomed the remnant Indian societies, but also introduced long and often bitter competition between different types of European farming. The dry grasslands that once supported the buffalo could just as well support herds of cattle on the open range, raised to feed the eastern cities. So the range lands often became crop-farms. In the dry years that followed soil deterioration and erosion began, becoming a major problem in the early decades of the present century.

With their markets in the cities of the east and in Europe, the plains farmers were caught in a vice

between the desiccation of their farms and the boom and slump of their markets. By the 1930s agricultural depression led to massive foreclosing on mortgaged lands, and when the dust-storms of eroded top-soil came the people were driven away – the 'Okies' of Woody Guthrie and John Steinbeck who fled to California. Much farmed land subsequently reverted to ranching.

Farming prospects improved during the later 1930s, when the New Deal brought better price structures. New approaches to farming practice, including dry farming (cropping only one year out of several), contour ploughing, diversification beyond basic grains, and widespread irrigation that was linked to the creation of a vast network of dams and reservoirs, all transformed the plains. Nevertheless these areas are marginal to semi-desert, remaining highly susceptible to periodic changes in precipitation over a wide area: thus a poor snowfall on the Rockies may mean insufficient water for irrigation the following summer. Coupled with worldwide fluctuations in the cereals market (on which Mid-West farmers still depend heavily), farming on the plains remains very risky.

The growth of industry: In the Gulf Coast states, petroleum provides a radically different basis for prosperity. Since the exploitation of oil reserves in the early years of the century Oklahoma, Texas and Louisiana have shifted from a dependence on agriculture (notably wheat, cattle, rice and sugar production) to the refining and petrochemical industries. Oil has transformed Dallas–Fort Worth into a major US conurbation, now larger than the twin-cities of Minneapolis–St Paul, which were once the chief urban focus of the agricultural economy of the upper Mississippi. At the meeting of the High Plains and the Rocky Mountains, Denver changed from a small elevated railhead town to a wealthy state capital (and further to a smog-ridden metropolis) in response to mineral wealth and the growth of aerospace industries.

Further north the cities of the central USA are great trading centres, dependent on local agriculture for their prosperity. Wholesaling and the transshipping of produce have been crucial since the days of the railheads, but cities like St Louis, Kansas City

and Chicago have been able to diversify far beyond their original role to become major manufacturing centres. Chicago, for example, is the main midwestern focus of the steel industries. Nowadays the interstate freeway system supplements and has partly replaced the railway networks, and air passenger traffic has increased rapidly.

From the air the landscape between the Mississippi and the Rockies is one of quilted farmlands and vast reservoirs, blending into wheatlands with extensive grasslands. Almost all the original vegetation is long gone, and most people now live in the cities, but the landscape still reflects the critical importance of agriculture past and present.

The West

The western USA is a complex mountain and plateau system, rich in scenic beauty and natural history, bordered by a rugged coast that starts in the semi-deserts of the south and ends in the rain-soaked forests of the north. Americans appreciate their far west; for long the final frontier of a youthful, expanding nation, it is still the goal of tens of thousands of immigrants each year and the vacation dream of many more: tourism is the most widespread industry.

Landscape and vegetation: Topographically the west is a land of high mountain ranges divided by high plateaus and deep valleys. The grain of the country runs north-west to south-east, at a right-angle to the crustal pressures that produced it, and

The Florida peninsula enjoys the warmest winters of the United States mainland and, with a winter rainfall minimum, the region is an ideal winter holiday resort. The lowest-ever recorded temperature is 1°C [34°F]. Summer is hot and humid with prevailing southerly winds and thundery rain. Hurricanes may affect the region in late summer and partially account for the high rainfall in September and October. Daily sunshine is 7.5–9 hours.

189

the highest mountains – the Rocky Mountains of a thousand legends – form a spectacular eastern flank. The southern Rockies of Colorado and New Mexico, remnants of an ancient granite plateau, are carved by weathering into ranges of spectacular peaks; Colorado alone has over 1,000 mountains of 3,000 m [10,000 ft] or more. Rising from dry, sandy, cactus-and-sagebrush desert, their lower slopes carry grey piñon pines and juniper scrub, with darker spruce, firs and pines above. At the timberline grow gnarled bristlecone pines, some 3,000 and more years old. Between the ranges 'parks' of mixed forest and grassland support deer and other game in summer grazing. To the south-west are the dry, colourful sandstones of the Colorado Plateau, dotted with cactus and deeply gouged by the Colorado River; to the north lies the Wyoming Basin, a rangeland of rich volcanic soil that once grazed herds of bison, and now supports sheep and cattle. The central Rocky Mountains, towering over western Wyoming, Idaho and Montana, include a number of snow-capped peaks of over 4,000 m [13,000 ft]; their eastern outliers, the Bighorn Mountains, rise 3,000 m [10,000 ft] almost sheer above the surrounding grasslands. These are the Rockies of the tourists; each year thousands of people visit the many national parks and reserves in the splendid heartland of the Cordilleras. The scenery is matchless, the forests, grasslands, alpine tundras and marshes are ecologically fascinating, and the wild animals are reasonably accessible. There is every chance for tourists to see bison, wapiti, mule deer, moose, black and brown bears, beavers and a host of smaller mammals and birds.

West of the Rockies, beyond the dry plateau scrublands of Arizona, Utah and Nevada, a double chain of mountains runs parallel to the coast from Mexico to Canada. In the arid, sun-baked south they form the desert landscape on either side of the Gulf of California. At Los Angeles they merge, parting again to form the Sierra Nevada and the Coastal Ranges that face each other across the Great Valley of central California. They rejoin in the Klamath Mountains, then continue north on either side of a broad valley – to the west as a lowly coastal chain, to the east as the magnificently forested Cascade Range. By keeping rain away from the interior, these mountains create the arid landscapes of the central Cordilleras.

Climate and agriculture: In the damp winters and dry summers of southern California the coastal mountains support semi-desert scrub; the Sierra Nevada, rising far above them, is relatively well-watered and forested. In the early days of settlement the long, bone-dry summers made farming – even ranching – difficult in the central valley of California. But the peaks of Sierra Nevada, accumulating thick blankets of snow in winter, now provide a reservoir for summer irrigation. Damming and water channelling have made the semi-deserts and dry rangelands bloom all over southern California, which now grows temperate and tropical fruits, vegetables, cotton and other thirsty crops in abundance – despite severe drought from the late 1980s.

Through northern California and Oregon, where annual rainfall is higher and summer heat less intense, the coastal mountains are clothed in forests of tall cedars and firs; notable among them are stands of giant redwood cedars, towering well over 100 m [330 ft]. In coastal Washington Douglas firs, grand firs, Sitka spruce and giant *arborvitae* are the spectacular trees, rivalling the famous giant red-

woods. Forests of giant conifers cover the Cascade Range too, providing the enormous stocks of timber on which the wealth of the American north-west was originally based.

Settlement and development: The Indian cultures of western America included hunting, fishing, seed-gathering and primitive irrigation farming. Some were semi-nomadic, others settled, living mostly in small, scattered communities. The first European colonists, spreading northwards from New Spain (Mexico) in the 1760s, made little impact on the Indians. But their forts and missions (which included San Diego, Los Angeles and San Francisco) attracted later settlers who proved more exploitative. From the 1840s pressures increased with the arrival of land-hungry Americans, both by sea and along wagon trails from the east. After a brief struggle, the south-west was sold to the USA; almost immediately the gold rushes brought new waves of adventurers and immigrants.

The Oregon coast, though visited by Spanish, British and Russian mariners in search of furs from the 16th century onwards, was first settled by American fur traders in 1811. Immigration began during the 1830s, the famous Oregon Trail across Wyoming and Idaho from the Mississippi coming into full use during the 1840s. After the establishment of the 49th parallel as the boundary between Canada and the USA, Oregon Territory (including Washington, Idaho and part of Montana) became part of the USA. Here in the north-west the forests and rangelands were equally vital to Indians and to settlers, and many battles were fought before the Indians were subdued and confined in tribal reserves.

Now the wagon trails are major highways, the staging posts, mission stations and isolated forts transformed into cities. Gold-mining, once the only kind of mining that mattered, has given way to the delving and processing of a dozen lesser metals, from copper to molybdenum. Fish-canning, food processing, electronics and aerospace are major sources of employment. The movie industry is based in Los Angeles, but this urban cluster now has a broad economy based on high-technology industries. The mountain states – once far behind in economic development – have caught up with the rest of the USA. But the enduring beauty of the western mountains remains.

Denver is at an altitude of over 1,500 m [5,000 ft]. The winters are chilly with snow, the summers pleasantly warm. The daily range is quite high; January's daily daytime average being 6°C [43°F], and the night -10°C [14°F]. Precipitation is low with a maximum in April–May, rain falling on ten days in any month. Sunshine levels are high with an average of over six hours a day in all months, with over nine hours in the summer months.

Economy

The years following the Civil War (1861–5) saw the firm establishment of the USA as the world's leading industrial society. Still attracting enormous numbers of emigrants from Europe, its agricultural and industrial output grew at unprecedented rates to the end of the century and beyond.

Agriculture: Stimulated by education, research and new, sophisticated machinery, agriculture developed into a highly mechanized industry for food production and processing. Chicago's agricultural machinery industries transformed the farmers' lives with mass-produced ploughs, tractors, seed drills, reapers and binders. Only a generation after the pioneering days, farmers found themselves tightly integrated into an economic system with such factors as mortgages, availability of spare parts, freight prices and world markets at least as crucial to the success of their efforts as climate and soil.

To the east of the western mountains farming was established in a zonal pattern which remains intact – though much modified – today, a pattern reflecting both the possibilities offered by climate and soils, and the inclinations and national origins of the settlers who first farmed the lands. In the north, from Minnesota to New England, lies a broad belt where dairy farming predominates, providing milk, butter and cheese for the industrial cities. Spring wheat is grown further west, where the climate is drier. The eastern and central states from Nebraska to Ohio form the famous corn belt – immensely productive land, formerly prairie and forest, where corn (maize) is the main crop.

Now much extended by the development of new, more tolerant strains, corn production has spread into belts on either side. No longer principally human food, except in the poorer areas of the south, corn is grown mainly for feeding to cattle and pigs, which supply the meat-packing industries. Soya beans, oats and other food and fodder crops grow in the corn belt, with wheat and dairy farming prominent along the northern border.

Southwards again, from Oklahoma and Kansas to Virginia, stretches a broad belt of mixed farming where winter wheat and corn alternate as the dominant cereals. In the warmer southern states lies the former 'cotton-belt' where cotton and tobacco were once the most widespread crops; both are now concentrated into small, highly-productive areas where mechanical handling is possible, and the bulk of the land is used for a wide variety of other crops from vegetables to fruit and peanuts.

Throughout American farming there has been a tendency to shift from small-scale operations to large, from labour-intensive to mechanized, and from low-capital to high-capital investment. The main centres of production are now concentrated in the western plains: much of the land originally farmed by the Pilgrim Fathers and other early settlers is now built over, or has reverted to attractive second-growth forest. By concentrating effort in this

These subtropical islands are cooled by the moisture-laden north-east trades. Temperatures remain high throughout the year, ranging from 26°C [79°F] in the warmest month to 22°C [72°F] in the coolest. Rainfall varies greatly throughout these mountainous islands. Mt Waialeale on Kauai has a rainfall of 12,000 mm [472 in], while Puako on the leeward side of Hawaii receives less than 250 mm [10 in]. The lofty volcanoes Mauna Kea and Mauna Loa are frequently snow-covered.

HAWAII

Most recent and most southerly of the United States, Hawaii is an archipelago of eight large and over 100 smaller volcanic islands in mid-Pacific, 3,850 km [2,400 mls] south-west of California. Only on the main island are there currently active volcanoes. High rainfall, warmth and rich soils combine to provide a wealth of year-round vegetation; originally forested, the islands are still well covered with trees and shrubs, but now provide commercial crops of sugar cane, cereals, forage for cattle, and a wide range of fruit and vegetables.

Originally settled by Polynesians and visited by James Cook in 1778, Hawaii became a port-of-call for trans-Pacific shipping and a wintering station for New England whalers, but retained its independent status until annexed by the USA in 1898. Only about 2% of its people are full-blooded Polynesians; the rest are of Chinese, Japanese, Korean, Philippine and Caucasian origins. About 80% live on the islands of Oahu, over half of them in the capital city of Honolulu. Agriculture, fishing and food processing are the main industries, though defence and tourism are also important.

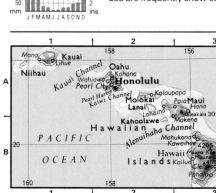

ALASKA

In 1867 the USA bought Alaska from the Tsarist government of Russia for a mere $7 million. More extensive than the south-western lands acquired from Mexico, Alaska remained a territory for over 90 years, becoming America's largest state in 1959. Geographically it forms the north-western end of the Western Cordilleras; peaks in the main Alaska Range rise to over 6,000 m [20,000 ft], and the southern 'panhandle' region is a drowned fjordland backed by ice-capped mountains. A gold rush in the 1880s stimulated the later development of other mineral resources – notably copper and, especially, oil. Alaska is the first real test of the USA's resolve to balance economic development and conservation; the six largest US national parks are in Alaska. Some farming is possible on the southern coastal lowlands; the interior tablelands are tundra-covered and rich in migrant birds and mammals.

The climate of the southern coastal regions of Alaska is drier and more extreme than might be expected from its maritime position. From November to May, winds are mainly easterly and winters are cold and dry, though the ports remain ice-free. In summer, south-westerly winds increase in frequency, giving a late summer rainfall maximum. Northwards, beyond the Alaskan Range, the climate becomes drier and bitterly cold in winter.

...vay, America has become a leading producer of meat, dairy foods, soya beans, corn, oats, wheat, barley, cotton, sugar and many other crops, both for home consumption and export.

Resources and industry: The spread of prosperity throughout a very broad spectrum of the community generated new consumer industries, to satisfy the demands of a large middle class for ever-increasing standards of comfort and material welfare. America became the pioneer of massive-scale industrial production of everything from thumb-tacks to automobiles. With almost every material needed for production available within its own boundaries, or readily gained through trading with neighbours, its mining and extractive industries have been heavily exploited from the start.

For several generations coal formed the main source of power and the basis of industrial prosperity. Anthracite from eastern Pennsylvania, good bituminous and coking coals from the Appalachians, Indiana, Illinois, Colorado and Utah are still in demand, and enormous reserves remain. Oil, first drilled in Pennsylvania in 1859, was subsequently found in several major fields underlying the midwest, the eastern and central mountain states, the Gulf of Mexico, California and Alaska. Home consumption of petroleum products has grown steadily; though the US remains a major producer, it is also by far the world's greatest consumer, and has for long been a net importer of oil. Natural gas too is found in abundance, usually in association with oil, and is moved to the main consumer areas through an elaborate, transcontinental network of pipes.

Today the USA is a major producer of iron and steel, mica, molybdenum, uranium and many other primary materials, and a major consumer and exporter of a wide range of manufactured goods. But though the USA remains the world's greatest economic power, its position was being threatened by Japan into the 1990s.

Population: The USA has one of the most diverse populations of any nation in the world. Until about 1860, with the exception of the native Indians and the southern blacks, the population was largely made up by immigrants of British (and Irish) origin, with small numbers of Spanish and French. After the Civil War, however, there was increasing immigration from the countries of central and south-eastern Europe – Italy, the Balkans, Poland, Scandinavia and Russia. This vast influx of Europeans, numbering about 30,000,000 between 1860 and 1920, was markedly different in culture and language from the established population. More recently there have been lesser influxes of Japanese, Chinese, Filipinos, Cubans and Puerto Ricans, with large numbers of Mexicans. Although there are strong influences and pressures towards Americanization, these groups have tended to establish social and cultural enclaves within US society.

The major westwards movement of population through the last century was replaced after 1900 by more subtle but no less important shifts of population away from rural areas and into the cities. Today there is further movement from the old, industrial centres and the tired, outmoded cities that flourished early in the century, away from the ageing buildings and urban dereliction, especially in the north and east, to new centres elsewhere.

The cities that gain population are mostly peripheral, on the Great Lakes and the coasts. The south is especially favoured for its warmth (particularly by retired people) and its closeness to the major source of energy in the USA – petroleum. Development of southern petrochemical and electronic industries has helped to relieve rural poverty and given new economic life, though partly at the expense of the north. However, Chicago and the eastern conurbations – New York, Boston, Philadelphia, Baltimore and Washington – still remain pre-eminent as the centres of US commercial life.

Since its earliest inception from the 13 colonies, the USA has led the world in industrial, economic and social innovation, creating problems through sheer ebullience and solving them – more or less – through inventiveness and enterprise, and with massive, wealth-bringing resources of energy and materials. The United States today continues to enjoy one of the highest material standards of living ever known, and continues to produce what may well be its greatest asset of all – a highly skilled, literate and imaginative population ■

COUNTRY: United States of America

AREA: 9,372,610 sq km [3,618,765 sq mls]

POPULATION: 249,975,000

CAPITAL (Population): Washington, D.C. (3,734,000)

GOVERNMENT: Federal republic with a bicameral legislature

ETHNIC GROUPS: White 85%, Black 12%, other races 3%

LANGUAGES: English (official), Spanish and over 30 others

RELIGIONS: Protestant 55%, Roman Catholic 30%, Jewish 3%, Eastern Orthodox 2%, Muslim 2%

NATIONAL DAY: 4 July; Declaration of Independence by Congress (1776)

CURRENCY: United States $ = 100 cents

ANNUAL INCOME PER PERSON: $21,700

SOURCE OF INCOME: Agriculture 2%, industry 33%, services 65%

MAIN PRIMARY PRODUCTS: Cereals, cotton, tobacco, soya beans, fruit, potatoes, oilseeds, sugar cane, livestock, timber, oil and natural gas, coal, copper, lead, iron ore, zinc, molybdenum, silver, gold

MAIN INDUSTRIES: Iron and steel, vehicles, chemicals, telecommunications, aeronautics and space, electronics, computers, textiles, paper, fishing, agriculture, mining

MAIN EXPORTS: Machinery and transport equipment 43%, chemicals 10%, food, beverages and tobacco 9%, crude materials 8%

MAIN EXPORT PARTNERS: Canada 24%, Japan 11%, Mexico 6%, UK 6%, Germany 5%

MAIN IMPORTS: Machinery and transport equipment 44%, clothing, footwear and manufactured articles 16%, paper, textiles, diamonds, iron and steel, non-ferrous metals 13%, mineral fuels 11%, foodstuffs 6%

MAIN IMPORT PARTNERS: Japan 21%, Canada 18%, Germany 7%, Taiwan 6%, Mexico 5%, UK 4%

EDUCATIONAL EXPENDITURE: 7% of national budget

DEFENCE: 27.1% of national budget

TOTAL ARMED FORCES: 2,124,900

TOURISM: 28,787,000 visitors per year

POPULATION DENSITY: 27 per sq km [70 per sq ml]

URBAN POPULATION: 74%

INFANT MORTALITY: 8 per 1,000 live births

LIFE EXPECTANCY: Female 80 yrs, male 73 yrs

ADULT LITERACY: 96%

PRINCIPAL CITIES (Population): New York 18,087,000 Los Angeles 14,532,000 Chicago 8,066,000 San Francisco 6,253,000 Philadelphia 5,899,000 Detroit 4,665,000 Boston 4,172,000

MEXICO

The stripes on the Mexican flag were inspired by the French tricolour and date from 1821. The emblem of the eagle, snake and cactus is based on an ancient Aztec legend about the founding of Mexico City. The design was adopted for the Olympic year, 1968.

Due to its elevation of over 2,000 m [6,500 ft], temperatures at Mexico City are some 9°C [16°F] lower than on the Gulf coast, though the annual range is about the same. But the daily range of temperature is far greater on the plateau and frost and snow are not unknown. Rainfall on the plateau is markedly seasonal and decreases northwards to under 250 mm [10 in] where the country widens. From June to September there is rain on 21–27 days per month.

The world's largest and most populous Spanish-speaking nation, Mexico has a faster-growing population than any other big country: between 1960 and 1980 it doubled, growing at an unprecedented 3.5% a year. It is thus an astonishingly young society; the average Mexican is a 17-year-old, and 75% of the people are under 30.

The combination of a stable and very high birth rate (now about 32 per thousand) and a declining and now low death rate (about five per thousand) is the main cause of this population explosion. Mexico City (population 1 million in 1930, 8.7 million in 1970, 16.6 million in 1985) is already the most populous in the Americas and estimated to be the world's largest by 2000, overtaking Tokyo and staying well ahead even of São Paulo.

Landscape and vegetation

Mexico is a land of great physical variety. The northern, emptier, half is open basin-and-range country of the Mesa Central. The land rises southwards from the Rio Grande (Rio Bravo del Norte) at the US border, averaging about 2,600 m [8,500 ft] above sea level in the middle, where it is crowned by many snow-capped volcanic cones, Orizaba (5,750 m [18,865 ft]) in the east being the highest. Though an active earthquake zone, this is the most densely settled part of the country. The Mesa Central ends equally dramatically in the west, where the Sierra Madre Occidental rise to over 4,000 m [13,120 ft], and in the east, where the Sierra Madre Oriental form a backcloth to the modest coastal plain bordering the Gulf of Mexico. In the far north-west is the isolated, 1,220 km [760 ml] mountain-cored peninsula of Baja California.

Mountains dominate southern Mexico, broken only by the low, narrow isthmus of Tehuantepec, which is crossed by railways and roads linking the Gulf ports with Salina Cruz on the Pacific. The flat, low-lying limestone Yucatan peninsula in the southeast is an exception in a country where half the land is over 1,000 m [3,280 ft] above sea level, and a quarter has slopes of over 25 degrees. Deserts characterize the north-west, and tropical rainforest is the natural vegetation of Tehuantepec; over 70% of the country is arid or semi-arid and irrigation is mandatory for agriculture.

Economy

Agriculture occupies half the population but contributes less than a third of the economic product contributed by manufacturing, with metals also important – the country is the world's leading producer of silver. Fresh petroleum discoveries during the 1970s from massive reserves in Tabasco and Campeche have turned Mexico into the world's fourth biggest producer, much of it exported to the USA, but the economy is now very diverse with food processing, textiles, forestry and tourism all making significant progress. Only an estimated 15–20% of the nation's mineral wealth has been exploited, with precious metals comprising almost half the value of total known mineral reserves.

While the century after independence in 1821 was characterized by political chaos, climaxing in the violent revolution of 1910–21, the post-revolutionary period was steady by Latin American standards, with the PRI in power for more than six decades from 1929 and instituting crucial land reforms in the 1930s. The economy has been dominated by this

COUNTRY: United Mexican States

AREA: 1,958,200 sq km [756,061 sq mls]

POPULATION: 86,154,000

CAPITAL (Population): Mexico City (18,748,000)

GOVERNMENT: Federal republic

ETHNIC GROUPS: Mestizo 55%, Amerindian 29%, European

LANGUAGES: Spanish (official) 92%, and 59 native dialects

RELIGIONS: Roman Catholic 93%, Protestant 3%

NATIONAL DAY: 16 September

CURRENCY: Peso = 100 centavos

ANNUAL INCOME PER PERSON: $2,490

SOURCE OF INCOME: Agriculture 9%, industry 35%, services 56%

MAIN PRIMARY PRODUCTS: Wheat, maize, coffee, sorghum, cattle, sugar, cotton, silver, copper, sulphur, coal, lead, iron, gold, oil, natural gas

MAIN INDUSTRIES: Oil refining, natural gas, mining, agriculture, aluminium, vehicles, textiles, pottery

MAIN EXPORTS: Crude petroleum 38%, engines and vehicle parts 24%, forestry products 15%, energy products 8%, machinery 3%, coffee 2%, shrimps 2%

MAIN EXPORT PARTNERS: USA 64%, Japan 6%, Germany 3%

MAIN IMPORTS: Machinery and equipment 32%, vehicles and parts 23%, industrial materials 18%, other consumer goods 11%, foodstuffs 6%

MAIN IMPORT PARTNERS: USA 62%, Japan 6%, Germany 6%

EDUCATIONAL EXPENDITURE: 12% of national budget

DEFENCE: 1.4% of national budget

TOTAL ARMED FORCES: 141,500

TOURISM: 5,407,000 visitors per year

ROADS: 225,684 km [151,053 mls]

RAILWAYS: 19,906 km [12,441 mls]

POPULATION DENSITY: 44 per sq km [114 per sq ml]

URBAN POPULATION: 73%

POPULATION GROWTH: 2.2% per year

INFANT MORTALITY: 41 per 1,000 live births

LIFE EXPECTANCY: Female 74 yrs, male 67 yrs

POPULATION PER DOCTOR: 1,242

ADULT LITERACY: 90%

PRINCIPAL CITIES (Population): Mexico City 18,748,000 Guadalajara 2,587,000 Monterrey 2,335,000 Puebla de Zaragoza 1,218,000

PRE-COLUMBIAN CIVILIZATIONS

The pre-Columbian civilizations of Central America flourished for centuries before the Spanish conquest and this heritage plays a strong role in fostering Mexican national identity today.

The Olmecs, the classical cultures of Teotihuacan, the Zapotecs and the Toltecs all left remarkable architectural monuments in the Mexican landscape, but the two outstanding cultures were those of the Maya and the Aztecs. The Maya civilization was the most brilliant, flourishing from the 3rd to the 10th centuries from the Yucatan to Honduras.

The Aztec empire was at its height when Mexico succumbed to the Spanish *conquistadores* in 1519. Originally an insignificantly nomadic tribe, the Aztecs invaded central Mexico in the 13th century and founded their island-city of Tenochtitlán in Lake Texcoco in 1325. During the 15th century they conquered neighbouring states and drew tribute from an empire extending from the Pacific to the Gulf of Mexico and into northern Central America.

Many of the great pre-Columbian centres survive as archaeological sites today. The stepped pyramid and rectangular courtyard are particularly characteristic.

egime since oil was nationalized in 1938, enjoying uge growth in the 1970s, when living standards ose considerably, but running into massive debt crises in the 1980s.

Mexico has since pursued the idea of a trading rea with Canada and the US, but rural-urban migration and high unemployment – probably around 40% in many cities – remain the biggest domestic problems. Above all, there is the emigration across the world's busiest border: hundreds of thousands of Mexicans cross into the USA each year, many of them staying as illegal immigrants ■

BELIZE

The badge shows loggers bearing axes and oars, tools employed in the industry responsible for developing Belize. The flag is commonly displayed without the badge – a simple white disc on a royal blue background.

COUNTRY: Belize

AREA: 22,960 sq km [8,865 sq mls]

POPULATION: 188,000

CAPITAL (Population): Belmopan (4,500)

GOVERNMENT: Constitutional monarchy with a bicameral National Assembly

ETHNIC GROUPS: Creole 40%, Mestizo (Spanish Maya) 33%, Mayan Indian 9%, Garifuna (Black Carib Indian) 8%, White 4%, East Indian 2%

LANGUAGES: English (official); 'Creole' spoken, Spanish 32%, Indian and Carib languages 28%

RELIGIONS: Roman Catholic 62%, Protestant 29%

NATIONAL DAY: 21 September; Independence Day (1981)

CURRENCY: Belize $ = 100 cents

ANNUAL INCOME PER PERSON: $1,970

POPULATION DENSITY: 8 per sq km [21 per sq ml]

LIFE EXPECTANCY: Female 75 yrs, male 68 yrs

ADULT LITERACY: 93%

Larger than El Salvador but with only 3.5% of its population, Belize is a sparsely populated enclave on the Caribbean coast of Central America. The northern half is low-lying swamp, the south a high corrugated plateau, while offshore lies the world's second biggest coral reef.

Formerly British Honduras, it enjoyed a boom after independence, with processing of citrus fruits and tourism helping to allay the dependency on timber, bananas and sugar, though the latter still accounts for 30% of export earnings. There is also the prospect of an end to the nagging dispute with Guatemala, which initially claimed all of Belizean territory. Over a quarter of the population lives in Belize City, replaced as the capital by Belmopan in 1970 following hurricane damage ■

GUATEMALA

The simple design of Guatemala's flag was adopted in 1871, but its origins date back to the Central American Federation (1825–39) formed with Honduras, El Salvador, Nicaragua and Costa Rica after the break from Spanish rule in 1821.

GUATEMALA

Temperature

Precipitation
1316mm
52in

J F M A M J J A S O N D

Its position between seas and with a mountainous spine gives a variety of climates. In the lowlands, temperatures are between 25–30°C [77-86°F], but at Guatemala City (1,500 m [5,000 ft]), the extremes are 17°C [63°F] in January and 22°C [72°F] in May. On the Caribbean coast, with the trade winds always blowing onshore, rainfall is high in all months. Rainfall is also high on the Pacific slopes, but inland there is a dry season, almost arid, in January and February.

COUNTRY: Republic of Guatemala

AREA: 108,890 sq km [42,042 sq mls]

POPULATION: 9,197,000

CAPITAL (Population): Guatemala City (2,000,000)

GOVERNMENT: Republic with a unicameral legislature

ETHNIC GROUPS: Mayaquiche Indian 55%, Ladino (Mestizo) 42%

LANGUAGES: Spanish (official) 40%, 20 Indian dialects

RELIGIONS: Roman Catholic 75%, Protestant 23%

NATIONAL DAY: 15 September; Independence Day

CURRENCY: Guatemalean quetzel = 100 centavos

ANNUAL INCOME PER PERSON: $900

MAIN PRIMARY PRODUCTS: Petroleum, iron, lead, nickel

MAIN EXPORTS: Coffee, bananas, sugar, cardamom

MAIN IMPORTS: Mineral fuels, chemicals, machinery and transport equipment, manufactured goods

DEFENCE: 15% of national budget

POPULATION DENSITY: 84 per sq km [219 per sq ml]

LIFE EXPECTANCY: Female 67 yrs, male 62 yrs

ADULT LITERACY: 55%

Most populous of the Central American countries, Guatemala's Pacific coastline, two and a half times longer than the Caribbean coast, is backed by broad alluvial plains, formed of material washed down from the towering volcanoes that front the ocean. These include extinct Tajumulco (4,217 m [13,830 ft]), the highest peak in Central America.

The plains have been used for commercial-scale agriculture only since the 1950s, when malaria was brought under control and roads were built; cattle and cotton are now more important than the traditional banana crop. Lower mountain slopes, up to about 1,500 m [5,000 ft], yield most of the country's best coffee.

While Indians are in the majority, society and government are run on autocratic, often repressive lines by the mestizos of mixed Indian and European stock. The Indians were the principal victims of the army's indiscriminate campaign against left-wing URNG guerrillas in the early 1980s – the acceleration of a policy in place since the 1950s. The 'low-

intensity' civil war that followed was still smouldering when a UN-mediated ceasefire became operative in neighbouring El Salvador in February 1992. This influence, allied to the government's sudden recognition of Belizean independence in 1991 (Guatemala had claimed the entire territory), would benefit a nation whose 'defence' spending takes 15% of the budget, and whose human rights record is appalling. As in El Salvador, Washington's stance is vitally important: in keeping with all the Central American republics (except Nicaragua) the US is crucial to the economy – in Guatemala's case accounting for more than 40% of trade ■

NORTH AND CENTRAL AMERICA

HONDURAS

Officially adopted in 1949, the flag of Honduras is based on that of the Central American Federation (*see Guatemala*). Honduras left the organization in 1838, but in 1866 added the five stars to the flag to express a hope for a future federation.

On the northern coast the average temperatures are between 26–28°C [79–82°F]. At Tegucigalpa (1,000 m [3,250 ft]), these are reduced to 20–24°C [68–75°F], and on the higher land are even lower. The diurnal temperature range can be as much as 15°C [27°F]. The sheltered mountain valleys receive a moderate rainfall of 1,000–1,500 mm [39–59 in], but the coasts and mountains get in excess of 2,000 mm [79 in]. The wet season is May–October.

Second largest of the Central American countries, Honduras has a small population: indeed, it is five times as large as neighbouring El Salvador – its opponent in the 'Soccer War' of 1969, triggered by illegal Salvadorean immigration – but has fewer people.

Some 80% of Honduras is mountainous, with peaks of more than 2,500 m [8,000 ft] in the west. The mountain ranges are metalliferous: lodes of gold drew the first Spanish *conquistadores* to found Tegucigalpa, the capital, in 1524, and silver is still an important export. Mining contributes more to the economy than it does in any other Central American state. However, the state has a short 124 km [80 ml] frontage on the Pacific in the Gulf of Fonseca, and

the limited lowlands around the Gulf form some of the prime cotton lands of the country.

Most of Honduras has a seasonal climate, relatively dry between November and May. Traditional cattle-ranching, employing cowboys, is as much in evidence as agriculture. The aromatic pine forests of the east are being consumed by new paper mills on the hot, rain-soaked Caribbean coast. The lower alluvium-filled valleys of the rivers draining into the Caribbean have been reclaimed and the forest replaced by orderly banana plantations.

Honduras was the original 'banana republic' – the world's leading exporter in the interwar years. Today it remains an important crop, accounting for nearly a quarter of exports, with production dom-

inated by two US companies, though coffee (40% is now the largest earner. Dependent on these cash crops, it is the region's least industrialized country.

It is also the most reliant on the US for trade – quite a claim in Central America: 56% of its imports and 49% of its exports are with the Americans. Aid from the US is crucial, partly in return for service rendered; strategically important to Washington, Honduras allowed the US-backed 'Contra' rebels to operate from its territory against the Communist revolutionary Sandinista government in Nicaragua throughout the 1980s, and in 1990 – following the Sandinista's defeat in the elections – signed a peace agreement with the pro-American government of Violeta Chamorro. Less enthusiastically, the Honduran Army also collaborated with US efforts to defeat left-wing guerillas in El Salvador.

After a short civil war in the 1920s a series of military regimes ruled Honduras until 1980, when civilians took over; the country has since had a series of democratically elected pro-American centre-right governments, but with the military retaining considerable influence ■

COUNTRY: Republic of Honduras
AREA: 112,090 sq km [43,278 sq mls]
POPULATION: 5,105,000
CAPITAL (Population): Tegucigalpa (605,000)
GOVERNMENT: Republic with one legislative house
ETHNIC GROUPS: Mestizo 90%, Amerindian 7%, Black (including Black Carib) 2%, White 1%
LANGUAGES: Spanish (official), Black Carib (Garifuna), English Creole, Miskito
RELIGIONS: Roman Catholic 97%
NATIONAL DAY: 15 September; Independence Day (1821)
CURRENCY: Honduran lempira = 100 centavos
POPULATION DENSITY: 46 per sq km [118 per sq ml]

EL SALVADOR

The original flag, the 'Stars and Stripes', was replaced in 1912 by the current one. The blue and white stripes are a common feature of the flags of Central American countries who gained their independence from Spain at the same time in 1821.

COUNTRY: Republic of El Salvador
AREA: 21,040 sq km [8,124 sq mls]
POPULATION: 5,252,000
CAPITAL (Population): San Salvador (973,000)
GOVERNMENT: Republic with a unicameral legislature
ETHNIC GROUPS: Mestizo 89%, Indian 9%, White 1%
LANGUAGES: Spanish (official)
RELIGIONS: Christian (Roman Catholic 92%)
NATIONAL DAY: 15 September; Independence Day (1821)
CURRENCY: Colón = 100 centavos
ANNUAL INCOME PER PERSON: $1,100
POPULATION DENSITY: 250 per sq km [647 per sq ml]
LIFE EXPECTANCY: Female 69 yrs, male 64 yrs
ADULT LITERACY: 72%

The only Central American country without a Caribbean coast, El Salvador is also the smallest and the most densely populated; pressure on agricultural land, combined with civil war, has led to widespread emigration. The Pacific coastal plain is narrow and backed by a volcanic range averaging about 1,200 m [4,000 ft] in altitude. El Salvador has over 20 volcanoes, some still active, and crater lakes occupying a fertile central plain 400 to 800 m [1,300 to 2,600 ft] above sea level. Urban and rural populations in this belt account for 60% of the total.

This fertile zone also produces 90% of the coffee and tobacco, and most of the maize and sugar – the foundations of the agricultural economy, with coffee usually accounting for over half the total value of

exports. The towns are centres of manufacturing for the domestic market. Inland the frontier with Honduras is marked by mountain ranges which reach heights of 2,000 m [6,560 ft]; previously forested and empty, they are now attracting migrants desperate for agricultural land.

El Salvador was plagued by conflict from the early 1970s and by full-blown civil war from 1980 when the political left joined revolutionary guerrillas against the US-backed extreme right-wing government. During the next 12 years, more than 75,000 people were killed (most of them civilians) and hundreds of thousands were made homeless as the regime received $4 billion in aid from the US in abetting the 55,000-strong Salvadorean Army and notorious death squads. After 19 months of UN-mediated talks the two sides agreed complicated terms at the end of 1991 and there appeared to be real prospects of peace for a country left in disarray: unemployment, for example, stood at more than 50% of the workforce ■

NICARAGUA

Nicaragua's flag, adopted in 1908, is identical to that of the Central American Federation (*see Guatemala*) to which it once belonged. Except for a difference in the shading of the blue and the motif, it is also the same as the flag of El Salvador.

COUNTRY: Republic of Nicaragua
AREA: 130,000 sq km [50,193 sq mls]
POPULATION: 3,871,000
CAPITAL (Population): Managua (682,000)
GOVERNMENT: Multiparty republic
ETHNIC GROUPS: Mestizo 69%, White 14%, Black 8%
LANGUAGES: Spanish (official), Indian, Creole
RELIGIONS: Christian (Roman Catholic 87%)
NATIONAL DAY: 15 September; Independence Day
CURRENCY: New córdoba = 100 centavos
ANNUAL INCOME PER PERSON: $800
MAIN PRIMARY PRODUCTS: Silver, gold, gypsum, lead
MAIN INDUSTRIES: Agriculture, mining, textiles
MAIN EXPORTS: Coffee, cotton, sugar and bananas
MAIN IMPORTS: Agricultural goods, oil products
POPULATION DENSITY: 30 per sq km [77 per sq ml]
LIFE EXPECTANCY: Female 68 yrs, male 65 yrs
ADULT LITERACY: 87%

Largest and least densely populated of the Central American countries, Nicaragua's eastern half is almost empty. The Caribbean plain is extensive, and the coast is a mixture of lagoons, sandy beaches and river deltas with shallow water and sand-bars offshore. With over 750 cm [300 in] of rain in some years, it is forested and rich in a tropical fauna including crocodiles, turtles, deer, pumas, jaguars and monkeys. Cut off from the populous west of Nicaragua, it was for two centuries the British protectorate of the Miskito Coast, with Bluefields (San Juan del Norte) as the largest settlement.

Inland the plain gives way gradually to mountain ranges broken by basins and fertile valleys. In the west and south they overlook a great depression which runs from the Gulf of Fonseca south-eastwards and contains Lakes Managua and Nicaragua. Nicaragua (8,264 sq km [3,191 sq mls]) is the largest lake in Central America; though only 20 km [12.5 mls] from the Pacific, it drains to the Caribbean by the navigable San Juan River and formed an important route across the isthmus before the Panama Canal was built. The capital city,

Managua, and other major centres are here, as is much of Nicaragua's industrial development; so are the cotton fields and coffee plantations that provide the country's chief cash crops and exports (23% and 36% respectively).

Forty volcanoes, many active, rise above the lakes; San Cristobál (1,745 m [5,725 ft]) is the highest, still-smoking Momotombo the most spectacular. Earthquakes are common and Managua was virtually destroyed in 1931 and 1972.

Nicaragua has been in a state of civil war almost continuously since the 1960s. In 1979, after a 17-year campaign, the long domination of the corrupt Somoza family (who controlled 40% of the economy) was ended by a popular uprising led by the Sandanista National Liberation Front (FSLN), who went on to win democratic power in 1985. Meanwhile, the US trained and supplied Contra guerrillas from bases in Honduras and imposed a trade embargo, pushing Nicaragua into increasing dependence on Cuba and the Soviet Union.

A ceasefire agreed in 1989 was followed the next year by electoral defeat for Daniel Ortega's Sandanistas at the hands of the US-backed coalition of Violeta Chamorro. The win was due mainly to the state of the economy, which had been reduced to crisis point by a combination of US sanctions and government incompetence; but while the two sides were forced into working uneasily together to try and put the country back on its feet with the benefit of conditional US aid, fighting frequently broke out between former Contra rebels and ex-Sandanistas, notably away from the capital ■

COSTA RICA

Dating from 1848, Costa Rica's national flag is based on the blue/white/blue sequence of the flag of the Central American Federation (*see Guatemala*), but with an additional red stripe in the centre.

San José is just over 1,000 m [3,250 ft], and its annual average temperature is 20°C [68°F]; on the Pacific or Caribbean coasts this rises to over 27°C [81°F]. December and January are the coolest months, and May the warmest. The north-east trade winds blow all the year along the Caribbean coast bringing high rainfall in excess of 3,000 mm [118 in]. This is lower in the mountains and along the Pacific coast. There is a marked dry season from December to April.

In many ways the exception among the Central American republics, Costa Rica ('rich coast') has become the most European of the republics of the isthmus, with the best educational standards, a long life expectancy, the most democratic and stable system of government, the highest per capita gross domestic product, and the least disparity between the poor and the rich. The abolition of the armed forces in 1948 – it has only 750 civil guards – meant there has been no familiar military regime and its neutral stance has enabled the country to play the role of broker in many regional disputes.

Three mountain ranges form the skeleton of the country. In the south-east the Talamanca ranges rise to 3,837 m [12,585 ft] in Chirripo Grande; further north and west the Central Cordillera includes volcanic Irazú (3,432 m [11,260 ft]) and Poas (2,705 m [8,875 ft]), both active in recent decades; Miravalles (2,020 m [6,627 ft]) is one of four active volcanoes in the Cordillera de Guanacaste.

Coffee grown in the interior has been a corner-stone of the economy since 1850; in this century bananas have become a second, and together they supply nearly half of Costa Rica's overseas earnings. The capital, San José, stands in the fertile Valle Central, in the economic heartland of the country. Drier Guanacaste, in the far north-west, is an important cattle-raising region ■

COUNTRY: Republic of Costa Rica
AREA: 51,100 sq km [19,730 sq mls]
POPULATION: 2,994,000
CAPITAL (Population): San José (284,000)
GOVERNMENT: Multiparty republic
ETHNIC GROUPS: White 87%, Mestizo 7%
LANGUAGES: Spanish (official), Creole, Indian
RELIGIONS: Christian (Roman Catholic 92%)
NATIONAL DAY: 15 September; Independence Day (1821)
CURRENCY: Costa Rican colón = 100 céntimos
MAIN PRIMARY PRODUCTS: Gold, salt, haematite
ANNUAL INCOME PER PERSON: $1,910
DEFENCE: No armed forces since 1948
POPULATION DENSITY: 59 per sq km [152 per sq ml]
LIFE EXPECTANCY: Female 78 yrs, male 73 yrs
ADULT LITERACY: 94%

SAN JOSE
Temperature
Precipitation 1798mm 71in

NORTH AND CENTRAL AMERICA

CUBA

First designed in 1849, Cuba's flag, the 'Lone Star' banner, was not officially adopted until the island finally gained its independence from Spain in 1901. The red triangle represents the Cuban people's bloody struggle for independence.

Cuba is encircled by the warm ocean current which is the beginning of what becomes the Gulf Stream. It is just within the tropics and has high temperatures: 22°C [72°F] in January and 28°C [82°F] in August. The highest temperature ever recorded is 36°C [97°F] and the lowest 10°C [50°F]. Rainfall is heavier on the northern side of the island and falls in a marked wet season from May to October. That season can also experience hurricanes.

As large as all the other Caribbean islands put together, Cuba is only 193 km [120 mls] across at its widest, but stretches for over 1,200 km [750 mls] from the Gulf of Mexico to the Windward Passage. Though large, it is the least mountainous of all the Greater Antilles.

Sugar cane remains the outstandingly important cash crop, as it has done throughout the century, and Cuba is the world's third largest producer behind the giants of Brazil and India. It uses over 1 million hectares (2.5 million acres), more than half the island country's cultivated land, and accounts for more than 75% of exports.

Before the 1959 Revolution the cane was grown on large estates, many of them owned by US companies or individuals, but after these were nationalized the focus of production shifted eastwards to Guayabal, with the USSR and Eastern European countries replacing the USA as the main market. Cattle raising and rice cultivation have also been encouraged to help diversify the economy, while Cuba is also a significant exporter of minerals.

A colony until 1898, Cuba took on many Spanish immigrants during the early years of independence. Since the Revolution that deposed the right-wing dictator Fulgencio Batista and brought Fidel Castro to power in 1959 – when 600,000 people fled the island, many of them to Florida – rural development has been fostered in a relatively successful bid to make the quality of life more homogeneous throughout the island. Havana, the chief port and capital, was particularly depopulated.

Cuba's relationship with the US, who secured its independence from Spain but bolstered the corrupt regimes before the Revolution, has always been crucial. In 1961, US-backed 'exiles' attempted to invade at the Bay of Pigs, and relations worsened still further the following year when the attempted installation of Soviet missiles on Cuban soil almost led to global war. A close ally of the USSR, Castro has encouraged left-wing revolutionary movements in Latin America and aided Marxist governments in Africa, while emerging as a Third World leader.

The rapid changes in Eastern Europe and the USSR from 1989 to 1991 have left Cuba isolated as a hardline Marxist state in the Western Hemisphere and the disruption of trade has severely affected the economy of a country heavily dependent on subsidized Soviet oil and aid. This undermines Castro's considerable social achievements, but a new Cuba is almost inevitable given the new wind of change in the Socialist world – and his advancing years. Early in 1992, for example, Cuban state radio called for an end to the 30-year-old trade embargo imposed by the US government ■

COUNTRY: Republic of Cuba
AREA: 110,860 sq km [42,803 sq mls]
POPULATION: 10,609,000
CAPITAL (Population): Havana (2,059,000)
GOVERNMENT: Socialist republic
ETHNIC GROUPS: White 66%, Mulatto 22%, Black 12%
LANGUAGES: Spanish (official)
RELIGIONS: Roman Catholic 40%, Protestant 3%
NATIONAL DAY: 1 January; Day of Liberation (1959)
CURRENCY: Peso = 100 centavos
ANNUAL INCOME PER PERSON: $3,000
MAIN PRIMARY PRODUCTS: Sugar cane, nickel, cobalt, copper, chrome, tobacco, citrus fruits, rice
MAIN INDUSTRIES: Agriculture, mining, food processing, tobacco, fishing, textiles, chemicals
DEFENCE: 10% of national budget
POPULATION DENSITY: 96 per sq km [248 per sq ml]
LIFE EXPECTANCY: Female 77 yrs, male 73 yrs
ADULT LITERACY: 91%
PRINCIPAL CITIES (Population): Havana 2,059,000 Santiago de Cuba 380,000 Camagüey 275,000

PANAMA

The Panamanian flag dates from the break with Colombia in 1903. Blue stands for the Conservative Party, red for the Liberal Party and white for the hope of peace. The red star represents law and order and the blue star 'public honesty'.

Less than 60 km [37 mls] wide at its narrowest point, the isthmus of Panama not only links Central and South America but also, via its famous Canal, the Atlantic and Pacific Oceans. Most of the country, including some 750 offshore islands, lies below 700 m [2,300 ft], sweltering daily in tropical heat and high humidity, with heavy downpours marking the May–December rainy season.

Many Panamanians live within about 20 km [12 mls] of the Canal Zone, a quarter of them in the capital city and 80% of the country's GDP originates here. This includes revenues from free trade, the open-registry merchant fleet (some 12,000 ships), and 'offshore' finance facilities. With exports of bananas (25% of total), shrimps (19%) and mahogany, not to mention substantial US aid, these have given Panama the highest standard of living in Central America – though Western confidence in

the economy took a dive after the crisis of 1989, when the US invaded to depose General Noriega.

The Panama Canal is 82 km [51 mls] long from deep water at either end, 65 km [40 mls] long from coast to coast. Three sets of locks at each end lift vessels to the elevated central section 26 m [85 ft] above sea level, which includes Gatun Lake and the 13 km [8 ml] Gaillard Cut through the continental divide.

Though an American-built railway crossed the isthmus in 1855, it was a French company under Ferdinand de Lesseps that began cutting the Canal in 1880, but engineering problems and deaths from disease stopped operations after ten years. In 1903 the province of Panama declared independence from Colombia and granted the USA rights in perpetuity over a 16 km [10 ml] wide Canal Zone. Work on the present Canal began a year later, and it was finally opened for shipping in 1914.

In 1980 there were some 13,000 transits through the Canal – over 36 ships per day – carrying twice the total cargo of 1960. Now running close to capacity, the Canal cannot take fully-laden ships of over about 80,000 tonnes, and an alternative Panama Seaway is under discussion. From 1979 sovereignty of the Canal Zone was restored to Panama, and the Canal itself reverts at the end of the century ■

COUNTRY: Republic of Panama
AREA: 77,080 sq km [29,761 sq mls]
POPULATION: 2,418,000
CAPITAL (Population): Panama City (625,000)
GOVERNMENT: Multiparty republic
ETHNIC GROUPS: Mestizo and Mulatto 59%, Black 14%, White 12%, Amerindian 7%
LANGUAGES: Spanish (official)
RELIGIONS: Roman Catholic 89%, Protestant 6%, Muslim 4%
NATIONAL DAY: 3 November; Independence Day (1821)
CURRENCY: Balboa = 100 cents
ANNUAL INCOME PER PERSON: $1,830
LIFE EXPECTANCY: Female 75 yrs, male 71 yrs
ADULT LITERACY: 88%

JAMAICA

Jamaica's distinctive flag dates from independence from Britain in 1962. The gold stands for the country's natural resources and sunshine, the green for its agriculture and hope for the future and black for the nation's hardships.

KINGSTON

Precipitation
801 mm
32 in

The mountains of eastern Jamaica exert a strong influence on rainfall. Kingston, on the south coast and in the lee of the mountains, has 800 mm [31 in] and a dry season from December to April, while Port Antonio, on the windward north-east coast, has 3,500 mm [138 in] and no dry season. The annual total is very variable, mainly due to the irregularity of hurricane rains in August and September. At Kingston, rain falls on about 55 days per year, with sunshine levels at around eight hours per day.

Third largest of the Caribbean islands and the most populous in the English-speaking 'West Indies', Jamaica has a central range culminating in Blue Mountain Peak (2,256 m [7,402 ft]), from which it declines westwards. Called Xaymaca ('land of wood and water') by the Arawak Indians, half the country lies above 300 m [1,000 ft] and moist south-east trade winds bring rain to the mountains.

The 'cockpit country' in the north-west of the island is an inaccessible limestone area of steep broken ridges and isolated basins. These offered a refuge to escaped slaves prior to emancipation in 1838. Elsewhere the limestone has weathered to

bauxite, an ore of aluminium. Bauxite overlies a quarter of the island; mined since 1952, most is exported as ore, about one-fifth as alumina, making Jamaica the world's third producer and accounting for over 38% of exports. Tourism and bauxite production, Jamaica's two most important industries, comprise almost two-thirds of foreign earnings.

Sugar, a staple product since the island became British in 1655, first made Jamaica a prized imperial possession, and the African slaves imported to work the plantations were the forefathers of much of the present population. But the plantations disappeared and the sugar market collapsed in the 19th century;

today sugar contributes only about 10% of the country's foreign earnings.

Michael Manley's democratic socialist experiment in the 1970s was followed by a modest growth in the 1980s; but unemployment and underemployment are currently rife, and many Jamaicans leave their country each year to work abroad, mainly in the USA, Canada and the UK ■

COUNTRY: Jamaica
AREA: 10,990 sq km [4,243 sq mls]
POPULATION: 2,420,000
CAPITAL (Population): Kingston (525,000)
GOVERNMENT: Constitutional monarchy
ETHNIC GROUPS: Black 76%, Afro-European 15%, East Indian and Afro-East Indian 3%, White 3%
LANGUAGES: English (official), English Creole, Hindi, Chinese, Spanish
RELIGIONS: Protestant 70%, Roman Catholic 8%
NATIONAL DAY: 7 August; Independence Day (1962)
CURRENCY: Jamaican $ = 100 cents
ANNUAL INCOME PER PERSON: $1,510
MAIN PRIMARY PRODUCTS: Bauxite, sugar, bananas
MAIN INDUSTRIES: Mining, agriculture, tourism, sugar

COPYRIGHT. GEORGE PHILIP LTD.

HAITI

Although the colours, first used in 1803, are said to represent the country's African heritage, the design of Haiti's flag derives from that of France, to which it once belonged. The present version was first used in 1843 and restored in 1986.

Port-au-Prince is in a relatively sheltered part of the island, but elsewhere altitude and aspect affect the climate. The temperatures along the coast are high with little annual variation from the maxima, July–August. The island is always under the influence of the north-east trade winds which bring rainfall totals of over 2,500 mm [98 in] along the northern coasts. These figures are lower in the south and west. Hurricanes can strike between August and November.

Occupying the western third of Hispaniola, the Caribbean's second largest island, Haiti is mainly mountainous with a long, indented coast. Most of the country is centred around the Massif du Nord, with the narrow Massif de la Hotte forming the southern peninsula. In the deep bight between the two lies the chief port and capital, Port-au-Prince. Haiti has few natural resources and most of the workforce is engaged on the land, with coffee the only significant cash crop and accounting for 17% of the country's meagre exports. Two-thirds of the population, however, lives at or below the poverty line, subsisting on agriculture and fishing.

Ceded to France in 1697, a century before the rest of Hispaniola, Haiti developed as a sugar-producing colony. Once the richest part of the Caribbean, it is now the poorest nation in the Western Hemisphere. For nearly two centuries, since a slave revolt made it the world's first independent black state in 1804, it has been bedevilled by military coups, government corruption, ethnic violence and political instability, including a period of US control from 1915 to 1934.

The appalling regime of François Duvalier ('Papa Doc'), president from 1957 and declaring himself 'President for Life' in 1964, was especially brutal, but that of his son Jean-Claude ('Baby Doc'), president from 1971, was little better; both used their murderous private militia, the Tontons Macoutes, to conduct a reign of terror. In 1986 popular unrest finally forced Duvalier to flee the country, and the military took over. After another period of political chaos and economic disaster – not helped by the suspension of US aid between 1987 and 1989 – the country's first multiparty elections were held in December 1990, putting in office a radical Catholic priest, Father Jean-Bertrand Aristide, on a platform of sweeping reforms. But with the partisans of the old regime, including the Tontons Macoutes, still powerful, the military took control in September 1991, forcing Aristide to flee (to Venezuela) after only seven

COUNTRY: Republic of Haiti
AREA: 27,750 sq km [10,714 sq mls]
POPULATION: 6,486,000
CAPITAL (Population): Port-au-Prince (1,144,000)
GOVERNMENT: Military regime (constitution suspended)
ETHNIC GROUPS: Black 95%, Mulatto 5%
LANGUAGES: French (official) 10%, Haitian Creole 88%
RELIGIONS: Christian (Roman Catholic 75%), Voodoo
CURRENCY: Gourde = 100 centimes
ANNUAL INCOME PER PERSON: $370

months of government. Tens of thousands of exiles followed in the ensuing weeks, heading mainly for the US naval base at Guantánamo Bay, in Cuba, in the face of a wave of savage repression, but the American government returned the 'boat people' to Port-au-Prince. Military intervention (as in Panama in 1989) was considered by the Organization of American States, but they instead imposed a trade embargo, inflicting further hardship on an already impoverished Haitian population ∎

DOMINICAN REPUBLIC

The Dominican Republic's flag dates from 1844, when the country finally gained its independence from both Spain and Haiti. The design developed from Haiti's flag, adding a white cross and rearranging the position of the colours.

COUNTRY: Dominican Republic
AREA: 48,730 sq km [18,815 sq mls]
POPULATION: 7,170,000
CAPITAL (Population): Santo Domingo (1,313,000)
GOVERNMENT: Multiparty republic
ETHNIC GROUPS: Mulatto 73%, White 16%, Black 11%
LANGUAGES: Spanish (official)
RELIGIONS: Christian (Roman Catholic 93%)
CURRENCY: Dominican peso = 100 centavos

Second largest of the Caribbean nations in both area and population, the Dominican Republic shares the island of Hispaniola with Haiti, occupying the eastern two-thirds. Of the steep-sided mountains that dominate the island, the country includes the northern Cordillera Septentrional, the huge Cordillera Central (rising to Pico Duarte, at 3,175 m [10,417 ft] the highest peak in the Caribbean), and the southern Sierra de Bahoruco. Between them and to the east lie fertile valleys and lowlands, including the Vega Real and the coastal plains where the main sugar plantations are found. Typical of the area, the Republic is hot and humid close to sea level, while cooler conditions prevail in the mountains; rainfall is heavy, especially in the north-east.

Columbus 'discovered' the island and its Amerindian population (soon to be decimated) on 5 December 1492; the city of Santo Domingo, now the capital and chief port, was founded by his brother Bartholomew four years later and is the oldest in the Americas. For long a Spanish colony, Hispaniola was initially the centrepiece of their empire but later it was to become its poor relation. In 1795 it became French, then Spanish again in 1809, but in 1821 (then called Santo Domingo) it won independence. Haiti held the territory from 1822 to 1844, when on restoring sovereignty it became the Dominican Republic. Growing American influence culminated in occupation from 1916 to 1924, followed by a long period of corrupt dictatorship. Since

a bitter war was ended by US military intervention in 1965, a precarious fledgling democracy has survived violent elections under the watchful eye of Washington.

In the 1980s, growth in industry (exploiting vast hydroelectric potential), mining (nickel, bauxite, gold and silver) and tourism have augmented the traditional agricultural economy based on sugar (still a fifth of exports), coffee, cocoa, tobacco and fruit. This highly Americanized Hispanic society is, however, far from stable ∎

TURKS AND CAICOS ISLANDS

A group of 30 islands (eight of them inhabited), lying at the eastern end of the Grand Bahama Bank, north of Haiti, the Turks and Caicos are composed of low, flat limestone terrain with scrub, marsh and swamp providing little agriculture over their 430 sq km [166 sq mls]. Previously claimed by France and Spain, they have been British since 1766, administered with Jamaica from 1873 to 1959 and a separate Crown Colony since 1973. A third of the 10,000 population, mainly of mixed Afro-European descent, lives in the capital of Cockburn Town on Grand Turk. Tourism has recently overhauled fishing as the main industry. Offshore banking facilities are also expanding ∎

CAYMAN ISLANDS

The Cayman Islands comprise three low-lying islands covering 259 sq km [100 sq mls], south of Cuba, with the capital Georgetown (population 12,000, in a total of 27,000) on the biggest, Grand Cayman. A dependent territory of Britain (Crown Colony since 1959), they were occupied mainly with farming and fishing until the 1960s, when an economic revolution transformed them into the world's biggest offshore financial centre, offering a secret tax haven to 18,000 companies and 450 banks. The flourishing luxury tourist industry (predominantly from US sources) now accounts for more than 70% of its official GDP and foreign earnings, while a property boom has put beachfront prices on Grand Cayman among the world's highest. An immigrant labour force, chiefly Jamaican, constitutes about a fifth of the population – similar to European and black groups; the rest are of mixed descent ∎

BAHAMAS

The black hoist triangle symbolizes the unity of the Bahamian people and their resolve to develop the island's natural resources. The golden sand and blue sea of the islands are depicted by the yellow and aquamarine stripes.

A coral-limestone archipelago of 29 inhabited low-lying islands, plus over 3,000 uninhabited cays, reefs and rocks, centred on the Grand Bahama Bank off eastern Florida and Cuba, the Bahamas has developed close ties with the USA since 1973.

Over 90% of its 3 million visitors a year are Americans, and tourism now accounts for more than half the nation's revenues, involving some 40% of the workforce. Offshore banking, financial services and a large 'open registry' merchant fleet also offset imports (including most foodstuffs), giving the country a relatively high standard of living. The remainder of the non-administrative population works mainly in traditional fishing and agriculture, notably citrus fruit production.

Though the Bahamas is an independent democracy, it is also élitist. Relations with the US were strained when it was used as a tax haven for drug traffickers in the 1980s, with government ministers implicated in drug-related corruption ■

The pleasant subtropical climate is the tourist attraction of the region. Sea breezes keep the temperatures below 30°C [86°F], but they seldom fall below 15°C [59°F]. In the summer the average temperature is around 27°C [80°F] and in the winter 21°C [70°F]. There is moderate rainfall of about 1,270 mm [50 in], falling with a maximum in the summer months from May to October. Hurricanes, which have in the past been disastrous, occur July–November.

COUNTRY: Commonwealth of the Bahamas
AREA: 13,880 sq km [5,359 sq mls]
POPULATION: 253,000
CAPITAL (Population): Nassau (135,000)
GOVERNMENT: Constitutional democratic monarchy
ETHNIC GROUPS: Black 73%, Mixed 14%, White 13%
LANGUAGES: English (official), English Creole 80%
RELIGIONS: Christian 95%
CURRENCY: Bahamian $ = 100 cents
ANNUAL INCOME PER PERSON: $11,510
LIFE EXPECTANCY: Female 74 yrs, male 68 yrs

PUERTO RICO

Puerto Rico fought with Cuba for independence from Spain and their flags are almost identical. The island is a dependent territory of the United States and the flag, adopted in 1952, is flown only with the American 'Stars and Stripes'.

Ceded by Spain to the USA in 1898, Puerto Rico ('rich port') became a self-governing commonwealth in free political association with the USA after a referendum in 1952. Though this gave the island a considerable measure of autonomy, American influence stretches well beyond its constitutional roles in defence and immigration. Full US citizens, Puerto Ricans pay no federal taxes – but nor do they vote in US congressional or presidential elections. Debate over the exact status of the country subsided in the 1970s, the compromise apparently accepted as a sensible middle way between the extremes of being the 51st state of the US or com-

pletely independent, but resurfaces with the boom years, a referendum in December 1991 narrowly rejecting a proposal to guarantee 'the island's distinct cultural identity' – a result interpreted as a move towards statehood. Meanwhile, free access to the US has relieved the growing pressure created by one of the greatest population densities in the New World, with New York traditionally the most popular destination.

Easternmost of the major Greater Antilles, Puerto Rico is mountainous, with a narrow coastal plain; Cerro de Punta (1,338 m [4,389 ft]) is the highest peak. Flat ground for agriculture is scarce, mainly devoted to cash crops like sugar, coffee, bananas and, since the arrival of Cuban refugees, tobacco, as well as tropical fruits, vegetables and various spices.

However, the island is now the most industrialized and urban nation in the Caribbean – nearly half the population lives in the San Juan area – with chemicals constituting 36% of exports and metal products (based on deposits of copper) a further 17%. Manufacturing, dominated by US companies attracted by tax exemptions, and tourism are now

COUNTRY: Commonwealth of Puerto Rico
AREA: 8,900 sq km [3,436 sq mls]
POPULATION: 3,599,000
CAPITAL (Population): San Juan (1,816,000)
GOVERNMENT: Republic with bicameral legislature
ETHNIC GROUPS: Spanish 99%, Negro, Indian
LANGUAGES: Spanish and English (both official)
RELIGIONS: Christian, mainly Roman Catholic
CURRENCY: US$ = 100 cents
ANNUAL INCOME PER PERSON: $6,470

The climate is hot and wet, but there are no great extremes of temperature; the records are 34°C [93°F] and 17°C [63°F]. Of course, altitude lowers the temperatures. Annual temperature range is low. The winds from the north-east or east, blowing over a warm sea, give high rainfall, falling on over 200 days in the year. Every month except February and March has in excess of 100 mm [4 in] of rain per month on average.

the two growth sectors in a country where the standard of living (while low in US terms) is nevertheless the highest in Latin America outside the island tax havens, and rising ■

BRITISH VIRGIN ISLANDS

Like their larger American neighbours, the British Virgin Islands were 'discovered' by Columbus in 1493. Most northerly of the Lesser Antilles, they comprise four low-lying islands of note and 36 islets and cays, covering a total of 153 sq km [59 sq mls]. The largest island, Tortola, contains over three-quarters of the total population of 13,000, more than a third of which lives in the capital Road Town. Dutch from 1648 but British since 1666, they are now a British dependency enjoying (since 1977) a

strong measure of self-government. Though an increasing rival to the Caymans and the Turks and Caicos in offshore banking from 1985, tourism is the country's main source of income ■

US VIRGIN ISLANDS

The US Virgin Islands were Spanish from 1553, Danish from 1672 and, for a sum of US$25 million, American from 1917 – Washington wishing to protect the approaches to the newly-built Panama

Canal. As an 'unincorporated territory', the residents have been US citizens since 1927, and from 1973 have elected a delegate to the House of Representatives. The 68 islands (dominated by the three largest – St Thomas, St Croix and St John) total 340 sq km [130 sq mls] and host a population of 117,000, more than 100,000 of them split almost evenly between St Croix and St Thomas, home of the capital Charlotte Amalie. The ethnic breakdown is about 80% black and 15% white. Tourism is now the main industry, notably cruise ships but also airborne day-trippers from the USA to the duty-free shops of St Thomas. The islands have the highest density of hotels and 'condominiums' in the Caribbean ■

ANGUILLA

Deriving its name from its 'discovery' in 1493 by Columbus – *anguil* is Spanish for eel – Anguilla is indeed long and thin, a low coral atoll covered with poor soil and scrub, measuring 96 sq km [37 sq mls]. First colonized by Britain in 1690 and long administered with St Kitts and Nevis, the island was subject to intervention by British troops in 1969 to restore legal government following its secession from the self-governing federation in 1967. Its position as a separate UK dependent territory (colony) was confirmed in 1971 and formalized in 1980.

Of the 8,000 population – largely of African descent and English-speaking – about a quarter lives in the capital of The Valley. The main source of revenue is now tourism ■

ST CHRISTOPHER AND NEVIS

The first West Indian islands to be colonized by Britain (1623 and 1628), St Christopher and Nevis became independent in 1983. The federation comprises two well-watered volcanic islands, mountains rising on both to around 1,000 m [3,300 ft], and about 20% forested. St Christopher is usually shortened to St Kitts; Nevis derives its name from Columbus (1493), to whom the cloud-covered peaks were reminiscent of Spanish mountains (*nieves* meaning snow). Thanks to fine beaches tourism has replaced sugar, nationalized in 1975 and still producing 57% of exports, as the main earner ■

ANTIGUA AND BARBUDA

Antigua and Barbuda are strategically situated islands linked by Britain after 1860; gaining internal self-government in 1967 and independence in 1981. They rely heavily on tourism, though some attempts at diversification (notably Sea Island cotton) have been successful. Run by the Antiguan Labour Party almost without break since 1956, its white-owned sugar industry – accounting for most of exports in the 1960s – was closed down in 1971. Only 1,500 people live on the game reserve island of Barbuda, where lobster fishing is the main occupation. Antigua is untypical of the Leewards in that despite its height it has no rivers or forests; Barbuda, by contrast, is a well-wooded low coral atoll ■

MONTSERRAT

Colonized from 1632 by Britain, which brought in Irish settlers, Montserrat (though still a UK dependent territory) has been self-governing since 1960. The island measures 101 sq km [39 sq mls] and has a population of 12,500, nearly a quarter living in the capital, Plymouth; 96% are of African descent.

Though tourism is the mainstay of the economy it is supported by exports of electronic components, Sea Island cotton, fruit and vegetables; unusually for the Caribbean, it is almost self-sufficient in food. Cotton was once the main industry, but new ones have moved in under generous tax concessions ■

GUADELOUPE

Slightly the larger of France's two Caribbean overseas departments, Guadeloupe comprises seven islands including Saint-Martin and Saint-Barthélemy to the north-west. Over 90% of the area, however, is taken up by Basse-Terre, which is volcanic – Soufrière (1,467 m [4,813 ft]) is the highest point in the Lesser Antilles – and the smaller Grande-Terre, made of low limestone; the two are separated by a narrow sea channel called Rivière-Salée (Salt River). The commercial centre of Pointe-à-Pitre (population 25,000) is on Grande-Terre. Food is the biggest import (22%, much of it from France), bananas (50%) the biggest export, followed by wheat flour, sugar, rum and aubergines. French aid has helped create a reasonable standard of living, but despite this and thriving tourism – much of it from France and the USA – unemployment is high. Though sharing an identical history to Martinique, Guadeloupe has a far stronger separatist movement, which sporadically resorts to acts of terrorism ■

DOMINICA

Dominica has been an independent republic (the Commonwealth of Dominica) since 1978, after 11 years as a self-governing UK colony; Britain and France fought long over the island, ownership decided in 1805 by a ransom of £12,000 (then US$53,000). The population of 82,000 is over 90% African and 6% mixed, with small Asian and white minorities and a settlement of about 500 mainly mixed-blood Carib Indians. Predominantly Christian (80% Catholic), most people speak French patois, though English is the official language.

A mountainous ridge forms the island's spine, as it is from this central region that the main rivers flow to the indented coast; 'Boiling Lake' is located in the south. Though rich soils support dense vegetation, less than 10% is cultivated; bananas account for 48% of exports, coconut-based soaps for 25%. Much food is imported, and future prospects for a relatively poor Caribbean island depend a good deal on the development of luxury tourism ■

MARTINIQUE

Martinique was 'discovered' by Columbus in 1493, colonized by France from 1635 and, apart from brief British interludes, has been French ever since. It became an overseas department in 1946 – enjoying the same status and representation as *départéments* – and, like Guadeloupe, was made an administrative region in 1974. Despite a more homogenous population than its neighbour, the island has a less vociferous independence movement – though in the 1991 elections the separatists made substantial gains, winning 19 of the 41 seats in the provincial assembly.

Martinique comprises three groups of volcanic hills and the intervening lowlands. The highest peak is Mt Pelée, notorious for its eruption of 1902, when in minutes it killed all the inhabitants of St Pierre (estimated at about 28,000) except one – a prisoner saved by the thickness of his cell.

Bananas (40%), rum and pineapples are the main agricultural exports, but tourism (mainly French and American) is the biggest earner. The

The small islands of the Caribbean all have very similar climates with a small range of temperature, high humidity, especially in summer, and a high annual rainfall with a summer maximum. The summer rainfall is mainly in the form of thundery showers, which build up in the afternoon, but in winter the rain tends to be lighter and more prolonged. Hurricanes may occur in August and September, when the sea is at its warmest.

COUNTRY: Overseas department of France
AREA: 1,100 sq km [425 sq mls]
POPULATION: 341,000
CAPITAL (Population): Fort-de-France (100,000)

industrial sector includes cement, food processing and oil refining, using Venezuelan crude; oil products account for 14% of exports. French government expenditure is higher than on Guadeloupe, at some 70% of GDP, helping provide jobs and retain a better standard of living than its northern compatriot ■

ST LUCIA

First settled by the British in 1605, St Lucia changed hands between Britain and France 14 times before finally being ceded formally in 1814. Internally self-governing as 'Associated State of the UK' from 1967, it gained full independence in 1979. A mountainous, forested island of extinct volcanoes – graphically represented on its flag – St Lucia boasts a huge variety of plant and animal life. To the south of its highest point of Mt Gimie (949 m [3,114 ft]) lies the Qualibou, an area containing 18 lava domes and seven craters. In the west are the

Pitons, rising from the sea to over 750 m [2,460 ft].

Though not poor, St Lucia is still overdependent on bananas (71% of exports), a crop easily hit by hurricane and disease. It is supported by coconuts, coconut products and cocoa, though clothing is the second export, and the free port of Vieux Fort has attracted modern industries. Cruise liners deliver tourists to Castries, and the Grande Cul de Sac Bay to the south is one of the deepest tanker ports on the continent, used mainly for trans-shipment of oil ■

COUNTRY: Saint Lucia
AREA: 622 sq km [240 sq mls]
POPULATION: 151,000
CAPITAL (Population): Castries (53,000)

ST VINCENT AND THE GRENADINES

St Vincent and the Grenadines comprise the main island (consisting 89% of the area and 95% of the population) and the Northern Grenadines, of which the largest are Bequia, Mustique and Canouan, with Union the furthest south. 'Discovered' in 1498, St Vincent was settled in the 16th century and became a British colony with the Treaty of Versailles in 1783, after a century of conflict with France, often supported by the Caribs – the last of whom were deported to Honduras after the Indian War of 1795–7. The colony became self-governing

in 1969 and independent in 1979.

St Vincent is a mountainous, volcanic island that receives heavy rainfall and boasts luxuriant vegetation. Soufrière (1,178 m [3,866 ft]), which last erupted in the year of independence, is one of two active volcanoes in the eastern Caribbean – Mt Pelée is the other. Less prosperous than its Commonwealth neighbours, there are nevertheless prosperous pockets, notably Mustique and Bequia, where beautiful clean waters have fostered tourism ■

COUNTRY: Saint Vincent and the Grenadines
AREA: 388 sq km [150 sq mls]
POPULATION: 116,000
CAPITAL (Population): Kingstown (34,000)

GRENADA

The most southern of the Windward Islands, the country of Grenada also includes the Southern Grenadines, principally Carriacou. Formally British since 1783, a self-governing colony from 1967 and independent in 1974, it went Communist after a bloodless coup in 1979 when Maurice Bishop established links with Cuba. After Bishop was executed by other Marxists in 1983, the US (supported by some Caribbean countries) sent in troops to restore democracy, and since the invasion the ailing econ-

omy has been heavily reliant on American aid.

Grenada is known as 'the spice island of the Caribbean' and is the world's leading producer of nutmeg, its main crop. Cocoa, bananas and mace also contribute to exports, but attempts to diversify the economy from an agricultural base have been largely unsuccessful. In the early 1990s there were signs that the tourist industry was finally making a recovery after the debilitating events of 1983 ■

COUNTRY: Grenada
AREA: 344 sq km [133 sq mls]
POPULATION: 85,000
CAPITAL (Population): St George's (29,000)

St Martin is divided into the northern two-thirds (Saint-Martin, French and administered as part of Guadeloupe), and the southern third (St Maarten, Dutch and part of the Netherlands Antilles) ■

BARBADOS

The flag was adopted on independence from Britain in 1960. The trident had been part of the colonial badge of Barbados and was retained as the centre to its flag. The gold stripe represents beaches and the blue stripes the sea and sky.

The most eastern Caribbean country, and first in line for the region's seasonal hurricanes, Barbados is underlain with limestone and capped with coral. Mt Hillaby (340m [1,115ft]), the highest point, is fringed by marine terraces marking stages in the island's emergence from the sea. Soils are fertile and deep, easily cultivated except in the eroded Scotland district of the north-east.

Barbados became British in 1627 and sugar production, using African slave labour, began soon afterwards. Cane plantations take up most of the cropped land (over half the total), but at 17% now contributes far less than previously to exports. Manufactures now constitute the largest exports, though tourism is the growth sector and the leading industry (430,000 visitors in 1988), and is the most likely future for this relatively prosperous but extremely overcrowded island; at 593 per sq km [1,536 per sq ml], it is the most densely populated rural society in the world (42% urban). Despite political stability and advanced welfare and education services, emigration (as from many West Indian countries) is high, notably to the US and the UK ■

COUNTRY: Barbados
AREA: 430 sq km [166 sq mls]
POPULATION: 255,000
CAPITAL (Population): Bridgetown (7,466)
GOVERNMENT: Constitutional monarchy with a bicameral legislature
ETHNIC GROUPS: Black 92%, White 3%, Mulatto 3%
LANGUAGES: English (official), Creole 90%
RELIGIONS: Protestant 65%, Roman Catholic 4%
NATIONAL DAY: 30 November; Independence Day (1966)
CURRENCY: Barbados $ = 100 cents
ANNUAL INCOME PER PERSON: $6,540
POPULATION DENSITY: 593 per sq km [1,536 per sq ml]
LIFE EXPECTANCY: Female 78 yrs, male 72 yrs
ADULT LITERACY: 98%

TRINIDAD AND TOBAGO

The islands of Trinidad and Tobago have flown this flag since independence from Britain in 1962. Red stands for the people's warmth and vitality, black for their strength, and white for their hopes and the surf of the sea.

The annual temperature range is very small (2°C [4°F]), as would be expected of a coastal location only 10° from the Equator. By day the temperature rises rapidly, setting off heavy showers during the afternoon in the rainy season, but the sky clears in the evenings, which feel pleasantly cool. The wettest months are in summer, when the inter-tropical rainbelt reaches its most northerly extent and lies close to Trinidad. Sunshine levels are fairly regular at 7–8 hours per day.

Furthest south of the West Indies, Trinidad is a rectangular island situated just 16km [10mls] off Venezuela's Orinoco delta. Tobago is a detached extension of its Northern Range of hills, lying 34km [21mls] to the north-east. Trinidad's highest point is Cerro Aripe (940m [3,085ft]) in the rugged, forested Northern Range; the capital, Port of Spain, nestles behind the hills on the sheltered west coast.

'Discovered' by Columbus in 1498, Trinidad was later planted for sugar production by Spanish and French settlers before becoming British in 1797. Black slaves worked the plantations until emancipation in 1834, when Indian and some Chinese indentured labourers were brought in. Indian influence is still strong in many villages, with African in others. Tobago was competed for by Spain, Holland and France before coming under British control in 1814, joining Trinidad to form a single colony in 1899. Independence came in 1962 and a republic was established in 1976, though Tobago is pushing for internal self-government.

Oil has been the lifeblood of the nation's economy throughout the 20th century, giving the island a relatively high standard of living, and (with petrochemicals) still accounts for over 70% of exports. Falling prices in the 1980s had a severe effect, however, only partly offset by the growth of tourism and continued revenues from asphalt – the other main resource (occurring naturally) – and gas.

Trinidad experienced a sharp political change in 1986, when after 30 years the People's National Movement was voted out and the National Alliance for Reconstruction coalition took office. After five years of instability the PNM was returned by a landslide, in December 1991, but it faced 22% unemployment and mounting economic problems ■

COUNTRY: Republic of Trinidad and Tobago
AREA: 5,130 sq km [1,981 sq mls]
POPULATION: 1,227,000
CAPITAL (Population): Port of Spain (60,000)
GOVERNMENT: Republic with a bicameral legislature
ETHNIC GROUPS: Black 43%, East Indian 40%, Mixed 16%, White 1%, Chinese 1%
LANGUAGES: English (official)
RELIGIONS: Christian 49%, Hindu 24%, Muslim 9%
NATIONAL DAY: 31 August; Independence Day (1962)
CURRENCY: Trinidad and Tobago $ = 100 cents
ANNUAL INCOME PER PERSON: $3,470
POPULATION DENSITY: 239 per sq km [619 per sq ml]
LIFE EXPECTANCY: Female 74 yrs, male 69 yrs

NETHERLANDS ANTILLES

The Netherlands Antilles consists of two very different island groups – Curaçao and Bonaire, off the coast of Venezuela, and Saba, St Eustacius and the southern part of St Maarten, at the northern end of the Leeward Islands, some 800km [500mls] away. With Aruba, they formed part of the Dutch East Indies, in 1954 attaining internal self-government as constitutional equals with the Netherlands and Surinam. Curaçao is politically dominant in the federation; it is the largest island, accounting for nearly 45% of the total of 933 sq km [383 sq mls] and 80% of the population of 189,000, almost half of it in the capital Willemstad. The people – mainly mulatto, Creole-speaking and Catholic – are well off by Caribbean standards, enjoying the benefits of an economy buoyed by tourism, offshore banking and oil refining (from Venezuela), mostly for export to the Netherlands, more than the traditional orange liqueur ■

ARUBA

A flat limestone island and the most western of the Lesser Antilles, Aruba measures 193 sq km [75 sq mls]. Incorporated into the Netherlands Antilles in 1845, Aruba held a referendum in 1977, which supported autonomy. With Dutch agreement (in 1981) it separated from the Antilles on 1 January 1986, and full independence is due ■

SOUTH AMERICA

SOUTH AMERICA

Occupying 12% of the Earth's land surface, South America has three structural parts – the Andes Mountains, the river basins and plains, and the ancient eastern highlands. The Andes run almost the entire length of the continent for about 8,000 km [5,000 mls]. Glaciers and snow-fields grace many of the peaks, some of which rise to over 6,500 m [21,000 ft]; Aconcagua (6,960 m [22,834 ft]), in Argentina, is the highest mountain outside Asia. West of the Andes lies a narrow coastal strip, except in the far south and on Tierra del Fuego ('Land of Fire').

Three vast river basins lie to the east of the Andes: the llanos of Venezuela, drained by the Orinoco, the Amazon Basin (occupying 40% of the continent), and the great Paraguay-Paranà-Uruguay Basin that empties into the River Plate estuary. The highlands are the rolling Guiana Highlands of the north, and the more extensive Brazilian plateau that fills and gives shape to South America's eastern bulge. Both are of hard crystalline rock, geologically much older than the Andes, and their presence helps to explain the wanderings and meanderings of the great river systems.

South America has great climatic variety, due partly to the wide latitudinal extent but also to the great range in altitude; 80% falls within the tropics, but height may temper the tropical climate considerably – for example in the Altiplano of Bolivia. The natural flora and fauna are equally varied. Long isolation from the rest of the world allowed a great variety of plants and animals to evolve, and this natural variety has not yet been reduced significantly by human pressures. Electric eels, carnivorous piranha fish, manatees, river dolphins, amphibious boa constrictors, sloths, anteaters, armadillos, several kinds of marsupials, camel-like guanacos and llamas, rheas, Andean condors and humming-birds are some of the many indigenous animals.

Many of the plants found useful to man – potato, cassava, quinoa, squashes, sweet potato, cacao, pineapple and rubber, for example – were originally South American, and the vast forests of the Amazon and Andes may yet contain more. Pressures on the natural fauna and flora are growing, however, in a continent that is, so far, weak on conservation.

South America is prodigal, too, with mineral wealth. Silver and gold were the first attractions but petroleum, iron, copper and tin are also plentiful, and many reserves have yet to be exploited. The people – who could still prove Latin America's greatest resource – include a rich mix of original Amerindians, Spanish and Portuguese colonial immigrants, African slaves, and a later generation of immigrants and refugees from the turmoils of Europe. Though large and growing fast, the population is still small compared with the vast potential of the continent.

Latin America is generally held to include all the nations of mainland Central America and the Caribbean islands where the Spanish culture is strong ■

BUENOS AIRES Capital Cities

SOUTH AMERICA

CLIMATIC REGIONS

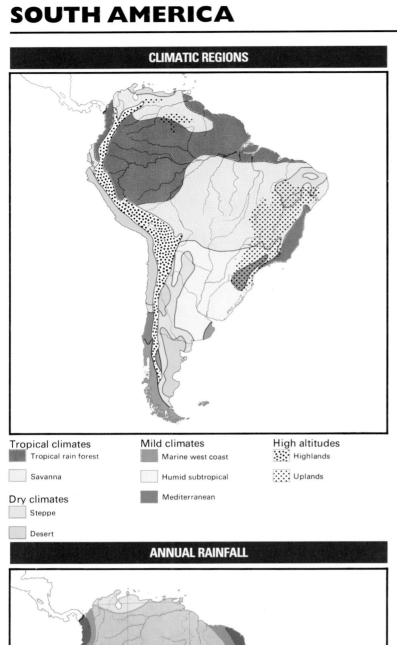

Tropical climates
- Tropical rain forest
- Savanna

Dry climates
- Steppe
- Desert

Mild climates
- Marine west coast
- Humid subtropical
- Mediterranean

High altitudes
- Highlands
- Uplands

NATURAL VEGETATION

Equator

Amazon

Andes

Atacama Desert

Tropic of Capricorn

Brazilian Highlands

Pampas

Patagonia

- Tropical rain forest
- Tropical thorn forest
- Temperate rain forest
- Evergreen trees and shrubs
- Grassland and savanna
- Steppe and scrub
- Desert
- Alpine and high plateau

ANNUAL RAINFALL

Equator

Tropic of Capricorn

ins.	mm
120	3000
80	2000
40	1000
20	500
10	250

POPULATION

Equator

• = 100,000 people

LAND USE

LAND USE

Other land 16·2%
Arable land and permanent crops 5·9%
Permanent pasture 25·2%
Woods and forests 52·7%

Total land area 1 753.7 million hectares
(4 333·4 million acres)

LAND USE

- Arable land
- Fruit trees, vineyards and plantations
- Permanent pasture
- Woods and forests
- Rough grazing
- Non-productive land

LIVESTOCK

- Cattle
- Sheep

CROPS

⟱ Bananas		◇ Sugar cane	
ʘ Cacao		▲ Tea	
◆ Citrus fruits		⊤ Tobacco	
○ Coffee		▽ Vines	
✻ Cotton		׀׀׀ Wheat	
׀׀׀ Maize			
○ Rice		⇀ Principal fishing areas	

MINERALS

○ Bauxite	Cr	Chrome
▲ Copper	Mn	Manganese
◇ Diamonds	Mo	Molybdenum
△ Gold	Ni	Nickel
◆ Iron ore		POWER
◆ Lead and zinc	▲	Coalfields
◆ Saltpetre	◼	Oilfields
▽ Silver	◼	Gasfields
● Tin	◼	Hydro-electric power
Sb Antimony		

Projection: Lambert's Equivalent Azimuthal

West from Greenwich

COPYRIGHT GEORGE PHILIP LTD.

SOUTH AMERICA

COLOMBIA

Colombia's colours – showing the (yellow) land of the nation separated by the (blue) sea from the tyranny of Spain, whose rule the people fought with their (red) blood – are shared by Ecuador and Venezuela. The blue is darker than her neighbours'.

Colombia is split by the northern Andes. Their altitude fundamentally changes the tropical climate of the country, lowering temperatures and increasing rainfall and with permanent snow at the higher levels. Temperatures are high with little annual variation. Rainfall is high, very high on the Pacific coast, but it is drier on the Caribbean coast and in the Magdalena Valley, which experience dry seasons.

Christopher Columbus sighted the country that would bear his name in 1499, and the Spanish conquest of the territory began ten years later. The nation gained independence from Spain after a decade of conflict in 1819, and since the 19th century the two political parties, the pro-clerical, centralizing Conservatives and the anti-clerical, federal-oriented Liberals, have regularly alternated in power. Their rivalry led to two brutal civil wars (1899–1902 and 1949–57), in which some 400,000 people lost their lives: the 1950s conflict, known as 'La Violencia', claimed 280,000 of them. In 1957 the two parties agreed to form a coalition, and this fragile arrangement – threatened by right-wing death squads, left-wing guerillas and powerful drug cartels – lasted until the Liberal President Virgilio Barco Vargas was elected by a record margin in 1986. Even by the violent standards of South America, however, Colombia remains politically unstable.

Landscape and agriculture

The Andes cross Colombia from south to north, fanning out into three ranges with two intervening valleys. In the west the low Cordillera Occidental rises from the hot, forested Pacific coastal plain. Almost parallel to it, and separated by the Cauca Valley, is the much higher Cordillera Central; the high peaks of this range, many of them volcanic, rise to over 5,000 m [16,400 ft].

To the east, across the broad valley of the Magdalena River, lies the more complex Cordillera Oriental, which includes high plateaus, plains, lakes and basins; the capital city, Bogotá, is situated on one of the plateaus, at a height of 2,610 m [8,563 ft]. North-west of the mountains lies the broad Atlantic plain, crossed by many rivers. The Andean foothills to the east, falling away into the Orinoco and Amazon basins and densely covered with rainforest (albeit rapidly diminishing), occupy about two-thirds of the total area of the country. Less than 2% of the population, mainly cattle-rangers and Indians, live east of the mountains.

Little of the country is under cultivation, but much of the land is very fertile and is coming into use as roads improve. The range of climate for crops is extraordinary and the agricultural colleges have different courses for 'cold-climate farming' and 'warm-climate farming'. The rubber tree grows wild and fibres are being exploited, notably the 'fique', which provides all the country's requirements for sacks and cordage. Colombia is the world's second biggest producer of coffee, which grows mainly in the Andean uplands, while bananas, cotton, sugar and rice are important lowland products. Colombia imports some food, though the country has the capacity to be self-sufficient. Drugs, however, may be the country's biggest industry: it was reported in 1987 that cocaine exports earn Colombia more than its main export, coffee.

Industry

Colombia was the home of El Dorado, the legendary 'gilded one' of the Chibcha Indians, but today the wealth is more likely to be coal or oil. The country has the largest proven reserves of coal in Latin America (18 billion tonnes) and is South America's biggest exporter. Gold, silver, iron ore, lead, zinc, mercury, emeralds (90% of world production) and other minerals are plentiful, and hydroelectric power is increasingly being developed. Petroleum is an important export and source of foreign exchange; large reserves have been found in the north-eastern areas of Arauca and Vichada and in 1991 proven reserves were put at 1.3 billion barrels. Early in 1992 BP stepped up its exploration programme among speculation that its new finds, north-east of Bogotá, were among the world's biggest.

There is compulsory social security funded by employees, employers and the government, but the benefits are not evenly spread. Education spending accounts for nearly 20% of the national budget.

Attempts are being made to broaden the industrial base of the economy to counter the decline in domestic demand and the recession being experienced by its neighbours. Foreign investment will be essential, but to achieve this the Liberal government – convincing winners in the 1991 elections – must first defeat the drug barons and the habitual violence that pervades the nation ■

COUNTRY: Republic of Colombia

AREA: 1,138,910 sq km [439,733 sq mls]

POPULATION: 32,987,000

CAPITAL (Population): Bogotá (4,185,000)

GOVERNMENT: Unitary republic with bicameral legislature

ETHNIC GROUPS: Mestizo 68%, White 20%, Amerindian 7%, Black 5%

LANGUAGES: Spanish (official), over 100 Indian languages and dialects spoken

RELIGIONS: Roman Catholic 95%

NATIONAL DAY: 20 July; Independence Day (1819)

CURRENCY: Peso = 100 centavos

ANNUAL INCOME PER PERSON: $1,240

MAIN PRIMARY PRODUCTS: Coal, natural gas, petroleum, silver, gold, iron ore, emeralds

MAIN INDUSTRIES: Iron, cement, petroleum industries, vehicles, food processing, paper

MAIN EXPORTS: Coffee 43%, crude petroleum 8%, bananas 6%, cotton 3%, coal, emeralds

MAIN EXPORT PARTNERS: USA 40%, Germany, Netherlands, Japan

MAIN IMPORTS: Machinery 28%, chemicals 18%, vehicles 13%

MAIN IMPORT PARTNERS: USA 36%, Japan, Venezuela, Germany, Brazil

POPULATION DENSITY: 29 per sq km [75 per sq ml]

INFANT MORTALITY: 42 per 1,000 live births

LIFE EXPECTANCY: Female 68 yrs, male 64 yrs

ADULT LITERACY: 88% (Indians 60%)

PRINCIPAL CITIES (Population): Bogotá 4,185,000 Medellín 1,506,000 Cali 1,397,000 Barranquilla 920,000

THE DRUGS TRADE

Colombia is notorious for its illegal export of cocaine, and several reliable estimates class the drug as the country's most lucrative source of foreign exchange as kilo after kilo feeds the seemingly insatiable demand from the US and, to a lesser extent, Western Europe. In addition to the indigenous crop (willingly grown by well-off peasants, though in a neo-feudal setting), far larger amounts of leaf are smuggled in from Bolivia and Peru for refining, processing and 're-export'. US agencies estimated that in 1987 retail sales of South American cocaine totalled $22 billion – earning about $2 billion for the producers.

Violence, though focused on the drug capitals of Medellín and Cali, is endemic, with warfare between both rival gangs and between producers and the authorities an almost daily occurrence.

Assassinations of civil servants, judicial officials, police officers or anyone attempting to investigate, control or end the rule of the multimillionaire drug barons are commonplace.

In February 1990, as part of President George Bush's $10.6 billion 'war on drugs', the governments of these three Andean states – Colombia, Bolivia and Peru – joined forces with the US Drug Enforcement Agency in a concentrated attempt to clamp down on the production and distribution of cocaine. But while early results from Bolivia were encouraging, the situation in Colombia if anything hardened, despite the brave attempts of politicians, administrators and police in many areas to break the socio-economic stranglehold of the drug cartels. By 1992 the crackdown was in serious danger of complete failure.

VENEZUELA

The seven stars on the tricolour (*see Colombia and Ecuador*) represent the provinces forming the Venezuelan Federation in 1811. The shield in the coat of arms depicts a wheatsheaf (for unity), weapons (for victory) and a wild horse (for liberty).

CARACAS

Temperature

Precipitation
836mm
33in

The country has a tropical climate. There is little variation in temperature from month to month, but there are marked wet and dry seasons, the rain falling from May to November. The north-east trade winds leave little rain in the coastal lowlands, but the total increases when they hit the mountains. The monthly temperature of Caracas on the northern coast is between 19 and 22°C [66-72°F], but this is much lower on the higher land. Some of the northern Andean peaks have permanent snow.

Sighted by Columbus in 1498, the country was visited by Alonzo de Ojeda and Amerigo Vespucci in 1499, when they named it Venezuela ('Little Venice'). It was part of the Spanish colony of New Granada until 1821 when it became independent, first in federation with Colombia and Ecuador and then, from 1830, as a separate independent republic under the leadership of Simón Bolivar. Between 1830 and 1945 the country was governed mainly by dictators; after frequent changes of president a new constitution came into force in 1961 and since then a fragile civilian-rule democracy has been enjoyed, resting on widespread repression and corruption – almost endemic in South America – with all presidents completing their term of office, despite periodic violence.

Landscape

In the north and north-west of Venezuela, where 90% of the population lives, the Andes split to form two ranges separated from each other by the Maracaibo basin. At 5,007 m [16,427 ft] snow-capped Merida is the highest of several tall peaks in the area. Above 3,000 m [10,000 ft] are the *paramos* – regions of grassland vegetation where Indian villagers live; temperatures are mild and the land is fertile. By contrast, Maracaibo swelters in tropical heat alongside the oilfields that for half a century have produced Venezuela's wealth.

The mountains running west to east behind the coast from Valencia to Trinidad have a separate geological history and gentler topography. Between the ranges are fertile alluvial basins, with many long-established market towns. Caracas, the teeming capital, was one such town before being expanded and modernized on the back of the 1970s oil boom. It now has to take a rapidly swelling population and is fringed with the shanties of hopeful immigrants from poor rural areas.

South of the mountains are the *llanos* of the Orinoco – mostly a vast savanna of trees and grasslands

that floods, especially in the west, during the April-to-October rains. This is now cattle-raising country. The Orinoco itself rises on the western rim in the Guiana Highlands, a region of high dissected plateaus made famous as the site of Arthur Conan Doyle's *Lost World*, and dense tropical forest makes this still a little-known area.

Not far to the north, however, lies Cerro Bolivar, where iron ore is mined and fed to the steel mills of Ciudad Guayana, a new industrial city built on the Orinoco since 1960. The smelting is powered by hydroelectricity from the nearby Caroni River, and a new deep-water port allows 60,000-tonne carriers to take surplus ore to world markets.

Oil made Venezuela a rich country, but the wealth was always distributed very unevenly and concentrated in the cities – hence the rapid urbanization that made 17 out of every 20 Venezuelans a city dweller and left enormous areas of the country unpopulated. Before the coming of oil, Venezuela was predominantly agricultural, the economy based on coffee, cocoa and cattle.

Commercially-viable reserves of oil were found in Venezuela in 1914, and by the 1930s the country had become the world's first major oil exporter – the largest producer after the USA. The industry was nationalized in 1976 but by 1990 there were signs of dangerous dependence on a single commodity controlled by OPEC and in plentiful supply, while large foreign debt saw austerity measures that triggered a violent reaction from many Venezuelans.

Before the development of the oil industry Venezuela was predominantly an agricultural country, but 85% of export earnings are now from oil and some of the profits from the industry help to fund developments in agriculture and other industries. Gold, nickel, iron ore, copper and manganese are also found and aluminium production has increased following further discoveries of bauxite.

Agriculture can supply only 70% of the country's needs. Only 5% of the arable land is cultivated and

COUNTRY: Republic of Venezuela
AREA: 912,050 sq km [352,143 sq mls]
POPULATION: 19,735,000
CAPITAL (Population): Caracas (3,247,000)
GOVERNMENT: Republic with bicameral legislature
ETHNIC GROUPS: Mestizo 67%, White 21%, Black 10%, Amerindian 2%
LANGUAGES: Spanish (official), 30 Amerindian languages and dialects also spoken
RELIGIONS: Roman Catholic 94%
NATIONAL DAY: 5 July; Independence Day (1811)
CURRENCY: Bolívar = 100 centivos
ANNUAL INCOME PER PERSON: $2,560
MAIN PRIMARY PRODUCTS: Food, oil, bauxite
MAIN INDUSTRIES: Oil refining, steel manufacture, food processing, textiles, vehicles
EXPORTS: $670 per person
MAIN EXPORTS: Petroleum 85%, bauxite 9%, iron ore
MAIN EXPORT PARTNERS: USA 49%, Germany, Japan, Italy, Brazil, Canada
IMPORTS: $407 per person
MAIN IMPORTS: Food, chemicals, manufactured goods
MAIN IMPORT PARTNERS: USA 44%, Germany, Japan, Netherlands
DEFENCE: 5.8% of national budget
TOURISM: 317,300 visitors per year
POPULATION DENSITY: 22 per sq km [56 per sq ml]
INFANT MORTALITY: 33 per 1,000 live births
LIFE EXPECTANCY: Female 74 yrs, male 68 yrs
ADULT LITERACY: 86%
PRINCIPAL CITIES (Population): Caracas 3,247,000 Maracaibo 1,295,000 Valencia 1,135,000 Maracay 857,000 Barquisimeto 718,000

much of that is pasture. The chief crops are sugar cane, coffee, bananas, maize and oranges; there is also substantial dairy and beef production. It is thought that more than 10,000 head of cattle are smuggled into Colombia each month.

Venezuela is still the richest country in South America but now plans to diversify away from the petroleum industry, and foreign investment is being actively encouraged. Demographically stable, with a growing middle class and a proven record in economic planning, it has every chance of increasing its prosperity further in a world economic upturn ∎

THE ANGEL FALLS

Called Cherun-Meru by the local Indians, and first known to Europeans in 1910, the world's highest waterfall was 'rediscovered' in 1937 when an American airman called Jimmy Angel flew his small plane into the Guiana Highlands in eastern Venezuela in search of gold – but found instead a natural wonder nearly 20 times the height of Niagara, plunging down from the plateau of Auyán Tepuí, the 'Devil's Mountain'.

Today light aircraft follow his route to take tourists to falls that tumble a total of 979 m [3,212 ft] on the Rio Carrao.

ECUADOR

Shared in different proportions by Colombia and Venezuela, Ecuador's colours were used in the flag created by the patriot Francisco de Miranda in 1806 and flown by Simón Bolívar, whose armies also liberated Peru and Bolivia.

QUITO

Temperature

Precipitation
1233mm
49in

Ecuador lies on the Equator, but it is bisected by the high Andes which significantly lower the expected high temperatures. Although offshore there is the cold Peruvian Current, the coastal temperatures are 23–25°C [73-77°F] throughout the year. At Quito, inland at 2,500 m [8,200 ft] this drops to 14–15°C [57–59°F]. There are permanent snowfields and glaciers nearby. Rainfall is low in the extreme south west, but generally heavy, and very heavy in the east. There is a dry season June to September.

distinct regions – the coastal plain (Costa), the Andes, and the eastern alluvial plains of the Oriente.

The coastal plain, averaging 100 km [60 mls] wide, is a hot, fertile area of variable rainfall. Recently cleared of forests and largely freed of malaria, it is now good farmland where banana farms, coffee and cocoa plantations and fishing are the main sources of income, with the country's commercial centre of Guayaquil a flourishing port.

The Andes form three linked ranges across the country, with several of the central peaks rising above 5,000 m [16,400 ft]. Quito, an old city rich in art and architecture from a colonial past, has a backdrop of snow-capped mountains, among them Cotopaxi – at 5,896 m [19,340 ft] the world's highest active volcano – and Chimborazo (6,267 m [20,556 ft]). The Oriente, a heavily forested upland, is virtually unexploited except for recent developments of oil and natural gas.

Ecuador's economy was based on the export of bananas, for which the country was world leader, and is still the biggest exporter, but this changed from 1972 when oil was first exploited with the opening of the trans-Andean pipeline linking with the tanker-loading port of Esmeraldas. Petroleum and derivatives account for about 40% of export earnings, after peaking at 66% in 1985.

Shortage of power limits much development in the manufacturing industry – even in the mid-1980s only 60% of the population had use of electricity. During the 1970s the manufacture of textiles, cement and pharmaceuticals grew, as did food processing, but there is little heavy industry. Fishing has been affected by the warm water current (El Niño) and there is now an emphasis on greater investment and using much more new technology.

Changes in demand for oil and an earthquake in March 1987, which disrupted much of industry, led the government to suspend payment of interest on its overseas debt, then cancel all debt repayment for the rest of the year. A strict economic recovery programme was put into place and a rescheduling of debt payments agreed in 1989.

COUNTRY: Republic of Ecuador
AREA: 283,560 sq km [109,483 sq mls]
POPULATION: 10,782,000
CAPITAL (Population): Quito (1,110,248)
GOVERNMENT: Unitary republic with unicameral legislature
ETHNIC GROUPS: Mestizo 55%, Amerindian 25%, White 10%, Black 10%
LANGUAGES: Spanish 93% (official), Quechua
RELIGIONS: Roman Catholic 90%, Protestant 6%
NATIONAL DAY: 10 August; Independence of Quito (1809)
CURRENCY: Sucre = 100 centavos
ANNUAL INCOME PER PERSON: $960
MAIN PRIMARY PRODUCTS: Silver, gold, copper, zinc
MAIN INDUSTRIES: Petroleum, agriculture, textiles
MAIN EXPORTS: Petroleum and derivatives, seafood, bananas, coffee, cocoa
MAIN IMPORTS: Fuels, lubricants, transport equipment, inputs and capital equipment for industry
DEFENCE: 12% of national budget
POPULATION DENSITY: 38 per sq km [98 per sq ml]
LIFE EXPECTANCY: Female 69 yrs, male 65 yrs
ADULT LITERACY: 85%

The Incas of Peru conquered Ecuador in the 15th century but in 1532 a colony was founded by the Spaniards in the territory, then called Quito. Independence from Spain was achieved in 1822, when it became part of Gran Colombia, and full independence followed in 1830. Today the country's democracy remains intact.

Ecuador's name comes from the Equator, which divides the country unequally; Quito, the capital, lies just within the southern hemisphere. There are three

The Galápagos Islands lie across the Equator 970 km [610 mls] west of Ecuador (of which they form a province), and consist of six main islands and over 50 smaller ones; all are volcanic, some of them active, but only four are inhabited.

Discovered by the Spanish in 1535 but annexed by Ecuador in 1832, the archipelago became famous after the visit of Charles Darwin in 1835 when he collected crucial evidence for his theory of natural selection. The islands contain a large variety of unique endemic species of flora and fauna ■

PERU

Flown since 1825, the flag's colours are said to have come about when the Argentine patriot General Jos de San Martin, arriving to liberate Peru from Spain in 1820, saw a flock of red and white flamingoes flying over his marching army.

LIMA

Temperature

Precipitation
45mm
2in

Peru has a great variety of climates; its northern border touches the Equator, over half the country is astride the high Andes and the prevailing winds from the south-west blow over the cold Peruvian Current of the Pacific. Desert conditions prevail along the foothills of the Andes. The rainfall increases with altitude, with snow-covered peaks. In the tropical north-eastern lowlands there are high temperatures and high rainfall.

Largest of the Andean states, Peru is spread over coastal plain, mountains and forested Amazon lowlands in the interior. It was formerly the homeland of Inca and other ancient civilizations, and has a history of human settlement stretching back over 10,500 years. The last Inca empire ended in the 16th century with the arrival of the Spaniards, who made Peru the most important of their viceroyalties in South America.

The coastal plain is narrow and generally arid, cooled by sea breezes from the offshore Humboldt Current. Occasionally it suffers violent rainstorms, associated with shifts in the pattern of surface waters. Rivers that cut through the foothills provide water for irrigated agriculture, mainly of cotton, rice and sugar cane. The middle slopes of the Andes – the Quechua, at heights of 2,000 to 3,500 m [6,500 to 11,500 ft] – are warm-temperate and fairly well

watered. These areas supported the main centres of Indian population in the Inca empire.

Above stand the higher reaches of the Andes, extending westwards in cold inhospitable tablelands at 4,000 to 4,800 m [13,000 to 15,700 ft], cultivated up to 4,200 m [13,700 ft] by peasant farmers and grazed by their sheep, alpacas, llamas and vicuñas. The snowy peaks of the high Andes rise to over 6,000 m [19,500 ft]. Though close to the Pacific Ocean, most of the rivers that rise here eventually drain into the Amazon. Their descent to the lowlands is through the *montaña*, a near-impenetrable maze of valleys, ridges and plains, permanently soaked by rain and thickly timbered. Beyond extend the Amazon lowlands – hot, wet and clad mainly in dense tropical rainforest. Occupying half the country, they are thinly inhabited by Indians.

Lima was developed as the Spanish colonial cap-

ital, and through its port of Callao passed much of the trade of Spanish settlers; 19th-century exports included guano (bird-droppings, valuable as an agricultural fertilizer) from the offshore islands, and wild rubber. Peru gained independence from Spain in 1824, but difficulties of communication, political strife, earthquakes and other natural disasters, and a chronically unbalanced economy have dogged the country's development.

Today Peru faces many economic, social and

THE ANDES

Created 200 million years ago by the collision of the Nasca plate and the land mass of South America – and still moving at about 12.5 mm [0.5 in] each year – the Andes mountain system extends along the entire west side of the continent from the coast of the Caribbean to Tierra del Fuego for over 6,400 km [4,000 mls], making it the world's longest chain.

It is the highest range outside the Himalayas and Argentina's Cerro Aconcagua, at 6,960 m [22,834 ft], is the highest peak outside Asia. Argentina shares with Chile four of the ten highest summits. In the middle section there are two main chains and elsewhere three, with the breadth exceeding 800 km [500 mls] to the north of latitude 20°S. Altogether the range has 54 peaks over 6,100 m [20,000 ft].

Many of South America's rivers, including the Orinoco, Negro, Amazon and Madeira, rise in the Andes, and the range is home to the continent's largest lake, Titicaca, which lies on the Peru–Bolivia border at 3,812 m [12,506 ft]. The Andes contains numerous volcanoes and is subject almost everywhere to violent earthquakes. Many volcanoes are still active and Cotopaxi in north-central Ecuador is usually regarded as the world's highest (5,896 m [19,457 ft]).

The condor, symbol of the mountains and the world's largest vulture, is now down to a few hundred, despite attempts by several Andean countries – backed by the United States – to increase its dwindling numbers.

In 1910 the Andes were tunnelled, linking the Chilean and Argentine railways by the 3 km [2 ml] long tunnel at an altitude of 3,200 m [10,500 ft], south-west of Aconcagua.

---

political problems. Agricultural production has failed to keep up with population, so wheat, rice, meat and other staple foods are imported. Cotton, coffee and sugar are exported. Peru is the leading producer of coca, the shrub used in the illegal production of cocaine, and earnings were thought to be in excess of US$3 billion in the 1980s.

Peru once had the largest fish catch in the world and there are 70 canning factories. Anchoveta was the main target, but fishing was halted from 1976 until 1982 because of depleted stocks. In 1983 a warm current known as 'El Niño' ruined the fishing but recovery followed from 1986.

Several metals are exported – Peru is third in world silver production, fifth in zinc and sixth in lead, though copper is its most important earner – but industrial unrest has reduced production. Exports of oil are growing, however, providing much-needed foreign capital for industrial development, now forthcoming after a lull following Peru's limiting of debt repayment in 1985. Peru's inflation rate – 3,400% in 1989 and a staggering 7,480% in 1990 – settled down to 200% in 1991, the year that many state industries were liberalized.

The economic problems facing Peru are coupled with the terrorist activity by the Sendero Luminoso

---

COUNTRY: Republic of Peru

AREA: 1,285,220 sq km [496,223 sq mls]

POPULATION: 22,332,000

CAPITAL (Population): Lima (4,605,000)

GOVERNMENT: Unitary republic with bicameral legislature

ETHNIC GROUPS: Quechua 47%, Mestizo 32%, White 12%

LANGUAGES: Spanish and Quechua (both official), Aymara

RELIGIONS: Roman Catholic 92%

NATIONAL DAY: 28 July; Independence Day (1821)

CURRENCY: Inti = 100 céntimos = 1,000 soles

ANNUAL INCOME PER PERSON: $1,160

MAIN PRIMARY PRODUCTS: Iron ore, silver, zinc, tungsten, petroleum, gold, copper, lead, tin, molybdenum

MAIN INDUSTRIES: Food processing, textiles, copper smelting, forestry, fishing

EXPORTS: $170 per person

MAIN EXPORTS: Copper 19%, petroleum and derivatives 10%, lead 9%, zinc 8%, fishmeal 8%, coffee 5%

MAIN EXPORT PARTNERS: USA 34%, Japan 10%, Belgium 4%, Germany 4%

IMPORTS: $84 per person

MAIN IMPORTS: Fuels, machinery, chemicals, food, tobacco

MAIN IMPORT PARTNERS: USA 27%, Argentina 9%, Brazil 6%

TOURISM: 350,000 visitors per year

POPULATION DENSITY: 17 per sq km [45 per sq ml]

INFANT MORTALITY: 76 per 1,000 live births

LIFE EXPECTANCY: Female 67 yrs, male 63 yrs

ADULT LITERACY: 80%

PRINCIPAL CITIES (Population): Lima 4,605,000 Arequipa 592,000 Trujillo 491,000 Chiclayo 395,000

('Shining Path') which began in 1980. This is a Maoist group also connected with the illegal trade in drugs, and the government has taken strong action. Over 23,000 people have been killed since their activities began, and damage to the economy is estimated at more than $20 billion. The government, however, is among Latin America's most repressive.

To add to Peru's problems, the country suffered the worst cholera outbreak in the Americas this century early in 1991, with some 2,500 deaths. While the disease spread to neighbouring nations, trading partners were reluctant to import vulnerable Peruvian food products ■

THE INCA CIVILIZATION

The empire of the Incas, centring on Cuzco in the Peruvian highlands, developed from millennia of earlier Andean civilizations that included the Chavin, the Nazca and the Tiahuanaco. The Incas began their conquests about 1350 AD, and by the end of the 15th century their empire extended from central Chile to Ecuador. Perhaps some 10 million people owed allegiance to it when it fell to the Spanish *conquistadores* in 1532.

The empire was military and theocratic, with the sun as the focus of worship. Temples and shrines were created for sun worship; the Sun Temple at Cuzco had a circumference of 350 m [1,148 ft], and many other buildings were equally massive. The people were skilled farmers, using elaborate irrigation systems and terraced fields.

Gold and silver were particularly valued by the Incas for ornamentation. They were prized also by the *conquistadores*, who looted them from every corner of the empire and quickly set the Indians to mining more. Fragments of Inca culture and beliefs remain among the Quechua-speaking peoples of Peru and Bolivia.

SOUTH AMERICA

GUYANA

This striking design, adopted by Guyana on independence from Britain in 1966, has colours representing the people's energy building a new nation (red), their perseverance (black), minerals (yellow), rivers (white) and forests (green).

Temperatures along the coast are high with an annual variation of only a few degrees; there is a daily range of about 10°C [18°F]. Temperatures are lower on the higher land of the south and west. The north-east trade winds blow constantly, and so the rainfall is high, falling on over 200 days in the year, in a longer and heavier wet season, May–August, and a lesser, January–December. The rainfall decreases southwards and inland, where the dry season extends from September–February.

COUNTRY: Co-operative Republic of Guyana
AREA: 214,970 sq km [83,000 sq mls]
POPULATION: 796,000
CAPITAL (Population): Georgetown (188,000)
GOVERNMENT: Republic with unicameral legislature
ETHNIC GROUPS: Asian Indian 51%, Black 29%, Mulatto 13%, Amerindian 4%
LANGUAGES: English (official), Hindi, Urdu and Amerindian dialects
RELIGIONS: Hindu 34%, Protestant 34%, Roman Catholic 18%, Sunni Muslim 9%
NATIONAL DAY: 23 February; Republic Day (1970)
CURRENCY: Guyana $ = 100 cents
ANNUAL INCOME PER PERSON: $370
POPULATION DENSITY: 4 per sq km [10 per sq ml]
LIFE EXPECTANCY: Female 74 yrs, male 69 yrs
ADULT LITERACY: 75%

The 'land of many waters' was settled by the Dutch between 1616 and 1621. The territory was ceded to Britain in 1814, and in 1831 British Guiana was formed. Independent since 1966, Guyana – the only English-speaking country in South America – became a republic in 1970. It is largely uninhabited and 95% of the population live within a few kilometres of the coast, leaving the interior virtually empty.

The vast interior, covering 85% of the land area, includes low forest-covered plateaus, the wooded Rupununi savannas, meandering river valleys, and the spectacular Roraima Massif on the Venezuela-Brazil border. The coastal plain is mainly artificial, reclaimed from the tidal marshes and mangrove swamps by dykes and canals.

Land reclamation for sugar and cotton planting began in the 18th century under Dutch West India Company rule, using slave labour, and continued through the 19th century after the British took over, with indentured Asian labour replacing slaves after emancipation. Today sugar remains the main plantation crop, with production largely mechanized, most of it in the lower Demerara River area.

The Asian community, however, who make up about half the total Guyanan population, are involved in rice growing. Bauxite mining and alumina production are well-established industries, combining with sugar production to provide 80% of the country's overseas earnings. But neither sugar nor rice provide year-round work and unemployment remains a stubborn problem. The economy, which is 80% state-controlled, entered a prolonged economic crisis in the 1970s, and in the early 1980s the situation was exacerbated by the decline in the production and price of bauxite, sugar and rice. Following unrest, the government sought to replace Western aid by turning for help to socialist countries. During the late 1980s Western aid and investment were again sought, but by 1989 the social and economic difficulties had led to the suspension of foreign assistance ∎

SURINAM

Adopted on independence from the Dutch in 1975, Surinam's flag features the colours of the main political parties, the yellow star symbolizing unity and a golden future. The red is twice the width of the green, and four times that of the white.

COUNTRY: Republic of Suriname
AREA: 163,270 sq km [63,039 sq mls]
POPULATION: 422,000
CAPITAL (Population): Paramaribo (192,000)
GOVERNMENT: Republic with unicameral legislature
ETHNIC GROUPS: Asian Indian 37%, Creole 31%, Indonesian 14%, Black 9%, Amerindian 3%
LANGUAGES: Dutch (official), English
RELIGIONS: Hindu 27%, Roman Catholic 23%, Sunni Muslim 20%, Protestant 19%
NATIONAL DAY: 25 November
CURRENCY: Surinam guilder = 100 cents
ANNUAL INCOME PER PERSON: $3,050
LIFE EXPECTANCY: Female 73 yrs, male 68 yrs
ADULT LITERACY: 65%

Although Spaniards visited as early as 1499, Surinam was first settled by British colonists in 1651. In 1667 it was ceded to Holland in exchange for Nieuw-Amsterdam, now New York, and was confirmed as a Dutch colony, called Dutch Guiana, in 1816.

Surinam has a coastline of 350 km [218 mls] of Amazonian mud and silt, fringed by extensive mangrove swamps. Behind lies an old coastal plain of sands and clays, bordering a stretch of sandy savanna. The heavily forested interior uplands further to the south are part of the Guiana Highlands, whose weathered soils form the basis of the crucial bauxite industry.

Surinam's hot, steamy climate grows an abundance of bananas, citrus fruits and coconuts for export, with rice and many other tropical commodities for home consumption. Plantations were initially worked by African slaves, later by Chinese and East Indian indentured labour. Bauxite and its derivatives, shrimps and bananas are the main exports, but though 92% of the land is covered by forest – the world's highest figure – little is commercially exploited. There is also considerable potential for expansion of tourism.

In 1980 there was a military coup and later, in 1982, after the execution of 15 opposition leaders and the banning of all political parties, the Netherlands broke off relations and suspended all aid; however, following elections, the Netherlands agreed to resume aid in 1988. This was badly needed because of a rebellion of boschneger (bush negro), descendants of the African slaves; begun in 1986, this disrupted bauxite mining on which the country depends for much of its earnings ∎

FRENCH GUIANA

The official flag flown over 'Guyane' is the French tricolour. A French possession since 1676 (apart from 1809–17), the territory is treated as part of mainland France and its citizens send representatives to the Paris parliament.

COUNTRY: Department of French Guiana
AREA: 90,000 sq km [34,749 sq mls]
POPULATION: 99,000
CAPITAL (Population): Cayenne (38,000)
GOVERNMENT: Overseas department of France
ETHNIC GROUPS: Creole 42%, Chinese 14%, French 10%, Haitian 7%
LANGUAGES: French (official), Creole patois
RELIGIONS: Roman Catholic 80%, Protestant 4%
NATIONAL DAY: 14 July; National Day – Storming of the Bastille (1789)
CURRENCY: Franc = 100 centimes
ANNUAL INCOME PER PERSON: $2,500

The smallest country in South America, French Guiana has a narrow coastal plain comprising mangrove swamps and marshes, alternating with drier areas that can be cultivated; one such is the site of the capital, Cayenne. Inland, a belt of sandy savanna rises to a forested plateau.

A French settlement was established in 1604 by a group of merchant adventurers, and after brief periods of Dutch, English and Portuguese rule the territory finally became permanently French in 1817. In 1946 – a year after the closure of Devil's Island, the notorious convict settlement – its status changed to that of an overseas department of France, and in 1974 it also became an administrative region.

The economy is very dependent on France, both for budgetary aid and for food and manufactured goods. The French have also built a rocket-launching station near the coast at Kaurou. Timber is the most important natural resource; bauxite and kaolin have been discovered but are largely unexploited. Only 104 sq km [40 sq mls] of the land is under cultivation where sugar, cassava and rice are grown. Fishing, particularly for shrimps, much of which are exported, is a leading occupation, and tourism, though in its infancy, has as main attractions the Amerindian villages of the interior and the lush tropical scenery ■

BRAZIL

The sphere bears the motto 'Order and Progress' and its 23 stars, arranged in the pattern of the night sky over Brazil, represent the states and federal district. Green symbolizes the nation's forests, the yellow diamond its mineral wealth.

Brazil lies almost entirely within the tropics. The northern half of the country is dominated by the Amazon basin and, except for the highlands in the south-east, there are no mountains. The monthly temperatures are high – over 25°C [77°F] – and there is little annual variation. Brasilia has only a 4°C [7°F] difference between July and October; Rio has twice this range. The hottest part of the country is in the north-east. Frosts do occur in the eastern highlands and the extreme south of the country.

By any standard Brazil is a big country. Fifth largest in the world – and the sixth most populous – it covers nearly 48% of South America. Structurally, it has two main regions. In the north lies the vast Amazon Basin, once an inland sea and now drained by a river system that carries one-fifth of the Earth's running water. In the centre and south lies the sprawling bulk of the Brazilian Highlands, a huge extent of hard crystalline rock deeply dissected into rolling uplands. This occupies the heartland (Mato Grosso), and the whole western flank of the country from the bulge to the border of Uruguay.

Landscape

The Amazon River rises in the Peruvian Andes, close to the Pacific Ocean, and many of its tributaries are of similar origin. Several are wide enough to take boats of substantial draught (6 m [20 ft]) from the Andean foothills all the way to the Atlantic – a distance of 5,000 km [3,000 mls] or more.

The largest area of river plain lies in the upper part of the basin, along the frontier with Bolivia and Peru. Downstream the flood plain is relatively narrow, shrinking in width to a few kilometres where the basin drains between the Guiana Highlands in the north and the Brazilian Highlands in the south.

The undulating plateau of the northern highlands carries poor soils; here rainfall is seasonal, and the typical natural vegetation is a thorny scrub forest, used as open grazing for poor cattle herds. Further south scrub turns to wooded savanna – the *campo cerrado* vegetation that covers 2 million sq km [770,000 sq mls] of the interior plateau. It extends into the basin of the Paraná River and its tributaries, most of which start in the coastal highlands and flow east, draining ultimately into the Plate estuary. The Mato Grosso, on the border with Bolivia, is part of this large area and still mostly unexplored.

Conditions are better in the south, with more reliable rainfall. The south-east includes a narrow coastal plain, swampy in places and with abundant rainfall throughout the year; behind rises the Great Escarpment (820 m [2,700 ft]), first in a series of steps to the high eastern edge of the plateau. Over 60% of Brazil's population live in four southern and south-eastern states that account for only 17% of the total area.

History and politics

Brazil was 'discovered' by Pedro Alvarez Cabral on 22 April 1500 and gradually penetrated by Portuguese settlers, missionaries, explorers and prospectors during the 17th and 18th centuries. Many of the semi-nomadic indigenous Indians were enslaved for plantation work or driven into the interior, and some 4 million African slaves were introduced, notably in the sugar-growing areas of the north-east.

Little more than a group of rival provinces, Brazil began to unite in 1808 when the Portuguese royal court, seeking refuge from Napoleon, transferred from Lisbon to Rio de Janeiro. The eldest surviving son of King Joãs VI of Portugal was chosen as 'Perpetual Defender' of Brazil by a national congress. In 1822 he proclaimed the independence of the country and was chosen as the constitutional emperor with the title Pedro I. He abdicated in 1831 and was succeeded by his son Pedro II, who ruled for nearly 50 years and whose liberal policies included the gradual abolition of slavery (1888).

A federal system was adopted for the United States of Brazil in the 1881 constitution and Brazil

RIO DE JANEIRO AND SAO PAULO

Much of Brazil's population is concentrated in a relatively small and highly developed 'corner' in the south-east of the country. Rio de Janeiro, discovered by the Portuguese in 1502, lies in a magnificent setting, stretching for 20 km [12 mls] along the coast between mountain and ocean. Though no longer the capital, it remains the focus of Brazil's cultural life, attracting visitors with the world's greatest pre-Lent festival at carnival time.

São Paulo, its early growth fuelled by the coffee boom of the late 19th century, is the most populous city in the southern hemisphere. Estimates state that the 1985 total of 15.5 million will increase to 23.6 million by the year 2000. In both cities the gap between rich and poor is all too evident, the sprawling shanty towns (*favelas*) standing in sharp contrast to sophisticated metropolitan centres.

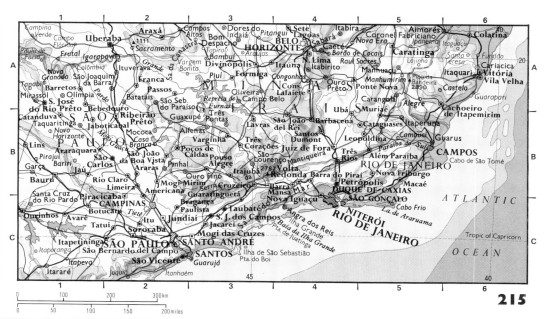

THE AMAZONIAN RAINFOREST

The world's largest and ecologically most important rainforest it was still being destroyed at an alarming rate in the 1980s, with somewhere between 1.5% and 4% disappearing each year in Brazil alone. Opening up the forest for many reasons – logging, mining, ranching, peasant resettlement – the Brazilian authorities did little in real terms when confronted with a catalogue of indictments: decimation of a crucial world habitat; pollution of rivers; destruction of thousands of species of fauna and flora, especially medicinal plants; and the brutal ruination of the lives of the last remaining Amerindian tribes.

Once cut off from the world by impenetrable jungle, hundreds of thousand of Indians have been displaced in the provinces of Rondonia and Acre, principally by loggers and landless migrants, and in Para by mining, dams for HEP and ranching for beef cattle. It is estimated that five centuries ago the Amazon rainforest supported some 2 million Indians in more than 200 tribes; today the number has shrunk to a pitiful 50,000 or so, and many of the tribes have disappeared altogether.

A handful have been relatively lucky – the Yanomani, after huge international support, won their battle in 1991 for a reserve three times the size of Belgium – but for the majority their traditional lifestyle has vanished forever.

At Manaus, in the centre of the Amazonian basin, there is little difference between the temperature of the warmest month, October (29°C [84°F]), and the coolest, April (27°C [81°F]). The temperatures are not extremely high and the highest recorded was 37°C [99°F]; the lowest was 18°C [64°F]. Rainfall totals are high in this region, especially December–March, with a distinct dry season from June to September, when rain falls on only 5–10 days per month on average.

MANAUS
Precipitation 1811mm 71in

---

became a republic in 1889. Until 1930 the country experienced strong economic expansion and prosperity, but social unrest in 1930 resulted in a major revolt and from then until 1945 the country was under the control of President Vargas, who established a strong corporate state similar to that of fascist Italy, although Brazil entered World War II on the side of the Allies. Democracy, often corrupt, prevailed from 1956 to 1964 and from 1985; between were five military presidents of illiberal regimes.

A new constitution came into force in October 1988 – the eighth since independence from the Portuguese in 1822 – which transferred powers from the president to congress and paved the way for a return to democracy in 1990. Today the country comprises 23 states, each with its own directly elected governor and legislature, three territories and the Federal District of Brasília.

Economy and resources

For many decades following the early settlements Brazil was mainly a sugar-producing colony, with most plantations centred on the rich coastal plains of the north-east. Later the same areas produced cotton, cocoa, rice and other crops. In the south, colonists penetrated the interior in search of slaves and minerals, especially gold and diamonds; the city of Ouro Prêto in Minas Gerais was built, and Rio de Janeiro grew as the port for the region.

During the 19th century São Paulo state became the centre of a huge coffee-growing industry; and while the fortunes made in mining helped to develop Rio de Janeiro, profits from coffee were invested in the city of São Paulo. Immigrants from Italy and Germany settled in the south, introducing farming into the fertile valleys in coexistence with the cattle-ranchers and gauchos of the plains.

The second half of the 19th century saw the development of the wild rubber industry in the Amazon Basin, where the city of Manaus, with its world-famous opera house, served as a centre and market; though Manaus lies 1,600 km [1,000 mls]

from the mouth of the Amazon, rubber collected from trees in the hinterland could be shipped out directly to world markets in ocean-going steamers. Brazil enjoyed a virtual monopoly of the rubber trade until the early 20th century, when Malaya began to compete, later with massive success.

Vast mineral resources exist, particularly in Minas Gerais and the Amazon area; they include bauxite, tin, iron ore, manganese, chrome, nickel, uranium, platinum and industrial diamonds. Brazil is the world's leading exporter of iron ore and there are reserves of at least 18,000 million metric tons including the world's biggest at Carajás. Discoveries of new reserves of minerals are frequently being made. The world's largest tin mine is situated in the Amazon region, 50% of the world's platinum is in Brazil, and 65% of the world's supply of precious stones are produced within the country.

The demand for energy has increased rapidly over the years and over a quarter of imports are for crude petroleum. An alternative energy was developed from 1976 made from sugar cane and cassava called ethanol (combustible alcohol) with the aim of reducing demand for petroleum, and in the eight years to 1987, some 3.5 million cars were manufactured to take this fuel; falling oil prices later made this uneconomic. Large investments have been made in hydroelectricity – 93% of the country's electricity is now from water – and the Itaipú HEP station on the Paraná, shared with Paraguay, is the world's largest.

Brazil is one of the world's largest farming countries, and agriculture employs 35% of the population and provides 40% of her exports. The main agricultural exports are coffee, sugar, soyabeans, orange juice concentrates (80% of world total), beef, cocoa, poultry, sisal, tobacco, maize and cotton. While Brazil is no longer the leading exporter of coffee – a position now held by Colombia – the country is the world's biggest producer, as it is for sugar cane, bananas, oranges, sisal and castor oil.

The Amazon Basin is gradually being opened for the controversial exploitation of forests and mines, with Santarém a new focus of agriculture in a frontier land. There are 35 deep-water ports in Brazil and the two main oil terminals at São Sebastião and Madre de Jesus are being expanded. Though river transport now plays only a minor part in the movement of goods, for many years rivers gave the only access to the interior, and there are plans to link the Amazon and the Upper Paraná to give a navigable waterway across central Brazil.

A network of arterial roads is being added, replacing the 19th-century railways which have been used to take primary products to markets on the coast. Road transport now accounts for 70% of freight and 97% of passenger traffic.

Population

In 1872 Brazil had a population of about 10 million. By 1972 this had increased almost tenfold, and 1989 saw a figure of 147.4 million Brazilians – with a projected increase to 200 million by the end of the century. Of the economically active population (55 million in 1985), 15 million were engaged in agriculture, 9 million in the service industries, 8 million in manufacturing, 5 million in the wholesale and retail trade, and 3 million in construction.

On 21 April 1960 Rio de Janeiro ceased to be the capital and inland the new city of Brasília, built from 1956 onwards, in many ways encapsulated

---

RIO DE JANEIRO
Precipitation 1086mm 43in

Rio de Janeiro experiences a high rainfall and a marked dry season May–August – rain falling on only about 20 days from June to August – but not so marked as inland. Most of Brazil has moderate rainfall, but there are very heavy totals at the mouth of the Amazon and in the headwaters of the Amazon and on the south-east coast below the highlands. There is an arid zone in the north-east. At Rio the sun shines for 5–7 hours per day.

COUNTRY: Federative Republic of Brazil

AREA: 8,511,970 sq km [3,286,472 sq mls]

POPULATION: 153,322,000

CAPITAL (Population): Brasilia (1,577,000)

GOVERNMENT: Federal republic with bicameral legislature

ETHNIC GROUPS: White 53%, Mulatto 22%, Mestizo 12%, Black 11% (Indian 0.1%)

LANGUAGES: Portuguese (official), others

RELIGIONS: Roman Catholic 87%, Protestant 8%

NATIONAL DAY: 7 September; Independence Day (1822)

CURRENCY: Cruzado = 100 centavos

ANNUAL INCOME PER PERSON: $2,680

SOURCE OF INCOME: Agriculture 9%, industry 43%, services 49%

MAIN PRIMARY PRODUCTS: Coal, iron ore, manganese, gold, bauxite, copper, diamonds, petroleum

MAIN INDUSTRIES: Steel, petrochemicals, vehicles, chemicals, machinery, consumer goods, cement, offshore oil, shipping, timber

EXPORTS: $233 per person

MAIN EXPORTS: Transport equipment 12%, soya beans 9%, coffee 8%, iron ore 7%, machinery 6%, footwear 5%

MAIN EXPORT PARTNERS: USA 27%, Japan 6%, Netherlands 6%, Germany 4%, Italy 5%

IMPORTS: $124 per person

MAIN IMPORTS: Primary products 33%, capital goods 26%, oil and oil products 25%

MAIN IMPORT PARTNERS: USA 20%, Germany 9%, Japan 6%, Saudi Arabia 6%

TOTAL ARMED FORCES: 320,000

TOURISM: 1,800,000 visitors per year

ROADS: 1,675,040 km [1,046,900 mls]

RAILWAYS: 29,901 km [18,688 mls]

POPULATION DENSITY: 18 per sq km [45 per sq ml]

URBAN POPULATION: 77%

POPULATION GROWTH: 2.1% per year

BIRTHS: 28 per 1,000 population

DEATHS: 8 per 1,000 population

INFANT MORTALITY: 57 per 1,000 live births

LIFE EXPECTANCY: Female 69 yrs, male 64 yrs

POPULATION PER DOCTOR: 1,080

ADULT LITERACY: 80%

PRINCIPAL CITIES (Population): São Paulo 16,832,000 Rio de Janeiro 11,141,000 Belo Horizonte 3,446,000 Recife 2,945,000 Pôrto Alegre 2,924,000 Salvador 2,362,000 Fortaleza 2,169,000 Curitiba 1,926,000 Brasilia 1,577,000 Nova Iguaçu 1,325,000

both the spirit and the problems of contemporary Brazil – a sparkling, dramatic, planned city, deliberately planted in the unpopulated uplands of Goías as a gesture of faith; modern, practical and beautiful, but still surrounded by the shanties of poverty and – beyond them – the challenge of an untamed wilderness. So much of the nation's wealth is still held by the élites of the cities, particularly those of the south-east, and despite grandiose development

plans aimed at spreading prosperity throughout the country and despite the international image of fun-loving carnivals, the interior remains poor and underpopulated.

Although possessing great reserves, Brazil has not made the big jump from developing to developed country. The boom of 'the miracle years' from 1968 to 1973, when the economy grew at more than 10% per annum, was not sustained. Indeed, falls in

commodity prices and massive borrowing to finance large and often unproductive projects have combined to make Brazil the world's biggest debtor nation; despite paying back $69 billion between 1985 and 1991 – a huge drain on any economy – there was still over $120 billion owed. Inflation during 1990 was nearly 3,000% – down to under 400% in 1991 – and mismanagement and corruption still afflicted administration ■

THE AMAZON

Though not the world's longest river – 6,430 km [3,990 mls] – the Amazon is easily the mightiest, discharging some 180,000 cu.m/sec [6,350,000 cu.ft/sec] into the Atlantic, more than four times the volume of its nearest rival, the Zaïre. The flow is so great that silt discolours the water up to 200 km [125 mls] out to sea.

The Amazon starts its journey in the Andes of Peru – only 150 km [95 mls] from the Pacific – at Lake Villafro, head of the Apurímac branch of the Ucayali, which then flows north to join the other main headstream, the Marañón. Navigable to ocean-going vessels of 6,000 tonnes up to the Peruvian jungle port of Iquitos, some 3,700 km [2,300 mls] from the sea, it then flows east briefly forming the Peru-Colombian border – before entering Brazil. Here it becomes the Solimões before joining the Negro (itself 18 km [11 mls] wide) at Manaus.

Along with more than 1,000 significant tributaries, seven of them more than 1,600 km [1,000 mls] long, the Amazon drains the largest river basin in the world – about 7 million sq km [2.7 million sq mls] – nearly two-fifths of South America and an area more than twice the size of India.

SOUTH AMERICA

BOLIVIA

Dating from liberation in 1825, the tricolour has been used as both national and merchant flag since 1988. The red stands for Bolivia's animals and the army's courage, the yellow for mineral resources and the green for agriculture.

COUNTRY: Republic of Bolivia
AREA: 1,098,580 sq km [424,162 sq mls]
POPULATION: 7,400,000
CAPITAL (Population): La Paz (993,000)
GOVERNMENT: Unitary republic with bicameral legislature
ETHNIC GROUPS: Mestizo 31%, Quechua 25%, Aymara 17%, White 15%
LANGUAGES: Spanish (official), Aymara, Quechua
RELIGIONS: Roman Catholic 94%
NATIONAL DAY: 6 August; Independence Day (1825)
CURRENCY: Boliviano = 100 centavos
ANNUAL INCOME PER PERSON: $620
MAIN PRIMARY PRODUCTS: Tin, sugar cane, rice, cotton
MAIN INDUSTRIES: Agriculture, manufacturing, tin mining
POPULATION DENSITY: 7 per sq km [17 per sq ml]
LIFE EXPECTANCY: Female 58 yrs, male 54 yrs
ADULT LITERACY: 63%

Although within the tropics, La Paz lies at 3,625 m [11,893 ft] on the Bolivian plateau and temperatures are clearly affected by altitude. The annual range is very small (1°C [2°F]), but temperatures rise rapidly by day and fall sharply at night in the clear air; the diurnal range is very large (10–15°C [18–27°F]), with frequent night frost in winter. Rainfall, which is often thundery, occurs mainly in summer. From April to October, rain falls on less than ten days per month.

THE ALTIPLANO

A high, rolling plateau 3,600 m [12,000 ft] above sea level on the Peruvian border of Bolivia, the Altiplano stretches 400 km [250 mls] north to south between the eastern and western cordilleras of the Andes. Surrounded by high, snow-capped peaks, at its north end lies Lake Titicaca, the highest navigable body of water in the world and according to Indian legend the birthplace of the Inca civilization. To the south are smaller lakes, and extensive salt flats representing old lake beds. Though tropical in latitude the Altiplano is cold, windswept and bleak, by any standards a harsh environment, yet over half the population of Bolivia, including a high proportion of native Indians, make it their home.

The natural vegetation is grassland merging at high levels to *puna* – small bushes and trees forming a hash scrubland. Summer rains and winter snows bring enough moisture to support grass, and llama and alpaca, from guanaco-like ancestors, are herded to provide meat and wool for the peasant farmers.

By far the larger of South America's two land-locked countries, Bolivia is made up of a wide stretch of the Andes and a long, broad Oriente – part of the south-western fringe of the Amazon basin. The western boundary is the High Cordillera Occidental, crowned by Sajama at 6,520 m [21,400 ft] and many other volcanic peaks. To the east lies the Altiplano, a high plateau which in prehistoric times was a great lake. Eastwards again rises the majestic Cordillera Real, where Illimani, a glacier-covered peak of 6,462 m [21,200 ft] forms a backdrop to La Paz (The Peace), the world's highest capital. In the transmontane region to the north and east lies the huge expanse of the Oriente – foothills and plains extending from the semi-arid Chaco of the south-east through the savanna-like llanos of the centre to the high, wetter forests of the northern plains.

In pre-Conquest days Bolivia was the homeland of the Tiahuanaco culture (7th–11th centuries AD) and was later absorbed into the Inca empire; Quechua, the Inca language, is still spoken by large Amerindian minorities that constitute the highest proportion of any South American country. Famous for its silver mines, the high Andean area was exploited ruthlessly by the Spanish *conquistadores*; the mine at Potosí, discovered in 1545, proved the richest in the world, and Upper Peru (today's highland Bolivia) was for two centuries one of the most densely populated of Spain's American colonies. In 1824 the local population seized their independence, naming the country after Simón Bolívar, hero of other South American wars of independence. When the era of silver passed, the economy flagged and the country began to lose ground to its neighbours. The Pacific coast was lost to Chile and Peru in 1884 and large tracts of the Oriente were ceded to Brazil (1903) and Paraguay (1935).

Today Bolivia is the poorest of the South American republics, though it has abundant natural resources with large reserves of petroleum, natural gas and many mineral ores. Lack of investment both in these areas and in the agricultural sector do not help the comparatively poor development, but new irrigation schemes in the south-western Oriente may improve local production of staple foods. Over half the working population is engaged in agriculture,

but mining still contributes significantly to the country's wealth. However, Bolivia, once the world's leading tin producer, now ranks fifth with just 7% of a rapidly dwindling total. Today's main export may well be coca and refined coccaine, which almost certainly employs 5% of the population; the government, with US help and co-operation with neighbours, is trying to stifle the growing industry.

The collapse of the tin market was linked to the record inflation of 1985 – figures vary between 12,000% and over 20,000%, and the 1980–8 average was the world's worst at 483% – though the rates were more stable by the end of the decade. So, too, in a nation renowned for its political volatility (192 coups in 156 years from independence to 1981), was the government, desperately trying to lift Bolivia to the standards of its neighbours ■

PARAGUAY

Paraguay's tricolour is the only national flag with different sides. On the obverse the state emblem, illustrated here, displays the May Star to commemorate liberation from Spain (1811); the reverse shows the treasury seal – a lion and staff.

In South America between 20° and 30°S, there is a prominent summer wet season. The rain is often heavy and can yield as much as 20 mm [0.8 in] per day in Asunción. Summers throughout the plains of Paraguay are very hot and humid, whereas winters are mild and relatively dry. Much of the winter rain is associated with surges of cold air from the Southern Ocean, which can give surprisingly low temperatures, especially in the south of the country.

A landlocked nation, Paraguay is bounded mainly by rivers – the Paraná (South America's second longest) in the south and east, the Pilcomayo in the south-west, and the Paraguay and Apa rivers in the north-west. The middle reach of the Paraguay, navigable for vessels of 1,700 tonnes to Asunción, 1,610 km [1,000 mls] from the sea, divides the country unequally. The eastern third, an extension of the Brazilian plateau at a height of 300 to 600 m [1,000 to 2,000 ft] is densely forested with tropical hardwoods. The western two-thirds is the Northern

Chaco, a flat, alluvial plain rising gently from the damp, marshy Paraguay river valley to semi-desert scrubland along the western border.

Paraguay was settled in 1537 by Spaniards attracted by the labour supply of the native Guarani Indians – and the chance of finding a short cut to the silver of Peru. Forming part of the Rio de la Plata Viceroyalty from 1766, Paraguay broke free in 1811 and achieved independence from Buenos Aires in 1813. For over a century the country struggled for nationhood, torn by destructive internal strife and

conflict with neighbouring states: in 1865–70, war against Brazil, Argentina and Uruguay cost the country more than half its 600,000 people and

BOLIVIA, PARAGUAY, URUGUAY

was followed by political and economic stability.

In 1954 General Stroessner seized power and assumed the presidency. During his dictatorship there was considerable economic growth, particularly in the 1970s, and great emphasis was placed on developing hydroelectricity: by 1976 Paraguay was self-sufficient in electric energy as a result of the completion of the Acaray complex, and a second HEP project (the world's largest) started production in 1984 at Itaipú – a joint $20 billion venture with Brazil to harness the Paraná. Paraguay was now generating 99.8% of its electricity from water-power, and another construction on the Paraná – in the south at Yacyreta (near Encarnación) and involving the world's longest dam – was commissioned.

However, demand slackened and income declined, making it difficult for Paraguay to repay foreign debts incurred on the projects, and high inflation and balance of payments problems followed. The economy is being adjusted and as there are no significant mineral sources a return to an agricultural base is planned for the 1990s.

Hopefully, this will be happening under the umbrella of democracy. Stroessner's regime was a particularly unpleasant variety of despotism, and he ruled with an ever-increasing disregard for human rights during nearly 35 years of fear and fraud before being deposed by his own supporters in 1989. The speeches about reform from his successor, General Andrés Rodríguez, sounded somewhat hollow, but

COUNTRY: Republic of Paraguay
AREA: 406,750 sq km [157,046 sq mls]
POPULATION: 4,277,000
CAPITAL (Population): Asunción (729,000)
GOVERNMENT: Unitary republic
ETHNIC GROUPS: Mestizo 90%, Amerindian 3%
LANGUAGES: Spanish (official) 6%, Guarani 40%
RELIGIONS: Roman Catholic 96%
NATIONAL DAY: 14 May; Independence Day (1811)
CURRENCY: Guarani = 100 centimos
ANNUAL INCOME PER PERSON: $1,110
MAIN PRIMARY PRODUCTS: Timber, cattle, limestone, kaolin, gypsum
MAIN INDUSTRIES: Agriculture, manufacturing
MAIN EXPORTS: Cotton, soya, oil seeds, timber
MAIN IMPORTS: Petroleum and petroleum products, chemicals, machinery, transport and electrical equipment
POPULATION DENSITY: 11 per sq km [27 per sq ml]
LIFE EXPECTANCY: Female 70 yrs, male 65 yrs
ADULT LITERACY: 81%

at the end of 1991 Paraguayans did indeed go to the polls to elect a constituent assembly which would frame a new constitution incorporating a multiparty system. At the same time the country was given what amounted to a virtual clean bill of health by international human rights organizations. The choice was whether to institute austerity measures to sort out the economy – or stick to the safe policies of the past ∎

much of its territory. At a time when most other South American countries were attracting European settlers and foreign capital for development, Paraguay remained isolated and forbidding. Some territory was regained after the Chaco Wars against Bolivia in 1929–35, and in 1947 a period of civil war

URUGUAY

Displayed since 1830, the stripes represent the nine provinces of Uruguay on independence from Spain two years earlier. The blue and white and the May Sun derive from the flag originally employed by Argentina in the colonial struggle.

After Surinam, Uruguay is the smallest South American state, a low-lying rolling country of tall prairie grasses and riparian woodlands with the highest land less than 600 m [2,000 ft] above sea level. The Atlantic coast and River Plate estuary are fringed with lagoons and sand dunes; the centre of the country is a low plateau, rising in the north towards the Brazilian border. The Uruguay River forms the western boundary, and is navigable as far as the falls at Salto, 300 km [186 mls] from the Plate.

Originally little more than the hinterland to the Spanish base at Montevideo, Uruguay formed a buffer area between northern Portuguese and western Spanish territories. Though independent in 1828, internal struggles and civil war intervened before the country developed a basis for prosperity. European immigrants settled the coast and the valley of the Uruguay River, farming the lowlands and leaving the highlands for stock-rearing.

Meat processing, pioneered at Fray Bentos in the 1860s, was the start of a meat-and-hide export industry that, boosted by railways to Montevideo and later by refrigerated cargo ships, established the nation's fortunes. Today a modern and moderately prosperous country, Uruguay still depends largely on exports of animal products – mostly meat, wool and dairy produce – for her livelihood.

Farming is thus the main industry, though four out of five Uruguayans are urban-living and almost half live in the capital. Morever, although more than 90% of Uruguay's land could be used for agriculture, only 10% of it is currently under cultivation. The manufacturing industry today is largely centred on food processing and packing, though with a small domestic market the economy has diversified into cement, chemicals, leather, textiles and steel. Uruguay's trading patterns are changing, too, in an

attempt to avoid reliance on Brazil and Argentina, and in 1988 trade agreements with China and USSR were signed. With inadequate supplies of coal, gas and oil, the nation depends on HEP (90%) for its energy, and exports electricity to Argentina.

Since 1828 Uruguay has been dominated by two political parties – Colorados (Liberals) and Blancos (Conservatives – and from 1904 has been unique in constitutional innovations aimed at avoiding a dictatorship. The early part of the 20th century saw the development of a pioneering welfare state which in turn encouraged extensive immigration. From 1973 until 1985, however, the country was under a strict

COUNTRY: Eastern Republic of Uruguay
AREA: 177,410 sq km [68,498 sq mls]
POPULATION: 3,094,000
CAPITAL (Population): Montevideo (1,248,000)
GOVERNMENT: Unitary state with bicameral legislature
ETHNIC GROUPS: White 88%, Mestizo 8%, Black 4%
LANGUAGES: Spanish (official)
RELIGIONS: Christian (Roman Catholic) 60%, Protestant 3%, Jewish 2%
NATIONAL DAY: 25 August; National Independence Day
CURRENCY: Peso = 100 centisimos
ANNUAL INCOME PER PERSON: $2,560
MAIN PRIMARY PRODUCTS: Rice, meat, fruit, fish
MAIN INDUSTRIES: Meat processing, food processing, light engineering, cement, chemicals, textiles, steel
MAIN EXPORTS: Hides and leather, meat, wool, dairy products, rice, fish
MAIN IMPORTS: Fuels, metals, machinery, vehicles
DEFENCE: 10% of national budget
POPULATION DENSITY: 17 per sq km [45 per sq ml]
LIFE EXPECTANCY: Female 75 yrs, male 68 yrs
ADULT LITERACY: 94%

The plains around the estuary of the River Plate have a very even distribution of rainfall throughout the year. Much of the rain is associated with the advance of cold air from the Southern Ocean, which may be accompanied by a Pampero Sucio, a violent squall with rain and thunder followed by cooler, sunny weather. Near to the ocean, summers are pleasantly warm and winters less cold than at similar latitudes in the northern hemisphere.

military regime accused of appalling human rights abuses, and by 1990 it was still adjusting again to civilian government. President Lacalle's first task was to try and reduce the dependency on events in Brazil and Argentina, Uruguay's huge neighbours ∎

SOUTH AMERICA

CHILE

Inspired by the US Stars and Stripes, the flag was designed by an American serving with the Chilean Army in 1817 and adopted that year. White represents the snow-capped Andes (to the east), blue the sky and red the blood of the nation's patriots.

Chile has nearly every type of climate because of its latitudinal extent and the Andes in the east. In northern Chile is the arid Atacama Desert. Rainfall increases southwards and central Chile has a Mediterranean-type climate of a dry season, November to March, a hot summer and warm winter. Monthly temperatures are never below 5°C [41°F]. In the south, westerly winds all the year bring storms and high rainfall. Except in the mountains, Chile does not often experience very low temperatures.

Extending in an extraordinary shape down the west coast of South America from latitude 17°30'S, well inside the tropics, to 55°50'S at Cape Horn, Chile falls into three parallel zones based on the longitudinal folding of the Andes.

From the Bolivian border in the north down as far as 27°S runs an extension of the high plateau of Bolivia. Several volcanic peaks of more than 6,000 m [19,680 ft] mark the edge of the western cordilleras. South of Ojos del Salado the ranges narrow and steepen, then gradually reduce in height as they approach Cape Horn.

The parallel coastal ranges create a rolling, hilly belt, rising to 3,000 m [10,000 ft] or more in the north but generally much lower. Between this belt and the Andes runs the sheltered and fertile central valley, most clearly marked southwards from Santiago; over 60% of the population live in an 800 km [500 ml] stretch of land here.

A Spanish colony from the 16th century, Chile developed as a mining enterprise in the north and a series of vast ranches, or haciendas, in the fertile central region. After Chile finally freed itself from Spanish rule in 1818 mining continued to flourish in the north, and in the south Valparaiso developed as a port with the farmlands of the southern valley exporting produce to California and Australia.

The first Christian Democrat president was elected in 1964, but in 1970 he was replaced by President Allende; his administration, the world's first democratically elected Marxist government, was overthrown in a CIA-backed military coup in 1973 and General Pinochet took power as dictator, banning all political activity in a repressive regime. A new constitution took effect from 1981, allowing for an eventual return to democracy, and free elections finally took place in 1989. President Aylwin took office in 1990, but Pinochet secured continued office as commander-in-chief of the armed forces.

Chile's economy continues to depend on agriculture, fishing and, particularly, mining: the country is the world's leading copper producer (17% of total) and copper accounts for nearly half of all export earnings. Magellanes, the southernmost region that includes Cape Horn and Tierra del Fuego (shared with Argentina), has oilfields that produce about half the country's needs. When the military

took over in 1973 inflation was running at about 850%, despite government controls, and Pinochet reintroduced a market economy and abandoned agricultural reform. Economic decline began in 1981 – brought about, in part, by low world prices for minerals and primary products in general – but in the 1990s economic recovery was in prospect ∎

COUNTRY: Republic of Chile

AREA: 756,950 sq km [292,258 sq mls]

POPULATION: 13,386,000

CAPITAL (Population): Santiago (4,858,000)

GOVERNMENT: Return to democracy after military rule

ETHNIC GROUPS: Mestizo 92%, Amerindian 7%

LANGUAGES: Spanish (official)

RELIGIONS: Roman Catholic 80%, Protestant 6%

NATIONAL DAY: 18 September; Independence Day (1810)

CURRENCY: Peso = 100 centavos

ANNUAL INCOME PER PERSON: $1,940

MAIN PRIMARY PRODUCTS: Copper, coal, petroleum, natural gas, gold, lead, iron ore

MAIN INDUSTRIES: Food processing, wine, forestry, iron and steel, copper, cement

DEFENCE: 11% of national budget

TOURISM: 560,000 visitors per year

POPULATION DENSITY: 18 per sq km [46 per sq ml]

LIFE EXPECTANCY: Female 76 yrs, male 69 yrs

PRINCIPAL CITIES (Population): Santiago 4,858,000 Concepción 394,000 Viña del Mar 316,000

ARGENTINA

The 'celeste' and white stripes, symbol of independence since 1810 around the city of Buenos Aires, became the national flag in 1816 and influenced other Latin American countries. A May Sun, not in general use, was added two years later.

Argentina, stretching from the tropics almost into Antarctica, with the high Andes to the west and lying in the narrow neck of land between the two oceans, experiences many climates. The north is subtropical, with temperatures around 20°C [68°F] in June and 25°C [77°F] in January. The south is temperate, with May–August above freezing and 10°C [50°F] in January or February. Rainfall is heaviest in the subtropical north-east and in Patagonia.

Largest of the Spanish-speaking countries of Latin America, but still less than a third of the size of Brazil, Argentina forms a wedge-shaped country from the Tropic of Capricorn to Tierra del Fuego. The western boundary lies high in the Andes, including basins, ridges and peaks of 6,000 m [19,685 ft] in the north. South of the latitude 27°S the ridges merge into a single high cordillera, the highest point being Aconcagua at 6,960 m [22,834 ft], the tallest mountain in the western hemisphere; south of 39°S the Patagonian Andes are lower, but include glaciers and volcanoes. Eastern Argentina is a series of alluvial plains, stretching from the Andean foothills to the sea. The Gran Chaco in the north slopes gradually towards the valley of the Paraná River, from the high desert in the foothills to lowland swamp forest. Further south are the extensive pampas grasslands, damp and fertile near Buenos Aires, drier but still productive elsewhere. Southwards again the pampas give way to the rougher and less hospitable plateaus of Patagonia.

Formerly a dependency of Peru, Argentina ('land of silver') was settled first in the north-west around Salta and San Miguel de Tucumán with strong links to Lima. This area is unusual today in retaining a largely mestizo (mixed Indian and Spanish) population, a remnant of colonial times. In 1776 Argentina, Uruguay, Paraguay and southern Bolivia were disengaged from Peru to form a separate viceroyalty, with its administrative centre in Buenos Aires. After a long war of independence the United Provinces of the Rió de la Plata achieved self-government under Simón Bolívar, but Uruguay, Bolivia and Paraguay separated between 1814 and 1828; it took many years of warfare and turbulence before Argentina emerged as a national entity in 1816, united and centred on Buenos Aires.

Early prosperity, based on stock-raising and farming, was boosted from 1870 by a massive influx of European immigrants, particularly Italians and Spaniards for whom the Argentine was a real alternative to the USA. They settled lands recently cleared of Indians and often organized by huge land companies. Britain provided much of the capital and some of the immigrants; families of English and Welsh sheep farmers, still speaking their own languages, are identifiable in Patagonia today. Development of a good railway network to the ports, plus steamship services to Europe and refrigerated vessels, helped to create the strong meat, wool and wheat economy that carried Argentina through its formative years and into the 20th century.

Politics and economy

A military coup in 1930 started a long period of military intervention in the politics of the country. The period from 1976 – the so-called 'dirty war' – saw the torture, wrongful imprisonment and murder ('disappearance') of up to 15,000 people by the military, and up to 2 million people fled the country. In 1982 the government, blamed for the poor state of the economy, launched an ill-fated invasion of the Falkland Islands (Islas Malvinas), a territory they had claimed since 1820. Britain regained possession later that year by sending an expeditionary force, and President Galtieri resigned. Constitutional rule was restored in 1983 under President Raúl Alfonsín, though the military remained influential. The country's economic problems – with their classic Latin American causes of reliance on certain commodities, big borrowing ($62 billion foreign debt) and maladministration – were inherited by his Peronist successor, Carlos Menem, in 1989. His austerity programme took Argentina through inflation rates of 3,084% and 2,314% down to 85% in 1991 – stable money by previous standards.

His policies of economic liberalization and reduction of state involvement may work. Certainly Argentina is one of the richest of South America's countries in terms of natural resources, and its population – though remarkably urban, with 85% living in towns and cities – is not growing at anything like the rates seen in most of Africa and Asia. The population, predominantly European and mainly middle-class, nevertheless relies on an economic base that is agricultural: Argentina's farming industry exports wheat, maize, sorghum and soya beans as well as enormous quantities of meat, and produces sugar, oilseed, fruit and vegetables for home consumption. The chief industries, too, are based on food products, and the government aims to switch to manufacturing from agricultural processing. The manufacturing base is around Buenos Aires, where more than a third of the population live, and there is a strong computer industry. Argentina is nearly self-sufficient in petroleum production and has copper and uranium reserves ■

COUNTRY: Argentine Republic

AREA: 2,766,890 sq km [1,068,296 sq mls]

POPULATION: 32,322,000

CAPITAL (Population): Buenos Aires (10,728,000)

GOVERNMENT: Federal republic

ETHNIC GROUPS: European 85%, Mestizo, Amerindian

LANGUAGES: Spanish (official) 95%, Italian, Guarani

RELIGIONS: Roman Catholic 93%, Protestant 2%

NATIONAL DAY: 10 July; Independence Day (1816)

CURRENCY: Peso = 100 centavos

ANNUAL INCOME PER PERSON: $2,370

MAIN PRIMARY PRODUCTS: Coal, cattle, petroleum, natural gas, zinc, lead, silver

MAIN INDUSTRIES: Food processing, wine, cotton yarn, cement, iron and steel, vehicles

EXPORTS: $286 per person

MAIN EXPORTS: Vegetable products 43%, textiles and manufactures 4%

MAIN EXPORT PARTNERS: Netherlands 10%, Brazil 9%, USA 8%

IMPORTS: $167 per person

MAIN IMPORTS: Machinery 23%, chemicals and petrochemicals 21%, mineral products 13%

MAIN IMPORT PARTNERS: USA 17%, Brazil 14%, Germany 11%, Bolivia 7%, Japan 7%

DEFENCE: 6% of national budget

TOURISM: 1,600,000 visitors per year

POPULATION DENSITY: 12 per sq km [30 per sq ml]

INFANT MORTALITY: 29 per 1000 live births

LIFE EXPECTANCY: Female 75 yrs, male 68 yrs

ADULT LITERACY: 95%

PRINCIPAL CITIES (Population): Buenos Aires 10,728,000 Córdoba 1,055,000 Rosario 1,016,000 Mendoza 668,000 La Plata 611,000

THE PAMPAS

'Pampa' is a South American Indian word describing a flat, featureless expanse: the pampas are the broad, grassy plains that stretch between the eastern flank of the Andes and the Atlantic Ocean. Geologically they represent outwash fans of rubble, sand, silt and clay, washed down from the Andes by torrents and redistributed by wind and water. Fine soils cover huge expanses of pampas, providing good deep soils in the well-watered areas, but scrub and sandy desert where rainfall and ground-water are lacking.

Early Spanish settlers introduced horses and cattle, and later the best areas of pampas were enclosed for cattle ranching and cultivation. Now the pampas are almost entirely converted to rangelands growing turf-grasses (vehicles have mostly replaced the gauchos) or to huge fields producing alfalfa, maize, wheat and flax.

BERMUDA

Comprising about 150 small islands, the coral caps of ancient submarine volcanoes rising over 4,000 m [13,000 ft] from the ocean floor, Bermuda is situated 920 km [570 mls] east of Cape Hatteras in North Carolina. Some 20 are inhabited, the vast majority of the population living on the biggest island of Great Bermuda, 21 km [13 mls] long and connected to the other main islands by bridges and causeways. The capital, Hamilton, stands beside a deep harbour on Great Bermuda.

Uninhabited when discovered by the Spaniard Juan Mermúdez in 1503, the islands were taken over by the British more than a century later (following a shipwreck) and slaves brought in from Virginia to work the land. Today over 60% of the population is of African descent. The pleasant climate, coral sand beaches, historic buildings and pastel-coloured townships attract nearly 600,000 tourists each year, mainly from the USA; but if tourism is the mainstay of the economy, the islands are also a tax haven for overseas companies and individuals.

Food and energy needs dominate imports, while (legal) drugs and medicines account for 57% of exports – though services are the main earners, offsetting a large deficit and giving the islanders an annual per capita income of US$25,000 (1989), the third highest in the world.

Bermuda remains Britain's oldest colony, but with a long tradition of self-government; the parliament dates from 1603. Ties with the US are strong, however, and in 1941 part of the islands was leased for 99 years by Washington for naval and air bases. The government is in regular discussions with the US, UK and Canada over constitutional change, but public opinion continues to oppose moves towards independence ■

Surrounded by the Atlantic and within the tropics has given Bermuda a mild and equable climate. There is no high land to give appreciable climatic variations. The annual average temperature is mild at about 22°C [72°C], with 10°C [18°F] difference between August (27°C [81°F]) and February (17°C [63°F]). Frosts are unknown and every month has recorded a temperature higher than 27°C [81°F]. Rainfall is around 1,400 mm [55 in], evenly distributed throughout the year.

COUNTRY: British colony
AREA: 53 sq km [20 sq mls]
POPULATION: 61,000
CAPITAL (Population): Hamilton (3,000)
ETHNIC GROUPS: Black 61%, White 37%
CURRENCY: Bermuda $ = 100 cents

CAPE VERDE

An archipelago of ten large and five small islands, divided into the Barlavento (windward) and Sotavento (leeward) groups, Cape Verde lies 560 km [350 mls] off Dakar. They are volcanic and mainly mountainous, with steep cliffs and rocky headlands; the highest, Fogo, rises to 2,829 m [9,281 ft] and is active. The islands are tropical, hot for most of the year and mainly dry at sea level. Higher ground is cooler and more fertile, producing maize, groundnuts, coffee, sugar cane, beans and fruit when not subject to the endemic droughts that have killed 75,000 people since 1900. Poor soils and the lack of surface water prohibit development.

Portuguese since the 15th century – and used chiefly as a provisioning station for ships and an assembly point for slaves in the trade from West Africa – the colony became an overseas territory in 1951 and independent in 1975. Linked with Guinea-Bissau in the fight against colonial rule, its Socialist single-party government flirted with union in 1980, but in 1991 the ruling PAICV was soundly trounced in the country's first multiparty elections by a newly legalized opposition, the Movement for Democracy.

Cape Verde's meagre exports comprise mainly bananas (36%) and tuna fish (30%), but it has to import much of its food. The only significant minerals are salt and *pozzolana*, a volcanic rock used in making cement. Much of the population's income comes from foreign aid and remittances sent home by the 600,000 Cape Verdeans who work abroad – nearly twice the native population; in the last severe drought (1968–82), some 40,000 emigrated to Portugal alone. Tourism is still in its infancy – only 2,000 visitors a year – lagging well behind the Azores, Madeira and the Canaries. Economic problems are compounded by tens of thousands of Angolan refugees ■

The oceanic situation of the islands has the effect of tempering a tropical climate. The temperature range is from 27°C [81°F] in September to 23°C [73°F] in February. Rainfall totals vary through the islands. Praia is nearly at the most southerly point in the islands and is one of the wettest regions, but its total is meagre. Rain falls in August– October and the rest of the year is arid. Nearly all the islands have over 3,000 hours of sunshine in the year.

COUNTRY: Republic of Cape Verde
AREA: 4,030 sq km [1,556 sq mls]
POPULATION: 370,000
CAPITAL (Population): Praia (58,000)
ETHNIC GROUPS: Mixed 71%, Black 28%, White 1%
LANGUAGES: Portuguese (official)
RELIGIONS: Roman Catholic 97%, Protestant 2%
NATIONAL DAY: 5 July; Independence Day (1975)
CURRENCY: Cape Verde escudo = 100 centavos
ANNUAL INCOME PER PERSON: $890
MAIN PRIMARY PRODUCTS: Maize, coffee, sugar, fruit
POPULATION DENSITY: 92 per sq km [238 per sq ml]
LIFE EXPECTANCY: Female 65 yrs, male 61 yrs
ADULT LITERACY: 47%

AZORES

Part of the Mid-Atlantic Ridge, the Azores are nine large and several small islands situated about 1,200 km [745 mls] west of Lisbon. They divide into three widely separated groups: São Miguel (759 sq km [293 sq mls] out of a total area of 2,247 sq km [868 sq mls]) and Santa Maria are the most easterly; 160 km [100 mls] to the north-west is the central cluster of Terceira, Graciosa, São Jorge, Pico and Faial; another 240 km [150 mls] to the north-west are Flores and the most isolated significant island of Corvo.

Of relatively recent volcanic origin, the islands are mostly mountainous, with high cliffs and narrow beaches of shell gravel or dark volcanic sand. Small-scale farming and fishing are the main occupations, with fruit, wine and canned fish exported (mostly to Portugal), but tourism is an increasingly important sector of the economy.

The variation between the hottest and coldest months is usually only about 10°C [18°F], January–March being 14°C [57°F] and August 23°C [73°F]. Night temperatures rarely fall below 10°C [50°F] and the all-time record is only 29°C [84°F]. There is ample rain all the year, but December–March have over 150 mm [6 in] per month on average. Santa Cruz is on the most westerly island and is wetter than the other islands.

The Azores have been Portuguese since the mid-15th century; there were no indigenous people, and its present population of 260,000 is mostly of Portuguese stock. Since 1976 they have been governed as three districts of Portugal, comprising an autonomous region. The capital is Ponta Delgada (population 21,000) on the island of São Miguel, which hosts more than half the total population ■

MADEIRA

Madeira is the largest of the group of picturesque volcanic islands of that name lying 550 km [350 mls] from the Moroccan coast and 900 km [560 mls] south-west of the national capital, Lisbon. Porto Santo and the uninhabited Ilhas Selvagens and Desertas complete the group, with a total area of 813 sq km [314 sq mls], of which Madeira itself contributes 745 sq km [288 sq mls].

With a warm temperate climate and good soils, Madeira was originally forested, but early settlers cleared the uplands for plantations. The islands form an autonomous region of Portugal ■

CANARY ISLANDS

The Canary Islands comprise seven large islands and numerous small volcanic islands situated off southern Morocco, the nearest within 100 km [60 mls] of the mainland. The 'inshore' islands of Lanzarote and Fuerteventura are low-lying, while the western group, including Gran Canaria and Tenerife, are more mountainous, the volcanic cone of Pico de Teide rising to 3,718 m [12,198 ft].

The islands, totalling 7,273 sq km [2,807 sq mls] in area, have a subtropical climate, dry at sea level but damp on higher ground. Soils are fertile, supporting farming and fruit growing, mainly by large-scale irrigation. Industries include food and fish processing, boat-building and crafts.

Known to ancient European civilizations as the Fortunate Islands, the picturesque Canaries are today a major destination for both winter and summer tourists. Claimed by Portugal in 1341, they were ceded to Spain in 1479 and since 1927 have been divided into two provinces under the name of their respective capitals, Las Palmas de Gran Canaria (at

On the coasts of these islands in the Atlantic, the climate is of a Mediterranean type – low rainfall falling on only a few days in the winter months, frosts unknown and the midday temperatures usually 20–25°C [68–77°F]. But most of the islands rise to central peaks of great height, high enough to carry snow throughout the year. There is thus a climatic variation from coast to peak, giving rise to a vegetation that ranges from arid to fairly dense stands of forest. Daily sunshine is 5–9 hours.

372,000 population Spain's eighth biggest city) and Santa Cruz de Tenerife (population 191,000). The former (56% of the area) includes Gran Canaria, Lanzarote and Fuerteventura, the latter (44%) includes Tenerife, La Palma, Gomera and Hierro. The total population of the islands is 1,700,000 ■

GREENLAND

Recognized by geographers as the world's largest island (the Australian mainland being considered a continental land mass), Greenland is almost three times the size of the second largest, New Guinea. However, more than 85% of the land is covered in continuous permafrost, an ice-cap with an average depth of about 1,500 m [5,000 ft], and though there are a few sandy and clay plains in the ice-free areas, settlement is confined to the rocky coasts.

The first recorded European to visit this barren desert was Eirike Raudi (Eric the Red), a Norseman from Iceland who settled at Brattahlid in 982. It was he who named the place Greenland – to make it sound attractive to settlers. Within four years, more than 30 ships had ferried pioneers there, founding a colony which would last five centuries.

Greenland became a Danish possession in 1380 and, eventually, an integral part of the Danish kingdom in 1953. After the island was taken into the EC in 1973 – despite a majority vote against by Greenlanders – a nationalist movement developed and in 1979, after another referendum, a home rule was introduced, with full internal self-government following in 1981. In 1985 Greenland withdrew from the EC, halving the Community's territory.

The economy still depends substantially on subsidies from Denmark, which remains its chief trading partner. The main rural occupations are sheep-rearing and fishing – with shrimps, prawns and molluscs contributing over 60% of exports. The only major manufacturing is fish canning, which has drawn many Eskimos to the towns; few now follow the traditional life of nomadic hunters.

Altitude and latitude affect the climate of Greenland. Godthåb on the warmer south-west coast has over seven months with average temperatures below freezing. Similar temperatures have been recorded in all months. On the inland ice and in the north, the coldest average can be as low as –25 to –40°C [–13 to –40°F]. Precipitation is moderate in the south at around 1,000 mm [39 in], but this declines to less than 250 mm [10 in] in the north.

Most Greenlanders (a mixture of Inuit Eskimo and Danish extraction) live precariously between the primitive and the modern; in the towns rates of alcoholism, venereal disease and suicide are all high. Yet the nationalist mood prevails, buoyed by abundant fish stocks, lead and zinc (15% of exports) from Uummannaq in the north-west, untapped uranium in the south, possible oil in the east – and the increase in organized, often adventure-oriented tourism. Independence is a daunting task, as the Danes point out: the island is nearly 50 times the size of the mother country with only 1% of the population – figures which make Mongolia, the world's least densely populated country, look almost crowded ■

COUNTRY: Self-governing division of Denmark
AREA: 2,175,600 sq km [839,999 sq mls]
POPULATION: 57,000

FALKLAND ISLANDS

Comprising two main islands and over 200 small islands, the Falkland Islands lie 480 km [300 mls] from South America. Windswept, virtually treeless, covered with peat moorland and tussock grass, the rolling landscape rises to two points of about 700 m [2,300 ft] – Mt Usborne in East Falkland and Mt Adam in West Falkland. Over half the population lives in (Port) Stanley, the capital situated in a sheltered inlet on East Falkland.

Discovered in 1592 by the English navigator John Davis, the Falklands were first occupied nearly 200 years later – by the French (East) in 1764 and the British (West) in 1765. The French interest, bought by Spain in 1770, was assumed by Argentina when it gained independence in 1806, and the Argentinians retained their settlements there. The British, who had withdrawn on economic grounds back in 1774, had never relinquished their claim, and in 1832 they returned to dispossess the Argentine settlers and start a settlement of their own – one that became a Crown Colony in 1892.

The prospect of rich offshore oil and gas deposits from the 1970s aggravated the long-standing dispute, and in 1982 Argentine forces invaded the islands (Islas Malvinas in Spanish) and expelled the Governor. Two months later – after the loss of 725 Argentinians and 225 Britons – the UK regained possession. Anglo-Argentine diplomatic relations were restored in 1990, but the UK refuses to enter discussions on sovereignty.

Life has since been based on the presence of a large British garrison, but in normal times the economy is dominated by sheep-farming, almost the only industry, with over 40% of exports comprising high-grade wool, mostly to Britain. The UK government

There is a constant westerly wind blowing in from over a cold sea, with gales many times a month. Rainfall is not high and is spread throughout the year, falling on about 150 days, 50 of them as snow, which rarely settles. The wettest months are December and July. The average summer temperature is not high at 10°C [50°F] – the highest ever recorded being only 24°C [75°F], but the winter minimum is not below freezing. The known coldest was –11°C [12°F].

is also funding a fishing development programme and helping with tourism.

South Georgia and **South Sandwich Island** ceased to be Falklands dependencies in 1985, though they are administered via Stanley. They have had no permanent population since 1966 ■

COUNTRY: British Dependent Territory
AREA: 12,170 sq km [4,699 sq mls]
POPULATION: 2,000

ASCENSION stands in isolation on the Mid-Atlantic Ridge, a triangular volcanic island of 88 sq km [34 sq mls], with a single high peak, Green Mountain (859 m [2,817 ft]), surrounded by hot low-lying ash and lava plains. The mountain climate is cool and damp enough to support a farm, which supplies vegetables for the local community of about 1,500. Ascension has no native population. Administered from St Helena since 1922, its inhabitants are British, St Helenian or American, many of them involved in telecommunications, satellite research and servicing a mid-ocean airstrip ■

ST HELENA is an isolated rectangular, slab-sided island of old volcanic rocks, well off the main line of the Mid-Atlantic Ridge and measuring 122 sq km [47 sq mls]. A tableland deeply dissected by valleys, it has steep cliffs and ridges. The population of about 7,000, mainly of East Indian descent, produce potatoes and other vegetables and raise cattle, sheep and goats on smallholdings. Cultivable land is scarce and many are unemployed. St Helena, a British colony since 1834 and the administrative centre for six of the UK's South Atlantic islands, is heavily dependent on subsidies ■

TRISTAN DA CUNHA is the largest of four scattered islands towards the southern end of the Mid-Atlantic Ridge, a volcanic cone of 2,060 m [6,760 ft], ringed by a lava plain that drops steeply to the sea; a narrow strip of flat ground accommodates the settlement of about 300 inhabitants. The Nightingale and Inaccessible Islands are small, uninhabited islands nearby; Gough Island, 400 km [250 mls] to the south-east, is a craggy, forested island some 13 km [8 mls] long; its only settlement is a weather station. Like Ascension, all are administered as dependencies of St Helena ■

INDEX TO
COUNTRY
MAPS

HOW TO USE THE INDEX

The index contains the names of all the principal places and features shown on the country maps. Each name is followed by an additional entry in italics giving the country or region within which it is located. The alphabetical order of names composed of two or more words is governed primarily by the first word and then by the second. This is an example of the rule:

Ba Don, *Vietnam*	**125**	**C4**
Ba Ria, *Vietnam*	**125**	**G4**
Baa, *Indonesia*	**129**	**F11**
Bab el Mandeb, *Red Sea* .	**132**	**E8**
Babahoyo, *Ecuador*	**212**	**C1**

Physical features composed of a proper name (Erie) and a description (Lake) are positioned alphabetically by the proper name. The description is positioned after the proper name and is usually abbreviated:

Erie, L., *N.Amer.*	**180**	**E11**

Where a description forms part of a settlement or administrative name, however, it is always written in full and put in its true alphabetical position:

Lake City, *U.S.A.*	**191**	**H15**

Names beginning with M' and Mc are indexed as if they were spelled Mac. Names beginning St. are alphabetized under Saint, but Sankt, Sint, Sant', Santa and San are all spelt in full and are alphabetized accordingly. If the same place name occurs two or more times in the index and all are in the same country, each is followed by the name of the administrative subdivision in which it is located. The names are placed in the alphabetical order of the subdivisions. For example:

Clinton, *Iowa, U.S.A.*	**191**	**D12**
Clinton, *Mass., U.S.A.* ...	**189**	**A6**
Clinton, *Okla., U.S.A.*	**190**	**G9**

The number in bold type which follows each name in the index refers to the number of the page where that feature or place will be found.

The letter and figure which are in bold type immediately after the page number give the imaginary grid square on the map page, within which the feature is situated. This is formed by joining the black ticks outside each map frame. It does not relate to the latitude nor longitude except in the case of the physical maps of the continents.

In some cases the feature itself may fall within the specified square, while the name is outside. Rivers carry the symbol ➝ after their names. A solid square ■ follows the name of a country while, an open square □ refers to a first order administrative area.

Abbreviations used in the index

A.C.T. — Australian Capital Territory
Afghan. — Afghanistan
Ala. — Alabama
Alta. — Alberta
Amer. — America(n)
Arch. — Archipelago
Ariz. — Arizona
Ark. — Arkansas
Atl. Oc. — Atlantic Ocean
B. — Baie, Bahia, Bay, Bucht, Bugt
B.C. — British Columbia
Bangla. — Bangladesh
Barr. — Barrage
Bos. & H. — Bosnia and Herzegovina
C. — Cabo, Cap, Cape, Coast
C.A.R. — Central African Republic
C. Prov. — Cape Province
Calif. — California
Cent. — Central
Chan. — Channel
Colo. — Colorado
Conn. — Connecticut
Cord. — Cordillera
Cr. — Creek
Czech. — Czechoslovakia
D.C. — District of Columbia
Del. — Delaware
Dep. — Dependency
Des. — Desert
Dist. — District
Dj. — Djebel
Domin. — Dominica
Dom. Rep. — Dominican Republic
E. — East

El Salv. — El Salvador
Eq. Guin. — Equatorial Guinea
Fla. — Florida
Falk. Is. — Falkland Is.
G. — Golfe, Golfo, Gulf, Guba, Gebel
Ga. — Georgia
Gt. — Great, Greater
Guinea-Biss. — Guinea-Bissau
H.K. — Hong Kong
H.P. — Himachal Pradesh
Hants. — Hampshire
Harb. — Harbor, Harbour
Hd. — Head
Hts. — Heights
I.(s). — Île, Ilha, Insel, Isla, Island, Isle
Ill. — Illinois
Ind. — Indiana
Ind. Oc. — Indian Ocean
Ivory C. — Ivory Coast
J. — Jabal, Jebel, Jazira
Junc. — Junction
K. — Kap, Kapp
Kans. — Kansas
Kep. — Kepulauan
Ky. — Kentucky
L. — Lac, Lacul, Lago, Lagoa, Lake, Limni, Loch, Lough
La. — Louisiana
Liech. — Liechtenstein
Lux. — Luxembourg
Mad. P. — Madhya Pradesh
Madag. — Madagascar
Man. — Manitoba
Mass. — Massachusetts

Md. — Maryland
Me. — Maine
Medit. S. — Mediterranean Sea
Mich. — Michigan
Minn. — Minnesota
Miss. — Mississippi
Mo. — Missouri
Mont. — Montana
Mozam. — Mozambique
Mt.(e). — Mont, Monte, Monti, Montaña, Mountain
N. — Nord, Norte, North, Northern, Nouveau
N.B. — New Brunswick
N.C. — North Carolina
N. Cal. — New Caledonia
N. Dak. — North Dakota
N.H. — New Hampshire
N.I. — North Island
N.J. — New Jersey
N. Mex. — New Mexico
N.S. — Nova Scotia
N.S.W. — New South Wales
N.W.T. — North West Territory
N.Y. — New York
N.Z. — New Zealand
Nebr. — Nebraska
Neths. — Netherlands
Nev. — Nevada
Nfld. — Newfoundland
Nic. — Nicaragua
O. — Oued, Ouadi
Occ. — Occidentale
O.F.S. — Orange Free State
Okla. — Oklahoma
Ont. — Ontario

Or. — Orientale
Oreg. — Oregon
Os. — Ostrov
Oz. — Ozero
P. — Pass, Passo, Pasul, Pulau
P.E.I. — Prince Edward Island
Pa. — Pennsylvania
Pac. Oc. — Pacific Ocean
Papua N.G. — Papua New Guinea
Pass. — Passage
Pen. — Peninsula, Péninsule
Phil. — Philippines
Pk. — Park, Peak
Plat. — Plateau
P-ov. — Poluostrov
Pt. — Point
Pta. — Ponta, Punta
Pte. — Pointe
Qué. — Québec
Queens. — Queensland
R. — Rio, River
R.I. — Rhode Island
Ra.(s). — Range(s)
Raj. — Rajasthan
Reg. — Region
Rep. — Republic
Res. — Reserve, Reservoir
S. — San, South, Sea
Si. Arabia — Saudi Arabia
S.C. — South Carolina
S. Dak. — South Dakota
S.I. — South Island
S. Leone — Sierra Leone
Sa. — Serra, Sierra
Sask. — Saskatchewan

Scot. — Scotland
Sd. — Sound
Sev. — Severnaya
Sib. — Siberia
Sprs. — Springs
St. — Saint, Sankt, Sint
Sta. — Santa, Station
Ste. — Sainte
Sto. — Santo
Str. — Strait, Stretto
Switz. — Switzerland
Tas. — Tasmania
Tenn. — Tennessee
Tex. — Texas
Tg. — Tanjung
Trin. & Tob. — Trinidad & Tobago
U.A.E. — United Arab Emirates
U.K. — United Kingdom
U.S.A. — United States of America
Ut. P. — Uttar Pradesh
Va. — Virginia
Vdkhr. — Vodokhranilishche
Vf. — Vîrful
Vic. — Victoria
Vol. — Volcano
Vt. — Vermont
W. — Wadi, West
W. Va. — West Virginia
Wash. — Washington
Wis. — Wisconsin
Wlkp. — Wielkopolski
Wyo. — Wyoming
Yorks. — Yorkshire

Ashdod, *Israel* 96 D1
Ashdown Forest, *U.K.* 45 E4
Asheville, *U.S.A.* 191 F14
Ashford, *Australia* 171 B8
Ashford, *U.K.* 45 E6
Ashikaga, *Japan* 120 A8
Ashkhabad, *Turkmenistan* 90 K3
Ashland, *Ky., U.S.A.* 191 E14
Ashland, *Wis., U.S.A.* 191 C11
Ashmûn, *Egypt* 139 B4
Ashqelon, *Israel* 96 D1
Ashton, *S. Africa* 163 H3
Ashuanipi, L., *Canada* 187 H13
Ashurstwood, *U.K.* 45 E4
Asia, Kepulauan, *Indonesia* 129 B15
Asidonhoppo, *Surinam* 214 D4
Asifabad, *India* 106 F4
Asike, *Indonesia* 129 E18
Asilah, *Morocco* 136 A4
Asinara, *Italy* 67 F1
Asinara, G. dell', *Italy* 67 F2
Asino, *Russia* 90 H9
Asīr □, *Si. Arabia* 99 E3
Asir, Ras, *Somali Rep.* 145 A3
Aşkale, *Turkey* 82 D3
Askham, *S. Africa* 163 D3
Askja, *Iceland* 38 C4
Asl, *Egypt* 139 B5
Asmār, *Afghan.* 104 C6
Asmara = Asmera, *Ethiopia* 144 B3
Asmera, *Ethiopia* 144 B3
Asni, *Morocco* 136 D3
Aspiring, Mt., *N.Z.* 175 H2
Assa, *Morocco* 136 F2
Assam □, *India* 107 C6
Assen, *Neths.* 50 B5
Assini, *Ivory C.* 148 E6
Assiniboia, *Canada* 186 J4
Assisi, *Italy* 67 D5
Aştārā, *Azerbaijan* 82 D9
Asti, *Italy* 67 B2
Astipálaia, *Greece* 71 F6
Aston Clinton, *U.K.* 45 B1
Astorga, *Spain* 63 B3
Astoria, *U.S.A.* 190 B2
Astrakhan, *Russia* 81 G8
Asturias, *Spain* 63 A3
Asunción, *Paraguay* 219 B2
Aswa →, *Uganda* 156 B3
Aswân, *Egypt* 139 E5
Aswân High Dam = Sadd el Aali, *Egypt* 139 E5
Asyût, *Egypt* 139 C4
Asyûti, Wadi →, *Egypt* 139 C4
At Ţafilah, *Jordan* 98 B2
At Ţā'if, *Si. Arabia* 99 D3
Atacama, Desierto de, *Chile* 220 C3
Atakpamé, *Togo* 150 D2
Atalaya, *Peru* 213 D3
Atami, *Japan* 120 B8
Atapupu, *Indonesia* 129 F12
Atâr, *Mauritania* 140 C1
Atara, *Russia* 91 E14
Atasu, *Kazakhstan* 90 J6
Atauro, *Indonesia* 129 F12
Atbara, *Sudan* 143 B5
Atbara →, *Sudan* 143 B5
Atbasar, *Kazakhstan* 90 H6
Atbashi, *Kirghizia* 93 C8
Atbashi, Khrebet, *Kirghizia* 93 C7
Atchafalaya B., *U.S.A.* 191 J12
Atchison, *U.S.A.* 191 E10
Atebubu, *Ghana* 149 C2
Ath, *Belgium* 51 C2
Athabasca, *Canada* 186 H5
Athabasca →, *Canada* 186 G6
Athabasca, L., *Canada* 186 G6
Athenry, *Ireland* 46 H1
Athens = Athínai, *Greece* 71 D3
Athens, *U.S.A.* 191 G14
Athiéme, *Benin* 150 D2
Athienou, *Cyprus* 95 B2
Athínai, *Greece* 71 D3
Athlone, *Ireland* 46 H2
Athos, *Greece* 71 B4
Athy, *Ireland* 46 H3
Ati, *Chad* 142 D2
Atiak, *Uganda* 156 A2
Atico, *Peru* 213 F4
Atimonan, *Phil.* 130 E3
Atka, *Russia* 91 D16
Atka, *U.S.A.* 193 B1
Atlanta, *U.S.A.* 191 G14
Atlantic City, *U.S.A.* 189 D5
Atlantic Ocean 222
Atlas Mts. = Haut Atlas, *Morocco* 136 C5
Atlin, *Canada* 186 E3
Atsuta, *Japan* 121 B7
Attawapiskat →, *Canada* 187 J10
Attendorn, *Germany* 59 B3
Attleboro, *U.S.A.* 189 A6
Attock, *Pakistan* 105 B5
Attopeu, *Laos* 125 D4
Aube →, *France* 55 C7
Aube □, *France* 55 C6
Aubel, *Belgium* 51 C5
Auburn, *U.S.A.* 189 A3
Aubusson, *France* 55 E5
Auch, *France* 55 G4
Auchi, *Nigeria* 151 E3
Auckland, *N.Z.* 175 B5
Auckland Is., *Pac. Oc.* 176 K5
Aude □, *France* 55 H6
Aude →, *France* 55 H6

Augrabies Falls, *S. Africa* 163 E3
Augsburg, *Germany* 58 F4
Augusta, *Italy* 67 K7
Augusta, *Ga., U.S.A.* 191 G15
Augusta, *Maine, U.S.A.* 191 B18
Augustów, *Poland* 77 A6
Auna, *Nigeria* 151 C2
Aunis, *France* 55 E3
Auponhia, *Indonesia* 129 D12
Aur, P., *Malaysia* 126 D3
Aurangabad, *Bihar, India* 106 C6
Aurangabad, *Maharashtra, India* 106 F2
Aurillac, *France* 55 F6
Aurora, *S. Africa* 163 G2
Aurora, *U.S.A.* 191 D12
Aus, *Namibia* 162 D2
Austerlitz = Slavkov, *Czech.* 76 C5
Austin, *Minn., U.S.A.* 191 D11
Austin, *Tex., U.S.A.* 190 J9
Austral Seamount Chain, *Pac. Oc.* 176 H8
Australia ■, *Oceania* 168
Australian Alps, *Australia* 171 G7
Australian Capital Territory □, *Australia* 171 F7
Austria ■, *Europe* 61
Autun, *France* 55 D7
Auvergne, *France* 55 F6
Auxerre, *France* 55 C6
Avallon, *France* 55 D7
Avaré, *Brazil* 215 C1
Aveiro, *Portugal* 63 D1
Avellaneda, *Argentina* 221 C5
Avellino, *Italy* 67 F6
Aversa, *Italy* 67 F6
Aveyron □, *France* 55 G6
Avignon, *France* 55 G7
Ávila, *Spain* 63 D4
Avilés, *Spain* 63 A3
Avoca →, *Australia* 171 F4
Avon →, *Australia* 170 B2
Avondale, *Zimbabwe* 161 B4
Avranches, *France* 55 C3
'Awālī, *Bahrain* 100 C3
Awash, *Ethiopia* 144 D3
Awaso, *Ghana* 149 D1
Awbārī, *Libya* 138 C2
Awgu, *Nigeria* 151 F4
Awjilah, *Libya* 138 B5
Axarfjörður, *Iceland* 38 A4
Axel Heiberg I., *Canada* 186 A9
Axim, *Ghana* 149 E1
Axminster, *U.K.* 46 L6
Ayaantang, *Eq. Guin.* 153 B2
Ayabaca, *Peru* 213 B2
Ayabe, *Japan* 120 B5
Ayacucho, *Argentina* 220 F5
Ayacucho, *Peru* 213 E3
Ayaguz, *Kazakhstan* 90 K8
Ayamonte, *Spain* 63 G2
Ayan, *Russia* 91 F16
Ayaviri, *Peru* 213 E4
Âybak, *Afghan.* 104 B5
Ayenngé, *Togo* 150 D2
Áyios Evstrátios, *Greece* 71 C4
Aylesbury, *U.K.* 45 B1
Aylesford, *U.K.* 45 D5
Aylmer, L., *Canada* 186 E7
Ayn Zālah, *Iraq* 102 A3
Ayni, *Tajikistan* 93 E2
Ayon, Ostrov, *Russia* 91 B16
Ayr, *U.K.* 46 E5
Aytos, *Bulgaria* 73 B5
Ayu, Kepulauan, *Indonesia* 129 C15
Ayutla, *Guatemala* 196 C1
Ayutla, *Mexico* 194 F5
Ayvalık, *Turkey* 94 B1
Az Zabdānī, *Syria* 97 C2
Az Zahrān, *Si. Arabia* 99 C6
Az Zarqā, *Jordan* 98 A2
Az Zubayr, *Iraq* 102 E6
Azamgarh, *India* 106 C6
Azare, *Nigeria* 151 B6
A'zāz, *Syria* 97 A3
Azbine = Aïr, *Niger* 141 B4
Azemmour, *Morocco* 136 C3
Azerbaijan ■, *Asia* 82 D8
Azilal, *Morocco* 136 C4
Azogues, *Ecuador* 212 D1
Azores, *Atl. Oc.* 223 C4
Azov, *Russia* 81 G6
Azov Sea = Azovskoye More, *Europe* 81 G5
Azovskoye More, *Europe* 81 G5
Azovy, *Russia* 90 E7
Azrou, *Morocco* 136 B4
Azúa de Compostela, *Dom. Rep.* 200 B3
Azuaga, *Spain* 63 F3
Azuay □, *Ecuador* 212 D1
Azuero, Pen. de, *Panama* 197 E5
Azul, *Argentina* 220 F5

B

Ba Don, *Vietnam* 125 C4
Ba Ngoi = Cam Lam, *Vietnam* 125 F5
Ba Ria, *Vietnam* 125 G4
Ba Xian, *China* 116 C3
Baa, *Indonesia* 129 F11

Baarle Nassau, *Belgium* 51 A4
Baarn, *Neths.* 50 D4
Bab el Mandeb, *Red Sea* 132 E8
Babahoyo, *Ecuador* 212 C1
Babakin, *Australia* 170 B3
Babana, *Nigeria* 151 C1
Babar, *Indonesia* 129 F14
Babi Besar, P., *Malaysia* 126 D3
Babine L., *Canada* 186 G3
Babo, *Indonesia* 129 D15
Bābol, *Iran* 103 B3
Baboua, *C.A.R.* 142 B1
Babura, *Nigeria* 151 A5
Babuyan Chan., *Phil.* 130 B3
Babuyan I., *Phil.* 130 A3
Babuyan Is., *Phil.* 130 B3
Babylon, *Iraq* 102 D4
Bac Kan, *Vietnam* 125 A3
Bac Ninh, *Vietnam* 125 B3
Bac-Phan, *Vietnam* 125 A3
Bac Quang, *Vietnam* 125 A3
Bacan, *Indonesia* 129 F13
Bacan, Kepulauan, *Indonesia* 129 C13
Bacarra, *Phil.* 130 B2
Bacău, *Romania* 75 B5
Bachelina, *Russia* 90 G7
Back →, *Canada* 186 E8
Baco, Mt., *Phil.* 130 F2
Bacolod, *Phil.* 130 H4
Bacuag, *Phil.* 130 H5
Bacuk, *Malaysia* 126 A2
Bad Ischl, *Austria* 61 B4
Bad Lands, *U.S.A.* 190 D8
Badagara, *India* 107 F0
Badagri, *Nigeria* 151 F1
Badajoz, *Spain* 63 E2
Badakhshān □, *Afghan.* 104 B6
Badalona, *Spain* 63 C9
Badampahar, *India* 106 E7
Badas, *Brunei* 127 B1
Badas, Kepulauan, *Indonesia* 128 C5
Baddo →, *Pakistan* 105 E2
Bade, *Indonesia* 129 F18
Baden, *Austria* 61 B5
Baden, *Switz.* 60 A3
Baden-Baden, *Germany* 58 F2
Baden-Württemberg □, *Germany* 58 F3
Badgastein, *Austria* 61 B3
Bādghīsāt □, *Afghan.* 104 C2
Badin, *Pakistan* 105 F4
Badulla, *Sri Lanka* 110 C2
Baeza, *Ecuador* 212 B2
Baeza, *Spain* 63 F5
Bafatá, *Guinea-Biss.* 146 D2
Baffin B., *Canada* 187 C10
Baffin I., *Canada* 187 D10
Bafia, *Cameroon* 153 D2
Bafilo, *Togo* 150 C2
Bafing →, *Mali* 140 F2
Bafliyūn, *Syria* 97 A3
Bafq, *Iran* 103 C4
Bafoulabé, *Mali* 140 E2
Bafoussam, *Togo* 150 C2
Bafwasende, *Zaïre* 155 B5
Bagamoyo, *Tanzania* 158 C3
Bagan Datoh, *Malaysia* 126 C1
Bagan Serai, *Malaysia* 126 B1
Baganga, *Phil.* 130 K6
Bagansiapiapi, *Indonesia* 128 B3
Bagdarin, *Russia* 91 H13
Bagé, *Brazil* 217 K5
Baghdād, *Iraq* 102 C4
Bagherhat, *Bangla.* 111 D1
Baghlān, *Afghan.* 104 C5
Baghlān □, *Afghan.* 104 B5
Bagshot, *U.K.* 45 D1
Baguio, *Phil.* 130 D2
Bahadurabad Ghat, *Bangla.* 111 B1
Bahamas ■, *N. Amer.* 201
Baharampur, *India* 106 D8
Baharîya, El Wâhât al, *Egypt* 139 C3
Bahawalpur, *Pakistan* 105 D5
Bahía = Salvador, *Brazil* 217 F8
Bahía □, *Brazil* 217 E8
Bahía, Is. de la, *Honduras* 196 B3
Bahía Blanca, *Argentina* 220 F4
Bahía de Caráquez, *Ecuador* 212 B1
Bahía Honda, *Cuba* 198 B2
Bahía Negra, *Paraguay* 219 A2
Bahr el Ahmar □, *Sudan* 143 B5
Bahr el Ghazâl □, *Sudan* 143 E2
Bahr Salamat →, *Chad* 142 E2
Bahr Yûsef →, *Egypt* 139 C4
Bahraich, *India* 106 B5
Bahrain ■, *Asia* 100
Bahret Assad, *Syria* 97 A3
Baia Mare, *Romania* 75 A3
Baie Comeau, *Canada* 187 J13
Baihe, *Taiwan* 117 B2
Ba'ijī, *Iraq* 102 B3
Baikal, L. = Baykal, Oz., *Russia* 91 J12
Baile Atha Cliath = Dublin, *Ireland* 46 H3
Bailundo, *Angola* 160 C3
Bainbridge, *U.S.A.* 191 H14
Baing, *Indonesia* 129 F11
Bā'ir, *Jordan* 98 B2
Baird Mts., *U.S.A.* 193 A4
Bairin Youqi, *China* 116 A4
Bairin Zuoqi, *China* 116 A4
Bairnsdale, *Australia* 171 H6

Bais, *Phil.* 130 H4
Baissa, *Nigeria* 151 E6
Baitadi, *Nepal* 109 A1
Baixo-Alentejo, *Portugal* 63 F1
Baiyin, *China* 113 E7
Baja, *Hungary* 74 C3
Baja, Pta., *Mexico* 194 B1
Baja California, *Mexico* 194 A1
Bajimba, Mt., *Australia* 171 B9
Bajoga, *Nigeria* 151 C6
Bakala, *C.A.R.* 142 B3
Bakchar, *Russia* 90 G8
Bakel, *Senegal* 146 B3
Baker, *U.S.A.* 190 C4
Baker, L., *Canada* 186 E8
Baker I., *Pac. Oc.* 176 F6
Baker Lake, *Canada* 186 E8
Baker Mt., *U.S.A.* 190 A3
Baker's Dozen Is., *Canada* 187 H11
Bakersfield, *U.S.A.* 190 F2
Bākhtarān, *Iran* 103 B2
Bakkafjörður, *Iceland* 38 B5
Bakkagerði, *Iceland* 38 B6
Bakony Forest = Bakony Hegyseg, *Hungary* 74 B2
Bakony Hegyseg, *Hungary* 74 B3
Bakori, *Nigeria* 151 B4
Bakouma, *C.A.R.* 142 B4
Baku, *Azerbaijan* 82 C9
Bālā Morghāb, *Afghan.* 104 C2
Balabac I., *Phil.* 130 J1
Balabalangan, Kepulauan, *Indonesia* 128 D9
Balaghat, *India* 106 E4
Balaguer, *Spain* 63 B8
Balaklava, *Australia* 171 E1
Balakovo, *Russia* 81 D8
Balashov, *Russia* 81 E7
Balasore = Baleshwar, *India* 106 E7
Balāt, *Egypt* 139 D3
Balaton, *Hungary* 74 B2
Balayan, *Phil.* 130 E2
Balboa, *Panama* 197 E5
Balbriggan, *Ireland* 46 G3
Balcarce, *Argentina* 220 F5
Balchik, *Bulgaria* 73 B5
Balclutha, *N.Z.* 175 J2
Balcombe, *U.K.* 45 E3
Bald Hd., *Australia* 170 D3
Bald I., *Australia* 170 D3
Baldock, *U.K.* 45 A3
Baldwinsville, *U.S.A.* 189 A3
Baldy Peak, *U.S.A.* 190 G5
Baleares, Is., *Spain* 65 B4
Balearic Is. = Baleares, Is., *Spain* 65 B4
Baler, *Phil.* 130 D3
Baler Bay, *Phil.* 130 D3
Balfate, *Honduras* 196 C3
Bali, *Cameroon* 153 D1
Bali, *Indonesia* 128 F8
Bali □, *Indonesia* 128 F8
Balık Gölü, *Turkey* 82 D5
Balıkeşir, *Turkey* 94 B1
Balikpapan, *Indonesia* 128 C9
Baling, *Malaysia* 126 A1
Balintang Channel, *Phil.* 130 A3
Balkan Mts. = Stara Planina, *Bulgaria* 73 B2
Balkh □, *Afghan.* 104 B4
Balkhash, *Kazakhstan* 90 K7
Balkhash, Ozero, *Kazakhstan* 90 K7
Ballarat, *Australia* 171 G4
Ballesteros, *Phil.* 130 B3
Ballidu, *Australia* 170 A2
Ballina, *Australia* 171 B9
Ballina, *Ireland* 46 G1
Ballymena, *U.K.* 46 F3
Balmoral, *Australia* 171 G3
Balmoral, *U.K.* 46 C6
Balonne →, *Australia* 171 B7
Balrampur, *India* 106 B5
Balranald, *Australia* 171 E4
Balsas →, *Mexico* 194 E4
Balta, *Russia* 82 A5
Balta, *Ukraine* 81 F2
Baltic Sea, *Europe* 34 G10
Baltim, *Egypt* 139 A4
Baltimore, *U.S.A.* 189 D3
Baluchistan □, *Pakistan* 105 E2
Balygychan, *Russia* 91 D16
Balzar, *Ecuador* 212 C1
Bam, *Iran* 103 D5
Bama, *Nigeria* 151 B7
Bamako, *Mali* 140 F3
Bamba, *Mali* 140 D5
Bambari, *C.A.R.* 142 B3
Bamberg, *Germany* 58 E4
Bambey, *Senegal* 146 B1
Bambili, *Zaïre* 155 A5
Bamenda, *Cameroon* 153 D1
Bāmiān □, *Afghan.* 104 C4
Bamiancheng, *China* 116 A6
Bampūr, *Iran* 103 D5

Ban Kantang, *Thailand* 123 L4
Ban Khe Bo, *Vietnam* 125 C3
Ban Khun Yuam, *Thailand* 122 E3
Ban Mae Sot, *Thailand* 122 F3
Ban Me Thuot, *Vietnam* 125 F5
Ban Phai, *Thailand* 123 F5
Ban Thateng, *Laos* 125 D4
Banaba, *Kiribati* 176 F5
Banalia, *Zaïre* 155 B5
Banam, *Cambodia* 125 F3
Banamba, *Mali* 140 E3
Bananal, I. do, *Brazil* 217 E6
Banaras = Varanasi, *India* 106 C5
Bancroft, *Canada* 185 B3
Band-e Torkestān, *Afghan.* 104 C2
Banda, *India* 106 C4
Banda, Kepulauan, *Indonesia* 129 E14
Banda Aceh, *Indonesia* 128 A1
Banda Banda, Mt., *Australia* 171 C9
Banda Elat, *Indonesia* 129 E15
Banda Is. = Banda, Kepulauan, *Indonesia* 129 E14
Banda Sea, *Indonesia* 129 E14
Bandai-San, *Japan* 121 F7
Bandama →, *Ivory C.* 148 E5
Bandanaira, *Indonesia* 129 E14
Bandar = Machilipatnam, *India* 107 E3
Bandar 'Abbās, *Iran* 103 E4
Bandar-e Anzalī, *Iran* 103 A2
Bandar-e Khomeyni, *Iran* 103 D2
Bandar-e Lengeh, *Iran* 103 E4
Bandar-e Rig, *Iran* 103 D3
Bandar-e Torkeman, *Iran* 103 B4
Bandar Maharani, *Malaysia* 126 D2
Bandar Penggaram, *Malaysia* 126 D2
Bandar Seri Begawan, *Brunei* 127 A3
Bandawe, *Malawi* 158 B2
Bandeira, Pico da, *Brazil* 215 A5
Bandiagara, *Mali* 140 E4
Bandırma, *Turkey* 94 A1
Bandon, *Ireland* 46 K1
Bandundu, *Zaïre* 155 D2
Bandung, *Indonesia* 128 F5
Banes, *Cuba* 198 C6
Banff, *Canada* 186 H5
Banff, *U.K.* 46 B6
Banfora, *Burkina Faso* 149 B1
Bang Hieng →, *Laos* 125 D3
Bang Lamung, *Thailand* 123 H4
Bang Saphan, *Thailand* 123 J4
Bangala Dam, *Zimbabwe* 161 D4
Bangalore, *India* 107 F3
Banggai, Kepulauan, *Indonesia* 129 D12
Banggi, P., *Malaysia* 126 A8
Banghāzi, *Libya* 138 A4
Bangka, *Sulawesi, Indonesia* 129 B12
Bangka, *Sumatera, Indonesia* 128 D5
Bangka, Selat, *Indonesia* 128 D5
Bangkalan, *Indonesia* 128 E7
Bangkinang, *Indonesia* 128 C3
Bangko, *Indonesia* 128 D3
Bangkok, *Thailand* 123 H4
Bangladesh ■, *Asia* 111
Bangolo, *Ivory C.* 148 C3
Bangor, *U.K.* 46 F4
Bangor, *U.S.A.* 191 B18
Bangued, *Phil.* 130 C2
Bangui, *C.A.R.* 142 C3
Bangui, *Phil.* 130 B2
Bangweulu, L., *Zambia* 161 B4
Bani, *Dom. Rep.* 200 B3
Bani, Djebel, *Morocco* 136 C3
Banī Walīd, *Libya* 138 A3
Bania, *Ivory C.* 148 B6
Baninah, *Libya* 138 A4
Bāniyās, *Syria* 97 B2
Banja Luka, *Bos.-H., Yug.* 72 B5
Banjarmasin, *Indonesia* 128 D8
Banjarnegara, *Indonesia* 128 F6
Banjul, *Gambia* 146 C1
Banket, *Zimbabwe* 161 B4
Bankipore, *India* 106 C6
Banks I., *Canada* 186 B7
Banks Pen., *N.Z.* 175 G4
Banks Str., *Australia* 172 A3
Bankura, *India* 106 D7
Banna, *Phil.* 130 C2
Banningville = Bandundu, *Zaïre* 155 D2
Bannockburn, *Zimbabwe* 161 D3
Bannu, *Pakistan* 105 B4
Banská Bystrica, *Czech.* 76 C6
Banská Štiavnica, *Czech.* 76 C6
Banstead, *U.K.* 45 D3
Banswara, *India* 106 D2
Bantayan, *Phil.* 130 G4
Bantry, *Ireland* 46 K1
Banyak, Kepulauan, *Indonesia* 128 B1
Banyo, *Cameroon* 153 C2
Banyuwangi, *Indonesia* 128 F8
Banzyville = Mobayi, *Zaïre* 155 A3
Bao Vista, *C. Verde Is.* 222 B3
Baode, *China* 116 C1
Baoding, *China* 116 C3
Baoji, *China* 113 E7
Baokang, *China* 116 F1
Baoshan, *China* 112 H6

Djeneïene

236

Fort Trinquet = Bir Mogrein, Mauritania 140 B2
Fort Vermilion, Canada .. 186 F5
Fort Wayne, U.S.A. 191 D13
Fort William, U.K. 46 C4
Fort Worth, U.S.A. 191 H10
Fort Yukon, U.S.A. 193 A5
Fortaleza, Brazil 217 C9
Forth, Firth of, U.K. 46 D6
Foshan, China 113 H9
Fougamou, Gabon 154 C1
Fougères, France 55 C3
Foul Pt., Sri Lanka 110 B3
Foum Assaka, Morocco .. 136 E2
Foum Zguid, Morocco .. 136 E3
Foumban, Cameroon 153 D1
Foundiougne, Senegal 146 B1
Fouriesburg, S. Africa 163 E7
Fournaise, Piton de la, Réunion 166 C3
Fouta Djalon, Guinea 147 A3
Foux, Cap-à-, Haiti 200 A1
Foveaux Str., N.Z. 175 J2
Foxe Basin, Canada 187 E10
Foxe Chan., Canada 187 E10
Foxe Pen., Canada 187 E11
Foxton, N.Z. 175 E5
Franca, Brazil 215 A2
France ■, Europe 55
Frances, Australia 171 G3
Francés Viejo, C., Dom. Rep. 200 A3
Franceville, Gabon 154 C2
Franche-Comté, France ... 55 D8
Francisco de Orellana, Ecuador 212 B2
Francistown, Botswana .. 162 B6
François L., Canada 186 G3
Franeker, Neths. 50 A4
Frankado, Djibouti 145 A2
Frankfort, S. Africa 163 D7
Frankfort, Ind., U.S.A. .. 191 E13
Frankfort, Ky., U.S.A. .. 191 F14
Frankfurt am Main, Germany 58 E2
Frankfurt an der Oder, Germany 58 C6
Fränkische Alb, Germany . 58 E4
Frankland →, Australia .. 170 D2
Franklin, U.S.A. 189 B1
Franklin, L., U.S.A. 190 D4
Franklin B., Canada 186 C6
Franklin D. Roosevelt L., U.S.A. 190 A4
Franklin Mts., Canada .. 186 D5
Franklin Str., Canada .. 186 C8
Frankston, Australia 171 H5
Frant, U.K. 45 E4
Frantsa Iosifa, Zemlya, Russia 90 A9
Franz, Canada 187 K10
Franz Josef Land = Frantsa Iosifa, Zemlya, Russia .. 90 A9
Fraser →, Canada 186 H3
Fraserburg, S. Africa 163 G3
Fraserburgh, U.K. 46 B7
Fray Bentos, Uruguay .. 219 C1
Fredericia, Denmark 42 C2
Frederick, U.S.A. 189 D3
Fredericksburg, U.S.A. .. 191 E16
Fredericton, Canada 187 K14
Frederikshåb, Greenland . 224 D1
Frederikshavn, Denmark .. 42 A3
Fredonia, U.S.A. 189 A1
Fredrikstad, Norway 40 F2
Freeport, Bahamas 201 A1
Freeport, N.Y., U.S.A. .. 189 C5
Freeport, Tex., U.S.A. .. 191 J10
Freetown, S. Leone 147 C2
Freibourg = Fribourg, Switz. 60 C2
Freiburg, Germany 58 G2
Freising, Germany 58 F4
Freistadt, Austria 61 A4
Fréjus, France 55 G9
Fremantle, Australia 170 B1
Fremont, U.S.A. 191 E10
French Cr. →, U.S.A. .. 189 B1
French Guiana ■, S. Amer. 214
French Terr. of Afars & Issas = Djibouti ■, Africa 145
Fresnillo, Mexico 194 D4
Fresno, U.S.A. 190 F2
Freycinet Pen., Australia .. 172 C3
Fria, Guinea 147 B2
Fria, C., Namibia 162 A1
Fribourg, Switz. 60 C2
Fribourg □, Switz. 60 C2
Friedrichshafen, Germany . 58 G3
Friendly Is. = Tonga ■, Pac. Oc. 174
Friesland □, Neths. 50 B4
Frigate, Seychelles 166 B3
Frimley, U.K. 45 D1
Frio, C., Brazil 206 E5
Friuli-Venezia Giulia □, Italy 67 A5
Frobisher B., Canada 187 E12
Frobisher Bay = Iqaluit, Canada 187 E12
Frobisher L., Canada 186 G6
Frome, U.K. 171 C2
Frome Downs, Australia .. 171 C2
Front Range, U.S.A. 190 E7
Frosinone, Italy 67 E5
Frostburg, U.S.A. 189 D2

Frunze = Bishkek, Kirghizia 93 A7
Frutigen, Switz. 60 C2
Frýdek-Místek, Czech. 76 B6
Fu Xian, China 116 C5
Fucheng, China 116 D3
Fuchou = Fuzhou, China .. 116 J4
Fuchū, Japan 120 C3
Fuchun Jiang →, China .. 116 G5
Fuding, China 116 J5
Fuente Ovejuna, Spain .. 63 C4
Fuentes de Oñoro, Spain .. 63 D3
Fuerte →, Mexico 194 C2
Fuerte Olimpo, Paraguay . 219 A2
Fuerteventura, Canary Is. . 223 C3
Fuga I., Phil. 130 B3
Fugou, China 116 F2
Fuhai, China 112 B4
Fuji, Japan 120 B8
Fuji-San, Japan 120 B8
Fujian □, China 113 H10
Fujinomiya, Japan 120 B8
Fujisawa, Japan 120 B8
Fukien = Fujian □, China . 113 H10
Fukuchiyama, Japan 120 B5
Fukui, Japan 120 A6
Fukui □, Japan 120 A6
Fukuoka, Japan 120 D1
Fukuoka □, Japan 120 D1
Fukushima, Japan 121 F7
Fukuyama, Japan 120 C4
Fulda, Germany 58 D3
Fulda →, Germany 58 D3
Fulton, U.S.A. 189 A3
Funabashi, Japan 120 B9
Funafuti, Pac. Oc. 176 F6
Funchal, Madeira 223 A2
Fundación, Colombia 210 A1
Fundão, Portugal 63 D2
Fundy, B. of, Canada 187 K14
Funing, China 116 F5
Funing, China 116 F2
Funiu Shan, China 116 B1
Funsi, Ghana 149 A1
Funtua, Nigeria 151 B4
Fuping, China 116 C2
Furnas, Reprêsa de, Brazil . 215 A3
Furneaux Group, Australia 172 A3
Furqlus, Syria 97 C3
Fürth, Germany 58 E4
Fury and Hecla Str., Canada 187 D10
Fusagasuga, Colombia .. 210 C1
Fushan, China 116 D5
Fushun, China 116 B6
Fuwa, Egypt 139 A4
Fuxin, China 116 B5
Fuyang, Anhui, China 116 F3
Fuyang, Zhejiang, China .. 116 G5
Fuyuan, China 113 A12
Fuzhou, China 116 J4
Fyn, Denmark 42 C2

G

Gaanda, Nigeria 151 C7
Gabarin, Nigeria 151 B6
Gabela, Angola 160 C2
Gabès, Tunisia 138 C2
Gabès, G. de, Tunisia 138 C2
Gabon ■, Africa 154
Gaborone, Botswana 162 D5
Gabrovo, Bulgaria 73 B3
Gadag, India 107 E2
Gadarwara, India 106 D4
Gadsden, U.S.A. 191 G13
Gafsa, Tunisia 138 C1
Gagnoa, Ivory C. 148 D4
Gagnon, Canada 187 H13
Gagra, Georgia 82 A2
Gahini, Rwanda 156 A2
Gai Xian, China 116 B6
Gainesville, Fla., U.S.A. . 191 J15
Gainesville, Ga., U.S.A. . 191 G14
Gairdner, L., Australia .. 168 D3
Gal Oya Res., Sri Lanka .. 110 C3
Galachipa, Bangla. 111 D3
Galana →, Kenya 157 E3
Galangue, Angola 160 D3
Galashiels, U.K. 46 E6
Galați, Romania 75 C6
Galdhøpiggen, Norway .. 40 E1
Galela, Indonesia 129 B13
Galera Point, Trin. & Tob. . 204 A3
Galesburg, U.S.A. 191 E12
Galets →, Réunion 166 A1
Gali, Georgia 82 A3
Galich, Russia 81 A6
Galicia □, Spain 63 B2
Galilee = Hagalil, Israel .. 96 B2
Galilee, Sea of = Yam Kinneret, Israel 96 B3
Gallabat, Sudan 143 D5
Galle, Sri Lanka 110 D2
Gállego →, Spain 63 C7
Gallinas, Pta., Colombia .. 210 A2
Gallípoli, Italy 67 G9
Gällivare, Sweden 40 C4
Gallup, U.S.A. 190 G6
Gallyaaral, Uzbekistan .. 93 D1
Galong, Australia 171 E7
Galveston, U.S.A. 191 J11
Gálvez, Argentina 221 A4
Galway, Ireland 46 H1
Galway B., Ireland 46 H1

Gamawa, Nigeria 151 B6
Gamay, Phil. 130 F5
Gambaga, Ghana 149 A2
Gambia ■, W. Afr. 146
Gambia →, W. Afr. 132 B2
Gambier Is., Australia 171 F1
Gamboma, Congo 154 C3
Gammouda, Tunisia 138 B2
Gand = Ghent, Belgium .. 51 B2
Ganda, Angola 160 D2
Gandak →, India 106 C7
Gandava, Pakistan 105 E3
Gander, Canada 187 H15
Ganderowe Falls, Zimbabwe 161 B3
Gandhi Sagar, India 106 C2
Gandi, Nigeria 151 A3
Gandole, Nigeria 151 D6
Ganedidalem = Gani, Indonesia 129 C13
Ganga →, India 106 E9
Ganganagar, India 106 A2
Gangara, Niger 141 C4
Gangaw, Burma 122 D1
Ganges = Ganga →, India 106 E9
Gangtok, India 106 B8
Gani, Indonesia 129 C13
Gannett Pk., U.S.A. 190 D6
Gansu □, China 112 D6
Ganta, Liberia 148 C2
Gantheaume, C., Australia 171 F1
Ganyu, China 116 E4
Ganzhou, China 113 H9
Gao'an, China 116 H3
Gaomi, China 116 D5
Gaoping, China 116 E2
Gaoua, Burkina Faso 149 B1
Gaoual, Guinea 147 A2
Gaoxiong, Taiwan 117 C2
Gaoyou, China 116 F4
Gaoyou Hu, China 116 F4
Gaoyuan, China 116 D6
Gap, France 55 F8
Gapan, Phil. 130 D2
Gar, China 112 F1
Garachiné, Panama 197 E6
Garanhuns, Brazil 217 D9
Garawe, Liberia 148 E3
Garba Tula, Kenya 157 C3
Gard □, France 55 G7
Garda, L. di, Italy 67 A3
Garden City, U.S.A. 190 F8
Gardez, Afghan. 104 D5
Gardner, U.S.A. 189 A6
Gare Tigre, Fr. Guiana .. 214 C6
Gargano, Mte., Italy 67 E7
Garies, S. Africa 163 F1
Garigliano →, Italy 67 F6
Garissa, Kenya 157 D4
Garissa □, Kenya 157 D4
Garkida, Nigeria 151 C7
Garko, Nigeria 151 B5
Garm, Tajikistan 93 E3
Garonne →, France 55 F3
Garoua, Cameroon 153 B2
Garrison Res. = Sakakawea, L., U.S.A. 190 B8
Garry, L., Canada 186 E8
Garsen, Kenya 157 E4
Garut, Indonesia 128 F5
Garvie Mts., N.Z. 175 H2
Garwa = Garoua, Cameroon 153 B2
Gary, U.S.A. 191 D13
Garzê, China 112 F6
Garzón, Colombia 210 D1
Gasan Kuli, Turkmenistan . 90 K2
Gascogne, France 55 G4
Gascony = Gascogne, France 55 G4
Gascoyne →, Australia .. 168 C1
Gashaka, Nigeria 151 E6
Gashua, Nigeria 151 A6
Gaspé, Canada 187 J14
Gaspé, C. de, Canada .. 187 J14
Gaspé, Pén. de, Canada .. 187 J14
Gassol, Nigeria 151 D6
Gata, C., Cyprus 95 C1
Gata, C. de, Spain 63 B4
Gata, Sierra de, Spain .. 63 D3
Gateshead, U.K. 46 F7
Gaths, Zimbabwe 161 D4
Gâtinais, France 55 C6
Gattaran, Phil. 130 B3
Gatun, L., Panama 197 E4
Gatyana, S. Africa 163 G7
Gauhati, India 106 C9
Gawilgarh Hills, India .. 106 E3
Gawler, Australia 171 F2
Gaxun Nur, China 112 C6
Gaya, India 106 C6
Gaya, Niger 141 D2
Gaya, Nigeria 151 B5
Gaziantep, Turkey 94 C5
Gazli, Uzbekistan 90 K4
Gbanga, Liberia 148 C2
Gbekebo, Nigeria 151 F2
Gboko, Nigeria 151 E5
Gbongan, Nigeria 151 E2
Gcuwa, S. Africa 163 G7
Gdańsk, Poland 77 A3
Gdańska, Zatoka, Poland . 77 A3

Gdov, Russia 81 A3
Gdynia, Poland 77 A3
Gebe, Indonesia 129 C14
Gebeit Mine, Sudan 143 A5
Gebel Musa, Egypt 139 C6
Gedaref, Sudan 143 C5
Gede, Tanjung, Indonesia . 128 E4
Gedser, Denmark 42 D3
Geel, Belgium 51 B4
Geelong, Australia 171 H4
Geili, Sudan 143 C4
Geita, Tanzania 158 B1
Gejiu, China 112 H6
Gela, Italy 67 K6
Geladi, Ethiopia 144 E5
Gelderland □, Neths. 50 D5
Geldermalsen, Neths. .. 50 E4
Geldern, Germany 59 A1
Geldrop, Neths. 50 F4
Geleen, Neths. 50 G4
Gelehun, S. Leone 147 C3
Gelsenkirchen, Germany . 58 C1
Gemas, Malaysia 126 D2
Gembloux, Belgium 51 C4
Gemena, Zaïre 155 A3
Gemert, Neths. 50 E4
Gemsa, Egypt 139 C5
Geneina, Gebel, Egypt .. 139 B5
General Acha, Argentina . 220 F4
General Alvear, Argentina . 220 E3
General Cabrera, Argentina 221 B1
General MacArthur, Phil. . 130 G5
General Pico, Argentina .. 221 C2
General Pinto, Argentina . 221 C3
General Santos, Phil. 130 L5
General Viamonte, Argentina 221 C4
General Villegas, Argentina 221 C3
Genesee →, U.S.A. 189 A2
Geneva, U.S.A. 189 A3
Geneva = Genève, Switz. . 60 D1
Geneva, L. = Léman, Lac, Switz. 60 C1
Genève, Switz. 60 D1
Geng, Afghan. 104 F1
Genil →, Spain 63 F4
Genk, Belgium 51 B5
Gennargentu, Mti. del, Italy 67 G2
Genoa = Génova, Italy .. 67 C2
Genoa, Australia 171 G7
Génova, Italy 67 C2
Génova, G. di, Italy 67 C2
Genyem, Indonesia 129 D18
Geographe B., Australia .. 170 C1
Geokchay, Azerbaijan .. 82 C5
George, S. Africa 163 H4
George →, Canada 187 G13
George, L., N.S.W., Australia 171 F7
George, L., S. Austral., Australia 171 G2
George, L., Uganda 156 C1
George, L., U.S.A. 191 J15
George Town, Malaysia .. 126 B1
Georgetown, Canada 185 D1
Georgetown, Gambia 146 C2
Georgetown, Guyana 214 B2
Georgetown, U.S.A. 191 J16
Georgia □, U.S.A. 191 H15
Georgia ■, Asia 82 B4
Georgiu-Dezh = Liski, Russia 81 E6
Georgiyevka, Kazakhstan . 93 A7
Gera, Germany 58 D4
Geraardsbergen, Belgium . 51 C2
Geraldton, Australia 168 H9
Gereshk, Afghan. 104 F2
Gerik, Malaysia 126 B1
Gerlogubu, Ethiopia 144 E5
Germany ■, Europe 58
Germiston, S. Africa 163 C7
Gerona, Spain 63 B9
Gerrards Cross, U.K. 45 C1
Gers □, France 55 G4
Gévaudan, France 55 F6
Geysir, Iceland 38 C3
Ghaghara →, India 106 C6
Ghana ■, W. Afr. 149
Gharb el Istiwa'iya □, Sudan 143 F3
Gharbiya, Es Sahrâ' el, Egypt 139 C2
Ghard Abû Muharik, Egypt 139 C3
Ghardaïa, Algeria 137 B4
Ghârib, G., Egypt 139 C5
Ghârib, Râs, Egypt 139 B5
Gharyân, Libya 138 A2
Ghat, Libya 138 C1
Ghawdex = Gozo, Malta . 69 A1
Ghazal, Bahr el →, Chad . 142 D1
Ghazâl, Bahr el →, Sudan 143 E3
Ghazaouet, Algeria 137 A3
Ghaziabad, India 106 A3
Ghazipur, India 106 C6
Ghaznî, Afghan. 104 D5
Ghaznî □, Afghan. 104 D5
Ghent, Belgium 51 B2
Ghot Ogrein, Egypt 139 A1
Ghowr □, Afghan. 104 D3
Ghugus, India 106 F4
Ghūrīān, Afghan. 104 D1
Gia Lai = Pleiku, Vietnam . 125 E5

Gia Nghia, Vietnam ...... 125 F
Giarabub = Al Jaghbūb, Libya .... 138 B
Giarre, Italy .... 67 J
Gibara, Cuba .... 198 C
Gibraltar, Europe ...... 63 H
Gibraltar, Str. of, Medit. S. 34 H
Gidole, Ethiopia ...... 144 E
Giessen, Germany ...... 58 D
Gifatin, Geziret, Egypt .. 139 C
Gifu, Japan .... 120 B
Gifu □, Japan .... 120 A
Gijón, Spain .... 63 A
Gila →, U.S.A. .... 190 G
Gilbert Is., Kiribati ...... 176 F
Gilf el Kebîr, Hadabat el, Egypt .... 139 D
Gilgandra, Australia .... 171 D
Gilgil, Kenya .... 157 D
Gilgit, India .... 107 A
Gillingham, U.K. ...... 45 D
Gilmore, Australia ...... 171 F
Gimbi, Ethiopia .... 144 D
Gin →, Sri Lanka ...... 110 D
Gingin, Australia ...... 170 B
Ginir, Ethiopia .... 144 E
Ginowan, Japan ...... 121 D
Girardot, Colombia .... 210 C
Giresun, Turkey .... 94 B
Girga, Egypt .... 139 D
Giridih, India .... 106 D
Girilambone, Australia .. 171 C
Giro, Nigeria .... 151 B
Gironde □, France ...... 55 F
Gironde →, France .... 55 E
Gisborne, N.Z. .... 175 D
Gisenyi, Rwanda ...... 156 A
Gissarskiy, Khrebet, Tajikistan .... 93 B
Gitega, Burundi .... 156 B
Giurgiu, Romania ...... 75 D
Giza = El Gîza, Egypt .. 139 B
Gizhiga, Russia 91 C1
Gizhiginskaya Guba, Russia 91 D1
Giżycko, Poland ...... 77 A
Gjirokastër, Albania .... 70 D
Gjoa Haven, Canada .... 186 D
Glace Bay, Canada 187 J1
Gladstone, Australia .... 171 E
Gláma, Iceland .... 38 B
Glåma →, Norway .... 40 F
Glarus, Switz. .... 60 B
Glasgow, U.K. .... 46 E
Glauchau, Germany .... 58 D
Gleiwitz = Gliwice, Poland 77 E
Glen Innes, Australia .... 171 B
Glencoe, S. Africa ...... 163 E
Glendale, U.S.A. ...... 190 G
Glendale, Zimbabwe .... 161 B
Glendive, U.S.A. ...... 190 B
Glenelg, Australia ...... 171 H
Glenelg →, Australia .. 171 H
Glenmorgan, Australia .. 171 A
Glenorchy, Australia .... 172 C
Glenreagh, Australia .... 171 C
Glens Falls, U.S.A. ...... 191 C
Glenwood, U.S.A. ...... 192 E
Gliwice, Poland .... 77 E
Globe, U.S.A. .... 190 G
Głogów, Poland .... 77 D
Gloucester, Australia .... 171 D
Gloucester, U.K. ...... 46 K
Gloversville, U.S.A. .... 189 A
Glückstadt, Germany .... 58 A
Gmünd, Austria .... 61 A
Gmunden, Austria ...... 61 B
Gniezno, Poland .... 77 B
Gnowangerup, Australia . 170 C
Go Cong, Vietnam ...... 125 G
Goa □, India .... 107 E
Goa, India .... 107 E
Goalen Hd., Australia .. 171 F
Goalpara, India .... 106 C
Goaso, Ghana .... 149 D
Goba, Ethiopia .... 144 E
Goba, Mozam. .... 159 D
Gobabis, Namibia ...... 162 C
Gobi, Asia .... 84 D
Goch, Germany .... 59 A
Gochas, Namibia ...... 162 D
Godalming, U.K. ...... 45 D
Godavari →, India .... 107 E
Godhavn, Greenland .... 224 C
Godhra, India .... 106 D
Gods →, Canada ...... 186 H
Gods L., Canada ...... 186 H
Godstone, U.K. .... 45 D
Godthåb, Greenland .... 224 D
Godwin Austen = K2, Mt., Pakistan .... 105 A
Goeie Hoop, Kaap die = Good Hope, C. of, S. Africa .... 163 H
Goeree, Neths. .... 50 E
Goes, Neths. .... 50 F
Gogra = Ghaghara →, India .... 106 C
Goiânia, Brazil .... 217 F
Goiás, Brazil .... 217 E
Goiás □, Brazil .... 217 E
Goirle, Neths. .... 50 E
Gojra, Pakistan .... 105 C
Gold Coast, Australia .... 171 A
Gold Coast, W. Afr. .... 132 D
Golden B., N.Z. ...... 175 D
Golden Gate, U.S.A. .... 190 F

Montebello, *Canada* 185 B4
Montecristi, *Ecuador* 212 C1
Montego Bay, *Jamaica* 199 A2
Montemorelos, *Mexico* 194 C5
Montenegro □,
  Montenegro, Yug. 72 D6
Montepuez, *Mozam.* 159 B3
Monterey, *U.S.A.* 190 E2
Monteria, *Colombia* 210 B1
Monterrey, *Mexico* 194 C5
Montes Claros, *Brazil* 217 F7
Montevideo, *Uruguay* 219 D2
Montgomery = Sahiwal,
  Pakistan 105 C5
Montgomery, *U.K.* 46 J6
Montgomery, *U.S.A.* 191 H13
Monthey, *Switz.* 60 D1
Montilla, *Spain* 63 F4
Montluçon, *France* 55 E6
Montoro, *Spain* 63 F4
Montpelier, *Idaho, U.S.A.* . 190 D5
Montpelier, *Vt., U.S.A.* . . 191 C17
Montpellier, *France* 55 G7
Montréal, *Canada* 185 B5
Montreuil, *France* 55 A5
Montreux, *Switz.* 60 C1
Montrose, *U.S.A.* 190 E6
Montserrat, *W. Indies* 202 E3
Montuiri, *Spain* 65 B4
Monveda, *Zaire* 155 B4
Monywa, *Burma* 122 D2
Monza, *Italy* 67 A2
Monze, *Zambia* 161 D3
Monzón, *Spain* 63 B8
Mooi River, *S. Africa* 163 E8
Moolawatana, *Australia* . . . 171 C2
Mooliabeenee, *Australia* . . . 170 A3
Moonie, *Australia* 171 A8
Moonie →, *Australia* 171 B7
Moonta, *Australia* 171 E1
Moora, *Australia* 170 A1
Moore →, *Australia* 170 B1
Moorefield, *U.S.A.* 189 D2
Moorhead, *U.S.A.* 191 C10
Mooroopna, *Australia* 171 G5
Moorreesburg, *S. Africa* . . 163 H2
Moose Jaw, *Canada* 186 J6
Moosehead L., *U.S.A.* . . 191 B17
Moosomin, *Canada* 186 J7
Moosonee, *Canada* 187 J11
Mopeia Velha, *Mozam.* . . . 159 C2
Mopti, *Mali* 140 E4
Moquegua, *Peru* 213 F4
Mora, *Sweden* 40 F3
Moradabad, *India* 106 A4
Morafenobe, *Madag.* 165 C1
Moramanga, *Madag.* 165 C2
Morant Bay, *Jamaica* 199 C6
Morant Pt., *Jamaica* 199 C6
Moratuwa, *Sri Lanka* 110 D1
Morava →, *Czech.* 76 D5
Moravian Hts. =
  Ceskomoravská
  Vrchovina, *Czech.* 76 B4
Morawhanna, *Guyana* 214 A1
Moray Firth, *U.K.* 46 B5
Morbihan □, *France* 55 C2
Morden, *Canada* 186 K8
Mordovian Republic □,
  Russia 81 C7
Morea, *Australia* 171 G3
Morea, *Greece* 34 H11
Moreau →, *U.S.A.* 190 C8
Moree, *Australia* 171 B7
Morelia, *Mexico* 194 E4
Morella, *Spain* 63 D8
Morena, Sierra, *Spain* 63 F4
Moreton I., *Australia* 171 A9
Morgan, *Australia* 171 E2
Morgan City, *U.S.A.* . . . 191 J12
Morgantown, *U.S.A.* 189 D1
Morgenzon, *S. Africa* 163 D8
Morges, *Switz.* 60 C1
Moriki, *Nigeria* 151 A3
Morioka, *Japan* 121 D7
Morlaix, *France* 55 C2
Mormugao, *India* 107 E2
Mornington, *Australia* 171 H5
Moro G., *Phil.* 130 K4
Morobe, *Papua N. G.* 173 C2
Morocco ■, *N. Afr.* 136
Morococha, *Peru* 213 D3
Morogoro, *Tanzania* 158 C3
Morombe, *Madag.* 165 D1
Morón, *Argentina* 221 C5
Morón, *Cuba* 198 B4
Morón, *Spain* 63 G4
Mörön →, *Mongolia* 113 A7
Morona-Santiago □,
  Ecuador 212 D2
Morondava, *Madag.* 165 D1
Morondo, *Ivory C.* 148 B4
Moroni, *Comoros Is.* 166 A1
Moronou, *Ivory C.* 148 D5
Morotai, *Indonesia* 129 B14
Moroto, *Uganda* 156 B3
Moroto Summit, *Kenya* . . . 157 B1
Morphou, *Cyprus* 95 B1
Morphou Bay, *Cyprus* 95 B1
Morrelganj, *Bangla.* 111 D2
Morristown, *U.S.A.* 191 F14
Morrumbene, *Mozam.* . . . 159 E2
Morshansk, *Russia* 81 D6

Mortlake, *Australia* 171 H4
Morundah, *Australia* 171 F5
Moruya, *Australia* 171 F7
Morvan, *France* 55 D7
Morwell, *Australia* 171 H5
Moscos Is., *Burma* 122 G3
Moscow = Moskva, *Russia* . . 81 C5
Moscow, *U.S.A.* 190 B4
Mosel →, *Europe* 55 C8
Moselle = Mosel →,
  Europe 55 C8
Moselle □, *France* 55 B8
Moses Lake, *U.S.A.* 190 B3
Mosgiel, *N.Z.* 175 J3
Moshi, *Tanzania* 158 B3
Mosjøen, *Norway* 40 C3
Moskva, *Russia* 81 C5
Moskva →, *Russia* 81 C5
Mosquera, *Colombia* 210 D1
Mosquitia, *Honduras* 196 C5
Mosquitos, G. de los,
  Panama 197 E4
Moss Vale, *Australia* 171 F8
Mossaka, *Congo* 154 C3
Mossburn, *N.Z.* 175 J2
Mosselbaai, *S. Africa* 163 H4
Mossendjo, *Congo* 154 C1
Mossgiel, *Australia* 171 E5
Mossoró, *Brazil* 217 C9
Mossuril, *Mozam.* 159 B3
Most, *Czech.* 76 A3
Mosta, *Malta* 69 B2
Mostaganem, *Algeria* 137 A3
Mostar, *Bos.-H., Yug.* . . . 72 D5
Mostefa, Rass, *Tunisia* . . . 138 A3
Mosul = Al Mawşil, *Iraq* . . 102 A3
Mosulpo, *S. Korea* 118 J4
Motagua →, *Guatemala* . . 196 C2
Motherwell, *U.K.* 46 D5
Motihari, *India* 106 B6
Motueka, *N.Z.* 175 E4
Mouanda, *Gabon* 154 C2
Moûdhros, *Greece* 71 C5
Moudjeria, *Mauritania* . . . 140 D2
Moudon, *Switz.* 60 C1
Mouila, *Gabon* 154 C1
Moulamein, *Australia* 171 F4
Moulins, *France* 55 E6
Moulmein = Maulamyaing,
  Burma 122 F3
Moulouya, O. →, *Morocco* . 136 A6
Moundou, *Chad* 142 F1
Mount Barker, *S. Austral.,*
  Australia 171 F2
Mount Barker, *W. Austral.,*
  Australia 170 D2
Mount Darwin, *Zimbabwe* . 161 B4
Mount Fletcher, *S. Africa* . 163 F7
Mount Gambier, *Australia* . 171 H3
Mount Hope, *Australia* . . . 171 D5
Mount Isa, *Australia* . . . 168 H11
Mount Lofty Ra., *Australia* . 171 E2
Mount Margaret, *Australia* . 171 A4
Mount Maunganui, *N.Z.* . . 175 C6
Mount Morris, *U.S.A.* . . . 189 A2
Mount Vernon, *Ind., U.S.A.* 191 F12
Mount Vernon, *N.Y., U.S.A.* 189 B5
Mourdi, Dépression du,
  Chad 142 B3
Mourdiah, *Mali* 140 E3
Mouri, *Ghana* 149 E2
Mourne Mts., *U.K.* 46 G4
Mouscron, *Belgium* 51 C1
Moussoro, *Chad* 142 D1
Moutier, *Switz.* 60 B2
Moutong, *Indonesia* 129 C11
Moyale, *Kenya* 157 A4
Moyamba, *S. Leone* 147 C3
Moyen Atlas, *Morocco* . . . 136 C5
Moyobamba, *Peru* 213 C2
Moyyero →, *Russia* 91 E11
Mozambique =
  Moçambique, *Mozam.* . . 159 B3
Mozambique ■, *Africa* . . . 159
Mozambique Chan., *Africa* . 132 J8
Mozyr, *Belorussia* 81 D3
Mpanda, *Tanzania* 158 C1
Mpika, *Zambia* 161 B5
Mpumalanga, *S. Africa* . . . 163 F8
Mpwapwa, *Tanzania* 158 C2
Mrimina, *Morocco* 136 E3
Msaken, *Tunisia* 138 B2
Msambansovu, *Zimbabwe* . 161 A3
Msoro, *Zambia* 161 C5
Mtilikwe →, *Zimbabwe* . . . 161 D4
Mtubatuba, *S. Africa* 163 E9
Muang Chiang Rai,
  Thailand 123 E4
Muang Lamphun, *Thailand* 122 E4
Muarabungo, *Indonesia* . . 128 C3
Muaraenim, *Indonesia* . . . 128 C3
Muarajuloi, *Indonesia* . . . 128 C8
Muarakaman, *Indonesia* . . 128 C9
Muaratebo, *Indonesia* . . . 128 C3
Muaratembesi, *Indonesia* . 128 D3
Muaratewe, *Indonesia* . . . 128 C8
Mubarraz = Al Mubarraz,
  Si. Arabia 99 C6
Mubende, *Uganda* 156 C1
Mubi, *Nigeria* 151 C7
Muconda, *Angola* 160 C4
Mudanjiang, *China* 113 B12
Mudgee, *Australia* 171 D7

Mudon, *Burma* 122 F3
Mufulira, *Zambia* 161 B3
Muğla, *Turkey* 94 C1
Mugu, *Nepal* 109 A2
Muhammad, Râs, *Egypt* . . 139 C6
Muhammad Qol, *Sudan* . . 143 A6
Mühlhausen, *Germany* . . . 58 D3
Muir, L., *Australia* 170 D2
Mukah, *Malaysia* 126 C6
Mukawwa, *Egypt* 139 E6
Mukden = Shenyang, *China* 116 B6
Mukhtuya = Lensk, *Russia* . 91 G13
Mukinbudin, *Australia* . . . 170 A3
Mukomuko, *Indonesia* . . . 128 D3
Muktsar Bhatinda, *India* . . 107 B2
Mulde →, *Germany* 58 C5
Mulgrave, *Canada* 187 K15
Mulhacén, *Spain* 63 G5
Mülheim, *Germany* 58 C1
Mulhouse, *France* 55 C9
Mull, *U.K.* 46 D4
Mullaittvu, *Sri Lanka* 110 A2
Mullengudgery, *Australia* . 171 D6
Muller, Pegunungan,
  Indonesia 128 C8
Mullingar, *Ireland* 46 G2
Mullumbimby, *Australia* . . 171 B9
Multan, *Pakistan* 105 D5
Mumbwa, *Zambia* 161 C3
Mun →, *Thailand* 123 G5
Muna, *Indonesia* 129 E11
München, *Germany* 58 F4
München-Gladbach =
  Mönchengladbach,
  Germany 58 D1
Munchŏn, *N. Korea* 118 D4
Muncie, *U.S.A.* 191 E13
Münden, *Germany* 58 D3
Mungallala Cr. →,
  Australia 171 A6
Mungbere, *Zaire* 155 B5
Munger, *India* 106 C7
Mungindi, *Australia* 171 B7
Munhango, *Angola* 160 C4
Munich = München,
  Germany 58 F4
Munku-Sardyk, *Russia* . . . 91 J11
Munsan, *S. Korea* 118 E4
Munshiganj, *Bangla.* 111 C2
Münster, *Germany* 58 C2
Muntadgin, *Australia* 170 B3
Muntok, *Indonesia* 128 D4
Munyak, *Uzbekistan* 90 J4
Munzer Dağlari, *Turkey* . . . 82 D1
Muon Pak Beng, *Laos* . . . 125 B1
Mupa, *Angola* 160 E3
Muping, *China* 116 D5
Muqdisho, *Somali Rep.* . . 145 C2
Mur →, *Austria* 61 C6
Muranda, *Rwanda* 156 A1
Murang'a, *Kenya* 157 D2
Murashi, *Russia* 81 A4
Murban, *U.A.E.* 101 C2
Murchison Falls =
  Kabarega Falls, *Uganda* . 156 B1
Murchison Rapids, *Malawi* . 158 E2
Murcia, *Spain* 63 F7
Murcia □, *Spain* 63 F6
Mureş →, *Romania* 75 B1
Mureşul = Mureş →,
  Romania 75 B1
Murgab, *Tajikistan* 93 F7
Muriaé, *Brazil* 215 B5
Muriel Mine, *Zimbabwe* . . 161 B4
Müritz See, *Germany* 58 B5
Murka, *Kenya* 157 E3
Murmansk, *Russia* 90 B5
Muro, *Spain* 65 A4
Murom, *Russia* 81 C6
Muroran, *Japan* 121 C7
Muroto-Misaki, *Japan* . . . 120 D5
Murray →, *Australia* 190 E5
Murray →, *Australia* 171 F2
Murray Bridge, *Australia* . . 171 F2
Murraysburg, *S. Africa* . . . 163 G5
Murrumbidgee →,
  Australia 171 E4
Murrumburrah, *Australia* . . 171 E7
Murrurundi, *Australia* 171 D8
Mursala, *Indonesia* 128 B2
Murtoa, *Australia* 171 G4
Murwara, *India* 106 D4
Murwillumbah, *Australia* . . 171 B9
Mürzzuschlag, *Austria* . . . 61 B6
Muş, *Turkey* 94 B6
Musa Khel, *Pakistan* 105 C4
Mûsa Qal'eh, *Afghan.* . . . 104 D3
Musaffargarh, *Pakistan* . . . 105 D5
Musala, *Bulgaria* 73 C2
Musan, *N. Korea* 118 A5
Musay'īd, *Qatar* 100 D3
Muscat = Masqat, *Oman* . . 101 B3
Muscat & Oman =
  Oman ■, *Asia* 101
Musgrave Ra., *Australia* . . 168 C3
Mushie, *Zaïre* 155 D2
Mushin, *Nigeria* 151 F1
Musi →, *Indonesia* 128 D4
Muskegon, *U.S.A.* 191 D13
Muskegon →, *U.S.A.* . . . 191 D13
Muskogee, *U.S.A.* 191 G10
Muslimiyah, *Syria* 97 A3
Musmar, *Sudan* 143 B5
Musoma, *Tanzania* 158 A1
Musselshell →, *U.S.A.* . . . 190 B6

Mustang, *Nepal* 109 A3
Musudan, *N. Korea* 118 C5
Muswellbrook, *Australia* . . 171 D8
Mût, *Egypt* 139 D3
Mutaray, *Russia* 91 G11
Mutare, *Zimbabwe* 161 C5
Muting, *Indonesia* 129 F18
Mutriba, *Kuwait* 100 A1
Mutsamudu, *Comoros Is.* . 166 B2
Mutsu-Wan, *Japan* 121 C7
Muxima, *Angola* 160 B2
Muy Muy, *Nic.* 197 B2
Muya, *Russia* 91 H13
Muzaffarabad, *Pakistan* . . 105 A6
Muzaffarnagar, *India* 106 A3
Muzaffarpur, *India* 106 C7
Muzhi, *Russia* 90 E7
Muzkol, Khrebet, *Tajikistan* 93 F6
Muztag, *China* 112 E3
Mvuma, *Zimbabwe* 161 C4
Mvurwi, *Zimbabwe* 161 B4
Mwanza, *Tanzania* 158 B1
Mwanza, *Zaïre* 155 E5
Mweka, *Zaïre* 155 D3
Mwenezi, *Zimbabwe* 161 E4
Mwenga, *Zaïre* 155 D6
Mweru, L., *Zambia* 161 A4
Mweza Range, *Zimbabwe* . 161 D3
Mwinilunga, *Zambia* 161 B2
My Tho, *Vietnam* 125 G4
Myanaung, *Burma* 122 E2
Myanmar = Burma ■, *Asia* 122
Myaungmya, *Burma* 122 F2
Mycenae = Mikinai, *Greece* 71 D3
Myeik Kyunzu, *Burma* . . . 122 H3
Myingyan, *Burma* 122 D2
Myitkyina, *Burma* 122 B3
Mymensingh, *Bangla.* . . . 111 B2
Mýrdalsjökull, *Iceland* . . . 38 D3
Mysore = Karnataka □,
  India 107 F2
Mysore, *India* 107 F2
Mývatn, *Iceland* 38 B4
Mzimba, *Malawi* 158 B2
Mzimkulu →, *S. Africa* . . . 163 F8
Mzimvubu →, *S. Africa* . . 163 G8
Mzuzu, *Malawi* 158 B2

N

N' Dioum, *Senegal* 146 A2
Naab →, *Germany* 58 F4
Naaldwijk, *Neths.* 50 D2
Naas, *Ireland* 46 H3
Nababiep, *S. Africa* 163 F1
Naberezhnyye Chelny,
  Russia 82 C9
Nabeul, *Tunisia* 138 A3
Nabire, *Indonesia* 129 D16
Nabiswera, *Uganda* 156 B2
Nablus = Nābulus, *Jordan* . 98 A1
Naboomspruit, *S. Africa* . . 163 B7
Nabua, *Phil.* 130 F4
Nābulus, *Jordan* 98 A1
Nacaome, *Honduras* 196 D3
Nachingwea, *Tanzania* . . . 158 D3
Nackara, *Australia* 171 D2
Nacogdoches, *U.S.A.* . . . 191 H11
Nacozari, *Mexico* 194 A2
Nadiad, *India* 106 D1
Nador, *Morocco* 136 A6
Nadur, *Malta* 69 A2
Nadym, *Russia* 90 E8
Nadym →, *Russia* 90 E8
Nafada, *Nigeria* 151 B6
Nag Hammâdi, *Egypt* 139 D5
Naga, *Phil.* 130 F4
Nagaland □, *India* 107 C6
Nagano, *Japan* 120 A7
Nagano □, *Japan* 120 A7
Nagaoka, *Japan* 121 F6
Nagappattinam, *India* . . . 107 F3
Nagar Parkar, *Pakistan* . . . 105 F4
Nagasaki, *Japan* 120 D1
Nagasaki □, *Japan* 120 D1
Nagaur, *India* 106 B2
Nagercoil, *India* 107 G3
Nagorno-Karabakh,
  Azerbaijan 82 D7
Nagornyy, *Russia* 91 G14
Nagoya, *Japan* 120 B6
Nagpur, *India* 106 E4
Nagua, *Dom. Rep.* 200 A3
Nagykanizsa, *Hungary* . . . 74 C2
Nagykörös, *Hungary* 74 B4
Naha, *Japan* 121 J8
Nahanni Butte, *Canada* . . 186 E5
Nahîya, Wadi →, *Egypt* . . 139 B4
Nain, *Canada* 187 G13
Nainpur, *India* 106 D4
Naira, *Indonesia* 129 E14
Nairn, *U.K.* 46 B5
Nairobi, *Kenya* 157 D2
Naivasha, *Kenya* 157 D2
Naivasha, L., *Kenya* 157 D2
Najd, *Si. Arabia* 99 C4
Najibabad, *India* 106 A4
Najin, *N. Korea* 118 A4
Naju, *S. Korea* 118 H4
Nakfa, *Ethiopia* 144 B3

Nakhichevan, *Azerbaijan* . . 82 D6
Nakhl, *Egypt* 139 B5
Nakhodka, *Russia* 91 J17
Nakhon Phanom, *Thailand* 123 F6
Nakhon Ratchasima,
  Thailand 123 G5
Nakhon Sawan, *Thailand* . 123 G4
Nakhon Si Thammarat,
  Thailand 123 K4
Nakina, *Canada* 187 K10
Nakskov, *Denmark* 42 D3
Naktong →, *S. Korea* 118 G5
Nakuru, *Kenya* 157 D2
Nakuru □, *Kenya* 157 D2
Nal →, *Pakistan* 105 F2
Nalchik, *Russia* 82 A5
Nalerigu, *Ghana* 149 A3
Nalón →, *Spain* 63 A3
Nālūt, *Libya* 138 A2
Nam-ch'on, *N. Korea* 118 E3
Nam Co, *China* 112 F4
Nam Dinh, *Vietnam* 125 B4
Nam-Phan, *Vietnam* 125 G4
Nam Phong, *Thailand* . . . 123 F5
Nam Tha, *Laos* 125 B1
Namacurra, *Mozam.* 159 C3
Namak, Daryācheh-ye, *Iran* 103 B3
Namaland, *Namibia* 162 D2
Namangan, *Uzbekistan* . . . 93 C5
Namapa, *Mozam.* 159 B3
Namaqualand, *S. Africa* . . 163 F1
Namasagali, *Uganda* 156 C2
Namatanai, *Papua N. G.* . . 173 A3
Namber, *Indonesia* 129 C16
Nambucca Heads, *Australia* 171 C9
Nameh, *Indonesia* 128 B9
Namib Desert =
  Namibwoestyn, *Namibia* . 162 C2
Namibe, *Angola* 160 D2
Namibia ■, *Africa* 162
Namibwoestyn, *Namibia* . . 162 C2
Namlea, *Indonesia* 129 D13
Nampa, *U.S.A.* 190 C4
Nampula, *Mozam.* 159 B3
Namrole, *Indonesia* 129 D13
Namtu, *Burma* 122 C3
Namtumbo, *Russia* 91 E14
Namur, *Belgium* 51 D4
Namur □, *Belgium* 51 D4
Namutoni, *Namibia* 162 A2
Namwala, *Zambia* 161 C3
Namwŏn, *S. Korea* 118 G4
Nan, *Thailand* 123 E4
Nanaimo, *Canada* 186 H3
Nanam, *N. Korea* 118 B5
Nanango, *Australia* 171 A9
Nanao, *Japan* 121 F5
Nanchang, *China* 116 H3
Nancheng, *China* 116 J3
Nanching = Nanjing, *China* 116 F4
Nanchong, *China* 113 F7
Nancy, *France* 55 C8
Nanded, *India* 106 F3
Nandewar Ra., *Australia* . . 171 C8
Nandi □, *Kenya* 157 C1
Nandurbar, *India* 106 E2
Nanga Parbat, *Pakistan* . . 105 A6
Nangapinoh, *Indonesia* . . 128 C7
Nangarhár □, *Afghan.* . . . 104 D6
Nangatayap, *Indonesia* . . 128 C6
Nangeya Mts., *Uganda* . . . 156 A3
Nanjing, *China* 116 F4
Nanking = Nanjing, *China* . 116 F4
Nanning, *China* 113 J7
Nannup, *Australia* 170 C1
Nanpi, *China* 116 D3
Nanping, *China* 116 J4
Nansei-Shotō, *Japan* 121 J7
Nansen Sd., *Canada* 186 A9
Nantes, *France* 55 D3
Nanticoke, *U.S.A.* 189 B4
Nantong, *China* 116 F5
Nantucket I., *U.S.A.* 180 E12
Nanyang, *China* 116 F2
Nanyuan, *China* 116 C3
Nanyuki, *Kenya* 157 C2
Nanzhang, *China* 116 G1
Náo, C. de la, *Spain* 63 E8
Naoetsu, *Japan* 121 F6
Napa, *U.S.A.* 190 E2
Napanee, *Canada* 185 C3
Napier, *N.Z.* 175 D6
Naples = Nápoli, *Italy* . . . 67 F6
Napo □, *Ecuador* 212 B2
Napo →, *Peru* 213 B4
Nápoli, *Italy* 67 F6
Nappa Merrie, *Australia* . . 171 A3
Naqâda, *Egypt* 139 D5
Nara, *Mali* 140 E3
Nara, *Japan* 120 C6
Naracoorte, *Australia* 171 G3
Naradhan, *Australia* 171 E6
Narathiwat, *Thailand* 123 L5
Narayanganj, *Bangla.* . . . 111 C2
Narbonne, *France* 55 H6
Naremberg, *Australia* 170 B3
Nares Str., *N. Amer.* 180 A13
Narmada →, *India* 106 E1
Narman, *Turkey* 82 C3
Naro, *Ghana* 149 A3
Narodnaya, *Russia* 34 B18
Narok, *Kenya* 157 D2
Narok □, *Kenya* 157 D2
Narooma, *Australia* 171 G7

U

V

Yeovil

Z

DÉPARTEMENTS OF FRANCE

Queen Elizabeth Is.   Ellesmere I.   **Greenland**
180   160   140   120   100   80   60   40   20
80

Victoria I.   + North Magnetic Pole   **Baffin**   Arctic C
Bering Str.   Yukon   Gt. Bear L.   **Island**
60   Mt. McKinley   Mackenzie   Hudson Str.   Davis Str.   **Iceland**
Bering   6199   Gt. Slave L.   Labrador   C. Farewell
Sea   **Hudson**   **British**
Aleutian Is.   L. Winnipeg   **Bay**   **Isles**

Vancouver I.   Great   **Newfoundland**
40   Lakes   St. Lawrence   C. Race   **Ib**
      Missouri   Ohio   **Appalachian Mts.**   **P**
Mt. Whitney   Arkansas   C. Hatteras   **Azores**
4418   Mississippi   **Bermuda**   Str. of Gibraltar
Lower   Rio Grande   Tropic of C   **Atla**
California   **Gulf of**   Florida Str.   **ATLANTIC**   Canary Is.   **S**
20   **Mexico**   **Bahama**   C.Verde   **G**
Hawaiian Is.   Popocatepetl   **Cuba**   **Islands**   Is.   C. Verde
Mauna Kea   5452   Yucatan   **Greater**   **Hispaniola**
4202   Citlaltepetl   **Antilles**   **OCEAN**
     5700   Jamaica   **Lesser**   C. Palmas
P A C I F I C   **Caribbean Sea**   **Antilles**   **Gu**
Palmyra Is.   Orinoco   **Guiana Highlands**
Tabuaeran   Isthmus   Llanos   Roraima   C. Palmas
Kiritimati   of Panama   2772
0   Galapagos   Chimborazo   Negro   Equator
    Is.   6267   Amazon   C. de São Roque
Phoenix Is.   Selvas   **Ascension**
      Madeira   Tocantins
Tokelau Is.   Marquesas Is.   Mato Grosso   **St. Helena**
O C E A N   **Brazilian Highlands**
Samoa Is.   Society Is.   L. Titicaca   C. Frio
   Cook Is.   Tahiti   Tuamotu   Paraguay
     Archipelago   Gran Chaco   Tropic of Capr
20   Tonga   Tubuai Is.   Atacama   Paraná
   Is.   Pitcairn I.   Desert   Ojos del Salado   R. de la Plata
     Easter I.   6863   Negro   Tristan da C
Kermadec Is.   Aconcagua   Pampas
      6960   Patagonia
40   Chatham Is.   Falkland Is.   S. Georgia
      Tierra del Fuego
     Magellan's Str.   C. Horn
      Drake Passage
       Graham   **Antarctic**   Antarctic
       Land   **Peninsula**
60   Palmer   **Weddell Sea**
      Land   Caird Coast
Ross Sea   Ellsworth Land   40   Coats Land
  80   Byrd Land   100   80   60   West from Gree
180   160   140   120

HEIGHT OF LAND

m		ft
6 000		18 000
4 000		12 000
2 000		6 000
1 000		3 000
200		600
0		0

DEPTH OF SEA

m		ft
200		600
4 000		12 000
8 000		24 000